Real-Time Web Application Development

With ASP.NET Core, SignalR, Docker, and Azure

Rami Vemula

Apress®

Real-Time Web Application Development
Rami Vemula
Visakhapatnam, Andhra Pradesh, India

ISBN-13 (pbk): 978-1-4842-3269-9   ISBN-13 (electronic): 978-1-4842-3270-5
https://doi.org/10.1007/978-1-4842-3270-5

Library of Congress Control Number: 2017960937

Cover image by Freepik (`www.freepik.com`)

Managing Director: Welmoed Spahr
Editorial Director: Todd Green
Acquisitions Editor: Nikhil Karkal
Development Editor: Matthew Moodie
Technical Reviewer: Mohana Krishna G and Yogesh Sharma
Coordinating Editor: Prachi Mehta
Copy Editor: Sharon Wilkey

Distributed to the book trade worldwide by Springer Science + Business Media New York, 233 Spring Street, 6th Floor, New York, NY 10013. Phone 1-800-SPRINGER, fax (201) 348-4505, e-mail orders-ny@springer-sbm.com, or visit `www.springeronline.com`. Apress Media, LLC is a California LLC, and the sole member (owner) is Springer Science + Business Media Finance Inc (SSBM Finance Inc). SSBM Finance Inc is a **Delaware** corporation.

For information on translations, please e-mail rights@apress.com, or visit `http://www.apress.com/rights-permissions`.

Apress titles may be purchased in bulk for academic, corporate, or promotional use. eBook versions and licenses are also available for most titles. For more information, reference our Print and eBook Bulk Sales web page at `http://www.apress.com/bulk-sales`.

Any source code or other supplementary material referenced by the author in this book is available to readers on GitHub via the book's product page, located at `www.apress.com/978-1-4842-3269-9`. For more detailed information, please visit `http://www.apress.com/source-code`.

Printed on acid-free paper

Dedicated to my maternal grandmother, Kanaka Maha Lakshmi, and in loving memory of my grandparents—my maternal grandfather, Rowgi; my paternal grandfather, Venkaiah; and my paternal grandmother, Raghavamma

Contents

About the Author

Rami Vemula is a technology consultant who has more than seven years of experience in delivering scalable web and cloud solutions using Microsoft technologies and platforms, including ASP.NET MVC/Web API, .NET Core, ASP.NET Core, JQuery, C#, Entity Framework, SQL Server, and Azure. He is currently working for Deloitte India (Offices of the US) as a senior consultant, where he leads a team of talented developers. As a part of his work, he architects, develops, and maintains technical solutions for various clients in the public sector.

Although web technologies are his primary area of focus, he also has worked on other projects such as big data analytics using HDInsight, Universal Windows Platform apps, and more. Nowadays he is promoting open source technologies, platforms, and tools to build cross-platform solutions. He is also interested in providing streamlined DevOps integration flows through which development teams can achieve greater productivity.

He is a Microsoft Certified ASP.NET and Azure developer. He was a Microsoft ASP.NET MVP from 2011 to 2014 and an active trainer. In his free time, he enjoys answering technical questions at StackOverflow and forums.asp.net. He loves to share his technical experiences through his blog at http://intstrings.com/ramivemula. Apart from technology, his other interests include movies, drama, and theater arts.

He holds a master's degree in electrical engineering from California State University, Long Beach. He lives with his wife, child, and parents in Hyderabad, India.

You can reach Rami at rami.ramilu@gmail.com or https://twitter.com/RamiRamilu.

About the Technical Reviewers

Yogesh Sharma is a software engineer who loves to work at the cutting edge of web technologies. He focuses his time and effort on the development of software that can help other people learn. His most recent project involving the MEAN stack is an NLP system that is currently under active development. He completed his bachelor's degree in Information Technology at the Vidyalankar School of Information Technology in Mumbai. He currently works for Mphasis as a senior infrastructure engineer on Microsoft Azure Cloud Services. He can be reached at `www.linkedin.com/in/yogisharma24/`.

Mohana Krishna Gundumogula is a full-stack developer in a multinational software engineering firm. He is a Microsoft Certified Professional for Developing Microsoft SharePoint Server 2013 Core Solutions. His expertise includes Microsoft web technologies, collaborative platforms such as Microsoft SharePoint, cloud platforms such as Microsoft Azure, as well as the AngularJS and ReactJS frameworks.

Acknowledgments

I would like to thank my parents, Ramanaiah and RajaKumari; my wife, Sneha; my two-year-old daughter, Akshaya; and the rest of my family—aunts, uncles, cousins, and kids—for their patience and support throughout my life and for helping me achieve many wonderful milestones and accomplishments. Their consistent encouragement and guidance gave me strength to overcome all the hurdles and kept me moving forward.

I would like to thank my longtime friend Sanjay Mylapilli for always pushing me toward great heights and excellence. Thanks to Mahadevu Durga Prasad for always encouraging me to explore new opportunities. Special thanks to uncle VSN Sastry for believing in and supporting me.

I could not imagine achieving all this success and passion in my life without the coaching and help I've received from my mentors. I would like to thank Srikanth Pragada for introducing me to the world of .NET and teaching me how to deliver technical solutions with the utmost discipline. Special thanks to Venu Yerra and RK Vadlani of Idea Entity Tech Solutions for trusting me and giving me my first professional opportunity, where I was introduced to real-world problems and technical challenges.

My heartfelt thanks to Vishwas Lele, Rajesh Agarwal, and Nasir Mirza of Applied Information Sciences (AIS) for introducing me to Microsoft's Azure platform. The extensive training provided by Vishwas not only gave me experience in providing cloud optimized solutions but also changed the way I thought about architecting those solutions. Special thanks to Gaurav Mantri (Cerebrata) for introducing me to the fantastic world of cloud technology.

I would like to thank all my friends at Deloitte for having lengthy conversations about modern technologies and supporting me in reaching my goals.

Thanks to Nikhil Karkal, Prachi Mehta, Matt, and other amazing people at Apress for this wonderful opportunity and making this a memorable journey. Thanks to my technical reviewers, Yogesh and Mohana, for their valuable suggestions.

Sincere thanks to all my friends, especially C.O. Dinesh Reddy, to the developers and architects at Microsoft, and to the open source contributors who are working extensively to deliver great products, frameworks, and next-generation platforms that create various innovation opportunities. The consistent effort by Microsoft communities to keep documents up-to-date and provide prompt responses to technical queries is unprecedented.

Last but not least, I would like to thank all my readers for spending their time and effort in reading this book. Please feel free to share your feedback, which will help me to deliver better content in the future. I look forward to your comments and suggestions.

Introduction

In this modern era of technology, businesses strive to grow at a rapid pace by exploring technical opportunities that cater to a diverse customer base. With the evolution of the open source community, technologies are evolving at a faster cadence, and new ones are quickly emerging to bridge the gaps between platforms. While cloud platforms continued to advance in offering the most affordable and greatest computational power, the focus is being shifted to develop and deliver cross-platform solutions by leveraging a hybrid cloud infrastructure.

Real-Time Web Application Development with ASP.NET Core, SignalR, Docker, and Azure is going to take you through the journey of designing, developing and deploying a real-world web application by leveraging modern open source technologies. ASP.NET Core is the latest open source web framework from Microsoft that is capable of building cross-platform web applications, and SignalR enriches applications by enabling real-time communication between the server and clients. Material Design concepts will deliver the state-of-the-art look and feel for the application, which supports multiple devices with different form factors. Azure, Microsoft's cloud computing platform, is used in this book to demonstrate data storage and hosting capabilities.

Code version control using GitHub, along with Travis CI builds, will help developers, software engineers, system administrators, and architects in building a robust and reliable development ecosystem. Docker's container technology and its seamless integration with GitHub are used to package the application and provide continuous deployment to Azure's IaaS platform.

This book will empower you to gain deeper insights in developing cross-platform applications by combining various open source technologies. By the end of this book, you will be equipped to take on any real-world challenge and provide reliable solutions. The rich code samples from this book can be used to retrofit or upgrade existing ASP.NET Core applications.

This book will deep dive into the following topics:

- Designing and developing real-world ASP.NET Core applications with Materialize CSS and Azure Storage

- Implementing security and data persistence using OAuth 2.0 external social logins and Azure Storage

- Orchestrating real-time communication using SignalR

- Performing source version control with GitHub and continuous integration with the Travis CI build service

- Containerizing and providing continuous deployment using Docker and Azure Linux virtual machines

Chapter 1 will introduce you to the real-world Automobile Service Center application, which we are going to build throughout this book. Chapter 1 also discusses the technology stack and prerequisites that will be used in building the application along with its technical architecture. Chapters 2 through 5 will take you through the basic concepts of .NET Core, ASP.NET Core, Material Design techniques, Azure Table Storage and xUnit.net test cases. In Chapter 6, we will work on securing the application with ASP.NET Core Identity, and enabling customer authentication using Gmail and the OAuth 2.0 protocol.

Chapters 7 and 8 will discuss the implementation of master data, caching, exception handling, and logging. We will use Azure Table Storage to persist all the application data along with logs. In Chapters 9 and 10, we will develop the application pages using ASP.NET Core and related concepts including data validation and internationalization. We will implement real time communication and notifications for the application in Chapter 11 by using the SignalR framework and enable SMS notifications using the Twilio API.

In Chapter 12, we will integrate version control for application code at the GitHub repository via Git commands (and using Visual Studio). Continuous integration with a Travis build is described in Chapter 13 along with user notifications on successful/failed builds. Chapters 14 and 15 focus on containerization of application code using Docker and deploying it to Azure Linux virtual machines.

As a last note, I encourage you to extend the Automobile Service Center application to support functionalities such as used car sales, spare parts management, and financial accounting services. As the digital world is transforming itself into microservices to serve a global audience, there is a need for technologies to collaborate and deliver high-performance and scalable solutions. An optimistic collaboration and automation can happen if technologies are open source, cross-platform, easy to adapt, and cloud ready. This book narrates one of the most prospective collaborations; having said that, it is just the beginning of long journey.

CHAPTER 1

■ ■ ■

Designing a Modern Real-World Web Application

In this modern era of the digital world, technology is no longer an auxiliary system but an integral part of the entire social ecosystem. Our current-day sophisticated devices, along with cutting-edge technologies, have made the entire world into a global village. People from different parts of the world, in spite of their diversity, can collaborate and solve complex challenges. Over the past decade, the open source community has played a pivotal role in evolving technology and setting the pace for innovation.

The ever-changing cadence of technology and tools has prompted a new generation of developers and engineers to rely mostly on Internet resources to educate themselves and deliver solutions. Although that approach still works in delivering solutions, it doesn't help in providing a panoramic view of the software-building process. Although different software development life cycle (SDLC) methodologies follow different processes, the most important ones are detailing functional requirements, system design, implementation, testing, deployment, and maintenance. Except for the testing part, this book will provide a holistic view of the software development process using the latest open source technologies and tools.

In this chapter, you will learn the basic phases of the software development life cycle. We will simulate a real-world business use case through a fictitious US company, Automobile Service Center. We will brainstorm the typical day-to-day challenges faced by this company and propose prospective solutions through a web application that we'll build with the latest technologies throughout the rest of the book. We'll start by defining the technologies that we are going to use in building the application. Then we'll design the logical architecture followed by continuous integration and deployment pipeline of the application. Finally, we will conclude the chapter by exploring the software prerequisites for our development environment.

■ **Note** My primary motive in writing this book is to introduce you to the experience of end-to-end software application development using .NET Core, ASP.NET Core, SignalR, Docker, and Microsoft Azure. This book provides a high-level overview of software development methodologies, and a detailed exploration is beyond the scope of this book.

© Rami Vemula 2017   1
R. Vemula, *Real-Time Web Application Development*, https://doi.org/10.1007/978-1-4842-3270-5_1

Overview of Application Development Strategies and Processes

The incredible pace of the current generation's digital innovation is not only transforming the creative process, but also influencing the incubation period for the latest technologies. Because of so many technical options being available to solve any given unique business challenge, technologists need to be more careful than ever before in offering prospective solutions. The current marketplace requires any technical professional to be adept at three major tasks: exploring, understanding, and adopting.

Let's look at an example of creating a next-generation e-commerce application. To serve a large global audience, this application should be highly scalable and deliver optimistic performance, be available on various devices, support a rich and clean user experience, include real-time data analytics and reports, be cost-effective and easy to maintain, and more. To deliver this e-commerce solution, we could turn to a wide range of technical options. We could use the traditional ASP.NET MVC in combination with JQuery, SQL Server, HDInsight, and Power BI. Other options include a LAMP stack with Hadoop Spark or a MEAN stack with R-powered analytics. The list goes on. We must carefully evaluate all potential solutions and then continue with the design and development process.

Many proven methodologies in the software industry can help us in the various phases of application development. These methodologies can be considered as frameworks for planning and controlling the process of developing software. Popular methodologies include the waterfall model, rapid application development, agile software development, and the prototype model. Different software organizations and projects use different methodologies based on their engineering and operational criteria. In fact, some organizations use their own tailored hybrid development methodologies and processes. Regardless of which software methodology we follow, we have to adhere to certain phases that are common to all methodologies. We will follow these phases, depicted in Figure 1-1, throughout this book as we journey through application development.

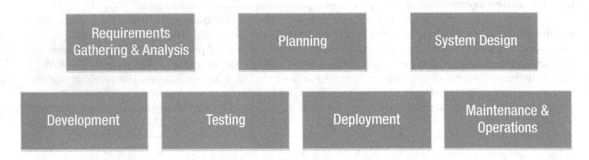

Figure 1-1. *Phases of the software development life cycle*

Requirements Gathering and Analysis

In this phase, we capture all the functional requirements of the software that we are planning to build. We create a brief functional specification document and then share it with all stakeholders.

Planning

During this phase, we start by augmenting staff and creating timelines for the project. Although it's not mandatory, we can organize all functionalities into logical groups and place them in different iterations, or *sprints*. We document the proposed project plan along with critical timelines as part of this phase's deliverables.

System Design

In this phase, we design the entire system's architecture. We have to list all technologies, tools, and commercial off-the-shelf (COTS) products that will be used during application development. The key deliverables of this phase are the specifications for the logical and physical architecture.

Development

The actual coding and development of the software is done during this phase. This phase may follow its own development strategies, such as test-driven development (TDD) or domain-driven development(DDD). In TDD, we write unit tests before developing the application code; so at first, all the unit tests will fail, and then we have to add or refactor application code to pass the unit tests. This is an iterative process that happens every time a new functionality is added or an existing one is modified.

Testing

During this phase, we integrate all the components of the software (for example, a web application might consume web API endpoints that are hosted differently, and these should be integrated as part of the testing phase). Then we test the application. The testing process usually comprises system integration testing (SIT) followed by user acceptance testing (UAT). Testing should be an iterative and ongoing activity that makes the application more stable and robust.

Deployment

Deployment activity includes all the procedures required for hosting the application on staging and production environments. Modern source-version-control systems support automated deployments to configured environments. Having said that, manual monitoring (for example, DEV, SIT, UAT, STAG, and PROD) should occur while promoting builds across various environments.

Maintenance and Operations

After the application is hosted and made available to the audience, unanticipated issues and errors (or even code-level exceptions) may arise, for multiple reasons. Maintenance is the phase when we closely monitor the hosted application for issues and then release hotfixes and patches to fix them. Operational tasks such as software upgrades on servers and backups of databases are performed as part of the maintenance activity.

As this book walks you through the end-to-end development of a web application, it will touch on every phase of application development except testing.

■ **Note**   As mentioned previously, it is not my intention to proclaim that the cited methodologies are the *only* widely accepted options. But the preceding application development phases are the most common and frequently used practices for software projects.

Introduction to the Automobile Service Center Application

In this book, we'll take a near-real-world business requirement and deliver an end-to-end technical solution. I believe that this type of demonstration will help you understand the concepts better because of their practical implementations. The step-by-step process of building the web application will help you remember the concepts you've learned in each chapter.

The Automobile Service Center is a fictitious US company that provides all types of car maintenance services to its customers. This company has more than 20 branches across the West Coast and serves more than 3,000 customers a day. It provides a personalized experience to its end customers in all areas related to car repairs and maintenance.

The Automobile Service Center provides car maintenance services in the following areas: Engine and Tires, Air Conditioning, Auto and Manual Transmissions, Electrical Systems, Batteries, Brakes, and Oil Changes. This Service Center also takes care of specific customer requests and complaints about the cars. At times it provides additional services including towing, pickup and drop, insurance, and financial-related offerings. This Service Center employs more than 1,500 professionals in various capacities. Most employees are service engineers who are responsible for the daily service operations, while other employees take care of responsibilities such as ordering spare parts, managing logistics, and running financial operations.

Today the Automobile Service Center is facing a major business challenge: maintaining good customer communication. The company lacks an affordable and reliable method of real-time communication with customers (for example, live chats between customers and service engineers, or e-mail/text notifications about service updates). A majority of customers want real-time service updates and automated service appointments. Currently, the company requires its customers to walk in to a Service Center branch and discuss the services with an available service engineer, who opens a service job card that documents the details. During the service work, all the communications between the service engineer and the customer occur through phone calls, and the points discussed are attached back to the job card. After the service is done, the customer pays the invoice amount, and the service engineer closes the job card. The Automobile Service Center has identified that this entire process is inefficient and is diminishing its brand value for the following reasons:

- Causes service delays because of a high dependency on the human factor

- Lack of transparency

- Creates opportunities for miscommunication

- Provides no precision in effort and estimations

- Doesn't enable the company to reach out to customers and promote great deals, discounts, and packages

Throughout this book, we'll help the Automobile Service Center overcome these challenges by creating a modern web application designed with cutting-edge technologies. By end of this book, we'll have a fully functional, production-ready web application, as shown in Figure 1-2.

Figure 1-2. Home page of the Automobile Service Center application

Throughout this book, we are going to use the same business use case and enhance the web application step-by-step. Let's get started by defining the scope of the application.

Scope of the Application

Any business challenge—whether it's simple or complex, big or small, mission-critical or optional—cannot be solved unless we have clear understanding of the functional requirements. Identifying the core features of an application is crucial for a successful implementation.

The Automobile Service Center application could have very complex requirements unless we carefully control them by defining their scope. Table 1-1 depicts the requirements of the Automobile Service Center application that are in the scope of this book's demonstration.

Table 1-1. *Scope of Work for Automobile Service Center Application*

Module	Functionality
User Administration	On the application's startup, an Admin user should be provisioned. Admin is a user who has access to the entire application and can manage other users; for example, provisioning service engineers. The Admin user can manage all customer information and the master data of the application.
	The application should be capable of allowing customers to log in by using their social media logins (for example, Gmail). On a user's first successful login, a local user account (specific to this application) should be created for moderation purposes.
	User management activities include customer registration, reminding users of or changing passwords, deactivating users (the Admin user can perform this action), signing out, assigning roles to service engineers and customers at registration.
	The Admin user should be able to provision other employees into the system.
Service Requests Management	The customer should be able to create a new service request. The Admin user should associate the service to a service engineer. Whenever the status of a service request changes, the customer should be notified via e-mail/text.
	Based on the service progress, the Admin user and service engineer can modify the job card details.
	The customer, service engineers, and Admin user should have respective dashboards displaying a summary of all activities and the latest updates.
Service Notifications	The customer, service engineer, and Admin user can view the summary of the job card.
	At any point during servicing, the customer, service engineer, and admin user can have two-way communication about the service progress and queries.
	The customer, service engineer, and Admin user can see the history of the job card (all the changes that have happened since the card's creation).
	The Admin user should be able to review services that are marked as completed by the service engineers.
	Note: Invoices and payment processing are beyond the scope of this book.
Promotions	The Admin user should be able to add details about new promotions and offers. Customers should receive real-time notifications with these details.
	Customers should be able to see all promotions and offers.

■ **Note**   The requirements for this application are limited so that the application remains easy for you to understand. The limited scope of requirements also gives me the liberty to emphasize the technological concepts.

Technologies Used in Building the Application

The fundamental power of the software industry comes from its diverse technical advancements and offerings. During the last few years, the substantial growth of cloud computing and open source communities contributed to a significant number of technical programming languages, frameworks, and platforms. It is always difficult to learn a technology for a particular requirement because that requires a lot of research and comparisons.

Microsoft open sourced its ASP.NET MVC, Web API, and Web Pages frameworks under the Apache 2.0 license. Microsoft also established the .NET Foundation, an independent organization that aims to improve open source software development and collaboration around the .NET Framework. *ASP.NET Core*, the latest release of ASP.NET under the .NET Foundation, is capable of building cross-platform web and cloud solutions.

In this book, we'll use ASP.NET Core (Long Term Support version, 1.0.3) in combination with C# to build our web application for the Automobile Service Center. *Materialize*, an open source CSS framework based on Material Design, is used to create CSS themes for the Automobile Service Center application. JQuery will be used throughout this book to perform the necessary client-side activities. The *SignalR* library will provide real-time, two-way communication between server and clients (browsers, in this case). The OAuth 2.0 protocol is used to enable single sign-on from various external social media identity providers such as Gmail, Twitter, and Facebook.

Microsoft Azure Storage is an enterprise-grade cloud storage service that provides reliable, scalable, and durable data-storage services. In this book, we'll primarily use Azure Table storage to store all application data in NoSQL format. Figure 1-3 shows all the technologies and platforms that we'll use in designing and developing the Automobile Service Center application.

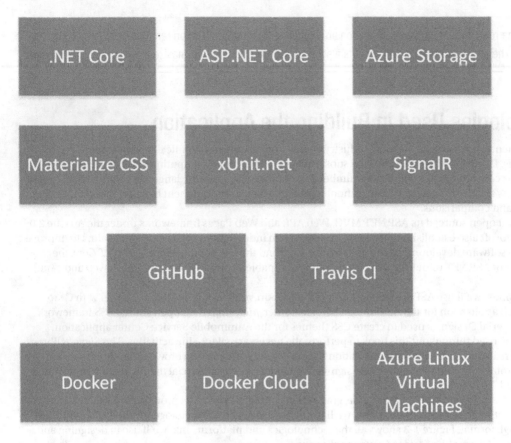

Figure 1-3. Technologies used in building our Automobile Service Center application

The Automobile Service Center application's code is versioned using *GitHub*, a distributed version-control and source-code management platform. To ensure code quality, we use *Travis CI* to build and test the source code from GitHub.

Docker is a container technology used to build software packages that can be deployed in any environment. The Automobile Service Center application is packaged using Docker by continuous integration with GitHub. *Docker Cloud*, which supports continuous deployment to any infrastructure, is used to deploy our web application containers to *Azure Linux Virtual Machines*.

Logical Architecture of the Application

The logical architecture is a design specification that depicts all the logical code components of the application and their interactions. Figure 1-4 illustrates the logical architecture of the Automobile Service Center technical solution.

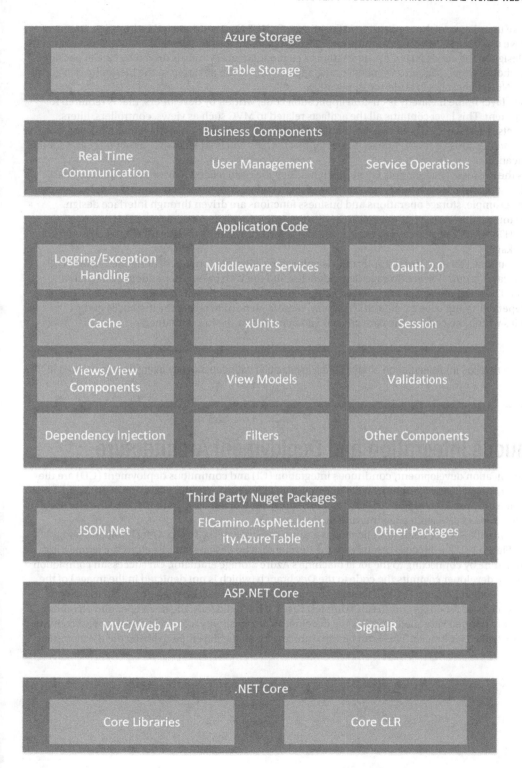

Figure 1-4. *Logical architecture of the Automobile Service Center technical solution*

The base foundation of the application is the Microsoft .NET Core runtime and its libraries. On top of .NET Core, we use the ASP.NET Core framework, which provides all the features related to web development. Microsoft designed the entire .NET Core ecosystem to be modular; everything is driven by NuGet packages, and we can choose which packages we need for the application. So the next step in the hierarchy is to get all the required NuGet packages to build the application.

The next layer in the hierarchy is custom application code, written by developers, that is required for web development. This layer contains all the artifacts related to MVC such as views, controllers, filters, and stylesheets. This layer also holds the key implementations such as session management, logging, and exception handling. This layer also houses the test project, which will hold all the xUnit.net test cases for the entire application.

Next is the Business Components layer, which holds all the code related to business requirements. This layer has a modular design by segregating the relevant code through interfaces into multiple physical projects. For example, storage operations and business functions are driven through interface design.

Azure Storage, the last layer of the hierarchy, is responsible for all data operations. This API is a C# wrapper for HTTP REST service calls to the Azure Storage infrastructure that's provided by Microsoft through a NuGet package.

The Automobile Service Center application is going to be a loosely coupled system; the Business Components layer requires Azure Storage dependencies, and the Web layer is dependent on business components. These dependencies are injected using dependency injection at runtime (ASP.NET Core supports dependency injection by default). This way, there is no need to create the instances of the dependencies within the code, as they are created and managed by the IoC containers.

■ **Note**   The detailed implementation steps of each layer, along with dependency injection, are covered in Chapter 2.

Continuous Integration and Deployment Architecture

In today's application development, continuous integration (CI) and continuous deployment (CD) are the key DevOps practices. These operations will prevent manual effort and repetitive tasks on every build, and thereby reduce the possibility of human error, improve the quality of the build, and increase the efficiency of the overall life cycle of developing, testing, and deploying.

The Automobile Service Center application is going to use the latest CI and CD technologies and tools, as shown in Figure 1-5. The process begins with the developer, who designs and develops the application on a local machine by connecting to the local machine's Azure Storage emulator. On successful completion of a feature, the developer commits the code to the Dev branch (which is not depicted in the image) of the GitHub source-code repository. On a successful commit, the Travis CI service triggers a build to validate the entire source code for errors and to run xUnit test cases. If the build fails, the developer and all other stakeholders are notified via e-mail, and it is the developer's responsibility to correct the error and commit the code back to the Dev branch. This is an iterative process for all the developers during the development phase.

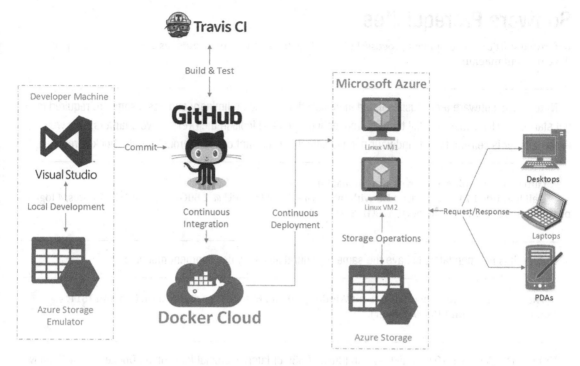

Figure 1-5. *Continuous integration and deployment architecture*

At a given logical time, when we decide to roll out the completed features to production servers, the Dev branch will be merged with the master branch. The Travis CI service builds again kicks off on master branch and validates the build. The same iterative process continues on the master branch as well.

■ **Note** The concepts described in this book are one way to achieve CI and CD. There are many ways to achieve CI and CD using different technologies. I advise developers to do thorough research and analysis of the contemporary CI and CD technologies and tools and to check their relevance in a project context before implementing these mission-critical strategies.

Deployments to production servers are triggered from the master branch. In this book, we use Docker technology to create application containers and deploy them to Azure Linux Virtual Machines. Whenever a merge or commit happens at the master branch at GitHub, Docker Cloud will take the latest source code, build a Docker image, create a Docker container, and finally push the container to the associated Azure Virtual Machine nodes.

■ **Note** The implementation details of CI and CD processes for an ASP.NET Core application are described in a later chapter.

Software Prerequisites

Before we start the development process, let's check all the software prerequisites and quickly set up the development machine.

■ **Note** The software prerequisites listed in this section are the preliminary and basic software required to get started. I will discuss in detail the required technologies and tools in their respective chapters. This way, every chapter is self-contained, and your need to search for relevant content throughout the book is reduced.

I am using the following development machine:

Dell Latitude E7450 x64-based PC with Intel Core i7-5600U CPU @ 2.60GHz, 2594MHz, 2 cores, 4 logical processors, 8GB physical memory, 476GB SSD hard drive.

■ **Note** It is not mandatory to have the same configuration as my development machine.

The operating system should be 64-bit Windows 10 Pro, Enterprise or Education (version 1511, November update, Build 10586 or later).

■ **Note** The Windows 10 OS Build version (Build 10586 or later) is crucial for running Docker on the Windows platform. One more important point is that Windows 10 Virtual Machine on Azure can't be used for Docker development because it doesn't support nested virtualization (at the time of writing this chapter).

Download and install Visual Studio Community 2017 from `www.visualstudio.com`. I am using the 15.1 (26403.7) release.

We need to install the following Visual Studio workloads: ASP.NET Web Development, Azure Development, and .NET Core Cross-Platform Development.

■ **Note** It is always advisable to sign into Visual Studio. Signing in will always sync your Visual Studio settings to your Microsoft account, and these settings can be retrieved later on any other machine by signing in with the same account. Starting from Visual Studio 2017, the new Roaming Extension Manager will keep track of all your favorite extensions across all development environments and sync them with Visual Studio sign-in.

We also need to have the following accounts created:

- GitHub (`https://github.com/`)

- Travis CI (`https://travis-ci.org/`): Associate Travis CI with GitHub by signing in with GitHub credentials.

- Docker (`www.docker.com`)

- Microsoft Azure Subscription (`https://azure.microsoft.com/`): Create a free Azure Account.

Other tools are required for development, including Docker for Windows, the latest .NET Core SDK, and the Azure Storage emulator. The details of these tools and SDKs are discussed in corresponding chapters.

Summary

In this chapter, you learned about the importance of, and paradigm shift toward, open source communities and cloud platforms in developing modern software applications. You also learned about the major software development strategies and procedures. Regardless of which software methodology we use, the basic processes remain the same, with a little tweak in implementation.

You were introduced to the business requirements of the fictitious Automobile Service Center. We defined the scope of the development work for the rest of the book.

You briefly looked at the technical stack—the combination of ASP.NET Core, SignalR, Azure Storage, GitHub, Travis CI, and Docker—which we are going to use to develop the application. We designed the logical architecture and CI/CD pipeline of the application. Finally, the chapter concluded with the details of the required environment and software prerequisites.

CHAPTER 2

■ ■ ■

The New Era of .NET Core

Over the last decade, the open source development model gained significant adoption and tremendous growth because of its ability to change and improve software products by making them available under a free license to the general public. The process of ideation and innovation in software development is at its peak because people around the world have been able to collaborate and create new products from open source code.

Microsoft's move toward the open source world started two years ago. Its strong commitment to the open source community was demonstrated by joining the Linux Foundation at the end of 2016. Microsoft's efforts— in adapting Linux on Azure Platform, running Bash on Windows, making the developer IDEs such as Visual Studio and VS Code available on various OSs, and enabling compatibility with SQL Server on Linux—made an extraordinary impact on open source communities and provided opportunities to create modern-day frameworks and tools. By far, Microsoft's decision to open source its .NET Framework was a game changer in the software industry, and .NET Core is the kickstarter of its open source journey.

In this chapter, you will learn the key features of .NET Core and ASP.NET Core, especially the advantages these frameworks offer compared to their predecessors. We will create an ASP.NET Core project that will serve as the baseline version of the Automobile Service Center application. You will learn the important project artifacts. You'll also see how to set up the configuration of the Automobile Service Center web project through the `Appsettings.json` file. Finally, we will conclude this chapter by exploring the new dependency injection system provided by the ASP.NET Core framework.

Introduction to .NET Core

.NET Core is an open source development platform maintained by Microsoft and the .NET community at GitHub under the .NET Foundation. (The .NET Foundation is an independent organization that supports open source development and collaboration around the .NET ecosystem.)

.NET Core possesses the following primary features:

- *Cross-platform*: Runs on Windows, macOS, and Linux. If the application's requirement is to run across multiple platforms, .NET Core is the obvious choice among Microsoft frameworks.

- *Compatible*: .NET Core is compatible with .NET Framework, Xamarin, and Mono, via the .NET Standard library.

- *Open source*: The .NET Core platform is open source under MIT and Apache 2 licenses.

- *Modular design*: In .NET Core, everything is a package. Unlike getting everything, even when it's not required for an application, we get only the required packages. All package dependencies can be retrieved from NuGet.

© Rami Vemula 2017

R. Vemula, *Real-Time Web Application Development*, https://doi.org/10.1007/978-1-4842-3270-5_2

- *Command-line-style development*: .NET Core is designed for the command-line interface (CLI). It provides command-line tools available on all supported platforms, enabling developers to build and test applications with a minimal installation on developer and production machines.

- *Container support*: .NET Core by default provides support to container technologies such as Docker.

- *Performance*: .NET Core is designed to deliver optimistic performance and high scalability for an application.

- *Microservices-oriented design*: .NET Core is built to support microservices and can easily get along with other microservices built using .NET Framework or Java, for example.

- *Side-by-side support to other .NET versions at an application level*: .NET Core supports easy, side-by-side installation of different versions on the same machine. This allows us to run multiple services on the same server, targeting different versions of .NET Core.

- *Microsoft support*: .NET Core is supported by Microsoft.

■ **Note**   Organizations should perform careful research and analysis before opting for .NET Core over .NET Framework.

As of now, .NET Core is a subset of .NET Framework, and not all the .NET Framework APIs are ported to .NET CoreFX libraries.

.NET Core doesn't support all the workloads, such as ASP.NET Web Forms or WPF.

.NET Core is relatively new, and most of the third-party NuGet packages and platforms don't support .NET Core yet.

Figure 2-1 shows the .NET ecosystem.

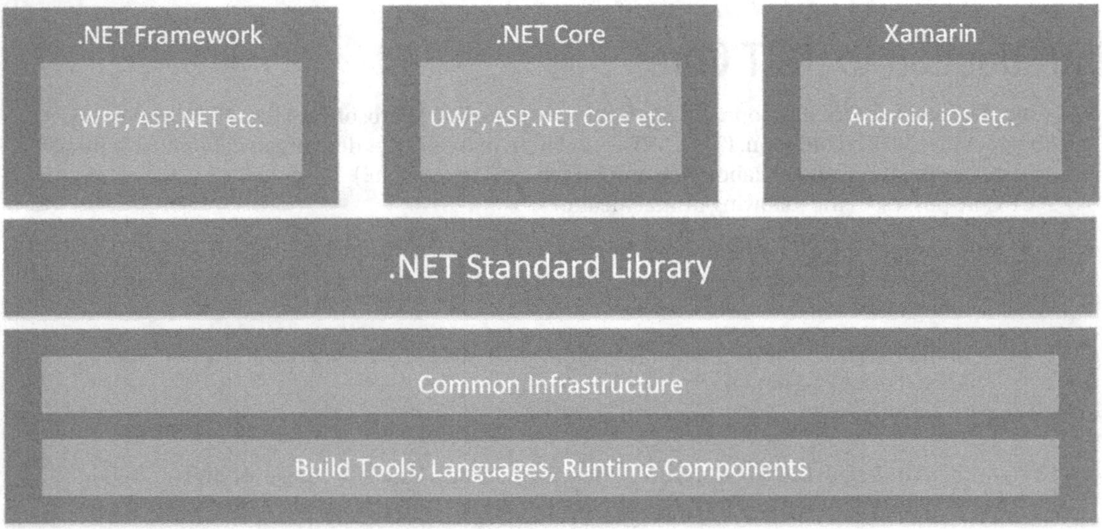

.NET Framework	.NET Core	Xamarin
WPF, ASP.NET etc.	UWP, ASP.NET Core etc.	Android, iOS etc.

.NET Standard Library

Common Infrastructure

Build Tools, Languages, Runtime Components

Figure 2-1.   *.NET ecosystem architecture*

In this architecture diagram, the bottom layer corresponds to languages and their compilers, runtime components (for example, JIT and garbage collectors), and build and CLI tools required to build any .NET application.

On top of that layer, we have the .NET Standard library, which is a specification of .NET APIs that make up a uniform set of contracts with underlying implementations for each .NET runtime. Typically, in a traditional .NET system, this layer constitutes most of the APIs from `mscorlib.dll`. If application code targets a version of.NET Standard, that application is guaranteed to run on any .NET runtime that implements that version.

The top layer consists of various runtimes of the .NET ecosystem (for example, .NET Core, .NET Framework, and Mono for Xamarin). The .NET Core runtime supports ASP.NET Core and Universal Windows Platform workloads. Similarly, the traditional .NET Framework runtime supports ASP.NET, WPF, and Windows Forms. The Mono runtime is used by Xamarin to build cross-platform mobile applications for Android and iOS platforms.

Introduction to ASP.NET Core

ASP.NET Core is a new, open source, cross-platform framework for building modern web applications. It is designed from the ground up to empower applications for the Web, IoT, cloud, and mobile services. As depicted in Figure 2-2, the other major advantage of an ASP.NET Core application is its ability to run on either .NET Core or the full .NET Framework. ASP.NET Core uses a modular design and is driven through NuGet packages, so rather than housing all the unwanted references, we need to get only the packages that are required for our application.

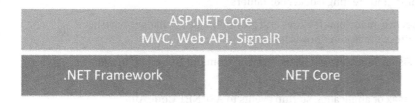

Figure 2-2. *Compatibility of ASP.NET Core with .NET Framework and .NET Core*

ASP.NET Core provides the following foundational improvements and capabilities when compared with the traditional .NET Framework–based ASP.NET Framework:

- *Open source*: ASP.NET Core is open source under the Apache 2 license.

- *Cross-platform support*: ASP.NET Core applications can be developed and run on Windows, macOS, and Linux.

- *Unified MVC and Web API approach*: In ASP.NET Core, both the MVC and Web APIs are driven with unified object model. A single namespace serves both the MVC and Web APIs, which removes confusion from older versions of ASP.NET.

- *Lightweight HTTP request pipeline*: Compared to previous versions of ASP.NET, most of the unwanted overhead has been removed from ASP.NET Core, resulting in a lightweight HTTP pipeline. We can construct the HTTP pipeline by using the default framework provided by middleware or through custom-developed middleware.

- *Modular design*: Starting with ASP.NET Core, there is no need to manage any unwanted packages or references in the project (there is no System.Web.dll). We need to get only those references that we want for the application. In fact, ASP.NET Core itself is a NuGet package.

- *Integration with client-side frameworks*: ASP.NET Core applications can easily integrate with client-side frameworks such as AngularJS, KnockoutJS, Gulp, Grunt, and Bower.

- *Improved performance*: ASP.NET Core's modular design and lightweight HTTP pipeline offer tremendous performance.

- *Dependency injection*: ASP.NET Core by default supports dependency injection.

- *Cloud-ready solutions*: ASP.NET Core solutions are optimized for cloud compatibility through an easy configuration system.

- *Runs on both .NET Framework and .NET Core*: ASP.NET Core applications can run on both .NET Framework and .NET Core runtimes. We have the flexibility of using traditional .NET Framework APIs that are not yet available in .NET Core. If the application is targeted for .NET Core runtime, it can support all the .NET Core versions available on the server.

- *Hosting*: Easy to self-host the ASP.NET Core application. It also supports IIS hosting.

- *Tooling*: ASP.NET Core applications can be built using Visual Studio Code, the Visual Studio IDE, or the .NET Core CLI. This new tooling enhances developer productivity in building, publishing, and creating Docker containers.

From a development perspective, many new features and groundbreaking changes have been introduced in ASP.NET Core. Some of the features are as follows.

- The ASP.NET Core Visual Studio project file is a rewrite from the ground up in a new format.

- There is no Global.asax or application startup events in ASP.NET Core. All configuration and streamlining of the HTTP pipeline is done at the Startup.cs class.

- Writing custom middleware is very easy in ASP.NET Core applications.

- The ASP.NET Core application is a pure console application. It has an application main entry point at the Program.cs file.

- ASP.NET Core uses a Kestrel server designed specifically for ASP.NET Core.

- The static content (such as JavaScript, stylesheets, and images) are now placed under the wwwroot folder of the application in ASP.NET Core.

- Bundling and minification is achieved through the bundleconfig.json file.

- The Roslyn compiler is used for in-memory compilation.

- Tag helpers and view components promote more robust, reusable, server-side HTML generation.

- Default support is provided for dependency injection, which can manage various object lifetime scopes.

- Attribute-based routing supports new controller and action tokens.

- Configuration based on `Appsettings.json`.

- New `_ViewImports.cshtml` file, which can be a common place for all namespaces across different views.

- New filter types and much better control on filter execution.

- Creating and managing unit tests is much easier.

- New way to manage secure information on development machine using user secrets.

- Better support for different caching providers.

- Data access using Entity Framework Core.

- Configuring authentication and authorization is easy using ASP.NET Core Identity.

- New improvement to internationalization, logging, and exception handling.

■ **Note**   We cover most of these ASP.NET Core features in subsequent chapters.

Versions and Roadmap of .NET Core and ASP.NET Core

The development of .NET Core and ASP.NET Core is happening at a rigorous pace. There are many reasons for this fast-paced development; because .NET Core is a relatively new market offering, a lot of effort is going toward stabilizing the framework and adding new features and APIs. At the same time, .NET Core is open source and has to extend its footprint to multiple OS distributions.

■ **Note**   My primary goal in writing this section is to help you understand the rapid cadence of .NET Core and familiarize you with the direction of its future releases. The complete release history of .NET Core, along with release notes, can be found at `https://github.com/dotnet/core/blob/master/release-notes/README.md`.

.NET Core has three major versions: 1.0., 1.1, and 2.0. The primary difference between .NET Core 1.0 and .NET Core 1.1 is the support for new operating system distributions and a new set of APIs added with the new .NET Standard. Both versions of .NET Core support side-by-side installation and adoption. .NET Core 2.0 targets .NET Standard 2.0, which has an extensive 32,000+ APIs. .NET Core 2 introduces a new development model to develop pages using Razor, which removes the dependency on ASP.NET controllers. There are lot of other performance improvements in .NET Core 2.0.

The rapid cadence in releasing new versions of .NET Core not only gave developers the flexibility of a new set of APIs, but also made them go through a roller coaster ride for the following reasons:

- The initial releases of .NET Core don't cover the exhaustive list of .NET Framework APIs.

- VS tooling is not fully feature rich, compared to regular .NET Framework development.

- Major changes occurred in the .NET project system, such as moving away from a Project.json-based approach to a csproj-based approach.

- Different versions of .NET Core support different OS distributions.

Similar to .NET Core, ASP.NET Core versions significantly improved over time. The following are some of the major changes in ASP.NET Core 2.0:

- Support for NET Standard 2.0.

- Microsoft.AspNetCore.All meta package, which will house all the packages required to build an ASP.NET Core application.

- Support for .NET Core 2.0 Runtime Store and automatic Razor view precompilation during publish.

- Performance improvements to the Kestrel server.

- New improvements to ASP.NET Core Identity.

- Enhancements to configuration, caching, Razor, diagnostics, and logging.

Developers should watch out for GitHub repositories of both .NET Core and ASP.NET Core for new changes and should plan development strategies in advance. One way to plan things for upcoming releases is to become familiar with the daily builds of the .NET Core SDK (which gives the latest up-to-date .NET Core runtime) and MyGet packages (which are, again, daily builds of packages, and NuGet houses stable versions) and do proof-of-concepts in order to understand what is coming in subsequent releases.

■ **Note**   Every developer should be aware that working with daily builds might result in unexpected behavior of an application. Bottlenecks can occur from VS tooling or the .NET Core CLI. Sporadic behavior could occur in the development environment, which might require uninstalling and reinstalling stable SDK versions and VS tooling.

Having said ups and downs, the recent releases of both .NET Core and ASP.NET Core are very stable, support numerous OS distributions, and offer an exhaustive set of APIs. The current releases were supported with great tooling from Visual Studio 2017 and the .NET Core CLI.

Creating the Automobile Service Center Application

In this section, we'll create an ASP.NET Core web application that will be used as the base solution for our Automobile Service Center application.

To get started with an ASP.NET Core application, we need the .NET Core SDK installed on a local machine.

By default, the .NET Core SDK will be installed with VS 2017. We can check the .NET Core SDK version as shown in Figure 2-3.

```
dotnet --version
```

■ Command Prompt

```
C:\>dotnet --version
1.0.3

C:\>
```

Figure 2-3. *dotnet version*

■ **Note** New versions of the .NET Core SDK will be released on a regular basis. Install the new version by downloading it from www.microsoft.com/net/download/core. Download the x64 version of Windows Installer as shown in Figure 2-4.

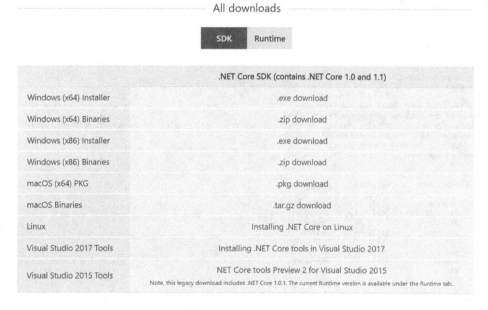

All downloads

| | SDK | Runtime |

	.NET Core SDK (contains .NET Core 1.0 and 1.1)
Windows (x64) Installer	.exe download
Windows (x64) Binaries	.zip download
Windows (x86) Installer	.exe download
Windows (x86) Binaries	.zip download
macOS (x64) PKG	.pkg download
macOS Binaries	.tar.gz download
Linux	Installing .NET Core on Linux
Visual Studio 2017 Tools	Installing .NET Core tools in Visual Studio 2017
Visual Studio 2015 Tools	NET Core tools Preview 2 for Visual Studio 2015 Note, this legacy download includes .NET Core 1.0.1. The current Runtime version is available under the Runtime tab.

Figure 2-4. *.NET Core downloads (at the time of writing)*

Examine the sample usage of the dotnet new command shown in Figures 2-5 and 2-6.

```
dotnet new --help
```

■ **Note** The initial run will populate the local package cache to improve performance.

```
c:\>dotnet new --help

Welcome to .NET Core!
---------------------
Learn more about .NET Core @ https://aka.ms/dotnet-docs. Use dotnet --help to see available commands or go to https://ak
a.ms/dotnet-cli-docs.

Telemetry
---------------
The .NET Core tools collect usage data in order to improve your experience. The data is anonymous and does not include c
ommand-line arguments. The data is collected by Microsoft and shared with the community.
You can opt out of telemetry by setting a DOTNET_CLI_TELEMETRY_OPTOUT environment variable to 1 using your favorite shel
l.
You can read more about .NET Core tools telemetry @ https://aka.ms/dotnet-cli-telemetry.

Configuring...
---------------------
A command is running to initially populate your local package cache, to improve restore speed and enable offline access.
 This command will take up to a minute to complete and will only happen once.
Decompressing 100% 8455 ms
Expanding 100% 83285 ms
Getting ready...
Template Instantiation Commands for .NET Core CLI.

Usage: dotnet new [arguments] [options]
```

Figure 2-5. *dotnet new command usage*

```
Usage: dotnet new [arguments] [options]

Arguments:
  template  The template to instantiate.

Options:
  -l|--list          List templates containing the specified name.
  -lang|--language   Specifies the language of the template to create
  -n|--name          The name for the output being created. If no name is specified, the name of the current directory is used.
  -o|--output        Location to place the generated output.
  -h|--help          Displays help for this command.
  -all|--show-all    Shows all templates

Templates                Short Name    Language    Tags
----------------------------------------------------------------------
Console Application      console       [C#], F#    Common/Console
Class library            classlib      [C#], F#    Common/Library
Unit Test Project        mstest        [C#], F#    Test/MSTest
xUnit Test Project       xunit         [C#], F#    Test/xUnit
ASP.NET Core Empty       web           [C#]        Web/Empty
ASP.NET Core Web App     mvc           [C#], F#    Web/MVC
ASP.NET Core Web API     webapi        [C#]        Web/WebAPI
Solution File            sln                       Solution

Examples:
    dotnet new mvc --auth None --framework netcoreapp1.1
    dotnet new classlib
    dotnet new --help

c:\>_
```

Figure 2-6. *dotnet new command usage*

Open VS 2017. Create a new solution with the name ASC.Solution, as shown in Figure 2-7.

Figure 2-7. *New Visual Studio solution*

Create a new ASP.NET Core Web Application Project with the name ASC.Web in the solution we created (right-click the solution and select Add New Project, as shown in Figure 2-8).

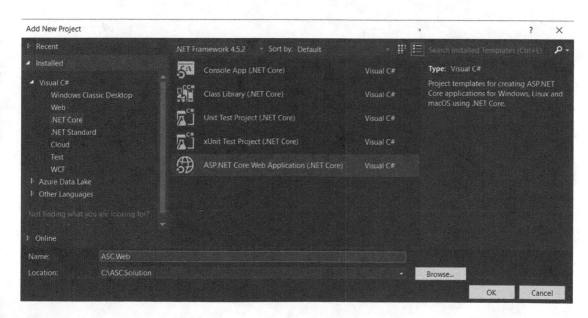

Figure 2-8. *New ASP.NET Core project in Visual Studio*

Click OK. A pop-up, shown in Figure 2-9, appears to allow the user to select the version of the ASP. NET Core framework and web template. Make sure to select ASP.NET Core 1.1 as the framework and Web Application template.

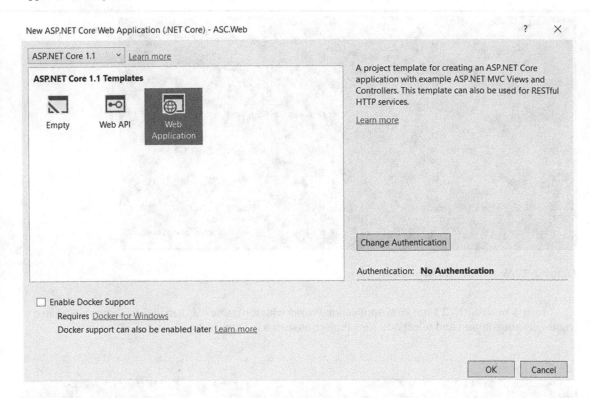

Figure 2-9. *ASP.NET Core framework version and template*

Click the Change Authentication button to access the Change Authentication dialog box. Change the Authentication mode from none to individual user accounts, as shown in Figure 2-10. Then click OK.

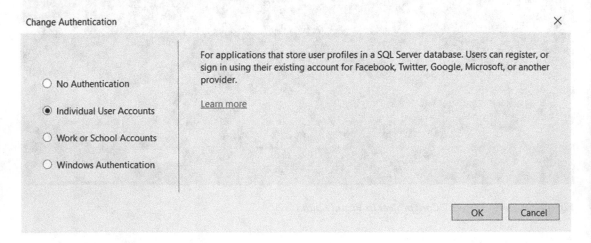

Figure 2-10. *Change authentication for the ASP.NET Core project*

After making sure all the settings are correct, click OK, and VS 2017 will create the web project that is shown in Figure 2-11.

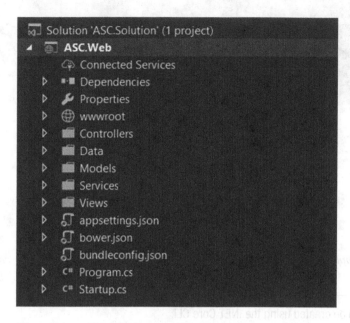

Figure 2-11. *ASP.NET Core project*

To run the web application, click IIS Express from the VS 2017 standard menu, as shown in Figure 2-12.

Figure 2-12. *Debug an ASP.NET Core project*

The application will be executed and opens in the default browser, as shown in Figure 2-13.

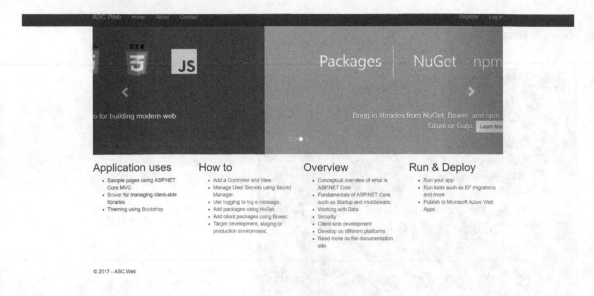

Figure 2-13. *Index page of ASP.NET Core application running from VS*

■ **Note**   A web application project can also be created using the .NET Core CLI.

To create a project by using the .NET Core CLI, we need to execute the following commands in order (make sure to run CMD as Administrator):

```
mkdir ASC.Solution
cd ASC.Solution
dotnet new sln --name ASC.Solution
dotnet new mvc --name ASC.Web --framework netcoreapp1.1 --auth Individual
dotnet sln add ASC.Web\ASC.Web.csproj
```

Here we create a directory and set it as the working directory for the command-line prompt. Using the .NET Core CLI, we then create a blank solution and an ASP.NET Core Web project with the MVC template, ASP.NET Core 1.1 framework, and authentication mode set to Individual. Finally, add the web project to the solution file, as shown in Figure 2-14.

```
c:\>mkdir ASC.Solution

c:\>cd ASC.Solution

c:\ASC.Solution>dotnet new sln --name ASC.Solution
Content generation time: 25.6502 ms
The template "Solution File" created successfully.

c:\ASC.Solution>dotnet new mvc --name ASC.Web --framework netcoreapp1.1 --auth Individual
Content generation time: 1237.3394 ms
The template "ASP.NET Core Web App" created successfully.

c:\ASC.Solution>dotnet sln add ASC.Web\ASC.Web.csproj
Project `ASC.Web\ASC.Web.csproj` added to the solution.

c:\ASC.Solution>▄
```

Figure 2-14. *Creating the ASP.NET Core project using the .NET Core CLI*

To run the application, we need to execute the following commands:

```
cd ASC.Web
dotnet restore
dotnet build
dotnet run
```

First we need to restore all the dependencies from nuget.org; this is a one-time activity that is required to resolve all dependencies. Then we build the application to make sure there are no errors. Finally, we run the application as shown in Figure 2-15.

```
C:\ASC.Solution>cd ASC.Web

C:\ASC.Solution\ASC.Web>dotnet restore
  Restoring packages for C:\ASC.Solution\ASC.Web\ASC.Web.csproj...
  Restoring packages for C:\ASC.Solution\ASC.Web\ASC.Web.csproj...
  Restore completed in 931.55 ms for C:\ASC.Solution\ASC.Web\ASC.Web.csproj.
  Restoring packages for C:\ASC.Solution\ASC.Web\ASC.Web.csproj...
  Restore completed in 757.47 ms for C:\ASC.Solution\ASC.Web\ASC.Web.csproj.
  Restoring packages for C:\ASC.Solution\ASC.Web\ASC.Web.csproj...
  Lock file has not changed. Skipping lock file write. Path: C:\ASC.Solution\ASC.Web\obj\project.assets.json
  Restore completed in 1.73 sec for C:\ASC.Solution\ASC.Web\ASC.Web.csproj.
  Restore completed in 773.81 ms for C:\ASC.Solution\ASC.Web\ASC.Web.csproj.

  NuGet Config files used:
      C:\Users\itsadmin\AppData\Roaming\NuGet\NuGet.Config
      C:\Program Files (x86)\NuGet\Config\Microsoft.VisualStudio.Offline.config

  Feeds used:
      https://api.nuget.org/v3/index.json
      C:\Program Files (x86)\Microsoft SDKs\NuGetPackages\

C:\ASC.Solution\ASC.Web>dotnet build
Microsoft (R) Build Engine version 15.1.548.43366
Copyright (C) Microsoft Corporation. All rights reserved.

  ASC.Web -> C:\ASC.Solution\ASC.Web\bin\Debug\netcoreapp1.1\ASC.Web.dll

Build succeeded.
    0 Warning(s)
    0 Error(s)

Time Elapsed 00:00:02.17

C:\ASC.Solution\ASC.Web>dotnet run
Hosting environment: Production
Content root path: C:\ASC.Solution\ASC.Web
Now listening on: http://localhost:5000
Application started. Press Ctrl+C to shut down.
```

Figure 2-15. *Restore, build, and run an ASP.NET Core application*

Navigate to http://localhost:5000 and you should see our application up and running.

■ **Note** By default, the .NET Core CLI always runs the application at port 5000. To change the default port, follow the tutorial at www.intstrings.com/ramivemula/articles/jumpstart-40-change-default-5000-port-of-dotnet-run-command/.

Understanding the ASP.NET Core Web Project Artifacts

The .NET Core project system is a rewrite compared to previous versions of .NET Framework. In the new .NET Core project system and especially in the ASP.NET Core project, we have a lot of new files (such as bundleconfig.json and Program.cs) that were added and old files (such as Global.asax) that were removed. In this section, we will demystify the project structure of ASP.NET Core web applications so you can understand the importance and relevance of each artifact.

Dependencies

The Dependencies node displays all the dependencies of the project. These dependencies are categorized into client-side Bower dependencies, NuGet package dependencies, and the actual .NET Core framework. All the dependencies will be restored initially when the project is created and loaded for the first time. Whenever the csproj file changes, dependencies will be restored automatically.

Properties and launchSettings.json

This node holds the profiles that are used to launch the project. Typically, for a web project, we have executable profiles based on IIS Express and the .NET Core CLI. The Properties node can be used to maintain web server settings such as Enable Authentication. Project-specific environment variables can be set by double-clicking the Properties node. Any changes to project settings will be saved to the launchSettings.json file.

wwwroot

The wwwroot folder contains all static files of the project. These include HTML, image, JavaScript, and CSS files. These files will be served to the user directly. Custom JQuery files will go into the js folder, and all JQuery library files will go into the lib folder.

Controllers

The Controllers folder will hold all the MVC/Web API controllers in the ASP.NET Core project. It is the same as a traditional ASP.NET MVC 4 project.

Data

The Data folder will hold all the code files related to the Entity Framework Database Context and migrations.

■ **Note**   As Individual Authentication mode is used while creating the project, the Data folder was created with the required ASP.NET Core Identity tables and migrations. During the course of this book, we are going to change the implementation to Azure Table Storage.

Models

All the web application View models are placed in this folder. A View model is typically used by the view for displaying data and submitting it.

Services

By default, all the custom interfaces and business logic will be created in this folder.

■ **Note** We will not use the Services folder to hold business logic. Instead, separate class libraries will be created for business and data storage operations.

Views

The Views folder holds all the cshtml files. It follows the same convention as does the traditional ASP.NET MVC 4 project, by placing views corresponding to a controller under the same folder with the controller name. Also, this folder holds shared views (such as partials) in the Shared folder. This folder contains a new file called _ViewImports.cshtml, which serves as a common place to add all namespaces that are used by all views, along with tag helpers. This folder contains _ViewStart.cshtml, which is used to execute the common view code at the start of each view's rendering.

appsettings.json

This file can be used to store configuration key/value pairs (just like appsettings in the web.config file of traditional ASP.NET projects) for the project. This file is also used to hold connection strings, log settings, and so forth.

bower.json

Client-side asset files (for example, JavaScript, stylesheets, images, and HTML) are managed through bower.json. By default, Bootstrap and JQuery files are loaded. The .bowerrc file holds the location (typically, wwwroot/lib) where Bower needs to save the downloaded packages.

bundleconfig.json

This file is used for the bundling and minification of JQuery and CSS files. In this file, we specify different input files and a corresponding output file. We need to refer to the BundlerMinifier.Core NuGet package and use dotnet bundle to trigger the bundle and minification operation.

Program.cs

Program.cs is the starting point of an ASP.NET Core web application. It contains the program entry point Static Void Main(), making the ASP.NET Core web application a truly console application. The ASP.NET Core application requires a host to start the application and manage the application's lifetime. Program.cs creates a new instance of WebHostBuilder, which is used to configure and launch the host. A Kestrel server is used to host the application. Finally, WebHostBuilder's Build method is called to create the host, and then the Run method is used to start it.

Startup.cs

Startup.cs configures the environment for the ASP.NET Core web application. In its constructor, it configures the configuration of the application. In its ConfigureServices method, framework services (for example, EF, MVC, and authentication) and custom services (business specific) will be added and resolved using dependency injection. One more method, Configure, is used to build the ASP.NET HTTP pipeline with middleware.

As we continue our journey of building a web application for the Automobile Service Center, we will explore more artifacts and new concepts of different .NET Core project types. We will also customize and modify most of the default artifacts to serve the Automobile Service Center application's business requirements.

Setting Up the Application Configuration

Before we deep-dive into the Automobile Service Center web application design and development, you need to understand some important concepts related to the ASP.NET Core web project. This way, you will get used to the new .NET Core project system and gain confidence in application development.

A configuration system is one of the important changes in the ASP.NET Core project. In previous versions of ASP.NET, web.config was primarily used to hold configurations in its appsettings section. In the new ASP.NET Core system, appsettings.json is used to hold the configurable values. Appsettings.json is a lightweight configuration file that stores all settings in JSON format; just as in web.config, we can have different configuration files for different environments. Accessing this configuration data can be done through the Options pattern, and ASP.NET Core provides default middleware to achieve this functionality.

■ **Note** In previous versions of ASP.NET, web.config supported transformations to different environments and build configurations. Similarly, in ASP.NET Core, we will have different JSON files for different environments and builds.

Listing 2-1 is the default appsettings.json file created by ASP.NET Core.

Listing 2-1. Default appsettings.json File

```
{
  "ConnectionStrings": {
    "DefaultConnection": "Default connection string"
  },
  "Logging": {
    "IncludeScopes": false,
    "LogLevel": {
      "Default": "Warning"
    }
  }
}
```

Update the appsettings.json file as shown in Listing 2-2.

Listing 2-2. Add a New JSON Setting to appsettings.json

```
{
  "AppSettings": {
    "ApplicationTitle" : "Automobile Service Center Application"
  },
  "ConnectionStrings": {
    "DefaultConnection": "Default connection string"
  },
```

```
  "Logging": {
    "IncludeScopes": false,
    "LogLevel": {
      "Default": "Warning"
    }
  }
}
```

To use the configuration settings, we have to make sure that the appsettings.json file is loaded to Configuration Builder, which is used to build the configuration of key/value-based settings. Go to the Startup.cs file, and make sure we have the lines in Listing 2-3 to load and run the Configuration Builder.

Listing 2-3. Load the appsettings.json File by Using the Configuration Builder

```
public Startup(IHostingEnvironment env)
    {
        var builder = new ConfigurationBuilder()
            .SetBasePath(env.ContentRootPath)
            .AddJsonFile("appsettings.json", optional: false, reloadOnChange: true)
            .AddJsonFile($"appsettings.{env.EnvironmentName}.json", optional: true);

        if (env.IsDevelopment())
        {
            builder.AddUserSecrets<Startup>();
        }

        builder.AddEnvironmentVariables();
        Configuration = builder.Build();
    }

    public IConfigurationRoot Configuration { get; }
```

We can get all the configuration settings in the form of strongly typed objects. Create a Configuration folder in the web project and place the ApplicationSettings class to hold the configuration values (Listing 2-4).

Listing 2-4. ApplicationSettings Class

```
namespace ASC.Web.Configuration
{
    public class ApplicationSettings
    {
        public string ApplicationTitle { get; set; }
    }
}
```

■ **Note**   Whereever we are planning to use the ApplicationSettings class, we have to resolve the dependency for ASC.Web.Configuration.

Now to make the instance of the ApplicationSettings class to hold the actual configuration values, we need to inject IOptions (basically, the Options pattern injected to every controller, view, and so forth) and configure the ApplicationSettings instance to hold the value from the AppSettings section of appsettings.json. Modify the ConfigureServices method of the Startup class as shown in Listing 2-5.

Listing 2-5. Configure Dependency Injection for IOptions Pattern

```
public void ConfigureServices(IServiceCollection services)
    {
        // Add framework services.
        services.AddDbContext<ApplicationDbContext>(options =>
        options.UseSqlServer(Configuration.GetConnectionString("DefaultConnection")));

        services.AddIdentity<ApplicationUser, IdentityRole>()
            .AddEntityFrameworkStores<ApplicationDbContext>()
            .AddDefaultTokenProviders();

        services.AddMvc();

        services.AddOptions();
        services.Configure<ApplicationSettings>(Configuration.GetSection("AppSettings"));

        // Add application services.
        services.AddTransient<IEmailSender, AuthMessageSender>();
        services.AddTransient<ISmsSender, AuthMessageSender>();
    }
```

To use the configuration in a view, inject the IOptions<ApplicationSettings> into the view as described in Listing 2-6. We will modify _Layout.cshtml to display the Automobile Service Center application name in navigation.

Listing 2-6. Inject IOptions<ApplicationSettings> into a View

```
@using Microsoft.Extensions.Options;
@using ASC.Web.Configuration;
@inject IOptions<ApplicationSettings> _configurationSettings
<!DOCTYPE html>
<html>
<head>
```

As shown in Listing 2-7, make the highlighted change in the Nav bar.

Listing 2-7. Updated Nav Bar

```
<nav class="navbar navbar-inverse navbar-fixed-top">
    <div class="container">
        <div class="navbar-header">
            <button type="button" class="navbar-toggle" data-toggle="collapse"
            data-target=".navbar-collapse">
                <span class="sr-only">Toggle navigation</span>
                <span class="icon-bar"></span>
                <span class="icon-bar"></span>
```

```
                    <span class="icon-bar"></span>
                </button>
                <a asp-area="" asp-controller="Home" asp-action="Index" class="navbar-brand">
                    @_configurationSettings.Value.ApplicationTitle
                </a>
            </div>
            <div class="navbar-collapse collapse">
                <ul class="nav navbar-nav">
                    <li><a asp-area="" asp-controller="Home" asp-action="Index">Home</a></li>
                    <li><a asp-area="" asp-controller="Home" asp-action="About">About</a></li>
                    <li><a asp-area="" asp-controller="Home" asp-action="Contact">Contact</a></li>
                </ul>
                @await Html.PartialAsync("_LoginPartial")
            </div>
        </div>
    </nav>
```

Run the application. You should see Automobile Service Center Application as the application name, as shown in Figure 2-16.

Figure 2-16. *Index page displaying application title through dependency injection*

To use the configuration in any controllers, we have to inject IOptions<ApplicationSettings> as shown in Listing 2-8.

Listing 2-8. Dependency Injection in Controllers

```
private IOptions<ApplicationSettings> _settings;
    public HomeController(IOptions<ApplicationSettings> settings)
    {
        _settings = settings;
    }

    public IActionResult Index()
    {
```

```
        // Usage of IOptions
        ViewBag.Title = _settings.Value.ApplicationTitle;
        return View();
    }
```

■ **Note**   Don't forget to add the using statement for Microsoft.Extensions.Options to resolve the IOptions<> pattern.

Now let's see how to maintain different configuration files for different environments. Create an appsettings JSON file (as shown in Listing 2-9) with the name appsettings.Production.json at the root of the project. This settings file will act as a production environment configuration.

Listing 2-9. appsettings.Production.json File

```
{
  "AppSettings": {
    "ApplicationTitle": "Automobile Service Center Production Application"
  },
  "Logging": {
    "IncludeScopes": false,
    "LogLevel": {
      "Default": "Debug",
      "System": "Information",
      "Microsoft": "Information"
    }
  }
}
```

Add the Production appsettings file to Configuration Builder, as shown in Listing 2-10. It will load the appsettings JSON file based on the environment variable that we set at the project properties. Configuration Builder will pick up both appsettings files (appsettings.json and appsettings. Production.json), and the second file settings will override the settings of the first one for the properties that are available in both; otherwise, the corresponding settings from each file will be persisted.

Listing 2-10. Add the appsettings.production.json File to Configuration Builder

```
        var builder = new ConfigurationBuilder()
        .SetBasePath(env.ContentRootPath)
        .AddJsonFile("appsettings.json", optional: false, reloadOnChange: true)
        .AddJsonFile($"appsettings.{env.EnvironmentName}.json", optional: true);
```

■ **Note**   Make sure to add environment variables to Configuration Builder by using builder. AddEnvironmentVariables(). These environment variables are used across the application at multiple places to get the desired functionality for specific environments. One example is the bundling and minification of JavaScript files; we usually bundle and minify them only in Production environments.

To set environment variables, right-click the web project and select Properties. Go to the Debug tab and set the `ASPNETCORE_ENVIRONMENT` variable to `Production`, as shown in Figure 2-17. Similarly, we can add any environment variables.

■ **Note**   Make sure to add environment variables for all profiles that will be used for debugging.

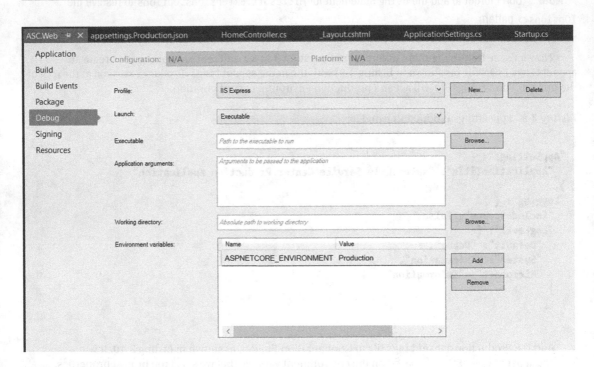

Figure 2-17. *Setting environment variables for an ASP.NET Core project*

Run the application. You should see the title updated from the `Production` configuration file, as shown in Figure 2-18.

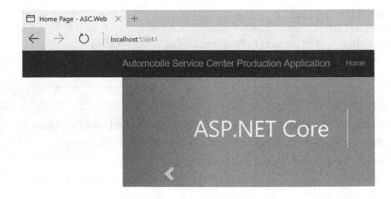

Figure 2-18. *Application updated with the title from the Production configuration*

Using Dependency Injection in the ASP.NET Core Application

Dependency injection (DI) is a software pattern through which a software application can achieve loosely coupled layers. Instead of directly creating objects at different layers of the application, dependency injection will inject the dependent objects in different ways (for example, constructor injection or property injection). This pattern uses abstractions (usually interfaces) and containers (it's essentially a factory that is responsible for providing instances of types) to resolve dependencies at runtime.

In previous ASP.NET versions, there was no built-in support for dependency injection. We used to get DI functionality through third-party frameworks such as Ninject and StructureMap. But starting from ASP.NET Core, we have built-in support for dependency injection (through the IServiceProvider interface).

In ASP.NET Core, the ConfigureServices method in Startup.cs is used to configure containers (as shown in Listing 2-11). By default, ASP.NET Core provides extensions to configure services such as Identity, Entity Framework, Authentication, and Caching. We can configure our custom business services by using any of the following extensions:

- *Transient*: A new instance of the object will be created every time a call is made for that type.

- *Scoped*: Only one instance of the object will be created, and it will be served for every call made for the type in the same request.

- *Singleton*: Only one instance of the object will be created, and it will be served for every call made for the type for all requests.

Listing. 2-11. Dependency Injection Container Configuration

```
// This method gets called by the runtime. Use this method to add services to the container.
public void ConfigureServices(IServiceCollection services)
{
    // Add framework services.
    services.AddDbContext<ApplicationDbContext>(options =>
    options.UseSqlite(Configuration.GetConnectionString("DefaultConnection")));

    services.AddIdentity<ApplicationUser, IdentityRole>()
        .AddEntityFrameworkStores<ApplicationDbContext>()
        .AddDefaultTokenProviders();

    services.AddOptions();
    services.Configure<ApplicationSettings>(Configuration.GetSection("AppSettings"));

    services.AddMvc();

    // Add application services.
    services.AddTransient<IEmailSender, AuthMessageSender>();
    services.AddTransient<ISmsSender, AuthMessageSender>();
}
```

In Listing 2-11, the Entity Framework Core is configured by using the AddDbContext extension, ASP.NET Core Identity is configured using the AddIdentity extension, configuration options are configured using the AddOptions extension, and MVC is configured by using the AddMvc extension. All these extension methods configure and add the services to the IServiceCollection collection. In a similar way, we can add our custom services (in Listing 2-11, we have configured IEmailSender and ISmsSender services). IServiceProvider is the default container provided by ASP.NET Core that is used to fetch the services at runtime.

Configured services can be accessed throughout the application in many ways. We can pass the dependencies through the constructor injection. We should define all dependencies as parameters in the constructor and later use them as shown in Listing 2-12.

Listing 2-12. Consuming Services Configured Using Dependency Injection

```
private IOptions<ApplicationSettings> _settings;
public HomeController(IOptions<ApplicationSettings> settings)
{
    _settings = settings;
}

public IActionResult Index()
{
    // Usage of IOptions
    ViewBag.Title = _settings.Value.ApplicationTitle;
    return View();
}
```

Another approach is to pass specific dependencies to Action methods. We have to explicitly use FromServices to tell ASP.NET Core that this parameter should be retrieved from configured services (see Listing 2-13).

Listing 2-13. Access Dependencies by Using the FromServices Attribute

```
public IActionResult Index([FromServices] IEmailSender emailSender)
{
    // Usage of IOptions
    ViewBag.Title = _settings.Value.ApplicationTitle;
    return View();
}
```

One more option for retrieving services is to use the RequestServices extension of HttpContext, as shown in Listing 2-14. It is not advisable to use this approach because it makes code less testable and is hard to maintain.

Listing 2-14. Usage of the RequestServices Extension of HttpContext

```
var emailService = this.HttpContext.RequestServices
                        .GetService(typeof(IEmailSender)) as IEmailSender;
```

We have to be careful in designing services that are configured for dependency injection. In the Automobile Service Center application, we are going to use dependency injection extensively to resolve all dependencies related to business and storage operations.

Summary

In this chapter, you learned about the .NET Core platform and its advantages. You briefly looked at the .NET Core platform architecture and key considerations to make before choosing .NET Core over .NET Framework. You also learned about the ASP.NET Core framework and its advantages. You learned about the new concepts and groundbreaking changes in ASP.NET Core as compared to previous versions of ASP.NET. You briefly looked at the history of .NET Core and ASP.NET Core, followed by proposed future changes and releases.

We created the base project for the Automobile Service Center web application by using both VS 2017 and the .NET Core SDK. We explored all the artifacts of the ASP.NET Core project system. You learned how to set up the basic configuration in an ASP.NET Core project and how to do transformation of configuration files based on environments. Finally, you looked at the dependency injection pattern and how ASP.NET Core leverages its new Service collection and Service provider to configure services and resolve dependencies at runtime.

References

1. https://docs.microsoft.com/en-us/dotnet/articles/standard/components

2. https://github.com/dotnet/core/blob/master/release-notes/README.md

3. https://github.com/dotnet/core/blob/master/roadmap.md

CHAPTER 3

■ ■ ■

Designing a Theme by Using Material Design

The success of any software application depends on many key factors. One prominent factor is the user experience and presentation. Lately, a significant drift has occurred in software design patterns: professionals and organizations are looking to deliver solutions by limiting page transitions with asynchronous server interactions. This paradigm demands a rich user experience—and without it, any application could easily fall apart by failing to meet expectations. Fortunately, today's browsers, along with the continuous innovation of the CSS and JQuery frameworks, are providing unprecedented visual presentations to end users.

The relevance and importance of jQuery-powered CSS frameworks has grown for multiple reasons. Here are some of the important ones:

- One-stop solution for supporting different devices

- Compatible with multiple browsers and platforms

- Design single-page applications

- Support for various application design models such as PhoneGap and Windows Store apps

In this chapter, we are going to walk through creating a good user experience by using Google's Material Design language. In the process of learning about Materialize CSS, we will create the CSS template for our Automobile Service Center application.

Responsive Design and New Approaches

This decade by far has experienced explosive growth in manufacturing smart devices to cater to various requirements. The evolution of laptops, smartphones, tablets, wearables, game consoles, and virtual reality devices has triggered challenges for developers to provide one-stop intuitive solutions that support most devices. *Responsive web design* is a new approach in designing a web solution to ensure that users have a good viewing experience no matter what type of device they're using. Responsive design primarily uses HTML along with CSS and JS languages to deliver optimized visual experiences for a specific device browser.

Responsive web design enables web applications to render efficiently on different devices, screen sizes, orientations, browsers, resolutions, and operating systems. Responsive design can be achieved using techniques such as media queries, fluid grids, and fluid images.

© Rami Vemula 2017

R. Vemula, *Real-Time Web Application Development*, https://doi.org/10.1007/978-1-4842-3270-5_3

Media queries let us design various layouts for the same web page for different media types such as screen, print, or handheld devices. Depending on the media type in conjunction with the width and height variants of the browser and device, we can configure the style, font, and other elements of the page. Using *fluid grid* design, all the elements are maintained in relative proportion to the base element. Instead of specifying the height and width in pixels, they are indicated in percentages with respect to the holding container. Images are not scalable by default, so they will fall apart when the screen size changes. The *fluid image* technique will ensure that images are resized proportionately based on screen size; using low-resolution images for smaller devices is suggested.

Fortunately, all of these techniques are provided by most CSS frameworks powered by JavaScript. Bootstrap is a popular open source front-end web framework that supports great responsive and mobile-first designs. It is often considered a pioneer in the marketplace. Other frameworks such as Foundation and Semantic UI offer similar capabilities. Most of these CSS frameworks use dynamic stylesheet languages such as LESS and SASS that are processed into CSS stylesheets. Dynamic stylesheet languages provide great advantages, including reusable CSS schemes for responsive designs, preprocessing capability for complex and large stylesheets, inheritance, and feature exports, and fewer HTTP requests required from the browser to the server.

Trends in responsive web design are evolving. Some of the key trends are as follows:

- *Precise and simple*: The main concept of the web application should be precise. It should be communicated in a simple and short message that's clearly communicated through the theme of the web application.

- *Great typography and icons*: Using great fonts and icons to present the content will always engage users.

- *Vibrant themes and unique presentation*: Most modern web applications use vibrant and new color combinations along with placing content in the right places.

- *Elegant design of input controls*: All HTML controls should have an elegant design provided by modern design techniques from, for example, Material Design.

- *Simplified navigation*: Easy-to-use navigation always yields good results

- *Content with infinite scrolling*: Users prefer getting information through a feed-based approach, like that of Facebook.

- *Push notifications*: Real-time notifications help users stay connected with the application.

Today's CSS frameworks are not only capable of providing these features but also support various application models. Mobile development frameworks such as Adobe PhoneGap and Sencha Touch use HTML, JS, and CSS to create typical mobile and tablet applications. Windows Store apps can be developed using HTML, JS, and CSS frameworks. In any development model, the responsive CSS frameworks play a pivotal role in the overall design and user experience.

Material Design is a visual design language developed by Google to focus more on the basic building blocks of visual representation and to enhance them by using animations, transitions, and shadow effects. The primary goals of Material Design are as follows:

- To create a visual language that produces a classic standard of design with innovative principles of technology.

- To develop a single uniform platform that provides a unified experience.

■ **Note**   Before Material Design came into the world, web applications were designed using flat design techniques. *Flat design* is not a multidimensional design technique and provides no textures, gradients, or shadows.

Material Design uses features such as tactical surfaces (multiple layers stacked up on one another), pixel density, and animations. In Material Design, typography, grids, space, scale, color, and imagery play a crucial role in the entire design. Elements are placed in defined spaces with a clear hierarchy and are bold in order to stand out in the design. Because of its multilayer structure, Material Design elements are easy to interact with; the animations surrounding elements give the feel of interacting with a real object. New open source CSS frameworks have been built using Material Design to offer responsive web design. These frameworks provide a very good user experience for end users when interacting with web applications.

In this book, we'll use one of the latest CSS frameworks that supports responsive web design and uses Material Design concepts.

About Materialize CSS

Materialize CSS is a modern, responsive, front-end framework based on Material Design. It was developed by a team of students from Carnegie Mellon University in 2014. It is an open source framework under the MIT License.

■ **Note**   More information about the Materialize CSS authors can be found at `http://materializecss.com/about.html`.

Just like Bootstrap, Materialize supports a 12-column responsive layout along with offsets. Materialize supports various navigation menus and has great support for mobile navigation through its drag-out menu. It uses Roboto font by default, which can be easily changed to any other font family. Materialize provides a good set of helpers to format, align, and render text on various devices. It also has, by default, responsive support for rendering media content such as images and videos.

Materialize CSS supports these additional features:

- Different form styles, buttons, and input controls. Built-in support for elements such as carousels, collapsible panels, feature discovery prompts, dialog boxes, tabs, and Scrollspy.

- Breadcrumbs to show the user's current location, and progress indicators to show the task status.

- Support for badges to show notifications, pushpins to fix positioning of messages, and cards to display different content from different objects.

- Different styles for collections and pagination.

- Great support for media content, and a wide range of iconography.

- Built-in support for modal pop-ups.

- Effects and transitions such as image parallax, fade in/out, and waves.

Materialize can be applied to a web application in two ways: via CSS/JS or SASS files.

■ **Note** Creating a stylesheet from Material Design is a lengthy and hard process. Materialize CSS fills that gap by providing a great stylesheet implementation. In this book, we are going to use Materialize CSS to style our Automobile Service Center application.

Materialize CSS Themes

So far, you have learned the concepts of Material Design and Materialize CSS. This section presents the Materialize themes that are designed using Materialize CSS. Fortunately, there was good early adoption of both Material Design and Materialize CSS by the open source community. As a result, several free and paid themes have been developed by leveraging Materialize CSS. For the Automobile Service Center application, we are going to use some of the open source developed themes and tailor them to our needs.

We are going to use the Parallax theme, shown in Figure 3-1, as the base theme for our Automobile Service Center application. The Parallax template, a free template offered by the Materialize CSS team, is the simplest template that we can start off with. We'll customize it based on the Automobile Service Center application's requirements.

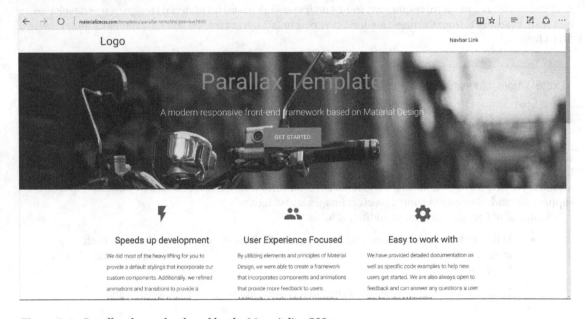

Figure 3-1. Parallax theme developed by the Materialize CSS team

---

■ **Note** The Parallax theme can be found at `http://materializecss.com/templates/parallax-template/preview.html`.

To support the Automobile Service Center application's functionalities, we are going to customize the template.

Using Materialize CSS in the Automobile Service Center Application

In this section, we will apply Materialize CSS themes to our Automobile Service Center application. Based on the requirements of our application, all the pages are divided into two categories: public pages and secured pages. *Public pages* are available to all users without a login requirement (authentication is not required). *Secured pages* are available only to authenticated users such as Administrator, Service Engineers and registered customers.

To get started, we will implement the Parallax theme in the public pages. Download the Parallax theme from http://materializecss.com/getting-started.html. Extract the zip contents to a folder as shown in Figure 3-2.

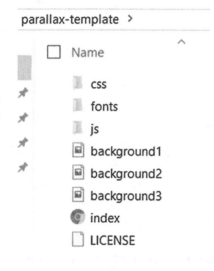

Figure 3-2. *Parallex theme contents*

Copy the following contents to the ASC.Web project:

1. All CSS files to the wwwroot/css directory. (Delete the default site.css provided as part of the solution.)

2. Fonts to the wwwroot/fonts directory.

3. All JS files to the wwwroot/js directory.

4. Background images to the wwwroot/images directory. (Delete the default banner SVG files.)

■ **Note**   I downloaded free background images from www.pexels.com/search/car/.

The logo is downloaded from www.iconfinder.com/icons/285807/auto_automobile_car_convertible_vehicle_icon#size=128.

The solution structure should be as shown in Figure 3-3.

Figure 3-3. *Visual Studio solution structure*

Public pages follow the design depicted in Figure 3-4. The top header, along with the Parallax container, goes into the top section of the layout file. The content page will be rendered immediately after the top section, using the standard ASP.NET MVC RenderBody. The footer section will be in the layout file.

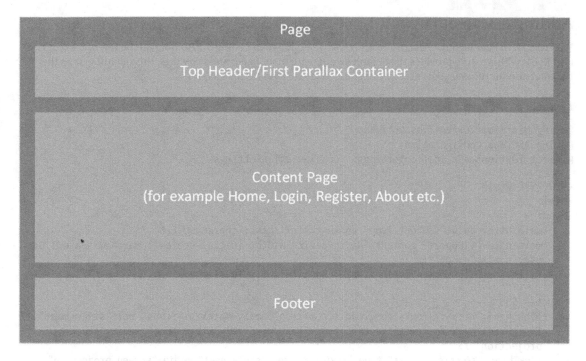

Figure 3-4. Public pages design

■ **Note**   For public screens, we are going to refer directly to minified CSS and JS files in layout.

As part of the ASP.NET Core Web Application template, JQuery is already added to the project as a Bower dependency. It can be found at `wwwroot/lib/jquery/dist/jquery.min.js`.

One more fantastic feature of ASP.NET Core is the capability to load different scripts for different environments, as shown in Listing 3-1. We are going to ignore this feature for the public pages design, as we are holding all the required files in the directory.

Listing 3-1. Loading JQuery Scripts Based on Environment Variables

```
<environment names="Development">
      <script src="~/lib/jquery/dist/jquery.js"></script>
</environment>
<environment names="Staging,Production">
     <script src="https://ajax.aspnetcdn.com/ajax/jquery/jquery-2.2.0.min.js"
            asp-fallback-src="~/lib/jquery/dist/jquery.min.js"
            asp-fallback-test="window.jQuery"
            crossorigin="anonymous"
            integrity="sha384-K+ctZQ+LL8q6tP7I94W+qzQsfRV2a+AfHIi9k8z8l9ggpc8X+Ytst4yBo/
                     hH+8Fk">
     </script>
</environment>
```

Adding a Master Layout

We create a master layout, _MasterLayout.cshtml, as shown in Listing 3-2, to hold all the references for CSS and JS files. This listing provides the default layout, with html, head, and body tags; this default acts as the base version for other layouts that we are going to create later in this chapter.

Listing 3-2. Master Layout

```
@using Microsoft.Extensions.Options;
@using ASC.Web.Configuration;
@inject IOptions<ApplicationSettings> _configurationSettings

<!DOCTYPE html>
<html>
<head>
    <meta http-equiv="Content-Type" content="text/html; charset=UTF-8" />
    <meta name="viewport" content="width=device-width, initial-scale=1, maximum-scale=1.0,
    user-scalable=no" />
    <title>@_configurationSettings.Value.ApplicationTitle</title>

    <!-- CSS -->
    <link href="https://fonts.googleapis.com/icon?family=Material+Icons" rel="stylesheet">
    <link href="~/css/materialize.css" type="text/css" rel="stylesheet" media="screen,
    projection" />
    <link href="~/css/style.css" type="text/css" rel="stylesheet" media="screen,projection" />

</head>
<body>
    <!-- Render Body -->
    @RenderBody()

    <script src="~/lib/jquery/dist/jquery.min.js"></script>
    <script src="~/js/materialize.min.js"></script>
    <script src="~/js/init.js"></script>

    @RenderSection("Scripts", required: false)
</body>
</html>
```

■ **Note** We can improve the physical structure of the solution and layout files by using areas. We will implement areas in subsequent chapters.

Replace the markup of _Layout.cshtml with the code in Listing 3-3 to reflect the Parallax theme. We have to specify _MasterLayout as the parent for this layout; by doing this, all the references from MasterLayout are inherited to Layout. The layout will have a navigation bar that points to the login and contact pages. The Parallax template's container is the next section, which will display the first background image.

The middle section of the layout will hold ASP.NET's RenderBody(), which will be used to render different content pages. The last section of the layout is the footer section, which will display three subsections: About Us, Additional Services, and Connect. The Additional Services subsection will hold links to various topics at the Automobile Service Center application, whereas Connect will point to the company's social media channels.

Listing 3-3. Layout.cshtml Design

```
@{
    Layout = "_MasterLayout";
}
<header>
    <nav class="white" role="navigation">
        <div class="nav-wrapper container">
            <a id="logo-container" href="#" class="brand-logo">
                <img class="responsive-img" src="~/images/logo.jpg" alt="Logo" />
            </a>
            <ul class="right hide-on-med-and-down">
                <li><a href="#">Login</a></li>
                <li><a href="#">Contact</a></li>
            </ul>
            <ul id="nav-mobile" class="side-nav">
                <li><a href="#">Login</a></li>
                <li><a href="#">Contact</a></li>
            </ul>
            <a href="#" data-activates="nav-mobile" class="button-collapse">
             <i class="material-icons">menu</i></a>
        </div>
    </nav>

    <div id="index-banner" class="parallax-container">
        <div class="section no-pad-bot">
            <div class="container">
                <br><br>
                <h1 class="header center teal-text text-lighten-2">Automobile Service Center</h1>
                <div class="row center">
                    <h5 class="header col s12 light ">Where Quality meets Safety</h5>
                </div>
                <div class="row center">
                    <a href="http://materializecss.com/getting-started.html" id="download-
                        button" class="btn-large waves-effect waves-light teal lighten-1">Get
                        Started</a>
                </div>
                <br><br>
            </div>
        </div>
        <div class="parallax"><img src="~/images/background1.jpg" alt="Unsplashed background
        img 1"></div>
    </div>
</header>

<!-- Render Body -->
<main>
    <div class="row margin-bottom-0px">
        <div class="col s12 padding-0px">
            @RenderBody()
        </div>
    </div>
</main>
```

```html
<!-- Footer -->
<footer class="page-footer teal">
    <div class="container">
        <div class="row">
            <div class="col l6 s12">
                <h5 class="white-text">About Us</h5>
                <p class="grey-text text-lighten-4">
                    Automobile Service Center is certified to perform car services. Our
                    workshop operations started in October 2010.
                    We primarily focus on providing better services to our customers, and as
                    a result of the hard work, we were awarded "Best Service" for 2008.
                </p>

            </div>
            <div class="col l3 s12">
                <h5 class="white-text">Additional Services</h5>
                <ul>
                    <li><a class="white-text" href="#!">Services</a></li>
                    <li><a class="white-text" href="#!">Finance</a></li>
                    <li><a class="white-text" href="#!">Used Cars</a></li>
                    <li><a class="white-text" href="#!">Insurance</a></li>
                    <li><a class="white-text" href="#!">Driving School</a></li>
                </ul>
            </div>
            <div class="col l3 s12">
                <h5 class="white-text">Connect</h5>
                <ul>
                    <li><a class="white-text" href="#!">Facebook</a></li>
                    <li><a class="white-text" href="#!">LinkedIn</a></li>
                    <li><a class="white-text" href="#!">Twitter</a></li>
                    <li><a class="white-text" href="#!">Youtube</a></li>
                </ul>
            </div>
        </div>
    </div>
    <div class="footer-copyright">
        <div class="container">
            Powered by <a class="brown-text text-lighten-3" href="http://materializecss.com">
            Materialize</a>
        </div>
    </div>
</footer>
```

The home page is going to be a static content page. Replace the code of Views/Home/Index.cshtml with the code shown in Listing 3-4. This static page will serve as the home page of the Automobile Service Center application. The first section of the Index page will have a container section that is divided into three subsections. Each subsection will display an icon followed by static content. These three subsections can be used primarily to display the core values of the Automobile Service Center application.

The next sections on the page are two Parallax containers that are lined up one after the other; each one of the containers will display a background image followed by static content. These sections can be used to display the Automobile Service Center's services and achievements.

Listing 3-4. Index.cshtml Design

```
<div class="container">
    <div class="section">
        <!--   Icon Section    -->
        <div class="row">
            <div class="col s12 m4">
                <div class="icon-block">
                    <h2 class="center brown-text"><i class="material-icons">group</i></h2>
                    <h5 class="center">Who we are</h5>
                    <p class="light">We believe in providing seamless and high-quality services
                        to our customers. Our customer-first approach will offer a unique
                        personalized experience that will bring more value to your car through a
                        smarter and quicker process. We are committed to great quality.</p>
                </div>
            </div>
            <div class="col s12 m4">
                <div class="icon-block">
                    <h2 class="center brown-text"><i class="material-icons">flash_on</i></h2>
                    <h5 class="center">Our Competency</h5>
                    <p class="light">By utilizing the elements and principles of modern
                        mechanical engineering, we are able to resolve complex technical challenges
                        through innovative solutions. Additionally, our service engineers are
                        highly qualified, with advanced training in automobile engineering.</p>
                </div>
            </div>
            <div class="col s12 m4">
                <div class="icon-block">
                    <h2 class="center brown-text"><i class="material-icons">settings</i></h2>
                    <h5 class="center">Easy to work with</h5>
                    <p class="light">We provide detailed information and predictive analysis
                        to help our customers understand their cars. We maintain continuous
                        communication and are always open to feedback. We are always avaiable
                        to answer our customers'  inquiries.</p>
                </div>
            </div>
        </div>
    </div>
</div>

<div class="parallax-container valign-wrapper">
    <div class="section no-pad-bot">
        <div class="container">
            <div class="row center">
                <h5 class="header col s12 light">Commited to delivering unprecendented
                    quality to our customers</h5>
            </div>
        </div>
    </div>
    <div class="parallax"><img src="~/images/background2.jpg" alt="Unsplashed background
    img 2"></div>
</div>
```

51

```
<div class="container">
    <div class="section">
        <div class="row">
            <div class="col s12 center">
                <h3><i class="mdi-content-send brown-text"></i></h3>
                <h4>Customer Value</h4>
                <p class="left-align light">Automobile Service Center has always been a
                value-driven company. Many of our values are based on years of research and
                commitment. Our values reflect the manner in which we run our business.
                We're proud of our professional ethics in dealing with our business
                partners, investors, employees, and customers. We provide customer-valued
                services built on our commitment to responsibility, sustainability,
                trust, openness, diversity, reliability, determination, credibility, and
                initiation. Our dedication in providing quality services is based on our
                great engineering-compliance model and industry-standard inspection and
                quality-control procedures.</p>
            </div>
        </div>
    </div>
</div>

<div class="parallax-container valign-wrapper">
    <div class="section no-pad-bot">
        <div class="container">
            <div class="row center">
                <h5 class="header col s12 light">Humility, Empathy, Hard Work, and Technology
                are our core drivers.</h5>
            </div>
        </div>
    </div>
    <div class="parallax"><img src="~/images/background3.jpg" alt="Unsplashed background
    img 3"></div>
</div>
```

Append the styles in Listing 3-5 to Style.css to support the logo image and small-screen resolution.

Listing 3-5. Styles

```css
/* Removes padding */
.padding-0px {
    padding: 0px !important;
}

/* Make logo fit in the header */
.nav-wrapper .brand-logo img {
    height: 64px;
}

@media (max-width: 600px) {
    .nav-wrapper .brand-logo img {
        height: 56px;
    }
}
```

Run the application (either from Visual Studio by pressing F5, or from the command-line prompt by typing dotnet run). The application will be launched and displayed in the browser, as shown in Figure 3-5.

Figure 3-5. *Automobile Service Center's home page*

■ **Note** Materialize CSS can also be included in the ASP.NET Core web project by using Bower.

This chapter focused mainly on theme design. We will design the rest of the application pages in later chapters as we cover relevant topics.

Designing a Layout for Secure Pages

So far, we have designed the templates for public pages. Now we will design the theme for secured pages. We will not use any prebuilt or open source templates for this theme. Instead, we'll use Materialize CSS and its JavaScript components to create a simple and responsive theme. The main concept behind this theme is to keep it simple and elegant, because the pages that are going to use this theme should highlight the data and functionality rather than confusing the user with a lot of moving parts and images. The secure page layout will be designed as shown in Figure 3-6.

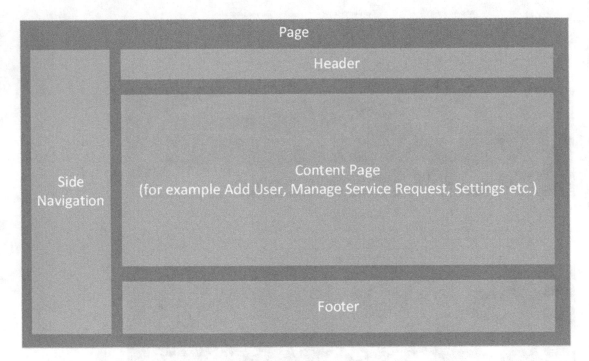

Figure 3-6. *Secure page design*

Create a new layout file with the name _SecureLayout.cshtml that will serve as the layout for all secured pages. As shown in Figure 3-6, we design the HTML in sections. As with Layout, we inherit SecureLayout from MasterLayout, as described in Listing 3-6.

The first section is the header section, which will display the title of the application. The header section is followed by the left-navigation section, which is again divided into two subsections. The first subsection will display the information related to the logged-in user. The second subsection will display the navigation menu, which will help the user navigate to different secure pages in the application.

The next section in the flow is the `RenderBody()` section, which will display the actual content page. The footer section is the last section in the secure layout, and is similar to the footer section that we designed for the public pages.

Listing 3-6. Secure Layout Design

```
@{
    Layout = "_MasterLayout";
}

<!-- Header -->
<header class="secureLayout">
    <nav class="top-nav blue-grey lighten-1">
        <div class="nav-wrapper row valign-wrapper">
            <div class="col s12 valign-wrapper">
                <a href="#" data-activates="nav-mobile" class="button-collapse top-nav full
                  hide-on-large-only white-text"><i class="material-icons">menu</i></a>
                <h5><a class="page-title">Automobile Service Center</a></h5>
            </div>
        </div>
    </nav>

    <!-- Side NavBar -->
    <ul id="nav-mobile" class="side-nav fixed">
        <li>
            <div class="userView">
                <div class="background blue-grey lighten-1"></div>
                <a href="#!user"><img class="circle" src="~/images/male.png"></a>
                <a href="#!name"><span class="white-text name">John Doe</span></a>
                <a href="#!email"><span class="white-text email">jdandturk@gmail.com</span></a>
            </div>
        </li>
        <li><a class="collapsible-header" href="#!"><i class="material-icons">dashboard</i>
          Dashboard</a></li>

        <li>
            <ul class="collapsible collapsible-accordion">
                <li>
                    <a class="collapsible-header">User Administration<i class="material-
                      icons">supervisor_account</i></a>
                    <div class="collapsible-body">
                        <ul>
                            <li><a href="#!">Customers<i class="material-icons">
                            account_box</i></a></li>
                            <li><a href="#!">Provision User<i class="material-icons">
                             person_add</i></a></li>
                            <li><a href="#!">Deactivate User<i class="material-icons">
                             remove_circle</i></a></li>
                        </ul>
                    </div>
                </li>
            </ul>
        </li>
```

```
        <li><a class="collapsible-header" href="#!"><i class="material-icons">perm_data_
        setting</i>Service Requests</a></li>
        <li><a class="collapsible-header" href="#!"><i class="material-icons">message</i>
        Service Notifications</a></li>
        <li><a class="collapsible-header" href="#!"><i class="material-icons">inbox</i>
        Promotions</a></li>
        <li><a class="collapsible-header" href="#!"><i class="material-icons">settings</i>
        Settings</a></li>
        <li><a class="collapsible-header" href="#!"><i class="material-icons">exit_to_app</i>
        Logout</a></li>
    </ul>
</header>

<!-- Render Body -->
<main class="secureLayout">
    <div class="row margin-bottom-0px">
        <div class="col s12">
            @RenderBody()
        </div>
    </div>
</main>

<!-- Footer -->
<footer class="page-footer blue-grey lighten-1 secureLayout">
    <div class="row">
        <div class="col l6 s12">
            <h5 class="white-text">About Us</h5>
            <p class="grey-text text-lighten-4">
                Automobile Service Center is certified Company to perform car services. Our
                Workshop operations started in the month of October, 2010.
                We primarily focus on providing better services to our customers, and as a
                result of the hard work we were awarded as the "Best Service" for the year
                2008 and that too within a short period of time.
            </p>

        </div>
        <div class="col l3 s12">
            <h5 class="white-text">Additional Services</h5>
            <ul>
                <li><a class="white-text" href="#!">Services</a></li>
                <li><a class="white-text" href="#!">Finance</a></li>
                <li><a class="white-text" href="#!">Used Cars</a></li>
                <li><a class="white-text" href="#!">Insurance</a></li>
                <li><a class="white-text" href="#!">Driving School</a></li>
            </ul>
        </div>
        <div class="col l3 s12">
            <h5 class="white-text">Connect</h5>
            <ul>
                <li><a class="white-text" href="#!">Facebook</a></li>
                <li><a class="white-text" href="#!">LinkedIn</a></li>
```

```
                    <li><a class="white-text" href="#!">Twitter</a></li>
                    <li><a class="white-text" href="#!">Youtube</a></li>
                </ul>
            </div>
        </div>
        <div class="footer-copyright row margin-bottom-0px">
            <div class="col s12">
                Powered by <a class="brown-text text-lighten-3" href="http://materializecss.com">
                Materialize</a>
            </div>
        </div>
    </div>
</footer>
```

Append the styles in Listing 3-7 to Style.css.

Listing 3-7. Styles

```css
/* Adjusting padding to display Side Nav */
header.secureLayout, main.secureLayout, footer.secureLayout {
    padding-left: 300px;
}

@media only screen and (max-width : 992px) {
    header.secureLayout, main.secureLayout, footer.secureLayout {
        padding-left: 0;
    }
}

/* Selected Menu Item style*/
.side-nav li.active {
    background-color: #f5f5f5;
}

.margin-bottom-0px {
    margin-bottom: 0px;
}
```

Create a Dashboard action in the home controller, as shown in Listing 3-8. This action is used to display a sample screen with the designed theme.

Listing 3-8. Dashboard Action in Home Controller

```csharp
    public IActionResult Dashboard()
    {
        return View();
    }
```

The Dashboard view is a simple view. For now, it just displays a message. The important part of the Dashboard view is that it inherits SecureLayout.

Listing 3-9. Dashboard View

```
@{
    Layout = "_SecureLayout";
}
<div class="section">
    <div class="row">
        <div class="col s12 m4" style="height: 500px;">
            Content Page will be displayed here.
        </div>
    </div>
</div>
```

■ **Note** I have downloaded free gender images from `www.iconfinder.com`.

Run the application (either from Visual Studio by pressing F5, or from the command-line prompt by typing `dotnet run`). The application will be launched. Navigate to /Home/Dashboard, and you should see the screen depicted in Figure 3-7.

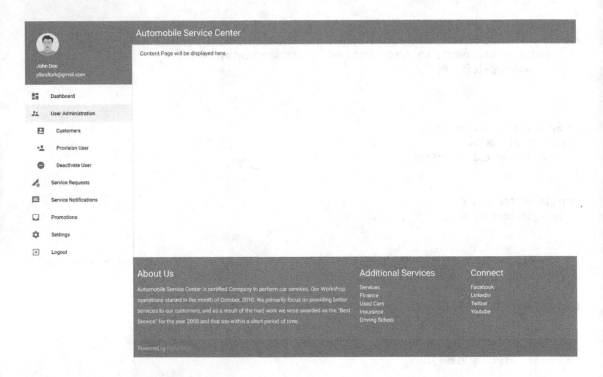

Figure 3-7. Dashboard view with secure layout

On mobile devices, the navigation will be hidden by default. Clicking the Menu icon will slide the navigation from the left portion of the screen, as shown in Figure 3-8.

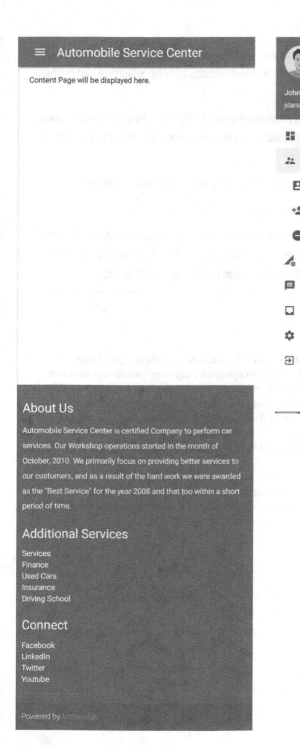

Figure 3-8. *Dashboard view in mobile devices*

■ **Note**   The main intention of this chapter is to familiarize you with designing themes via Material Design. Numerous other approaches and frameworks are available in the marketplace through which we can develop different user experiences.

I recommend that you do some research on modern CSS frameworks and JS libraries. As part of this learning exercise, I advise you to develop some themes to serve business requirements such as Patient Management System or Air Cargo System.

To learn more about Material Design, visit `https://material.io/guidelines/#introduction-goals`.

For Materialize CSS concepts, visit `http://materializecss.com/`.

We will be using Materialize CSS extensively in the Automobile Service Center application. We have already used the Parallax and Navbar components from Materialize CSS. Many other CSS and JS components are available from Materialize CSS that are used for relevant functionalities in subsequent chapters.

Summary

You started this chapter by learning about the importance and relevance of providing a great user experience and visual presentation. Responsive web design concepts can empower various application models, especially web applications that need to render efficiently on different devices and present different variations. The latest JavaScript-powered CSS frameworks offer great responsive web design solutions.

You also learned about Material Design, which is a visual design language developed by Google that enhances the user experience by providing basic building blocks of visual representation. You also explored Materialize CSS, which is the latest CSS framework developed by leveraging Material Design and responsive web design.

Material Design is widely accepted by the open source community, and free open source themes have been developed using Materialize CSS. For our Automobile Service Center application, we have customized the Parallax theme for its public pages. For the secured pages, we developed a theme using the Materialize CSS vertical Navbar, which will ensure responsive navigation on different devices.

Reference

1. `https://www.elegantthemes.com/blog/resources/how-to-test-your-wordpress-website-for-responsive-design`

CHAPTER 4

■ ■ ■

Overview of Azure Storage

Data is undoubtedly the most important output generated by a software product or platform. As the current generation quickly adapts to the new application development models based on numerous devices and technologies, generating enormous amounts of data is possible. Gone are the days when software professionals dealt with gigabytes of information. Present-day application models such as the Internet of Things (IoT) and event hubs have created new channels of large datasets ranging from terabytes to petabytes.

New collaborative business workflows between different organizations and professionals, changing demands of customers, and modern environmental conditions are increasing the need for quick data analysis and immediate action. Although prompt action is the primary goal, decisions are becoming increasingly complex as companies compete in the global marketplace. The new cloud infrastructure, along with Business Intelligence (BI) tools, help businesses process a high volume of data and generate complex reports that help in mission-critical decision making.

A smart application design should include resilient storage that offers the following important features:

- Scalability, durability, and redundancy

- High availability and disaster recovery

- Easy to manage and maintain

- Support for various data formats and heterogeneous application models

- Security with controlled access

- Cost-optimized environment for big-data solutions

- Seamless integration and migration options

These features are offered by most new database and storage systems. Compared to on-premises storage options, the new cloud computing platforms offer more features and reliable storage options at a very low cost. The Microsoft Azure Cloud platform provides numerous offerings for data storage, including databases, distributed file systems, binary data, queues, big-data platforms and extensions, and NoSQL databases.

This chapter presents the basic concepts of Azure Table storage and implements a simple CRUD (Create, Read, Update and Delete) operations. We will create a UnitOfWork pattern with a generic repository implementation of Azure Table storage that will provide a reusable and loosely coupled data access layer for the Automobile Service Center application.

© Rami Vemula 2017
R. Vemula, *Real-Time Web Application Development*, https://doi.org/10.1007/978-1-4842-3270-5_4

Introduction to Azure Storage

Azure Storage is a storage-as-a-service offering from Microsoft for modern applications that require scalable, durable, and highly available storage for their data. Developers can use Azure Storage to build large-scale applications targeting cloud, mobile, server, and desktop options. Using Azure Storage, we can store and process terabytes to petabytes of data to support the big-data scenarios required by scientific, financial analysis, and media applications. At the same time, Azure Storage attracts many small-business applications throughout the world because of its affordable pricing model, in which we pay only for the data we are storing and for the transactions we perform on it.

Azure Storage can be scaled massively to support high-volume transactions on large amounts of data. It uses an autopartitioning system that automatically load-balances the data by allocating appropriate resources to serve the requests.

Azure Storage supports diverse operating systems and a variety of programming languages for development. Azure Storage also exposes data resources via simple REST APIs, which are available to any client capable of sending and receiving data via HTTP/HTTPS. As shown in Figure 4-1, Azure storage supports various types of storage.

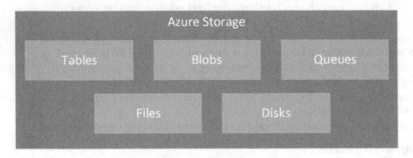

Figure 4-1. *Storage services offered by Azure Storage*

Blob storage is used to store unstructured object data. A blob can be of any type—for example, binary data such as a document or media file. *Table storage* is used to store structured datasets. Table storage is a NoSQL key/attribute data store, which allows for rapid development and fast access to large quantities of data. *Queue storage* provides reliable messaging for workflow processing and enables communication between components of cloud services. *File storage* is a service that offers shared storage for files in the cloud by using the standard Server Message Block (SMB) protocol. Applications running in Azure Virtual Machines or cloud services or from on-premises clients can mount a file share in the cloud and start using it. Legacy applications that typically rely on file shares can now easily migrate to Azure quickly and without any rework.

Azure Storage services are available in two types of performance tiers:

- A standard storage performance tier for storing tables, queues, files, blobs, and Azure virtual machine disks

- A premium storage performance tier for storing Azure virtual machine disks

The main advantage of Azure Premium Storage compared with Standard Storage is that it delivers high-performance, low-latency disk support for I/O-intensive operations running on Azure Virtual Machines. With Azure Premium Storage, you can attach multiple persistent data disks (SSD disks) to a virtual machine and configure them to deliver maximum I/O and performance.

■ **Note** We use Microsoft Azure Table as a persistence medium for the Automobile Service Center application. We can also use Azure SQL Database as the back end, but I opted to use Azure Storage to demonstrate a different design technique instead of the regular traditional SQL Server and Entity Framework combination.

By default, Storage account services are accessible to only the account owner. They also provide two private access keys, which are used for authentication by connected applications. The reason for having two keys, primary and secondary, is to prevent downtime for storage services, especially while we regenerate the keys (the secondary can be used while the primary is being regenerated). To allow controlled access to other users, a shared access signature (SAS) is used. There are two types of SAS keys: one at the service level (for access to a particular storage service such as Blob or Queue) and the other at the account level (for access to multiple storage services). An account-level SAS can delegate access to a service-level SAS with access modifiers such as read, write, and delete operations.

Azure Storage provides four replication options to support high availability:

- *Locally redundant storage*: Three copies of data are replicated within the same datacenter in the same region.

- *Zero redundant storage*: Data is replicated three times across two to three datacenters, either within a single region or across two regions.

- *Geo redundant storage*: Six copies of data are replicated across primary and secondary regions. In case of failure, all requests will be failed over to the secondary region.

- *Read-access geo redundant storage*: This is exactly similar to geo redundant storage, but it provides read access from both primary and secondary storage at the same time.

Azure storage services are consistently being upgraded from year to year to support enhancements with respect to size of the data, querying the data through the API, availability through different regions, security, migration and bulk copy.

Azure achieves scalability of storage services through partitioning logic. Whenever the size and load of a partition changes to a high value, that partition will be moved on to other machines that can deliver high throughput.

Azure Table storage holds data as collections of entities. *Entities* are similar to rows. An entity has a row key, partition key, and a set of properties; every property has both a type and a value. There is no fixed schema requirement for Azure Table storage. So two entities in the same table may have different sets of properties. A table may contain any number of entities.

PartitionKey and RowKey are system properties that are automatically included for every entity in a table, and they play a crucial role in partitioning. Azure Storage creates a partition of all entities in a consecutive range of the same partition-key value. The partition key is a unique identifier for the partition within a given table, specified by the PartitionKey property. The partition key forms the first part of an entity's primary key. The second part of the primary key is the RowKey. The RowKey is a unique identifier for an entity within a given partition. Together, the PartitionKey and RowKey uniquely identify every entity within a table.

RowKey and PartitionKey properties should be included in every insert, update, and delete operation. These properties are of the string type with a maximum allowed size of 1KB.

There is one more important property, Timestamp, which is used internally by Azure Storage to maintain optimistic concurrency. This property holds the last modified time of the entity. This property should not be set on insert or update operations (even if it is set, the value will be ignored).

Getting Started with Azure SDK and Storage Emulator

To use Azure Storage services for application development, we have the following prerequisites:

■ **Note** As stated in Chapter 1, create a Microsoft Azure subscription: (https://azure.microsoft.com/).

- Azure development prerequisites
- Azure Storage emulator

■ **Note** As shown in Chapter 1, we installed Azure SDKs and development tools as part of the VS 2017 installation.

Azure Storage emulator runs on the developer's local machine and provides a local environment that emulates the Azure Blob, Queue, and Table services for development purposes. Storage emulator is helpful during development, when we do not want to test the storage-related code against actual Azure Storage services.

To start a Storage emulator, execute the following commands, also shown in Figure 4-2:

```
cd C:\Program Files (x86)\Microsoft SDKs\Azure\Storage Emulator
AzureStorageEmulator.exe start
```

```
Select C:\WINDOWS\system32\cmd.exe

C:\Program Files (x86)\Microsoft SDKs\Azure\Storage Emulator>AzureStorageEmulator.exe start
Windows Azure Storage Emulator 5.0.0.0 command line tool
The storage emulator was successfully started.

C:\Program Files (x86)\Microsoft SDKs\Azure\Storage Emulator>cmd /K AzureStorageEmulator.exe help
Windows Azure Storage Emulator 5.0.0.0 command line tool
Usage:
    AzureStorageEmulator.exe init            : Initialize the emulator database and configuration.
    AzureStorageEmulator.exe start           : Start the emulator.
    AzureStorageEmulator.exe stop            : Stop the emulator.
    AzureStorageEmulator.exe status          : Get current emulator status.
    AzureStorageEmulator.exe clear           : Delete all data in the emulator.
    AzureStorageEmulator.exe help [command]  : Show general or command-specific help.

See the following URL for more command line help: http://go.microsoft.com/fwlink/?LinkId=392235

C:\Program Files (x86)\Microsoft SDKs\Azure\Storage Emulator>
```

Figure 4-2. *Azure Storage emulator*

To test the connectivity to Storage emulator, we will create a simple .NET Core console application, shown in Figure 4-3. Then we'll create a test table with sample data.

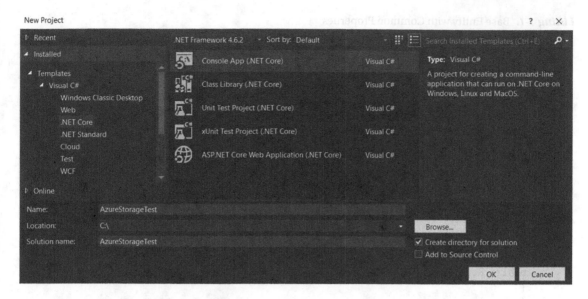

Figure 4-3. *.NET Core console application*

Once the solution is created in VS 2017, right-click the project and select the Manage NuGet Packages option. Search for the `WindowsAzure.Storage` NuGet package and install it as shown in Figure 4-4.

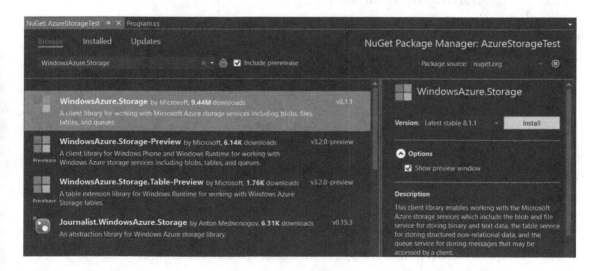

Figure 4-4. *Installing the WindowsAzure.Storage NuGet package*

Create a base type of Table Entity, which will hold common properties such as `CreatedDate`, `UpdatedDate`, `CreatedBy`, `UpdatedBy`, and `IsDeleted` shared by all entities (see Listing 4-1). These properties are useful for tracking the user account through which the entity is being inserted or modified. The `IsDeleted` property is useful for soft-deleting an entity.

Listing 4-1. Base Entity with Common Properties

```
public class BaseEntity : TableEntity
{
    public bool IsDeleted { get; set; }
    public DateTime CreatedDate { get; set; }
    public DateTime UpdatedDate { get; set; }
    public string CreatedBy { get; set; }
    public string UpdatedBy { get; set; }
}
```

Create a Book entity by inheriting BaseEntity, as shown in Listing 4-2. We'll use this entity to perform sample data operations against the Storage emulator.

Listing 4-2. Book Entity

```
public class Book : BaseEntity
{
    public Book()
    {
    }

    public Book(int bookid, string publisher)
    {
        this.RowKey = bookid.ToString();
        this.PartitionKey = publisher;
    }

    public int BookId { get; set; }
    public string BookName { get; set; }
    public string Author { get; set; }
    public string Publisher { get; set; }
}
```

Open the Program.cs file and add the namespaces shown in Listing 4-3 to support the storage operations API.

Listing 4-3. Azure Storage Namespaces

```
// Azure Storage Namespaces
using Microsoft.WindowsAzure.Storage;
using Microsoft.WindowsAzure.Storage.Table;
```

Next, we update the Main method to support Table storage operations as shown in Listing 4-4.

Listing 4-4. Main Method of .NET Core Console Application

```
class Program
{
    static void Main()
    {
        // Azure Storage Account and Table Service Instances
        CloudStorageAccount storageAccount;
        CloudTableClient tableClient;
```

```
        // Connnect to Storage Account
        storageAccount = CloudStorageAccount.Parse("UseDevelopmentStorage=true");

        // Create the Table 'Book', if it not exists
        tableClient = storageAccount.CreateCloudTableClient();
        CloudTable table = tableClient.GetTableReference("Book");
        table.CreateIfNotExistsAsync();

        // Create a Book instance
        Book book = new Book() { Author = "Rami", BookName = "ASP.NET Core With Azure",
        Publisher = "APress" };
        book.BookId = 1;
        book.RowKey = book.BookId.ToString();
        book.PartitionKey = book.Publisher;
        book.CreatedDate = DateTime.UtcNow;
        book.UpdatedDate = DateTime.UtcNow;

        // Insert and execute operations
        TableOperation insertOperation = TableOperation.Insert(book);
        table.ExecuteAsync(insertOperation);

        Console.ReadLine();
    }
}
```

We first create the instances of the Azure Storage account and Table service. Using the CloudStorageAcccount instance, we can connect to the Azure Storage account based on the connection string. In this sample, we get connected to a local storage emulator.

■ **Note**   UseDevelopmentStorage=true is the connection string to be used to perform storage operations on the Storage emulator.

We created a Book instance and saved it to table storage by using the ExecuteAsync method.

■ **Note**   CreateIfNotExisitsAsync and ExecuteAsync trigger asynchronous operations. The invoking method should be an async method with the return type of Task. Await should be used to suspend the execution of the invoking method until the awaited task completes.

Run the program, and it should execute successfully.

To explore the contents of Azure Storage, open the Cloud Explorer view in VS 2017, as shown in Figure 4-5.

Figure 4-5. *Visual Studio Cloud Explorer option*

You can see the inserted Book entity in the Cloud Explorer view, as shown in Figure 4-6.

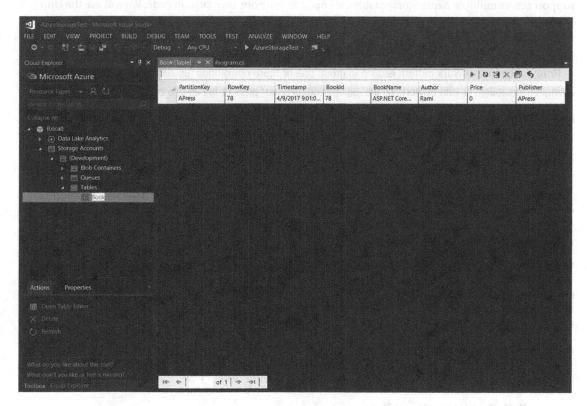

Figure 4-6. *Cloud Explorer displaying the Book entity from local storage*

■ **Note** Visual Studio's Cloud Explorer can connect with both an Azure Storage account and a local emulator. It can display tables, blobs, and queues.

Azure Table Storage Unit of Work Pattern

The atomicity, consistency, isolation, and durability (ACID) properties are considered the basic prerequisite for any storage platform. These properties ensure that storage will always be in a stable state and thereby provide reliable application design models. The sequence of storage operations that follows ACID properties can be labeled as a single logical operation called a transaction.

Different databases such as SQL Server and Oracle follow different approaches to provide transactional support to data operations. Azure Storage by default provides transaction support to entity groups with following key requirements:

1. All entities must have the same PartitionKey value.

2. An entity can appear only once in the transaction, and only one operation may be performed against it.

3. The transaction can include at most 100 entities, and its total payload may be no more than 4MB in size.

Azure storage has no support for transactions that span across multiple tables. To achieve transaction support across multiple Azure Storage tables, we need to write our own custom code. We will use the Unit of Work design pattern along with the Generic Repository pattern to build a simple transaction system for Azure Table Storage services.

■ **Note**   The Unit of Work pattern is used to group one or more operations (usually database operations) into a single transaction, or unit of work, so that all operations either pass or fail as one batch.

A normal repository class provides extension methods, usually for CRUD operations, for a given Table entity, whereas a generic repository can be used for all the entities to perform the same operations. This is useful in achieving reusable code.

We get started by creating an IRepository interface using generics. This interface defines the basic operations for inserting, updating, deleting, and reading data from Azure Table storage, as shown in Listing 4-5.

Listing 4-5. IRepository<T> Interface

```
using Microsoft.WindowsAzure.Storage.Table;
using System;
using System.Collections.Generic;
using System.Text;
using System.Threading.Tasks;

namespace ASC.DataAccess.Interfaces
{
    public interface IRepository<T> where T : TableEntity
    {
        Task<T> AddAsync(T entity);
        Task<T> UpdateAsync(T entity);
        Task DeleteAsync(T entity);
        Task<T> FindAsync(string partitionKey, string rowKey);
        Task<IEnumerable<T>> FindAllByPartitionKeyAsync(string partitionkey);
        Task<IEnumerable<T>> FindAllAsync();
        Task CreateTableAsync();
    }
}
```

Implement IRepository<T> onto Repository<T>, as shown in Listing 4-6. In the constructor of the Repository<T> class, we create the instances of CloudStorageAccount and CloudTableClient. We will also get the reference of CloudTable and hold it in a private variable.

■ **Note**   The constructor of Repository<T> will take the IUnitOfWork instance as a parameter. This is required to keep track of all storage operations performed using the repository, which will be used to roll back the entire transaction in case of exceptions. The ConnectionString that is required to create an instance of the Azure Storage instance is passed by using the UnitOfWork instance.

More details on IUnitOfWork are be discussed later in the chapter.

Listing 4-6. Respository<T> Class

```
using ASC.DataAccess.Interfaces;
using ASC.Models.BaseTypes;
using ASC.Utilities;
using Microsoft.WindowsAzure.Storage;
using Microsoft.WindowsAzure.Storage.Table;
using System;
using System.Collections.Generic;
using System.Threading.Tasks;
using System.Reflection;

namespace ASC.DataAccess
{
    public class Repository<T> : IRepository<T> where T : TableEntity, new()
    {
        private readonly CloudStorageAccount storageAccount;
        private readonly CloudTableClient tableClient;
        private readonly CloudTable storageTable;

        public IUnitOfWork Scope { get; set; }

        public Repository(IUnitOfWork scope)
        {
            storageAccount = CloudStorageAccount.Parse(scope.ConnectionString);

            tableClient = storageAccount.CreateCloudTableClient();
            CloudTable table = tableClient.GetTableReference(typeof(T).Name);

            this.storageTable = table;
            this.Scope = scope;
        }
    }
}
```

By default, transactions are not supported by Azure Table storage operations. If an exception occurs while performing insert/update/delete actions on multiple entities in one transaction, we have to revert the entire transaction so that Azure Table storage will not be left with partial entities. For the Automobile Service Center application, we will create custom rollback logic, as shown in Listing 4-7.

We will create a reverse action for every insert, update, and delete action and store the reverse action in a queue. In situations of transient exceptions, we have to execute all the reverse actions from the queue so that the committed entities will be rolled back.

The CreateRollbackAction method does the actual work of creating a rollback action—which is typically to delete for an insert, set the IsDeleted flag to false for a delete, or replace the updated entity with the original entity for an update operation.

Listing 4-7. Extended Respository<T> Class

```
private async Task<Action> CreateRollbackAction(TableOperation operation)
{
    if (operation.OperationType == TableOperationType.Retrieve) return null;

    var tableEntity = operation.Entity;
    var cloudTable = storageTable;
    switch (operation.OperationType)
    {
        case TableOperationType.Insert:
            return async () => await UndoInsertOperationAsync(cloudTable, tableEntity);
        case TableOperationType.Delete:
            return async () => await UndoDeleteOperation(cloudTable, tableEntity);
        case TableOperationType.Replace:
            var retrieveResult = await cloudTable.ExecuteAsync(TableOperation.
            Retrieve(tableEntity.PartitionKey, tableEntity.RowKey));
            return async () => await UndoReplaceOperation(cloudTable, retrieveResult.Result
            as DynamicTableEntity, tableEntity);
        default:
            throw new InvalidOperationException("The storage operation cannot be
            identified.");
    }
}

private async Task UndoInsertOperationAsync(CloudTable table, ITableEntity entity)
{
    var deleteOperation = TableOperation.Delete(entity);
    await table.ExecuteAsync(deleteOperation);
}

private async Task UndoDeleteOperation(CloudTable table, ITableEntity entity)
{
    var entityToRestore = entity as BaseEntity;
    entityToRestore.IsDeleted = false;

    var insertOperation = TableOperation.Replace(entity);
    await table.ExecuteAsync(insertOperation);
}

private async Task UndoReplaceOperation(CloudTable table, ITableEntity originalEntity,
ITableEntity newEntity)
{
    if (originalEntity != null)
    {
        if (!String.IsNullOrEmpty(newEntity.ETag)) originalEntity.ETag = newEntity.ETag;

        var replaceOperation = TableOperation.Replace(originalEntity);
        await table.ExecuteAsync(replaceOperation);
    }
}
```

As shown in Listing 4-8, we will implement the AddAsync, UpdateAsync, DeleteAsync, FindAsync, FindAllAsync, and FindAllByPartitionKeyAsync methods to create the respective TableOperation instance. FindAsync and FindAllAsync return a specific entity and all entities in a storage partition, respectively. The transaction's scope is limited to insert, update, and delete operations. So AddAsync, UpdateAsync, and DeleteAsync methods use a common ExecuteAsync method that will perform the insert, update, and delete actions and create a rollback action that will be stored in the queue of the IUnitOfWork instance. We will implement the CreateTableAsync method to create the table if it doesn't exist in Azure Storage.

Listing 4-8. Extended Respository<T> Class

```
public async Task<T> AddAsync(T entity)
{
    var entityToInsert = entity as BaseEntity;
    entityToInsert.CreatedDate = DateTime.UtcNow;
    entityToInsert.UpdatedDate = DateTime.UtcNow;

    TableOperation insertOperation = TableOperation.Insert(entity);
    var result = await ExecuteAsync(insertOperation);
    return result.Result as T;
}

public async Task<T> UpdateAsync(T entity)
{
    var entityToUpdate = entity as BaseEntity;
    entityToUpdate.UpdatedDate = DateTime.UtcNow;

    TableOperation updateOperation = TableOperation.Replace(entity);
    var result = await ExecuteAsync(updateOperation);
    return result.Result as T;
}

public async Task DeleteAsync(T entity)
{
    var entityToDelete = entity as BaseEntity;
    entityToDelete.UpdatedDate = DateTime.UtcNow;
    entityToDelete.IsDeleted = true;

    TableOperation deleteOperation = TableOperation.Replace(entityToDelete);
    await ExecuteAsync(deleteOperation);
}

public async Task<T> FindAsync(string partitionKey, string rowKey)
{
    TableOperation retrieveOperation = TableOperation.Retrieve<T>(partitionKey, rowKey);
    var result = await storageTable.ExecuteAsync(retrieveOperation);
    return result.Result as T;
}

public async Task<IEnumerable<T>> FindAllByPartitionKeyAsync(string partitionkey)
{
    TableQuery<T> query = new TableQuery<T>().Where(TableQuery.GenerateFilterCondition("Part
    itionKey", QueryComparisons.Equal, partitionkey));
```

```
    TableContinuationToken tableContinuationToken = null;
    var result = await storageTable.ExecuteQuerySegmentedAsync(query, tableContinuation
    Token);
    return result.Results as IEnumerable<T>;
}

public async Task<IEnumerable<T>> FindAllAsync()
{
    TableQuery<T> query = new TableQuery<T>();
    TableContinuationToken tableContinuationToken = null;
    var result = await storageTable.ExecuteQuerySegmentedAsync(query, tableContinuation
    Token);
    return result.Results as IEnumerable<T>;
}

public async Task CreateTableAsync()
{
    CloudTable table = tableClient.GetTableReference(typeof(T).Name);
    await table.CreateIfNotExistsAsync();
}

private async Task<TableResult> ExecuteAsync(TableOperation operation)
{
    var rollbackAction = CreateRollbackAction(operation);
    var result = await storageTable.ExecuteAsync(operation);
    Scope.RollbackActions.Enqueue(rollbackAction);
    return result;
}
```

The BaseEntity's properties are being set in the repository, so that there will not be any redundancy in the application code. In the Automobile Service Center application, the CreatedBy and UpdatedBy properties will be set from the logged-in user's identity.

■ **Note** In the Automobile Service Center application, we will pass the connection string from the configuration file through IOptions<ApplicationSettings>.

We will now create the IUnitOfWork interface shown in Listing 4-9, which will be the primary face for all storage interactions. IUnitOfWork will house all the instances of repositories and handle rollback operations in case of exceptions. IUnitOfWork holds the ConnectionString of Azure Table storage. IUnitOfWork is inherited from IDisposable.

Listing 4-9. IUnitOfWork Interface

```
using Microsoft.WindowsAzure.Storage.Table;
using System;
using System.Collections.Generic;
using System.Text;
using System.Threading.Tasks;
```

```
namespace ASC.DataAccess.Interfaces
{
    public interface IUnitOfWork : IDisposable
    {
        Queue<Task<Action>> RollbackActions { get; set; }
        string ConnectionString { get; set; }
        IRepository<T> Repository<T>() where T : TableEntity;
        void CommitTransaction();
    }
}
```

The IUnitOfWork interface is implemented on the UnitOfWork class, as shown in Listing 4-10. UnitOfWork implements both the IUnitOfWork interface and IDisposable (as IUnitOfWork is inherited from IDisposable). Implementing IDisposable helps UnitOfWork to fire the Dispose method at the time of exceptions. The constructor of the UnitOfWork implementation takes ConnectionString as a parameter that is initialized to the ConnectionString property of UnitOfWork; this ConnectionString is subsequently used in Repository<> to connect to Azure Table storage.

During disposition of UnitOfWork (the Dispose method), we check whether the UnitOfWork transaction was completed (based on the complete flag, which is set in the CommitTransaction method). If the transaction was completed, no action will be taken, and the rollback actions queue (this queue will be filled with rollback actions by the repositories) will be emptied. If the transaction was not completed, all the rollback actions will be executed from the queue. Once the disposition method is completed, we revert the complete flag to false, so that UnitOfWork can be used multiple times in the same scope.

The CommitTransaction method should be called to commit a transaction to Azure Table storage. Otherwise, the entire transaction will be rolled back.

UnitOfWork will also hold different repositories through the Repository<T> implementation. First it checks whether the requested repository is available in the pool of repositories (Dictionary<string, object>). If it is, we return the repository. If the repository is not present, we create a new instance of the repository, place it in the pool, and return it to the requestor.

Listing 4-10. UnitOfWork Class

```
using ASC.DataAccess.Interfaces;
using Microsoft.WindowsAzure.Storage.Table;
using System;
using System.Collections.Generic;
using System.Text;
using System.Threading.Tasks;

namespace ASC.DataAccess
{
    public class UnitOfWork : IUnitOfWork
    {
        private bool disposed;
        private bool complete;
        private Dictionary<string, object> _repositories;
        public Queue<Task<Action>> RollbackActions { get; set; }

        public string ConnectionString { get; set; }
        public UnitOfWork(string connectionString)
        {
```

```
        ConnectionString = connectionString;
        RollbackActions = new Queue<Task<Action>>();
}
public void CommitTransaction()
{
    complete = true;
}

~UnitOfWork()
{
    Dispose(false);
}

private void Dispose(bool disposing)
{
        if (disposing)
        {
            try
            {
                if (!complete) RollbackTransaction();
            }
            finally
            {
                RollbackActions.Clear();
            }
        }
        complete = false;
}

public void Dispose()
{
    Dispose(true);
    GC.SuppressFinalize(this);
}

private void RollbackTransaction()
{
    while (RollbackActions.Count > 0)
    {
        var undoAction = RollbackActions.Dequeue();
        undoAction.Result();
    }
}

public IRepository<T> Repository<T>() where T : TableEntity
{
    if (_repositories == null)
        _repositories = new Dictionary<string, object>();

    var type = typeof(T).Name;
```

```
        if (_repositories.ContainsKey(type)) return (IRepository<T>)_repositories[type];

        var repositoryType = typeof(Repository<>);

        var repositoryInstance =
            Activator.CreateInstance(repositoryType
                .MakeGenericType(typeof(T)), this);

        _repositories.Add(type, repositoryInstance);

        return (IRepository<T>)_repositories[type];
    }
  }
}
```

■ **Note**   The implementations of the generic repository and Unit of Work patterns that have been demonstrated so far are one of many possible implementations. Different projects may require different tailored approaches. The concept of creating a transaction scope was taken from Valery Mizonov [5].

To keep it simple, we created rollback actions only for insert, update, and delete operations on Table storage. Other table storage operations (for example, InsertOrReplace, InsertOrMerge, and Merge) are also widely used but beyond the scope of this book.

Sample CRUD Operations

In this section, we will update the console application that we created earlier in order to test the UnitOfWork implementation with the code from Listings 4-11 to 4-13. First, we create a new entity, as shown in Listing 4-11.

Listing 4-11. Create a New Entity

```
using (var _unitOfWork = new UnitOfWork("UseDevelopmentStorage=true;"))
{
    var bookRepository = _unitOfWork.Repository<Book>();
    await bookRepository.CreateTableAsync();

    Book book = new Book() { Author = "Rami", BookName = "ASP.NET Core With Azure",
    Publisher = "APress" };
    book.BookId = 1;
    book.RowKey = book.BookId.ToString();
    book.PartitionKey = book.Publisher;
    var data = await bookRepository.AddAsync(book);
    Console.WriteLine(data);

    _unitOfWork.CommitTransaction();
}
```

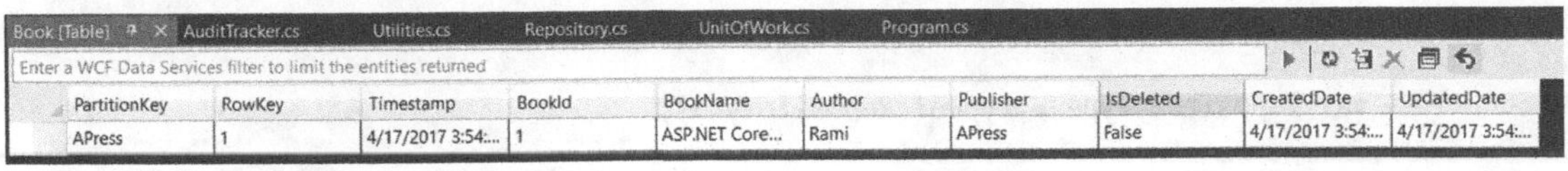

Figure 4-7. *Inserted Book entity in local storage*

■ **Note** The use of `Repository.CreateTableAsync()` will be automated in later chapters, so that there is no need to explicitly call this method to create a table.

To update an entity, we first find the entity and then update it, as shown in Listing 4-12.

Listing 4-12. Find an Entity and Update It

```
using (var _unitOfWork = new UnitOfWork("UseDevelopmentStorage=true;"))
{
    var bookRepository = _unitOfWork.Repository<Book>();
    await bookRepository.CreateTableAsync();
    var data = await bookRepository.FindAsync("APress", "1");
    Console.WriteLine(data);

    data.Author = "Rami Vemula";
    var updatedData = await bookRepository.UpdateAsync(data);
    Console.WriteLine(updatedData);

    _unitOfWork.CommitTransaction();
}
```

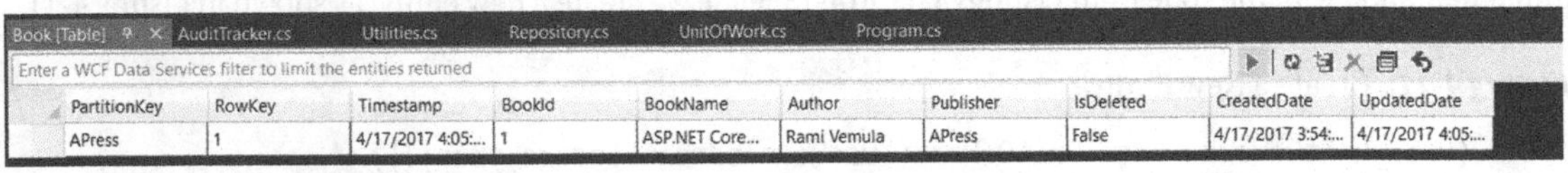

Figure 4-8. *Updated Book entity in local storage*

To delete an entity, we have to use the code in Listing 4-13. We throw an example to test the rollback action of IUnitOfWork. As a result of the exception occurring before committing IUnitOfWork, the entire delete transaction will be rolled back and the entity will be persisted.

Listing 4-13. Delete an Entity and Roll Back Transaction Support

```
using (var _unitOfWork = new UnitOfWork("UseDevelopmentStorage=true;"))
{
    var bookRepository = _unitOfWork.Repository<Book>();
    await bookRepository.CreateTableAsync();
    var data = await bookRepository.FindAsync("APress", "1");
    Console.WriteLine(data);
```

```
    await bookRepository.DeleteAsync(data);
    Console.WriteLine("Deleted");

    // Throw an exception to test rollback actions
    // throw new Exception();

    _unitOfWork.CommitTransaction();
}
```

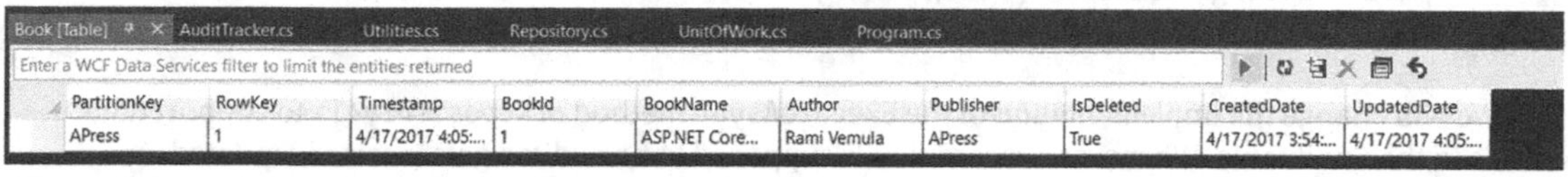
Book [Table]
AuditTracker.cs
Utilities.cs
Repository.cs
UnitOfWork.cs
Program.cs
Enter a WCF Data Services filter to limit the entities returned
PartitionKey
RowKey
Timestamp
BookId
BookName
Author
Publisher
IsDeleted
CreatedDate
UpdatedDate
APress
1
4/17/2017 4:05:...
1
ASP.NET Core...
Rami Vemula
APress
True
4/17/2017 3:54:...
4/17/2017 4:05:...

Figure 4-9. *Deleting an entity and rolling back the transaction*

■ **Note** To test rollback actions, uncomment the code that throws the exception. It will revert the delete operation.

Auditing Data Through Snapshots

The design of application data should incorporate seamless control over the entire life cycle of critical entities. At any given point in time, the system should be capable of identifying and analyzing all the changes that have happened for a particular entity since the point of its generation. This kind of auditing mechanism helps reinforce reliable data access, enforce secure channels to the data by identifying data thefts and inconsistent access, and track changes to important business data. In this section, we'll implement a robust audit mechanism to the `UnitOfWork` we created in the previous section.

We will create the `IAuditTracker` interface to identify the entities that are required to be audited. This interface should be implemented on all the entities that will participate in auditing. `IAuditTracker` is shown in Listing 4-14.

Listing 4-14. IAuditTracker Interface

```
public interface IAuditTracker
{
}
```

Now modify the `Book` entity to implement the preceding interface as shown in Listing 4-15.

Listing 4-15. Updated Book Entity with IAuditTracker Implementation

```
public class Book : BaseEntity, IAuditTracker
    {
        public Book()
        {
        }
```

```
        public Book(int bookid, string publisher)
        {
            this.RowKey = bookid.ToString();
            this.PartitionKey = publisher;
        }

        public int BookId { get; set; }
        public string BookName { get; set; }
        public string Author { get; set; }
        public string Publisher { get; set; }
    }
```

We will change the implementation of the ExecuteAsync method of Repository<T> to support data entries to the audit table. Whenever a record that is supposed to be audited gets inserted, updated, or deleted, an audit record will be entered into the audit table. We also need to update the CreateTableAsync method to create the audit table if the main entity supports audit snapshots, as shown in Listing 4-16.

Listing 4-16. CreateTableAsync and ExecuteAsync Methods with Audit Changes

```
        public async Task CreateTableAsync()
        {
            CloudTable table = tableClient.GetTableReference(typeof(T).Name);
            await table.CreateIfNotExistsAsync();

            if (typeof(IAuditTracker).IsAssignableFrom(typeof(T)))
            {
                var auditTable = tableClient.GetTableReference($"{typeof(T).Name}Audit");
                await auditTable.CreateIfNotExistsAsync();
            }
        }
private async Task<TableResult> ExecuteAsync(TableOperation operation)
        {
            var rollbackAction = CreateRollbackAction(operation);
            var result = await storageTable.ExecuteAsync(operation);
            Scope.RollbackActions.Enqueue(rollbackAction);

            // Audit Implementation
            if (operation.Entity is IAuditTracker)
            {
                // Make sure we do not use same RowKey and PartitionKey
                var auditEntity = ObjectExtension.CopyObject<T>(operation.Entity);
                auditEntity.PartitionKey = $"{auditEntity.PartitionKey}-{auditEntity.RowKey}";
                auditEntity.RowKey = $"{DateTime.UtcNow.ToString("yyyy-MM-ddTHH:mm:ss.fff")}";

                var auditOperation = TableOperation.Insert(auditEntity);
                var auditRollbackAction = CreateRollbackAction(auditOperation, true);

                var auditTable = tableClient.GetTableReference($"{typeof(T).Name}Audit");
                await auditTable.ExecuteAsync(auditOperation);

                Scope.RollbackActions.Enqueue(auditRollbackAction);
            }
```

```
        return result;
    }

    private async Task<Action> CreateRollbackAction(TableOperation operation, bool
    IsAuditOperation = false)
    {
        if (operation.OperationType == TableOperationType.Retrieve) return null;

        var tableEntity = operation.Entity;
        var cloudTable = !IsAuditOperation ? storageTable : tableClient.
        GetTableReference($"{typeof(T).Name}Audit");
        switch (operation.OperationType)
        {
            case TableOperationType.Insert:
                return async () => await UndoInsertOperationAsync(cloudTable, tableEntity);
            case TableOperationType.Delete:
                return async () => await UndoDeleteOperation(cloudTable, tableEntity);
            case TableOperationType.Replace:
                var retrieveResult = await cloudTable.ExecuteAsync(TableOperation.
                Retrieve(tableEntity.PartitionKey, tableEntity.RowKey));
                return async () => await UndoReplaceOperation(cloudTable,
                retrieveResult.Result as DynamicTableEntity, tableEntity);
            default:
                throw new InvalidOperationException("The storage operation cannot be
                identified.");
        }
    }
}
```

The audit table will be created with the name of the entity followed by the Audit word—for example, BookAudit. One more important point to remember is to make sure the audit records have different RowKeys and PartitionKeys because many audit records can exist for a given entity record. In our implementation, we use DateTime.UtcNow as the RowKey and a combination of the original entity's PartitionKey and RowKey as the PartitionKey for the audit record.

■ **Note** Audit records should also participate in rollback transaction actions. Otherwise, even if the main entity is not inserted, updated, or deleted, an audit record will be inserted into the audit table. This behavior creates data-integrity problems. So the CreateRollbackAction method has been changed to roll back audit entries.

We need to have an Object extension to create a copy of the entity, as shown in Listing 4-17. This is required to create a copy of the original entity and transform the copy as an audit record.

Listing 4-17. CopyObject<T> Method

```
using Newtonsoft.Json;
public static class ObjectExtension
{
    public static T CopyObject<T>(this object objSource)
    {
        var serialized = JsonConvert.SerializeObject(objSource);
```

```
        return JsonConvert.DeserializeObject<T>(serialized);
    }
}
```

When we execute the insert, update, and delete operations on the Book entity, audit records will be created, as shown in Figure 4-10.

	PartitionKey	RowKey	Timestamp	BookId	BookName	Author	Publisher	IsDeleted	CreatedDate	UpdatedDate
	APress-1	2017-04-17T15:...	4/17/2017 3:54:...	1	ASP.NET Core...	Rami	APress	False	4/17/2017 3:54:...	4/17/2017 3:54:...
	APress-1	2017-04-17T16:...	4/17/2017 4:05:...	1	ASP.NET Core...	Rami Vemula	APress	False	4/17/2017 3:54:...	4/17/2017 4:05:...
	APress-1	2017-04-17T16:...	4/17/2017 4:05:...	1	ASP.NET Core...	Rami Vemula	APress	True	4/17/2017 3:54:...	4/17/2017 4:05:...

Figure 4-10. Audit records for the Book entity

Create the Unit of Work Project in the Automobile Service Center Solution

The UnitOfWork and Repository<T> patterns that we have developed are being tested so far in a .NET Core console application. In this section, we will port this code to our Automobile Service Center solution.

Create a new .NET Core class library project called ASC.Models in the ASC.Solution, as shown in Figure 4-11. This project is going to hold all the Azure data models for the Automobile Service Center application that are used for persistence.

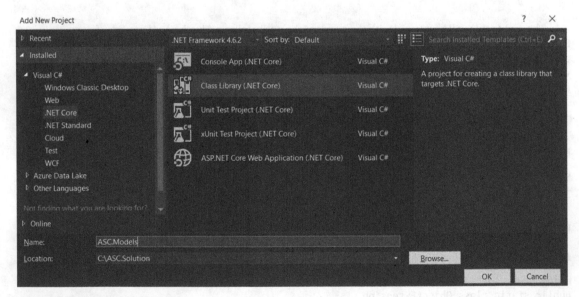

Figure 4-11. ASC.Models project

Right-click the ASC.Models project and select the Manage NuGet Packages option. Search for the WindowsAzure.Storage package and install it.

DOMAIN-DRIVEN DEVELOPMENT

There is a concept in domain-driven development that the core business models should be independent of any storage or platform. Having independent models helps achieve reusability across various types of applications without carrying storage dependencies. This concept is subjective in terms of the level of complexity and maintainability we want to achieve in a given application.

In terms of complexity, when we try to maintain business models independent of a storage platform, we have to introduce an extra layer of mappings. We have to create business models (independent of storage dependencies) and data access models (which will have storage dependencies), and introduce an extra layer to convert business models to data access models, and vice versa. This conversion is required for each and every data operation.

For the Automobile Service Center application, we are going to implement Azure Table storage's TableEntity on each and every model, so that they serve the common goal of data access and business operations. This way, there is no need to worry about the overhead of model conversion.

Create a folder named BaseTypes, and place BaseEntity and IAuditTracker in different class files. Create a folder named Models, where we are going to place all the models of the Automobile Service Center application (for now, leave it empty).

To place all the utility classes, we will create a new .NET Core class library project called ASC.Utilities to the ASC.Solution, as shown in Figure 4-12.

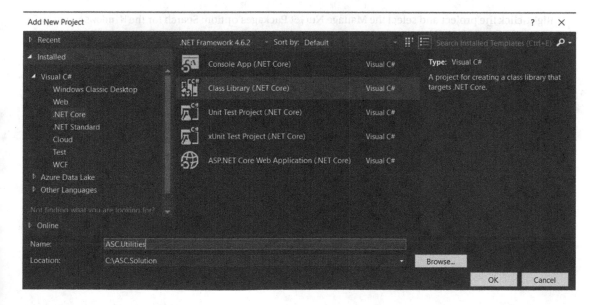

Figure 4-12. *ASC.Utilities project*

Right-click the project and select the Manage NuGet Packages option. Search for the Newtonsoft.Json package and install it.

Create a class file for ObjectExtensions and place the CopyObject<T> method code in it.

To place all the Repository<T> and UnitOfWork related code, create a new .NET Core class library project called ASC.DataAccess at ASC.Solution, as shown in Figure 4-13.

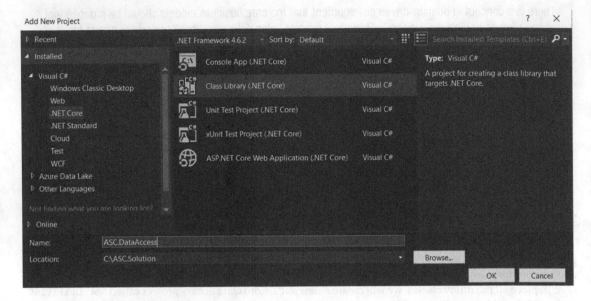

Figure 4-13. *ASC.DataAccess project*

Right-click the project and select the Manage NuGet Packages option. Search for the WindowsAzure. Storage package and install it.

Create an Interfaces folder and place the IUnitOfWork and IRepository<T> classes in different class files.

Add references to the ASC.Models and ASC.Utilities projects to ASC.DataAccess, as shown in Figure 4-14.

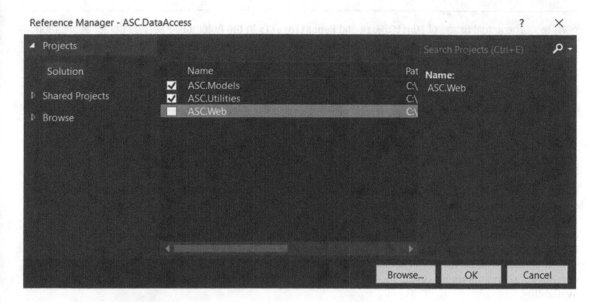

Figure 4-14. Adding ASC.Models and ASC.Utilities project references to the ASC.DataAccess project

Clean and rebuild the solution. The rebuild should be successful. The entire solution structure should be as shown in Figure 4-15.

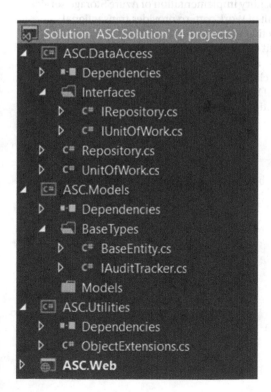

Figure 4-15. Updated ASC.Solution structure

■ **Note**   The actual usage of `IUnitOfWork` and `Repository<T>` in the Automobile Service Center application will be discussed in subsequent chapters as we start developing the screens by using business logic.

Business logic will be segregated into a different class library project that will consume `IUnitOfWork` and `Repository<T>` to perform operations on data.

Summary

In this chapter, you learned the importance of scalable, reliable, and resilient data storage for a robust application design. You explored the Microsoft Azure Cloud platform, which offers services such as databases, distributed file systems, binary data, queues, big-data platforms and extensions, and NoSQL databases. Azure Storage is a storage-as-a-service offering from Microsoft that consists of queues, tables, blobs, disks, and files.

You learned about the performance tiers of Azure Storage, along with security options. You also looked at replication options such as local, zero, geo, and read-access geo redundant storage to support high availability.

You installed an Azure Storage emulator, which provides a local development environment by emulating storage services. Using the emulator, you developed a simple console application that performed a simple CRUD operations. You also used Visual Studio's Storage Explorer to explore storage entities.

You learned the common properties for an Azure Storage entity, such as `PartitionKey` and `RowKey`. You developed a Unit of work pattern using the generic repository implementation of Azure Storage services through the `WindowsAzure.Storage` NuGet package. The Unit of Work pattern provides transactional support, which ensures that all operations in a single transaction will be either committed or rolled back. The Unit of Work implementation was later extended to audit data tracking; the entire history of a given entity was tracked from the point of its generation.

The chapter concluded by creating different .NET Core class library projects at the Automobile Service Center solution and porting all the code related to the Unit of Work and repository to them. The practical use of the Unit of Work at the Automobile Service Center application will be detailed in later chapters.

Reference

1. `http://smallbusiness.chron.com/role-data-business-20405.html`

CHAPTER 5

■ ■ ■

Test-Driven Approach Using xUnit.net

Over the past decade, test-driven development (TDD) has become a widely accepted and key area in the software development process. In traditional development approaches, most design and technical gaps were usually identified during the post-development or testing phases. This would not only affect the quality of the application but also incur severe operational overhead for project timelines and business goals. TDD techniques help identify design and technical gaps up front, even before development of a particular functionality begins. TDD consists of small development iterations in which unit test cases are written for an application feature and then the actual development of the feature starts targeting the 100 percent pass rate of test cases.

The TDD approach has many advantages. Here are a few important highlights:

- TDD identifies design mishaps and edge cases at the early stages of development, thereby reducing the overall development time by reducing the need to redo work.

- Individual components can be tested, which provides better control over the quality of code.

- The quality of technical design will be improved, as unit testing promotes loosely coupled components.

- Understanding and maintaining legacy code can be much easier with unit tests.

- Automating unit tests along with build definitions ensures that the right code is in the repository.

- Unit tests can be considered documentation.

- The availability of new unit-testing frameworks make tests easy to write.

A good unit-test suite for an application should comprise the following standards:

- Unit tests should cover small and independent code blocks.

- One test case should have one assertion, which should be confined to the test under execution. In rare cases, a maximum of two assertions should be made.

- Unit tests should be independent of the infrastructure, which means they should not have any physical dependencies such as databases or file systems.

- The code that we write in test classes should not be included in the regular application code.

© Rami Vemula 2017
R. Vemula, *Real-Time Web Application Development*, https://doi.org/10.1007/978-1-4842-3270-5_5

- Unit tests should be able to run independently using test runners and should support automation.

- Proper test data stubs should be created and used to test various scenarios of parameterized tests.

- Unit tests should use mocking frameworks to inject dependencies such as web services or the data access layer. Fake implementations should be created for APIs, such as a session or cache, which are frequently used and should persist for subsequent tests.

- Unit tests should be integrated as part of the build process, and reports should be generated for code coverage metrics.

This chapter presents the basic concepts of test-driven development with the xUnit.net framework. In the process, we will define the standards for the Automobile Server Center application and develop sample xUnit tests. We will use MOQ as the mocking framework through which we will mock actual Azure Storage service calls.

Test-Driven Development Life Cycle

Test-driven development primarily comprises three phases, illustrated in Figure 5-1. These phases repeat in cycles for every change in the functional requirement. The phases are as follows:

1. Test-case generation
2. Application code development
3. Code optimization

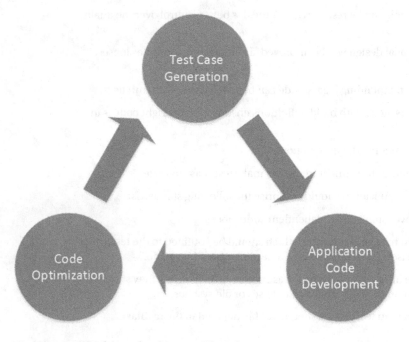

Figure 5-1. *Test-driven development life cycle*

During *test-case generation*, a developer first writes the test cases targeting a business requirement by using frameworks such as xUnit. These test cases need not necessarily cover the entire functionality, but should drive some of the goals of end functional results. These test cases should be developed before getting started with application code. After test cases are completed, they are executed with an expectation that all will fail. The main intention of this phase is to ensure that the functional requirements are captured in the form of test cases.

Application code development is the next phase; a developer starts writing application code to meet the objectives of the test cases developed in the previous phase. This phase ensures that the developer writes only code that is required for passing the test cases and doesn't end up writing unwanted code. When the application code is ready, the test cases are again executed with the expectation that all test cases will pass.

In the *code optimization* phase, the application code is refactored to meet coding standards and improve performance to target production readiness. Test cases are executed again, and if any of the test cases fails, the application code should be fixed accordingly.

After the code optimization phase, a new set of test cases should be developed in order to implement any missing functionalities. The entire process therefore occurs repetitively until all functionality is achieved.

Understanding xUnit.net

xUnit.net is a free, open source, community-based, unit-testing tool for the .NET Framework and .NET Core. Developed by James Newkirk and Brad Wilson, xUnit is the latest technology for unit testing in C#, F#, VB.NET, and other .NET languages. It is part of the .NET Foundation and operates under its code of conduct. xUnit.net provides an exhaustive API for writing unit test cases, and its test runner can be easily integrated with Visual Studio and automated build systems including TFS and Travis.

xUnit has a lot of advantages compared to its contemporaries such as MSTest and NUnit:

- Can run tests under isolation by creating a new instance per test

- Provides more control over the Test class and Test method execution

- Has great extensibility support, as we can extend the default attributes and assertions more easily than in other frameworks

- Has good support for passing multiple datasets to the same test by using parameterized tests

- Promotes writing clean and maintainable tests

- Encourages writing tests by using default language features instead of relying on a framework

- Has good support for asserting exceptions

- Has faster performance than other frameworks

- Doesn't require extra files such as vsmdi to keep track of tests

- Requires no dependency on the file system for test execution

xUnit can be used in any application by installing it via NuGet. Visual Studio has good compatibility with the xUnit runner, which is used to run xUnit tests. All we need to do is to install the xUnit runner from NuGet.

■ **Note** Other frameworks such as NUnit and MSTest are available as alternatives to xUnit, but they fall short in some of the aforementioned key advantages. The current innovation and new features of xUnit are driven by its open source community, which clearly makes xUnit stand out among its competitors.

Getting Started with xUnit.net and MOQ

In this section, we will write simple xUnit test cases for our Automobile Service Center application. To get started, we will focus on writing unit tests for the home controller. To follow the standard of keeping unit-test code separate from application code, we'll create a new .NET Core class library named ASC.Tests, as shown in Figure 5-2.

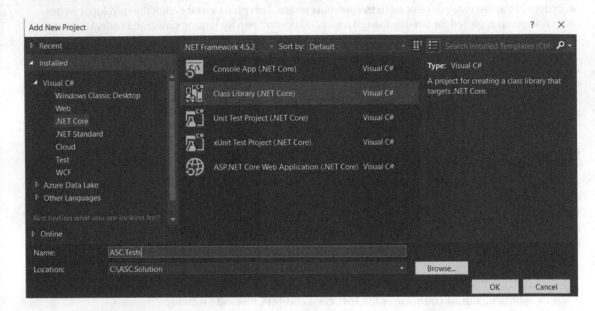

Figure 5-2. *Creating the ASC.Tests project in ASC.Solution*

Install xUnit NuGet as shown in Figure 5-3.

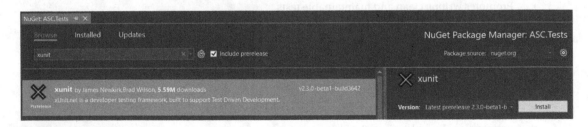

Figure 5-3. *Installing the xUnit NuGet package in the ASC.Tests project*

■ **Note** We will install the latest versions of both xUnit and the xUnit Visual Studio runner.

To run xUnit tests in Visual Studio, we need the xUnit Visual Studio test runner. Install `xUnit.Runner.VisualStudio` from NuGet as shown in Figure 5-4.

Figure 5-4. *Installing the xUnit test runner on the ASC.Tests project*

Because we need to test the home controller, add a reference to the `ASC.Web` project to the `ASC.Tests` project, as shown in Figure 5-5.

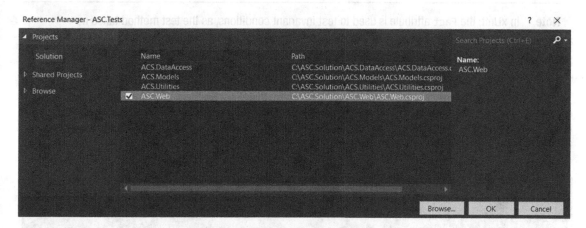

Figure 5-5. *Adding ASC.Web Project references on the ASC.Tests project*

Create a new class file named `HomeControllerTests`. This class is going to hold all the tests related to the home controller. Based on the functional specifications, we understand that the home page should return a type of `ViewResult`, should not return any model, and should contain no validation errors. The basic template to cover these scenarios can be written as shown in Listing 5-1.

Listing 5-1. Template of HomeController Tests

```
using System;
using ASC.Web.Controllers;
using Xunit;

namespace ASC.Tests
{
    public class HomeControllerTests
    {
```

```
    [Fact]
    public void HomeController_Index_View_Test()
    {
    }


    [Fact]
    public void HomeController_Index_NoModel_Test()
    {
    }


    [Fact]
    public void HomeController_Index_Validation_Test()
    {
    }
  }
}
```

■ **Note**   In xUnit, the Fact attribute is used to test invariant conditions, as the test method takes no arguments. The Theory attribute, on the other hand, tests the same test for multiple variant conditions by passing different data to the test method as arguments.

The naming convention is self-explanatory: ControllerName_ActionName_TestCondition_Test. For simplicity, we will complete the View test, followed by the Model and Validation tests. To test action methods in the home controller, we need to create an instance of HomeController in the unit test. We get the error shown in Figure 5-6 when we try to create an instance of HomeController.

Figure 5-6. *Compile error while creating HomeController instance*

It is complaining that no arguments of type IOptions are passed to the HomeController constructor. If we look at the HomeController constructor, we see the IOptions argument being passed, as shown in Listing 5-2.

Listing 5-2. HomeController Constructor

```
private IOptions<ApplicationSettings> _settings;
public HomeController(IOptions<ApplicationSettings> settings)
{
    _settings = settings;
}
```

■ **Note** Refer to "Setting Up the Application Configuration" in Chapter 2. We are using ASP.NET Core's dependency injection to inject the `appsettings.json` configuration via the `IOptions` pattern.

We have a lot of possible resolutions for this issue, including the following: -

- Read the actual `appsettings.json` configuration file from the web project and pass `IOptions<ApplicationSettings>` to the `HomeController` instance.

- Create mock data for `IOptions<ApplicationSettings>` and pass it to the `HomeController` instance.

- Refactor the `HomeController` code so that `IOptions<ApplicationSettings>` is not a constructor injection but instead uses property injection. In unit tests, resolve `IOptions<ApplicationSettings>` with the right sample data and assign it to the property.

As we've discussed in this chapter, unit tests should be independent of the infrastructure and should have minimum dependency on the file system. So we can rule out the first option. Also, constructor injection is a well-known practice for resolving dependencies, which rules out the third option.

Mocking the dependencies will ease up both infrastructure dependencies and forceful refactoring of application code. To create mocks in .NET Core, we use MOQ, a popular mocking framework for .NET applications. Install the MOQ NuGet package on the ASC.Tests project, as shown in Figure 5-7.

Figure 5-7. *Installing the MOQ framework on the ASC.Tests project*

Once installed, the MOQ API can be leveraged by importing the MOQ namespace. We need to import `Microsoft.Extensions.Options` and `ASC.Web.Configuration` to use the `IOptions<>` and `ApplicationSettings` classes.

In the constructor, we create an instance of `Mock<IOptions<>>` and set up the mock to return a new instance of `ApplicationSettings`. Then in the unit test, we pass the mock object to the `HomeController` instance, as shown in Listing 5-3.

Listing 5-3. Using MOQ to Resolve the `IOptions<>` Dependency

```
xxusing System;
using ASC.Web.Controllers;
using Xunit;
using Moq;
using Microsoft.Extensions.Options;
using ASC.Web.Configuration;
```

```
namespace ASC.Tests
{
    public class HomeControllerTests
    {
        private readonly Mock<IOptions<ApplicationSettings>> optionsMock;
        public HomeControllerTests()
        {
            // Create an instance of Mock IOptions
            optionsMock = new Mock<IOptions<ApplicationSettings>>();
            // Set IOptions<> Values property to return ApplicationSettings object
            optionsMock.Setup(ap => ap.Value).Returns(new ApplicationSettings {
            ApplicationTitle = "ASC" });
        }

        [Fact]
        public void HomeController_Index_View_Test()
        {
            // Home controller instantiated with Mock IOptions<> object
            var controller = new HomeController(optionsMock.Object);
        }

        [Fact]
        public void HomeController_Index_NoModel_Test() { }
        [Fact]
        public void HomeController_Index_Validation_Test() { }
    }
}
```

To run our tests, we need to have the Microsoft.TestPlatform.TestHost and Microsoft.NET.Test.Sdk NuGet packages.

Figure 5-8. *Installing the Microsoft.TestPlatform.TestHost NuGet package on the ASC.Tests project*

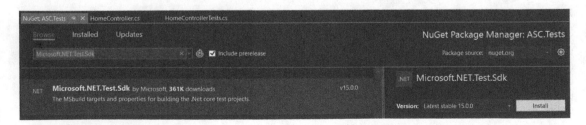

Figure 5-9. *Installing the Microsoft.NET.Test.Sdk NuGet package on the ASC.Tests project*

Open Visual Studio's Test Explorer to discover all the unit tests. Then run all the tests, as shown in Figures 5-10 and 5-11.

Figure 5-10. *Opening Test Explorer in Visual Studio*

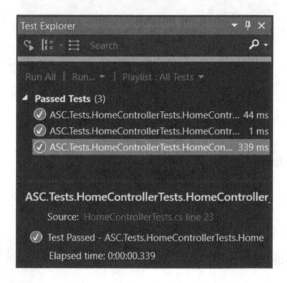

Figure 5-11. *Discovering and running all xUnit test cases from Test Explorer*

To demonstrate a failed test result, expect a `JsonResult` instead of `ViewResult` and rerun the tests. The test should fail, as shown Figure 5-12.

Figure 5-12. *Failed test assertion*

Complete the other two pending tests, as shown in Listing 5-4.

Listing 5-4. HomeController Tests

```
[Fact]
    public void HomeController_Index_NoModel_Test()
    {
        var controller = new HomeController(optionsMock.Object);
        // Assert Model for Null
        Assert.Null((controller.Index() as ViewResult).ViewData.Model);
    }

    [Fact]
    public void HomeController_Index_Validation_Test()
    {
        var controller = new HomeController(optionsMock.Object);
        // Assert ModelState Error Count to 0
        Assert.Equal(0, (controller.Index() as ViewResult).ViewData.ModelState.ErrorCount);
    }
```

Rerun the tests. All of them should pass, as shown in Figure 5-13.

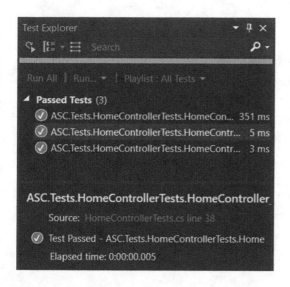

Figure 5-13. *All tests have passed*

We can also run the unit test cases from a command-line prompt. Open CMD, navigate to the test project directory, and execute the dotnet test command, as shown in Figure 5-14.

■ Command Prompt

```
C:\ASC.Solution\ASC.Tests>dotnet test
Build started, please wait...
Build completed.

Test run for C:\ASC.Solution\ASC.Tests\bin\Debug\netcoreapp1.1\ASC.Tests.dll(.NETCoreApp,Version=v1.1)
Microsoft (R) Test Execution Command Line Tool Version 15.0.0.0
Copyright (c) Microsoft Corporation.  All rights reserved.

Starting test execution, please wait...
[xUnit.net 00:00:00.8291804]    Discovering: ASC.Tests
[xUnit.net 00:00:00.9670068]    Discovered:  ASC.Tests
[xUnit.net 00:00:00.9762014]    Starting:    ASC.Tests
[xUnit.net 00:00:01.4299336]    Finished:    ASC.Tests

Total tests: 3. Passed: 3. Failed: 0. Skipped: 0.
Test Run Successful.
Test execution time: 2.9755 Seconds


C:\ASC.Solution\ASC.Tests>_
```

Figure 5-14. *Executing xUnit test cases from the command prompt*

Similarly, if there are any failed tests, they are also reported in CMD, as shown in Figure 5-15.

```
Command Prompt                                                         —    □    ×

C:\ASC.Solution\ASC.Tests>dotnet test
Build started, please wait...
Build completed.
Test run for C:\ASC.Solution\ASC.Tests\bin\Debug\netcoreapp1.1\ASC.Tests.dll(.NETCoreApp,Version=v1.1)
Microsoft (R) Test Execution Command Line Tool Version 15.0.0.0
Copyright (c) Microsoft Corporation.  All rights reserved.

Starting test execution, please wait...
[xUnit.net 00:00:01.6340305]   Discovering: ASC.Tests
[xUnit.net 00:00:01.7787796]   Discovered:  ASC.Tests
[xUnit.net 00:00:01.7883151]   Starting:    ASC.Tests
[xUnit.net 00:00:02.3114810]     ASC.Tests.HomeControllerTests.HomeController_Index_View_Test [FAIL]
[xUnit.net 00:00:02.3129256]       Assert.IsType() Failure
[xUnit.net 00:00:02.3130011]       Expected: Microsoft.AspNetCore.Mvc.JsonResult
[xUnit.net 00:00:02.3130425]       Actual:   Microsoft.AspNetCore.Mvc.ViewResult
[xUnit.net 00:00:02.3141265]       Stack Trace:
[xUnit.net 00:00:02.3156267]          C:\ASC.Solution\ASC.Tests\HomeControllerTests.cs(26,0): at ASC.Tests.HomeController
Tests.HomeController_Index_View_Test()
[xUnit.net 00:00:03.4011778]   Finished:    ASC.Tests
Failed   ASC.Tests.HomeControllerTests.HomeController_Index_View_Test
Error Message:
 Assert.IsType() Failure
Expected: Microsoft.AspNetCore.Mvc.JsonResult
Actual:   Microsoft.AspNetCore.Mvc.ViewResult
Stack Trace:
   at ASC.Tests.HomeControllerTests.HomeController_Index_View_Test() in C:\ASC.Solution\ASC.Tests\HomeControllerTests.cs
:line 26

Total tests: 3. Passed: 2. Failed: 1. Skipped: 0.
Test Run Failed.
Test execution time: 6.4147 Seconds
```

Figure 5-15. *Failed test cases display at the command prompt*

■ **Note**   We have written only a few unit test cases to demonstrate how to get started with xUnit. It is always advisable to write multiple unit test cases to cover all functionality. The recommended process includes the following steps:

1. Complete functional analysis of the screen or component that has to be developed.

2. Write functional test-case documents that outline all the scenarios that have to be tested as part of development completion sign-off.

3. Write xUnit test cases.

4. Develop application code and follow the iterative process as suggested in the "Test-Driven Development Life Cycle" section.

5. After the screen or component development is completed, evaluate the functional test-case document along with the xUnit test cases, and sign off on the development completion report.

As mentioned in Chapter 1, different organizations might follow different approaches, but the core essence of meeting the functional requirements and achieving code quality remains the same.

Setting Up Session-State Middleware and Its Unit-Testing Fake

So far in this chapter, you have seen how to write unit-test cases and use the MOQ framework to resolve dependencies with mock data. The MOQ framework helps us achieve unit-test cases that are independent of the infrastructure and typical system dependencies. But in some scenarios, setting the mock data might be too cumbersome and might require a lot of code for all the dependent types. For example, if a controller action is heavily dependent on session and cache providers, then creating all session and cache keys with relevant mock data is time-consuming and hard to maintain. In these scenarios, we can create fake implementations of target types, so that unit tests will use these fake implementations instead of actual providers. In the Automobile Service Center application, we will use session state to demonstrate a fake implementation.

Session state is the most common API used by almost all present-day web applications to hold and retrieve user-specific information that is common to multiple pages and shared among different requests. Previously, applications retrieved this user-specific information from their persistence medium (for example, a database) every time a new request was made and a new page was visited by the same user. This is not a scalable and recommended approach because of the unnecessary database hits required to fetch the same information. To solve this problem, session state is used to hold and retrieve data between requests for a given user.

In previous versions of ASP.NET, session management is straightforward by using `HttpSessionState`. But in an ASP.NET Core MVC application, it is not straightforward. We have to include and configure `ISession` middleware to the `request-response` pipeline. In ASP.NET Core, `ISession` exposes a new API to support saving and retrieving objects from the session state.

Install the `Microsoft.AspNetCore.Session` NuGet package on the ASC.Web project, as shown in Figure 5-16.

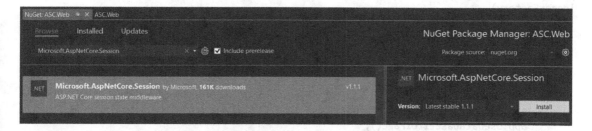

Figure 5-16. *Installing the Microsoft.AspNetCore.Session NuGet package on the ASC.Web project*

Open `Startup.cs` and add the distributed memory cache and session middleware at the `ConfigureServices` method, as shown in Listing 5-5. `ISession` needs `IDistributedCache` to store and retrieve items to a persistent medium. `AddDistributedMemoryCache` is used to store items in the server memory.

Listing 5-5. Adding Session and Distributed Memory Cache Services in Startup Class

```
public void ConfigureServices(IServiceCollection services)
{
    // Add framework services.
    services.AddDbContext<ApplicationDbContext>(options =>
        options.UseSqlite(Configuration.GetConnectionString("DefaultConnection")));

    services.AddIdentity<ApplicationUser, IdentityRole>()
        .AddEntityFrameworkStores<ApplicationDbContext>()
        .AddDefaultTokenProviders();

    services.AddOptions();
    services.Configure<ApplicationSettings>(Configuration.GetSection("AppSettings"));
    services.AddDistributedMemoryCache();
    services.AddSession();
    services.AddMvc();

    // Add application services.
    services.AddTransient<IEmailSender, AuthMessageSender>();
    services.AddTransient<ISmsSender, AuthMessageSender>();
}
```

Now configure the HTTP pipeline to use the session, as shown in Listing 5-6.

Listing 5-6. Adding Session to HTTP Pipeline

```
public void Configure(IApplicationBuilder app, IHostingEnvironment env, ILoggerFactory
loggerFactory)
{
    loggerFactory.AddConsole(Configuration.GetSection("Logging"));
    loggerFactory.AddDebug();

    if (env.IsDevelopment())
    {
        app.UseDeveloperExceptionPage();
        app.UseDatabaseErrorPage();
        app.UseBrowserLink();
    }
    else
    {
        app.UseExceptionHandler("/Home/Error");
    }
    app.UseSession();
    app.UseStaticFiles();

    app.UseIdentity();

    // Add external authentication middleware below. To configure them, please see https://
    go.microsoft.com/fwlink/?LinkID=532715
```

```
app.UseMvc(routes =>
{
    routes.MapRoute(
        name: "default",
        template: "{controller=Home}/{action=Index}/{id?}");
});
}
```

By default in an ASP.NET Core application, saving and retrieving complex objects is not straightforward (the ISession API supports only Int32 and String types through SetInt32, SetString, GetInt32, and GetString). We have to serialize the complex object and save it to the session; while retrieving the object from the session, we have to deserialize it. We will be using JSON serialization (using the Newtonsoft. Json NuGet package), which is light and easy to use. Create the SessionExtensions helper class in ASC. Utilities to help the application code perform the aforesaid functionality.

To get the ISession API in the ASC.Utilities project, we need to add the Microsoft.AspNetCore. Session NuGet package reference, as shown in Figure 5-17.

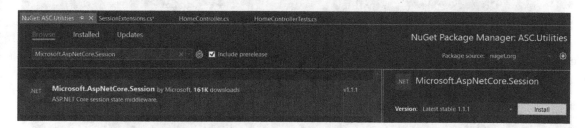

Figure 5-17. *Adding the Microsoft.AspNetCore.Session NuGet package to the ASC.Utilities project*

After adding the session reference, update the SessionExtensions helper class, as shown in Listing 5-7.

Listing 5-7. SessionExtensions Helper Class

```
using Microsoft.AspNetCore.Http;
using Newtonsoft.Json;
using System.Text;

namespace ASC.Utilities
{
    public static class SessionExtensions
    {
        public static void SetSession(this ISession session, string key, object value)
        {
            session.Set(key, Encoding.ASCII.GetBytes(JsonConvert.SerializeObject(value)));
        }

        public static T GetSession<T>(this ISession session, string key)
        {
            byte[] value;
            if (session.TryGetValue(key, out value))
            {
```

```
            return JsonConvert.DeserializeObject<T>(Encoding.ASCII.GetString(value));
        }
        else
        {
            return default(T);
        }
    }
}
```

To use these extensions in the ASC.Web project, we need to add the ASC.Utilities project reference to the ASC.Web project, as shown in Figure 5-18.

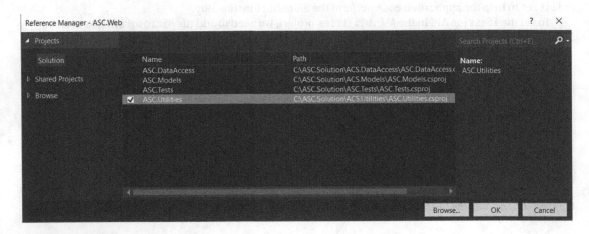

Figure 5-18. *Adding the* ASC.Utilities *project reference to the* ASC.Web *project*

We will modify the Index action of HomeController to use the session and store an arbitrary key and value for the demonstration, as shown in Listing 5-8.

Listing 5-8. Session Usage in the Index Action of HomeController

```
public IActionResult Index()
{
    // Set Session
    HttpContext.Session.SetSession("Test", _settings.Value);
    // Get Session
    var settings = HttpContext.Session.GetSession<ApplicationSettings>("Test");
    // Usage of IOptions
    ViewBag.Title = _settings.Value.ApplicationTitle;
    return View();
}
```

Run the unit-test cases. All the tests will fail at the same line where we are setting the session variable, as shown in Figure 5-19.

Figure 5-19. *Failing tests caused by session dependency*

Tests are failing because `HttpContext` is null. Unit tests run the `Index` action of `HomeController` just like any other normal C# method, so none of the default web features that are typically populated by the web server (like IIS) are going to be available under test execution. As `HttpContext` itself is null, obviously `Session` is not available.

To solve this problem, we will create a fake implementation of `ISession` in the unit-test project and assign it to a mock `HttpContext`. Finally, we will associate the mock `HttpContext` to the controller instance and execute the tests. Create a new folder in the `ASC.Tests` project named `TestUtilities` and create a class called `FakeSession` that will implement the `ISession` interface, as shown in Listing 5-9.

Listing 5-9. Fake Session Implementation in the ASC.Tests Project

```
public class FakeSession : ISession
{
    public bool IsAvailable => throw new NotImplementedException();
    public string Id => throw new NotImplementedException();
    public IEnumerable<string> Keys => throw new NotImplementedException();
    private Dictionary<string, byte[]> sessionFactory = new Dictionary<string, byte[]>();

    public void Clear()
    {
        throw new NotImplementedException();
    }
```

103

```csharp
    public Task CommitAsync()
    {
        throw new NotImplementedException();
    }

    public Task LoadAsync()
    {
        throw new NotImplementedException();
    }

    public void Remove(string key)
    {
        throw new NotImplementedException();
    }

    public void Set(string key, byte[] value)
    {
        if (!sessionFactory.ContainsKey(key))
            sessionFactory.Add(key, value);
        else
            sessionFactory[key] = value;
    }

    public bool TryGetValue(string key, out byte[] value)
    {
        if (sessionFactory.ContainsKey(key) && sessionFactory[key] != null)
        {
            value = sessionFactory[key];
            return true;
        }
        else
        {
            value = null;
            return false;
        }
    }
}
```

Here we have created a simple Dictionary<string, byte []> that will serve our purpose of holding session data. We have implemented two methods, Set and TryGetValue, which are primarily used to save and retrieve values from the session, respectively (in our implementation, it is Dictionary). The next step is to create a mock HttpContext and assign FakeSession to the mock HttpContext's Session property, as shown in Listing 5-10.

Listing 5-10. Setting Fake Session to Mock HttpContext

```csharp
private readonly Mock<IOptions<ApplicationSettings>> optionsMock;
private readonly Mock<HttpContext> mockHttpContext;
public HomeControllerTests()
{
```

```
// Create an instance of Mock IOptions
optionsMock = new Mock<IOptions<ApplicationSettings>>();
mockHttpContext = new Mock<HttpContext>();
// Set FakeSession to HttpContext Session.
mockHttpContext.Setup(p => p.Session).Returns(new FakeSession());

// Set IOptions<> Values property to return ApplicationSettings object
optionsMock.Setup(ap => ap.Value).Returns(new ApplicationSettings { Application
Title = "ASC" });
}
```

To use the mock HttpContext in unit tests, we have to set ControllerContext.HttpContext with the mock HttpContext instance, as shown in Listing 5-11.

Listing 5-11. Setting Mock HttpContext Instance to Controller Context

```
[Fact]
public void HomeController_Index_View_Test()
{
    // Home controller instantiated with Mock IOptions<> object
    var controller = new HomeController(optionsMock.Object);
    controller.ControllerContext.HttpContext = mockHttpContext.Object;

    Assert.IsType(typeof(ViewResult), controller.Index());
}
```

Similarly, assign it in other tests and run all the test cases. All tests should pass without any exceptions. Now we will write a new test case to check that the session contains at least one value. To reuse the session extensions from the ASC.Utilities project, add a reference of it in ASC.Tests.

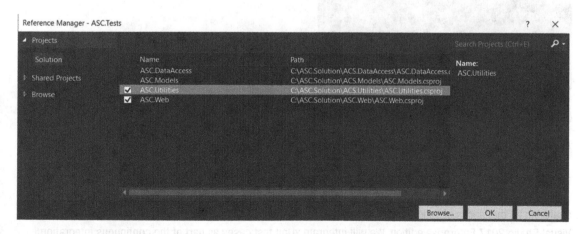

Figure 5-20. Adding a ASC.Utilities project reference to the ASC.Tests project

Write a new test case, as shown in Listing 5-12, to check the session value based on the key Test.

Listing 5-12. Test Case to Test the Session Value

```
[Fact]
public void HomeController_Index_Session_Test()
{
    var controller = new HomeController(optionsMock.Object);
    controller.ControllerContext.HttpContext = mockHttpContext.Object;

    controller.Index();

    // Session value with key "Test" should not be null.
    Assert.NotNull(controller.HttpContext.Session.GetSession<ApplicationSettings>("Test"));
}
```

Execute all the tests. All will pass, as shown in Figure 5-21.

Figure 5-21. *Successful execution of xUnit test cases*

■ **Note**   A code coverage report is one more important metric for achieving clean and stable code by analyzing all the blocks of code that are covered as part of unit tests. Code coverage results are available in Visual Studio 2017 Enterprise edition. We will integrate xUnit test cases as part of the continuous integration and deployment workflow, which we will cover later in this book.

Summary

You started this chapter by learning about unit testing and its significance in the software development life cycle. Test-driven development is always recommended in order to achieve a high level of functional correctness of the system. It is also useful in enhancing code quality and reusability. TDD promotes software coding standards and ensures that the design is loosely coupled with dependencies.

You became familiar with best practices for writing unit tests; for example, unit tests should be modular and independent, and should achieve high code coverage. You also learned about the TDD life cycle, which consists of test-case generation, application code development, and code optimization phases.

You explored the xUnit.net open source framework, which provides an API for developing unit-test cases. You started by writing simple xUnit test cases in the Automobile Service Center application and extended the tests to support mocking dependencies through the MOQ framework. You extended the Automobile Service Center application with session capabilities and created a fake implementation of ISession to demonstrate the ease of using fakes in unit tests for frequently used web-server-related APIs.

In subsequent chapters, we will include unit tests as part of the build's automation process, as a first check to ensure build quality.

CHAPTER 6

■ ■ ■

Securing the Application with ASP.NET Core Identity and the OAuth 2.0 Protocol

Sophisticated advancements in technology have yielded great results for many industries through numerous innovations and data analytics. The gradual rise of big-data analytics, machine learning, and the Internet of Things (IoT) have transformed the traditional ways of data acquisition, transformation, and analysis, and created new horizons in predictive analysis. The growing importance of data in making business decisions is creating not only technical challenges but also severe security threats.

Data can be secured via methodologies and tools at various layers of the entire system, such as Network, Server, Applications, Physical Storage, and Users. Information at these layers can be secured in various ways; for example, firewalls can be used as a defense strategy at the Network layer, Secure Sockets Layer can be leveraged at the Server layer, access control lists can be prepared and applied for users, authentication and authorization concepts are implemented at the Application layer, and encryption and data masking can make physical data devices more secure.

This chapter focuses on securing our Automobile Service Center application by implementing authentication and authorization. *Authentication* is the process of identifying the individual who is trying to access information. *Authorization* validates the authenticated user's access to the secured information by assigning access roles to users. Fortunately, ASP.NET Core has a very strong Identity system through which functionalities such as registration, login, changing/resetting a password, and logout can be achieved easily. ASP.NET Identity has built-in compatibility for OAuth integration with external providers including Gmail. We use external providers in the Automobile Service Center for authenticating external customers.

The key advantages of ASP.NET Identity are as follows:

- Can be used across all ASP.NET frameworks such as MVC and Web Forms, and can easily be consumed by applications through NuGet packages.

- Provides developers more control over the structure of user logins and authentication information that is persisted.

- Has built-in support for integration with external identity providers including Gmail, Facebook, Microsoft and Twitter.

- Can be easily extended to various data stores such as NoSQL databases.

© Rami Vemula 2017
R. Vemula, *Real-Time Web Application Development*, https://doi.org/10.1007/978-1-4842-3270-5_6

- Has default support for role-provider and claims-based authentication.

- Offers compatibility with OWIN-based applications.

- Provides great support for unit testing.

In subsequent sections, you will learn key concepts of ASP.NET Identity along with its practical implementation in the Automobile Service Center application.

Creating and Setting Up the Admin Account

As part of the Automobile Service Center application's requirements, an Admin account should be created and set up for the application. The Admin should have access to the entire site and should be able to manage data throughout the entire application. The Admin should also create and manage service engineers. In this section, you will learn how to get started with ASP.NET Core Identity, evaluate all the necessary artifacts, and create an Admin account on the application's first run.

The Automobile Service Center Visual Studio solution was created in Chapter 1 by enabling individual user accounts for authentication. This option creates the default code that is required to perform authentication and authorization against a SQL Server Database (SQL Server is the default option). For our Automobile Service Center application, we need to tweak this implementation to use the same code base against Microsoft Azure Table storage.

AccountController is an important component of the entire authentication code base and is created by default by Visual Studio. It consists of the following APIs and methods:

- UserManager: This is part of the Microsoft.AspNetCore.Identity API provided by Microsoft, and it provides the APIs for managing users in a persistence store.

- SigninManager: This is part of the Microsoft.AspNetCore.Identity API provided by Microsoft, and it provides the APIs to manage sign-in operations for users from different sources.

- IEmailSender, ISmsSender, and ILogger:

  - IEmailSender is used by AccountController to send e-mail for account confirmation and password resets.

  - ISmsSender is used for two-factor authentication.

  - ILogger is used to log messages and information about the user sign-in process.

- Action methods: AccountController has default controller actions that are used to perform various authentication-related activities. Actions are used for the following: Registration, Login, Logout, External Sources Login, Forgot Password, Reset Password, Two-Factor Authentication, and Send and Verify Codes.

Other files created by Visual Studio include models to support AccountController. These models are placed under the Models/AccountViewModels folder. The corresponding views for AccountController are placed in the Views/Account folder.

The default implementation of ASP.NET Identity works with SQL Server instances. Microsoft is still working on providing Entity Framework Core support to the Azure Table storage provider; it is currently listed in the EF Core roadmap as a high-priority item (see https://github.com/aspnet/EntityFramework/wiki/Roadmap). For our Automobile Service Center implementation, we'll use the Identityazuretable NuGet package, which is developed by David Melendez at GitHub.

Identityazuretable abstracts Azure Table storage requests and responses made for authentication from developers. We will configure ASP.NET Identity to use Identityazuretable's Azure Table store at Startup.cs (basically, instead of configuring SQL Server to Identity, we will configure Azure Table storage through an Identityazuretable implementation for the Automobile Service Center application), so that AccountController's UserManager and SigninManager will work seamlessly without any change.

Open the ASC.Web project and install the ElCamino.AspNetCore.Identity.AzureTable NuGet package, as shown in Figure 6-1.

Figure 6-1. *Installing the ElCamino.AspNetCore.Identity.AzureTable NuGet package to the ASC.Web project*

Open the ApplicationUser class and remove the Identity.EntityFrameworkCore reference, shown in Listing 6-1.

Listing 6-1. Identity.EntityFrameworkCore reference

```
using Microsoft.AspNetCore.Identity.EntityFrameworkCore;
```

Add a reference to ElCamino.AspNetCore.Identity.AzureTable.Model, as shown in Listing 6-2. This change is required to make sure that we are not using the IdentityUser instance that we got from Entity Framework Core and at the same time to generate proper keys for Azure table entities.

Listing 6-2. ElCamino.AspNetCore.Identity.AzureTable.Model reference

```
using ElCamino.AspNetCore.Identity.AzureTable.Model;

namespace ASC.Web.Models
{
    // Add profile data for application users by adding properties to the ApplicationUser class
    public class ApplicationUser : IdentityUser
    {
    }
}
```

Now change ApplicationDbContext to inherit from IdentityCloudContext, as shown in Listing 6-3. This change is required to make sure that we use CloudTable and CloudTableClient instances.

Listing 6-3. Inherit ApplicationDbContext from IdentityCloudContext

```
using ElCamino.AspNetCore.Identity.AzureTable;
using ElCamino.AspNetCore.Identity.AzureTable.Model;

namespace ASC.Web.Data
{
    public class ApplicationDbContext : IdentityCloudContext
    {
        public ApplicationDbContext() : base() { }
        public ApplicationDbContext(IdentityConfiguration config) : base(config) { }
    }
}
```

Let's modify the Startup class to configure ASP.NET Core Identity to use the modified ApplicationDbContext and Azure Storage. Remove the `Microsoft.AspNetCore.Identity.EntityFrameworkCore` reference, and add the `ElCamino.AspNetCore.Identity.AzureTable.Model` reference, as shown in Listing 6-4.

Listing 6-4. ElCamino.AspNetCore.Identity.AzureTable.Model reference

```
using ElCamino.AspNetCore.Identity.AzureTable.Model;
```

Change the `ConfigureServices` method of the Startup class, as shown in Listing 6-5. We configure Azure Table stores for ASP.NET Core Identity, and the configuration is pulled from the `appsettings.json` file.

Listing 6-5. Configure Azure Table stores for ASP.NET Core Identity

```
public void ConfigureServices(IServiceCollection services)
{
    // Add Elcamino Azure Table Identity services.
    services.AddIdentity<ApplicationUser, IdentityRole>((options) =>
    {
        options.User.RequireUniqueEmail = true;
    })
    .AddAzureTableStores<ApplicationDbContext>(new Func<IdentityConfiguration>(() =>
    {
        IdentityConfiguration idconfig = new IdentityConfiguration();
        idconfig.TablePrefix = Configuration.GetSection("IdentityAzureTable:IdentityConfigur
        ation:TablePrefix").Value;
        idconfig.StorageConnectionString = Configuration.GetSection
        ("IdentityAzureTable:IdentityConfiguration:StorageConnectionString").Value;
        idconfig.LocationMode = Configuration.GetSection("IdentityAzureTable:
        IdentityConfiguration:LocationMode").Value;
        return idconfig;
    }))
    .AddDefaultTokenProviders()
    .CreateAzureTablesIfNotExists<ApplicationDbContext>();

    services.AddOptions();
    services.Configure<ApplicationSettings>(Configuration.GetSection("AppSettings"));

    services.AddSession();
    services.AddMvc();
```

```
    // Add application services.
    services.AddTransient<IEmailSender, AuthMessageSender>();
    services.AddTransient<ISmsSender, AuthMessageSender>();
}
```

Add the Azure Table storage ConnectionString settings to the appsettings.json file, as shown in Listing 6-6.

Listing 6-6. Azure Table storage ConnectionString settings

```
{
  "AppSettings": {
    "ApplicationTitle": "Automobile Service Center Application"
  },
  "ConnectionStrings": {
    "DefaultConnection": "UseDevelopmentStorage=true;"
  },
  "IdentityAzureTable": {
    "IdentityConfiguration": {
      "TablePrefix": "ASC",
      "StorageConnectionString": "UseDevelopmentStorage=true;",
      "LocationMode": "PrimaryOnly"
    }
  },
  "Logging": {
    "IncludeScopes": false,
    "LogLevel": {
      "Default": "Warning"
    }
  }
}
```

Now that we have configured the ASC.Web project to the Identityazuretable package, we will provision the Admin user on the application run through custom middleware. Create a StorageDataSeed.cs class in the Data folder of the ASC.Web project. Create an interface that will serve as a contract for data seeding to Azure Storage, as shown in Listing 6-7. It takes UserManager, SigninManager, and IOptions<> to seed the data.

Listing 6-7. IIdentitySeed Interface

```
public interface IIdentitySeed
{
    Task Seed(UserManager<ApplicationUser> userManager, RoleManager<IdentityRole>
    roleManager, IOptions<ApplicationSettings> options);
}
```

In the same class, implement the IIdentitySeed interface, as shown in Listing 6-8. The IdentitySeed class will implement the IIdentitySeed interface. The Seed method first gets all the comma-separated roles from the IOptions<> instance and splits the roles string by comma. It then iterates all the roles and make sure the roles are created in Azure Storage (if they don't already exist). Then it checks for an Admin user; if an Admin user is not present, it will create the user with the specified configuration and attach that user to the Admin role. Two claims—Email and IsActive—are attached to the user. Email is used to read the user's e-mail, and IsActive will be used in the future to deactivate a user in the system.

113

Listing 6-8. IdentitySeed Class

```
public class IdentitySeed : IIdentitySeed
{
    public async Task Seed(UserManager<ApplicationUser> userManager,
    RoleManager<IdentityRole> roleManager, IOptions<ApplicationSettings> options)
    {
        // Get All comma-separated roles
        var roles = options.Value.Roles.Split(new char[] { ',' });

        // Create roles if they don't exist
        foreach (var role in roles)
        {
            if (!await roleManager.RoleExistsAsync(role))
            {
                IdentityRole storageRole = new IdentityRole
                {
                    Name = role
                };
                IdentityResult roleResult = await roleManager.CreateAsync(storageRole);
            }
        }

        // Create admin if he doesn't exist
        var admin = await userManager.FindByEmailAsync(options.Value.AdminEmail);
        if (admin == null)
        {
            ApplicationUser user = new ApplicationUser
            {
                UserName = options.Value.AdminName,
                Email = options.Value.AdminEmail,
                EmailConfirmed = true
            };

            IdentityResult result = await userManager.CreateAsync(user, options.Value.
            AdminPassword);
            await userManager.AddClaimAsync(user, new System.Security.Claims.Claim("http://
            schemas.xmlsoap.org/ws/2005/05/identity/claims/emailaddress", options.Value.
            AdminEmail));
            await userManager.AddClaimAsync(user, new System.Security.Claims.
            Claim("IsActive", "True"));

            // Add Admin to Admin roles
            if (result.Succeeded)
            {
                await userManager.AddToRoleAsync(user, "Admin");
            }
        }
    }
}
```

As we are reading the Admin information from IOptions<>, make sure to specify the configuration in the appsettings.json file, as shown in Listing 6-9.

Listing 6-9. Admin User Configuration in appsettings.json file

```
"AppSettings": {
  "ApplicationTitle": "Automobile Service Center Application",
  "AdminEmail": "asc.superuser@gmail.com",
  "AdminName":  "Admin",
  "AdminPassword": "P@ssw0rd",
  "Roles":  "Admin,User"
},
```

■ **Note**   The use of the Gmail e-mail address is for the sake of this demonstration. In the real world, we would use organization accounts for registration and communication.

Update the ApplicationSettings class with new properties to hold the configuration related to Admin, as shown in Listing 6-10.

Listing 6-10. Updated ApplicationSettings class

```
public class ApplicationSettings
{
    public string ApplicationTitle { get; set; }
    public string AdminEmail { get; set; }
    public string AdminName { get; set; }
    public string AdminPassword { get; set; }
    public string Roles { get; set; }
}
```

Resolve the dependency of IIdentitySeed in the Configure method of the Startup class, as shown in Listing 6-11.

Listing 6-11. Resolving IIdentitySeed dependency in Startup class

```
// Add application services.
services.AddTransient<IEmailSender, AuthMessageSender>();
services.AddTransient<ISmsSender, AuthMessageSender>();
services.AddSingleton<IIdentitySeed, IdentitySeed>();
```

■ **Note**   For more information on dependency injection in an ASP.NET Core application, refer to "Using Dependency Injection in the ASP.NET Core Application" in Chapter 2.

Finally, call the IIdentitySeed's Seed method in the Configure method, as shown in Listing 6-12. We pass IIdentitySeed as a parameter to the Configure method and invoke the Seed method.

Listing 6-12. Invoke IIdentitySeed's Seed method

```
public async void Configure(IApplicationBuilder app,
    IHostingEnvironment env,
    ILoggerFactory loggerFactory,
    IIdentitySeed storageSeed)
{
    loggerFactory.AddConsole(Configuration.GetSection("Logging"));
    loggerFactory.AddDebug();

    if (env.IsDevelopment())
    {
        app.UseDeveloperExceptionPage();
        app.UseDatabaseErrorPage();
        app.UseBrowserLink();
    }
    else
    {
        app.UseExceptionHandler("/Home/Error");
    }
    app.UseSession();
    app.UseStaticFiles();
    app.UseIdentity();

    app.UseMvc(routes =>
    {
        routes.MapRoute(
            name: "default",
            template: "{controller=Home}/{action=Index}/{id?}");
    });

    await storageSeed.Seed(app.ApplicationServices.GetService<UserManager
    <ApplicationUser>>(),
        app.ApplicationServices.GetService<RoleManager<IdentityRole>>(),
        app.ApplicationServices.GetService<IOptions<ApplicationSettings>>());
}
```

■ **Note**   IApplicationBuilder.ApplicationServices is the service container that will hold all the services in the scope of the application. By using its GetService<T>, we can retrieve a specific service from the service container based on type.

Run the application. You should see that Roles and Admin are created at the Azure Storage emulator as specified in the appsettings.json file. These three tables should be created:

- ASCAspNetRoles: Stores all roles. Figure 6-2 shows this table in Cloud Explorer on Visual Studio.

- ASCAspNetUsers: Stores all users and their claims and role associations. Figure 6-3 shows this table in Cloud Explorer on Visual Studio.

116

- ASCAspNetIndex: This table is used internally by Identityazuretable to query users. When the user ID is unknown, the AspNetIndex table is queried first, either by the user's e-mail (UserStore.FindByEmailAsync method) or by external login information (UserStore.FindAsync method) to get the user's ID. A query by user ID can then complete the user information. See Figure 6-4.

PartitionKey	RowKey	Timestamp	KeyVersion	Name	NormalizedName
A	R_ADMIN	5/7/2017 11:47:...	1.66	Admin	ADMIN
U	R_USER	5/7/2017 11:47:...	1.66	User	USER

Figure 6-2. *ASCAspNetRoles Azure table*

PartitionKey	RowKey	Timestamp	KeyVersion	ClaimType	ClaimValue	Id	RoleName	UserName	NormalizedEmail	Norm
U_ADMIN	C_HTTP_3A_2F_...	5/7/2017 11:47:...	1.66	http://schemas....	asc.superuser@...	e2ee7d26-c39e...				
U_ADMIN	C_ISACTIVE_TRUE	5/7/2017 11:47:...	1.66	IsActive	True	7bc8e880-bb65...				
U_ADMIN	R_ADMIN	5/7/2017 11:47:...	1.66			535db8b5-7e26...	ADMIN			
U_ADMIN	U_ADMIN	5/7/2017 11:47:...	1.66					Admin	ASC.SUPERUSE...	ADM

Figure 6-3. *ASCAspNetUsers Azure table*

PartitionKey	RowKey	Timestamp	Id	KeyVersion
E_ASC.SUPERUS...	U_ADMIN	5/7/2017 11:47:...	U_ADMIN	1.66

Figure 6-4. *ASCAspNetIndex Azure table*

Creating Login and Logout Screens

Now that we have an Admin created in the system, he should be able to log in to the system and perform his activities. In this section, we will create pages for login and logout functionalities. But before creating a login page, we have to segregate our controllers into secure and anonymous controllers. Create two controllers, BaseController and AnonymousController, in the Controllers folder. Decorate BaseController with the Authorize attribute, as shown in Listing 6-13, so that any action inside this controller, or in any controllers that are inherited from this BaseController, are completely secured. AnonymousController will not have the Authorize attribute, as shown in Listing 6-14. Having these controllers will help us share common functionalities across pages in future development.

Listing 6-13. BaseController

BaseController:

```
using Microsoft.AspNetCore.Authorization;
using Microsoft.AspNetCore.Mvc;

namespace ASC.Web.Controllers
{
    [Authorize]
    public class BaseController : Controller
    {
    }
}
```

Listing 6-14. AnonymousController

AnonymousController:

```
using Microsoft.AspNetCore.Authorization;
using Microsoft.AspNetCore.Mvc;

namespace ASC.Web.Controllers
{
    public class AnonymousController : Controller
    {
    }
}
```

We will inherit HomeController from AnonymousController because we do not want any of these pages to be secured. Create a new controller named DashboardController that inherits from BaseController. Move the Dashboard action to DashboardController, as shown in Listing 6-15.

Listing 6-15. DashboardController

```
using Microsoft.AspNetCore.Mvc;
using Microsoft.Extensions.Options;
using ASC.Web.Configuration;

namespace ASC.Web.Controllers
{
    public class DashboardController : BaseController
    {
        private IOptions<ApplicationSettings> _settings;
        public DashboardController(IOptions<ApplicationSettings> settings)
        {
            _settings = settings;
        }
```

```
        public IActionResult Dashboard()
        {
            return View();
        }
    }
}
```

Because we moved the Dashboard action to the dashboard controller, we have to move Dashboard. cshtml to the Dashboard folder under Views. Create a new folder named Dashboard under the Views folder and then move Dashboard.cshtml.

HomeController is shown in Listing 6-16.

Listing 6-16. Updated HomeController

```
using Microsoft.AspNetCore.Mvc;
using Microsoft.Extensions.Options;
using ASC.Web.Configuration;
using ASC.Utilities;

namespace ASC.Web.Controllers
{

    public class HomeController : AnonymousController
    {
        private IOptions<ApplicationSettings> _settings;
        public HomeController(IOptions<ApplicationSettings> settings)
        {
            _settings = settings;
        }

        public IActionResult Index()
        {
            // Set Session Test
             HttpContext.Session.SetSession("Test", _settings.Value);
            // Get Session Test
             var settings = HttpContext.Session.GetSession<ApplicationSettings>("Test");

            // Usage of IOptions
            ViewBag.Title = _settings.Value.ApplicationTitle;
            return View();
        }

        public IActionResult About()
        {
            ViewData["Message"] = "Your application description page.";
            return View();
        }

        public IActionResult Contact()
        {
            ViewData["Message"] = "Your contact page.";
            return View();
        }
```

```
    public IActionResult Error()
    {
        return View();
    }
  }
}
```

■ **Note** Add the following RenderSection code at the end of _Layout.cshtml and _SecureLayout.cshtml to support the JQuery scripts section, to propagate the scripts section to the master layout.

@section Scripts{

```
@RenderSection("Scripts", required: false)
```

}

Now we will design a Login page indicating which users can log in to the system. Whenever an anonymous user tries to access any secure page in the application, that user will be redirected to this Login page. By default, a LoginViewModel, login action, and login view comes with AccountController. LoginViewModel, shown in Listing 6-17, is used to post the user-entered username and password to the POST action.

Listing 6-17. LoginViewModel

```
public class LoginViewModel
{
    [Required]
    [EmailAddress]
    public string Email { get; set; }

    [Required]
    [DataType(DataType.Password)]
    public string Password { get; set; }

    [Display(Name = "Remember me?")]
    public bool RememberMe { get; set; }
}
```

The GET action of the Login view is shown in Listing 6-18; this will sign out the user (if the user is already logged in) and return the Login view.

Listing 6-18. GET action of the Login view

```
[HttpGet]
[AllowAnonymous]
public async Task<IActionResult> Login(string returnUrl = null)
{
    // Clear the existing external cookie to ensure a clean login process
    await HttpContext.Authentication.SignOutAsync(_externalCookieScheme);

    ViewData["ReturnUrl"] = returnUrl;
    return View();
}
```

We will use the same action and view for the Automobile Service Center application, but change the look and feel of the page. Open Login.cshtml under the /Views/Account folder and change the HTML as shown in Listing 6-19.

We have used Materialize CSS to design the Login view. This view takes LoginViewModel from the GET action and uses asp-for on input elements to get strongly typed views. The traditional HTML form tag is used to post the information back to the POST action. All the validations on the page are performed on the client side by using JQuery's unobtrusive validation. Error messages are displayed using ASP.NET Core's asp-validation-summary attribute. Apart from displaying validation error messages in the summary, validation-failed controls will be highlighted in red.

■ **Note** A Forgot Password link has been placed in the Login view to help users reset their passwords. This Forgot Password functionality will be explained in the next section.

Listing 6-19. Login View

```
@using System.Collections.Generic
@using Microsoft.AspNetCore.Http
@using Microsoft.AspNetCore.Http.Authentication
@model LoginViewModel
@inject SignInManager<ApplicationUser> SignInManager
@{
    ViewData["Title"] = "Log in";
}
<div class="container">
    <div class="row">
        <div class="col s12 m6 offset-m3">
            <form asp-controller="Account" asp-action="Login" asp-route-returnurl="@
            ViewData["ReturnUrl"]" method="post">
                <div asp-validation-summary="All" class="text-danger"></div>

                <div class="row">
                    <div class="input-field col s12">
                        <input asp-for="Email" type="email" class="validate">
                        <label asp-for="Email" data-error="wrong" data-success="right">
                        Email</label>
                    </div>
                </div>

                <div class="row">
                    <div class="input-field col s12">
                        <input asp-for="Password" type="password" class="validate">
                        <label asp-for="Password" data-error="wrong" data-success="right">Password
                        </label>
                    </div>
                </div>

                <div class="row padding-left-10px">
                    <p>
                        <input asp-for="RememberMe" type="checkbox" class="filled-in" />
```

121

```
                        <label asp-for="RememberMe">@Html.DisplayNameFor(m => m.RememberMe)</label>
                </p>
            </div>

            <div class="row center">
                <button class="btn waves-effect waves-light" type="submit">
                Submit
                <i class="material-icons right">send</i>
                </button>
            </div>

            <div class="row center">
                <a asp-action="ForgotPassword">Forgot your password?</a>
            </div>
        </form>
    </div>
  </div>
</div>
```

Add the styles to `style.css`, as shown in Listing 6-20, to support validation styles and the Login page. These styles will make sure all the validation-failed controls will be highlighted in red.

Listing 6-20. Extended Style.css

```css
.padding-left-10px{
    padding-left: 10px;
}

.input-field .input-validation-error {
    border-bottom: 1px solid #FF4081;
    box-shadow: 0 1px 0 0 #FF4081;
}

.input-field .valid {
    border-bottom: 1px solid #00E676;
    box-shadow: 0 1px 0 0 #00E676;
}

.validation-summary-errors {
    color: #FF4081;
}
```

We also need to include JQuery's Validate and Unobtrusive scripts to perform client-side validations on a page. Make sure `_MasterLayout.cshtml` has JavaScript references, as shown in Listing 6-21.

Listing 6-21. JQuery's Validate and Unobtrusive scripts references

```html
<script src="~/lib/jquery/dist/jquery.min.js"></script>
<script src="~/lib/jquery-validation/dist/jquery.validate.js"></script>
<script src="~/lib/jquery-validation-unobtrusive/jquery.validate.unobtrusive.js"></script>
<script src="~/js/materialize.min.js"></script>
<script src="~/js/init.js"></script>
```

■ **Note**   To provide easier navigation to the Login page, modify `_Layout.cshtml` to point the Login link at the top of the navigation bar to the Login page:

```
<li><a href="/Account/Login">Login</a></li>
```

For easier navigation to the home page from anywhere in the application, update the URL of the Logo anchor tag:

```
<a id="logo-container" href="/" class ="brand-logo">

  <img class="responsive-img" src="~/images/logo.jpg" alt="Logo"/>

</a>
```

Run the application and navigate to the Login page. The page should be displayed as in Figure 6-5.

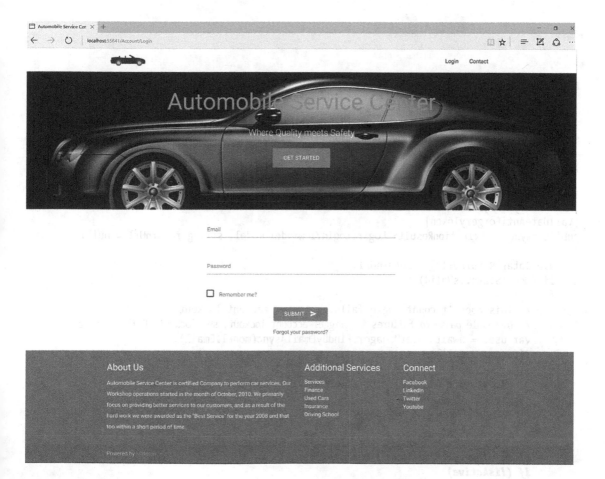

Figure 6-5. Login page

Validation error messages will be displayed, as shown in Figure 6-6.

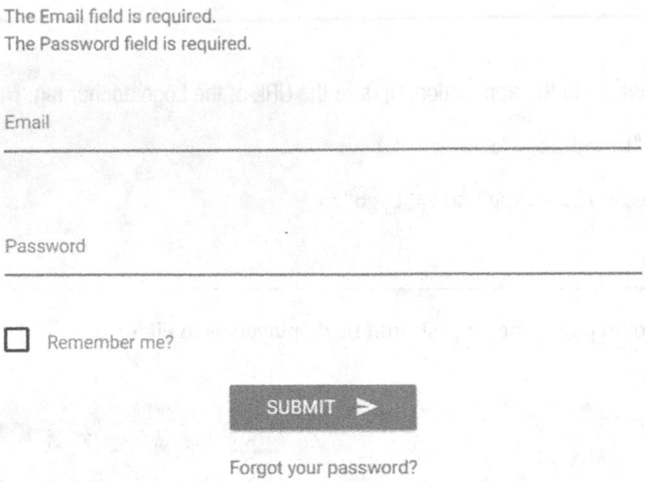

The Email field is required.
The Password field is required.

Email
_____

Password
_____

☐ Remember me?

SUBMIT ▶

Forgot your password?

Figure 6-6. *Validation error messages in the Login view*

The POST action of Login is also provided by default when we create the application. We need to make slight modifications to support proper redirection to the dashboard, as shown in Listing 6-22.

Listing 6-22. POST action of Login View

```
[HttpPost]
[AllowAnonymous]
[ValidateAntiForgeryToken]
public async Task<IActionResult> Login(LoginViewModel model, string returnUrl = null)
{
    ViewData["ReturnUrl"] = returnUrl;
    if (ModelState.IsValid)
    {
        // This doesn't count login failures toward account lockout
        // To enable password failures to trigger account lockout, set lockoutOnFailure: true
        var user = await _userManager.FindByEmailAsync(model.Email);
        if(user == null)
        {
            ModelState.AddModelError(string.Empty, "Invalid login attempt.");
            return View(model);
        }

        var isActive = Boolean.Parse(user.Claims.SingleOrDefault(p =>
        p.ClaimType == "IsActive").ClaimValue);
        if (!isActive)
        {
            ModelState.AddModelError(string.Empty, "Account has been locked.");
            return View(model);
        }
```

```
    var result = await _signInManager.PasswordSignInAsync(user.UserName, model.Password,
    model.RememberMe, lockoutOnFailure: false);

    if (result.Succeeded)
    {
        _logger.LogInformation(1, "User logged in.");
        if(!String.IsNullOrWhiteSpace(returnUrl))
            return RedirectToLocal(returnUrl);
        else
            return RedirectToAction("Dashboard", "Dashboard");
    }
    if (result.RequiresTwoFactor)
    {
        return RedirectToAction(nameof(SendCode), new { ReturnUrl = returnUrl,
        RememberMe = model.RememberMe });
    }
    if (result.IsLockedOut)
    {
        _logger.LogWarning(2, "User account locked out.");
        return View("Lockout");
    }
    else
    {
        ModelState.AddModelError(string.Empty, "Invalid login attempt.");
        return View(model);
    }
}
```

The POST action first validates the model. Then it checks whether there is a user in the system with the specified e-mail, and it also checks the IsActive claim for true or false. On a valid model state, SigninManager will validate the e-mail and password passed by the user against Azure Table storage. Upon a successful result, the user will be redirected to either the dashboard or to the requested page. The POST action also checks whether the logged-in user required two-factor authentication; if required, it will redirect to an action that will send the code to the user and initiate the two-factor authentication workflow. The POST action also validates whether the user account has been locked out because of consecutive wrong authentication information. For any other reason if the login fails, this action will return an Invalid Login attempt message.

If we enter any details incorrectly in either the Email or Password fields, we will get an error message, as shown in Figure 6-7.

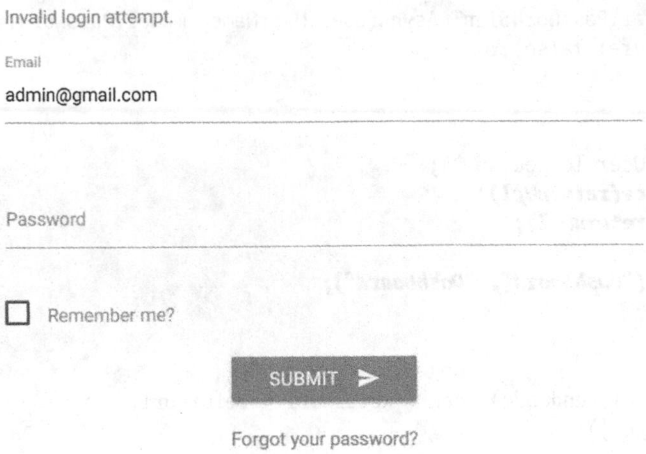

Invalid login attempt.

Email

admin@gmail.com

Password

☐ Remember me?

SUBMIT ➤

Forgot your password?

Figure 6-7. *Invalid Login Attempt*

■ **Note** We will use the `IsActive` claim flag for the `ApplicationUser` class to check whether the user is active in the system. Going forward in this book, we will implement the service engineer's login, and Admin can manage service engineers by activating and deactivating them.

The Remember Me field can be used to indicate whether the sign-in cookie should persist after the browser is closed, so that the user can get back to the secure pages in a new browser window.

Upon passing correct credentials, the user will be logged in and redirected to the dashboard, as shown in Figure 6-8.

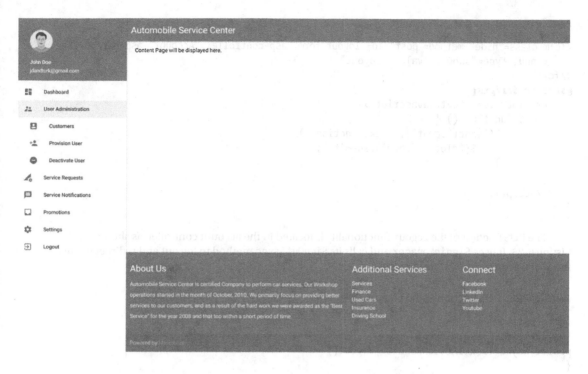

Figure 6-8. *Successful Login redirection to Dashboard view*

■ **Note**   The Dashboard page displays static content as of now. In subsequent sections, we will make that screen dynamically load data based on the logged-in user.

To implement logout functionality, we have to make changes to _SecureLayout.cshtml. Give an ID to the Logout anchor tag, as shown in Listing 6-23.

Listing 6-23. Logout anchor tag

```
<li><a class="collapsible-header" href="#!" id="ancrLogout"><i class="material-icons">
exit_to_app</i>Logout</a></li>
```

■ **Note**   All secure operations such as Logout, Reset Password, Forgot Password, and Edit Profile. should be POST operations. If these operations are based on GET requests, any malicious user or site can send these requests on an authenticated user's behalf, so always make POST requests for greater security.

Place a hidden form tag with asp-controller pointing to Account, and asp-action pointing to Logout in _SecureLayout.cshtml. We will trigger the submit event of this form tag upon a click of the Logout anchor tag. Handle the click event of the Logout anchor tag in JQuery in _SecureLayout.cshtml, as shown in Listing 6-24.

Listing 6-24. JQuery POST event on Logout

```
<form class="hide" method="post" id="logout_form" asp-controller="Account" asp-action="Logout">
    <input type="submit" value="Logout" />
</form>
@section Scripts{
    <script type="text/javascript">
        $(function () {
            $('#ancrLogout').click(function () {
                $('#logout_form').submit();
            });
        });
    </script>
}
```

The POST action of the Logout functionality is located in the account controller, as shown in
Listing 6-25. It uses SigninManager and calls its SignOutAsync method to log out and redirect the user to
the Index action of the home controller.

Listing 6-25. POST action of the Logout

```
[HttpPost]
[ValidateAntiForgeryToken]
public async Task<IActionResult> Logout()
{
    await _signInManager.SignOutAsync();
    _logger.LogInformation(4, "User logged out.");
    return RedirectToAction(nameof(HomeController.Index), "Home");
}
```

■ **Note** There is one problem with the Logout functionality. When the user logs out and clicks the browser's
Back button, the cached version of the web page will be displayed. Even though the user cannot perform any
action on the web page, still displaying the cached version might impact security. Many solutions are available
to solve this problem—for example, setting the cache expire headers to make sure the cached version of the
web page is invalidated by the browser. I took a different approach to resolve this problem, by using JQuery to
prevent the user from navigating to a previous page by clicking the browser's Back button. This feature applies
to the entire Automobile Service Center application.

Open the init.js file and change the code as shown in Listing 6-26. We will manipulate window.history to
always go forward instead of going back to the previous pages.

Listing 6-26. JQuery code to prevent navigation on browser back button click

```
(function ($) {
    $(function () {

        $('.button-collapse').sideNav();
        $('.parallax').parallax();

        //Prevent browser back and forward buttons.
        if (window.history && window.history.pushState) {
            window.history.pushState('forward', '', window.location.href);

            $(window).on('popstate', function (e) {
                window.history.pushState('forward', '', window.location.href);
                e.preventDefault();
            });
        }
        //Prevent right-click on entire window
        $(document).ready(function () {
            $(window).on("contextmenu", function () {
                return false;
            });
        });

    }); // end of document ready
})(jQuery); // end of jQuery name space
```

Retrieving User Information from ClaimsPrincipal

In the preceding section, we built all the pages required for authentication. In this section, we will retrieve logged-in user information from ClaimsPrincipal. This information can be fetched from HttpContext. User, which is of type ClaimsPrincipal. This property will be available all the time, until the user signs out from the system. The only problem with this approach is that whichever component uses the logged-in user information will be dependent on the HttpContext API from the Microsoft.AspNetCore.Mvc package. This unnecessary reference of the MVC package in all components can be addressed by using a simple class and a utility method. Create a class named ClaimsPrincipalExtensions in the ASC.Utilities project, as shown in Listing 6-27.

Listing 6-27. CurrentUser class

```
public class CurrentUser
    {
        public string Name { get; set; }
        public string Email { get; set; }
        public bool IsActive { get; set; }
        public string[] Roles { get; set; }
    }
```

Create an extension method for ClaimsPrincipal, as shown in Listing 6-28. It reads all the claims and returns the CurrentUser object.

Listing 6-28. ClaimsPrincipalExtensions class

```
public static class ClaimsPrincipalExtensions
{
    public static CurrentUser GetCurrentUserDetails(this ClaimsPrincipal principal)
    {
        if (!principal.Claims.Any())
            return null;

        return new CurrentUser
        {
            Name = principal.Claims.Where(c => c.Type == ClaimTypes.Name).Select(c =>
            c.Value).SingleOrDefault(),
            Email = principal.Claims.Where(c => c.Type == ClaimTypes.Email).Select(c =>
            c.Value).SingleOrDefault(),
            Roles = principal.Claims.Where(c => c.Type == ClaimTypes.Role).Select(c =>
            c.Value).ToArray(),
            IsActive = Boolean.Parse(principal.Claims.Where(c => c.Type == "IsActive").
            Select(c => c.Value).SingleOrDefault()),
        };
    }
}
```

We can use this extension in the ASC.Web project and convert ClaimsPrincipal to the CurrentUser object, thereby passing the CurrentUser object to any method that requires it. We are going to use this extension method in _SecureLayout.cshtml to display the logged-in user details.

To access HttpContext in views, we need to resolve the HttpContextAccessor dependency in the ConfigureServices method of the Startup class, as shown in Listing 6-29.

Listing 6-29. Resolve HttpContextAccessor dependency

```
services.AddSingleton<IHttpContextAccessor, HttpContextAccessor>();
```

We inject IHttpContextAccessor to _SecureLayout.cshtml, as shown in Listing 6-30. The GetCurrentUserDetails extension method is used to get details of the current user.

Listing 6-30. Retrieving User Details in Secure Layout

```
@using Microsoft.AspNetCore.Http
@using ASC.Utilities
@inject IHttpContextAccessor UserHttpContext

@{
    Layout = "_MasterLayout";
    var currentUser = UserHttpContext.HttpContext.User.GetCurrentUserDetails();
}
```

Change the HTML of _SecureLayout.cshtml to display user details, as shown in Listing 6-31.

Listing 6-31. Display user details

```
<div class="userView">
    <div class="background blue-grey lighten-1"></div>
    <a href="#!user"><img class="circle" src="~/images/male.png"></a>
    <a href="#!name"><span class="white-text name">@currentUser.Name</span></a>
    <a href="#!email"><span class="white-text email">@currentUser.Email</span></a>
</div>
```

■ **Note**   We will display a generic logged-in user avatar. This functionality can be extended to display user photo.

Run the application and log in as Admin. The Admin details are displayed, as shown in Figure 6-9.

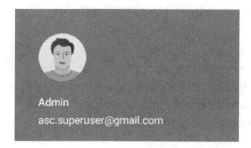

Figure 6-9. *Displaying logged-in Admin user details*

Resetting a Password Through MailKit E-mail Library Integration

In this section, we will implement the Reset Password page through which a logged-in user can reset his/her password. Whenever the user wants to reset password, an e-mail with a unique user-specific code embedded in a link will be sent to the user's e-mail. Upon clicking the link, the user will be able to reset password at the Automobile Service Center application. ASP.NET Core's account controller already has default code that is required to implement the Reset Password functionality, and we will slightly modify that code to meet the Automobile Service Center application's requirements. We will start by adding the Reset Password menu item in the left navigation bar for the logged-in user in _SecureLayout.cshtml. Add the Reset Password link under the Settings menu, as shown in Listing 6-32.

Listing 6-32. Reset Password Link in Left Menu

```
<li><a class="collapsible-header" href="#!"><i class="material-icons">perm_data_setting
</i>Service Requests</a></li>
        <li><a class="collapsible-header" href="#!"><i class="material-icons">message</i>
        Service Notifications</a></li>
        <li><a class="collapsible-header" href="#!"><i class="material-icons">inbox</i>
        Promotions</a></li>
```

```
<li>
    <ul class="collapsible collapsible-accordion">
        <li>
            <a class="collapsible-header">Settings<i class="material-
                icons">settings</i></a>
            <div class="collapsible-body">
                <ul>
                    <li><a class="collapsible-header" href="#!" id="ancrResetPassword">
                        Reset Password<i class="material-icons">lock_outline</i></a></
                        li>
                </ul>
            </div>
        </li>
    </ul>
</li>
    <li><a class="collapsible-header" href="#!" id="ancrLogout"><i class="material-
icons">exit_to_app</i>Logout</a></li>
```

■ **Note**   For a demonstration of e-mail capabilities, we will use Gmail's SMTP server to send e-mail. I created a sample e-mail address, autoservicectrnew@gmail. This account will be used to get authenticated at Gmail's SMTP server and to send e-mail from the application. We will use the MailKit client library and its rich set of C# APIs to send e-mail.

To use Gmail's SMTP server, we need to allow access to less-secure apps at the time of development. Navigate to https://myaccount.google.com/lesssecureapps?pli=1 and turn on the Allow Less Secure Apps option.

Less secure apps

Some apps and devices use less secure sign-in technology, which makes your account more vulnerable. You can **turn off** access for these apps, which we recommend, or **turn on** access if you want to use them despite the risks. Learn more

Allow less secure apps: ON

Figure 6-10.   *Allowing less-secure applications at the Google account*

Install MailKit to the ASC.Web project, as shown in Figure 6-11.

Figure 6-11. *Installing the MailKit NuGet package to the ASC.Web project*

Update the Appsettings.json file to hold the SMTP Server and Port configuration, as shown in Listing 6-33.

Listing 6-33. SMTP Configuration in appsettings.json file

```
"AppSettings": {
  "ApplicationTitle": "Automobile Service Center Application",
  "AdminEmail": "ascadmin@mailinator.com",
  "AdminName": "Admin",
  "AdminPassword": "P@ssw0rd",
  "Roles": "Admin,User",

  "SMTPServer": "smtp.gmail.com",
  "SMTPPort": "465",
  "SMTPAccount": "autoservicenternew@gmail.com",
  "SMTPPassword": "************"
},
```

Add SMTP configuration properties to the ApplicationSettings class, as shown in Listing 6-34, so that SMTP configuration will also be available through the site, just like other configuration settings.

Listing 6-34. Updated ApplicationSettings class with SMTP configuration

```
public class ApplicationSettings
{
    public string ApplicationTitle { get; set; }
    public string AdminEmail { get; set; }
    public string AdminName { get; set; }
    public string AdminPassword { get; set; }
    public string Roles { get; set; }

    public string SMTPServer { get; set; }
    public int SMTPPort { get; set; }
    public string SMTPAccount { get; set; }
    public string SMTPPassword { get; set; }
}
```

An ASP.NET Core application by default comes with a template to send e-mail and texts for Identity operations. AuthMessageSender is the class, located in the Service folder under the ASC.Web project. Listing 6-35 shows the default code.

Listing 6-35. AuthMessageSender class

```
public class AuthMessageSender : IEmailSender, ISmsSender
{
    public Task SendEmailAsync(string email, string subject, string message)
    {
        // Plug in your email service here to send an email.
        return Task.FromResult(0);
    }

    public Task SendSmsAsync(string number, string message)
    {
        // Plug in your SMS service here to send a text message.
        return Task.FromResult(0);
    }
}
```

We will modify the SendEmailAsync method to use Gmail's SMTP server and send e-mail. Listing 6-36 shows the updated code. The SendEmailAsync method first creates a MimeMessage with the logged-in user's e-mail. Using MailKit's SmtpClient, a connection is opened to the specified SMTP server and gets authenticated with the e-mail and password provided in the appsettings configuration. SmtpClient sends the message and then disconnects form the SMTP server.

Listing 6-36. Updated AuthMessageSender class with MailKit API

```
using ASC.Web.Configuration;
using MailKit.Net.Smtp;
using Microsoft.Extensions.Options;
using MimeKit;
using System.Threading.Tasks;

namespace ASC.Web.Services
{
    public class AuthMessageSender : IEmailSender, ISmsSender
    {
        private IOptions<ApplicationSettings> _settings;
        public AuthMessageSender(IOptions<ApplicationSettings> settings)
        {
            _settings = settings;
        }

        public async Task SendEmailAsync(string email, string subject, string message)
        {
            var emailMessage = new MimeMessage();
            emailMessage.From.Add(new MailboxAddress(_settings.Value.SMTPAccount));
            emailMessage.To.Add(new MailboxAddress(email));
            emailMessage.Subject = subject;
            emailMessage.Body = new TextPart("plain") { Text = message };
```

```
using (var client = new SmtpClient())
{
    await client.ConnectAsync(_settings.Value.SMTPServer, _settings.Value.
    SMTPPort, false);
    await client.AuthenticateAsync(_settings.Value.SMTPAccount, _settings.Value.
    SMTPPassword);
    await client.SendAsync(emailMessage);
    await client.DisconnectAsync(true);

    }
}

    public Task SendSmsAsync(string number, string message)
    {
        // Plug in your SMS service here to send a text message.
        return Task.FromResult(0);
    }
    }
}
```

Now we will modify the account controller's ResetPassword action, which will call the AuthMessageSender's SendEmailAsync method and send an e-mail to the user with the Reset Password link, as shown in Listing 6-37. The Reset Password action will find the logged-in user based on the e-mail from HttpContext.User and generates a unique code that serves as a password-reset token. This token is appended to the URL generated from the account controller and Reset Password action. Finally, an e-mail is sent to the user, and a confirmation view is displayed to the user.

Listing 6-37. InitiateResetPassword action

```
[HttpPost]
[AllowAnonymous]
public async Task<IActionResult> InitiateResetPassword()
{
    // Find User
    var userEmail = HttpContext.User.GetCurrentUserDetails().Email;
    var user = await _userManager.FindByEmailAsync(userEmail);

    // Generate User code
    var code = await _userManager.GeneratePasswordResetTokenAsync(user);
    var callbackUrl = Url.Action(nameof(ResetPassword), "Account", new { userId = user.Id,
    code = code }, protocol: HttpContext.Request.Scheme);

    // Send Email
    await _emailSender.SendEmailAsync(userEmail, "Reset Password",
        $"Please reset your password by clicking here: <a href='{callbackUrl}'>link</a>");
    return View("ResetPasswordEmailConfirmation");
}
```

The Reset Password action is triggered by the Reset Password anchor click of the left navigation menu. Because this is a POST action, we need to include a hidden form in _SecureLayout.cshtml, as shown in Listing 6-38. This form is posted to the account controller by using a JQuery click event (similar to the Logout event).

Listing 6-38. JQuery event of Reset Password Link

```
<form class="hide" method="post" id="resetPassword_form" asp-controller="Account"
asp-action="InitiateResetPassword">
</form>

@section Scripts{
@RenderSection("Scripts", required: false)
    <script type="text/javascript">
        $(function () {
            $('#ancrLogout').click(function () {
                $('#logout_form').submit();
            });

            $('#ancrResetPassword').click(function () {
                $('#resetPassword_form').submit();
            });
        });
    </script>
}
```

The Reset Password Confirmation view is a simple view that displays the message shown in Listing 6-39.

■ **Note** Add the following styles, which are used by some of the Reset Password views:

```
.margin-top-50px{

  margin-top: 50px;

}

.margin-bottom-50px{

  margin-bottom: 50px;

}
```

Listing 6-39. Reset Password Confirmation view

```
@{
    ViewData["Title"] = "Reset Password Confirmation";
    Layout = "_Layout";
}

<div class="row">
    <div class="col s12">
        <div class="card-panel orange lighten-1 margin-bottom-50px margin-top-50px">
            <span class="white-text">
                Please check your email to reset your password.
            </span>
        </div>
    </div>
</div>
```

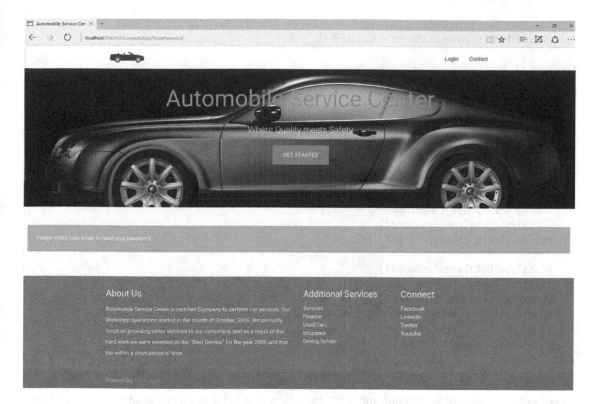

Figure 6-12. *Reset Password confirmation page*

After the preceding action, the user receives an e-mail and clicks the unique URL that is included in the e-mail (see Figure 6-13).

Figure 6-13. *E-mail received by the user about the Reset Password action*

The user will be redirected to the Reset Password action of the account controller, which will present a view through which the user can change her password. The Reset Password action is shown in Listing 6-40.

Listing 6-40. *ResetPassword action*

```
[HttpGet]
[AllowAnonymous]
public IActionResult ResetPassword(string code = null)
{
    return code == null ? View("Error") : View();
}
```

To collect the e-mail and new password, we define the ResetPasswordViewModel in the AccountViewModels folder, as shown in Listing 6-41.

Listing 6-41. ResetPasswordViewModel class

```
public class ResetPasswordViewModel
{
    [Required]
    [EmailAddress]
    public string Email { get; set; }

    [Required]
    [StringLength(100, ErrorMessage = "The {0} must be at least {2} and at max {1}
     characters long.", MinimumLength = 6)]
    [DataType(DataType.Password)]
    public string Password { get; set; }

    [DataType(DataType.Password)]
    [Display(Name = "Confirm password")]
    [Compare("Password", ErrorMessage = "The password and confirmation password do not match.")]
    public string ConfirmPassword { get; set; }

    public string Code { get; set; }
}
```

The Reset Password view cshtml is as shown in Listing 6-42. The Reset Password view collects the user's e-mail and new password information and POSTs the information to the Reset Password POST action of the account controller.

At the time of execution, this view looks like in Figure 6-14.

Listing 6-42. Reset Password view

```
@model ResetPasswordViewModel
@{
    ViewData["Title"] = "Reset password";
    Layout = "_Layout";
}

<div class="container">
    <div class="row">
        <div class="col s12 m6 offset-m3">
            <form asp-controller="Account" asp-action="ResetPassword" method="post"
              class="form-horizontal">
                <div asp-validation-summary="All" class="text-danger"></div>
                <input asp-for="Code" type="hidden" />
                <div class="row">
                    <div class="input-field col s12">
                        <input asp-for="Email" type="email" class="validate">
                        <label asp-for="Email" data-error="wrong" data-success="right">Email
                          </label>
                    </div>
                </div>
```

```
        <div class="row">
            <div class="input-field col s12">
                <input asp-for="Password" type="password" class="validate">
                <label asp-for="Password" data-error="wrong" data-success="right">
                Password</label>
            </div>
        </div>

        <div class="row">
            <div class="input-field col s12">
                <input asp-for="ConfirmPassword" type="password" class="validate">
                <label asp-for="ConfirmPassword" data-error="wrong" data-success="right">
                Confirm Password</label>
            </div>
        </div>

        <div class="row center">
            <button class="btn waves-effect waves-light" type="submit">
                Submit
                <i class="material-icons right">Reset</i>
            </button>
        </div>

        <div class="row center">
            <a asp-action="ForgotPassword">Forgot your password?</a>
        </div>
    </form>
  </div>
 </div>
</div>
```

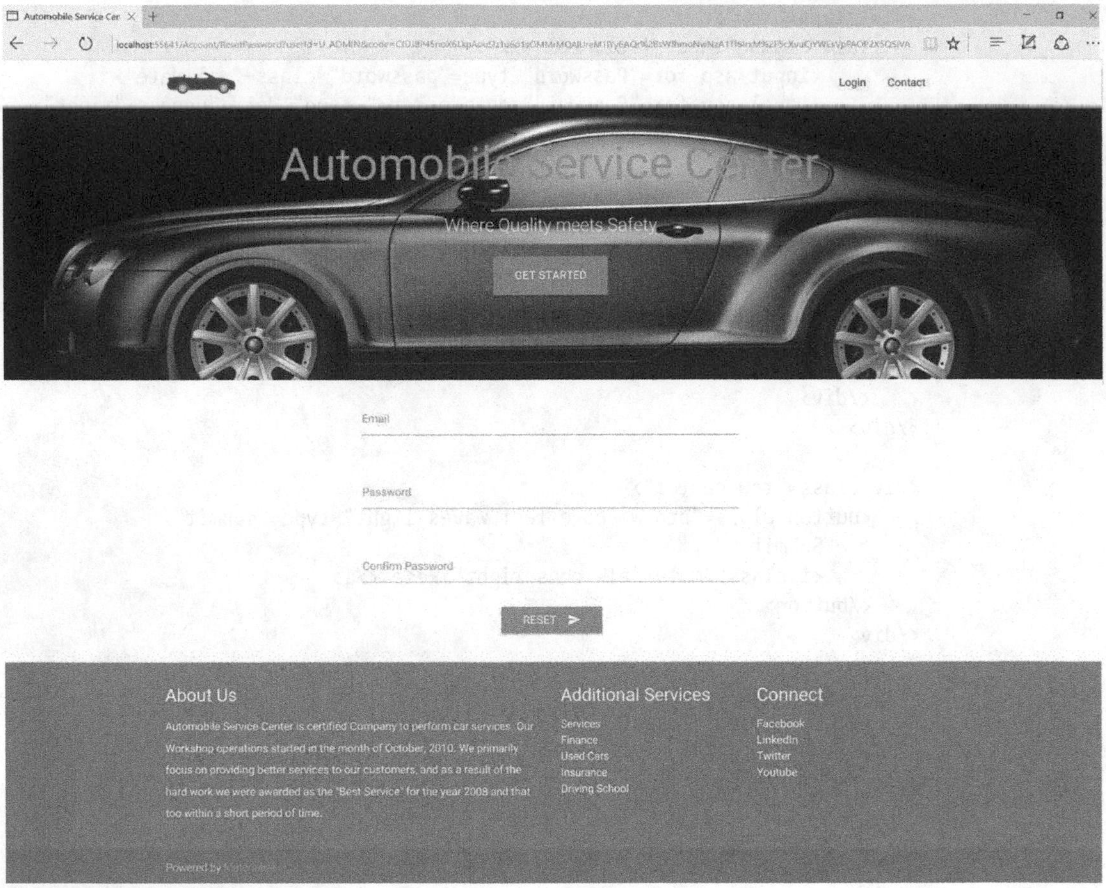

Figure 6-14. *Reset Password view*

Validation messages in the Reset Password view are displayed, as shown in Figure 6-15.

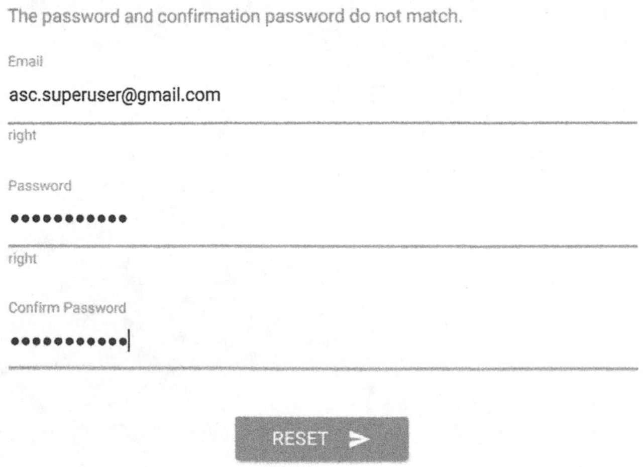

Figure 6-15. *Validation messages in the Reset Password view*

The POST action of ResetPassword is as shown in Listing 6-43. In this action, we first query the user based on the e-mail address provided in the form. If the user is found, we will reset the password by calling UserManager's ResetPasswordAsync method. After the password has been reset, we will forcefully sign out and redirect the user to the Reset Password Confirmation action.

Listing 6-43. POST action of Reset Password

```
[HttpPost]
[AllowAnonymous]
[ValidateAntiForgeryToken]
public async Task<IActionResult> ResetPassword(ResetPasswordViewModel model)
{
    if (!ModelState.IsValid)
    {
        return View(model);
    }
    var user = await _userManager.FindByEmailAsync(model.Email);
    if (user == null)
    {
        // Don't reveal that the user does not exist
        return RedirectToAction(nameof(AccountController.ResetPasswordConfirmation),
        "Account");
    }
    var result = await _userManager.ResetPasswordAsync(user, model.Code, model.Password);
    if (result.Succeeded)
    {
        if(HttpContext.User.Identity.IsAuthenticated)
        await _signInManager.SignOutAsync();

        return RedirectToAction(nameof(AccountController.ResetPasswordConfirmation),
        "Account");
    }
    AddErrors(result);
    return View();
}
```

■ **Note** Forcibly logging out the user after a successful password entry ensures that any trace of the old password is removed.

The Reset Password Confirmation action is shown in Listing 6-44.

Listing 6-44. Reset Passwork Confirmation action

```
[HttpGet]
[AllowAnonymous]
public IActionResult ResetPasswordConfirmation()
{
    return View();
}
```

The Reset Password Confirmation view is shown in Listing 6-45; this view will present the Login link to the user. Upon clicking the link, the user will be redirected to the Login page, and can use the new password and login to the system, as shown in Figure 6-16.

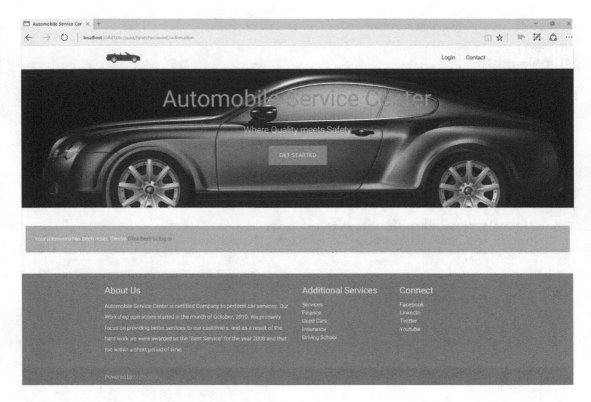

Figure 6-16. *Reset Password confirmation view*

Listing 6-45. Reset Password Confirmation view

```
@{
    ViewData["Title"] = "Reset password confirmation";
}

<div class="row">
    <div class="col s12">
        <div class="card-panel orange lighten-1 margin-bottom-50px margin-top-50px">
            <span class="white-text">
                Your password has been reset. Please <a asp-controller="Account"
                asp-action="Login">Click here to log in</a>.
            </span>
        </div>
    </div>
</div>
```

■ **Note**   All the Reset Password action methods of the account controller are made anonymous endpoints to achieve code reusability for supporting other functionalities such as Forgot Password.

Developing a Forgot Password Option

In this section, we will develop the Forgot Password functionality for the Automobile Service Center application. We will reuse most of the Reset Password functionality code and artifacts. The main difference between the Forgot and Reset Password pages is that Reset Password is used by users who are already authenticated, whereas Forgot Password will be used by users who have an account but forgot their password. We already placed the Forgot Password link on the Login page; the link points to the ForgotPassword action of the account controller. The ForgotPassword action is shown in Listing 6-46.

Listing 6-46. ForgotPassword action

```
[HttpGet]
        [AllowAnonymous]
        public IActionResult ForgotPassword()
        {
            return View();
        }
```

■ **Note**   The ForgotPassword action is a GET call compared with the ResetPassword action, because Forgot Password is available for all anonymous users.

The Forgot Password cshtml is shown in Listing 6-47. It will collect the user's e-mail address and send that information in a POST operation to the Forgot Password POST action of the account controller.

Listing 6-47. Forgot Password view

```
@model ForgotPasswordViewModel
@{
    ViewData["Title"] = "Forgot your password?";
}
<div class="container">
    <div class="row">
        <div class="col s12 m6 offset-m3">
            <form asp-controller="Account" asp-action="ForgotPassword" method="post"
              class="form-horizontal">
                <div asp-validation-summary="All" class="text-danger"></div>
                <div class="row">
                    <div class="input-field col s12">
                        <input asp-for="Email" type="email" class="validate">
                        <label asp-for="Email" data-error="wrong" data-success="right">
                          Email</label>
                    </div>
                </div>
                <div class="row center">
```

```
                <button class="btn waves-effect waves-light" type="submit">
                    Reset
                    <i class="material-icons right">send</i>
                </button>
            </div>
        </form>
    </div>
</div>
</div>
```

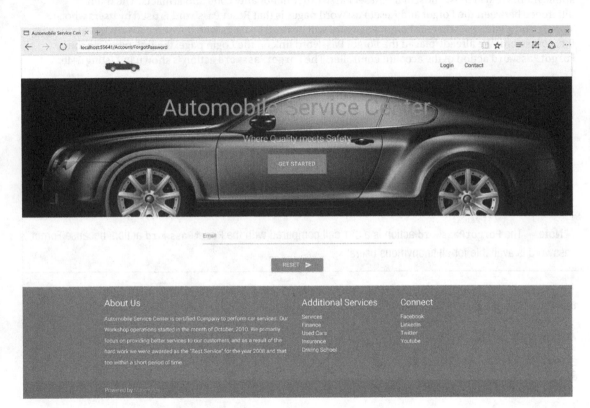

Figure 6-17. *Forgot Password view*

The POST action of Forgot Password first validates whether a user in the system is associated with the e-mail address and then checks whether the e-mail is verified by the user. If all validations pass, an e-mail with a unique user-specific link will be sent to the user, and an e-mail-confirmation view is displayed. The Forgot Password POST action is shown in Listing 6-48.

Listing 6-48. POST action of Forgot Password

```
[HttpPost]
[AllowAnonymous]
[ValidateAntiForgeryToken]
public async Task<IActionResult> ForgotPassword(ForgotPasswordViewModel model)
{
```

```
if (ModelState.IsValid)
{
    var user = await _userManager.FindByEmailAsync(model.Email);
    if (user == null || !(await _userManager.IsEmailConfirmedAsync(user)))
    {
        // Don't reveal that the user does not exist or is not confirmed
        return View("ResetPasswordEmailConfirmation");
    }

    // Send an email with this link
    var code = await _userManager.GeneratePasswordResetTokenAsync(user);
    var callbackUrl = Url.Action(nameof(ResetPassword), "Account", new { userId = user.
    Id, code = code }, protocol: HttpContext.Request.Scheme);
    await _emailSender.SendEmailAsync(model.Email, "Reset Password",
        $"Please reset your password by clicking here: <a href='{callbackUrl}'>link</a>");
    return View("ResetPasswordEmailConfirmation");
}

// If we got this far, something failed, redisplay form
return View(model);
}
```

Starting from this point, the user should follow exactly the same steps required to reset a password. The user should click the Reset Password link from the e-mail, which will prompt the user to enter an e-mail and new password. Upon submitting the new password, the user will be prompted to log in to the system by using that new password.

■ **Note**   Refer to the detailed steps indicated previously in the "Resetting a Password Through MailKit E-mail Library Integration" section of this chapter.

Creating and Managing Service Engineers

The Automobile Service Center employs service engineers with different capabilities to perform maintenance and repairs on customers' cars. Previously, we set up an Admin user who can be considered a superuser to all other roles. In this section, we will extend Admin's capabilities to set up service engineers under the Engineer role. In short, the functional requirements for this section are as follows:

1. The administrator sets up a service engineer under the Engineer role with a password.

2. The service engineer will be given a password via an e-mail.

3. The service engineer logs in to the system and changes his password, and then continues his daily activities.

4. For service engineers who are no longer associated with the Automobile Service Center, the administrator can mark them as Inactive.

We will first add the Engineer role to the system, as well as a test Service Engineer account that we'll associate with Engineer role. To set up an Engineer role on the system, we will append the existing role's configuration setting in the `appsettings.json` file, as shown in Listing 6-49. We will also set the default credentials of the Service Engineer test account in the same `appsettings.json` file.

Listing 6-49. Service engineer test account configuration in appsettings.json file

```json
"AppSettings": {
  "ApplicationTitle": "Automobile Service Center Application",
  "AdminEmail": "asc.superuser@gmail.com",
  "AdminName": "Admin",
  "AdminPassword": "P@ssw0rd",
  "EngineerEmail": "asc.superengineer@gmail.com",
  "EngineerName": "Engineer",
  "EngineerPassword": "P@ssw0rd",
  "Roles": "Admin,User,Engineer",

  "SMTPServer": "smtp.gmail.com",
  "SMTPPort": "587",
  "SMTPAccount": "autoservicenternew@gmail.com",
  "SMTPPassword": "********"
},
```

■ **Note** The Service Engineer test account is created purely for testing purposes. This account has no business or technical relevance.

Update the `ApplicationSettings` class to hold the new configuration settings, as shown in Listing 6-50.

Listing 6-50. Updated ApplicationSettings class with service engineer test account properties

```csharp
public class ApplicationSettings
{
    public string ApplicationTitle { get; set; }
    public string AdminEmail { get; set; }
    public string AdminName { get; set; }
    public string AdminPassword { get; set; }
    public string EngineerEmail { get; set; }
    public string EngineerName { get; set; }
    public string EngineerPassword { get; set; }
    public string Roles { get; set; }

    public string SMTPServer { get; set; }
    public int SMTPPort { get; set; }
    public string SMTPAccount { get; set; }
    public string SMTPPassword { get; set; }
}
```

To support different roles at the C# programming level, we will add a Roles enum to the system. Create a `Constants` class file at the `ASC.Models` project in the `BaseTypes` folder. The `Roles` enum is shown in Listing 6-51.

Listing 6-51. Roles enum

```
namespace ASC.Models.BaseTypes
{
    public static class Constants
    {
    }

    public enum Roles
    {
        Admin, Engineer, User
    }
}
```

■ **Note**   Having a Constants class always helps application development to centralize the commonly used strings and other settings. A developer should be aware of the practice that all the environment-related settings should go into appsettings.json, and any setting related to C# code should go into the Constants class.

Add the ASC.Models project reference to the ASC.Web project.

Now we will extend the IdentitySeed class to support the new Engineer role and the Service Engineer test account. As we are already iterating all the comma-separated roles and inserting them one by one to storage, no additional code or modifications are required to set up the Engineer role.

The highlighted code in Listing 6-52 describes how to set up a Service Engineer account. Similar to provisioning an administrator account, we first verify whether any user with a specified e-mail exists; if that user doesn't exist, we create the user and associated Email claim with that user. Finally, we associate the account with the Engineer role.

Listing 6-52. Updated IdentitySeed class to provision service engineer test account

```
public class IdentitySeed : IIdentitySeed
{
    public async Task Seed(UserManager<ApplicationUser> userManager,
    RoleManager<IdentityRole> roleManager, IOptions<ApplicationSettings> options)
    {
    // Get All comma-separated roles
        var roles = options.Value.Roles.Split(new char[] { ',' });

        // Create roles if they don't exist
        foreach (var role in roles)
        {
            if (!await roleManager.RoleExistsAsync(role))
            {
                IdentityRole storageRole = new IdentityRole
                {
                    Name = role
                };
                IdentityResult roleResult = await roleManager.CreateAsync(storageRole);
            }
        }
```

```
// Create admin if he doesn't exist
var admin = await userManager.FindByEmailAsync(options.Value.AdminEmail);
if (admin == null)
{
    ApplicationUser user = new ApplicationUser
    {
        UserName = options.Value.AdminName,
        Email = options.Value.AdminEmail,
        EmailConfirmed = true,
        LockoutEnabled = false
    };

    IdentityResult result = await userManager.CreateAsync(user, options.Value.
    AdminPassword);
    await userManager.AddClaimAsync(user, new System.Security.Claims.Claim("http://
    schemas.xmlsoap.org/ws/2005/05/identity/claims/emailaddress", options.Value.
    AdminEmail));
    await userManager.AddClaimAsync(user, new System.Security.Claims.Claim("IsActive", "True"));

    // Add Admin to Admin roles
    if (result.Succeeded)
    {
        await userManager.AddToRoleAsync(user, Roles.Admin.ToString());
    }
}

// Create a service engineer if he doesn't exist
var engineer = await userManager.FindByEmailAsync(options.Value.EngineerEmail);
if (engineer == null)
{
    ApplicationUser user = new ApplicationUser
    {
        UserName = options.Value.EngineerName,
        Email = options.Value.EngineerEmail,
        EmailConfirmed = true,
        LockoutEnabled = false
    };

    IdentityResult result = await userManager.CreateAsync(user, options.Value.
    EngineerPassword);
    await userManager.AddClaimAsync(user, new System.Security.Claims.Claim("http://
    schemas.xmlsoap.org/ws/2005/05/identity/claims/emailaddress", options.Value.
    EngineerEmail));
    await userManager.AddClaimAsync(user, new System.Security.Claims.
    Claim("IsActive", "True"));

    // Add Service Engineer to Engineer role
    if (result.Succeeded)
    {
        await userManager.AddToRoleAsync(user, Roles.Engineer.ToString());
    }
}
```

> ■ **Note** To test the preceding changes, we need to clear the previously created Azure development storage tables.

Run the application. You should see the users set up as shown in Figure 6-18.

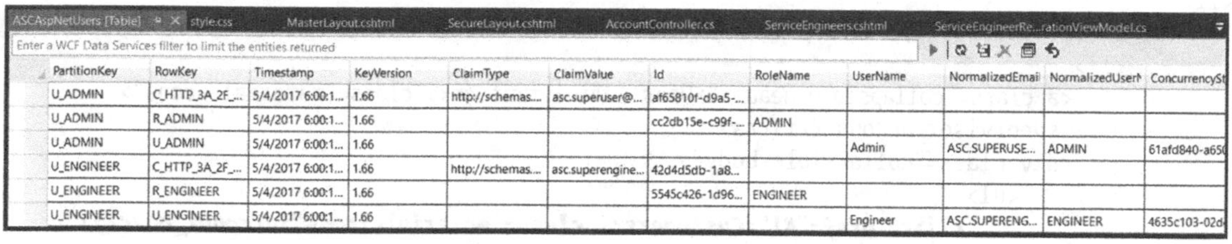

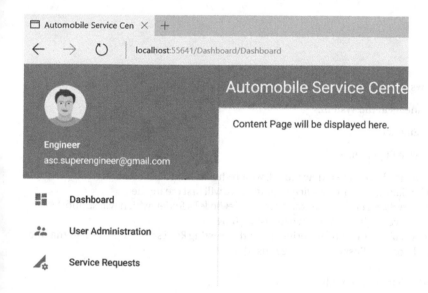

PartitionKey	RowKey	Timestamp	KeyVersion	ClaimType	ClaimValue	Id	RoleName	UserName	NormalizedEmail	NormalizedUser	ConcurrencySt
U_ADMIN	C_HTTP_3A_2F_...	5/4/2017 6:00:1...	1.66	http://schemas...	asc.superuser@...	af65810f-d9a5-...					
U_ADMIN	R_ADMIN	5/4/2017 6:00:1...	1.66			cc2db15e-c99f-...	ADMIN				
U_ADMIN	U_ADMIN	5/4/2017 6:00:1...	1.66					Admin	ASC.SUPERUSE...	ADMIN	61afd840-a65(
U_ENGINEER	C_HTTP_3A_2F_...	5/4/2017 6:00:1...	1.66	http://schemas...	asc.superengine...	42d4d5db-1a8...					
U_ENGINEER	R_ENGINEER	5/4/2017 6:00:1...	1.66			5545c426-1d96...	ENGINEER				
U_ENGINEER	U_ENGINEER	5/4/2017 6:00:1...	1.66					Engineer	ASC.SUPERENG...	ENGINEER	4635c103-02d(

Figure 6-18. *User records in the ASCAspNetUsers Azure table*

Quickly, we will check the newly created service engineer login in our application. As shown in Figure 6-19, the dashboard view will be displayed to the service engineer user.

Figure 6-19. *Service engineer dashboard view*

> ■ **Note** So far, the process of setting up a service engineer is useful only at the time that the application is first set up. But in reality, employees will leave organizations, and new employees will join, so we still need to create a front-end user interface to set up and manage service engineers. This functionality should be available to only the Admin user.

As the next step, we will add new functionalities to Admin so he can manage and set up service engineers from the front-end user interface rather than from the back end. Modify _SecureLayout.cshtml to add the Service Engineers menu item, as shown in Listing 6-53. This menu item will navigate the user to the account controller's ServiceEngineers action, which we will create in the next step.

Listing 6-53. Service Engineers menu item in left navigation

```
<li>
    <ul class="collapsible collapsible-accordion">
        <li>
            <a class="collapsible-header">User Administration<i class="material-icons">
             supervisor_account</i></a>
            <div class="collapsible-body">
                <ul>
                    <li><a href="#!">Customers<i class="material-icons">account_box</i>
                     </a></li>
                    <li><a href="#!">Deactivate Customer<i class="material-icons">remove_
                     circle</i></a></li>
                    <li><a asp-controller="Account" asp-action="ServiceEngineers">Service
                     Engineers<i class="material-icons">person_add</i></a></li>
                </ul>
            </div>
        </li>
    </ul>
</li>
```

The Service Engineers views should provide the following capabilities to Admin:

1. List all Service Engineers in the system.

2. Add a new Service Engineer.

3. Edit an existing Service Engineer.

To support these features, we need to create a view model, which should hold a list of Service Engineers, and a model to add/update an existing Service Engineer. We will first create the ServiceEngineerRegistrationViewModel class under the AccountViewModels folder, which will support adding or updating an existing Service Engineer, as shown in Listing 6-54. ServiceEngineerRegistrationViewModel will be inherited from the existing RegisterViewModel so that the properties Email, Password, and Confirm Password can be reused.

Listing 6-54. ServiceEngineerRegistrationViewModel class

```
namespace ASC.Web.Models.AccountViewModels
{
    public class ServiceEngineerRegistrationViewModel : RegisterViewModel
    {
        public string UserName { get; set; }
        public bool IsEdit { get; set; }
        public bool IsActive { get; set; }
    }
}
```

Now we will create `ServiceEngineerViewModel` under the `AccountViewModels` folder, as shown in Listing 6-55, which will wrap a list of Service Engineers along with `ServiceEngineerRegistrationViewModel`.

Listing 6-55. ServiceEngineerViewModel class

```
namespace ASC.Web.Models.AccountViewModels
{
    public class ServiceEngineerViewModel
    {
        public List<ApplicationUser> ServiceEngineers { get; set; }
        public ServiceEngineerRegistrationViewModel Registration { get; set; }
    }
}
```

Now that we have our view model ready, we will add the `ServiceEngineers` action in the account controller, as shown in Listing 6-56. We get all the users based on the Engineer role and return the view.

Listing 6-56. GET action of Service Engineers

```
[HttpGet]
        public async Task<IActionResult> ServiceEngineers()
        {
            var serviceEngineers = await _userManager.GetUsersInRoleAsync(Roles.Engineer.
            ToString());

            // Hold all service engineers in session
            HttpContext.Session.SetSession("ServiceEngineers", serviceEngineers);

            return View(new ServiceEngineerViewModel
            {
                ServiceEngineers = serviceEngineers == null ? null : serviceEngineers.ToList() ,
                Registration = new ServiceEngineerRegistrationViewModel() { IsEdit = false }
            });
        }
```

We will construct our view in two sections. The top section will display a list of service engineers, with an Edit option against each engineer. The bottom section will be the details section, which displays the details of the service engineer who is in edit mode. The details section can also be used to create a new service engineer.

We will use a JQuery plug-in called DataTables that is highly flexible in displaying content in list format and comes by default with advanced interaction controls such as pagination, sorting, and filtering for any HTML table.

■ **Note** More details about the JQuery DataTables plug-in can be found at `https://datatables.net/`.

To get started with DataTables, we need to refer its JQuery and CSS files in our solution. We will add those scripts from DataTables' content-delivery network, as shown in Listing 6-57.

Listing 6-57. JQuery DataTables scripts and CSS references

```
@using Microsoft.Extensions.Options;
@using ASC.Web.Configuration;
@inject IOptions<ApplicationSettings> _configurationSettings

<!DOCTYPE html>
<html>
<head>
    <meta http-equiv="Content-Type" content="text/html; charset=UTF-8" />
    <meta name="viewport" content="width=device-width, initial-scale=1, maximum-scale=1.0,
    user-scalable=no" />
    <title>@_configurationSettings.Value.ApplicationTitle</title>

    <!-- CSS -->
    <link href="https://fonts.googleapis.com/icon?family=Material+Icons" rel="stylesheet">
    <link href="https://cdn.datatables.net/1.10.15/css/jquery.dataTables.min.css"
     type="text/css" rel="stylesheet" media="screen,projection" />
    <link href="~/css/materialize.css" type="text/css" rel="stylesheet" media="screen,projection" />
    <link href="~/css/style.css" type="text/css" rel="stylesheet" media="screen,projection" />
</head>
<body>
    <!-- Render Body -->
    @RenderBody()

    <script src="~/lib/jquery/dist/jquery.min.js"></script>
    <script src="~/lib/jquery-validation/dist/jquery.validate.js"></script>
    <script src="~/lib/jquery-validation-unobtrusive/jquery.validate.unobtrusive.js"></script>
    <script src="~/js/materialize.min.js"></script>
    <script src="https://cdn.datatables.net/1.10.15/js/jquery.dataTables.min.js"></script>
    <script src="~/js/init.js"></script>

    @RenderSection("Scripts", required: false)
</body>
</html>
```

Create the Service Engineers view, as shown in Listing 6-58. An HTML table has been defined, and all the service engineers are iterated and rendered in the same table. By default, we will show Email, Username, IsActive, and Edit action columns in the table. If no service engineers are available, instead of displaying the table, a No Records Available message will be rendered. The details section of the view contains a form tag with the required elements for e-mail, password, active flags. By default, we will not give Admin an option to change the e-mail of the user. We also maintain hidden fields in the form to identify information such as type of operation and e-mail.

The view also contains JQuery code that is primarily used to configure DataTables by initializing it with page size and length options. We also set the required styles for DataTables. In JQuery code, we hide the IsActive column by default because we will not show a Boolean flag for the IsActive column; instead we will show green tick or red X.

We will also handle the reset button functionality in JQuery, through which the user changes will be discarded. Finally, an Edit click event is handled in which we will populate the details section with the information of the service engineer who is in edit mode. JQuery code is also used to populate the e-mail hidden field (which is by default disabled on the user interface) upon click of the Submit button.

Listing 6-58. Service Engineers view with JQuery code

```
@model ServiceEngineerViewModel
@{
    Layout = "_SecureLayout";
}

<div class="row"></div>
<div class="row padding-top-20px">

    <div class="row z-depth-3">
        <div class="section white-text padding-left-10px blue-grey lighten-1">
            <h5>Users</h5>
        </div>
        <div class="divider"></div>
        <div class="col s12 padding-bottom-15px">
            @if (Model.ServiceEngineers != null)
            {
                @* Display List of Service Engineers *@
                <table class="highlight centered" id="tblServiceEngineers">
                    <thead>
                        <tr>
                            <th data-field="Email">Email</th>
                            <th data-field="UserName">Name</th>
                            <th data-field="IsActive">Is Active</th>
                            <th data-field="IsActiveImg">Is Active</th>
                            <th data-field="Actions">Edit User</th>
                        </tr>
                    </thead>
                    <tbody>
                        @foreach (var user in Model.ServiceEngineers)
                        {
                            <tr>
                                <td>@user.Email</td>
                                <td>@user.UserName</td>
                                <td>@(Boolean.Parse(user.Claims.SingleOrDefault(p =>
                                p.ClaimType == "IsActive").ClaimValue))</td>
                                <td><img src="@(Boolean.Parse(user.Claims.SingleOrDefault
                                (p => p.ClaimType == "IsActive").ClaimValue) ? "/images/
                                green_tick.png" : "/images/red_cross.png")" /></td>
                                <td><i class="small material-icons edit cursor-hand">mode_
                                edit</i></td>
                            </tr>
                        }
                    </tbody>
                </table>
            }
            else
            {
                @* In case of No records, display no records message *@
                <div class="card blue-grey lighten-1">
                    <div class="card-content white-text">
```

```
                    <span class="card-title">No Service Engineers!!!</span>
                    <p>
                         No Service Engineers found, please add a Service Engineer to system.
                    </p>
                </div>
            </div>
        }
    </div>
</div>

<div class="row"></div>

@* Details Section *@
<div class="row z-depth-3">
    <div class="col s12 padding-0px">
        <div class="section white-text padding-left-10px blue-grey lighten-1">
            <h5>Service Engineer Details</h5>
        </div>
        <div class="divider"></div>
        <form asp-controller="Account" asp-action="ServiceEngineers" method="post"
         class="col s12" id="fromUser">
            <input type="hidden" asp-for="Registration.IsEdit" />
            <input type="hidden" asp-for="Registration.Email"/>
            <div class="input-field col s4">
                <input asp-for="Registration.Email" id="Input_Registration_Email" />
                <label asp-for="Registration.Email"></label>
            </div>
            <div class="input-field col s4">
                <input asp-for="Registration.UserName" class="validate" />
                <label asp-for="Registration.UserName"></label>
            </div>
            <div class="input-field col s4">
                <input asp-for="Registration.Password" class="validate" />
                <label asp-for="Registration.Password"></label>
            </div>
            <div class="input-field col s4">
                <input asp-for="Registration.ConfirmPassword" class="validate" />
                <label asp-for="Registration.ConfirmPassword"></label>
            </div>
            <div class="input-field col s4">
                <div class="switch">
                    <label>
                        Is Active
                        <input asp-for="Registration.IsActive" class="validate" />
                        <span class="lever"></span>
                    </label>
                </div>
            </div>
            <div class="input-field col s4 right-align">
                <button class="btn waves-effect waves-light btnSubmit" type="submit"
                 name="action">
```

154

```
                    Create
                    <i class="material-icons right">send</i>
                </button>
                <button class="btn waves-effect waves-light reset  red lighten-1"
                 type="button" name="action">
                    Reset
                </button>
            </div>
            <div class="row col s12 right-align" asp-validation-summary="All"></div>
        </form>

    </div>
    <div class="row"></div>

  </div>

</div>

@section Scripts{
    <script>
        $(document).ready(function () {
            // Initialize DataTable to show list of Engineers
            var table = $('#tblServiceEngineers').DataTable({
                'pageLength': 3,
                // Number of records to be displayed per page
                'lengthMenu': [[3, 5, 10, -1], [3, 5, 10, 'All']]
            });

            // Set Styles for DataTable and Number of Records to be displayed in drop-down
            $('#tblServiceEngineers').css("width", "100%");
            $('select[name="tblServiceEngineers_length"]').material_select();

            // Get the column API object
            var isActiveColumn = table.column(2);
            isActiveColumn.visible(false);

            // Handle Reset fucntionality
            $(document).on("click", ".reset", function () {
                $('#fromUser')[0].reset();
                $('#Input_Registration_Email').removeAttr('disabled');
                $('.btnSubmit').text('Create');
                $('#Registration_IsEdit').val('False');
            });

            // This is required to disable Email filed on Server-side model validation failure.
            if ($('#Registration_IsEdit').val() === 'True') {
                $('#Input_Registration_Email').attr('disabled', 'disabled');
            }

            // On click of Edit icon, populate the details section with details of service engineer
            $(document).on('click', '.edit', function () {
```

```
            var user = $('#tblServiceEngineers').DataTable().row($(this).parents('tr')).data();

            $('#Registration_IsEdit').val('True');

            $('#Input_Registration_Email').val(user[0]);
            $('#Input_Registration_Email').attr('disabled', 'disabled');

            $('#Registration_UserName').val(user[1]);
            $('#Registration_UserName').addClass('valid');

            $('#Registration_IsActive').prop('checked', user[2] === 'True' ? true : false);

            $('.btnSubmit').text('Save');
            Materialize.updateTextFields();
        });

        // Set hidden Email field to correct value from UI field
        // This is required for
        $(document).on('click', '.btnSubmit', function () {
            $('#Registration_Email').val($('#Input_Registration_Email').val());
            Materialize.updateTextFields();
        });

    });
    </script>
}
```

Styles in Listing 6-59 are added to style.css to support the Service Engineers view.

Listing 6-59. Extended Style.css

```
.padding-bottom-15px{
    padding-bottom : 15px !important;
}

.cursor-hand{
    cursor: pointer
}
```

■ **Note** Add the following images to the images folder under wwwroot to show active and inactive service engineers:

The POST action of Service Engineers is shown in Listing 6-60. It takes the entire ServiceEngineerViewModel as an input parameter, but it uses primarily ServiceEngineerRegistrationViewModel of the model to edit or create a new service engineer. The POST action is very simple; it first checks for model validations. If there are model validations, the POST action will return the same Service Engineers view with all validation error messages.

If there are no validation errors and if the IsEdit flag is true, then the Service Engineer is first updated with the given username. The IsActive status is updated to the IsActive claim of the user at Azure Storage.

■ **Note**   The IsActive claim is used to toggle the user activation. During the login process, this claim will be checked to make sure the user who is trying to log in is an active user. Along with this check, the IsLockedOut check will also be present at the time of login to prevent the user from logging in if that account is locked out.

If the IsEdit flag is false, a new user is created with the given details and password and is added to the Engineer role. The IsActive claim for a new user is set to the value that the Admin selects on the user interface.

Finally, an e-mail is sent to the user with e-mail and password details used to create/modify the account.

Listing 6-60. POST action of Service Engineers view

```
[HttpPost]
[ValidateAntiForgeryToken]
public async Task<IActionResult> ServiceEngineers(ServiceEngineerViewModel serviceEngineer)
{
    serviceEngineer.ServiceEngineers = HttpContext.Session.GetSession<List<ApplicationUser>>
    ("ServiceEngineers");
    if (!ModelState.IsValid)
    {
        return View(serviceEngineer);
    }

    if (serviceEngineer.Registration.IsEdit)
    {
        // Update User
        var user = await _userManager.FindByEmailAsync(serviceEngineer.Registration.Email);
        user.UserName = serviceEngineer.Registration.UserName;
        IdentityResult result = await _userManager.UpdateAsync(user);

        if (!result.Succeeded)
        {
            result.Errors.ToList().ForEach(p => ModelState.AddModelError("", p.Description));
            return View(serviceEngineer);
        }

        // Update Password
        var token = await _userManager.GeneratePasswordResetTokenAsync(user);
        IdentityResult passwordResult = await _userManager.ResetPasswordAsync(user, token,
        serviceEngineer.Registration.Password);
```

```
        if (!passwordResult.Succeeded)
        {
            passwordResult.Errors.ToList().ForEach(p => ModelState.AddModelError("",
            p.Description));
            return View(serviceEngineer);
        }

        // Update claims
        user = await _userManager.FindByEmailAsync(serviceEngineer.Registration.Email);
        var isActiveClaim = user.Claims.SingleOrDefault(p => p.ClaimType == "IsActive");
        var removeClaimResult = await _userManager.RemoveClaimAsync(user,
            new System.Security.Claims.Claim(isActiveClaim.ClaimType, isActiveClaim.
            ClaimValue));
        var addClaimResult = await _userManager.AddClaimAsync(user,
            new System.Security.Claims.Claim(isActiveClaim.ClaimType, serviceEngineer.
            Registration.IsActive.ToString()));
}
else
{
        // Create User
        ApplicationUser user = new ApplicationUser
        {
            UserName = serviceEngineer.Registration.UserName,
            Email = serviceEngineer.Registration.Email,
            EmailConfirmed = true
        };

        IdentityResult result = await _userManager.CreateAsync(user, serviceEngineer.
        Registration.Password);
        await _userManager.AddClaimAsync(user, new System.Security.Claims.Claim("http://
        schemas.xmlsoap.org/ws/2005/05/identity/claims/emailaddress", serviceEngineer.
        Registration.Email));
        await _userManager.AddClaimAsync(user, new System.Security.Claims.Claim("IsActive",
        serviceEngineer.Registration.IsActive.ToString()));

        if (!result.Succeeded)
        {
            result.Errors.ToList().ForEach(p => ModelState.AddModelError("",
            p.Description));
            return View(serviceEngineer);
        }

        // Assign user to Engineer Role
          var roleResult = await _userManager.AddToRoleAsync(user, Roles.Engineer.
          ToString());
        if (!roleResult.Succeeded)
        {
            roleResult.Errors.ToList().ForEach(p => ModelState.AddModelError("",
            p.Description));
            return View(serviceEngineer);
        }
}
```

```
if (serviceEngineer.Registration.IsActive)
{
    await _emailSender.SendEmailAsync(serviceEngineer.Registration.Email,
        "Account Created/Modified",
        $"Email : {serviceEngineer.Registration.Email} /n Passowrd : {serviceEngineer.
        Registration.Password}");
}
else
{
    await _emailSender.SendEmailAsync(serviceEngineer.Registration.Email,
        "Account Deactivated",
        $"Your account has been deactivated.");
}

    return RedirectToAction("ServiceEngineers");
}
```

Run the application and log in as Admin. You should see Service Engineers navigation menu item in the left navigation bar, as shown in Figure 6-20.

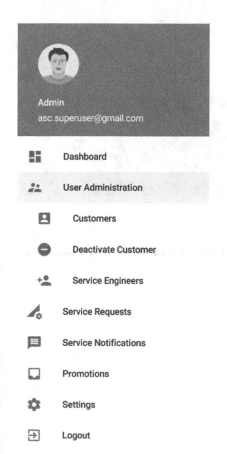

Figure 6-20. *Service Engineers menu option in the left navigation bar*

Click the Service Engineers menu item. The Service Engineer test account will be displayed, as shown in Figure 6-21.

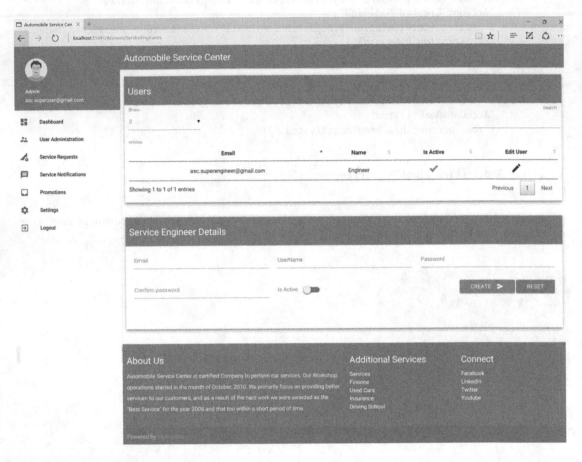

Figure 6-21. *Service Engineers view*

Click the Edit User button. The details of the Service Engineer will be populated in the details section, as shown in Figure 6-22.

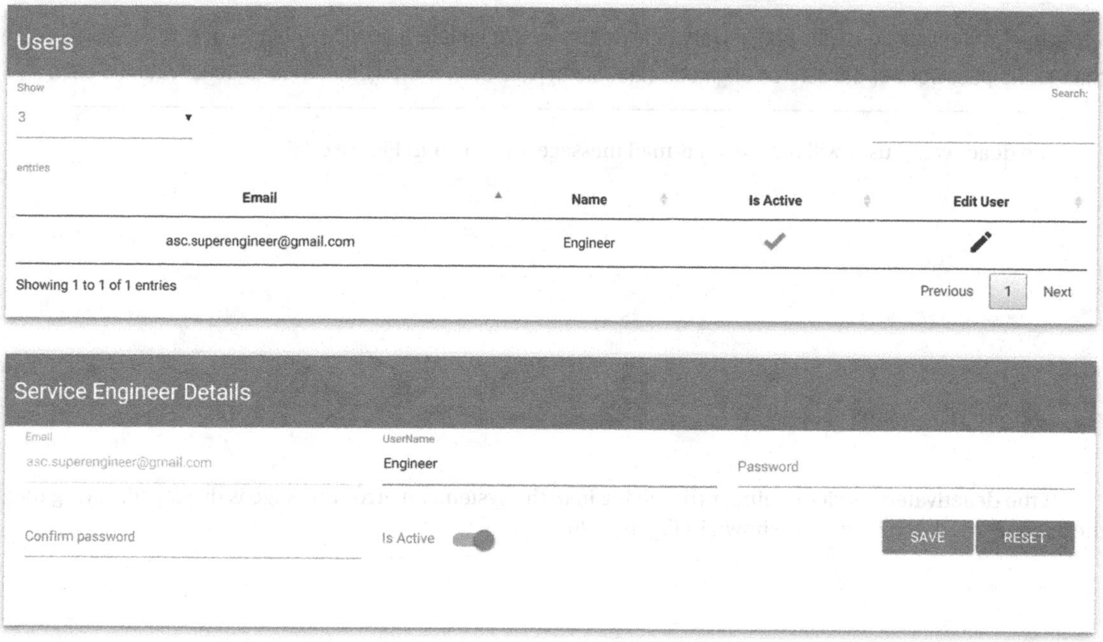

Users

Show

3 ▼

Search:

entries

Email	▲	Name	⇕	Is Active	⇕	Edit User	⇕
asc.superengineer@gmail.com		Engineer		✓		✎	

Showing 1 to 1 of 1 entries

Previous 1 Next

Service Engineer Details

Email
asc.superengineer@gmail.com

UserName
Engineer

Password

Confirm password

Is Active 🔵

SAVE   RESET

Figure 6-22. *Service Engineer Details section populated with details based on the edit operation*

Change the password and click Save. Now try to log in on any other browser with the new password for the edited service engineer, and the login should be successful. At the same time, the service engineer should receive an e-mail message with the new password, as shown in Figure 6-23.

Account Created/Modified   Inbox   x

autoservicenternew@gmail.com
to me ▾

7:23 PM (6 minutes ago)

Email : asc.superengineer@gmail.com /n Passowrd : P@ssw0rd!@#

Figure 6-23. *Account Created/Modified e-mail message for the service engineer*

Again, edit the same service engineer and turn off the Is Active flag, as shown in Figure 6-24. Click Save.

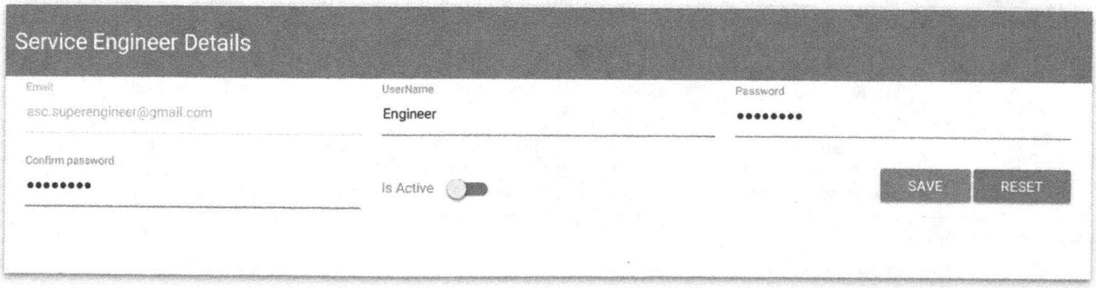

Service Engineer Details

Email
asc.superengineer@gmail.com

UserName
Engineer

Password
••••••••

Confirm password
••••••••

Is Active ⚪

SAVE   RESET

Figure 6-24. *Deactivating a service engineer*

■ **Note**   In the context of this book, every time Admin tries to update a service engineer, it is mandatory to set change the password of the service engineer. This rule applies even if the Admin tries to deactivate the user.

The deactivated user will receive an e-mail message, as shown in Figure 6-25.

Figure 6-25. *Deactivation e-mail message to the service engineer*

If the deactivated service engineer tries to log in to the system, an error message is displayed, saying that the account has been locked, as shown in Figure 6-26.

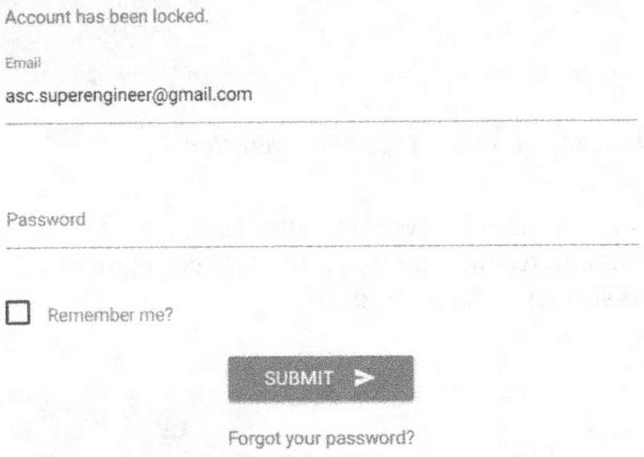

Account has been locked.

Email

asc.superengineer@gmail.com

Password

☐ Remember me?

SUBMIT ➤

Forgot your password?

Figure 6-26. *Deactivation message displayed for the service engineer*

If we look at the Service Engineers grid, we will have updated Is Active status, as shown in Figure 6-27.

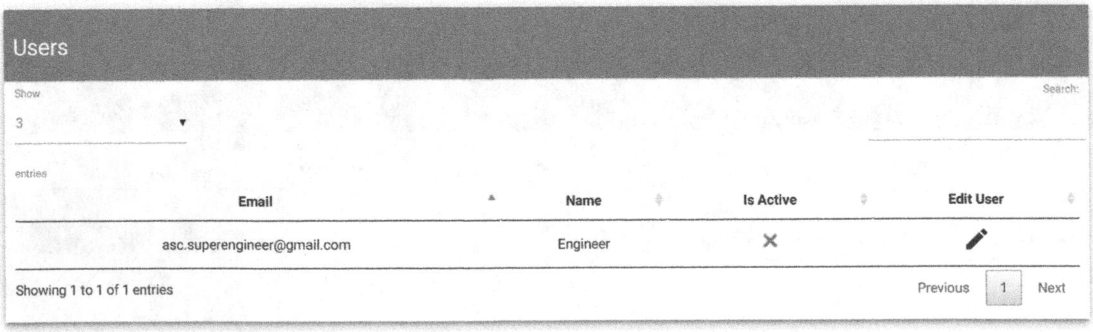

Email		Name	Is Active	Edit User
asc.superengineer@gmail.com		Engineer	✕	✎

Users

Show
3 ▾
entries

Search:

Showing 1 to 1 of 1 entries

Previous 1 Next

Figure 6-27. *Updated details of the service engineer in the data table*

In a similar way, a deactivated service engineer can be reactivated. Upon reactivation, an e-mail message with the new password will be sent to the service engineer, which he can use to access the system. Now we will add a new service engineer to the system, as shown in Figure 6-28. Click Save.

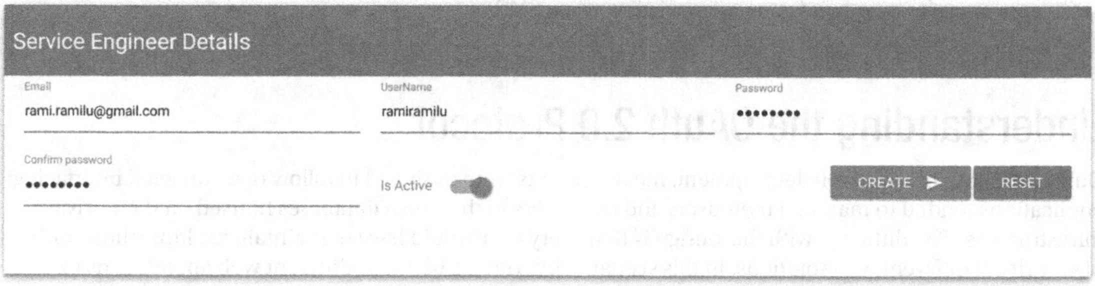

Service Engineer Details

Email	UserName	Password
rami.ramilu@gmail.com	ramiramilu	●●●●●●●●

Confirm password			
●●●●●●●●	Is Active	CREATE ➤	RESET

Figure 6-28.

The new user should get an e-mail message with e-mail and password credentials. He can use those credentials and access the system. The Service Engineers grid will be updated with new user details, as shown in Figure 6-29.

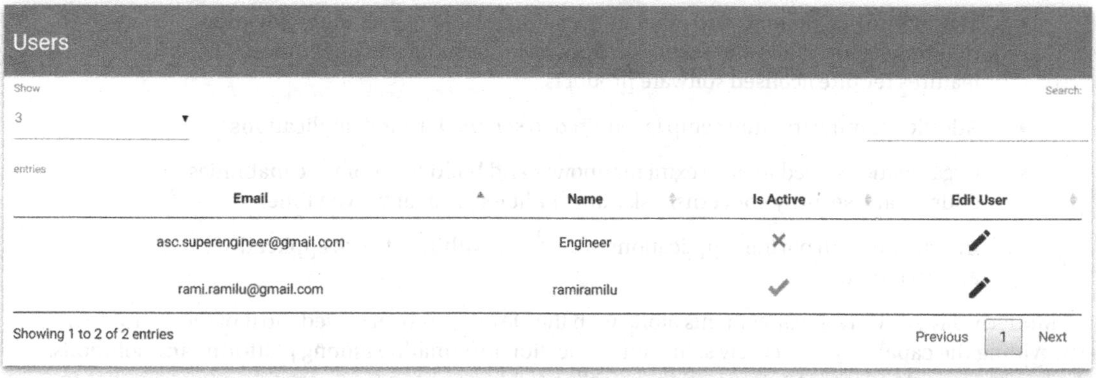

Users

Show

3

▼

entries

Search:

Email ▲	Name ⬍	Is Active ⬍	Edit User ⬍
asc.superengineer@gmail.com	Engineer	✕	✐
rami.ramilu@gmail.com	ramiramilu	✓	✐

Showing 1 to 2 of 2 entries   Previous 1 Next

Figure 6-29. Service Engineers table updated with new service engineer details

Service engineer management is available only to the Admin of the Automobile Service Center. So we need to restrict other roles from accessing the Service Engineer's actions in the account controller. Add the Authorize attribute on top of the actions that are accessible to only Admin, as shown in Listing 6-61.

Listing 6-61. Grant authorization to Admin role

```
[Authorize(Roles = "Admin")]
```

■ **Note** User management is a vast topic with many possible technical implementations. This chapter introduces you to the concepts of authentication, authorization, and user management. To broaden your understanding beyond the scope of this chapter, I suggest you practice with topics such as generating one-time passwords or performing two-factor authentication using SMS.

Understanding the OAuth 2.0 Protocol

During the days of early web development, most solutions were designed to follow disconnected interfacing; applications tended to maintain their users and customers in their own databases housed on their private infrastructure. The difficulty with this design is that every user would have to maintain multiple thumbprints of security at different web solutions. In this scenario, interfacing between different web applications to create custom workflows is always a challenge because of the different security protocols and practices followed by these applications.

Today, most applications tend to *not* store user information in their own data stores for the following reasons:

- User management is always prone to security threats and identity theft. To mitigate these risks, organizations need to spend hefty dollar amounts to hire security consultants.

- Maintaining credentials and other information related to user authentication requires secure vaults and secure certificates for hashing and encryption. These features require licensed software products.

- Additional infrastructure setup is required to secure data and applications.

- Organizations need to have extra manpower and build technology capabilities to address any security concerns, risks, and audit issues at any given time.

- Interfacing with partner applications and others within network applications is always tedious.

Modern-day software advancements along with the OAuth protocol solved most of these problems by providing the capability to securely share authentication information among platforms and solutions. OAuth is an open standard for authorization typically used by applications to provide other web sites or applications secure, authorized access to customer information without giving those sites or applications any passwords. This mechanism is used by companies such as Google, Facebook, Microsoft, and Twitter to permit users to share information about their accounts with third-party applications or web sites.

The journey of OAuth 1.0 began in 2006 by Blaine Cook, who was later joined by Chris Messina and Larry Halff. The OAuth 1.0 protocol was published as RFC 5849 in April 2010. The OAuth 2.0 framework was published as RFC 6749, and the Bearer Token Usage as RFC 6750 in October 2012. The main differences between OAuth 1.0 and 2.0 are as follows:

- Better support for non-browser-based applications.

- Client applications no longer require the usage of cryptography.

- Less complicated.

- Short-lived tokens with long-lived authorizations.

- Improved performance.

OAuth 2.0 has four major parties:

- *Resource owner*: Typically, a user in the system.

- *Resource server*: A server hosting protected data of the user.

- *Client*: Application requesting access to a resource server.

- *Authorization server*: A server issuing access token to the client. This token will be used for the client to request the resource server.

The authorization server issues tokens to client applications. Tokens are of two types: access tokens and refresh tokens. An *access token* is a short-lived token with a defined scope that is used by the client application to access user information on the resource server. The access token should be sent in every request to the resource server though an authorization request header. The *refresh token*, on the other hand, is only sent to the authorization server for renewing the access token when it has expired. The OAuth 2.0 authorization flow is depicted in Figure 6-30.

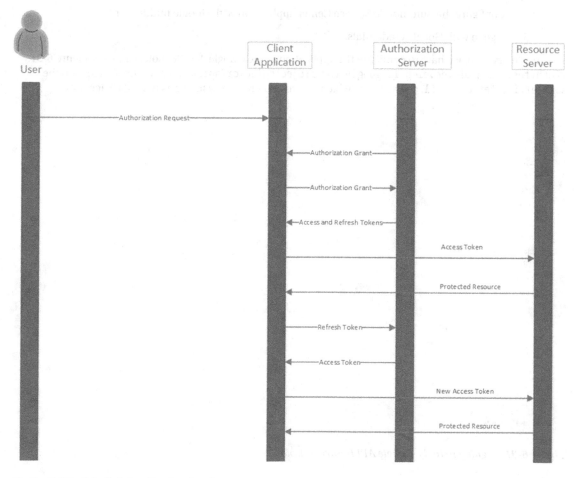

Figure 6-30. *OAuth 2.0 authorization flow*

■ **Note** More details on the OAuth 2.0 protocol can be found at `https://oauth.net/2/`.

For our Automobile Service Center application, we are going to use the OAuth 2.0 protocol to enable authorization of customers from Google.

Using a Gmail Authentication Provider for Customer Authentication

In this section, we will integrate the Automobile Service Center application with a Google identity provider through the OAuth 2.0 protocol. We need to follow these steps to integrate the Gmail authentication provider with `ASC.Web`:

1. Create an application at the Google API Console.

2. Configure the Automobile Service Center application with Google middleware.

3. Sign in with Google credentials.

As the first step, we have to configure the application at the Google API Console, shown in Figure 6-31. Visit `https://console.developers.google.com/projectselector/apis/library`, and sign in with the `autoservicenternew@gmail.com` account, which we created previously to use as the SMTP account.

Figure 6-31. Signing in to the Google API library console

The Google API Manager Library page opens, as shown in Figure 6-32. Click the Create button.

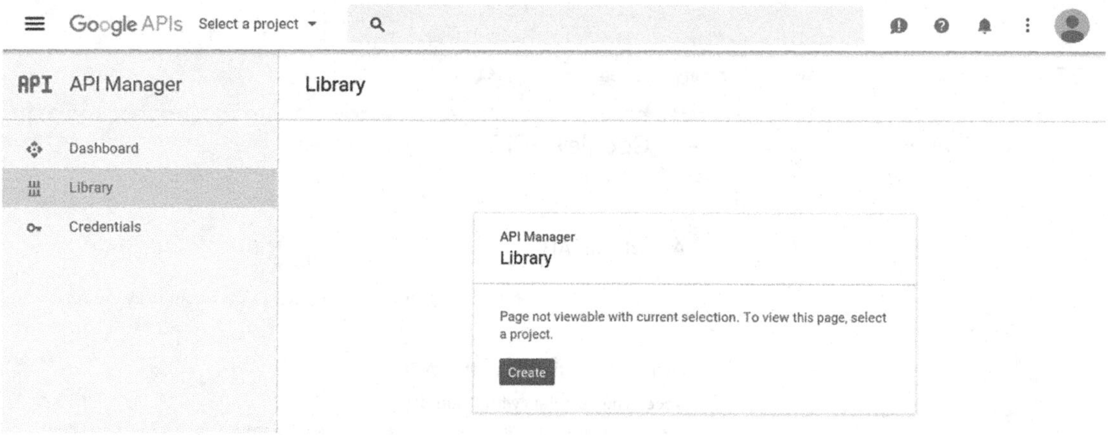

Figure 6-32. *Google API Manager*

Enter a name for the application, as shown in Figure 6-33, and click Create.

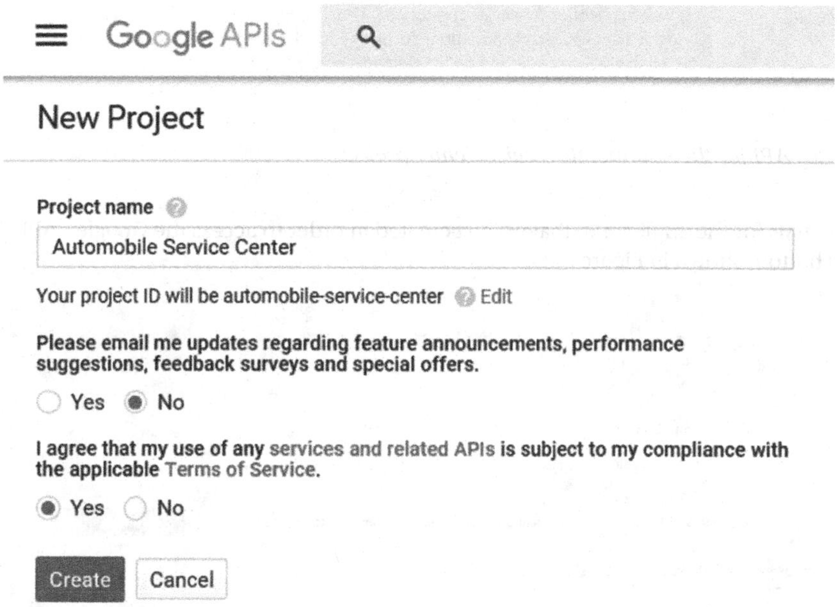

Figure 6-33. *Creating a project at the Google library console*

Once the project is created, search for *Google+ API* in the search bar and select the appropriate result. The Google+ API is used for accessing user data through the OAuth 2.0 protocol. Click Enable to get access to the Google+ API, as shown in Figure 6-34.

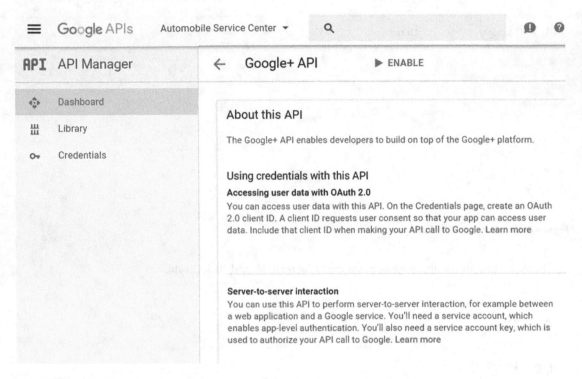

Figure 6-34. *Enabling Google+ API for the Automobile Service Center project*

We have to create credentials for the application that we just created in order to access the Google+ API. Click the Create Credentials button, shown in Figure 6-35.

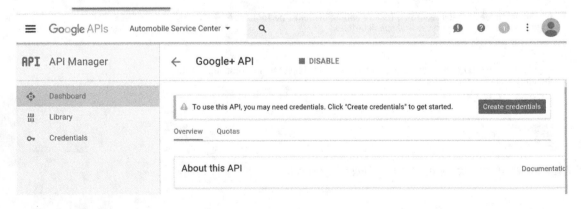

Figure 6-35. *Creating credentials to consume the Google+ API*

We need to specify the kind of credentials we need for our application. As shown in Figure 6-36, we configure our credentials for a Web Server to access User Data from the Google+ API and then click the What Credentials Do I Need? button.

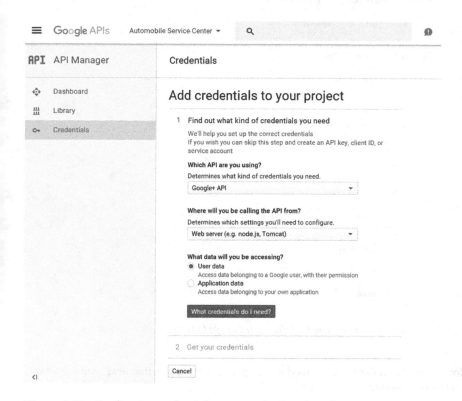

Figure 6-36. *Configuring credentials to access the Google+ API*

As shown in Figure 6-37, give a name to the client and enter the URL of the application, followed by `signin-google`.

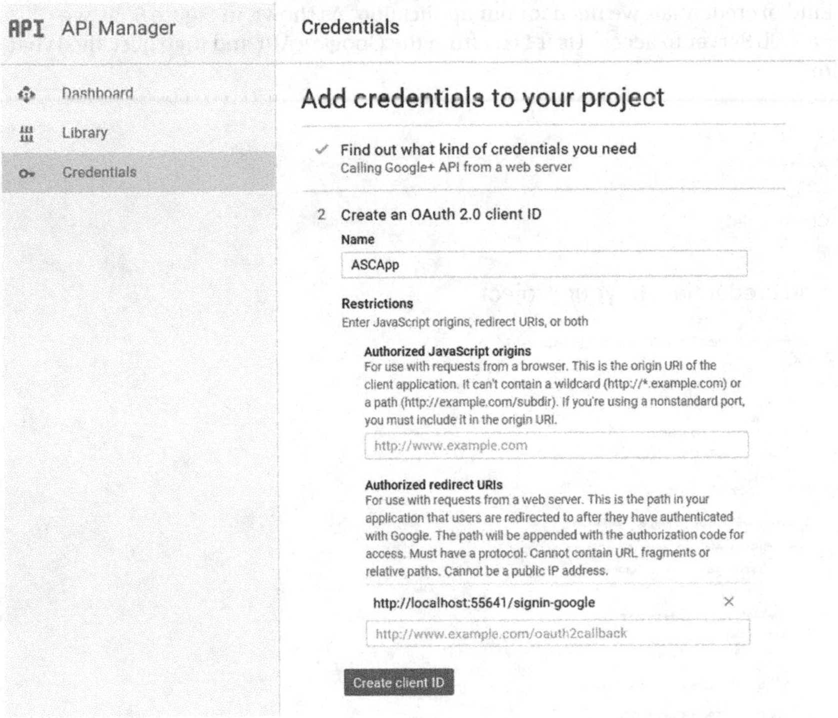

Figure 6-37. *Configuring the Automobile Service Center URL with Google OAuth 2.0*

As the last step before we create credentials, we need to set up a consent screen that users will see when they accept the consent at Google, as shown in Figure 6-38.

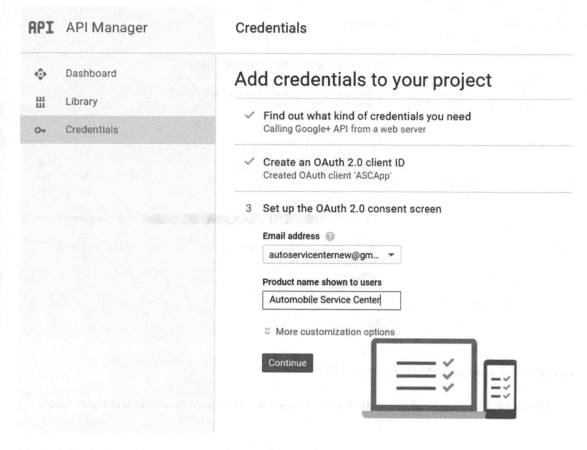

Figure 6-38. *Setting up a consent screen for Google+ OAuth 2.0*

Google will create a Client ID that allows us to download credentials in JSON format, as shown in Figure 6-39. Download the JSON file and verify the contents of file. You should find `client_id` and `client_secret` properties with values. These are the important values that are required to configure the `ASC.Web` project.

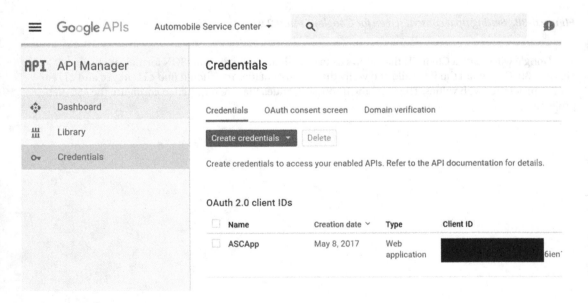

RPI API Manager

Credentials

◈ Dashboard
Ⴤ Library
o↝ Credentials

Add credentials to your project

✓ Find out what kind of credentials you need
   Calling Google+ API from a web server

✓ Create an OAuth 2.0 client ID
   Created OAuth client 'ASCApp'

✓ Set up the OAuth 2.0 consent screen

4 Download credentials

   Client ID ████████████████████████apps.googleusercontent.com

   Download this credential information in JSON format. This is always available for you on the credentials page.

   [Download] I'll do this later

[Done] Cancel

Figure 6-39. *Downloading the JSON credentials file*

Finally, click Done. All credentials are displayed in the Credentials section, as shown in Figure 6-40.

≡ Google APIs   Automobile Service Center ▾   Q   ❶

RPI API Manager

Credentials

◈ Dashboard
Ⴤ Library
o↝ Credentials

Credentials   OAuth consent screen   Domain verification

[Create credentials ▾] [Delete]

Create credentials to access your enabled APIs. Refer to the API documentation for details.

OAuth 2.0 client IDs

	Name	Creation date ✓	Type	Client ID
☐	ASCApp	May 8, 2017	Web application	████████████6ien⁁

Figure 6-40. *Created credentials at the Google console*

Now that we have a client ID and client secret, we should configure our Automobile Service Center application with Google authentication middleware. Prior to that, create the Google section in the appsettings.json file and copy the client ID and secret values as shown in Listing 6-62.

Listing 6-62. Google identity configuration in appsettings.json file

```
"Google" :{
  "Identity": {
    "ClientId": "*********************",
    "ClientSecret": "**************"
  }
},
```

■ **Note** Usually, we will not store sensitive information in the appsettings.json file because it will reside in a source version-control repository and is accessible to everyone who has access to code. We can use Azure Key Vault to store sensitive information and access it in a secure way.

For the sake of simplicity, we will use the appsettings.json file of the ASC.Web project to store the client ID and secret information.

Install the Microsoft.AspNetCore.Authentication.Google NuGet package, as shown in Figure 6-41, to the ASC.Web project that supports Google OAuth 2.0 authentication workflows.

Figure 6-41. *Installing the Microsoft.AspNetCore.Authentication.Google NuGet package to the ASC.Web project*

Configure the Google middleware in the Configure method of the Startup class, as shown in Listing 6-63. Make sure to configure the Google middleware after configuring Identity services.

Listing 6-63. Configure Google authentication in Startup class

```
public async void Configure(IApplicationBuilder app,
    IHostingEnvironment env,
    ILoggerFactory loggerFactory,
    IIdentitySeed storageSeed)
{
    loggerFactory.AddConsole(Configuration.GetSection("Logging"));
    loggerFactory.AddDebug();
```

```
if (env.IsDevelopment())
{
    app.UseDeveloperExceptionPage();
    app.UseDatabaseErrorPage();
    app.UseBrowserLink();
}
else
{
    app.UseExceptionHandler("/Home/Error");
}

app.UseSession();
app.UseStaticFiles();
app.UseIdentity();

app.UseGoogleAuthentication(new GoogleOptions()
{
    ClientId = Configuration["Google:Identity:ClientId"],
    ClientSecret = Configuration["Google:Identity:ClientSecret"]
});

app.UseMvc(routes =>
{
    routes.MapRoute(
        name: "default",
        template: "{controller=Home}/{action=Index}/{id?}");
});

await storageSeed.Seed(app.ApplicationServices.GetService<UserManager<ApplicationUs
er>>(),
    app.ApplicationServices.GetService<RoleManager<IdentityRole>>(),
    app.ApplicationServices.GetService<IOptions<ApplicationSettings>>());
}
```

Now we need to change Login.cshtml to include a button that will trigger Google authentication. Modify Login.cshtml as shown in Listing 6-64. We first get all the external authentication providers by using the GetExternalAuthenticationSchemes method of SignInManager and then iterate them and create the required buttons to trigger external authentication. As we only configured Google authentication to the Automobile Service Center application, we will be getting only a Google Sign-in button. The button is wrapped in a form that will post to the ExternalLogin action of AccountController, which will initiate the authentication request with the external provider. Necessary style changes are made to make the view appealing to users.

Listing 6-64. External authentication providers buttons on Login page

```
@using System.Collections.Generic
@using Microsoft.AspNetCore.Http
@using Microsoft.AspNetCore.Http.Authentication
@model LoginViewModel
@inject SignInManager<ApplicationUser> SignInManager
@{
```

```
    ViewData["Title"] = "Log in";
}
<div class="container">
    <div class="row">
        <div class="col s12 m5 offset-m2">
            <form asp-controller="Account" asp-action="Login" asp-route-
              returnurl="@ViewData["ReturnUrl"]" method="post">
                <div asp-validation-summary="All" class="text-danger"></div>

                <div class="row">
                    <div class="input-field col s12">
                        <input asp-for="Email" type="email" class="validate">
                        <label asp-for="Email" data-error="wrong" data-success="right">
                        Email</label>
                    </div>
                </div>

                <div class="row">
                    <div class="input-field col s12">
                        <input asp-for="Password" type="password" class="validate">
                        <label asp-for="Password" data-error="wrong" data-success="right">
                        Password</label>
                    </div>
                </div>

                <div class="row padding-left-10px">
                    <p>
                        <input asp-for="RememberMe" type="checkbox" class="filled-in" />
                        <label asp-for="RememberMe">@Html.DisplayNameFor(m => m.RememberMe)
                        </label>
                    </p>
                </div>

                <div class="row center">
                    <button class="btn waves-effect waves-light" type="submit">
                        Submit
                        <i class="material-icons right">send</i>
                    </button>
                </div>

                <div class="row center">
                    <a asp-action="ForgotPassword">Forgot your password?</a>
                </div>
            </form>
        </div>
        <div class="col s12 m4 offset-m1">
            <h5>Login using External Providers.</h5>
            <div class="divider"></div>
                @{
```

```
var loginProviders = SignInManager.GetExternalAuthenticationSchemes().ToList();
if (loginProviders.Count != 0)
{
    <form asp-controller="Account" asp-action="ExternalLogin" asp-
    route-returnurl="@ViewData["ReturnUrl"]" method="post" class="form-
    horizontal">
        <div>
            <p>
                @foreach (var provider in loginProviders)
                {
                    <button type="submit" class="btn btn-
                    default" name="provider" value="@provider.
                    AuthenticationScheme" title="Log in using your
                    @provider.DisplayName account">@provider.
                    AuthenticationScheme</button>
                }
            </p>
        </div>
    </form>
}
    }
    </div>

    </div>

</div>
```

Run the application and navigate to the Login view. You should see the login screen shown in Figure 6-42.

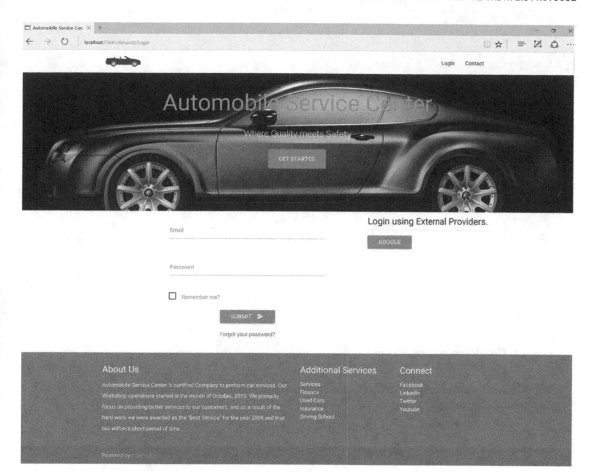

Figure 6-42. *Login view with Google authentication button*

Click the Google button. It will post the form to the `ExternalLogin` post action of `AccountController`, as shown in Listing 6-65. The post action will first fetch the properties of the external authentication provider and then redirect to the provider's login page, as shown in Figure 6-43. It will also hold the callback action to which the redirection should happen on successful login at the external authentication provider.

Listing 6-65. POST action of external login

```
[HttpPost]
[AllowAnonymous]
[ValidateAntiForgeryToken]
public IActionResult ExternalLogin(string provider, string returnUrl = null)
{
    // Request a redirect to the external login provider.
    var redirectUrl = Url.Action(nameof(ExternalLoginCallback), "Account", new { ReturnUrl =
    returnUrl });
    var properties = _signInManager.ConfigureExternalAuthenticationProperties(provider,
    redirectUrl);
    return Challenge(properties, provider);
}
```

Figure 6-43. *Google provider login page*

The account I used to sign in has two-factor authentication enabled at Gmail. As a result, I got a two-factor authentication prompt, as shown in Figure 6-44.

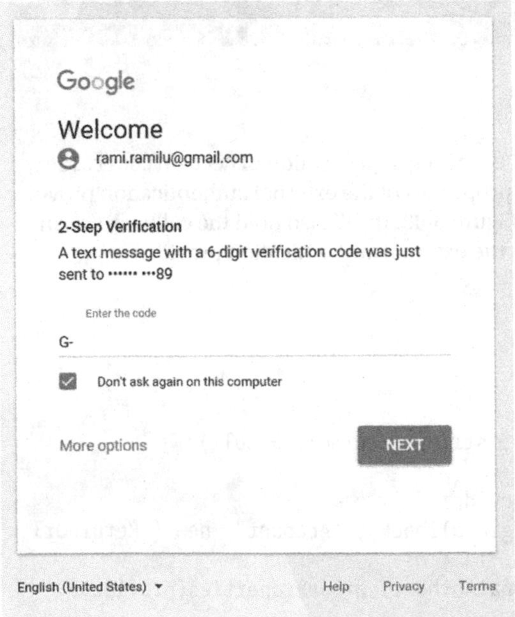

Figure 6-44. *Google two-factor authentication screen*

On successful login at the external authentication provider, the browser will be redirected to the callback URL mentioned in the previous action. The code for the callback action is shown in Listing 6-66. The code first gets the login information of the user from the external login; if it is null, the user is redirected back to the login action. If the login information is a valid object, we need to check whether the received information already exists in our table storage. If the information exists, then based on the status of the login (for example, it requires two-factor authentication), we redirect the user to the secure URL; otherwise, we redirect the user to the registration confirmation view.

Listing 6-66. External login callback

```
[HttpGet]
[AllowAnonymous]
public async Task<IActionResult> ExternalLoginCallback(string returnUrl = null, string
remoteError = null)
{
    if (remoteError != null)
    {
        ModelState.AddModelError(string.Empty, $"Error from external provider:
        {remoteError}");
        return View(nameof(Login));
    }
    var info = await _signInManager.GetExternalLoginInfoAsync();
    if (info == null)
    {
        return RedirectToAction(nameof(Login));
    }

    // Sign in the user with this external login provider if the user already has a login.
    var result = await _signInManager.ExternalLoginSignInAsync(info.LoginProvider, info.
    ProviderKey, isPersistent: false);
    if (result.Succeeded)
    {
        _logger.LogInformation(5, "User logged in with {Name} provider.", info.
        LoginProvider);
        return RedirectToAction("Dashboard", "Dashboard");
    }
    if (result.RequiresTwoFactor)
    {
        return RedirectToAction(nameof(SendCode), new { ReturnUrl = returnUrl });
    }
    if (result.IsLockedOut)
    {
        return View("Lockout");
    }
    else
    {
        // If the user does not have an account, then ask the user to create an account.
        ViewData["ReturnUrl"] = returnUrl;
        ViewData["LoginProvider"] = info.LoginProvider;
        var email = info.Principal.FindFirstValue(ClaimTypes.Email);
```

```
    return View("ExternalLoginConfirmation", new ExternalLoginConfirmationViewModel
    { Email = email });
}
}
```

The External Login Confirmation view is a very simple view with just one input field, which will be prepopulated with the e-mail information of the authenticated user from the external provider, as shown in Listing 6-67. The External Login Confirmation view is shown in Figure 6-45.

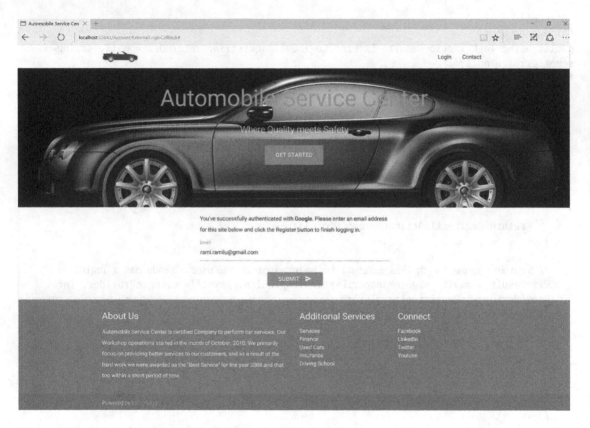

Figure 6-45. *External Authentication Confirmation view*

■ **Note**   Most external authenticated providers forward basic user information in the form of claims to the requested application. The application can therefore uniquely identify a user based on the claims and create a local user account with the information received from the external provider.

Listing 6-67. External login confirmation view

```
@model ExternalLoginConfirmationViewModel
@{
    ViewData["Title"] = "Register";
}

<div class="container">
    <div class="row">
        <div class="col s12 m6 offset-m3">
            <form asp-controller="Account" asp-action="ExternalLoginConfirmation" asp-route-
            returnurl="@ViewData["ReturnUrl"]" method="post" class="form-horizontal">
                <div asp-validation-summary="All" class="text-danger"></div>
                <p class="text-info">
                    You've successfully authenticated with <strong>@ViewData["LoginProvider
                    "]</strong>.
                    Please enter an email address for this site below and click the Register
                    button to finish
                    logging in.
                </p>

                <div class="row">
                    <div class="input-field col s12">
                        <input asp-for="Email" type="email" class="validate">
                        <label asp-for="Email" data-error="wrong" data-
                        success="right">Email</label>
                    </div>
                </div>

                <div class="row center">
                    <button class="btn waves-effect waves-light" type="submit">
                    Submit
                    <i class="material-icons right">send</i>
                    </button>
                </div>
            </form>
        </div>
    </div>
</div>
```

Upon clicking Submit, e-mail will be posted to the `ExternalLoginConfirmation` post action, as shown in Listing 6-68, where it will first validate the model and then verify the login information from the external provider. If the login information is null, we redirect to a failure view. On successful login information, the user will be created at Azure Table storage, and just as with service engineers, Email and `IsActive` claims are added to the user account. Then the user will be added to the User role and saved to storage. As the user is from an external authentication provider, his login information is attached to the user information and signs in to the system through `SignInManager`'s `SignInAync` method. Finally, the user is redirected to the dashboard controller's `Dashboard` action.

Listing 6-68. POST action of External login confirmation

```
[HttpPost]
[AllowAnonymous]
[ValidateAntiForgeryToken]
public async Task<IActionResult> ExternalLoginConfirmation(ExternalLoginConfirmationViewMod
el model, string returnUrl = null)
{
    if (ModelState.IsValid)
    {
        // Get the information about the user from the external login provider
        var info = await _signInManager.GetExternalLoginInfoAsync();
        if (info == null)
        {
            return View("ExternalLoginFailure");
        }
        var user = new ApplicationUser { UserName = model.Email, Email = model.Email,
        EmailConfirmed = true };
        var result = await _userManager.CreateAsync(user);

        await _userManager.AddClaimAsync(user, new System.Security.Claims.Claim
        ("http://schemas.xmlsoap.org/ws/2005/05/identity/claims/emailaddress", user.Email));
        await _userManager.AddClaimAsync(user, new System.Security.Claims.Claim
        ("IsActive", "True"));

        if (!result.Succeeded)
        {
            result.Errors.ToList().ForEach(p => ModelState.AddModelError("",
            p.Description));
            return View("ExternalLoginConfirmation", model);
        }

        // Assign user to Engineer Role
        var roleResult = await _userManager.AddToRoleAsync(user, Roles.User.ToString());
        if (!roleResult.Succeeded)
        {
            roleResult.Errors.ToList().ForEach(p => ModelState.AddModelError("", p.Description));
            return View("ExternalLoginConfirmation", model);
        }

        if (result.Succeeded)
        {
            result = await _userManager.AddLoginAsync(user, info);
            if (result.Succeeded)
            {
                await _signInManager.SignInAsync(user, isPersistent: false);
                _logger.LogInformation(6, "User created an account using {Name} provider.",
                 info.LoginProvider);
                return RedirectToAction("Dashboard", "Dashboard");
            }
        }
    }
```

```
        AddErrors(result);
    }

    ViewData["ReturnUrl"] = returnUrl;
    return View(model);
}
```

The Dashboard view for the user looks like Figure 6-46.

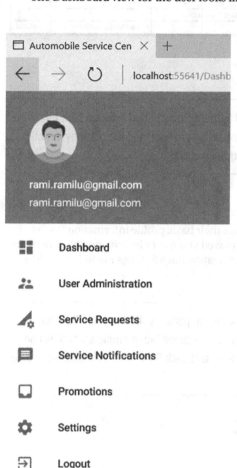

Figure 6-46. *Customer Dashboard view*

Figure 6-47 shows records that are created at Azure Table storage for a user who is authenticated from external providers. The one extra record is for the login information retrieved from external authentication. All other records resemble those for Service Engineers and Admin.

U_RAMI.RAMIL...	C_HTTP_3A_2F_...	5/10/2017 6:41:...	1.66	http://schemas....	rami.ramilu@g...	e0166760-5aae...				
U_RAMI.RAMIL...	C_ISACTIVE_TRUE	5/10/2017 6:41:...	1.66	IsActive	True	1ea2ac73-4e6e...				
U_RAMI.RAMIL...	L_GOOGLE_103...	5/10/2017 6:41:...	1.66			6692485f-6b66...				
U_RAMI.RAMIL...	R_USER	5/10/2017 6:41:...	1.66			55bd8188-2e5d...	USER			
U_RAMI.RAMIL...	U_RAMI.RAMIL...	5/10/2017 6:41:...	1.66					rami.ramilu@g...	RAMI.RAMILU...	RAMI.RAMILU

Figure 6-47. *ASCAspNetUser table records for customer login*

■ **Note**   The advantage with the preceding approach of external authentication is that now the user has two options to log in to the system: one by using the Google authentication provider, and the other by directly signing in at the Automobile Service Center application by resetting the password.

Exercise 1

Create a page for an authenticated user that will help users change their basic profile information (for example, username). Ensure that the updated information is displayed at the user information section of the page. Navigation to this screen should be enabled from the left navigation bar's Settings menu item (add a new submenu item called Profile).

■ **Note**   A solution to this problem can be found with source code accompanied with this book. Run the code and log in as a customer. Click the Profile navigation item from the Settings tab. A profile section will be displayed with the username in an editable field. Update the username and click Save. The username should be updated in Azure Storage, and the same screen will be refreshed.

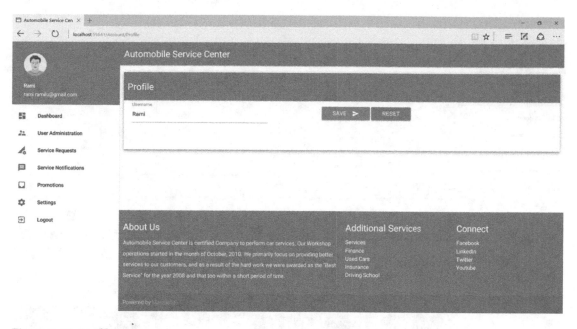

Figure 6-48. Profile view

Exercise 2

Create a page to list all the customers in the system in a tabular format (just as for Service Engineers). Provide an option to deactivate/reactivate a customer in the system. Ensure that deactivated customers cannot sign in to the system (show the invalid login message at the time of login).

■ **Note**   A solution to this problem can be found with source code accompanied with this book. Run the code and log in as Admin. Click the Customers tab under User Administration. All customers will be listed, and now Admin can deactivate a customer. In the provided solution, the Deactivate Customer link has been removed from the left navigation because it is a redundant functionality that is solved on the same page of the customers listing.

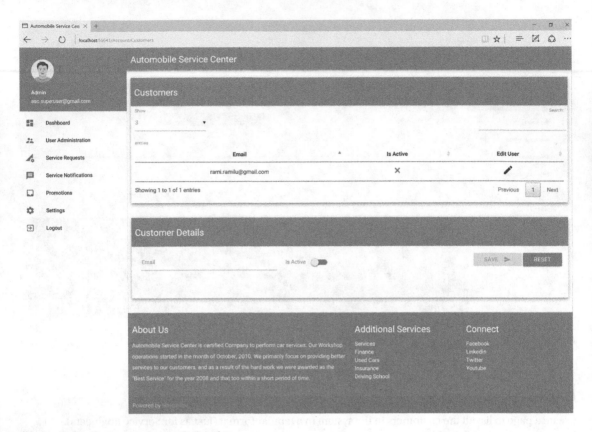

Figure 6-49. *Customer management view*

Exercise 3

Just as we enabled integrating the Google authentication provider with the Automobile Service Center application (users were able to log in to the system by using their Google credentials), we should enable Twitter and Facebook providers.

■ **Note** For more information on how to accomplish this exercise, visit `https://docs.microsoft.com/en-us/aspnet/core/security/authentication/social/`.

Summary

You started this chapter by learning about data security and the key advantages of ASP.NET Identity, through which we can achieve robust security for an ASP.NET web application. You explored the artifacts and APIs provided by default by an ASP.NET Core application. You set up an Admin account for the Automobile Service Center application by using `ElCamino.AspNetCore.Identity.AzureTable.Model`, an open source NuGet package that supports Azure Table storage as a back end for ASP.NET Core Identity. You also configured the default Admin account from the `appsettings` configuration.

You customized the Login and Logout screens that are provided by default by the ASP.NET Core Visual Studio template. A custom extension class has been written to retrieve logged-in user information from claims and display it on the secure layout. You also completed the Reset Password functionality and integrated it with the MailKit e-mail Library to send an e-mail to users with a password reset link and thereby allow them to reset their password securely.

You introduced the Engineer role to the system and developed a page to support managing service engineers. Using this page, an Admin can add, modify, and deactivate a Service Engineer account. All these functionalities are achieved through custom claims attached to the user identity and stored in Azure Table storage. Whenever the Admin performs an action on a Service Engineer, he will be via e-mail. Login page code has been changed accordingly to support service engineer deactivation, so that a deactivated user cannot log in to the system.

We got familiar with OAuth 2.0 Protocol and understood the concepts and flow of authorization between different parties. We configured Automobile Service Center to support authentication from Google OAuth provider. This functionality is primarily used by customers to login in to the system and on successful authentication a local account is created and associated with user role. A customer can reset the password for his newly created local account and use either Google's or local account credentials to access Automobile Service Center application.

References

1. https://docs.microsoft.com/en-us/aspnet/core/security/
    authentication/social/

2. https://docs.microsoft.com/en-us/aspnet/core/security/
    authentication/social/google-logins

■■■

CHAPTER 7

Master Data Management Using Azure Table Storage

Any real-world application deals with data in three formats: transactional data, batch-processing data, and master data. Transactional data is data that is accumulated through day-to-day user transactions, and batch-processing data is from different integrations. *Master data* is the fine-tuned information that will be consumed by any application in a given technical solution ecosystem. Typically, it is referential data that serves the following purposes:

- Master data allows only predefined sets of values in business-critical functions.

- It will act as a common referential point for integrating various systems.

- It helps data storage to always be in a consistent state by maintaining data integrity.

Designing master data for any application should focus on two important criteria. The first criteria is that master data management should enable data to be easily included or excluded. Preferably, a user interface should be designed that system administrators can use to manage data.

The second important criteria focuses on the scalability and performance of master data operations. Because this data is widely used by numerous applications in the ecosystem, frequent queries will occur to retrieve master data from storage; these queries will result in redundant fetch operations as the same data is retrieved again and again. A good caching mechanism should be implemented to hold the master data, and this cache should be invalidated if master data is modified. For the Automobile Service Center application, we will use Azure Redis Cache to hold master data at the application tier.

The Automobile Service Center is dependent on certain data types such as Vehicle Types, Statuses, Vehicle Manufacturers, and Vehicle Models. This information is required from day 1 of the application going live. In this chapter, you will learn key concepts for managing master data in the Automobile Service Center application.

Managing Master Data in Azure Tables

Master data in the Automobile Service Center application will be stored in two tables: `MasterDataKey` and `MasterDataValue`. The MasterDataKey table stores all the keys; for example, `State`, `County`, `Vehicle`, and `Manufacturer`. `MasterDataValue` stores all the values for the respective keys; for example, `California` and `Oregon` for `State`; and `Sacramento` and `Orange` for `County`. Both tables are stored in Azure Table storage and are accessed by using the Unit of Work pattern (which we used in Chapter 4).

First, we need to add the `IUnitOfWork` dependency to the `ASC.Web` project. Add the `ASC.DataAccess` project reference to the `ASC.Web` project, as shown in Figure 7-1.

© Rami Vemula 2017

R. Vemula, *Real-Time Web Application Development*, https://doi.org/10.1007/978-1-4842-3270-5_7

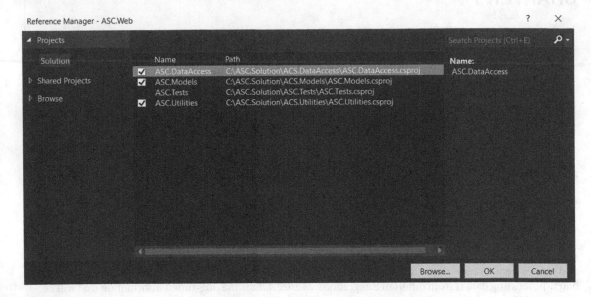

Figure 7-1. Adding the ASC.DataAccess project reference to the ASC.Web project

Add IUnitOfWork to IServiceCollection in the ConfigureServices method of the Startup class, as shown in Listing 7-1. We pass the default connection string from the appsettings configuration.

Listing 7-1. Resolving IUnitOfWork dependency

```
services.AddScoped<IUnitOfWork>(p => new UnitOfWork(Configuration.GetSection("ConnectionStri
ngs:DefaultConnection").Value));
```

■ **Note** We resolve the IUnitOfWork dependency as scoped because we want to have a single instance of IUnitOfWork in the entire request cycle. We cannot have a singleton instance of IUnitOfWork because it will be shared across all users, and having a singleton instance would create mishaps in commit and rollback transactions.

We have to update DefaultConnection in the ConnectionStrings section of the appsettings configuration file to UseDevelopmentStorage=true;, which points to the local Azure Table storage. Later in the chapters, we will point it to the actual Azure Table storage connection string.

Create two entities in the Models folder of the ASC.Models project, as shown in Listings 7-2 and 7-3. MasterDataKey is the entity that will hold all the keys of the master data such as State and County. The RowKey of the entity is going to be uniquely identified by using Guid, and PartitionKey is going to be name of the key. MasterDataValue is the entity that will hold the values of master keys. In both entities, we have the IsActive property, which can be used to turn on/off the entity status in business operations. Finally, we have the Name property, which is going to hold the name of the entity.

Listing 7-2. MasterDataKey Entity

```
using ASC.Models.BaseTypes;
using System;

namespace ASC.Models.Models
{
    public class MasterDataKey : BaseEntity, IAuditTracker
    {
        public MasterDataKey() { }

        public MasterDataKey(string key)
        {
            this.RowKey = Guid.NewGuid().ToString();
            this.PartitionKey = key;
        }
        public bool IsActive { get; set; }
        public string Name { get; set; }
    }
}
```

Listing 7-3. MasterDataValue Entity

```
using ASC.Models.BaseTypes;
using System;

namespace ASC.Models.Models
{
    public class MasterDataValue : BaseEntity, IAuditTracker
    {
        public MasterDataValue() { }
        public MasterDataValue(string masterDataPartitionKey, string value)
        {
            this.PartitionKey = masterDataPartitionKey;
            this.RowKey = Guid.NewGuid().ToString();
        }
        public bool IsActive { get; set; }
        public string Name { get; set; }
    }
}
```

As you saw in Chapter 4, we need to call IRepository's CreateTableAsync method to create a table at Azure Table storage. It is too tedious to call the CreateTableAsync method for all entities that we are going to create from now on. We will automate the process by updating the Configure method of the Startup class in the ASC.Web project. First, we need to inject the IUnitOfWork dependency into the Configure method. We will iterate all the types from the ASC.Models.Models namespace of the ASC.Models assembly. With each model, we will create an instance of the repository through reflection and call the CreateTableAsync method, as shown in Listing 7-4, which will create the table in Azure Table storage. This way, when we add new entities in the ASC.Models.Models namespace, they will be automatically created at Azure Storage.

Listing 7-4. Create Azure tables based on types present in ASC.Models

```
public async void Configure(IApplicationBuilder app,
    IHostingEnvironment env,
    ILoggerFactory loggerFactory,
    IIdentitySeed storageSeed,
    IMasterDataCacheOperations masterDataCacheOperations,
    IUnitOfWork unitOfWork)
{
    loggerFactory.AddConsole(Configuration.GetSection("Logging"));
    loggerFactory.AddDebug();

    if (env.IsDevelopment())
    {
        app.UseDeveloperExceptionPage();
        app.UseDatabaseErrorPage();
        app.UseBrowserLink();
    }
    else
    {
        app.UseExceptionHandler("/Home/Error");
    }

    app.UseSession();
    app.UseStaticFiles();
    app.UseIdentity();

    app.UseGoogleAuthentication(new GoogleOptions()
    {
        ClientId = Configuration["Google:Identity:ClientId"],
        ClientSecret = Configuration["Google:Identity:ClientSecret"]
    });

    app.UseMvc(routes =>
    {
        routes.MapRoute(
            name: "default",
            template: "{controller=Home}/{action=Index}/{id?}");
    });

    await storageSeed.Seed(app.ApplicationServices.GetService<UserManager<ApplicationUser>>(),
        app.ApplicationServices.GetService<RoleManager<IdentityRole>>(),
        app.ApplicationServices.GetService<IOptions<ApplicationSettings>>());

    var models = Assembly.Load(new AssemblyName("ASC.Models")).GetTypes().Where(type =>
    type.Namespace == "ASC.Models.Models");
    foreach (var model in models)
    {
        var repositoryInstance = Activator.CreateInstance(typeof(Repository<>).
        MakeGenericType(model), unitOfWork);
```

```
        MethodInfo method = typeof(Repository<>).MakeGenericType(model).GetMethod("CreateTa
        bleAsync");
        method.Invoke(repositoryInstance, new object[0]);
    }

    await masterDataCacheOperations.CreateMasterDataCacheAsync();
}
```

We will segregate all business logic in a different .NET Core class library. Create a new .NET Core class library project named ASC.Business, as shown in Figure 7-2.

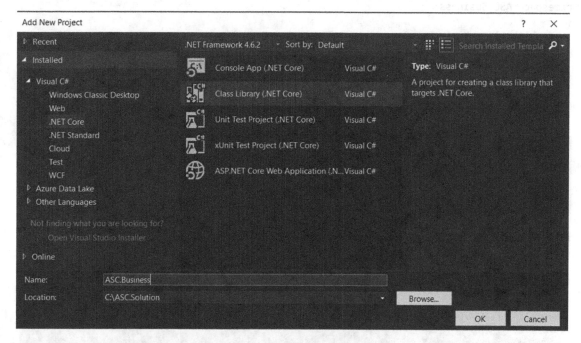

Figure 7-2. *Creating a .NET Core class library named ASC.Business*

■ **Note** In a multilayered architecture, a web project will call a business class, which will internally call the Unit of Work operations. This segregation of code helps achieve code reusability at all layers.

Create a folder named Interfaces in the ASC.Business project. This folder will hold all the business interfaces. Create an IMasterDataOperations interface in this folder, and its MasterDataOperations implementation in the root of the ASC.Business project, as shown in Listings 7-5 and 7-6.

Listing 7-5. IMasterDataOperations interface

```
using System;
using System.Collections.Generic;
using System.Text;
```

```
namespace ASC.Business.Interfaces
{
    public interface IMasterDataOperations
    {
    }
}
```

Listing 7-6. MasterDataOperations class

```
using ASC.Business.Interfaces;

namespace ASC.Business
{
    public class MasterDataOperations : IMasterDataOperations
    {
    }
}
```

The structure of the project is shown in Figure 7-3.

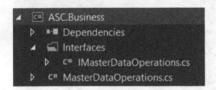

Figure 7-3. *Logical structure of the ASC.Business project*

Because the business project needs to interact with Azure Storage, we need to add references of both the ASC.DataAccess and ASC.Models projects to the ASC.Business project, as shown in Figure 7-4.

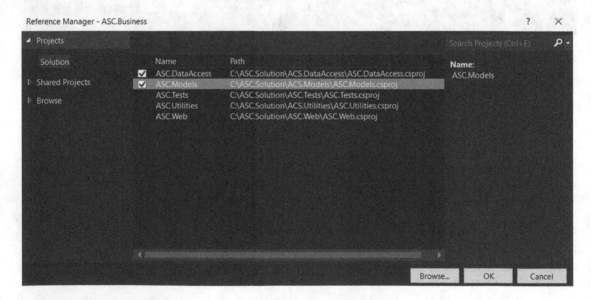

Figure 7-4. *Adding the ASC.DataAccess and ASC.Models project references to the ASC.Business project*

194

We will add the actual implementations to MasterDataOperations in order to support retrieving, adding, and modifying operations to both MasterDataKey and MasterDataValue. IMasterDataOperations is shown in Listing 7-7.

Listing 7-7. Updated IMasterDataOperations interface

```
using ASC.Models.Models;
using System.Collections.Generic;
using System.Threading.Tasks;

namespace ASC.Business.Interfaces
{
    public interface IMasterDataOperations
    {
        Task<List<MasterDataKey>> GetAllMasterKeysAsync();
        Task<List<MasterDataKey>> GetMaserKeyByNameAsync(string name);
        Task<bool> InsertMasterKeyAsync(MasterDataKey key);
        Task<bool> UpdateMasterKeyAsync(string orginalPartitionKey, MasterDataKey key);

        Task<List<MasterDataValue>> GetAllMasterValuesByKeyAsync(string key);
        Task<List<MasterDataValue>> GetAllMasterValuesAsync();
        Task<MasterDataValue> GetMasterValueByNameAsync(string key, string name);
        Task<bool> InsertMasterValueAsync(MasterDataValue value);
        Task<bool> UpdateMasterValueAsync(string originalPartitionKey, string originalRowKey,
        MasterDataValue value);
    }
}
```

MasterDataOperations is shown in Listing 7-8. MasterDataOperations has all methods that can be used to read, create, and update both MasterDataKey and MasterDataValue entities. This class uses an IUnitOfWork instance that is injected through constructor dependency. We use the IUnitOfWork instance to fetch repositories and perform all operations on them. Finally, we will commit all transactions by using IUnitOfWork's CommitTransaction method.

■ **Note**   Refer to Chapter 4 for implementation and usage details of the Unit of Work. The IUnitOfWork dependency is resolved at the ASC.Web project, which will be injected through the constructor to MasterDataOperations.

Listing 7-8. Updated MasterDataOperations class

```
using System.Collections.Generic;
using ASC.Business.Interfaces;
using ASC.Models.Models;
using ASC.DataAccess.Interfaces;
using System.Threading.Tasks;
using System.Linq;
```

```
namespace ASC.Business
{
    public class MasterDataOperations : IMasterDataOperations
    {
        private readonly IUnitOfWork _unitOfWork;
        public MasterDataOperations(IUnitOfWork unitOfWork)
        {
            _unitOfWork = unitOfWork;
        }

        public async Task<List<MasterDataKey>> GetAllMasterKeysAsync()
        {
            var masterKeys = await _unitOfWork.Repository<MasterDataKey>().FindAllAsync();
            return masterKeys.ToList();
        }

        public async Task<List<MasterDataKey>> GetMaserKeyByNameAsync(string name)
        {
            var masterKeys = await _unitOfWork.Repository<MasterDataKey>().FindAllBy
            PartitionKeyAsync(name);
            return masterKeys.ToList();
        }

        public async Task<bool> InsertMasterKeyAsync(MasterDataKey key)
        {
            using (_unitOfWork)
            {
                await _unitOfWork.Repository<MasterDataKey>().AddAsync(key);
                _unitOfWork.CommitTransaction();
                return true;
            }
        }

        public async Task<List<MasterDataValue>> GetAllMasterValuesByKeyAsync(string key)
        {
            var masterKeys = await _unitOfWork.Repository<MasterDataValue>().FindAllBy
            PartitionKeyAsync(key);
            return masterKeys.ToList();
        }

        public async Task<MasterDataValue> GetMasterValueByNameAsync(string key, string name)
        {
            var masterValues = await _unitOfWork.Repository<MasterDataValue>().
            FindAsync(key, name);
            return masterValues;
        }

        public async Task<bool> InsertMasterValueAsync(MasterDataValue value)
        {
            using (_unitOfWork)
            {
                await _unitOfWork.Repository<MasterDataValue>().AddAsync(value);
```

```
            _unitOfWork.CommitTransaction();
            return true;
        }
    }

    public async Task<bool> UpdateMasterKeyAsync(string orginalPartitionKey,
    MasterDataKey key)
    {
        using (_unitOfWork)
        {
            var masterKey = await _unitOfWork.Repository<MasterDataKey>().
            FindAsync(orginalPartitionKey, key.RowKey);
            masterKey.IsActive = key.IsActive;
            masterKey.IsDeleted = key.IsDeleted;
            masterKey.Name = key.Name;

            await _unitOfWork.Repository<MasterDataKey>().UpdateAsync(masterKey);
            _unitOfWork.CommitTransaction();
            return true;
        }
    }

    public async Task<bool> UpdateMasterValueAsync(string originalPartitionKey, string
    originalRowKey, MasterDataValue value)
    {
        using (_unitOfWork)
        {
            var masterValue = await _unitOfWork.Repository<MasterDataValue>().
            FindAsync(originalPartitionKey, originalRowKey);
            masterValue.IsActive = value.IsActive;
            masterValue.IsDeleted = value.IsDeleted;
            masterValue.Name = value.Name;

            await _unitOfWork.Repository<MasterDataValue>().UpdateAsync(masterValue);
            _unitOfWork.CommitTransaction();
            return true;
        }
    }

    public async Task<List<MasterDataValue>> GetAllMasterValuesAsync()
    {
        var masterValues = await _unitOfWork.Repository<MasterDataValue>().
        FindAllAsync();
        return masterValues.ToList();
    }
}
}
```

To consume business project methods in the web project, we need to add the reference of ASC.Business to the ASC.Web project, as shown in Figure 7-5.

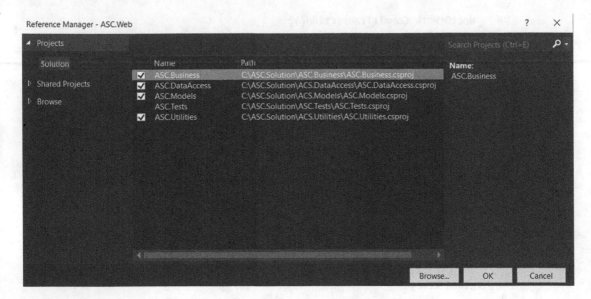

Figure 7-5. *Adding the ASC.Business project reference to the ASC.Web project*

We will resolve the IMasterDataOperations dependency by adding it to the services in the ConfigureServices method of the Startup class, as shown in Listing 7-9.

Listing 7-9. Resolving the IMasterDataOperations dependency

```
services.AddScoped<IMasterDataOperations, MasterDataOperations>();
```

Now we will create two pages in the ASC.Web project, through which Admin can manage the MasterDataKey and MasterDataValue entities. First, we will create a new controller named MasterDataController, as shown in Listing 7-10, and inject IMasterDataOperations through the controller's constructor.

Listing 7-10. MasterDataController

```
using Microsoft.AspNetCore.Mvc;
using Microsoft.AspNetCore.Authorization;
using ASC.Business.Interfaces;

namespace ASC.Web.Controllers
{
    [Authorize(Roles = "Admin")]
    public class MasterDataController : BaseController
    {
        private readonly IMasterDataOperations _masterData;
        public MasterDataController(IMasterDataOperations masterData)
        {
            _masterData = masterData;
        }
    }
}
```

We will create new view models named `MasterKeysViewModel` and `MasterDataKeyViewModel`, which will be used by both the controller and view to display a list of master keys and to add/update a new/existing master key. Create a folder named `MasterDataViewModels` under the `Models` folder of the `ASC.Web` project, and place the view models as shown in Listing 7-11.

Listing 7-11. MasterKeysViewModel class

```
using ASC.Models.Models;
using System.Collections.Generic;
using System.ComponentModel.DataAnnotations;

namespace ASC.Web.Models.MasterDataViewModels
{
    public class MasterKeysViewModel
    {
        public List<MasterDataKeyViewModel> MasterKeys { get; set; }
        public MasterDataKeyViewModel MasterKeyInContext { get; set; }
        public bool IsEdit { get; set; }
    }
}
```

`MasterDataKeyViewModel` is shown in Listing 7-12.

Listing 7-12. MasterDataKeyViewModel class

```
using System.ComponentModel.DataAnnotations;

namespace ASC.Web.Models.MasterDataViewModels
{
    public class MasterDataKeyViewModel
    {
        public string RowKey { get; set; }
        public string PartitionKey { get; set; }
        public bool IsActive { get; set; }

        [Required]
        public string Name { get; set; }
    }
}
```

■ **Note** We use `AutoMapper` to map business models to our web view models. `AutoMapper` is an object-to-object mapper that uses a fluent configuration API to define an object-to-object mapping strategy.

Install the `AutoMapper` and `AutoMapper.Extensions.Microsoft.DependencyInjection` NuGet packages to the `ASC.Web` project, as shown in Figures 7-6 and 7-7.

Figure 7-6. *Installing the AutoMapper NuGet package to the ASC.Web project*

Figure 7-7. *Installing the AutoMapper.Extensions.Microsoft.DependencyInjection NuGet package to the ASC.Web project*

Add AutoMapper to the ASP.NET Core services in the ConfigureServices method of the Startup class, as shown in Listing 7-13.

Listing 7-13. Add AutoMapper service

```
services.AddAutoMapper();
```

We inject AutoMapper through the constructor of MasterDataController, and in the GET action we map the list of MasterDataKey to the list of MasterDataKeyViewModel. In the POST action, we will map MasterDataKeyViewModel to MasterDataKey and save it to Azure Table storage.

Create a class in the Models folder of the ASC.Web project named MappingProfile, which will have AutoMapper mappings for MasterDataKey and MasterDataKeyViewModel, as shown in Listing 7-14.

Listing 7-14. Automapper's MappingProfile class

```
using ASC.Models.Models;
using ASC.Web.Models.MasterDataViewModels;
using AutoMapper;

namespace ASC.Web.Models
{
    public class MappingProfile : Profile
    {
        public MappingProfile()
        {
            CreateMap<MasterDataKey, MasterDataKeyViewModel>();
            CreateMap<MasterDataKeyViewModel, MasterDataKey>();
        }
    }
}
```

The GET and POST actions to manage master keys are shown in Listing 7-15. The GET action gets all the master keys and transforms MasterDataKey to MasterDataKeyViewModel and passes the model to MasterKeys.cshtml. The POST action first validates the model and then based on IsEdit flag it will either update or insert a master key.

Listing 7-15. GET and POST actions of Master Keys

```
using Microsoft.AspNetCore.Mvc;
using Microsoft.AspNetCore.Authorization;
using ASC.Business.Interfaces;
using System.Threading.Tasks;
using ASC.Utilities;
using ASC.Models.Models;
using System.Collections.Generic;
using System.Linq;
using ASC.Web.Models.MasterDataViewModels;
using System;
using AutoMapper;

namespace ASC.Web.Controllers
{
    [Authorize(Roles = "Admin")]
    public class MasterDataController : BaseController
    {
        private readonly IMasterDataOperations _masterData;
        private readonly IMapper _mapper;
        public MasterDataController(IMasterDataOperations masterData, IMapper mapper)
        {
            _masterData = masterData;
            _mapper = mapper;
        }

        [HttpGet]
        public async Task<IActionResult> MasterKeys()
        {
            var masterKeys = await _masterData.GetAllMasterKeysAsync();
            var masterKeysViewModel = _mapper.Map<List<MasterDataKey>, List<MasterDataKey
            ViewModel>>(masterKeys);

            // Hold all Master Keys in session
            HttpContext.Session.SetSession("MasterKeys", masterKeysViewModel);

            return View(new MasterKeysViewModel
            {
                MasterKeys = masterKeysViewModel == null ? null : masterKeysViewModel.ToList(),
                IsEdit = false
            });
        }
```

```
[HttpPost]
[ValidateAntiForgeryToken]
public async Task<IActionResult> MasterKeys(MasterKeysViewModel masterKeys)
{
    masterKeys.MasterKeys = HttpContext.Session.GetSession<List<MasterDataKeyView
    Model>>("MasterKeys");
    if (!ModelState.IsValid)
    {
        return View(masterKeys);
    }

    var masterKey = _mapper.Map<MasterDataKeyViewModel, MasterDataKey>(masterKeys.
    MasterKeyInContext);
    if (masterKeys.IsEdit)
    {
        // Update Master Key
        await _masterData.UpdateMasterKeyAsync(masterKeys.MasterKeyInContext.
        PartitionKey, masterKey);
    }
    else
    {
        // Insert Master Key
        masterKey.RowKey = Guid.NewGuid().ToString();
        masterKey.PartitionKey = masterKey.Name;
        await _masterData.InsertMasterKeyAsync(masterKey);
    }

    return RedirectToAction("MasterKeys");
    }
  }
}
```

In MasterKeys.cshtml, Admin can create a new master key or edit an existing one. Create a folder named MasterData in the Views folder, and place MasterKeys.cshtml as shown in Listing 7-16.

An HTML table has been defined, and all the master keys are iterated and rendered in the same table. By default, we will show RowKey, Name, IsActive, and Edit action columns in the table. If no master keys are available, no record message will be displayed in the table. The details section of the view contains a form tag with the required elements for RowKey, PartitionKey, Name, and Active flags. By default, we will not give Admin an option to change the RowKey of the master key. We also maintain hidden fields in the form to identify information such as type of operation (Create or Update) and PartitionKey.

The view also contains JQuery code that is primarily used to configure DataTable by initializing it with page size and length options. We also set the required styles of DataTable. In JQuery code, we also hide the IsActive column by default because we will not show a Boolean flag for the IsActive column; instead, we will show a green tick or red X. The PartitionKey column is also hidden by default.

We will also handle the reset button functionality in JQuery, through which users can discard their changes. Finally, an Edit click event is handled, in which we will populate the details section with the information of the master key that is in edit mode. JQuery code is also used to populate the RowKey and PartitionKey hidden fields, which are used by the POST action to identity the entity that is being edited.

Listing 7-16. Master Keys View with JQuery code

```
@model ASC.Web.Models.MasterDataViewModels.MasterKeysViewModel
@{
    Layout = "_SecureLayout";
}

<div class="row"></div>
<div class="row padding-top-20px">

    <div class="row z-depth-3">
        <div class="section white-text padding-left-10px blue-grey lighten-1">
            <h5>Master Keys</h5>
        </div>
        <div class="divider"></div>
        <div class="col s12 padding-bottom-15px">
            @if (Model.MasterKeys != null)
            {
                @* Display List of Master Keys *@
                <table class="highlight centered" id="tblMasterKeys">
                    <thead>
                        <tr>
                            <th data-field="RowKey">Row Key</th>
                            <th data-field="PartitionKey">Partition Key</th>
                            <th data-field="Name">Name</th>
                            <th data-field="IsActive">Is Active</th>
                            <th data-field="IsActiveImg">Is Active</th>
                            <th data-field="Actions">Edit</th>
                        </tr>
                    </thead>
                    <tbody>
                        @foreach (var masterKey in Model.MasterKeys)
                        {
                            <tr>
                                <td>@masterKey.RowKey</td>
                                <td>@masterKey.PartitionKey</td>
                                <td>@masterKey.Name</td>
                                <td>@masterKey.IsActive</td>
                                <td><img src="@(masterKey.IsActive ? "/images/green_tick.
                                png" : "/images/red_cross.png")" /></td>
                                <td><i class="small material-icons edit cursor-hand">mode_
                                edit</i></td>
                            </tr>
                        }
                    </tbody>
                </table>
            }
            else
```

```
        {
            @* In case of No records, display no records message *@
            <div class="card blue-grey lighten-1">
                <div class="card-content white-text">
                    <span class="card-title">No Service Engineers!!!</span>
                    <p>
                        No Master Keys found, please add a Master Key to system.
                    </p>
                </div>
            </div>
        }
    </div>
</div>

<div class="row"></div>

@* Details Section *@
<div class="row z-depth-3">
    <div class="col s12 padding-0px">
        <div class="section white-text padding-left-10px blue-grey lighten-1">
            <h5>Master Key Details</h5>
        </div>
        <div class="divider"></div>
        <form asp-controller="MasterData" asp-action="MasterKeys" method="post"
        class="col s12" id="formMasterKey">
            <div class="row">
                <input type="hidden" asp-for="IsEdit" />
                <input type="hidden" asp-for="MasterKeyInContext.RowKey" />
                <input type="hidden" asp-for="MasterKeyInContext.PartitionKey" />
                <div class="input-field col s4">
                    <input asp-for="MasterKeyInContext.RowKey" id="Input_MasterKey_
                    RowKey" disabled="disabled" />
                    <label asp-for="MasterKeyInContext.RowKey"></label>
                </div>
                <div class="input-field col s4">
                    <input asp-for="MasterKeyInContext.Name" class="validate" />
                    <label asp-for="MasterKeyInContext.Name"></label>
                </div>
                <div class="input-field col s4">
                    <div class="switch">
                        <label>
                            Is Active
                            <input asp-for="MasterKeyInContext.IsActive"
                            class="validate" />
                            <span class="lever"></span>
                        </label>
                    </div>
                </div>
                </div>
```

```
                <div class="row">
                    <div class="input-field col s12 right-align">
                        <button class="btn waves-effect waves-light btnSubmit"
                        type="submit" name="action">
                            Create
                            <i class="material-icons right">send</i>
                        </button>
                        <button class="btn waves-effect waves-light reset  red
                        lighten-1" type="button" name="action">
                            Reset
                        </button>
                    </div>
                    <div class="row col s12 right-align" asp-validation-summary="All">
                    </div>
                </div>
</form>

        </div>
        <div class="row"></div>

    </div>

</div>

@section Scripts{
    <script>
        $(document).ready(function () {
            // Initialize DataTable to show list of Engineers
            var table = $('#tblMasterKeys').DataTable({
                'pageLength': 3,
                // Number of records to be displayed per page
                'lengthMenu': [[3, 5, 10, -1], [3, 5, 10, 'All']]
            });

            // Set Styles for DataTable and Number of Records to be displayed in dropdown
            $('#tblMasterKeys').css("width", "100%");
            $('select[name="tblMasterKeys_length"]').material_select();

            // Get the column API object
            var partitionKeyColumn = table.column(1);
            partitionKeyColumn.visible(false);

            var isActiveColumn = table.column(3);
            isActiveColumn.visible(false);

            // Handle Reset functionality
            $(document).on("click", ".reset", function () {
                $('#formMasterKey')[0].reset();
                $('.btnSubmit').text('Create');
                $('#IsEdit').val('False');
            });
```

```
            // On click of Edit icon, populate the details section with details of service engineer
            $(document).on('click', '.edit', function () {
                var user = $('#tblMasterKeys').DataTable().row($(this).parents('tr')).data();

                $('#IsEdit').val('True');
                // Map Row Key
                $('#MasterKeyInContext_RowKey').val(user[0]);
                $('#Input_MasterKey_RowKey').val(user[0]);
                // Map Partition Key
                $('#MasterKeyInContext_PartitionKey').val(user[1]);
                // Map Name
                $('#MasterKeyInContext_Name').val(user[2]);
                $('#MasterKeyInContext_Name').addClass('valid');
                // Map IsActive
                $('#MasterKeyInContext_IsActive').prop('checked', user[3] === 'True' ?
                true : false);

                $('.btnSubmit').text('Save');
                Materialize.updateTextFields();
            });

        });
    </script>
}
```

Modify SecureLayout to support navigation to the MasterKeys view, as shown in Listing 7-17.

Listing 7-17. Master Keys menu item in left navigation

```
<li>
    <ul class="collapsible collapsible-accordion">
        <li>
            <a class="collapsible-header">Master Data<i class="material-icons">
            perm_data_setting</i></a>
            <div class="collapsible-body">
                <ul>
                    <li><a asp-controller="MasterData" asp-action="MasterKeys"
                    class="collapsible-header">Master Keys<i class="material-icons">data_
                    usage</i></a></li>
                    <li><a class="collapsible-header" href="#!"
                    id="ancrResetPassword">Master Values<i class="material-icons">settings_
                    system_daydream</i></a></li>
                </ul>
            </div>
        </li>
    </ul>
</li>
```

Run the application and login as Admin. You should see the Master Data section in the left navigation menu, as shown in Figure 7-8.

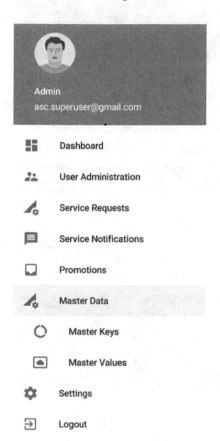

Figure 7-8. *Master Data section in the left navigation menu*

Click the Master Keys menu item. You should see the Master Keys view, as shown in Figure 7-9.

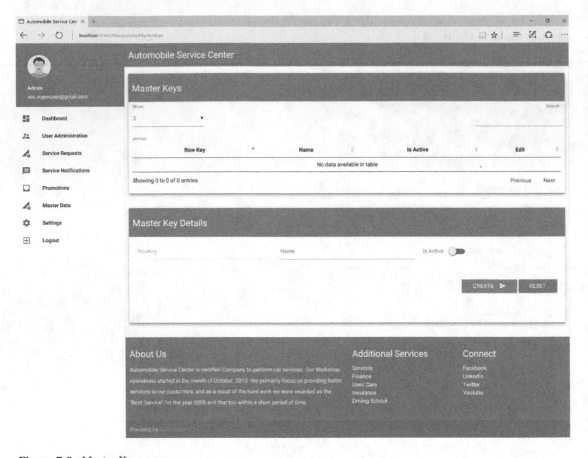

Figure 7-9. *Master Keys page*

Enter a Master Key value (for example, Status), set Is Active to True, and click Create. We should have a master key created in Azure Storage, and the grid will be updated as shown in Figure 7-10.

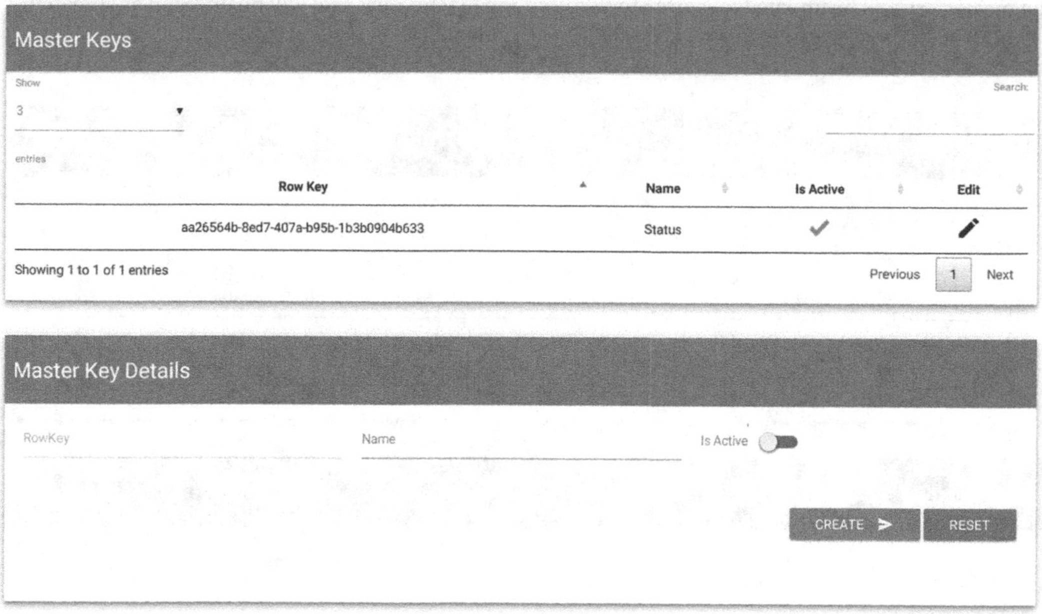

Figure 7-10. *Newly added master key in the Master Keys table*

Click the Edit icon. Change the value of the Master Key name from Status to any other value, and then click Save, as shown in Figure 7-11.

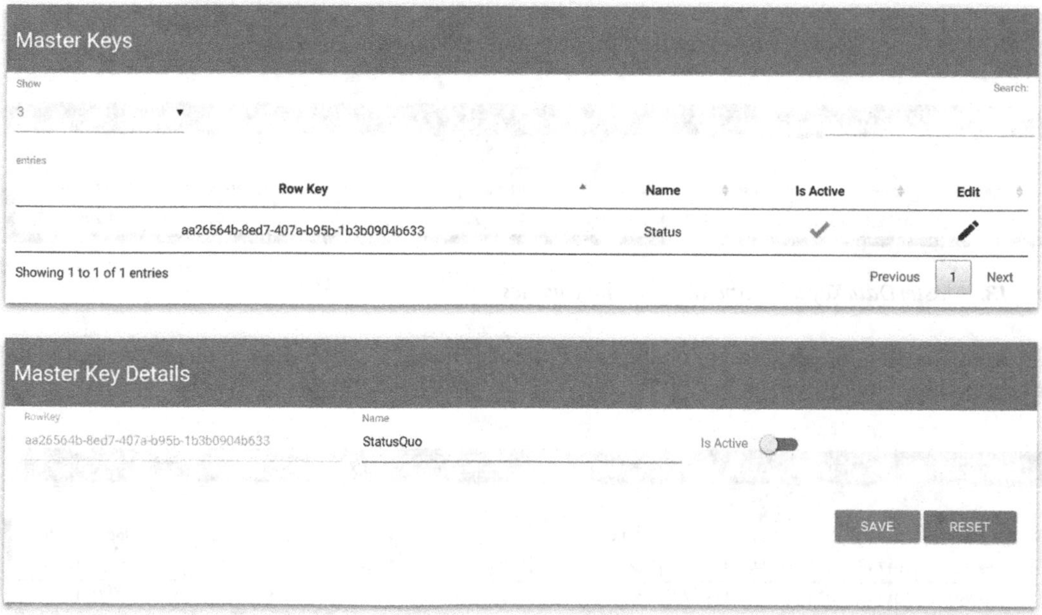

Figure 7-11. *Edit operation on the master key*

The master key will be updated in Azure Storage, and the Master Keys grid will be updated as shown in Figure 7-12.

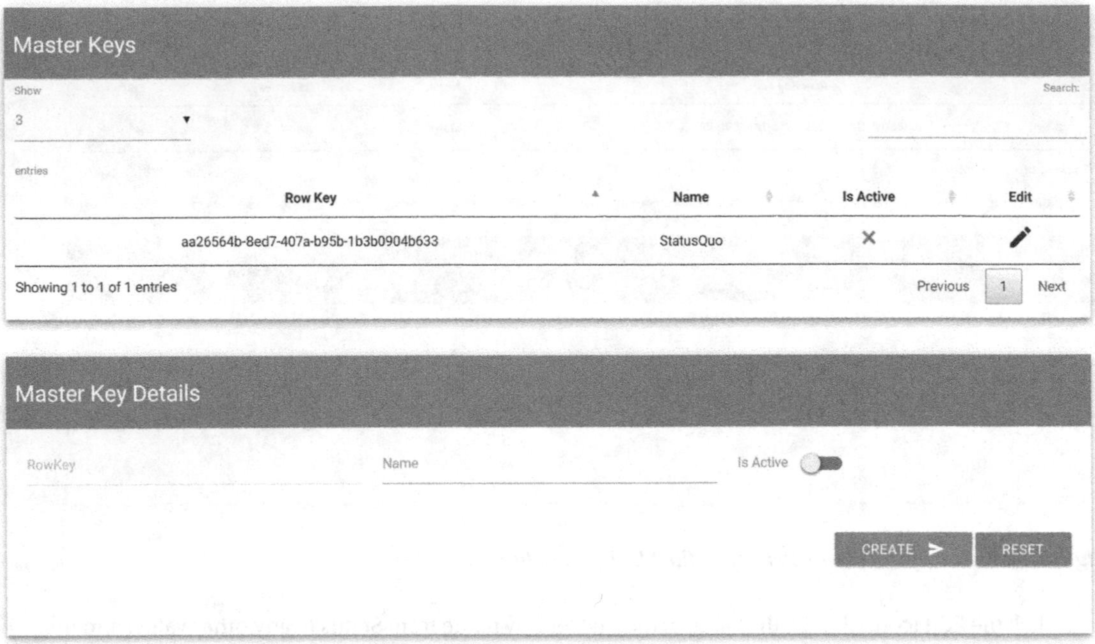

Figure 7-12. *Edit operation on master key*

If we look at Azure Storage, we will see the updated value, as shown in Figure 7-13.

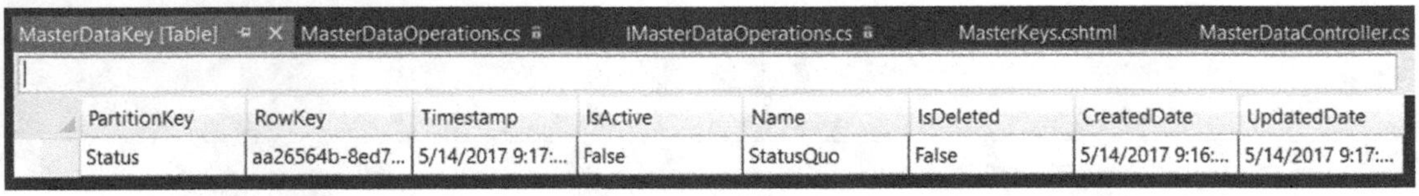

PartitionKey	RowKey	Timestamp	IsActive	Name	IsDeleted	CreatedDate	UpdatedDate
Status	aa26564b-8ed7...	5/14/2017 9:17:...	False	StatusQuo	False	5/14/2017 9:16:...	5/14/2017 9:17:...

Figure 7-13. *MasterDataKey table updated with new values*

Because we enabled `IAuditTracker` on the `MasterDataKey` entity, we should see audit entries for the master key, as shown in Figure 7-14.

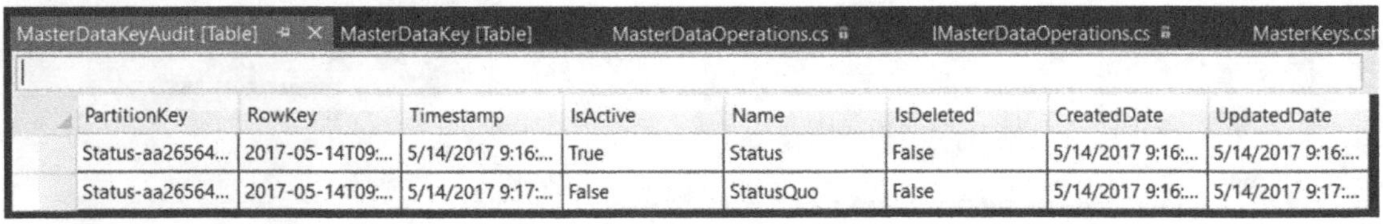

PartitionKey	RowKey	Timestamp	IsActive	Name	IsDeleted	CreatedDate	UpdatedDate
Status-aa26564...	2017-05-14T09:...	5/14/2017 9:16:...	True	Status	False	5/14/2017 9:16:...	5/14/2017 9:16:...
Status-aa26564...	2017-05-14T09:...	5/14/2017 9:17:...	False	StatusQuo	False	5/14/2017 9:16:...	5/14/2017 9:17:...

Figure 7-14. *MasterDataKeyAudit records*

■ **Note**   To learn more about implementing `IAuditTracker`, refer to the "Auditing Data Through Snapshots" section of Chapter 4.

Now we will create a page to manage master values for a given master key. First, we will create new view models named `MasterValuesViewModel` and `MasterDataValueViewModel` in the `MasterDataViewModels` folder of the `ASC.Web` project. These view models will be used by both controller and view to display list of master values based on a master key and add/update a new/existing master value.

`MasterDataValueViewModel` is shown in Listing 7-18.

Listing 7-18. MasterDataValueViewModel class

```
using System.ComponentModel.DataAnnotations;

namespace ASC.Web.Models.MasterDataViewModels
{
    public class MasterDataValueViewModel
    {
        public string RowKey { get; set; }
        [Required]
        [Display(Name = "Partition Key")]
        public string PartitionKey { get; set; }
        public bool IsActive { get; set; }

        [Required]
        public string Name { get; set; }
    }
}
```

Similarly, `MasterValuesViewModel` is shown in Listing 7-19.

Listing 7-19. MasterValuesViewModel class

```
using System.Collections.Generic;

namespace ASC.Web.Models.MasterDataViewModels
{
    public class MasterValuesViewModel
    {
        public List<MasterDataValueViewModel> MasterValues { get; set; }
        public MasterDataValueViewModel MasterValueInContext { get; set; }
        public bool IsEdit { get; set; }
    }
}
```

We need to create the necessary `AutoMapper` mappings for `MasterDataValueViewModel` to the `MasterDataValue` business model to support data transformation from page to business methods. Add mappings in the `MappingProfile` class, as shown in Listing 7-20.

211

Listing 7-20. Updated AutoMapper's MappingProfile class

```
using ASC.Models.Models;
using ASC.Web.Models.MasterDataViewModels;
using AutoMapper;

namespace ASC.Web.Models
{
    public class MappingProfile : Profile
    {
        public MappingProfile()
        {
            CreateMap<MasterDataKey, MasterDataKeyViewModel>();
            CreateMap<MasterDataKeyViewModel, MasterDataKey>();
            CreateMap<MasterDataValue, MasterDataValueViewModel>();
            CreateMap<MasterDataValueViewModel, MasterDataValue>();
        }
    }
}
```

■ **Note**   We will follow a different approach in displaying and modifying data related to master values. We will take AJAX-based JSON data to bind master values to a `DataTable` based on the selected master key.

To support AJAX-based JSON data, we need two actions. The first action is to render the view with all master keys in a `select` tag. Upon selecting a master key in the `select` tag, we will need to make an AJAX call to the server to fetch all the related master values associated with the master key. The second action is used to fetch the master values based on the master key, as shown in Listing 7-21.

Listing 7-21. Action methods of Master Values

```
[HttpGet]
public async Task<IActionResult> MasterValues()
{
    // Get All Master Keys and hold them in ViewBag for Select tag
    ViewBag.MasterKeys = await _masterData.GetAllMasterKeysAsync();

    return View(new MasterValuesViewModel
    {
        MasterValues = new List<MasterDataValueViewModel>(),
        IsEdit = false
    });
}

[HttpGet]
public async Task<IActionResult> MasterValuesByKey(string key)
{
    // Get Master values based on master key.
    return Json(new { data = await _masterData.GetAllMasterValuesByKeyAsync(key) });
}
```

■ **Note** By default, ASP.NET Core MVC serializes JSON data by using camel casing. To prevent that, we need to add the following configuration to MVC in the ConfigureServices method of the Startup class:

Services.AddMc().AddJsonOptions(options => options.SerializerSettings.ContractResolver = newDefaultContactResolver ());

The POST action of master values is a simple action that is similar to the POST action of master keys, as shown in Listing 7-22. The POST action will first validate ModelState, and if it passes, it will either update or insert based on the IsEdit flag passed from the user interface. Finally, it will send a JSON true response back to the user interface.

Listing 7-22. POST action of Master Values

```
[HttpPost]
[ValidateAntiForgeryToken]
public async Task<IActionResult> MasterValues(bool isEdit, MasterDataValueViewModel
masterValue)
{
    if (!ModelState.IsValid)
    {
        return Json("Error");
    }

    var masterDataValue = _mapper.Map<MasterDataValueViewModel,
    MasterDataValue>(masterValue);
    if (isEdit)
    {
        // Update Master Value
        await _masterData.UpdateMasterValueAsync(masterDataValue.PartitionKey,
        masterDataValue.RowKey, masterDataValue);
    }
    else
    {
        // Insert Master Value
        masterDataValue.RowKey = Guid.NewGuid().ToString();
        await _masterData.InsertMasterValueAsync(masterDataValue);
    }

    return Json(true);
}
```

We will now create the view for master values, as shown in Listing 7-23. This view will have two sections. The top section will have a select tag with all master keys populated from the ViewBag data. This section also holds the empty Table tag, which will be populated with master values based on the selected master key.

The bottom section of the view is a typical details section. This details section will be populated based on the edit operation made in the top section of the table. The details section also holds a select tag for PartitionKey, which is again prepopulated with all master keys from the ViewBag data. This is used to associate a particular master value to a master key at the time of creation. The user can perform insert or update operations in this section for a specific master value.

During an edit operation, the user cannot modify the RowKey and PartitionKey associated with a master value. In an insert operation, users cannot enter a RowKey because it is generated automatically with a unique GUID, but they can select a PartitionKey to associate the new master value that is about to be created.

Listing 7-23. Master values view

```
@model ASC.Web.Models.MasterDataViewModels.MasterValuesViewModel
@{
    Layout = "_SecureLayout";
}

<div class="row"></div>
<div class="row padding-top-20px">

    <div class="row z-depth-3">
        <div class="section white-text padding-left-10px blue-grey lighten-1">
            <h5>Master Values</h5>
        </div>
        <div class="divider"></div>
        <div class="col s4 padding-bottom-15px">
            <select id="ddlMasterKeys" asp-items="@(new SelectList(ViewBag.MasterKeys,
            "RowKey","PartitionKey"))">
                <option>--Select--</option>
            </select>
            <label>Partition Key</label>
        </div>
        <div class="col s12 padding-bottom-15px">
            @* Display List of Master Values *@
            <table class="highlight centered" id="tblMasterValues">
                <thead>
                    <tr>
                        <th data-field="RowKey">Row Key</th>
                        <th data-field="PartitionKey">Partition Key</th>
                        <th data-field="Name">Name</th>
                        <th data-field="IsActive">Is Active</th>
                        <th data-field="Actions">Edit</th>
                    </tr>
                </thead>
            </table>
        </div>
    </div>

    <div class="row"></div>

    @* Details Section *@
    <div class="row z-depth-3">
        <div class="col s12 padding-0px">
            <div class="section white-text padding-left-10px blue-grey lighten-1">
                <h5>Master Value Details</h5>
            </div>
            <div class="divider"></div>
```

```
<form asp-controller="MasterData" asp-action="MasterValues" method="post"
class="col s12" id="formMasterValue">
    <div class="row">
        <input type="hidden" asp-for="IsEdit" />
        <input type="hidden" asp-for="MasterValueInContext.RowKey" />
        <input type="hidden" asp-for="MasterValueInContext.PartitionKey" />
        <div class="input-field col s4">
            <input asp-for="MasterValueInContext.RowKey" id="Input_MasterKey_
            RowKey" disabled="disabled" />
            <label asp-for="MasterValueInContext.RowKey"></label>
        </div>
        <div class="input-field col s4">
            <select id="Select_MasterValueInContext_PartitionKey"
                    asp-for="MasterValueInContext.PartitionKey"
                    asp-items="@(new SelectList(ViewBag.MasterKeys,"RowKey",
                    "PartitionKey"))"
                    required="required">
                <option value="">--Select--</option>
            </select>
            <label>Partition Key</label>
        </div>
        <div class="input-field col s4">
            <input asp-for="MasterValueInContext.Name" class="validate" />
            <label asp-for="MasterValueInContext.Name"></label>
        </div>
    </div>
    <div class="row">
        <div class="input-field col s4">
            <div class="switch">
                <label>
                    Is Active
                    <input asp-for="MasterValueInContext.IsActive"
                    class="validate" />
                    <span class="lever"></span>
                </label>
            </div>
        </div>
        <div class="input-field col s8 right-align">
            <button class="btn waves-effect waves-light btnSubmit" type="button"
            name="action">
                Create
                <i class="material-icons right">send</i>
            </button>
            <button class="btn waves-effect waves-light reset  red lighten-1"
            type="button" name="action">
                Reset
            </button>
        </div>
        <div class="row col s12 right-align" asp-validation-summary="All"></div>
    </div>
</form>
```

```
        </div>
        <div class="row"></div>
    </div>
</div>
```

To support the Master Values view, we have JQuery code written in the view, as shown in Listing 7-24. The script consists of the following main concepts:

- *Anti-forgery request validation*: By default, ASP.NET MVC Core creates a request verification token and places in HTML. This token should be sent in all POST requests to the server to validate a request for forgery. This security flow happens seamlessly for normal POST operations, as the server posts hidden fields by default. But for AJAX POST operations, we need to explicitly get the hidden field value and pass it in the request headers. This is achieved as part of setting up the default for AJAX requests by using the $.ajaxSetup method.

- *Initialize DataTable*: The Master Values screen's DataTable is going to be based on the data sent in response to the AJAX request on the MasterValuesByKey action. We initialize DataTable by indicating the necessary AJAX endpoint and type of operation (GET, in this case). Then we configure the settings for page length and number of records per page. We define the columns that need to be displayed in DataTable. Finally, we define the custom render functions for the InActive and Actions columns.

- *Styles*: We set up the basic styles for the Material CSS Dropdown and DataTable.

- *Reset*: This function resets all the controls in the details section and enables the PartitionKey select tag, so that the user can proceed with creating the new master value.

- *Edit*: This function is invoked whenever the user clicks the Edit icon of any master value record in the DataTable. This function populates the details section with the details of the record that is the context of the edit operation. It also sets the hidden fields such as RowKey that will be used in the POST action for identifying the master value record that is being edited.

- *Master keys select change*: This event will be triggered whenever the user changes the master key option in the select tag. This event will reload the master values DataTable from Azure Storage by making an AJAX call to the MasterValuesByKey action with the selected master key.

- *Submit*: This function will be triggered whenever the users clicks the Save/Create button in the Details section. It will create a JQuery object of the master value (which is being created or modified) and send it to the MasterValues POST action through the AJAX call. Upon a successful POST operation, the master values DataTable is reloaded with the selected option in the master keys select tag.

■ **Note**   We need the following code to fire a mandatory validation on the select list. This is a known workaround for material select list.

```
$("select[required]").css({ display: "block", position: 'absolute', visibility: 'hidden' });
```

Listing 7-24. JQuery code on Master Values view

```
@section Scripts{
    <script>
        $(document).ready(function () {
            // Need to pass Verification Token to get Request Validated for Forgery
            var token = $('input[type=hidden][name=__RequestVerificationToken]',
            document).val();
            $.ajaxSetup({
                // Disable caching of AJAX responses
                cache: false,
                headers: { 'RequestVerificationToken': token }
            });

            // Initialize DataTable to show list of Master Values
            var table = $('#tblMasterValues').DataTable({
                // Make AJAX call based to get Master Values from Server
                'ajax': {
                    'url': '@Url.Action("MasterValuesByKey", "MasterData")',
                    'type': 'GET'
                },
                'pageLength': 3,
                // Number of records to be displayed per page
                'lengthMenu': [[3, 5, 10, -1], [3, 5, 10, 'All']],
                // Set Columns
                'columns': [
                    { 'data': 'RowKey' },
                    { 'data': 'PartitionKey' },
                    { 'data': 'Name' },
                    { 'data': 'IsActive' },
                    { 'data': 'Actions', }
                ],
                // Set Custom Column definitions and define their render HTML.
                "aoColumnDefs": [
                    {
                        "aTargets": [3],
                        "mData": "IsActive",
                        "mRender": function (data, type, full) {
                            if (data === true)
                                return '<img src="/images/green_tick.png" />';
                            else
                                return '<img src="/images/red_cross.png" />';
                        }
                    },
                    {
                        "aTargets": [4],
                        "mData": "Actions",
                        "mRender": function (data, type, full) {
                            return '<i class="small material-icons edit cursor-hand">
                            mode_edit</i>';
```

```
                }
            }
        ]
});

    // Set Styles for DataTable and Number of Records to be displayed in drop-down
    $('#tblMasterValues').css("width", "100%");
    $('select[name="tblMasterValues_length"]').material_select();
    $("select[required]").css({ display: "block", position: 'absolute', visibility:
    'hidden' });
    // Initialize Master Key Select
    $('select').material_select();

    // Handle Reset functionality
    $(document).on("click", ".reset", function () {
        $('#formMasterValue')[0].reset();
        $('.btnSubmit').text('Create');
        $('#IsEdit').val('False');

        // Remove Partition key disabled attribute
        $('#Select_MasterValueInContext_PartitionKey').material_select('destroy');
        $('#Select_MasterValueInContext_PartitionKey').removeAttr('disabled');
        $('#Select_MasterValueInContext_PartitionKey').material_select();

        // Remove the validation error messages.
        $('.validation-summary-valid').find("ul").html('');
    });

    // On click of Edit icon, populate the details section with details of service
    engineer
    $(document).on('click', '.edit', function () {
        var user = $('#tblMasterValues').DataTable().row($(this).parents('tr')).data();

        $('#IsEdit').val('True');
        // Map Row Key
        $('#MasterValueInContext_RowKey').val(user["RowKey"]);
        $('#Input_MasterKey_RowKey').val(user["RowKey"]);

        // Map Partition Key
        $('#MasterValueInContext_PartitionKey').val(user["PartitionKey"]);
        // Set Partition Key Dropdown and re-initialize Material Select
        $('#Select_MasterValueInContext_PartitionKey').material_select('destroy');
        $('#Select_MasterValueInContext_PartitionKey option:contains(' +
        user['PartitionKey'] + ')').prop('selected', true);
        $('#Select_MasterValueInContext_PartitionKey').attr('disabled', 'disabled');
        $('#Select_MasterValueInContext_PartitionKey').material_select();

        // Remove valid class for dropdownlist, as it is disabled
        $('.select-wrapper').removeClass('valid');
```

```
            // Map Name
            $('#MasterValueInContext_Name').val(user["Name"]);
            $('#MasterValueInContext_Name').addClass('valid');
            // Map IsActive
            $('#MasterValueInContext_IsActive').prop('checked', user["IsActive"] ===
            true ? true : false);

            $('.btnSubmit').text('Save');
            Materialize.updateTextFields();
        });

        // Dropdown change event
        $(document).on('change', '#ddlMasterKeys', function () {
            table.ajax.url('@Url.Action("MasterValuesByKey","MasterData")' + '?key=' +
            $('#ddlMasterKeys option:selected').text());
            table.ajax.reload();
        });

        // Save/Create Button Click Event
        $(document).on('click', '.btnSubmit', function () {
            var form = $("#formMasterValue");
            if ($(form).valid()) {
                // Create the POST Object
                var masterData = new Object();
                masterData.Name = $('#MasterValueInContext_Name').val();
                masterData.PartitionKey = $('#Select_MasterValueInContext_PartitionKey
                option:selected').text();
                masterData.IsActive = $('#MasterValueInContext_IsActive').is(':checked');

                if ($('#IsEdit').val())
                    masterData.RowKey = $('#MasterValueInContext_RowKey').val();

                // POST the data to server
                $.post('@Url.Action("MasterValues", "MasterData")',
                    { masterValue: masterData, isEdit: $('#IsEdit').val() },
                    function (data, status, xhr) {
                        table.ajax.url('@Url.Action("MasterValuesByKey","MasterData")' +
                        '?key=' + $('#ddlMasterKeys option:selected').text());
                        table.ajax.reload();
                    });

                // Reset the form
                $('.reset').click();

                // Remove valid class for materialize css dropdown, otherwise there is a
                CSS distortion
                $('.select-wrapper').removeClass('valid');
            }
        });
    });
</script>
}
```

Run the application and navigate to the Master Values screen by clicking the left navigation menu option, as shown in Figure 7-15.

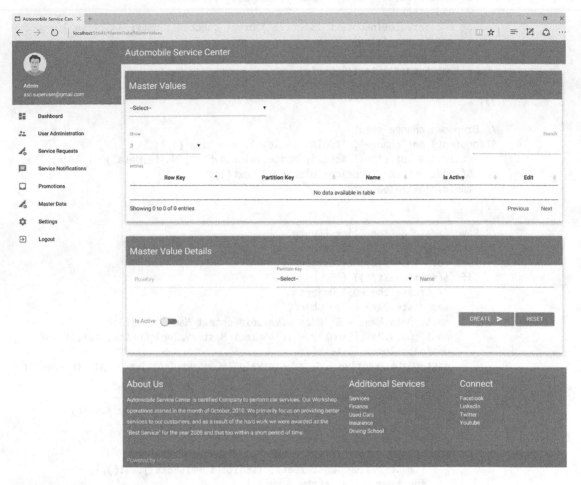

Figure 7-15. *Master Values screen*

Enter data into the Details section as shown in Figure 7-16 and click Create. Similarly, add other values such as InProgress and Completed.

Master Value Details
RowKey
Partition Key
Status
Name
Pending
Is Active
CREATE
RESET

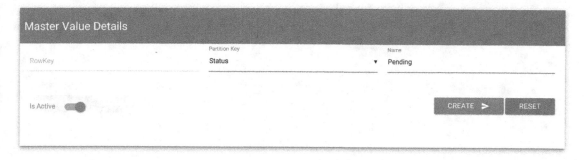

Figure 7-16. *Creating a new master value*

Select Status in the master keys select tag in the Master Values section. All the newly added values should be displayed in the table, as shown in Figure 7-17.

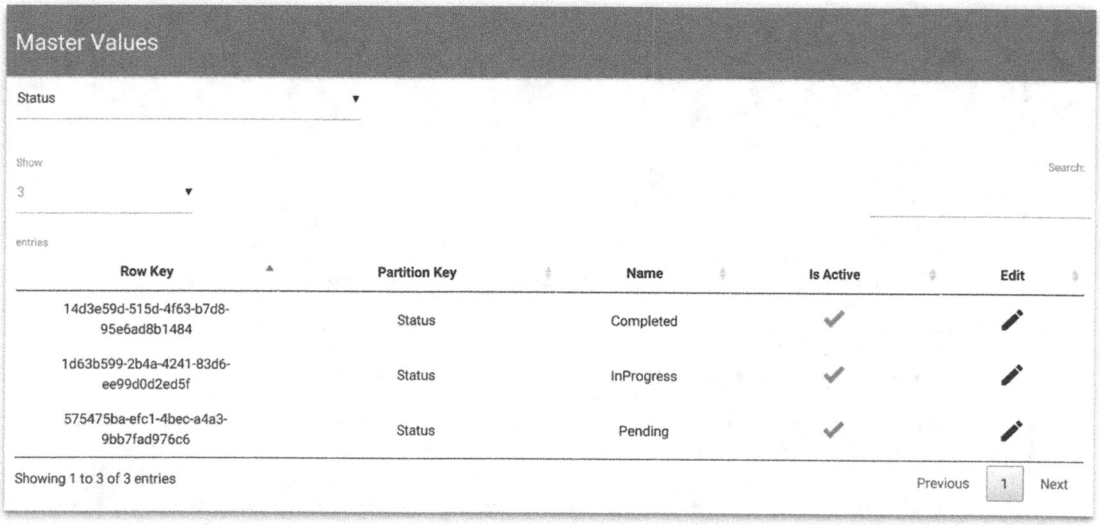

Master Values
Status
Show
3
entries
Search:
Row Key
Partition Key
Name
Is Active
Edit
14d3e59d-515d-4f63-b7d8-95e6ad8b1484
Status
Completed
1d63b599-2b4a-4241-83d6-ee99d0d2ed5f
Status
InProgress
575475ba-efc1-4bec-a4a3-9bb7fad976c6
Status
Pending
Showing 1 to 3 of 3 entries
Previous
1
Next

Figure 7-17. *Master Values section*

Click the Edit icon of the Pending value. The corresponding details should be visible in the details section, as shown in Figure 7-18.

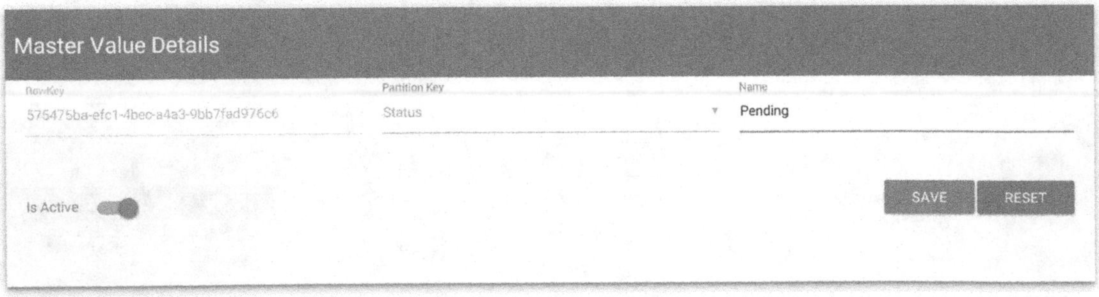

Figure 7-18. *Edit operation on the master value*

Update the Pending value to OnHold and click Save. The value should be updated, and the table should be refreshed, as shown in Figure 7-19.

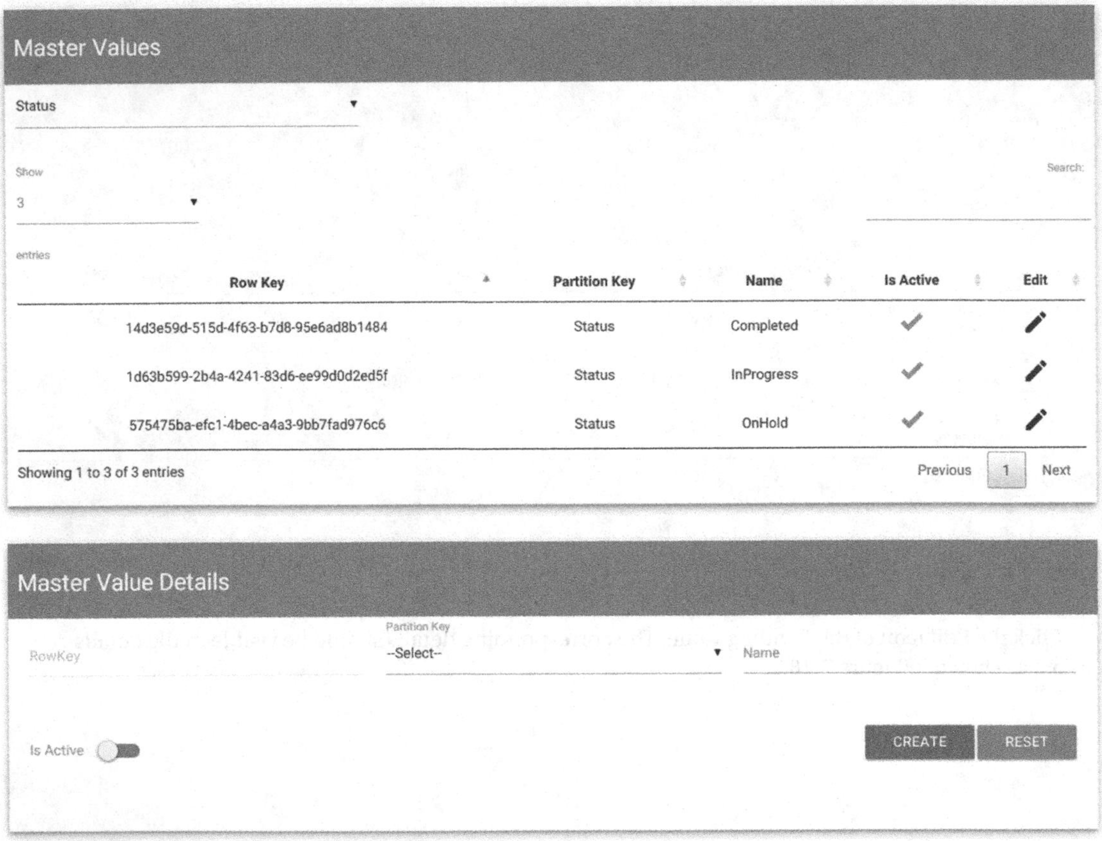

Figure 7-19. *Updated master value shown in the Master Values table*

Similarly, we can add values to any master key. Figure 7-20 shows the values associated with the County key.

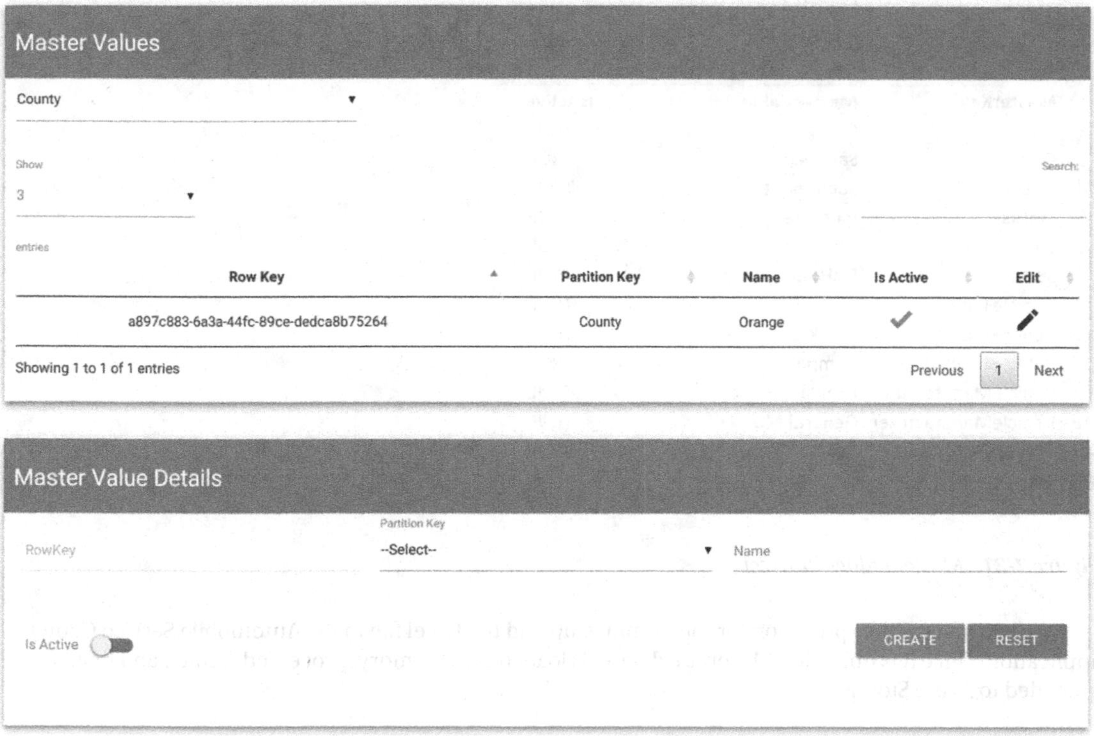

Figure 7-20. *Master Values table displaying values for the County key*

Importing Master Data to Azure Tables from Excel

In the previous section, you saw how an Admin can use custom-built web pages to manage master data. These pages are very useful for managing master data on a day-to-day basis, but they might not be helpful for initial data setup that requires migrating a large amount of master data to storage. Usually, administrators use Excel or CSV sheets to manage this static data, and almost all modern applications provide the capability to process data from Excel or other file types and store it. In this section, we are going to build a simple Excel parser through which an Admin can upload master data to Azure Storage in one attempt.

Prepare an Excel workbook, as shown in Figure 7-21, to hold the master data. The first column has the master keys, and the second column holds the master values. The third column has a Boolean value, marking the value for IsActive.

	A	B	C
1	**MasterKey**	**MasterValue**	**IsActive**
2	County	Orange	TRUE
3	County	San Diego	TRUE
4	County	Sacramento	TRUE
5	Status	InProgress	TRUE
6	Status	Completed	TRUE
7	Status	OnHold	TRUE
8	VehicleType	Car	TRUE
9	VehicleType	Truck	TRUE
10	VehicleType	Camper	TRUE
11	VehicleManufacturer	Honda	TRUE
12	VehicleManufacturer	General Motors	TRUE
13	VehicleManufacturer	Ford	TRUE
14			
15			

Figure 7-21. *Master values in Excel*

We will first create a provision for the Admin to upload the Excel file to the Automobile Service Center application. Once it is uploaded, the entire dataset is loaded into memory, processed further, and finally uploaded to Azure Storage.

■ **Note**   Paste the following image, which is used to open the File Upload dialog box, in the Images folder under the wwwroot.

We will modify MasterValues.cshtml to support the Excel upload. First, we will add the Excel icon as shown in Listing 7-25.

Listing 7-25. Excel icon on Master Values view

```
<div class="row z-depth-3">
    <div class="section white-text padding-left-10px blue-grey lighten-1">
        <h5>Master Values</h5>
    </div>
    <div class="divider"></div>
    <div class="col s4 padding-bottom-15px">
        <select id="ddlMasterKeys" asp-items="@(new SelectList(ViewBag.MasterKeys,
        "RowKey","PartitionKey"))">
            <option>--Select--</option>
        </select>
        <label>Partition Key</label>
    </div>
```

```
<div class="col s4 offset-s4 padding-bottom-15px right-align">
    <a class="modal-trigger waves-effect waves-light" href="#modal1">
        <img src="~/images/excel.png" />
    </a>
</div>
<div class="col s12 padding-bottom-15px">
    @* Display List of Master Values *@
    <table class="highlight centered" id="tblMasterValues">
        <thead>
            <tr>
                <th data-field="RowKey">Row Key</th>
                <th data-field="PartitionKey">Partition Key</th>
                <th data-field="Name">Name</th>
                <th data-field="IsActive">Is Active</th>
                <th data-field="Actions">Edit</th>
            </tr>
        </thead>
    </table>
</div>
</div>
```

Upon clicking the Excel icon, we will open a Materialize CSS modal dialog box with the file input tag. Listing 7-26 shows the Modal pop-up design, where we have one input file type tag and a button inside a form tag that we will use to post the file to the UploadExcel action of MasterDataController (we will code the UploadExcel action later in this section). We will use JQuery to POST the file to the server. The modal pop-up also contains a div to display all errors; this div will be hidden by default. Based on the success or failure of the file upload, we will toggle the visibility of this div. The modal pop-up also contains a div to show the progress bar that will display the progress of the Excel file processing.

Listing 7-26. Modal popup for excel file upload

```
<!-- Modal Structure -->
<div id="modal1" class="modal modal-fixed-footer">
    <div class="modal-content">
        <h4>Upload Excel</h4>
        <p>Upload the Excel file that contains all the master values.</p>
        <!-- Div to display Errors-->
        <div class="row hide divErrors">
            <div class="col s12">
                <div class="card-panel red lighten-1">
                    <span class="white-text errors"></span>
                </div>
            </div>
        </div>
        <!-- Div to display progress -->
        <div class="progress hide">
            <div class="indeterminate"></div>
        </div>
        <form action="UploadExcel" controller="MasterData" method="post">
            <div class="file-field input-field">
                <div class="btn">
                    <span>File</span>
```

```
                      <input type="file" id="files">
              </div>
              <div class="file-path-wrapper">
                      <input class="file-path validate" type="text">
              </div>
              <div class="input-field row right">
                      <button class="btn waves-effect waves-light btnUpload" type="button"
                      name="action">
                          Upload
                          <i class="material-icons right">send</i>
                      </button>
              </div>
          </div>
      </form>
  </div>
</div>
```

Finally, the modal pop-up is associated with the Excel icon by initializing the modal. Place the code from Listing 7-27 in JQuery code inside the document ready function.

Listing 7-27. Initialize Modal popup

```
// the "href" attribute of .modal-trigger must specify the modal ID that wants to be
triggered
$('.modal').modal();
```

Run the application and navigate to the Master Values view. You should see the Excel icon shown in Figure 7-22.

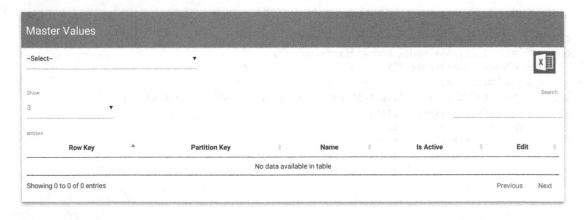

Figure 7-22. *Excel icon on Master Values view*

Click the Excel icon. A modal pop-up opens, as shown in Figure 7-23.

Figure 7-23. *Modal popup to upload excel file*

We will expand our business component to support bulk insert/update operations. Add the UploadBulkMasterData method to the IMasterDataOperations interface, as shown in Listing 7-28.

Listing 7-28. Updated IMasterDataOperations interface

```
Task<bool> UploadBulkMasterData(List<MasterDataValue> values);
```

Create the implementation of UploadBulkMasterData in the MasterDataOperations class, as shown in Listing 7-29. We will iterate all the master values. For each value, we first we check whether the associated master key of the master value is present in the storage. If it is not, we will create the master key. The same process is followed for the master value as well; we will first check whether the master value is present in storage, and if not, we will create the master value in storage.

Listing 7-29. UploadBulkMasterData method

```
public async Task<bool> UploadBulkMasterData(List<MasterDataValue> values)
{
    using (_unitOfWork)
    {
        foreach (var value in values)
        {
            // Find, if null insert MasterKey
            var masterKey = await GetMaserKeyByNameAsync(value.PartitionKey);
            if (!masterKey.Any())
            {
                await _unitOfWork.Repository<MasterDataKey>().AddAsync(new MasterDataKey()
```

```
                    {
                        Name = value.PartitionKey,
                        RowKey = Guid.NewGuid().ToString(),
                        PartitionKey = value.PartitionKey
                    });
            }

            // Find, if null Insert MasterValue
            var masterValuesByKey = await GetAllMasterValuesByKeyAsync(value.PartitionKey);
            var masterValue = masterValuesByKey.FirstOrDefault(p => p.Name == value.Name);
            if (masterValue == null)
            {
                await _unitOfWork.Repository<MasterDataValue>().AddAsync(value);
            }
            else
            {
                masterValue.IsActive = value.IsActive;
                masterValue.IsDeleted = value.IsDeleted;
                masterValue.Name = value.Name;

                await _unitOfWork.Repository<MasterDataValue>().UpdateAsync(masterValue);
            }
        }

        _unitOfWork.CommitTransaction();
        return true;
    }
}
```

Now we will set up the controller action that will process the uploaded Excel file. ASP.NET Core doesn't have built-in support to process Excel files. To achieve Excel file parsing, we will use the EPPlus.Core

NuGet package, which is an open source library that supports Excel parsing in .NET Core apps. Add the EPPlus.Core package reference to the ASC.Web project, as shown in Figure 7-24.

Figure 7-24. *Installing the EPPlus.Core NuGet ptackage to the ASC.Web project*

■ **Note**   EPPlus.Core is an unofficial port of the EPPlus library to .NET Core (see https://www.nuget.org/packages/EPPlus/).

Create a private method in `MasterDataController` that will parse the Excel file, as shown in Listing 7-30. This private method will return a processed list of `MasterDataValue` objects to the caller (which is going to be an `Action` method). `ParseMasterDataExcel` will read the Excel file into `MemoryStream`, and then create an `EPPlus ExcelPackage` object out of `MemoryStream`. It then iterates all the rows of the Excel worksheet and creates a list of `MasterDataValues` and returns the list to the caller.

Listing 7-30. ParseMasterDataExcel method

```
private async Task<List<MasterDataValue>> ParseMasterDataExcel(IFormFile excelFile)
{
    var masterValueList = new List<MasterDataValue>();
        using (var memoryStream = new MemoryStream())
    {
        // Get MemoryStream from Excel file
        await excelFile.CopyToAsync(memoryStream);
        // Create a ExcelPackage object from MemoryStream
        using (ExcelPackage package = new ExcelPackage(memoryStream))
        {
            // Get the first Excel sheet from the Workbook
            ExcelWorksheet worksheet = package.Workbook.Worksheets[1];
            int rowCount = worksheet.Dimension.Rows;

            // Iterate all the rows and create the list of MasterDataValue
            // Ignore first row as it is header
            for (int row = 2; row <= rowCount; row++)
            {
                var masterDataValue = new MasterDataValue();
                masterDataValue.RowKey = Guid.NewGuid().ToString();
                masterDataValue.PartitionKey = worksheet.Cells[row, 1].Value.ToString();
                masterDataValue.Name = worksheet.Cells[row, 2].Value.ToString();
                masterDataValue.IsActive = Boolean.Parse(worksheet.Cells[row, 3].
                Value.ToString());

                masterValueList.Add(masterDataValue);
            }
        }
    }
    return masterValueList;
}
```

■ **Note** Excel parsing logic can be made more generic to support any form of Excel file. But that code will deviate from the scope of our requirement, so I am refraining from creating a generic component for Excel file parsing.

Now we will create the POST action to which the Excel file will be posted from the page, as shown in Listing 7-31. The `UploadExcel` action reads all the files uploaded from `Request.Form.Files` collections. It then validates the files to contain a minimum of one file with length greater than zero. If validations are passed, the Excel file is parsed with the `EPPlus ExcelPackage` (as shown in the private method in Listing 7-30).

Upon successful parsing of the Excel file, we will pass the list of master values to the UploadBulkMasterData method of the MasterDataOperations business component. Once all keys and values are stored, we will return the result in a JSON message.

Listing 7-31. UploadExcel action

```
[HttpPost]
[ValidateAntiForgeryToken]
public async Task<IActionResult> UploadExcel()
{
    var files = Request.Form.Files;
    // Validations
    if (!files.Any())
    {
        return Json( new { Error = true, Text = "Upload a file" });
    }

    var excelFile = files.First();
    if(excelFile.Length <= 0)
    {
        return Json(new { Error = true, Text = "Upload a file" });
    }

    // Parse Excel Data
    var masterData = await ParseMasterDataExcel(excelFile);
    var result = await _masterData.UploadBulkMasterData(masterData);

    return Json(new { Success = result });
}
```

The UploadExcel POST action is called from the MasterValues view by using a JQuery AJAX POST operation, as shown in Listing 7-32. The JQuery click function processes all the files from the input file tag and creates a FormData object. It then displays the progress bar and makes an AJAX POST call to the UploadExcel action. Upon success of the AJAX call, the page will be refreshed; upon failure, the error messages will be displayed in a pop-up.

Listing 7-32. JQuery code to POST excel file to UploadExcel action

```
// Excel Upload
$(document).on('click', '.btnUpload', function () {
    // Get all files from input file tag
    var fileUpload = $("#files").get(0);
    var files = fileUpload.files;
    var data = new FormData();

    // Process the file and create FormData object
    $.each(files, function (i) {
        data.append(files[i].name, files[i]);
    });

    // Show progress bar
    $(".progress").removeClass("hide");
```

```
$.ajax({
    type: "POST",
    url: "/MasterData/UploadExcel",
    contentType: false,
    processData: false,
    data: data,
    success: function (message) {
        // Hide progress bar
        $(".progress").addClass("hide");

        if (message.Success) {
            // Reload the page on success
            window.location.reload();
        }

        if (message.Error) {
            // Show Errors
            $(".divErrors").removeClass("hide");
            $(".errors").html("");
            $(".errors").html(message.Text);
        }
    },
    error: function () { }
});
});
```

Run the application and navigate to the `MasterValues` action. Click the Excel icon and click Submit without selecting any file. You should see the error message displayed in the pop-up, as shown in Figure 7-25.

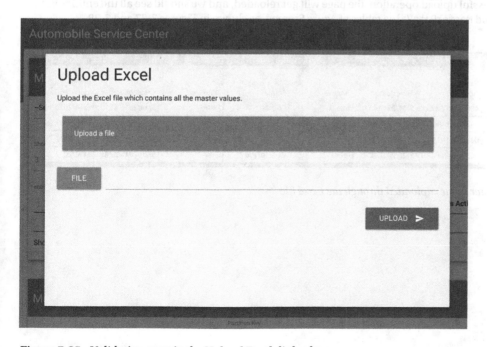

Figure 7-25. *Validation error in the Upload Excel dialog box*

Now select the Excel file that we created at the start of this section and click Upload. A progress bar showing the status of the upload is displayed, as shown in Figure 7-26.

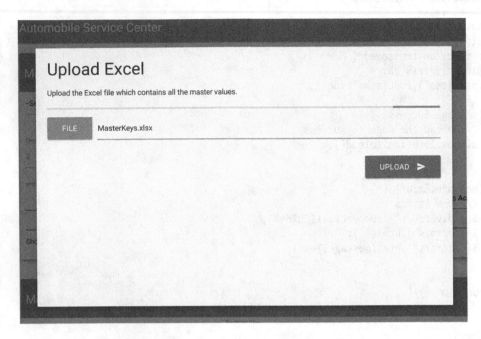

Figure 7-26. *Displaying a progress bar during Excel file processing*

Upon a successful upload operation, the page will get reloaded, and we should see all the entities in the `MasterDataKey` and `MasterDataValue` tables of Azure Storage, as shown in Figures 7-27 and 7-28.

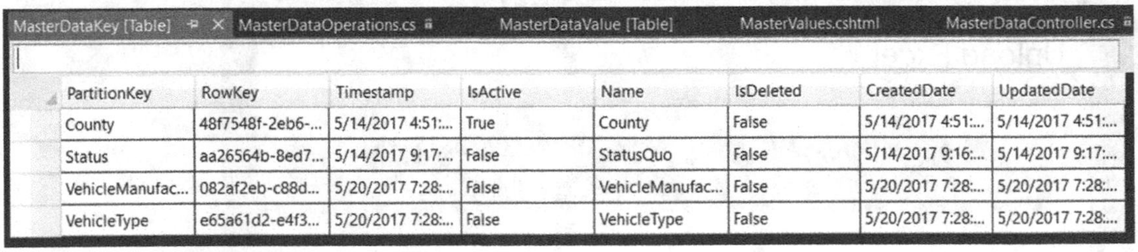

MasterDataKey [Table] ⊹ ✕	MasterDataOperations.cs		MasterDataValue [Table]	MasterValues.cshtml		MasterDataController.cs

	PartitionKey	RowKey	Timestamp	IsActive	Name	IsDeleted	CreatedDate	UpdatedDate
	County	48f7548f-2eb6-...	5/14/2017 4:51:...	True	County	False	5/14/2017 4:51:...	5/14/2017 4:51:...
	Status	aa26564b-8ed7...	5/14/2017 9:17:...	False	StatusQuo	False	5/14/2017 9:16:...	5/14/2017 9:17:...
	VehicleManufac...	082af2eb-c88d...	5/20/2017 7:28:...	False	VehicleManufac...	False	5/20/2017 7:28:...	5/20/2017 7:28:...
	VehicleType	e65a61d2-e4f3...	5/20/2017 7:28:...	False	VehicleType	False	5/20/2017 7:28:...	5/20/2017 7:28:...

Figure 7-27. *Master values uploaded through the Excel file*

PartitionKey	RowKey	Timestamp	IsActive	Name	IsDeleted	CreatedDate	UpdatedDate
County	0972e39a-b195...	5/20/2017 7:28:...	True	SanDiego	False	5/20/2017 7:26:...	5/20/2017 7:28:...
County	5a779d03-f8e6...	5/20/2017 7:28:...	True	Sacramento	False	5/20/2017 7:26:...	5/20/2017 7:28:...
County	5cf77cfd-ad4a-...	5/20/2017 7:28:...	True	Orange	False	5/20/2017 7:26:...	5/20/2017 7:28:...
Status	9e9e910f-55e1-...	5/20/2017 7:28:...	True	InProgress	False	5/20/2017 7:26:...	5/20/2017 7:28:...
Status	9f15a32a-3cf5-...	5/20/2017 7:28:...	True	Completed	False	5/20/2017 7:26:...	5/20/2017 7:28:...
Status	9fb3d28e-1c6b...	5/20/2017 7:28:...	True	Pending	False	5/20/2017 7:26:...	5/20/2017 7:28:...
VehicleManufac...	20d3a850-40dc...	5/20/2017 7:28:...	True	GeneralMotors	False	5/20/2017 7:26:...	5/20/2017 7:28:...
VehicleManufac...	210e0ea3-ab63...	5/20/2017 7:28:...	True	Ford	False	5/20/2017 7:26:...	5/20/2017 7:28:...
VehicleManufac...	eca31bca-0cd9...	5/20/2017 7:28:...	True	Honda	False	5/20/2017 7:26:...	5/20/2017 7:28:...
VehicleType	3a63b7f5-f0d4-...	5/20/2017 7:28:...	True	Truck	False	5/20/2017 7:26:...	5/20/2017 7:28:...
VehicleType	6b1018a6-1c73...	5/20/2017 7:28:...	True	Car	False	5/20/2017 7:26:...	5/20/2017 7:28:...
VehicleType	d079b851-ea0d...	5/20/2017 7:28:...	True	Camper	False	5/20/2017 7:26:...	5/20/2017 7:28:...

Figure 7-28. *Master keys uploaded through the Excel file*

■ **Note** For the Automobile Service Center application, we have used simple logic to maintain master data. In large applications, this management logic might differ, based on business requirements and operations.

Enabling Redis Memory Caching

The most frequent operation on master data by any application is a GET operation (fetching the master data from data storage and using it in the application). This operation can be redundant if the same master data is being used at multiple places in the application. In these scenarios, using a cache can improve the performance of the application by storing master data in memory to the server instead of obtaining data for every request from external resources such as databases, storage, or services.

■ **Note** A cache can be used for multiple purposes, not only to store master data, but also to store sessions. Instead of storing sessions in memory on a server, storing them in a cache can provide scalability of the application that is distributed across multiple servers.

Especially for cloud solutions, we should use a distributed cache instead of an in-memory cache because cloud platforms are virtualized and load-balanced.

In this section, we will use Azure Redis Cache to enable the caching mechanism for the Automobile Service Center application. Azure Redis Cache is a cache offering from Microsoft Azure that uses the open source Redis Cache framework (an in-memory data structure store).

Just as with Azure Storage emulator, we can use the Redis local installation to support cache implementation at development time on a local development machine. At the time of production, we can create a new Redis cache at Azure Redis Cache. Toggling between a development and production cache is going to be accomplished with a simple ConnectionString setting change.

First, we need to install Redis on a local machine. To do so, we need to install Chocolatey (a package manager for Windows). Open the command-line prompt in Administrator mode and run the following command, also shown in Figure 7-29:

```
@powershell -NoProfile -ExecutionPolicy Bypass -Command "iex ((New-Object System.
Net.WebClient).DownloadString('https://chocolatey.org/install.ps1'))" && SET
"PATH=%PATH%;%ALLUSERSPROFILE%\chocolatey\bin"
```

Figure 7-29. *Installing Chocolatey on a local machine*

Install Redis Cache by using the following command, as shown in Figure 7-30:

Administrator: Command Prompt

```
C:\Windows\system32>choco install redis-64
Chocolatey v0.10.5
Installing the following packages:
redis-64
By installing you accept licenses for the packages.
Progress: Downloading redis-64 3.0.503... 100%

redis-64 v3.0.503 [Approved]
redis-64 package files install completed. Performing other installation steps.
 ShimGen has successfully created a shim for redis-benchmark.exe
 ShimGen has successfully created a shim for redis-check-aof.exe
 ShimGen has successfully created a shim for redis-check-dump.exe
 ShimGen has successfully created a shim for redis-cli.exe
 ShimGen has successfully created a shim for redis-server.exe
 The install of redis-64 was successful.
  Software install location not explicitly set, could be in package or
  default install location if installer.

Chocolatey installed 1/1 packages. 0 packages failed.
 See the log for details (C:\ProgramData\chocolatey\logs\chocolatey.log).
```

Figure 7-30. *Installing Redis Cache on a local machine*

choco install redis-64

Start the Redis server on a local machine by running the following command, as shown in Figure 7-31:

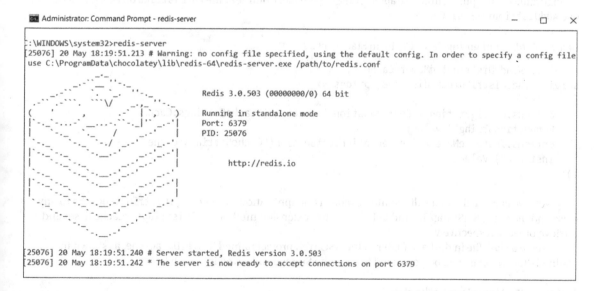

Figure 7-31. *Starting Redis Cache on a local machine*

Redis-server

Redis Cache is up and running. Now we will enable Redis Cache in the ASC.Web project by installing the Microsoft.Extensions.Caching.Redis NuGet package, as shown in Figure 7-32.

Figure 7-32. *Installing the Microsoft.Extensions.Cachine.Redis NuGtet package to the ASC.Web project*

Add the cache configuration to the appsettings.json file, as shown in Listing 7-33.

Listing 7-33. Cache configuration in appsettings.json file

```
"CacheSettings": {
  "CacheConnectionString": "localhost",
  "CacheInstance": "ASCInstance"
},
```

We need to add the Redis Cache service in the Startup class, as shown in Listing 7-34, with the configuration being pulled from the appsettings.json file. Comment the AddDistributedMemoryCache and use AddDistributedRedisCache.

Listing 7-34. Configuring Redis Cache in Startup class

```
//services.AddDistributedMemoryCache();
services.AddDistributedRedisCache(options =>
{
    options.Configuration = Configuration.GetSection("CacheSettings:Cache
    ConnectionString").Value;
    options.InstanceName = Configuration.GetSection("CacheSettings:Cache
    Instance").Value;
});
```

Now we can use the Redis distributed cache in our application by injecting IDistributedCache in any class and using the SetString/Set and GetString/Get extension methods of IDistributedCache to set and retrieve objects, respectively.

Create a class file in the Data folder of the ASC.Web project named MasterDataCache, as shown in Listing 7-35. This class will be populated from Azure Storage and saved in the cache.

Listing 7-35. MasterDataCache class

```
public class MasterDataCache
{
    public List<MasterDataKey> Keys { get; set; }
    public List<MasterDataValue> Values { get; set; }
}
```

■ **Note** Except in `MasterDataController`, which is primarily used to manage master data, we are going to use `MasterDataCache` throughout the application, wherever we have a requirement with master data.

We will create the `IMasterDataCacheOperations` interface in the same class file as `MasterDataCache`, as shown in Listing 7-36. `IMasterDataCacheOperations` has methods to perform the following cache-related operations:

- Creating all master data in the cache
- Retrieving the master data from the cache

Listing 7-36. IMasterDataCacheOperations interface

```
public interface IMasterDataCacheOperations
{
    Task<MasterDataCache> GetMasterDataCache();
    Task CreateMasterDataCache();
}
```

The implementation of `IMasterDataCacheOperations` is created in the same class file and is shown in Listing 7-37. `MasterDataCacheOperations` uses `IMasterDataOperations` methods and creates the `MasterDataCache` object and saves it to the cache. The `GetMasterDataCache` method will read `MasterDataCache` from the cache and return it to the caller. The retrieved master keys and values are filtered based on the `IsActive` flag before caching them.

■ **Note** We use JSON serialization to serialize the `MasterDataCache` object to the string before we store it to the cache. Similarly, we deserialize the string back to the `MasterDataCache` object after reading it back from the cache.

Listing 7-37. MasterDataCacheOperations class

```
public class MasterDataCacheOperations : IMasterDataCacheOperations
{
    private readonly IDistributedCache _cache;
    private readonly IMasterDataOperations _masterData;
    private readonly string MasterDataCacheName = "MasterDataCache";
    public MasterDataCacheOperations(IDistributedCache cache, IMasterDataOperations
    masterData)
    {
        _cache = cache;
        _masterData = masterData;
    }
```

```
public async Task CreateMasterDataCacheAsync()
{
    var masterDataCache = new MasterDataCache
    {
        Keys = (await _masterData.GetAllMasterKeysAsync()).Where(p => p.IsActive ==
        true).ToList(),
        Values = (await _masterData.GetAllMasterValuesAsync()).Where(p =>
        p.IsActive == true).ToList()
    };

    await _cache.SetStringAsync(MasterDataCacheName, JsonConvert.SerializeObject
    (masterDataCache));
}

public async Task<MasterDataCache> GetMasterDataCacheAsync()
{
    return JsonConvert.DeserializeObject<MasterDataCache>(await _cache.GetString
    Async(MasterDataCacheName));
}
}
```

To use the MasterDataCache API, we need to resolve IMasterDataCacheOperations in the ConfigureServices method of the Startup class, as shown in Listing 7-38.

Listing 7-38. Resolve the dependency of IMasterDataCacheOperations

```
services.AddSingleton<IMasterDataCacheOperations, MasterDataCacheOperations>();
```

As part of starting the application, we will invoke the CreateMasterDataCache method in the Configure method of the Startup class, as shown in Listing 7-39.

Listing 7-39. Updated Configure method of Startup class with MasterDataCacheOperations

```
public async void Configure(IApplicationBuilder app,
    IHostingEnvironment env,
    ILoggerFactory loggerFactory,
    IIdentitySeed storageSeed,
    IMasterDataCacheOperations masterDataCacheOperations,
    IUnitOfWork unitOfWork)
{
    loggerFactory.AddConsole(Configuration.GetSection("Logging"));
    loggerFactory.AddDebug();

    if (env.IsDevelopment())
    {
        app.UseDeveloperExceptionPage();
        app.UseDatabaseErrorPage();
        app.UseBrowserLink();
    }
```

```
else
{
    app.UseExceptionHandler("/Home/Error");
}

app.UseSession();
app.UseStaticFiles();
app.UseIdentity();

app.UseGoogleAuthentication(new GoogleOptions()
{
    ClientId = Configuration["Google:Identity:ClientId"],
    ClientSecret = Configuration["Google:Identity:ClientSecret"]
});

app.UseMvc(routes =>
{
    routes.MapRoute(
        name: "default",
        template: "{controller=Home}/{action=Index}/{id?}");
});

await storageSeed.Seed(app.ApplicationServices.GetService<UserManager<ApplicationUser>>(),
    app.ApplicationServices.GetService<RoleManager<IdentityRole>>(),
    app.ApplicationServices.GetService<IOptions<ApplicationSettings>>());

var models = Assembly.Load(new AssemblyName("ASC.Models")).GetTypes().Where
(type => type.Namespace == "ASC.Models.Models");
foreach (var model in models)
{
    var repositoryInstance = Activator.CreateInstance(typeof(Repository<>).
    MakeGenericType(model), unitOfWork);
    MethodInfo method = typeof(Repository<>).MakeGenericType(model).
    GetMethod("CreateTableAsync");
    method.Invoke(repositoryInstance, new object[0]);
}

    await masterDataCacheOperations.CreateMasterDataCacheAsync();
}
```

Run the application and navigate to any screen that we have developed so far. To check whether the cache has been created properly, open another command-line prompt and execute the following redis-cli commands, as shown in Figure 7-33. You should see the created master data cache.

```
redis-cli
keys *
hgetall ASCInstanceMasterDataCache
```

239

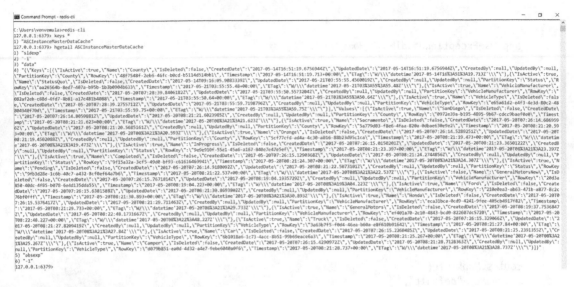

Figure 7-33. *Master data in the the Redis Cache console*

We can retrieve the master data cache in code by injecting `IMasterDataCacheOperations` to any controller or class and calling the `GetMasterDataCacheAsync` method.

■ **Note**   The Session implementation in ASP.NET Core requires `IDistributedCache` to be configured as a store for the Session save and retrieval. As we configured the Redis distributed cache for the entire application, even Session will use the Redis cache as its store.

Navigate to the Master Keys page after login. Now if we check keys in `redis-cli`, we will have a new one created for the session value for `MasterKeys` that we are storing in the `MasterValues` action, as shown in Figure 7-34.

```
127.0.0.1:6379> keys *
1) "ASCInstance7489443b-7533-a317-b593-61f5e176a8f2"
2) "ASCInstanceMasterDataCache"
127.0.0.1:6379> hgetall ASCInstance7489443b-7533-a317-b593-61f5e176a8f2
1) "sldexp"
2) "1200000000000"
3) "data"
4) "\x02\x00\x00\x01\xd8\xe1\x1d\xa2\x88\xdb\xcf\xff\x10M;\x18\xc8\x83M\xbd\x00\nMasterKeys\x00\x00\x01\xd0[{\"RowKey\":\"48f7548f-2eb6-46fc-b8cd-b5114d514bb1\",\"PartitionKey\":\"County\",\"IsActive\":true,\"N
ame\":\"County\"},{\"RowKey\":\"aa26564b-8ed7-407a-b95b-1b3b004b633\",\"PartitionKey\":\"Status\",\"IsActive\":true,\"Name\":\"StatusQuo\"},{\"RowKey\":\"082af2eb-c88d-4fd7-8b81-a17c481b4088\",\"PartitionKey\"
:\"VehicleManufacturer\",\"IsActive\":true,\"Name\":\"VehicleManufacturer\"},{\"RowKey\":\"e65a61d2-e4f3-4e3d-80c2-48804940f70d\",\"PartitionKey\":\"VehicleType\",\"IsActive\":true,\"Name\":\"VehicleType\"}]"
5) "absexp"
6) "-1"
127.0.0.1:6379>
```

Figure 7-34. *Session data in the Redis Cache console*

The last change that we have to make is to invalidate the cache whenever a master key or value changes or when a new master key or value is created. To invalidate the cache, we need to call the `CreateMasterDataCacheAsync` method from the POST actions of `MasterKeys`, `MasterValues`, and `UploadExcel`, which will re-create the cache once again with complete data from Azure Storage.

■ **Note** The code changes required to invalidate the cache at `MasterKeys`, `MasterValues`, and `UploadExcel` POST actions can be found in code samples accompanied with this book.

Summary

You started this chapter by learning about the types of data an application is going to deal with throughout its life cycle. Master data plays a crucial role in maintaining data integrity, and it acts as a common referential point for systems integration. For the Automobile Service Center application, you identified master keys (for example, Vehicle Types and Status) and their corresponding values.

You created master data entities that are used to persist master keys and values to Azure Storage. Later you created a class library to hold business logic for managing master data operations. You configured dependency injection at the web project for the business project and injected Unit of Work to the master data operations layer, through which you received a decoupling of layers. You then developed screens to manage master keys and master values, and in the process you used `AutoMapper` to map data models to view models.

Later in the chapter, you built a simple Excel parser by using the `EPPlus.Core` NuGet package, so an admin can upload master data to Azure Storage via an Excel file. You also developed a modal pop-up by using Materialize so an admin can upload an Excel file of master data to the server.

Finally, to improve application performance and remove redundant storage calls to master data, you enabled Redis Cache for the Automobile Service Center. The configuration for Redis Cache is stored in the `appsettings.json` file, which will be replaced with the Azure Redis Cache `ConnectionString`. Redis Cache will be used by the Automobile Service Center application not only to hold master data, but also to hold session values, as ASP.NET Core's session implementation is dependent on a distributed cache for storage.

CHAPTER 8

■ ■ ■

Logging and Exception Handling

Logging and exception-handling frameworks are key players that account for the robustness and reliability in the design of an application. The *logging framework* ensures that all key information, messages, and errors are logged to the persistent medium. The *exception-handling framework* ensures that users are presented with standard but meaningful error messages in case of system failure or unhandled exceptions.

Generally, exception-handling and logging frameworks go hand in hand, with the former handling exceptions, and the latter logging exception details to storage. The key advantages of having standard logging and exception-handling frameworks are as follows:

- Captures all system-generated and unhandled exceptions in one place and provides standard and user-friendly error messages

- Improves security of the system by not disclosing vulnerable exception details to end users

- Captures the user footprint in the application to help identify the most frequently used functionalities and improve the overall application experience

- Stores important information related to system integrations, which helps in troubleshooting and identifying issues in production

- Captures diagnostic information that helps improve performance of the system

For the Automobile Service Center, we are going to design a centralized exception-handling mechanism that will capture all exceptions at all levels through a global handler. Having a global handler helps get rid of redundant, traditional, try-catch exception-handling code that is otherwise required throughout the application.

We'll also create a unified logging framework for the Automobile Service Center application by using ASP.NET Core's logging features. We'll use a logging framework to log messages and exceptions to Azure Table storage. In the case of exceptions, a unique identification ID will be generated and communicated back to users for technical assistance.

Creating a Logging Framework

In this section, we will create a logging framework to log messages and exceptions to Azure Table storage. Log messages can be of different levels: Trace, Debug, Information, Warning, Error, and Critical, for example. We will tailor our logging framework to capture messages of specific levels.

We will start by creating Log and ExceptionLog entities in the ASC.Models project, as shown in Listings 8-1 and 8-2. These entities are similar to other entities we've created that are used to persist information in Azure Table storage. Both entities will have a Message property that is used to capture the message we want to log. ExceptionLog will have a Stacktrace property to hold the exception's stacktrace.

The RowKey of both entities is generated automatically through Guid, whereas the PartitionKey for the Log entity is going to be Log level, and for the ExceptionLog entity, it is going to be UTC DateTime.

Listing 8-1. Log entity

```
public class Log : BaseEntity
{
    public Log() { }
    public Log(string key)
    {
        this.RowKey = Guid.NewGuid().ToString();
        this.PartitionKey = key;
    }
    public string Message { get; set; }
}
```

Listing 8-2. ExceptionLog entity

```
public class ExceptionLog : BaseEntity
{
    public ExceptionLog() { }
    public ExceptionLog(string key)
    {
        this.RowKey = Guid.NewGuid().ToString();
        this.PartitionKey = DateTime.UtcNow.ToString();
    }
    public string Message { get; set; }
    public string Stacktrace { get; set; }
}
```

■ **Note** Log and ExceptionLog entities aren't inherited from IAuditTracker because we will not capture audit records for log entries.

Now we are going to write the business component methods for the Log and ExceptionLog entities. Create an ILogDataOperations interface in the Interfaces folder of the ASC.Business project, as shown in Listing 8-3.

Listing 8-3. ILogDataOperations interface

```
public interface ILogDataOperations
{
    Task CreateLogAsync(string category, string message);
    Task CreateExceptionLogAsync(string id, string message, string stacktrace);
}
```

We will create a LogDataOperations class that will implement the ILogDataOperations interface, as shown in Listing 8-4. LogDataOperations gets an instance of IUnitOfWork through dependency injection from the ASC.Web project. CreateExceptionLog will create an instance of the ExceptionLog entity based on the inputs and insert it into the ExceptionLog table of Azure Storage and commit the transaction. Similarly, CreateLog will insert the Log entity to the Log entity of Azure Storage.

Listing 8-4. LogDataOperations class

```
public class LogDataOperations : ILogDataOperations
{
private readonly IUnitOfWork _unitOfWork;
    public LogDataOperations(IUnitOfWork unitOfWork)
    {
        _unitOfWork = unitOfWork;
    }
    public async Task CreateExceptionLogAsync(string id, string message, string stacktrace)
    {
        using (_unitOfWork)
        {
            await _unitOfWork.Repository<ExceptionLog>().AddAsync(new ExceptionLog()
            {
                RowKey = id,
                PartitionKey = "Exception",
                Message = message,
                Stacktrace = stacktrace
            });

            _unitOfWork.CommitTransaction();
        }
    }
    public async Task CreateLogAsync(string category, string message)
    {
        using (_unitOfWork)
        {
            await _unitOfWork.Repository<Log>().AddAsync(new Log()
            {
                RowKey = Guid.NewGuid().ToString(),
                PartitionKey = category,
                Message = message
            });

            _unitOfWork.CommitTransaction();
        }
    }
}
```

Resolve the dependency of ILogDataOperations at the ASC.Web project, as shown in Listing 8-5.

Listing 8-5. Resolve the dependency of ILogDataOperations

```
services.AddScoped<ILogDataOperations, LogDataOperations>();
```

Now we will create the logger at the ASC.Web project to provide an interface for logging messages and exceptions. Create a folder with the name Logger in the ASC.Web project and create a class file named LogExtensions that will hold all log extension methods. Create the class AzureStorageLogger and implement ILogger of ASP.NET Core on the AzureStorageLogger class, as shown in Listing 8-6. We will use ILogger throughout the ASC.Web project to log messages and exceptions. AzureStorageLogger's constructor takes ILogDataOperations as one of its parameters, which it will use internally to persist log entries to Azure

Storage. The other parameters include the category name, which primarily holds the fully qualified method name that is creating the log entry, and a filter function to filter the log entries based on the category name and log level.

First we will focus on the Log method of the ILogger implementation. We use this method to check whether logging is enabled for a given log level and message category (which is in context of execution) by calling the IsEnabled method. This method simply executes the filter function that is passed in the filter parameter by passing the category name and log-level parameters. If logging is enabled for the given message, we will call ILogDataOperations' CreateLog or CreateExceptionLog method to perform actual storage logging.

The BeginScope method is used to group some log operations based on scope. We can attach the same data to each log that is created as part of the group. In the Automobile Service Center application, we do not have a requirement to group the log operations, so we simply return null in this method for now.

Listing 8-6. AzureStorageLogger class

```
public class AzureStorageLogger : ILogger
{
    private readonly string _categoryName;
    private readonly Func<string, LogLevel, bool> _filter;
    private readonly ILogDataOperations _logOperations;

    public AzureStorageLogger(string categoryName, Func<string, LogLevel, bool> filter,
    ILogDataOperations logOperations)
    {
        _categoryName = categoryName;
        _filter = filter;
        _logOperations = logOperations;
    }
    public IDisposable BeginScope<TState>(TState state)
    {
        return null;
    }

    public bool IsEnabled(LogLevel logLevel)
    {
        return (_filter == null || _filter(_categoryName, logLevel));
    }
    public void Log<TState>(LogLevel logLevel, EventId eventId, TState state, Exception
    exception, Func<TState, Exception, string> formatter)
    {
        if (!IsEnabled(logLevel))
            return;

        if (exception == null)
            _logOperations.CreateLogAsync(logLevel.ToString(), formatter(state, exception));
        else
            _logOperations.CreateExceptionLogAsync(eventId.Name, exception.Message,
            exception.StackTrace);
    }
}
```

We have to create the implementation of ILoggingProvider that is used to create the instance of ILogger types; in our case, this is the AzureStorageLogger type. AzureStorageLoggerProvider takes the filter function and ILogDataOperations as parameters to the constructor, which are eventually passed as parameters to the AzureStorageLogger instance. The CreateLogger method is used to create the instance of AzureStorageLogger, as shown in Listing 8-7.

Listing 8-7. AzureStorageLoggerProvider class

```
public class AzureStorageLoggerProvider : ILoggerProvider
{
    private readonly Func<string, LogLevel, bool> _filter;
    private readonly ILogDataOperations _logOperations;

    public AzureStorageLoggerProvider(Func<string, LogLevel, bool> filter,
    ILogDataOperations logOperations)
    {
        _logOperations = logOperations;
        _filter = filter;
    }

    public ILogger CreateLogger(string categoryName)
    {
        return new AzureStorageLogger(categoryName, _filter, _logOperations);
    }

    public void Dispose()
    {
    }
}
```

Finally, we will create an extension method to add AzureStorageLoggerProvider to the logger factory, as shown in Listing 8-8.

Listing 8-8. Extension method to add AzureStorageLoggerProvider to logger factory

```
public static class EmailLoggerExtensions
{
    public static ILoggerFactory AddAzureTableStorageLog(this ILoggerFactory factory,
    ILogDataOperations logOperations, Func<string, LogLevel, bool> filter = null)
    {
        factory.AddProvider(new AzureStorageLoggerProvider(filter, logOperations));
        return factory;
    }
}
```

■ **Note**   All the code from Listing 8-6 to Listing 8-8 is created in the same LogExtensions physical class file in the ASC.Web project.

To add the created AzureStorageLoggerProvider, we will call the AddAzureTableStorageLog method in the Configure method of the Startup class, as shown in Listing 8-9. The filter condition that we use will filter all log messages that are not generated from any of the namespaces that contain the word *Microsoft*, so that our log table will not be loaded up with messages generated by ASP.NET Core. Also, the same filter condition filters messages that fall under the Information log level and above.

■ **Note**   The default log levels and order of priority provided by ASP.NET Core are Trace = 0, Debug = 1, Information = 2, Warning = 3, Error = 4, Critical = 5, and None = 6.

Listing 8-9. Updated Configure method of Startup class with AddAzureTableStorageLog invocation

```
public async void Configure(IApplicationBuilder app,
    IHostingEnvironment env,
    ILoggerFactory loggerFactory,
    IIdentitySeed storageSeed,
    IMasterDataCacheOperations masterDataCacheOperations,
    ILogDataOperations logDataOperations,
    IUnitOfWork unitOfWork)
{
    //loggerFactory.AddConsole(Configuration.GetSection("Logging"));
    //loggerFactory.AddDebug();

    // Configure Azure Logger to log all events except the ones that are generated by
    // default by ASP.NET Core.
    loggerFactory.AddAzureTableStorageLog(logDataOperations,
        (categoryName, logLevel) => !categoryName.Contains("Microsoft") &&
        logLevel >= LogLevel.Information);

    if (env.IsDevelopment())
    {
        app.UseDeveloperExceptionPage();
        app.UseDatabaseErrorPage();
        app.UseBrowserLink();
    }
    else
    {
        app.UseExceptionHandler("/Home/Error");
    }

    app.UseSession();
    app.UseStaticFiles();
    app.UseIdentity();

    app.UseGoogleAuthentication(new GoogleOptions()
    {
        ClientId = Configuration["Google:Identity:ClientId"],
        ClientSecret = Configuration["Google:Identity:ClientSecret"]
    });
```

```
app.UseMvc(routes =>
{
    routes.MapRoute(
        name: "default",
        template: "{controller=Home}/{action=Index}/{id?}");
});

await storageSeed.Seed(app.ApplicationServices.GetService<UserManager<ApplicationUser>>(),
    app.ApplicationServices.GetService<RoleManager<IdentityRole>>(),
    app.ApplicationServices.GetService<IOptions<ApplicationSettings>>());

var models = Assembly.Load(new AssemblyName("ASC.Models")).GetTypes().Where(type =>
type.Namespace == "ASC.Models.Models");
    foreach (var model in models)
    {
        var repositoryInstance = Activator.CreateInstance(typeof(Repository<>).
        MakeGenericType(model), unitOfWork);
        MethodInfo method = typeof(Repository<>).MakeGenericType(model).
        GetMethod("CreateTableAsync");
        method.Invoke(repositoryInstance, new object[0]);
    }

    await masterDataCacheOperations.CreateMasterDataCacheAsync();
}
```

To use the logger that we created, change the account controller code as shown in Listing 8-10; we are injecting the logger into the constructor and associating it with the AccountController type.

Listing 8-10. Updated AccountController class with ILogger

```
private readonly UserManager<ApplicationUser> _userManager;
private readonly SignInManager<ApplicationUser> _signInManager;
private readonly IEmailSender _emailSender;
private readonly ISmsSender _smsSender;
private readonly string _externalCookieScheme;
private readonly ILogger<AccountController> _logger;

public AccountController(
    UserManager<ApplicationUser> userManager,
    SignInManager<ApplicationUser> signInManager,
    IOptions<IdentityCookieOptions> identityCookieOptions,
    IEmailSender emailSender,
    ISmsSender smsSender,
    ILogger<AccountController> logger)
{
    _userManager = userManager;
    _signInManager = signInManager;
    _externalCookieScheme = identityCookieOptions.Value.ExternalCookieAuthenticationScheme;
    _emailSender = emailSender;
    _smsSender = smsSender;
    _logger = logger;

}
```

By default, we have some log entries being made in `AccountController`, especially when users register into the system, log in to the system either from an external identity provider or through a username and password, or log out from the system. Sample code for logging normal information is shown in Listing 8-11.

Listing 8-11. LogInformation method usage

```
_logger.LogInformation(1, "User logged in.");
```

Run the application and log in to the system as the administrator and then log out. You should see the log messages shown in Figure 8-1.

	PartitionKey	RowKey	Timestamp	Message	IsDeleted	CreatedDate	UpdatedDate
	Information	c2837bd4-4202...	5/27/2017 7:44:...	User logged in.	False	5/27/2017 7:44:...	5/27/2017 7:44:53 AM
	Information	dd496d85-bc0c...	5/27/2017 7:44:...	User logged out.	False	5/27/2017 7:44:...	5/27/2017 7:44:55 AM

Log [Table] ⇥ ✕ AccountController.cs 🔒   LogExtensions.cs 🔒   LogDataOperations.cs 🔒   ILogDataOperations.cs 🔒

Enter a WCF Data Services filter to limit the entities returned

Figure 8-1. *Log entries created at Azure Table storage*

___

■ **Note**   We will test exception logging later in this chapter, when we implement global exception handling.

___

Capturing User Activity Through an Action Filter

Most modern web applications capture user activity on the site. Analyzing this data enables us to improve the user experience and provide better navigation and ease in operations. This data log also helps us find out what actions were performed by any user and when they were performed. We will implement this feature in our Automobile Service Center application through ASP.NET Core's Action filter.

Filters in ASP.NET Core MVC help us execute code for every request at a particular state in the request pipeline. There are five kinds of filters: authorization, resource, action, exception, and result filters.

As shown in Figure 8-2, *authorization filters* are used to determine whether the current user is authorized for the current request. These filters are executed first before any other filter. *Resource filters* are executed after the authorization filter. They can execute code before and after the rest of the filters. *Action filters* can run code immediately before and after an individual action method is called. *Exception filters* are used to handle unhandled exceptions at a global level. *Result filters* can run code immediately before and after the execution of individual action results.

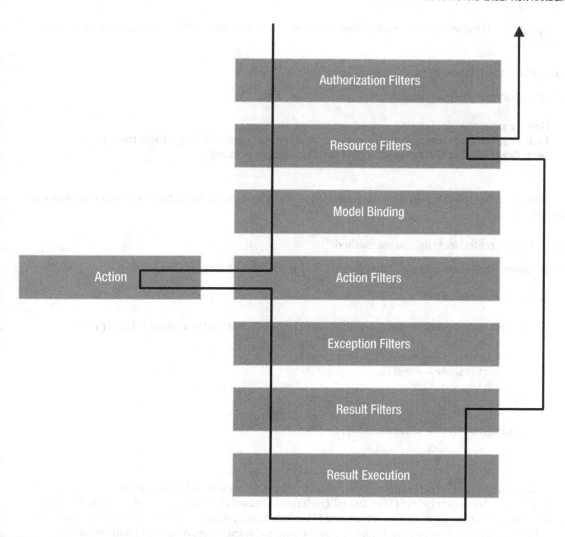

Figure 8-2. *Filter exececution flow*

First we will create a UserActivity entity in the ASC.Models project, as shown in Listing 8-12. The RowKey of the entity is going to be autogenerated by Guid, and the PartitionKey is going to be the e-mail of the user.

Listing 8-12. UserActivity entity

```
public class UserActivity : BaseEntity
{
    public UserActivity() { }
    public UserActivity(string email)
    {
        this.RowKey = Guid.NewGuid().ToString();
        this.PartitionKey = email;
    }
    public string Action { get; set; }
}
```

251

Update the ILogDataOperations interface to support the CreateUserActivity method, as shown in Listing 8-13.

Listing 8-13. Updated ILogDataOperations interface

```
public interface ILogDataOperations
{
    Task CreateLogAsync(string category, string message);
    Task CreateExceptionLogAsync(string id, string message, string stacktrace);
    Task CreateUserActivityAsync(string email, string action);
}
```

Update LogDataOperations with the implementation of the CreateUserActivity method, as shown in Listing 8-14.

Listing 8-14. CreateUserActivityAsync method

```
public async Task CreateUserActivityAsync(string email, string action)
{
    using (_unitOfWork)
    {
        await _unitOfWork.Repository<UserActivity>().AddAsync(new UserActivity()
        {
            RowKey = Guid.NewGuid().ToString(),
            PartitionKey = email,
            Action = action
        });

        _unitOfWork.CommitTransaction();
    }
}
```

Now we will create an action filter in the ASC.Web project. First create a folder named Filters and create a class with UserActivityFilter and inherit it from ActionFilterAttribute. We have to override the OnActionExecutionAsync method of ActionFilterAttribute, which is capable of executing the custom business logic asynchronously after the action method is executed. After the action execution, we will get an instance of ILogDataOperations from RequestServices of HttpContext and call the CreateUserActivityAsync method, which will create the user activity log at Azure Table storage, as shown in Listing 8-15.

Listing 8-15. UserActivityFilter class

```
public class UserActivityFilter : ActionFilterAttribute
{
    public override async Task OnActionExecutionAsync(ActionExecutingContext context,
    ActionExecutionDelegate next)
    {
        await next();
        var logger = context.HttpContext.RequestServices.GetService(typeof(ILogDataOperatio
        ns)) as ILogDataOperations;
```

```
    await logger.CreateUserActivityAsync(context.HttpContext.User.
    GetCurrentUserDetails().Email, context.HttpContext.Request.Path);
    }
}
```

As the final step, update the base controller with the UserActivityFilter attribute, as shown in Listing 8-16.

Listing 8-16. Update the base controller with the UserActivityFilter attribute

```
[Authorize]
[UserActivityFilter]
public class BaseController : Controller
{
}
```

■ **Note** We set up UserActivityFilter on BaseController because we want to capture the user activity only for secured pages.

Run the application and navigate to any of the secure pages. You should see user activity log messages, as shown in Figure 8-3.

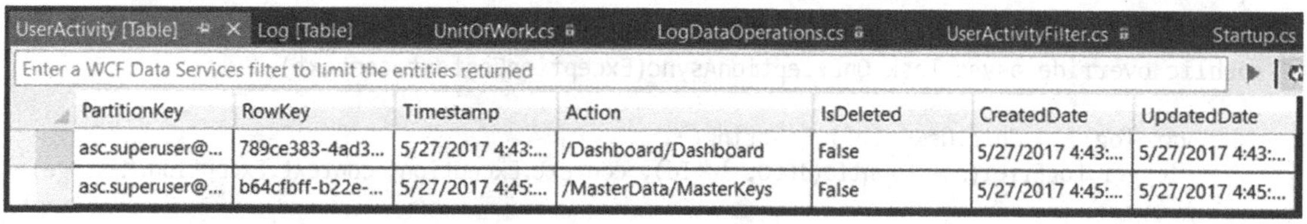

	PartitionKey	RowKey	Timestamp	Action	IsDeleted	CreatedDate	UpdatedDate
	asc.superuser@...	789ce383-4ad3...	5/27/2017 4:43:...	/Dashboard/Dashboard	False	5/27/2017 4:43:...	5/27/2017 4:43:...
	asc.superuser@...	b64cfbff-b22e-...	5/27/2017 4:45:...	/MasterData/MasterKeys	False	5/27/2017 4:45:...	5/27/2017 4:45:...

UserActivity [Table] ╪ ✕ Log [Table]   UnitOfWork.cs ☰   LogDataOperations.cs ☰   UserActivityFilter.cs ☰   Startup.cs
Enter a WCF Data Services filter to limit the entities returned   ▶ | ↻

Figure 8-3. *User activity entries in Azure Storage*

Implementing Global Exception Handling

In this section, we will develop a robust exception-handling mechanism for our Automobile Service Center application. By default, ASP.NET Core provides good exception-handling capabilities. We are going to extend that default framework to provide additional functionality that logs exceptions to Azure Table storage. We will handle all unhandled exceptions that occur in controller creation, model binding, action filters, action methods, or typically in an entire web project.

In ASP.NET Core, a developer exception page is configured by default in the Configure method of the Startup class, as shown in Listing 8-17. We can follow the same approach and handle exceptions in the / Home/Error controller action. But instead, we will create an exception filter and capture all exceptions. Comment out the highlighted lines shown in Listing 8-17.

Listing 8-17. Default exception handler in Configure method of Startup class

```
if (env.IsDevelopment())
{
    app.UseDeveloperExceptionPage();
    app.UseDatabaseErrorPage();
```

```
    app.UseBrowserLink();
}
else
{
    app.UseExceptionHandler("/Home/Error");
}
```

Create a class named CustomExceptionFilter in the Filters folder of the ASC.Web project. Inherit the class from ExceptionFilterAttribute, as shown in Listing 8-18. The ILogger instance is injected through the constructor that is used in the OnExceptionAsync method to log the exception details to Azure Table storage. Once an exception has been logged, a custom error view will be presented to the user. IModelMetadataProvider is also required to initiate ViewDataDictionary for the Error view.

Listing 8-18. CustomExceptionFilter class

```
public class CustomExceptionFilter : ExceptionFilterAttribute
{
    private readonly ILogger<CustomExceptionFilter> _logger;
    private readonly IModelMetadataProvider _modelMetadataProvider;
    public CustomExceptionFilter(ILogger<CustomExceptionFilter> logger,
    IModelMetadataProvider modelMetadataProvider)
    {
        _logger = logger;
        _modelMetadataProvider = modelMetadataProvider;
    }

    public override async Task OnExceptionAsync(ExceptionContext context)
    {
        var logId = Guid.NewGuid().ToString();
        _logger.LogError(new EventId(1000, logId), context.Exception, context.Exception.Message);

        var result = new ViewResult { ViewName = "CustomError" };
        result.ViewData = new ViewDataDictionary(_modelMetadataProvider, context.ModelState);
        result.ViewData.Add("ExceptionId", logId);
        context.Result = result;
    }
}
```

The CustomError view is a simple view, as shown in Listing 8-19. It checks whether the user is logged in. If the user is logged in, it uses _SecureLayout; otherwise, it uses _Layout to display a standard error message along with the ExceptionId.

Listing 8-19. CustomError view

```
@using Microsoft.AspNetCore.Http
@inject IHttpContextAccessor UserHttpContext
@{
    ViewData["Title"] = "Error";
    Layout = !UserHttpContext.HttpContext.User.Identity.IsAuthenticated ? "_layout" : "_
    SecureLayout";
}
```

```
<div class="row">
    <div class="col s12">
        <div class="card-panel orange lighten-1 margin-bottom-50px margin-top-50px">
            <span class="white-text">
                An error occurred while processing your request. Please contact customer
                service with following
                Ticket No. @ViewData["ExceptionId"]
            </span>
        </div>
    </div>
</div>
```

Now we need to add `CustomExceptionFilter` to the services collection in the `ConfigureServices` method of the `Startup` class, as shown in Listing 8-20.

Listing 8-20. Configure CustomExceptionFilter in Startup class

```
services.AddScoped<CustomExceptionFilter>();
```

■ **Note** Because `CustomExceptionFilter` is dependent on `ILogger`, we need to add `CustomExceptionFilter` to `IServiceCollection`.

Finally, add the filter to the filters collection in the `ConfigureServices` method of the `Startup` class, as shown in Listing 8-21.

Listing 8-21. Add CustomExceptionFilter to filters collection

```
services.AddMvc(o => { o.Filters.Add(typeof(CustomExceptionFilter)); })
        .AddJsonOptions(options => options.SerializerSettings.ContractResolver = new
DefaultContractResolver());
```

To test the exception logging, we will throw an exception in a `TestException` action in the `Dashboard` controller, as shown in Listing 8-22.

Listing 8-22. TestException action

```
public IActionResult TestException()
{
    var i = 0;
    // Should through Divide by zero error
    var j = 1 / i;
    return View();
}
```

Run the application, log in as an administrator, and navigate to /Dashboard/TestException. You should see the error page shown in Figure 8-4.

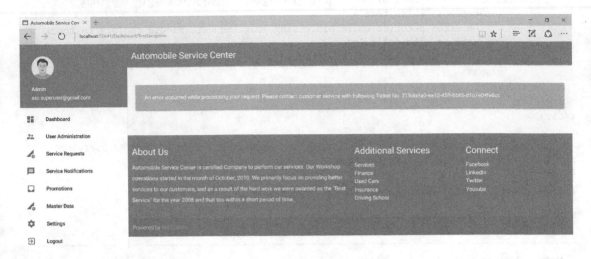

Figure 8-4. *Custom exception page*

Explore Azure Table storage for the ExceptionLog table. You should see exception log entries, as shown in Figure 8-5.

PartitionKey	RowKey	Timestamp	Message	Stacktrace	IsDeleted	CreatedDate	UpdatedDate
Exception	bb94177e-055e...	5/28/2017 7:20:...	Attempted to d...	at ASC.Web.Controller...	False	5/28/2017 7:20:...	5/28/2017 7:20:...

Figure 8-5. *Exception log entries in Azure Table storage*

■ **Note** We are not going to handle exceptions that occur in the Program and Startup classes. By default, when an exception occurs in these classes, the web host will exit and the application will not start. These exceptions should be identified as part of an initial sanity check that we perform immediately after the deployment.

Configuring Status Code Pages

Common problems for any web application are the requests sent for nonexistent pages or unauthorized modules. For such requests, the application should gracefully display an error page with standard information. ASP.NET Core provides built-in capabilities to handle error status responses such as 404 (Page Not Found). In this section, we will implement status code pages for our Automobile Service Center application.

First we will configure status code pages by using UseStatusCodePagesWithRedirects middleware in the Configure method of the Startup class, as shown in Listing 8-23. It will redirect to the home controller's Error action with the status code. The status code can be anywhere between 400 and 599.

Listing 8-23. Configure UseStatusCodePagesWithRedirects middleware

```
public async void Configure(IApplicationBuilder app,
    IHostingEnvironment env,
    ILoggerFactory loggerFactory,
    IIdentitySeed storageSeed,
    IMasterDataCacheOperations masterDataCacheOperations,
    ILogDataOperations logDataOperations,
    IUnitOfWork unitOfWork)
{
    // Configure Azure Logger to log all events except the ones that are generated by
    default by ASP.NET Core.
    loggerFactory.AddAzureTableStorageLog(logDataOperations,
        (categoryName, logLevel) => !categoryName.Contains("Microsoft") && logLevel >=
        LogLevel.Information);

    if (env.IsDevelopment())
    {
        // app.UseDeveloperExceptionPage();
        // app.UseDatabaseErrorPage();
         app.UseBrowserLink();
    }
    else
    {
        // app.UseExceptionHandler("/Home/Error");
    }

    app.UseStatusCodePagesWithRedirects("/Home/Error/{0}");
    app.UseSession();
    app.UseStaticFiles();
    app.UseIdentity();

    app.UseGoogleAuthentication(new GoogleOptions()
    {
        ClientId = Configuration["Google:Identity:ClientId"],
        ClientSecret = Configuration["Google:Identity:ClientSecret"]
    });

    app.UseMvc(routes =>
    {
        routes.MapRoute(
            name: "default",
            template: "{controller=Home}/{action=Index}/{id?}");
    });
```

```
await storageSeed.Seed(app.ApplicationServices.GetService<UserManager<ApplicationUser>>(),
    app.ApplicationServices.GetService<RoleManager<IdentityRole>>(),
    app.ApplicationServices.GetService<IOptions<ApplicationSettings>>());

var models = Assembly.Load(new AssemblyName("ASC.Models")).GetTypes().Where(type =>
type.Namespace == "ASC.Models.Models");
    foreach (var model in models)
    {

    var repositoryInstance = Activator.CreateInstance(typeof(Repository<>).
    MakeGenericType(model), unitOfWork);
    MethodInfo method = typeof(Repository<>).MakeGenericType(model).
    GetMethod("CreateTableAsync");
    method.Invoke(repositoryInstance, new object[0]);
    }

    await masterDataCacheOperations.CreateMasterDataCacheAsync();
}
```

The home controller's `Error` action is a simple action that will check for the status code and return an appropriate view, as shown in Listing 8-24.

Listing 8-24. Error action

```
public IActionResult Error(string id)
{
    if (id == "404")
        return View("NotFound");
    else
        return View();
}
```

■ **Note**   In Listing 8-24, we handled only the 404 status code. We can handle any other status codes similarly.

The Not Found view simply displays a standard message, as shown in Listing 8-25. It checks whether the user is logged in or anonymous, and then based on that, chooses an appropriate layout to render the view.

Listing 8-25. Not Found view

```
@using Microsoft.AspNetCore.Http
@inject IHttpContextAccessor UserHttpContext
@{
    ViewData["Title"] = "Error";
    Layout = !UserHttpContext.HttpContext.User.Identity.IsAuthenticated ? "_layout" :
    "_SecureLayout";
}

<div class="row">
    <div class="col s12">
        <div class="card-panel orange lighten-1 margin-bottom-50px margin-top-50px">
            <span class="white-text">
```

```
            Page not found.
        </span>
      </div>
    </div>
</div>
```

Run the application and go to any nonexistent URL. You should see an error page, as shown in Figure 8-6.

Figure 8-6. *Page Not Found error view*

■ **Note**   We are not going to log 404 status messages to Azure Table storage because these status codes can occur frequently, and this information has no business relevance.

For an authenticated user, you should see the page shown in Figure 8-7.

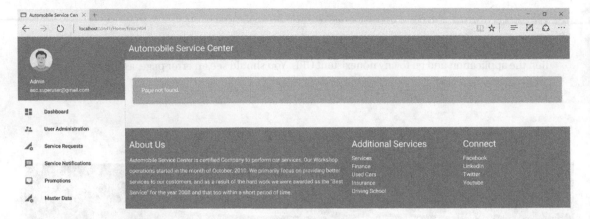

Figure 8-7. *Logged-in user Page Not Found error view*

In a similar way, we can get custom status code pages for a 401 Unauthorized Response. First, we need to make sure that Identity redirects to custom status code pages rather than to the default AccessDenied action; we need to make the code change to the Configure method of the Startup class, as shown in Listing 8-26.

Listing 8-26. Setting AutomaticChallenge to false

```
services.AddIdentity<ApplicationUser, IdentityRole>((options) =>
        {
                options.User.RequireUniqueEmail = true;
                options.Cookies.ApplicationCookie.AutomaticChallenge = false;
        })
```

Modify the Error action in the home controller to support unauthorized responses, as shown in Listing 8-27.

Listing 8-27. Updated Error action

```
public IActionResult Error(string id)
{
    if (id == "404")
        return View("NotFound");

    if (id == "401" && User.Identity.IsAuthenticated)
        return View("AccessDenied");
    else
        return RedirectToAction("Login", "Account");

        return View();
}
```

The Access Denied view is a simple view that displays a standard error message, as shown in Listing 8-28.

Listing 8-28. Access Denied view

```
@using Microsoft.AspNetCore.Http
@inject IHttpContextAccessor UserHttpContext
@{
    ViewData["Title"] = "Error";
    Layout = !UserHttpContext.HttpContext.User.Identity.IsAuthenticated ? "_layout" : "_
    SecureLayout";
}

<div class="row">
    <div class="col s12">
        <div class="card-panel orange lighten-1 margin-bottom-50px margin-top-50px">
            <span class="white-text">
                Access Denied.
            </span>
        </div>
    </div>
</div>
```

Run the application and log in as a customer. Try to access any secure page that is available only to the admin user. You should see the Access Denied screen shown in Figure 8-8.

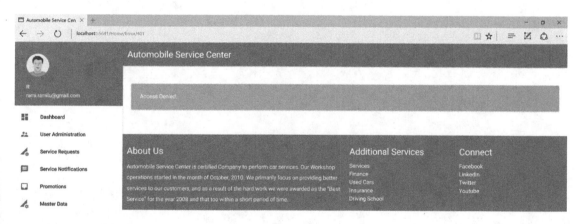

Figure 8-8. *Access Denied error view*

■ **Note**   After the preceding change, when an anonymous user tries to access an authorized page, the program will redirect him to the Login view. The user needs to submit his credentials to navigate to the dashboard.

Summary

You started this chapter by learning about the importance of logging and exception handling for any software application. Both exception-handling and logging frameworks make an application more robust, secure, and user-friendly by providing the required diagnostic and debugging information.

You proceeded to create a logging framework for our Automobile Service Center application by leveraging ASP.NET Core's default logging features. The logging framework takes an implementation of the Azure Storage repository as a dependency and uses it to store various types of logs to Azure Storage. The logging framework is configured in the Startup class and has been tested with the default log entries in the account controller.

You started off with user activity logging functionality by learning about the types of ASP.NET Core's action filters. Then you created a new Azure Storage entity and implemented the storage persistence method that is used to store user activity logs to Azure Storage. Finally, you created an action filter to log each and every URL requested by users, through a storage persistence method created earlier.

Exception handling for the Automobile Service Center is achieved through an Exception filter that displays a standard error page to end users with a unique ExceptionId. Later we configured status code pages through which any response status code between 400 and 599 can be handled by a custom action. For the Automobile Service Center application, we handled 404 Not Found and 401 Access Denied status codes and displayed their respective custom error pages.

CHAPTER 9

■ ■ ■

Creating Areas and Navigation by Using View Components

Often the development of web applications starts at a slow pace, with limited functionalities and fixed deliverables. But over the course of time, the complexity of technical components increases as more and more functional requirements arise and integration is needed between modules. With this ever-growing code, along with its complexity, projects can suffer from issues of code maintainability and version control. It is a recommended practice to have proper code structure and segregation of functionalities and technical components throughout the entire code base.

ASP.NET MVC *areas* are used to organize code based on related functionalities into different physical folders and namespaces. In an area, all logical components (such as the model, controller, and view) are kept in different folders, and the same namespace is used for all the related components. For our Automobile Service Center application, we are going to create separate areas for user account management, service requests, and configuration-related pages.

After the application code is segregated into different areas, the next biggest challenge for any application is to provide easy and seamless navigation throughout the site. The complexity in providing a good navigation flow is directly proportional to the user roles that are supported by the system, along with the overall functionalities (modules and submodules). In this chapter, we will develop a reusable navigational component for the Automobile Service Center's secure pages by using ASP.NET Core's view components.

ASP.NET Core has good support for bundling and minification, which are used to improve the page-load performance of a web application. *Bundling* combines multiple files into a single file, whereas *minification* performs optimizations on JS and CSS scripts. In this chapter, we will enable bundling and minification optimizations for the Automobile Service Center.

■ **Note** My main intention in this chapter is to show you how to handle project structure changes in the middle of development. Typically, areas should be implemented at the architectural design phase. I delayed our implementation of areas specifically to demonstrate design changes at the time of development.

© Rami Vemula 2017

R. Vemula, *Real-Time Web Application Development*, https://doi.org/10.1007/978-1-4842-3270-5_9

Implementing Areas for the Automobile Service Center Application

In this section, we will segregate the code of our Automobile Service Center application by using ASP.NET Core's areas feature. We will categorize the entire application code into the following modules:

- *User Account Management*: This module will hold all the code artifacts related to Automobile Service Center users such as service engineers.

- *Service Requests*: This module will hold all the code related to managing service requests, and communication between customers and service engineers.

- *Configuration*: All the screens related to configuration (for example, MasterData) will be held in this module.

Areas are primarily used for code segregation, but at the same time we should be careful about duplicating code to achieve proper segregation. For example, the error controller is common to all modules, so the ideal place for this controller and its associated views is still the common Controllers and Views folder. Following are the key points to remember while creating areas for our Automobile Service Center application:

- Anonymous pages and common user authentication pages (such as Login and Reset Password) are not included in areas.

- Common types (for example, view models related to user account management) are not included in areas.

- Base and anonymous controllers are exempted from areas.

- Shared views across modules are not included in areas.

- The Service Requests module will be developed in Chapters 10 and 11.

Create a new folder named Areas and then create three subfolders inside Areas that are named for the modules: Accounts, ServiceRequests, and Configuration. Create Controllers, **Models** and Views folders in all the modules, as shown in Figure 9-1.

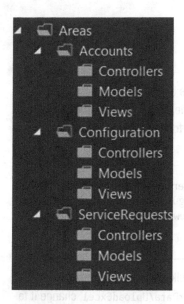

Figure 9-1. The areas folder structure for the Automobile Service Center application

---

■ **Note** In the Automobile Service Center application, we are not using Manage Controller and its related views and models. Delete the controller and its related artifacts.

Remove the ManageViewModels reference from the _ViewImports.cshtml file.

First, we will focus on the Configuration module. Cut and paste the MasterData controller to the Controllers subfolder under the Configuration area. Change the namespace as shown in Listing 9-1.

Listing 9-1. Configuration namespace

```
namespace ASC.Web.Areas.Configuration.Controllers
```

Decorate MasterDataController with the Area attribute, as shown in Listing 9-2.

Listing 9-2. Area attribute for configuration module

```
[Area("Configuration")]
[Authorize(Roles = "Admin")]
public class MasterDataController : BaseController
```

Make sure to copy the MasterData view models (including MappingProfile) to the Models folder of the Configuration area, and change the namespace for all master data models, as shown in Listing 9-3.

Listing 9-3. Configuration models namespace

```
namespace ASC.Web.Areas.Configuration.Models
```

■ **Note**   While moving the code, we will have to resolve certain dependencies by including using statements, or in some cases, removing old using statements. Resolving these dependencies is not detailed in this book. Most of the dependencies can be resolved by pressing the Ctrl+period (.) shortcut and then selecting the appropriate resolution.

Move the MasterData controller views from the Views/MasterData folder to the Configuration/Views folder. Make sure to change the fully qualified name (ASC.Web.Areas.Configuration.Models) of the model in each view to reflect the new namespace changes of the models. Copy _ViewImports.cshtml to the root of the Configuration/Views folder.

■ **Note**   One change is required in the MasterValues view, where we are bulk-uploading the data by using a Microsoft Excel file. Instead of having the URL hard-coded like /MasterData/UploadExcel, change it to @Url.Action("UploadExcel", "MasterData").

Before we make routing changes, build the entire ASC.Web project to make sure no compile errors are present.

We need to include areas in the route template in the Configure method of the Startup class, as shown in Listing 9-4. Here, a new route has been created to hold the area name in the route if it exists.

Listing 9-4. Routes configuration

```
app.UseMvc(routes =>
{
    routes.MapRoute(name: "areaRoute",
        template: "{area:exists}/{controller=Home}/{action=Index}");

    routes.MapRoute(
        name: "default",
        template: "{controller=Home}/{action=Index}/{id?}");
});
```

The folder structure should look like Figure 9-2.

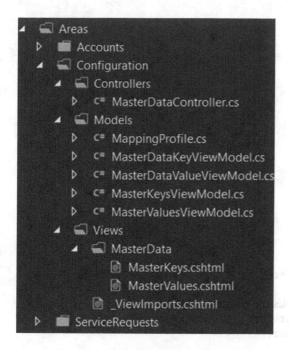

Figure 9-2. *The Configuration area's folder structure*

Run the application. You should see the home page as usual, without any errors.

Now we will move the code artifacts related to service engineers and customers to the Accounts module. Move the `ProfileViewModel`, `CustomerRegistrationViewModel`, `CustomersViewModel`, `ServiceEngineerRegistrationViewModel`, and `ServiceEngineerViewModel` models from the `Models/AccountViewModels` folder to the `Areas/Accounts/Models` folder. Change the namespace of the models as shown in Listing 9-5.

Listing 9-5. Accounts namespace

```
namespace ASC.Web.Areas.Accounts.Models
```

Create a new controller named `AccountController` in the `Accounts/Controllers` folder. Decorate the controller with the Area attribute and pass the relevant area name (in this case, it is `Account`). Inject the dependencies (for example, of `UserManager`) as shown in Listing 9-6.

Extract all the actions related to the profile, customers, and service engineers from the old account controller and place them in the newly created controller.

■ **Note**   The account controller that is present from the start of the application will be used for generic functionalities such as logging in, logging out, and resetting a password. The newly created account controller will be used to perform actions on customers, service engineers, and the profile.

Listing 9-6. Account module controller

```
using ASC.Models.BaseTypes;
using ASC.Utilities;
using ASC.Web.Areas.Accounts.Models;
using ASC.Web.Controllers;
using ASC.Web.Models;
using ASC.Web.Services;
using Microsoft.AspNetCore.Authorization;
using Microsoft.AspNetCore.Identity;
using Microsoft.AspNetCore.Mvc;
using Microsoft.Extensions.Options;
using System.Collections.Generic;
using System.Linq;
using System.Threading.Tasks;

namespace ASC.Web.Areas.Accounts.Controllers
{
    [Authorize]
    [Area("Account")]
    public class AccountController: BaseController
    {
        private readonly UserManager<ApplicationUser> _userManager;
        private readonly SignInManager<ApplicationUser> _signInManager;
        private readonly IEmailSender _emailSender;

        public AccountController(
            UserManager<ApplicationUser> userManager,
            SignInManager<ApplicationUser> signInManager,
            IOptions<IdentityCookieOptions> identityCookieOptions,
            IEmailSender emailSender)
        {
            _userManager = userManager;
            _signInManager = signInManager;
            _emailSender = emailSender;
        }

        [HttpGet]
        [Authorize(Roles = "Admin")]
        public async Task<IActionResult> ServiceEngineers()
        {
            // Code removed for brevity. This is moved from the other AccountController.
        }

        [HttpPost]
        [ValidateAntiForgeryToken]
        [Authorize(Roles = "Admin")]
        public async Task<IActionResult> ServiceEngineers(ServiceEngineerViewModel serviceEngineer)
        {
            // Code removed for brevity. This is moved from the other AccountController.
        }
```

```
[HttpGet]
[Authorize(Roles = "Admin")]
public async Task<IActionResult> Customers()
{
    // Code removed for brevity. This is moved from the other AccountController.
}

[HttpPost]
[ValidateAntiForgeryToken]
[Authorize(Roles = "Admin")]
public async Task<IActionResult> Customers(CustomersViewModel customer)
{
    // Code removed for brevity. This is moved from the other AccountController.
}

[HttpGet]
public async Task<IActionResult> Profile()
{
// Code removed for brevity. This is moved from the other AccountController.
}

[HttpPost]
[ValidateAntiForgeryToken]
public async Task<IActionResult> Profile(ProfileViewModel profile)
{
    // Code removed for brevity. This is moved from the other AccountController.
}

private void AddErrors(IdentityResult result)
{
    // Code removed for brevity. This is moved from the other AccountController.
}
    }
}
```

Create an Accounts folder under the Accounts/Views folder. Copy the Profile, Customers, and Service Engineers views from the normal Views folder to the Accounts/Views/Account folder. Change the namespace of the model to ASC.Web.Areas.Accounts.Models. Copy _ViewImports.cshtml to the root of the Accounts/Views folder. The Accounts area should look like in Figure 9-3.

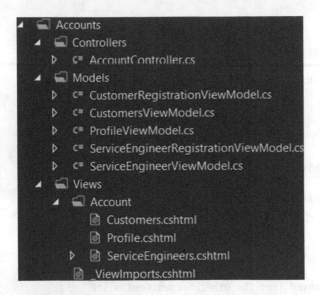

Figure 9-3. *The Accounts area's folder structure*

Finally, we will move code related to the dashboard to the ServiceRequests module. We have to move the dashboard controller to the ServiceRequests/Controllers folder. Decorate the controller with the Area attribute and pass the relevant area name (in this case, it is ServiceRequests). Change the namespace on the dashboard controller as shown in Listing 9-7.

Listing 9-7. ServiceRequests namespace

```
namespace ASC.Web.Areas.ServiceRequests.Controllers
```

Move the Dashboard view from the Views/Dashboard folder to the ServiceRequests/Views/Dashboard folder. Copy _ViewImports.cshtml to the root of the ServiceRequests /Views folder. The ServiceRequests area should look like Figure 9-4.

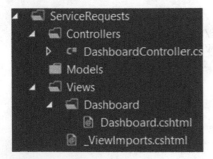

Figure 9-4. *The ServiceRequests area's folder structure*

As we have moved Dashboard to the ServiceRequests area, we need to handle the redirections to this action from different controllers by including the area in the route. Open both account controllers and find all the places where a request is redirected to the Dashboard action of the Dashboard controller and replace it with code shown in Listing 9-8.

Listing 9-8. Redirect to Dashboard action

```
return RedirectToAction("Dashboard", "Dashboard", new { Area = "ServiceRequests" });
```

The last change that we need to make is to fix the broken links in the left navigation bar by including the area in the anchor tags, as shown in Listing 9-9.

Listing 9-9. Updated left navigation by including Areas

```
<ul id="nav-mobile" class="side-nav fixed">
    <li>
        <div class="userView">
            <div class="background blue-grey lighten-1"></div>
            <a href="#!user"><img class="circle" src="~/images/male.png"></a>
            <a href="#!name"><span class="white-text name">@currentUser.Name</span></a>
            <a href="#!email"><span class="white-text email">@currentUser.Email</span></a>
        </div>
    </li>
    <li>
        <a asp-area="ServiceRequests" asp-controller="Dashboard" asp-action="Dashboard"
        class="collapsible-header"><i class="material-icons">dashboard</i>Dashboard</a>
    </li>
    <li>
        <ul class="collapsible collapsible-accordion">
            <li>
                <a class="collapsible-header">User Administration<i class="material-
                icons">supervisor_account</i></a>
                <div class="collapsible-body">
                    <ul>
                        <li><a asp-area="Accounts" asp-controller="Account" asp-
                        action="Customers">Customers<i class="material-icons">
                        account_box</i></a></li>
                        <li><a asp-area="Accounts" asp-controller="Account" asp-action="
                        ServiceEngineers">Service Engineers<i class="material-icons">
                        person_add</i></a></li>
                    </ul>
                </div>
            </li>
        </ul>
    </li>
    <li><a class="collapsible-header" href="#!"><i class="material-icons">perm_data_
    setting</i>Service Requests</a></li>
    <li><a class="collapsible-header" href="#!"><i class="material-icons">message</i>
    Service Notifications</a></li>
    <li><a class="collapsible-header" href="#!"><i class="material-icons">inbox</i>
    Promotions</a></li>
    <li>
        <ul class="collapsible collapsible-accordion">
```

271

```
        <li>
            <a class="collapsible-header">Master Data<i class="material-icons">
            perm_data_setting</i></a>
            <div class="collapsible-body">
                <ul>
                    <li><a asp-area="Configuration" asp-controller="MasterData"
                    asp-action="MasterKeys" class="collapsible-header">Master Keys
                    <i class="material-icons">data_usage</i></a></li>
                    <li><a asp-area="Configuration" asp-controller="MasterData"
                    asp-action="MasterValues" class="collapsible-header">Master Values
                    <i class="material-icons">settings_system_daydream</i></a></li>
                </ul>
            </div>
        </li>
    </ul>
</li>
<li>
    <ul class="collapsible collapsible-accordion">
        <li>
            <a class="collapsible-header">Settings<i class="material-icons">settings</
            i></a>
            <div class="collapsible-body">
                <ul>
                    <li><a asp-area="Accounts" asp-controller="Account" asp-action="Profile"
                    class="collapsible-header">Profile<i class="material-icons">
                    system_update_alt</i></a></li>
                    <li><a class="collapsible-header" href="#!"
                    id="ancrResetPassword">Reset Password<i class="material-icons">
                    lock_outline</i></a></li>
                </ul>
            </div>
        </li>
    </ul>
</li>
<li><a class="collapsible-header" href="#!" id="ancrLogout"><i class="material-
icons">exit_to_app</i>Logout</a></li>
</ul>
```

The Logout and Reset Password form tags are broken and need to be fixed as part of upgrading the areas. Open _SecureLayout.cshtml and update the form tags as shown in Listing 9-10.

Listing 9-10. Areas configuration in logout and reset password form tags

```
<form class="hide" method="post" id="logout_form" asp-area="" asp-controller="Account" asp-
action="Logout">
    <input type="submit" value="Logout" />
</form>

<form class="hide" method="post" id="resetPassword_form" asp-area="" asp-
controller="Account" asp-action="InitiateResetPassword">
</form>
```

Run the application and test all the functionalities that we have developed so far. Everything should work seamlessly, without errors.

Creating a Dynamic JSON-Driven Navigation Menu

In this section, we will create a dynamic left navigation menu for our Automobile Service Center application. So far, we have used a static left menu that has predefined menu items in _SecureLayout.cshtml. Although this approach works fine for small applications with a few pages, it won't work for larger applications because of the complex navigation requirements based on the roles of logged-in users.

For our Automobile Service Center application, we have modules such as Master Data and User Administration that are supposed to be accessible only to the admin user. Users with roles other than Admin should not be able to view those modules in navigation. We will use ASP.NET Core's view components feature to build a dynamic left navigation menu that supports user access levels. We will use a JSON file to hold all the configuration of menu items with user access mappings.

First, you'll learn about view components in ASP.NET Core. These components are primarily used to achieve reusable view code by leveraging the principle of separation of concerns. View components can be considered traditional ASP.NET MVC partial views, but these have overwhelming advantages in terms of data binding and testability features. The following are the key features of view components:

- View components can have their own business logic and parameters.

- These are not dependent on model binding, but only on the data that we pass to them.

- They can be easily testable.

- View components can render as chunks rather than as a whole response.

We will create a Navigation.json file (by using any text editor), as shown in Listing 9-11. Then we'll create a folder named Navigation in the ASC.Web project and place the Navigation.json file in it.

■ **Note**   We will use the ASC.Web project navigation folder to house the configuration of the JSON navigation menu items. But we will use the ASC.Utilities project to hold all navigation-related code artifacts. This way, it will be easy to share and reuse code across multiple projects. In addition, if we want to update any navigation menu items in the future, we can simply edit the Navigation.json file, and the changes will be reflected automatically on the web interface.

Listing 9-11. Navigation.json file

```
{
  "MenuItems": [
    {
      "DisplayName": "Dashboard",
      "MaterialIcon": "dashboard",
      "Link": "/ServiceRequests/Dashboard/Dashboard",
      "IsNested": false,
      "Sequence": 1,
      "UserRoles": [ "User", "Engineer", "Admin" ],
      "NestedItems": []
    },
```

```
{
    "DisplayName": "User Administration",
    "MaterialIcon": "supervisor_account",
    "Link": "",
    "IsNested": true,
    "Sequence": 2,
    "UserRoles": [ "Admin" ],
    "NestedItems": [
        {
            "DisplayName": "Customers",
            "MaterialIcon": "account_box",
            "Link": "/Accounts/Account/Customers",
            "IsNested": false,
            "Sequence": 1,
            "UserRoles": [ "Admin" ],
            "NestedItems": []
        },
        {
            "DisplayName": "Service Engineers",
            "MaterialIcon": "person_add",
            "Link": "/Accounts/Account/ServiceEngineers",
            "IsNested": false,
            "Sequence": 2,
            "UserRoles": [ "Admin" ],
            "NestedItems": []
        }
    ]
},
{
    "DisplayName": "Service Requests",
    "MaterialIcon": "perm_data_setting",
    "Link": "/ServiceRequests/Dashboard/Dashboard",
    "IsNested": false,
    "Sequence": 3,
    "UserRoles": [ "User", "Engineer", "Admin" ],
    "NestedItems": []
},
{
    "DisplayName": "Service Notifications",
    "MaterialIcon": "message",
    "Link": "/ServiceRequests/Dashboard/Dashboard",
    "IsNested": false,
    "Sequence": 4,
    "UserRoles": [ "User", "Engineer", "Admin" ],
    "NestedItems": []
},
{
    "DisplayName": "Promotions",
    "MaterialIcon": "inbox",
    "Link": "/ServiceRequests/Dashboard/Dashboard",
    "IsNested": false,
```

```
    "Sequence": 5,
    "UserRoles": [ "User", "Engineer", "Admin" ],
    "NestedItems": []
},
{
    "DisplayName": "Master Data",
    "MaterialIcon": "perm_data_setting",
    "Link": "",
    "IsNested": true,
    "Sequence": 6,
    "UserRoles": [ "Admin" ],
    "NestedItems": [
      {
        "DisplayName": "Master Keys",
        "MaterialIcon": "data_usage",
        "Link": "/Configuration/MasterData/MasterKeys",
        "IsNested": false,
        "Sequence": 1,
        "UserRoles": [ "Admin" ],
        "NestedItems": []
      },
      {
        "DisplayName": "Master Values",
        "MaterialIcon": "settings_system_daydream",
        "Link": "/Configuration/MasterData/MasterValues",
        "IsNested": false,
        "Sequence": 2,
        "UserRoles": [ "Admin" ],
        "NestedItems": []
      }
    ]
},
{
    "DisplayName": "Settings",
    "MaterialIcon": "settings",
    "Link": "",
    "IsNested": true,
    "Sequence": 7,
    "UserRoles": [ "User", "Engineer", "Admin" ],
    "NestedItems": [
      {
        "DisplayName": "Profile",
        "MaterialIcon": "system_update_alt",
        "Link": "/Accounts/Account/Profile",
        "IsNested": false,
        "Sequence": 1,
        "UserRoles": [ "User", "Engineer", "Admin" ],
        "NestedItems": []
      },
```

```json
      {
        "DisplayName": "Reset Password",
        "MaterialIcon": "lock_outline",
        "Link": "#!",
        "IsNested": false,
        "Sequence": 2,
        "UserRoles": [ "User", "Engineer", "Admin" ],
        "NestedItems": []
      }
    ]
  },
  {
    "DisplayName": "Logout",
    "MaterialIcon": "exit_to_app",
    "Link": "#!",
    "IsNested": false,
    "Sequence": 8,
    "UserRoles": [ "User", "Engineer", "Admin" ],
    "NestedItems": []
  }
  ]
}
```

The content of Navigation.json will hold all the menu items and the associated information. Each navigation menu item has the following properties:

- DisplayName: Text that needs to be displayed on the user interface.

- MaterialIcon: Icon from Material Design that needs to be displayed along with the display name.

- Link: URL to which the menu item should be redirected.

- IsNested: This property indicates whether the current menu item has child menu items. In the processing logic that we are going to come up with, if any menu item has child menu items, then the URL link of the parent will be ignored.

- Sequence: The display sequence of the menu items in the entire menu.

- UserRoles: User roles that are allowed to view the current menu item.

- NestedItems: If IsNested is True, the child navigation menu items will be stored in this array. Each child navigation item will share the same structure as any top-level menu item.

Ensure that you set the Content of the output directory to Copy Always for the Navigation.json file properties (right-click the file in Visual Studio and select Properties), as shown in Figure 9-5.

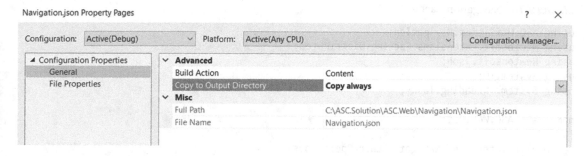

Figure 9-5. *Setting the Content option to Copy Always for the Navigation.json file*

Create a new folder named Navigation in the ASC.Utilities project. Create a new class named NavigationModels in this Navigation folder. We will create a NavigationMenuItem class that resembles the JSON structure, as shown in Listing 9-12. The NavigationMenu class will hold a list of NavigationMenuItem instances.

Listing 9-12. Navigation models

```
using System.Collections.Generic;

namespace ASC.Utilities.Navigation
{
    public class NavigationMenu
    {
        public List<NavigationMenuItem> MenuItems { get; set; }
    }

    public class NavigationMenuItem
    {
        public string DisplayName { get; set; }
        public string MaterialIcon { get; set; }
        public string Link { get; set; }
        public bool IsNested { get; set; }
        public int Sequence { get; set; }
        public List<string> UserRoles { get; set; }
        public List<NavigationMenuItem> NestedItems { get; set; }
    }
}
```

Now in the ASC.Web project, we will create the INavigationCacheOperations interface and its associated implementation, as shown in Listing 9-13. On initial startup of the application, we will call the CreateNavigationCacheAsync method to get the Navigation.json string and store it in a Redis cache. Then, on page-to-page navigation, instead of reading the navigation configuration from the JSON file again and again, we will get the JSON string from the Redis cache, deserialize it, and consume it in the menu view component (which we are going to create).

Listing 9-13. Navigation Cache

```
using ASC.Utilities.Navigation;
using Microsoft.Extensions.Caching.Distributed;
using Newtonsoft.Json;
using System.IO;
using System.Threading.Tasks;

namespace ASC.Web.Data
{
    public interface INavigationCacheOperations
    {
        Task<NavigationMenu> GetNavigationCacheAsync();
        Task CreateNavigationCacheAsync();
    }

    public class NavigationCacheOperations : INavigationCacheOperations
    {
        private readonly IDistributedCache _cache;
        private readonly string NavigationCacheName = "NavigationCache";
        public NavigationCacheOperations(IDistributedCache cache)
        {
            _cache = cache;
        }

        public async Task CreateNavigationCacheAsync()
        {
            await _cache.SetStringAsync(NavigationCacheName, File.ReadAllText("Navigation/
            Navigation.json"));
        }

        public async Task<NavigationMenu> GetNavigationCacheAsync()
        {
            return JsonConvert.DeserializeObject<NavigationMenu>(await _cache.GetStringAsync
            (NavigationCacheName));
        }
    }
}
```

Resolve the INavigationCacheOperations dependency in the ConfigureServices method of the Startup class, as shown in Listing 9-14.

Listing 9-14. Resolve the dependency of INavigationCacheOperations

```
services.AddSingleton<INavigationCacheOperations, NavigationCacheOperations>();
```

We will call the CreateNavigationCacheAsync method from the Configure method of the Startup class, as shown in Listing 9-15.

Listing 9-15. Create Navigation cache in Startup class

```
public async void Configure(IApplicationBuilder app,
    IHostingEnvironment env,
    ILoggerFactory loggerFactory,
    IIdentitySeed storageSeed,
    IMasterDataCacheOperations masterDataCacheOperations,
    ILogDataOperations logDataOperations,
    INavigationCacheOperations navigationCacheOperations,
    IUnitOfWork unitOfWork)
{
    loggerFactory.AddConsole();
    // Configure Azure Logger to log all events except the ones that are generated by
    default by ASP.NET Core.
    loggerFactory.AddAzureTableStorageLog(logDataOperations,
        (categoryName, logLevel) => !categoryName.Contains("Microsoft") && logLevel >=
        LogLevel.Information);

    if (env.IsDevelopment())
    {
        // app.UseDeveloperExceptionPage();
        // app.UseDatabaseErrorPage();
         app.UseBrowserLink();
    }
    else
    {
        // app.UseExceptionHandler("/Home/Error");
    }

    app.UseStatusCodePagesWithRedirects("/Home/Error/{0}");
    app.UseSession();
    app.UseStaticFiles();
    app.UseIdentity();

    app.UseGoogleAuthentication(new GoogleOptions()
    {
        ClientId = Configuration["Google:Identity:ClientId"],
        ClientSecret = Configuration["Google:Identity:ClientSecret"]
    });

    app.UseMvc(routes =>
    {
        routes.MapRoute(name: "areaRoute",
            template: "{area:exists}/{controller=Home}/{action=Index}");
        routes.MapRoute(
    name: "default",
            template: "{controller=Home}/{action=Index}/{id?}");
    });
```

```
await storageSeed.Seed(app.ApplicationServices.GetService<UserManager<ApplicationUser>>(),
    app.ApplicationServices.GetService<RoleManager<IdentityRole>>(),
    app.ApplicationServices.GetService<IOptions<ApplicationSettings>>());

var models = Assembly.Load(new AssemblyName("ASC.Models")).GetTypes().Where(type =>
type.Namespace == "ASC.Models.Models");
foreach (var model in models)
{
    var repositoryInstance = Activator.CreateInstance(typeof(Repository<>).
    MakeGenericType(model), unitOfWork);
    MethodInfo method = typeof(Repository<>).MakeGenericType(model).
    GetMethod("CreateTableAsync");
    method.Invoke(repositoryInstance, new object[0]);
}

await masterDataCacheOperations.CreateMasterDataCacheAsync();

await navigationCacheOperations.CreateNavigationCacheAsync();
}
```

Now we will start building the navigation view component. To get started, we need to install the Microsoft.AspNetCore.Mvc NuGet package to the ASC.Utilities project, as shown in Figure 9-6.

Figure 9-6. *Installing the Microsoft.AspNetCore.Mvc NuGet package to the ASC.Utilities project*

Create a class named LeftNavigationViewComponent under the Navigation folder of the ASC. Utilities project, as shown in Listing 9-16. This class will be inherited for ASP.NET Core's ViewComponent class, which is used to create view components. ViewComponent uses the Invoke method to process business logic; in our case, this method accepts a NavigationMenu instance and returns a view corresponding to left navigation by sorting the menu items in ascending order. ASC.Utilities.Navigation.LeftNavigation is used as a unique name for the left navigation view component.

Listing 9-16. Left Navigation view component

```
using Microsoft.AspNetCore.Mvc;
using System.Linq;

namespace ASC.Utilities.Navigation
{
    [ViewComponent(Name = "ASC.Utilities.Navigation.LeftNavigation")]
    public class LeftNavigationViewComponent : ViewComponent
    {
```

```
public IViewComponentResult Invoke(NavigationMenu menu)
{
    menu.MenuItems = menu.MenuItems.OrderBy(p => p.Sequence).ToList();
    return View(menu);
}
    }
}
```

We have to create a view named Default.cshtml in the ASC.Utilities project under Views/Shared/Components/LeftNavigation, as shown in Figure 9-7. As the project type is a class library, we do not have the option to add cshtml to the project; we have to create a physical file with the cshtml extension and include it in the project.

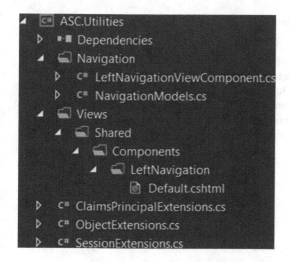

Figure 9-7. *The Default.cshtml file in the ASC.Utilities project*

Default.cshtml will be used by LeftNavigation to render the left navigation menu items.

■ **Note** As ASC.Utilities is a class library project, by default we will not get IntelliSense for Razor views. As per Microsoft, this feature is supported only from Visual Studio 2017 Update 3 Preview 2 (https://github. com/aspnet/Razor/issues/1136). We have to carefully construct the view without any errors.

Include `Default.cshtml` as an embedded resource in the `ASC.Utilities` project, as shown in Figure 9-8, so that the `ASC.Web` project can consume the left navigation view component and its associated view.

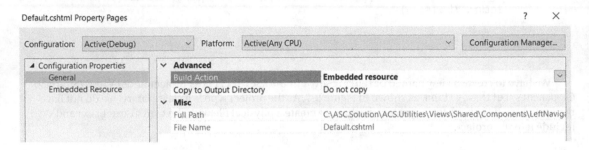

Figure 9-8. Including Default.cshtml as an embedded resource

The HTML of `Default.cshtml` is straightforward, as shown in Listing 9-17. We will iterate each menu item and check whether the logged-in user role is eligible to view the menu item. If it is not, we will go to processing the next menu item. For each menu item, if it has nested submenu items, then we will display an unordered list of parent menu items and insert the submenu items as anchors in the respective list item (only after checking for user access). If the menu item is not nested, we will render a list item with the anchor tag. To identify each menu item differently, we will give a different ID to anchor tags based on the display name.

Listing 9-17. Left Navigation menu HTML

```
@using Microsoft.AspNetCore.Http
@using ASC.Utilities
@model ASC.Utilities.Navigation.NavigationMenu
@inject IHttpContextAccessor UserHttpContext
@{
    var currentUser = UserHttpContext.HttpContext.User.GetCurrentUserDetails();
}
@foreach (var menuItem in Model.MenuItems)
{
    if (currentUser.Roles.Intersect(menuItem.UserRoles).Any())
    {
        if (menuItem.IsNested)
        {
            <li>
                <ul class="collapsible collapsible-accordion">
                    <li>
                        <a class="collapsible-header" id="@string.Format("ancr{0}",
                        menuItem.DisplayName.Replace(" ",""))">@menuItem.DisplayName<i
                        class="material-icons">@menuItem.MaterialIcon</i></a>
                        <div class="collapsible-body">
                            <ul>
                                @foreach (var subMenuItem in menuItem.NestedItems.OrderBy(p
                                => p.Sequence).ToList())
```

```
                    {
                        if (currentUser.Roles.Intersect(subMenuItem.UserRoles).Any())
                        {
                            <li><a href="@subMenuItem.Link" id="@string.Format
                            ("ancr{0}", subMenuItem.DisplayName.Replace(" ",""))">
                            @subMenuItem.DisplayName<i class="material-icons">
                            @subMenuItem.MaterialIcon</i></a></li>
                        }
                    }
                    </ul>
                </div>
            </li>
        </ul>
    </li>
    }
    else
    {
        <li>
            <a href="@menuItem.Link" id="@string.Format("ancr{0}",menuItem.DisplayName.
            Replace(" ",""))" class="collapsible-header"><i class="material-icons">@
            menuItem.MaterialIcon</i>@menuItem.DisplayName</a>
        </li>
    }
}
}
```

To consume the left navigation view component, we need to install the `Microsoft.Extensions.FileProviders.Embedded` NuGet package to the `ASC.Web` project, as shown in Figure 9-9.

Figure 9-9. *Installing the Microsoft.Extensions.FileProviders.Embedded NuGet package to the ASC.Web project*

Now we need to configure the Razor view engine to support views that are embedded resources in an external class library. We need to create a new `EmbeddedFileProvider` instance in the `ConfigureServices` method of the `Startup` class. The `EmbeddedFileProvider` instance will be associated with the `ASC.Utilities` namespace, and it should be added as one of the `FileProviders` to the Razor view engine, as shown in Listing 9-18.

Listing 9-18. Adding support to embedded views

```
public void ConfigureServices(IServiceCollection services)
    {
        // Code removed for brevity

        services.AddSession();
        services
            .AddMvc(o => { o.Filters.Add(typeof(CustomExceptionFilter)); })
            .AddJsonOptions(options => options.SerializerSettings.ContractResolver = new
            DefaultContractResolver());

        services.AddAutoMapper();

        // Add support to embedded views from ASC.Utilities project.
        var assembly = typeof(ASC.Utilities.Navigation.LeftNavigationViewComponent).
        GetTypeInfo().Assembly;
        var embeddedFileProvider = new EmbeddedFileProvider(assembly, "ASC.Utilities");
        services.Configure<RazorViewEngineOptions>(options =>
        {
            options.FileProviders.Add(embeddedFileProvider);
        });

        // Add application services.
        services.AddTransient<IEmailSender, AuthMessageSender>();
        // Code removed for brevity.
    }
```

Finally, we will render the view component in _SecureLayout.cshtml, as shown in Listing 9-19.

Listing 9-19. Rendering Left Navigation view component

```
<!-- Side NavBar -->
<ul id="nav-mobile" class="side-nav fixed">
    <li>
        <div class="userView">
            <div class="background blue-grey lighten-1"></div>
            <a href="#!user"><img class="circle" src="~/images/male.png"></a>
            <a href="#!name"><span class="white-text name">@currentUser.Name</span></a>
            <a href="#!email"><span class="white-text email">@currentUser.Email</span></a>
        </div>
    </li>
    @await Component.InvokeAsync("ASC.Utilities.Navigation.LeftNavigation", await
    navigationCache.GetNavigationCacheAsync())
</ul>
```

Run the application and navigate to the dashboard by signing in as Admin. You should see the left navigation menu, as shown in Figure 9-10.

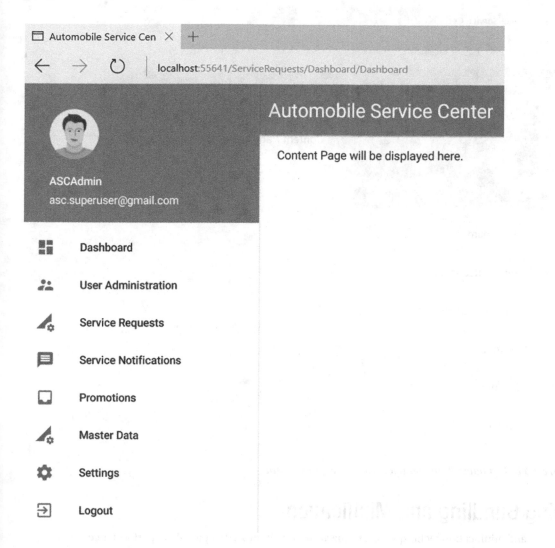

Figure 9-10. *Left menu navigation for the Admin login*

Now log in as a service engineer. You should see the left navigation menu shown in Figure 9-11.

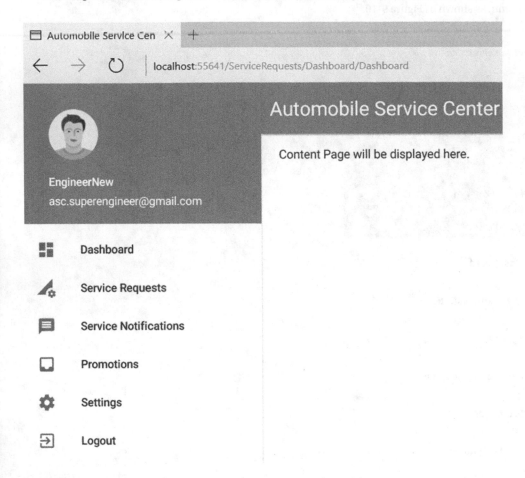

Figure 9-11. *Left navigation menu for a service engineer login*

Using Bundling and Minification

Bundling and minification techniques are primarily used to improve the page-load performance of a web application. *Bundling* combines multiple files into a single file, whereas *minification* performs optimizations on JS and CSS scripts (for example, removing unnecessary whitespace and comments, and renaming variables). We achieve the following key improvements with the help of bundling and minification:

- Reduced number of requests to the server for JavaScript and stylesheets

- Reduced size of JavaScript and stylesheets

■ **Note** Bundling and minification don't affect the actual code files in a Visual Studio solution. A new set of output files is created as part of the bundling and minification process, and the layout typically references the output files.

In this section, we will configure the Automobile Service Center application to use bundling and minification optimization in Production mode. We will not optimize JS and CSS files in Development mode because developers would be extensively using client-side development tools to debug and troubleshoot JS and CSS issues, and optimizing code would hamper the developer's debugging capabilities.

■ **Note** Before we start with bundling and minification, download DataTable CSS (`https://cdn. datatables.net/1.10.15/css/jquery.dataTables.min.css`) and DataTable JS (`https://cdn.datatables. net/1.10.15/js/jquery.dataTables.min.js`) and create the `jquery.dataTable.css` and `jquery. dataTables.js` files in the CSS and JS folders of the `wwwroot` directory.

We are making this change to ensure that all the CSS and JS files are merged into logical files through bundles.

Make sure to refer to the already minified JQuery validation libraries by changing `jquery.validate.js` to `jquery.validate.min.js`, and `jquery.validate.unobtrusive.js` to `jquery.validate.unobtrusive.min. js` in `_MasterLayout.cshtml`.

Open `_MasterLayout.cshtml` and make changes as shown in Listing 9-20. We primarily use the environment tag helper of ASP.NET Core, which can be used to include certain sections in the view based on the current application's environment settings. In Development mode, we configure the regular CSS and JS files that we have been using throughout the application so far. For now, leave the Staging and Production section empty; soon we will fill this section with bundled and minified file references. The Material Icons reference is configured to be common for all modes.

Listing 9-20. Usage of environment tag helper

```
@using Microsoft.Extensions.Options;
@using ASC.Web.Configuration;
@inject IOptions<ApplicationSettings> _configurationSettings

<!DOCTYPE html>
<html>
<head>
    <meta http-equiv="Content-Type" content="text/html; charset=UTF-8" />
    <meta name="viewport" content="width=device-width, initial-scale=1, maximum-scale=1.0,
    user-scalable=no" />
    <title>@_configurationSettings.Value.ApplicationTitle</title>

    <!-- CSS Files -->
    <link href="https://fonts.googleapis.com/icon?family=Material+Icons" rel="stylesheet">
    <environment names="Development">
        <link href="~/css/jquery.dataTables.css" type="text/css" rel="stylesheet"
        media="screen,projection" />
        <link href="~/css/materialize.css" type="text/css" rel="stylesheet"
        media="screen,projection" />
        <link href="~/css/style.css" type="text/css" rel="stylesheet"
        media="screen,projection" />
    </environment>
```

```
    <environment names="Staging,Production">
    </environment>
</head>
<body>
    <!-- Render Body -->
    @RenderBody()

    <!-- JS Files -->
    <environment names="Development">
        <script src="~/lib/jquery/dist/jquery.min.js"></script>
        <script src="~/lib/jquery-validation/dist/jquery.validate.min.js"></script>
        <script src="~/lib/jquery-validation-unobtrusive/jquery.validate.unobtrusive.min.js">
        </script>
        <script src="~/js/materialize.min.js"></script>
        <script src="~/js/jquery.dataTables.js"></script>
        <script src="~/js/init.js"></script>
    </environment>
    <environment names="Staging,Production">
    </environment>

    @RenderSection("Scripts", required: false)
</body>
</html>
```

Run the application. Because we've already configured the ASC.Web project to run in Development mode, everything should work as expected.

To get started with bundling and minification, we need to add the BundlerMinifier.Core package as a DotNetCliToolReference in the ASC.Web.csproj file. This package is primarily required to do the heavy lifting of bundling and minification of CSS, JS, and HTML files. Right-click the ASC.Web project in Visual Studio and select the Edit ASC.Web.csproj option, as shown in Figure 9-12.

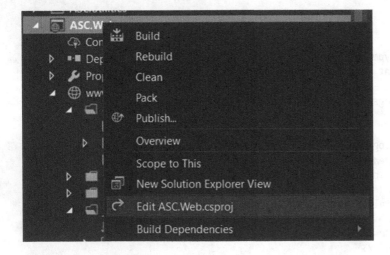

Figure 9-12. *The Edit option for the csproj file*

Add the BundlerMinifier.Core package, as shown in Listing 9-21.

Listing 9-21. Add BundlerMinifier.Core reference

```
<ItemGroup>
  <DotNetCliToolReference Include="BundlerMinifier.Core" Version="2.4.337" />
  <DotNetCliToolReference Include="Microsoft.EntityFrameworkCore.Tools.DotNet" Version="1.0.0" />
  <DotNetCliToolReference Include="Microsoft.Extensions.SecretManager.Tools" Version="1.0.0" />
  <DotNetCliToolReference Include="Microsoft.VisualStudio.Web.CodeGeneration.Tools"
    Version="1.0.0" />
</ItemGroup>
```

In ASP.NET Core, bundling and minification are configured in the bundleconfig.json file. Open this file and add the configuration shown in Listing 9-22. We are going to create one bundle for all CSS files with site.min.css as the bundle name. When it is generated, it will be placed in the same location (wwwroot/css) as the other CSS files.

We are going to create three bundles for JS files, one for JQuery libraries, one for third-party libraries such as DataTables, and one for custom application scripts such as init.js. We specify outputFileName with the location and bundle name (for example, wwwroot/js/jqueryBundle.min.js) for each bundle and then we specify the inputFiles with the files that need to be included in the bundle. We specify the optional configuration to turn on/off minification for each bundle by using the minify section.

Listing 9-22. bundleconfig.json file configuration

```
// Configure bundling and minification for the project.
// More info at https://go.microsoft.com/fwlink/?LinkId=808241
[
  {
    "outputFileName": "wwwroot/css/site.min.css",
    // An array of relative input file paths. Globbing patterns supported
    "inputFiles": [
      "wwwroot/css/jquery.dataTables.css",
      "wwwroot/css/materialize.css",
      "wwwroot/css/style.css"
    ]
  },
  {
    "outputFileName": "wwwroot/js/jqueryBundle.min.js",
    "inputFiles": [
      "wwwroot/lib/jquery/dist/jquery.js",
      "wwwroot/lib/jquery-validation/dist/jquery.validate.js",
      "wwwroot/lib/jquery-validation-unobtrusive/jquery.validate.unobtrusive.js"
    ],
    // Optionally specify minification options
    "minify": {
      "enabled": true
    }
  },
  {
```

```
    "outputFileName": "wwwroot/js/libraryBundle.min.js",
    "inputFiles": [
      "wwwroot/js/materialize.min.js",
      "wwwroot/js/jquery.dataTables.js"
    ],
    // Optionally specify minification options
    "minify": {
      "enabled": true
    }
  },
  {
    "outputFileName": "wwwroot/js/appBundle.min.js",
    "inputFiles": [
      "wwwroot/js/init.js"
    ],
    // Optionally specify minification options
    "minify": {
      "enabled": true
    }
  }
]
```

Now we will update _MasterLayout.cshtml with the bundleconfig.json outputFileName as shown in Listing 9-23. We will update the files to target only the Production and Staging section of the layout.

Listing 9-23. Update master layout with JQuery and CSS bundle files

```
@using Microsoft.Extensions.Options;
@using ASC.Web.Configuration;
@inject IOptions<ApplicationSettings> _configurationSettings

<!DOCTYPE html>
<html>
<head>
    <meta http-equiv="Content-Type" content="text/html; charset=UTF-8" />
    <meta name="viewport" content="width=device-width, initial-scale=1, maximum-scale=1.0,
    user-scalable=no" />
    <title>@_configurationSettings.Value.ApplicationTitle</title>

    <!-- CSS Files -->
    <link href="https://fonts.googleapis.com/icon?family=Material+Icons" rel="stylesheet">
    <environment names="Development">
        <link href="~/css/jquery.dataTables.css" type="text/css" rel="stylesheet"
        media="screen,projection" />
        <link href="~/css/materialize.css" type="text/css" rel="stylesheet"
        media="screen,projection" />
        <link href="~/css/style.css" type="text/css" rel="stylesheet"
        media="screen,projection" />
    </environment>
    <environment names="Staging,Production">
```

```html
        <link href="~/css/site.min.css" type="text/css" rel="stylesheet"
        media="screen,projection" />
    </environment>
</head>
<body>
    <!-- Render Body -->
    @RenderBody()

    <!-- JS Files -->
    <environment names="Development">
        <script src="~/lib/jquery/dist/jquery.min.js"></script>
        <script src="~/lib/jquery-validation/dist/jquery.validate.min.js"></script>
        <script src="~/lib/jquery-validation-unobtrusive/jquery.validate.unobtrusive.min.
        js"></script>
        <script src="~/js/materialize.min.js"></script>
        <script src="~/js/jquery.dataTables.js"></script>
        <script src="~/js/init.js"></script>
    </environment>
    <environment names="Staging,Production">
        <script src="~/js/jqueryBundle.min.js"></script>
        <script src="~/js/libraryBundle.min.js"></script>
        <script src="~/js/appBundle.min.js"></script>
    </environment>

    @RenderSection("Scripts", required: false)
</body>
</html>
```

As the last step of the bundling process, we need to automate the build process to make sure the bundle files are created on every build.

Edit the ASC.Web.csproj file and add the PreBuildScript section, as shown in Listing 9-24. The commands mentioned in the target node execute before the code build. The dotnet bundle clean command deletes the existing bundle artifacts, and dotnet bundle creates the new bundles.

Listing 9-24. PreBuildScript

```xml
<Target Name="PreBuildScript" BeforeTargets="Build">
  <Exec Command="dotnet bundle clean" />
  <Exec Command="dotnet bundle" />
</Target>
```

■ **Note** During development, developers can always remove these commands from their csproj files so that the regular dev builds will not take more time to finish.

Another way to run these commands is to use the command prompt. Navigate to the ASC.Web project directory from the command prompt and run both commands. Running commands manually will also yield the same results.

Now build the solution in Visual Studio. You should see all the bundles created, as shown in Figure 9-13.

Figure 9-13. *Created bundles in the Visual Studio solution*

Run the application either in Development mode or Production mode. The application should run without any errors.

Summary

You started this chapter by learning about the importance segregating code into modules by using ASP. NET Core's areas feature. For our Automobile Service Center application, you created User Account Management, Service Requests, and Configuration areas in Visual Studio Solution. First, you created the physical folders under the Areas folder, one for each module. Then, in each module you organized code into controllers, models, and views. Finally, you moved the existing source code to respective folders with appropriate namespaces.

Later in the chapter, you designed an easy-to-use and seamless left navigation menu system for our Automobile Service Center application. You created a JSON-based navigation configuration and loaded it into a Redis cache on application initialization. You then created an ASP.NET Core view component that renders the left navigation menu by using JSON configuration. The left navigation menu also supports restricted visibility of menu items based on the logged-in user role. As a last step, you configured the view component's view as an embedded resource and consumed it in the ASC.Web project's secure layout.

In the last section of the chapter, you implemented bundling and minification for our Automobile Service Center application. Bundling combines multiple files into a single file, whereas minification performs optimizations. You configured one CSS bundle and three JQuery bundles for the application and loaded them in the master layout based on environment variables (in Development mode, we load normal CSS and JQuery files, and for other modes we load bundles). You automated bundling and minification tasks by including pre-build commands for the ASC.Web project that will clean and regenerate bundles on every build.

CHAPTER 10

■ ■ ■

Forms and Validations

The main business motive behind designing Automobile Service Center application is to drive the car servicing business through transparent and highly efficient automated system which will provide seamless communication between customers and service engineers. Customers should be able to reach out to service engineers to raise the service requests and in return service engineers should respond back to customers on a timely basis with the specific details of service progress. To establish the aforesaid communication channel between business and customers, we need to design data input screens which are traditionally called Forms.

In this chapter, we will define a workflow for new service request which will be created by customer, monitored by Admin and organized by service engineers. We are going to create a service request form which will be used by customers to initiate new service requests. A common view to display list of associated service requests will be created which will display all the service requests based on user role.

We will create a service request detail view which will help customers, service engineers and admin to view the details of an on-going or completed service. Customers and Service Engineers can use service request details view to send and receive messages thereby sharing information and particulars about an on-going car service.

We will also focus on user input validations through ASP.NET Core's DataAnnotation attributes. Wherever custom validations are required, we will develop custom validation attributes by implementing ValidationAttribute and IClientModelValidator. Client side custom validations will be achieved by creating Unobtrusive JQuery adapters and attaching custom validation functions to JQuery validator framework.

Lastly we will implement internationalization for Automobile Service Center application to support different cultures and languages.

Service Request Workflow

In this section, we will define a custom workflow for Automobile Service Center application through which we can ensure highest level of transparency and good communication between customers and service engineers.

The workflow will be triggered when a customer submits a new service request for his automobile. The request lands up in Admin queue with status as 'New'. Admin then reviews the request and makes a decision to either assign the request to an available service engineer (by marking request status as 'Initiated') or to communicate back with customer for more information (based on the information, request status would be 'Pending' or 'Denied'). Service Engineer takes charge of servicing and continues with the operations, at this point, service request status would be 'InProgress'. On service completion, Service Engineer will flip the status to 'PendingCustomerApproval'. At this stage, customer can review his car and service request details and if he is pleased with the quality of service, he can mark the status as 'Completed' otherwise he can update the status to 'RequestForInformation'. Admin will monitor his service request queue for RequestForInformation tagged services and appropriately connects with customers to resolve any pending actions.

© Rami Vemula 2017

R. Vemula, *Real-Time Web Application Development*, https://doi.org/10.1007/978-1-4842-3270-5_10

Automobile Service Center Serive Request workflow is as shown in Figure 10-1.

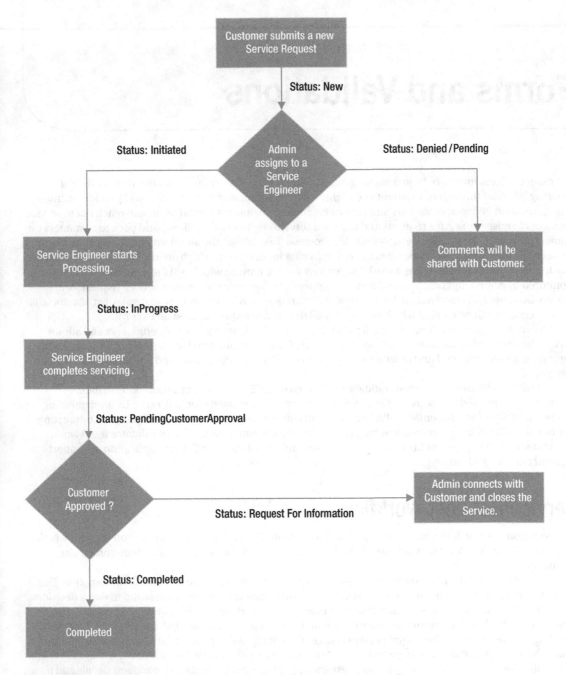

Figure 10-1. *Service Request workflow for Automobile Service Center application*

Service Request Form

In this section we will create Service Request form using which a customer can submit a new service request. Service Requests can also be created by Service Engineers and Admin because some customers may directly walk into service station and request for a new service.

■ **Note** In the scope of this book, we will implement a simple Service Request form, but in reality a service request form might be complex and large.

We will get start by creating an entity model in ASC.Models project as shown in Listing 10-1. ServiceRequest entity consists of properties which captures information like Vehicle Name, Vehicle type, Status, Services which are requested by customer, Service Engineer who is responsible for providing the services, Requested date and Date of completion. The RowKey of ServiceRequest entity is going to be a unique Guid value and PartitionKey will be the email address of the customer who is requesting the service.

Listing 10-1. ServiceRequest Entity

```
using ASC.Models.BaseTypes;
using System;

namespace ASC.Models.Models
{
    public class ServiceRequest : BaseEntity, IAuditTracker
    {
        public ServiceRequest() { }

        public ServiceRequest(string email)
        {
            this.RowKey = Guid.NewGuid().ToString();
            this.PartitionKey = email;
        }

        public string VehicleName { get; set; }
        public string VehicleType { get; set; }
        public string Status { get; set; }
        public string RequestedServices { get; set; }
        public DateTime? RequestedDate { get; set; }
        public DateTime? CompletedDate { get; set; }
        public string ServiceEngineer { get; set; }
    }
}
```

Now we will create IServiceRequestOperations interface in ASC.Business Project under Interfaces folder as shown in Listing 10-2. This interface will hold all the key methods which are used to insert and update a service request details in Azure Table storage.

Listing 10-2. IServiceRequestOperations interface

```
using ASC.Models.Models;
using System.Threading.Tasks;

namespace ASC.Business.Interfaces
{
    public interface IServiceRequestOperations
    {
        Task CreateServiceRequestAsync(ServiceRequest request);
        Task<ServiceRequest> UpdateServiceRequestAsync(ServiceRequest request);
        Task<ServiceRequest> UpdateServiceRequestStatusAsync(string rowKey, string
        partitionKey, string status);
    }
}
```

Create a class with name ServiceRequestOperations which will implement IServiceRequestOperations as shown in Listing 10-3. CreateServiceRequestAsync method will create a new service request at Azure table storage. UpdateServiceRequestAsync will update a service request details in Azure table storage. UpdateServiceRequestStatusAsync method will update the status of service request with the value passed in status parameter.

Listing 10-3. ServiceRequestOperations class

```
using ASC.Business.Interfaces;
using ASC.DataAccess.Interfaces;
using ASC.Models.Models;
using System;
using System.Threading.Tasks;

namespace ASC.Business
{
    public class ServiceRequestOperations : IServiceRequestOperations
    {
        private readonly IUnitOfWork _unitOfWork;
        public ServiceRequestOperations(IUnitOfWork unitOfWork)
        {
            _unitOfWork = unitOfWork;
        }
        public async Task CreateServiceRequestAsync(ServiceRequest request)
        {
            using (_unitOfWork)
            {
                await _unitOfWork.Repository<ServiceRequest>().AddAsync(request);
                _unitOfWork.CommitTransaction();
            }
        }
```

```
public async Task<ServiceRequest> UpdateServiceRequestAsync(ServiceRequest request)
{
    using (_unitOfWork)
    {
        await _unitOfWork.Repository<ServiceRequest>().UpdateAsync(request);
        _unitOfWork.CommitTransaction();

        return request;
    }
}

public async Task<ServiceRequest> UpdateServiceRequestStatusAsync(string rowKey,
string partitionKey, string status)
{
    using (_unitOfWork)
    {
        var serviceRequest = await _unitOfWork.Repository<ServiceRequest>().
        FindAsync(partitionKey, rowKey);

        if (serviceRequest == null)
            throw new NullReferenceException();

        serviceRequest.Status = status;

        await _unitOfWork.Repository<ServiceRequest>().UpdateAsync(serviceRequest);
        _unitOfWork.CommitTransaction();

        return serviceRequest;
    }
}
}
}
```

Resolve the dependency of IServiceRequestOperations in ConfigureServices method of Startup class at ASC.Web project as shown in Listing 10-4.

Listing 10-4. Resolve the dependency of IServiceRequestOperations

```
services.AddScoped<IServiceRequestOperations, ServiceRequestOperations>();
```

To support Controller actions and Views, we will create a class with name NewServiceRequestViewModel under Models folder of ServiceRequests area as shown in Listing 10-5. This is the view model which we will use in creating a new service request. The Required attribute makes the property mandatory in the model and Display attribute is used to give a name to the property which can be used for display purpose.

Listing 10-5. NewServiceRequestViewModel class

```
using System;
using System.ComponentModel.DataAnnotations;

namespace ASC.Web.Areas.ServiceRequests.Models
{
    public class NewServiceRequestViewModel
    {
        [Required]
        [Display(Name ="Vehicle Name")]
        public string VehicleName { get; set; }
        [Required]
        [Display(Name = "Vehicle Type")]
        public string VehicleType { get; set; }
        [Required]
        [Display(Name = "Requested Services")]
        public string RequestedServices { get; set; }
        [Required]
        [Display(Name = "Requested Date")]
        public DateTime? RequestedDate { get; set; }
    }
}
```

Create a class with name ServiceRequestMappingProfile under Models folder of ServiceRequests area as shown in Listing 10-6. ServiceRequestMappingProfile will be used to create AutoMapper map between ServiceRequest Azure Table Storage entity and NewServiceRequestViewModel which is ver useful in transforming business models with view models and vice versa.

Listing 10-6. AutoMapper mappings in ServiceRequestMappingProfile class

```
using ASC.Models.Models;
using AutoMapper;

namespace ASC.Web.Areas.ServiceRequests.Models
{
    public class ServiceRequestMappingProfile : Profile
    {
        public ServiceRequestMappingProfile()
        {
            CreateMap<ServiceRequest, NewServiceRequestViewModel>();
            CreateMap<NewServiceRequestViewModel, ServiceRequest>();
        }
    }
}
```

Now we will create two Enum types - MasterKeys and Status in Constants file of ASC.Models project as shown in Listing 10-7. These enums are useful in referencing master data keys in the project instead of hardcoding master data strings. Status Enum is used to refer to the status of service request. VehicleName and VehicleType keys are used to retrieve master data related to vehicles.

Listing 10-7. Enum types

```
public enum MasterKeys
{
    VehicleName, VehicleType
}

public enum Status
{
    New, Denied, Pending, Initiated, InProgress, PendingCustomerApproval,
    RequestForInformation, Completed
}
```

Create a new controller with name ServiceRequestController under ServiceRequests area as shown in Listing 10-8. ServiceRequestController constructor takes IServiceRequestOperations, IMapper and IMasterDataCacheOperations dependencies, which are used in controller actions.

ServiceRequestController got two actions, one for GET and another for POST operation. GET action is used to render the ServiceRequest view which is used to create a new service request. In GET action, we get required master data from Redis cache and hold it in ViewBag dictionary. This master data information is used to populate the select options on view.

On valid ModelState, POST action will save the new service request to Azure Table storage and redirects user to Dashboard on successful save operation.

■ **Note** Use Master Data management screens which we developed in Chapter 7 to setup reference data for Vehicle Names, Vehicle types and Status.

Listing 10-8. ServiceRequestController class

```
using Microsoft.AspNetCore.Mvc;
using ASC.Web.Controllers;
using ASC.Business.Interfaces;
using ASC.Models.Models;
using ASC.Utilities;
using System;
using System.Threading.Tasks;
using ASC.Web.Areas.ServiceRequests.Models;
using AutoMapper;
using ASC.Web.Data;
using System.Linq;
using ASC.Models.BaseTypes;

namespace ASC.Web.Areas.ServiceRequests.Controllers
{
    [Area("ServiceRequests")]
    public class ServiceRequestController : BaseController
    {
        private readonly IServiceRequestOperations _serviceRequestOperations;
        private readonly IMapper _mapper;
        private readonly IMasterDataCacheOperations _masterData;
```

```csharp
        public ServiceRequestController(IServiceRequestOperations operations, IMapper
        mapper, IMasterDataCacheOperations masterData)
        {
            _serviceRequestOperations = operations;
            _mapper = mapper;
            _masterData = masterData;
        }

        [HttpGet]
        public async Task<IActionResult> ServiceRequest()
        {
            var masterData = await _masterData.GetMasterDataCacheAsync();
            ViewBag.VehicleTypes = masterData.Values.Where(p => p.PartitionKey ==
            MasterKeys.VehicleType.ToString()).ToList();
            ViewBag.VehicleNames = masterData.Values.Where(p => p.PartitionKey ==
            MasterKeys.VehicleName.ToString()).ToList();
            return View(new NewServiceRequestViewModel());
        }

        [HttpPost]
        public async Task<IActionResult> ServiceRequest(NewServiceRequestViewModel request)
        {
            if (!ModelState.IsValid)
            {
                var masterData = await _masterData.GetMasterDataCacheAsync();
                ViewBag.VehicleTypes = masterData.Values.Where(p => p.PartitionKey ==
                MasterKeys.VehicleType.ToString()).ToList();
                ViewBag.VehicleNames = masterData.Values.Where(p => p.PartitionKey ==
                MasterKeys.VehicleName.ToString()).ToList();
                return View(request);
            }

            // Map the view model to Azure model
            var serviceRequest = _mapper.Map<NewServiceRequestViewModel,
            ServiceRequest>(request);

            // Set RowKey, PartitionKey, RequestedDate, Status properties
            serviceRequest.PartitionKey = HttpContext.User.GetCurrentUserDetails().Email;
            serviceRequest.RowKey = Guid.NewGuid().ToString();
            serviceRequest.RequestedDate = request.RequestedDate;
            serviceRequest.Status = Status.New.ToString();

            await _serviceRequestOperations.CreateServiceRequestAsync(serviceRequest);

            return RedirectToAction("Dashboard", "Dashboard", new { Area = "ServiceRequests" });
        }
    }
}
```

The service request cshtml is shown in Listing 10-9. It is a simple view where we display two select options for Vehicle type and name, a textarea for Requested services and a date picker for requested date. JQuery code is used to initialize date picker and select controls with Material design.

Listing 10-9. New service request view

```
@model ASC.Web.Areas.ServiceRequests.Models.NewServiceRequestViewModel
@using System.Globalization
@{
    Layout = "_SecureLayout";
}

<div class="row"></div>
<div class="row padding-top-20px">

    @* Details Section *@
    <div class="row z-depth-3">
        <div class="col s12 padding-0px">
            <div class="section white-text padding-left-10px blue-grey lighten-1">
                <h5>New Service Request</h5>
            </div>
            <div class="divider"></div>
            <form asp-controller="ServiceRequest" asp-action="ServiceRequest" method="post"
            class="col s12">
                <div class="row">
                    <div class="input-field col s4">
                        <select asp-for="VehicleName"
                                asp-items="@(new SelectList(ViewBag.VehicleNames,"RowKey","
                                Name"))"
                                class="" required="required">
                            <option value="">Please select one</option>
                        </select>
                        <label asp-for="VehicleName"></label>
                    </div>
                    <div class="input-field col s4">
                        <select asp-for="VehicleType"
                                asp-items="@(new SelectList(ViewBag.VehicleTypes,"RowKey","
                                Name"))"
                                class="validate" required="required">
                            <option value="">Please select one</option>
                        </select>
                        <label asp-for="VehicleType"></label>
                    </div>
                    <div class="input-field col s4">
                        <input asp-for="RequestedDate" type="date" class="datepicker" data-
                        value="@(Model.RequestedDate.HasValue ?
Model.RequestedDate.Value.ToString("dd MMMM, yyyy", CultureInfo.InvariantCulture) :
string.Empty)" />
                        <label asp-for="RequestedDate"></label>
                    </div>
                </div>
```

```
                <div class="row">
                    <div class="input-field col s8">
                        <textarea asp-for="RequestedServices" class="materialize-textarea
                        validate"></textarea>
                        <label asp-for="RequestedServices"></label>
                    </div>
                </div>
                <div class="row">
                    <div class="input-field col s12 right-align">
                        <button class="btn waves-effect waves-light btnSubmit" type="submit"
                        name="action">
                            Create
                            <i class="material-icons right">send</i>
                        </button>
                    </div>
                    <div class="row col s12 right-align" asp-validation-summary="All"></div>
                </div>
            </form>
        </div>
        <div class="row"></div>
    </div>
</div>

@section Scripts{
    <script>
        $(document).ready(function () {
            $('.datepicker').pickadate({
                selectMonths: true,
                selectYears: 15
            });
            $('select').material_select();
            $("select[required]").css({ display: "block", position: 'absolute',
            visibility: 'hidden' });
        });
    </script>
}
```

■ **Note**   We need following code to invoke mandatory validation on select list. This is a known workaround for material select list.

$("select[required]").css({ display: "block", position: 'absolute', visibility: 'hidden' });

One more important point to be remembered is to use data-value attribute which is required for Materialize Date picker to populate the date on page load. In listing 10-9, we are formatting date using 'dd MMM, yyyy' format to keep in sync with the default materialize date format.

To provide navigation to service request screen, we need to update Navigation.json file as shown in Listing 10-10 to reflect new menu item in left navigation.

Listing 10-10. Updated Navigation.json file to include Service Request view

```
{
  "DisplayName": "Service Requests",
  "MaterialIcon": "local_laundry_service",
  "Link": "",
  "IsNested": true,
  "Sequence": 3,
  "UserRoles": [ "User", "Engineer", "Admin" ],
  "NestedItems": [
    {
      "DisplayName": "New Service Request",
      "MaterialIcon": "insert_invitation",
      "Link": "/ServiceRequests/ServiceRequest/ServiceRequest",
      "IsNested": false,
      "Sequence": 1,
      "UserRoles": [ "User", "Engineer", "Admin" ],
      "NestedItems": []
    }
  ]
},
```

Run the application and login as any user, we should see left menu item as shown in Figure 10-2.

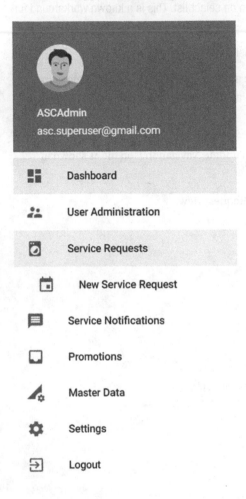

Figure 10-2. *New Service Request left navigation menu option*

Navigate to New Service Request Screen by clicking left navigation menu item. New Service Request screen will be displayed as shown in Figure 10-3.

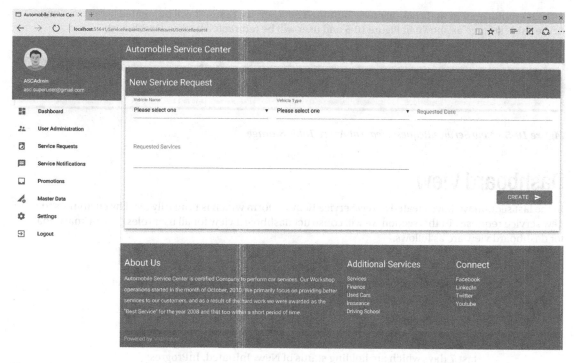

Figure 10-3. *New Service Request Screen*

If we do not enter any values and click on create, we will get validation error messages displayed as shown in Figure 10-4.

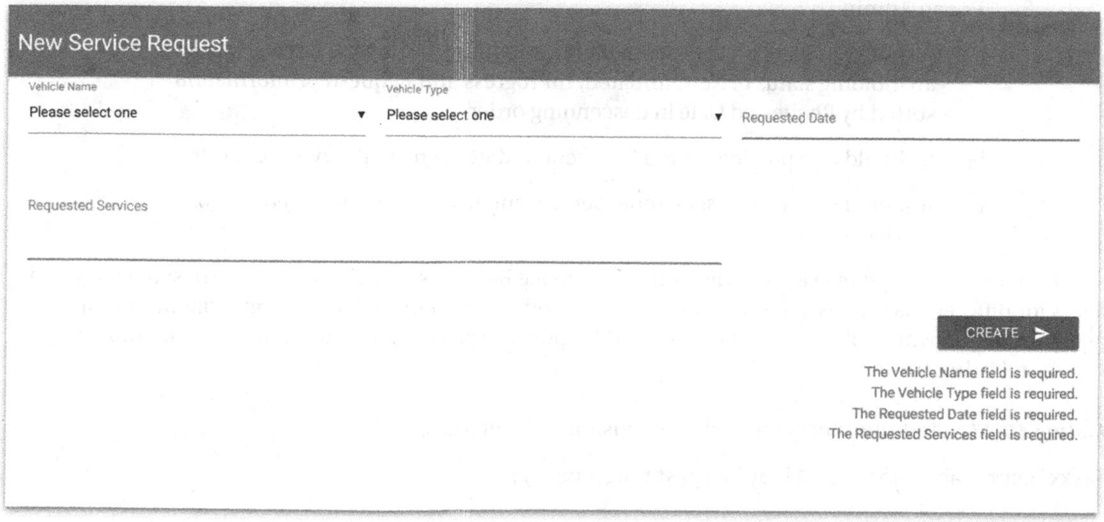

New Service Request

Vehicle Name
Please select one ▼

Vehicle Type
Please select one ▼

Requested Date

Requested Services

CREATE ➤

The Vehicle Name field is required.
The Vehicle Type field is required.
The Requested Date field is required.
The Requested Services field is required.

Figure 10-4. *Validation messages on Service Request screen*

Enter information and click on create button. A new Service Request will be created at ServiceRequest Azure Table storage as shown in Figure 10-5 and user will be redirected back to Dashboard.

Figure 10-5. *New Service Request create at Azure Table Storage*

Dashboard View

In the last section we have created a New Service Request form which is primarily used by customers to raise new service requests. In this section we will construct dashboard view for all user roles. The primary goals for dashboard view are as follows.

1. For a Customer

    a. It should provide list of his own service requests during the past one year sorted from latest to oldest.

2. For a Service Engineer

    a. It should provide list of his associated on-going service requests in last 7 days which are holding status of New, Initiated, InProgress and RequestForInformation and finally sorted by Requested Date in descending order.

    b. It should also provide the top 20 recent service updates of the service requests associated with him.

3. For an Admin

    a. It should provide list of on-going service requests during the last week which are holding status of New, Initiated, InProgress and RequestForInformation sorted by Requested Date in descending order.

    b. It should also provide the top 20 recent updates across all service requests.

    c. It should provide statistics about service engineer to his associated on-going service requests.

As a first step to get relevant information from Service Requests Azure Table Storage based on different filters for different user roles and status, we should extend IRepository and its implementation to support query execution with multiple conditions. Extend IRepository class to have FindAllByQuery method as shown in Listing 10-11.

Listing 10-11. FindAllByQuery method in IRepository<T> interface

```
Task<IEnumerable<T>> FindAllByQuery(string query);
```

Implement the FindAllByQuery method in Repository class as shown in Listing 10-12. FindAllByQuery method takes a string query parameter. The query is passed to ExecuteQuerySegmentedAsync method and finally results are returned to the calling method.

Listing 10-12. FindAllByQuery method

```
public async Task<IEnumerable<T>> FindAllByQuery(string query)
{
    TableContinuationToken tableContinuationToken = null;
    var result = await storageTable.ExecuteQuerySegmentedAsync(new TableQuery<T>().
    Where(query), tableContinuationToken);
    return result.Results as IEnumerable<T>;
}
```

Before getting started with the query generation, add the following constant values in Constants static class of ASC.Models project as shown in Listing 10-13. These constant values are useful in creating where clause ocnditions for Azure Table Storage.

Listing 10-13. Constants class

```
public static class Constants
{
    public const string Equal = "eq";
    public const string NotEqual = "ne";
    public const string GreaterThan = "gt";
    public const string GreaterThanOrEqual = "ge";
    public const string LessThan = "lt";
    public const string LessThanOrEqual = "le";
}
```

Now we need to create different queries which we can pass to FindAllByQuery repository method. Create a folder with name Queries in ASC.Models project. Create a static class inside Queries folder with name Queries and add GetDashboardQuery method to it which will create the necessary query to retrieve data for Dashboard as shown in Listing 10-14. The Dashboard query includes service requested date as the first clause and then checks for optional parameters of status, user email and service engineer email. User email and service engineer email clauses are used to retrieve the service requests which are only associated with them. The sample query would be as shown below.

(RequestedDate ge datetime'2016-06-24T03:39:09.4174760Z') and (Email eq 'intstrings@gmail.com') and (Status eq 'New'or Status eq 'InProgress'or Status eq 'Initiated'or Status eq 'RequestForInformation')

Listing 10-14. GetDashboardQuery method in Queries class

```
using ASC.Models.BaseTypes;
using Microsoft.WindowsAzure.Storage.Table;
using System;
using System.Collections.Generic;

namespace ASC.Models.Queries
{
    public class Queries
    {
        public static string GetDashboardQuery(DateTime? requestedDate,
            List<string> status = null,
            string email = "",
            string serviceEngineerEmail = "")
        {
```

```
        var finalQuery = string.Empty;
        var statusQueries = new List<string>();
        // Add Requested Date Clause
        if (requestedDate.HasValue)
        {
            finalQuery = TableQuery.GenerateFilterConditionForDate("RequestedDate",
            Constants.GreaterThanOrEqual, requestedDate.Value);
        }

        // Add Email clause if email is passed as a parameter
        if (!string.IsNullOrWhiteSpace(email))
        {
            finalQuery = !string.IsNullOrWhiteSpace(finalQuery) ?
                TableQuery.CombineFilters(finalQuery, TableOperators.And, TableQuery.Gen
                erateFilterCondition("PartitionKey", Constants.Equal, email)) :
                TableQuery.GenerateFilterCondition("PartitionKey", Constants.Equal,
                email);
        }

        // Add  Service Engineer Email clause if email is passed as a parameter
        if (!string.IsNullOrWhiteSpace(serviceEngineerEmail))
        {
            finalQuery = !string.IsNullOrWhiteSpace(finalQuery) ?
                TableQuery.CombineFilters(finalQuery, TableOperators.And, TableQuery.
                GenerateFilterCondition("ServiceEngineer", Constants.Equal,
                serviceEngineerEmail)) :
                TableQuery.GenerateFilterCondition("ServiceEngineer", Constants.Equal,
                serviceEngineerEmail);
        }

        // Add Status clause if status is passed a parameter.
        // Individual status clauses are appended with OR Condition
        if (status != null)
        {
            foreach (var state in status)
            {
                statusQueries.Add(TableQuery.GenerateFilterCondition("Status",
                Constants.Equal, state));
            }
            var statusQuery = string.Join(string.Format("{0} ", TableOperators.Or),
            statusQueries);

            finalQuery = !string.IsNullOrWhiteSpace(finalQuery) ?
                string.Format("{0} {1} ({2})", finalQuery, TableOperators.And,
                statusQuery) :
                string.Format("({0})", statusQuery);
        }

        return finalQuery;
    }
  }
}
```

We will add GetServiceRequestsByRequestedDateAndStatus method in IServiceRequestOperations as shown in Listing 10-15.

Listing 10-15. GetServiceRequestsByRequestedDateAndStatus method in IServiceRequestOperations interface

```
Task<List<ServiceRequest>> GetServiceRequestsByRequestedDateAndStatus
(DateTime? requestedDate,
    List<string> status = null,
    string email = "",
    string serviceEngineerEmail = "");
```

The GetServiceRequestsByRequestedDateAndStatus method implementation is shown in Listing 10-16. This method takes Requested Date as mandatory parameter and status, email, service EngineerEmail as optional parameters, it then calls GetDashboardQuery method of Queries class to get the constructed query and pass it to FindAllByQuery method of IRepository<ServiceRequest>. The results of the query execution are send back to the caller.

Listing 10-16. GetServiceRequestsByRequestedDateAndStatus method

```
public async Task<List<ServiceRequest>> GetServiceRequestsByRequestedDateAndStatus
(DateTime? requestedDate,
    List<string> status = null,
    string email = "",
    string serviceEngineerEmail = "")
{
    var query = Queries.GetDashboardQuery(requestedDate, status, email,
    serviceEngineerEmail);
    var serviceRequests = await _unitOfWork.Repository<ServiceRequest>().
    FindAllByQuery(query);
    return serviceRequests.ToList();
}
```

Now as we have the backend query logic ready, we will start with front end implementation in ASC.Web project. Create a DashboardViewModel under Models folder of ServiceRequests area as shown in Listing 10-17. The Dashboard view model will hold all the necessary properties which are required to display data on Dashboard, for example ServiceRequests are used display the recent service requests based on user roles and status.

Listing 10-17. DashboardViewModel class

```
using ASC.Models.Models;
using System.Collections.Generic;

namespace ASC.Web.Areas.ServiceRequests.Models
{
    public class DashboardViewModel
    {
        public List<ServiceRequest> ServiceRequests { get; set; }
    }
}
```

The existing Dashboard action code from Dashboard controller is modified as shown in Listing 10-18. ServiceRequestOperations and MasterDataCacheOperations dependencies are injected to Dashboard controller's constructor. Dashboard action will invoke GetServiceRequestsByRequestedDateAndStatus method with appropriate parameters based on user role. The return results are mapped to ServiceRequests property of DashboardViewModel and returned to the view.

Listing 10-18. Updated Dashboard action

```
private readonly IServiceRequestOperations _serviceRequestOperations;
private readonly IMasterDataCacheOperations _masterData;
public DashboardController(IServiceRequestOperations operations, IMasterDataCacheOperations
masterData)
{
    _serviceRequestOperations = operations;
    _masterData = masterData;
}

public async Task<IActionResult> Dashboard()
{
    // List of Status which were to be queried.
    var status = new List<string>
        {
            Status.New.ToString(),
            Status.InProgress.ToString(),
            Status.Initiated.ToString(),
            Status.RequestForInformation.ToString()
        };

    List<ServiceRequest> serviceRequests = new List<ServiceRequest>();

    if (HttpContext.User.IsInRole(Roles.Admin.ToString()))
    {
        serviceRequests = await _serviceRequestOperations.
        GetServiceRequestsByRequestedDateAndStatus(
            DateTime.UtcNow.AddDays(-7),
            status);
    }
    else if (HttpContext.User.IsInRole(Roles.Engineer.ToString()))
    {
        serviceRequests = await _serviceRequestOperations.
        GetServiceRequestsByRequestedDateAndStatus(
            DateTime.UtcNow.AddDays(-7),
            status,
            serviceEngineerEmail: HttpContext.User.GetCurrentUserDetails().Email);
    }
    else
    {
        serviceRequests = await _serviceRequestOperations.
        GetServiceRequestsByRequestedDateAndStatus(
            DateTime.UtcNow.AddYears(-1),
            email: HttpContext.User.GetCurrentUserDetails().Email);
    }
```

```
    return View(new DashboardViewModel { ServiceRequests = serviceRequests.
    OrderByDescending(p => p.RequestedDate).ToList()});
}
```

■ **Note** Currently we are building common dashboard feature to display Service Requests based on user role. The additional dashboard features for Admin and Service Engineer role will be developed in the later part of the chapter.

The next step is to modify the Dashboard.cshtml to reflect the service requests table. The dashboard view will primarily consists of a table which is populated through ServiceRequests property of DashboardViewModel. This table is initialized with JQuery DataTable so that we get the default pagination, sorting and filtering features.

The columns of Service request table are populated with customer email, status of service request, date on which service requested, email of service engineer who is handling the service. Status column is given color coding to differentiate status of service request. In the last column we have view icon which can be used navigate to corresponding service details page.

To get a reusable view, we will create a partial view for service requests DataTable. Create a view with name _ServiceRequestGrid.cshtml in Views/Shared folder (create a new folder with name Shared under Views folder of ServiceRequests area) of ServiceRequests area as shown in Listing 10-19. This partial view will take list of ServiceRequest as model and iterate each item to render in a tabular format. The name of the section and Id of the table are passed from the Dashboard page to uniquely identify the sections on the same dashboard view. _ServiceRequestGrid also uses one more parameter from ViewBag to check if the partial view is rendered for audit mode, in case of audit mode, an additional column of Requested Services along with other columns will be displayed to end user. If the content length of Requested Services property is more than 50 characters then we display a trimmed text of first 50 characters otherwise we will show the entire text.

Listing 10-19. Service Request List partial view

```
@model IEnumerable<ASC.Models.Models.ServiceRequest>
@using ASC.Models.BaseTypes
@{
    var isAudit = ViewBag.IsAudit;
}
<div class="row"></div>
<div class="row padding-top-20px">

    <div class="row z-depth-3">
        <div class="section white-text padding-left-10px blue-grey lighten-1">
            <h5>@ViewBag.SectionName</h5>
        </div>
        <div class="divider"></div>
        <div class="col s12 padding-bottom-15px">
            @* Display List of Service Requests *@
            <table class="highlight centered tblServiceRequests" id="@ViewBag.Id">
                <thead>
                    <tr>
                        <th data-field="RowKey">RowKey</th>
                        <th data-field="PartitionKey">PartitionKey</th>
                        <th data-field="PartitionKey">User</th>
```

```
                <th data-field="Status">Status</th>
                <th data-field="RequestedDate">Requested Date</th>
                <th data-field="ServiceEngineer">Service Engineer</th>
                @if (isAudit)
                {
                    <th data-field="RequestedServices">Requested Services</th>
                }
                <th data-field="Actions">View</th>
            </tr>
        </thead>
        <tbody>
            @foreach (var serviceRequest in Model)
            {
                <tr>
                    <td>@serviceRequest.RowKey</td>
                    <td>@serviceRequest.PartitionKey</td>
                    <td>
                        @(!serviceRequest.PartitionKey.Contains('-') ?
                    serviceRequest.PartitionKey :
                    serviceRequest.PartitionKey.Split(new char[] { '-' })[0])
                    </td>
                    <td>
                    @switch ((Status)Enum.Parse(typeof(Status), serviceRequest.
                    Status))
                    {
                        case Status.New:
                        case Status.Initiated:
                        case Status.InProgress:
                        case Status.Completed:
                            <div class="white-text teal lighten-1 center-align">
                                <span>@serviceRequest.Status</span>
                            </div>
                            break;
                        case Status.RequestForInformation:
                        case Status.Pending:
                        case Status.Denied:
                            <div class="white-text red lighten-1 center-align">
                                <span>@serviceRequest.Status</span>
                            </div>
                            break;
                        case Status.PendingCustomerApproval:
                            <div class="white-text orange lighten-1 center-align">
                                <span>@serviceRequest.Status</span>
                            </div>
                            break;
                        default:
                            break;

                    }
                    </td>
```

```
        <td>@(serviceRequest.RequestedDate == null ? "" : serviceRequest.
        RequestedDate.Value.ToString("dd/MM/yyyy") )</td>
        <td>@serviceRequest.ServiceEngineer</td>
        @if (isAudit)
        {
            var trimText = String.IsNullOrWhiteSpace(serviceRequest.
            RequestedServices) ?
                string.Empty :
                serviceRequest.RequestedServices.Length > 50 ?
                    string.Format("{0}...",serviceRequest.RequestedServices.
                    Substring(0, 50)) :
                    serviceRequest.RequestedServices;
            <td title="@serviceRequest.RequestedServices">@trimText</td>
        }
        <td><i class="small material-icons view cursor-hand">pageview</i></td>
    </tr>
    }
            </tbody>
        </table>
    </div>
    </div>
</div>
```

Update the Dashboard view as shown in Listing 10-20. In the view we call _ServiceRequestGrid partial view and pass ServiceRequests property from model. We also pass Service Requests as the name of the section, tblServiceRequests as Id and false for IsAudit. In JQuery code we initialize tblServiceRequests with DataTable and all select tags with material design.

Listing 10-20. Dashboard view

```
@model ASC.Web.Areas.ServiceRequests.Models.DashboardViewModel
@using ASC.Models.BaseTypes
@{
    Layout = "_SecureLayout";
}

<div class="row"></div>
@await Html.PartialAsync("_ServiceRequestGrid", Model.ServiceRequests, new
ViewDataDictionary(ViewData) {
    { "SectionName", "Service Requests" },
    { "Id", "tblServiceRequests" },
    { "IsAudit", false }
})

@section Scripts{
    <script>
        $(document).ready(function () {
            // Initialize DataTable to show list of Service Requests
            var table = $('#tblServiceRequests').DataTable({
                'pageLength': 3,
                // Number of records to be displayed per page
                'lengthMenu': [[3, 5, 10, -1], [3, 5, 10, 'All']],
```

```
            // Remove default Sorting
            'sorting': [],
            'columns': [{ "visible": false }, { "visible": false }, null, { "width":
            "20%" }, null, null, null]
        });
        // Set Styles for DataTable and Number of Records to be displayed dropdown
        $('.tblServiceRequests').css("width", "100%");
        $('select[name$="ServiceRequests_length"]').material_select();

    });
    </script>
}
```

Run the application, if admin login to the application he should service requests for past 7 days as shown in Figure 10-6.

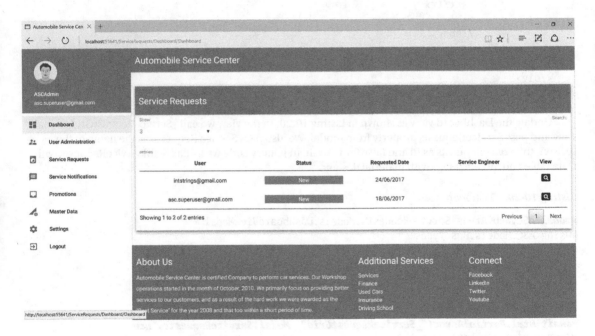

Figure 10-6. *Dashboard view on Admin login*

If a customer login to system, he should see his service requests as shown in Figure 10-7.

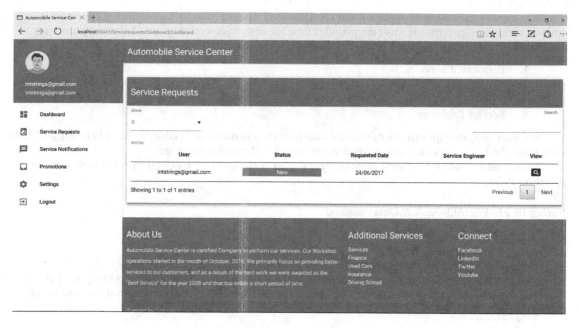

Figure 10-7. *Dashboard view on Customer login*

If a Service Engineer login to system, he should see service requests which are associated with him in last 7 days. As there are no service requests associated to service engineer, there will be no records displayed as shown in Figure 10-8.

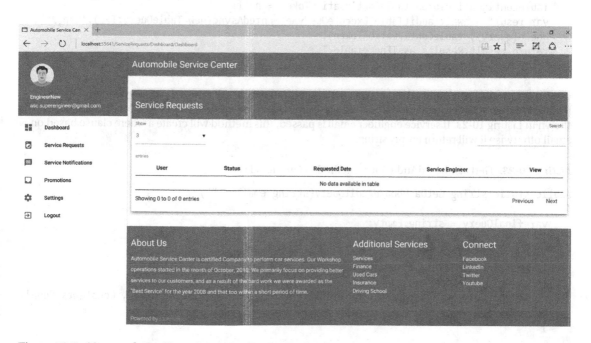

Figure 10-8. *No records Dashboard view for Service Engineer*

Now we will extend Dashboard for Admin and Service Engineer roles to display the top 20 recent updates to the Service requests. Over the period of time for any given service request following properties can change.

1. Requested Services

2. Status

3. Service Engineer

As we are already capturing all this information in ServiceRequestAudit table, we need to first query this table to get the top 20 service requests which are changed in chronological order.

We will get started by extending IRepository to expose a method which will query Audit table as shown in Listing 10-21.

Listing 10-21. FindAllInAuditByQuery method

```
Task<IEnumerable<T>> FindAllInAuditByQuery(string query);
```

Implement FindAllInAuditByQuery method on Repository class as shown in Listing 10-22. FindAllInAuditByQuery methods first gets the instance of audit CloudTable and executes the query (which is passed as a parameter to the method) by limiting the results to top 20. Finally it returns the results to the calling method.

Listing 10-22. FindAllInAuditByQuery method

```
public async Task<IEnumerable<T>> FindAllInAuditByQuery(string query)
{
    var auditTable = tableClient.GetTableReference($"{typeof(T).Name}Audit");
    TableContinuationToken tableContinuationToken = null;
    var result = await auditTable.ExecuteQuerySegmentedAsync(new TableQuery<T>().Take(20).
    Where(query), tableContinuationToken);
    return result.Results as IEnumerable<T>;
}
```

To get results from Audit table, we will create a method which will return the query similar to the Dashboard query. Create a method GetDashboardAuditQuery in Queries class of ASC.Models project as shown in Listing 10-23. If service engineer email is passed, this method will create a where clause based on email otherwise it will return empty string.

Listing 10-23. GetDashboardAuditQuery method in Queries class

```
public static string GetDashboardAuditQuery(string email = "")
{
    var finalQuery = string.Empty;

    // Add Email clause if email is passed as a parameter
    if (!string.IsNullOrWhiteSpace(email))
    {
        finalQuery = TableQuery.GenerateFilterCondition("ServiceEngineer", Constants.Equal,
        email);
    }

    return finalQuery;
}
```

Create GetServiceRequestsFromAudit method in IServiceRequestOperations interface as shown in Listing 10-24 which will server a business method to retrieve service request audit information.

Listing 10-24. GetServiceRequestsFormAudit method in IServiceRequestOperations interface

```
Task<List<ServiceRequest>> GetServiceRequestsFormAudit(string serviceEngineerEmail = "");
```

We need to implement GetServiceRequestsFromAudit method in ServiceRequestOperations as shown in Listing 10-25. GetServiceRequestsFromAudit calls GetDashboardAuditQuery to get the service request audit query and return the results to the invoking method.

Listing 10-25. GetServiceRequestsFormAudit method

```
public async Task<List<ServiceRequest>> GetServiceRequestsFormAudit(string
serviceEngineerEmail = "")
{
    var query = Queries.GetDashboardAuditQuery(serviceEngineerEmail);
    var serviceRequests = await _unitOfWork.Repository<ServiceRequest>().
    FindAllInAuditByQuery(query);
    return serviceRequests.ToList();
}
```

Now update the DashboardViewModel to hold the list of service requests from audit table as shown in Listing 10-26.

Listing 10-26. Updated DashboardViewModel class

```
using ASC.Models.Models;
using System.Collections.Generic;

namespace ASC.Web.Areas.ServiceRequests.Models
{
    public class DashboardViewModel
    {
        public List<ServiceRequest> ServiceRequests { get; set; }
        public List<ServiceRequest> AuditServiceRequests { get; set; }
    }
}
```

Update the Dashboard action from Dashboard controller to call GetServiceRequestsFromAudit method and pass the results back to view as shown in Listing 10-27.

Listing 10-27. Updated Dashboard action

```
        public async Task<IActionResult> Dashboard()
        {
            // List of Status which were to be queried.
            var status = new List<string>
                {
                    Status.New.ToString(),
                    Status.InProgress.ToString(),
```

```
                        Status.Initiated.ToString(),
                        Status.RequestForInformation.ToString()
            };

        List<ServiceRequest> serviceRequests = new List<ServiceRequest>();
        List<ServiceRequest> auditServiceRequests = new List<ServiceRequest>();
        if (HttpContext.User.IsInRole(Roles.Admin.ToString()))
        {
            serviceRequests = await _serviceRequestOperations.
            GetServiceRequestsByRequestedDateAndStatus(
                DateTime.UtcNow.AddDays(-7),
                status);

            auditServiceRequests = await _serviceRequestOperations.
            GetServiceRequestsFormAudit();
        }
        else if (HttpContext.User.IsInRole(Roles.Engineer.ToString()))
        {
            serviceRequests = await _serviceRequestOperations.
            GetServiceRequestsByRequestedDateAndStatus(
                DateTime.UtcNow.AddDays(-7),
                status,
                serviceEngineerEmail: HttpContext.User.GetCurrentUserDetails().Email);

            auditServiceRequests = await _serviceRequestOperations.
            GetServiceRequestsFormAudit(
                HttpContext.User.GetCurrentUserDetails().Email);
        }
        else
        {
            serviceRequests = await _serviceRequestOperations.
            GetServiceRequestsByRequestedDateAndStatus(
                DateTime.UtcNow.AddYears(-1),
                status,
                email: HttpContext.User.GetCurrentUserDetails().Email);
        }

var orderedAudit = auditServiceRequests.OrderByDescending(p => p.Timestamp).ToList();
        return View(new DashboardViewModel {
            ServiceRequests = serviceRequests.OrderByDescending(p => p.RequestedDate).
            ToList(),
            AuditServiceRequests = orderedAudit
        });
    }
```

Finally we will have to do modifications to the Dashboard.cshtml, we will add the same partial view which we added for Service Requests, but this time we will pass data from AuditServiceRequests property from Model and set IsAudit property to true as shown in Listing 10-28. We need to add a check to display the second partial view if user is in role of Admin or Engineer. In JQuery code, we will initialize the DataTable.

Listing 10-28. Updated Dashboard view

```
@model ASC.Web.Areas.ServiceRequests.Models.DashboardViewModel
@using Microsoft.AspNetCore.Http
@inject IHttpContextAccessor UserHttpContext
@using ASC.Models.BaseTypes
@{
    Layout = "_SecureLayout";
}

<div class="row"></div>
@await Html.PartialAsync("_ServiceRequestGrid", Model.ServiceRequests, new
ViewDataDictionary(ViewData) {
    { "SectionName", "Service Requests" },
    { "Id", "tblServiceRequests" },
    { "IsAudit", false }
})

@if (UserHttpContext.HttpContext.User.IsInRole(Roles.Admin.ToString()) ||
        UserHttpContext.HttpContext.User.IsInRole(Roles.Engineer.ToString()))
{
    @await Html.PartialAsync("_ServiceRequestGrid", Model.AuditServiceRequests,
    new ViewDataDictionary(ViewData) {
        { "SectionName", "Recent Updates" },
        { "Id", "tblAuditServiceRequests" },
    { "IsAudit", true }
})
}

@section Scripts{
    <script>
        $(document).ready(function () {
            // Initialize DataTable to show list of Service Requests
            var table = $('#tblServiceRequests').DataTable({
                'pageLength': 3,
                // Number of records to be displayed per page
                'lengthMenu': [[3, 5, 10, -1], [3, 5, 10, 'All']],
                // Remove default Sorting
                'sorting': [],
                'columns': [{ "visible": false }, { "visible": false }, null,
                { "width": "20%" }, null, null, null]
            });

            var table = $('#tblAuditServiceRequests').DataTable({
                'pageLength': 3,
                // Number of records to be displayed per page
                'lengthMenu': [[3, 5, 10, -1], [3, 5, 10, 'All']],
                // Remove default Sorting
                'sorting': [],
                'columns': [{ "visible": false }, { "visible": false }, null,
                { "width": "20%" }, null, null, null, null]
            });
```

```
        // Set Styles for DataTable and Number of Records to be displayed dropdown
        $('.tblServiceRequests').css("width", "100%");
        $('select[name$="ServiceRequests_length"]').material_select();


    });
    </script>
}
```

Run the application and login as admin or service engineer, we should see both the tables with service requests and audit information as shown in Figure 10-9. Now when a customer login and visits his dashboard, there will be only one table which displays his own service requests.

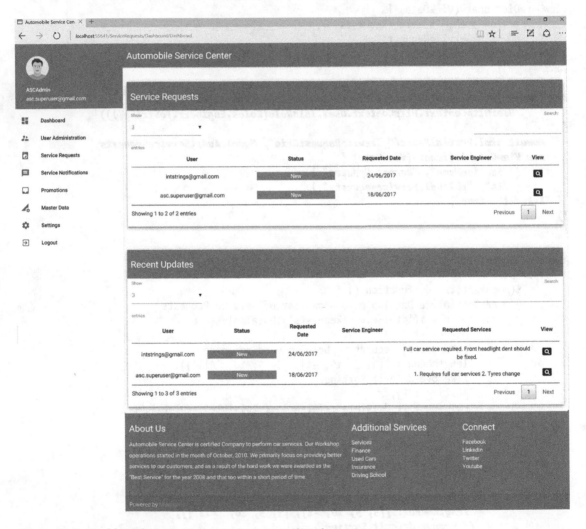

Figure 10-9. *Dashboard view with Service Request Audit information*

The last change which is required on dashboard view is to get statistics for admin role, where he can find the statistics about active service requests (which are in Initiated and InProgress status) are being handled by different service engineers. As we already have Repository methods in place, we need to come up with a query which will support to retrieve service requests which are in Initiated and InProgress status. Add GetDashboardServiceEngineersQuery method which will return query as shown in Listing 10-29. This method will take list of status as parameter and iterate all the statuses and finally return the concatenated where conditions to the invoking method.

Listing 10-29. GetDashboardServiceEngineersQuery method in Queries class

```
public static string GetDashboardServiceEngineersQuery(List<string> status)
{
    var finalQuery = string.Empty;
    var statusQueries = new List<string>();

    // Add Status clause if status is passed a parameter.
    foreach (var state in status)
    {
        statusQueries.Add(TableQuery.GenerateFilterCondition("Status", Constants.Equal,
        state));
    }
    finalQuery = string.Join(string.Format("{0} ", TableOperators.Or), statusQueries);

    return finalQuery;
}
```

Create GetActiveServiceRequests method in IServiceRequestOperations interface as shown in Listing 10-30 which will serve as business method.

Listing 10-30. GetActiveServiceRequests method in IRequestServiceOperations class

```
Task<List<ServiceRequest>> GetActiveServiceRequests(List<string> status);
```

We need to implement GetActiveServiceRequests method in ServiceRequestOperations as shown in Listing 10-31. GetActiveServiceRequests calls GetDashboardServiceEngineersQuery to get the active service request query and call repository's FindAllByQuery method which will return the results.

Listing 10-31. GetActiveServiceRequests method

```
public async Task<List<ServiceRequest>> GetActiveServiceRequests(List<string> status)
{
    var query = Queries.GetDashboardServiceEngineersQuery(status);
    var serviceRequests = await _unitOfWork.Repository<ServiceRequest>().
    FindAllByQuery(query);
    return serviceRequests.ToList();
}
```

Update the DashboardViewModel to hold the list of active service requests as shown in Listing 10-32.

Listing 10-32. Updated DashboardViewModel class

```
using ASC.Models.Models;
using System.Collections.Generic;

namespace ASC.Web.Areas.ServiceRequests.Models
{
    public class DashboardViewModel
    {
        public List<ServiceRequest> ServiceRequests { get; set; }
        public List<ServiceRequest> AuditServiceRequests { get; set; }
        public Dictionary<string,int> ActiveServiceRequests { get; set; }
    }
}
```

Update the Dashboard action from Dashboard controller to call GetActiveServiceRequests method and pass the results back to view as shown in Listing 10-33. All the results which are returned from the business components are grouped by service engineer property and then converted to Dictionary<string, int> which will contain total count of services against each service engineer. The dictionary is then assigned to the ActiveServiceRequests property of DashboardViewModel.

Listing 10-33. Updated Dashboard action

```
public async Task<IActionResult> Dashboard()
{
    // List of Status which were to be queried.
    var status = new List<string>
        {
            Status.New.ToString(),
            Status.InProgress.ToString(),
            Status.Initiated.ToString(),
            Status.RequestForInformation.ToString()
        };

    List<ServiceRequest> serviceRequests = new List<ServiceRequest>();
    List<ServiceRequest> auditServiceRequests = new List<ServiceRequest>();
    Dictionary<string, int> activeServiceRequests = new Dictionary<string, int>();
    if (HttpContext.User.IsInRole(Roles.Admin.ToString()))
    {
        serviceRequests = await _serviceRequestOperations.
        GetServiceRequestsByRequestedDateAndStatus(
            DateTime.UtcNow.AddDays(-7),
            status);

        auditServiceRequests = await _serviceRequestOperations.
        GetServiceRequestsFormAudit();

        var serviceEngineerServiceRequests = await _serviceRequestOperations.
        GetActiveServiceRequests(new List<string>
        {
            Status.InProgress.ToString(),
            Status.Initiated.ToString(),
        });
```

```
        if (serviceEngineerServiceRequests.Any())
        {
            activeServiceRequests = serviceEngineerServiceRequests
                .GroupBy(x => x.ServiceEngineer)
                .ToDictionary(p => p.Key, p => p.Count());
        }
    }
    else if (HttpContext.User.IsInRole(Roles.Engineer.ToString()))
    {
        serviceRequests = await _serviceRequestOperations.
        GetServiceRequestsByRequestedDateAndStatus(
            DateTime.UtcNow.AddDays(-7),
            status,
            serviceEngineerEmail: HttpContext.User.GetCurrentUserDetails().Email);

        auditServiceRequests = await _serviceRequestOperations.GetServiceRequestsFormAudit(
            HttpContext.User.GetCurrentUserDetails().Email);
    }
    else
    {
        serviceRequests = await _serviceRequestOperations.
        GetServiceRequestsByRequestedDateAndStatus(
            DateTime.UtcNow.AddYears(-1),
            status,
            email: HttpContext.User.GetCurrentUserDetails().Email);
    }

    var orderedAudit = auditServiceRequests.OrderByDescending(p => p.Timestamp).ToList();
    return View(new DashboardViewModel {
        ServiceRequests = serviceRequests.OrderByDescending(p => p.RequestedDate).ToList(),
        AuditServiceRequests = orderedAudit,
        ActiveServiceRequests = activeServiceRequests
    });
}
```

Now we need to extend Dashboard.cshtml to include active service requests statistics for admin role. Append Dashboard.cshtml with code show in Listing 10-34. It first checks if the logged-in user is an admin, if not then it will not render the statistics collection. For admin, it will iterate all the active service requests dictionary items and render using li tag. If there are no active services going, then a generic message will be shown to admin.

Listing 10-34. Service Engineers statistics markup code

```
@if (UserHttpContext.HttpContext.User.IsInRole(Roles.Admin.ToString()))
{
    <div class="row">
        <div class="col s6">
            <ul class="collection with-header height-300px overflow-y">
                <li class="collection-header"><h5>Active Service Engineers</h5></li>
                @if (Model.ActiveServiceRequests.Any())
                {
                    @foreach (var activeServiceRequest in Model.ActiveServiceRequests)
```

```
                {
                    <li class="collection-item">
                        <div>
                            <span class="new badge" data-badge-
                            caption="">@activeServiceRequest.Value</
                            span>@activeServiceRequest.Key
                        </div>
                    </li>
                }
                }
                else
                {
                    <li class="collection-item">
                        <div class="card-panel teal lighten-2 white-text">No Activer Service
                        Requests.</div>
                    </li>
                }
            </ul>
        </div>
    </div>
}
```

■ **Note**   Add the following styles to style.css to support vertical scroll bar for active service engineers section.

```
.height-300px{
    height: 300px;
}
.overflow-y{
    overflow-y: auto;

}
```

Run the application and login as admin, we should see the collection of service engineers and their active service requests as shown in Figure 10-10. When a customer or service engineer login to the system, they will not be able to see this section.

■ **Note**   For demonstration, I manually updated Service Engineer property with asc.superengineer@gmail.com account for couple of ServiceRequest entities in local development Azure Table Storage. I also updated the Status property of entities to InProgress and Initiated values.

Once testing is done, we need to revert the values to old values.

Figure 10-10. Active Service Engineers section in Dashboard view

In case if there are no active service requests, 'No Active Service Requests' message will be displayed for admin as shown in Figure 10-11.

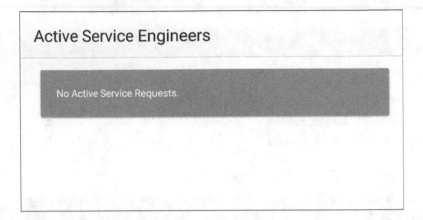

Figure 10-11. *No Active Service Requests message*

Service Request Details View

So far in this chapter, we have developed pages to create a new service request and a dashboard view which is common to all user roles but displays different information based on the role of logged in user. In both these pages we do not have an option to update a service request with new information or to change the status of service request. In this section we will create service request details view which can be used to view the details of a service along with options to update the information. User can navigate to service request details view from dashboard by clicking the view icon of a particular service.

First we will create a GET action with name ServiceRequestDetails in ServiceRequestController of ServiceRequests area as shown in Listing 10-35 which will return the Service Request Details view.

Listing 10-35. ServiceRequestDetails action

```
[HttpGet]
public async Task<IActionResult> ServiceRequestDetails(string id)
{
    return View();
}
```

Create a corresponding ServiceRequestDetails.cshtml in Views/ServiceRequest folder of ServiceRequests area as shown in Listing 10-36. For now, the view is blnak, we will add more display logic later in this section.

Listing 10-36. ServiceRequestDetails view

```
@{
    Layout = "_SecureLayout";
}

<div class="row"></div>
```

Now we will add the redirection from dashboard view to service request details view. Add the JQuery click event for View icon in Dashboard.cshtml as shown in Listing 10-37. In the click event, we will get the RowKey from the corresponding DataTable (either main service requests table or audit table) based on the view icon. We will then navigate to the service details action with the id of service request.

Listing 10-37. JQuery click event of view icon on Dashboard view

```
// On click of View icon, redirect to Service Request Details View based on RowKey
$(document).on('click', '.view', function () {
    var tableId = '#' + $(this).parents('table').attr('id');
    var serviceRequest = $(tableId).DataTable().row($(this).parents('tr')).data();

    // For Service Request Table, populate id with RowKey
    var id = serviceRequest[0];
    // For Service Request Audit Table, populate id by splitting the Partition key with '-'
    if (tableId.indexOf('Audit') >= 0)
        id = serviceRequest[1].substring(serviceRequest[1].indexOf('-') + 1,
        serviceRequest[1].length);

        window.location.href = '@Url.Action("ServiceRequestDetails",
                            "ServiceRequest",
                            new { Area = "ServiceRequests" })?Id=' + id;
});
```

In service request details view, we will display the details along with audit information of service request. To get both service request along with audit data, we need to construct the query which can be used to retrieve data from ServiceRequest Azure table storage. Add GetServiceRequestDetailsQuery and GetServiceRequestAuditDetailsQuery methods in Queries class of ASC.Models project as shown in Listing 10-38.

Listing 10-38. Service Request Details query methods in Queries class

```
public static string GetServiceRequestDetailsQuery(string id)
{
    return TableQuery.GenerateFilterCondition("RowKey", Constants.Equal, id);
}

public static string GetServiceRequestAuditDetailsQuery(string id)
{
    return TableQuery.GenerateFilterCondition("PartitionKey", Constants.Equal, id);
}
```

To get the service request and its audit details, we need to add GetServiceRequestByRowKey and GetServiceRequestAuditByPartitionKey methods in IServiceRequestOperations interface as shown in Listing 10-39. These methods will serve as business methods which will be invoked from Web project.

Listing 10-39. GetServiceRequestByRowKey and GetServiceRequestAuditByPartitionKey methods in IServiceRequestOperations interface

```
Task<ServiceRequest> GetServiceRequestByRowKey(string id);
Task<List<ServiceRequest>> GetServiceRequestAuditByPartitionKey(string id);
```

We need to implement GetServiceRequestByRowKey and GetServiceRequestAuditByPartitionKey methods in ServiceRequestOperations as shown in Listing 10-40. GetServiceRequestByRowKey calls GetServiceRequestDetailsQuery to get the details of service request query and return the results to the invoking method. GetServiceRequestAuditByPartitionKey calls GetServiceRequestAuditDetailsQuery to get the audit details of service request and return the results to the caller method.

Listing 10-40. GetServiceRequestByRowKey and GetServiceRequestAuditByPartitionKey methods

```
public async Task<ServiceRequest> GetServiceRequestByRowKey(string id)
{
    var query = Queries.GetServiceRequestDetailsQuery(id);
    var serviceRequests = await _unitOfWork.Repository<ServiceRequest>().
    FindAllByQuery(query);
    return serviceRequests.FirstOrDefault();
}

public async Task<List<ServiceRequest>> GetServiceRequestAuditByPartitionKey(string id)
{
    var query = Queries.GetServiceRequestAuditDetailsQuery(id);
    var serviceRequests = await _unitOfWork.Repository<ServiceRequest>().
    FindAllInAuditByQuery(query);
    return serviceRequests.ToList();
}
```

Create a new view model in ASC.Web project under ServiceRequests area with name UpdateServiceRequestViewModel by extending NewServiceRequestViewModel as shown in Listing 10-41. This view model is primarily used to update the service request information and it holds properties like RowKey, PartitionKey etc. which are not present in NewServiceRequestViewModel.

Listing 10-41. UpdateServiceRequestViewModel class

```
using System;
using System.ComponentModel.DataAnnotations;

namespace ASC.Web.Areas.ServiceRequests.Models
{
    public class UpdateServiceRequestViewModel : NewServiceRequestViewModel
    {
        public string RowKey { get; set; }
        public string PartitionKey { get; set; }
        [Required]
        [Display(Name = "Service Engineer")]
        public string ServiceEngineer { get; set; }
        [Required]
        [Display(Name = "Status")]
        public string Status { get; set; }
    }
}
```

Create the ServiceRequestDetailViewModel class in Models folder of ServiceRequests area as shown in Listing 10-42. For now, it will have two properties to hold data of service request and its corresponding audit information.

Listing 10-42. ServiceRequestDetailViewModel class

```
using ASC.Models.Models;
using System.Collections.Generic;

namespace ASC.Web.Areas.ServiceRequests.Models
{
    public class ServiceRequestDetailViewModel
    {
        public UpdateServiceRequestViewModel ServiceRequest { get; set; }
        public List<ServiceRequest> ServiceRequestAudit { get; set; }
    }
}
```

Update the AutoMapper's mappings in ServiceRequestMappingProfile class to support UpdateServiceRequestViewModel transformation to ServiceRequest model as vice versa as shown in Listing 10-43.

Listing 10-43. Updated ServiceRequestMappingProfile class

```
CreateMap<ServiceRequest, UpdateServiceRequestViewModel>();
CreateMap<UpdateServiceRequestViewModel, ServiceRequest>();
```

Update the ServiceRequest controller's ServiceRequestDetails action as shown in Listing 10-44. In the action, we are calling GetServiceRequestByRowKey and GetServiceRequestAuditByPartitionKey methods and getting service request related information. User access check is performed to make sure the logged in user is authorized to view the details of service request. Vehicle names and types are populated from master data cache, status is retrieved from Status Enum and all users in service engineer roles are fetched using UserManager<>. All the collections are stored in ViewBag to display in view. Finally ServiceRequestDetailViewModel is returned to the view.

Listing 10-44. Updated ServiceRequestDetails action

```
using Microsoft.AspNetCore.Mvc;
// Using Statements removed for brevity.

namespace ASC.Web.Areas.ServiceRequests.Controllers
{
    [Area("ServiceRequests")]
    public class ServiceRequestController : BaseController
    {
        private readonly IServiceRequestOperations _serviceRequestOperations;
        private readonly IMapper _mapper;
        private readonly IMasterDataCacheOperations _masterData;
        private readonly UserManager<ApplicationUser> _userManager;
        public ServiceRequestController(IServiceRequestOperations operations, IMapper
        mapper, IMasterDataCacheOperations masterData, UserManager<ApplicationUser>
        userManager)
        {
            _serviceRequestOperations = operations;
            _mapper = mapper;
```

```csharp
            _masterData = masterData;
            _userManager = userManager;
        }

// Code removed for brevity.

        [HttpGet]
        public async Task<IActionResult> ServiceRequestDetails(string id)
        {
            var serviceRequestDetails = await _serviceRequestOperations.
            GetServiceRequestByRowKey(id);

            // Access Check
            if (HttpContext.User.IsInRole(Roles.Engineer.ToString())
                && serviceRequestDetails.ServiceEngineer != HttpContext.User.
                GetCurrentUserDetails().Email)
            {
                throw new UnauthorizedAccessException();
            }

            if (HttpContext.User.IsInRole(Roles.User.ToString())
                && serviceRequestDetails.PartitionKey != HttpContext.User.
                GetCurrentUserDetails().Email)
            {
                throw new UnauthorizedAccessException();
            }

            var serviceRequestAuditDetails = await _serviceRequestOperations.
            GetServiceRequestAuditByPartitionKey(
                serviceRequestDetails.PartitionKey + "-" + id);

            // Select List Data
            var masterData = await _masterData.GetMasterDataCacheAsync();
            ViewBag.VehicleTypes = masterData.Values.Where(p => p.PartitionKey ==
            MasterKeys.VehicleType.ToString()).ToList();
            ViewBag.VehicleNames = masterData.Values.Where(p => p.PartitionKey ==
            MasterKeys.VehicleName.ToString()).ToList();
            ViewBag.Status = Enum.GetValues(typeof(Status)).Cast<Status>().Select(v =>
            v.ToString()).ToList();
            ViewBag.ServiceEngineers = await _userManager.GetUsersInRoleAsync(Roles.
            Engineer.ToString());

            return View(new ServiceRequestDetailViewModel
            {
                ServiceRequest = _mapper.Map<ServiceRequest, UpdateServiceRequestViewModel>(
                serviceRequestDetails),
                ServiceRequestAudit = serviceRequestAuditDetails.OrderByDescending(p =>
                p.Timestamp).ToList()
            });
        }
    }
}
```

Service Request Details view is a simple view which has two sections, the details section and audit section. In the details section, we show all the details related to service request, whereas in audit section we show a grid with all audit items.

In the details section, only admin can edit service engineer field. Whereas an admin or service engineer can edit status field (customer can edit status field only if status is PendingCustomerApproval). At any point of time, nobody can edit the basic information of a service request like Vehicle Name, Type and Requested Date. Requested Services can be changed at any time by customer, admin and service engineer.

All the controls in the details view are rendered with traditional HTML tags with asp-for bindings. Vehicle Name, Type and Requested Date are disabled using disabled attribute. RowKey, PartitionKey and RequestedDate are placed in hidden fields, so that they will be posted along with form in update operation. All the controls are placed inside a form which can be posted to server action on update button click. Audit details section is rendered using _ServiceRequestGrid partial view and passing ServiceRequestAudit parameter of ServiceRequestDetailViewModel model. DataTable, Select and Date picker controls are initialized with Materialize styles in JQuery. Service Request Details view is shown in Listing 10-45.

Listing 10-45. Service Request Details view

```
@model ASC.Web.Areas.ServiceRequests.Models.ServiceRequestDetailViewModel
@using Microsoft.AspNetCore.Http
@using ASC.Models.BaseTypes
@inject IHttpContextAccessor UserHttpContext
@{
    Layout = "_SecureLayout";
}


@{
    // Compute Service Engineer and Status Disable logic
    string serviceEngineerDisabled = null;
    if (!UserHttpContext.HttpContext.User.IsInRole(Roles.Admin.ToString()))
    {
        serviceEngineerDisabled = "disabled";
    }

    string statusDisabled = null;
    if (!UserHttpContext.HttpContext.User.IsInRole(Roles.Admin.ToString()) &&
        !UserHttpContext.HttpContext.User.IsInRole(Roles.Engineer.ToString()))
    {
        statusDisabled = "disabled";
    }

    // Customer can update the status only if the original status is Customer pending
        approval.
    if (UserHttpContext.HttpContext.User.IsInRole(Roles.User.ToString()) &&
    Model.ServiceRequest.Status == Status.PendingCustomerApproval.ToString())
    {
        statusDisabled = null;
        ViewBag.Status = new List<string> { "Completed", "RequestForInformation" };
    }
}
```

```
<div class="row"></div>
<div class="row padding-top-20px">

    @* Details Section *@
    <div class="row z-depth-3">
        <div class="col s12 padding-0px">
            <div class="section white-text padding-left-10px blue-grey lighten-1">
                <h5>Service Request Details</h5>
            </div>
            <div class="divider"></div>
            <form asp-controller="ServiceRequest" asp-action="UpdateServiceRequestDetails"
            method="post" class="col s12">
                <input type="hidden" asp-for="ServiceRequest.RowKey" />
                <input type="hidden" asp-for="ServiceRequest.PartitionKey" />
                <input type="hidden" asp-for="ServiceRequest.RequestedDate" />
                <div class="row">
                    <div class="input-field col s4">
                        <select asp-for="ServiceRequest.VehicleName"
                                asp-items="@(new SelectList(ViewBag.VehicleNames,"RowKey","
                                Name"))"
                                class="" required="required" disabled>
                            <option value="">Please select one</option>
                        </select>
                        <label asp-for="ServiceRequest.VehicleName"></label>
                    </div>
                    <div class="input-field col s4">
                        <select asp-for="ServiceRequest.VehicleType"
                                asp-items="@(new SelectList(ViewBag.VehicleTypes,"RowKey","
                                Name"))"
                                class="validate" required="required" disabled>
                            <option value="">Please select one</option>
                        </select>
                        <label asp-for="ServiceRequest.VehicleType"></label>
                    </div>
                    <div class="input-field col s4">
                        <input asp-for="ServiceRequest.RequestedDate" type="text"
                        disabled="disabled" class="datepicker"/>
                        <label asp-for="ServiceRequest.RequestedDate"></label>
                    </div>
                </div>
                <div class="row">
                    <div class="input-field col s8">
                        <textarea asp-for="ServiceRequest.RequestedServices"
                        class="materialize-textarea validate"></textarea>
                        <label asp-for="ServiceRequest.RequestedServices"></label>
                    </div>
                </div>
```

```html
<div class="row">
    <div class="input-field col s4">
        <select asp-for="ServiceRequest.ServiceEngineer"
                asp-items="@(new SelectList(ViewBag.ServiceEngineers,
                "Email", "Email"))"
                class="" required="required" disabled=@service
                EngineerDisabled>
            <option value="">Please select one</option>
        </select>
        <label asp-for="ServiceRequest.ServiceEngineer"></label>
    </div>
    <div class="input-field col s4">
        <select asp-for="ServiceRequest.Status"
                asp-items="@(new SelectList(ViewBag.Status))"
                class="validate" required="required"
                disabled=@statusDisabled>
            <option value="">Please select one</option>
        </select>
        <label asp-for="ServiceRequest.Status"></label>
    </div>
    <div class="input-field col s12 right-align">
        <button class="btn waves-effect waves-light btnSubmit" type="submit"
        name="action">
            Update
            <i class="material-icons right">send</i>
        </button>
    </div>
    <div class="row col s12 right-align" asp-validation-summary="All"></div>
    </div>
</form>

</div>
<div class="row"></div>
</div>

@await Html.PartialAsync("_ServiceRequestGrid", Model.ServiceRequestAudit, new
ViewDataDictionary(ViewData) {
    { "SectionName", "Recent Updates" },
    { "Id", "tblAuditServiceRequests" },
    { "IsAudit", true }
})
</div>

@section Scripts{
    <script>
        $(document).ready(function () {
            // Initialize DataTable to show list of Service Requests
            var table = $('.tblServiceRequests').DataTable({
                'pageLength': 3,
                // Number of records to be displayed per page
                'lengthMenu': [[3, 5, 10, -1], [3, 5, 10, 'All']],
```

```
                // Remove default Sorting
                'sorting': [],
                'columns': [{ "visible": false }, { "visible": false }, null,
                { "width": "20%" }, null, null, null, { "visible": false }]
        });

                // Set Styles for DataTable and Number of Records to be displayed dropdown
                $('.tblServiceRequests').css("width", "100%");
                $('select[name$="ServiceRequests_length"]').material_select();

                // Initialize DatePicker
                $('.datepicker').pickadate({
                    selectMonths: true,
                    selectYears: 15
                });

                // initialize Material Select
                $('select').material_select();
                $("select[required]").css({ display: "block", position: 'absolute',
                visibility: 'hidden' })
        });
    </script>
}
```

Create a POST action with name UpdateServiceRequestDetails in ServiceRequest controller as shown in Listing 10-46. The POST action will take UpdateServiceRequestViewModel as input and updates the service request using UpdateServiceRequestAsync method of IServiceRequestOperations. Action method will update Status and Service Engineer fields based on user role who is trying to update the values. Customer can only update the status of the service request only if it is in PendingCustomerApproval. On successful update, the control will be redirected to ServiceRequestDetails action with corresponding RowKey.

Listing 10-46. UpdateServiceRequestDetails action

```
[HttpPost]
public async Task<IActionResult> UpdateServiceRequestDetails(UpdateServiceRequestViewModel
serviceRequest)
{
    var originalServiceRequest = await _serviceRequestOperations.GetServiceRequestByRowKey(s
    erviceRequest.RowKey);
    originalServiceRequest.RequestedServices = serviceRequest.RequestedServices;

    // Update Status only if user role is either Admin or Engineer
    // Or Customer can update the status if it is only in Pending Customer Approval.
    if (HttpContext.User.IsInRole(Roles.Admin.ToString()) ||
        HttpContext.User.IsInRole(Roles.Engineer.ToString()) ||
        (HttpContext.User.IsInRole(Roles.User.ToString()) && originalServiceRequest.Status
        == Status.PendingCustomerApproval.ToString()))
    {
        originalServiceRequest.Status = serviceRequest.Status;
    }
```

```
// Update Service Engineer field only if user role is Admin
if (HttpContext.User.IsInRole(Roles.Admin.ToString()))
{
    originalServiceRequest.ServiceEngineer = serviceRequest.ServiceEngineer;
}

await _serviceRequestOperations.UpdateServiceRequestAsync(originalServiceRequest);

return RedirectToAction("ServiceRequestDetails", "ServiceRequest",
    new { Area = "ServiceRequests", Id = serviceRequest.RowKey });
}
```

Run the application and login as admin, navigate to any service request from dashboard by clicking the view icon. We should see service request details view as shown in Figure 10-12.

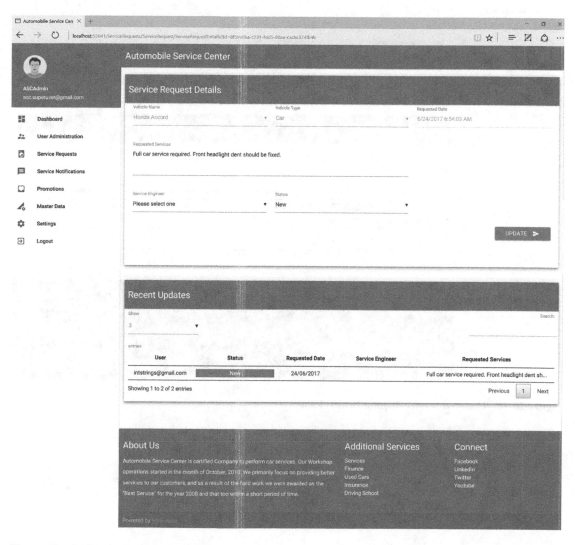

Figure 10-12. Service Request Details View

Assign a service engineer and change the status of service request from New to Initiated and click update button. Service Request details will be updated and redirected to the same service request details view. Updated service request details along with audit details are shown in Figure 10-13.

Figure 10-13. *Updated Service Request Details View*

When a service engineer logs in to the system, he should the initiated service request in his queue and can view details as shown in Figure 10-14.

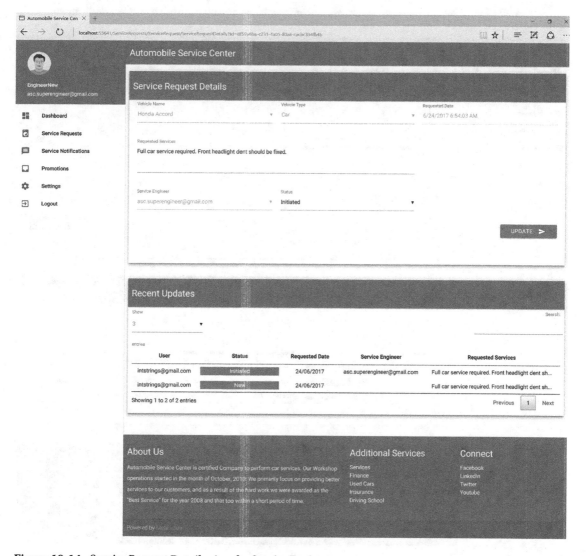

Figure 10-14. *Service Request Details view for Service Engineer*

Service engineer can change the status to InProgress and continue with the service request progress. When a customer logs into the system, he should see updated service request details as shown in Figure 10-15.

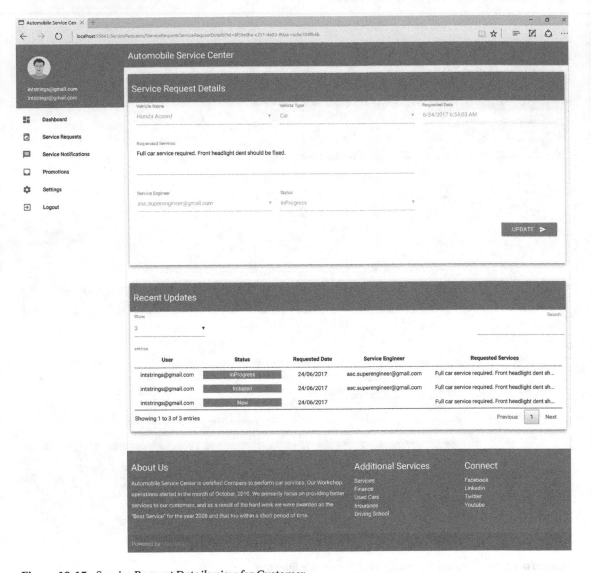

Figure 10-15. *Service Request Details view for Customer*

As time progress, service engineer might complete the all the services required and mark the status of service as PendingCustomerApproval. At this time when customer logs into the system, he should see the status field enabled with only two options Completed and RequestForInformation which are used to mark the service request as complete or seeking for more information. Customer can select any of the status and click on update and subsequent work flow from Admin and Service Engineer will kick off.

When an Admin logs in he will not be able to see the service request in his service requests queue (because of the service request status filter which we applied in Dashboard Service Requests table), but he can navigate to the service request from recent updates grid. Now he can perform actions on service request similar to pervious operations. In the same way service engineer can also update the status of the service request.

Figure 10-16. *Completed Service Request Details View*

Custom Validations using DataAnnotation Attributes

Data integrity and consistency are crucial factors for the success of any modern day application. With ever growing data interfaces and different channels for data acquisition and ingestion, maintaining data quality is a typical challenge faced by many applications. Furthermore the complex business requirements and complicated integrations add more risks to maintain consistent superior data quality conditions. The current day trend shows that many organizations spend more time and effort on data cleansing techniques than ever before to make sure the automated business decisions are accurate.

One way to mitigate the risk of data fragility is to design a good validation framework which will ensure all the data is thoroughly validated before making to business component methods. Fortunately ASP.NET Core provides a good validation attributes through which an application can validate data for type, size, format, range etc. This validation is typically called as Model Validation.

Following are some of the prominent DataAnnotation attributes provided by ASP.NET Core which can be decorated on top of any property of a model.

1. **Required**: Makes a property required.

2. **StringLength**: Validates that a string property has at most the given maximum length.

3. **Range**: Validates the property value falls within the given range.

4. **RegularExpression**: Validates that the data matches the specified regular expression.

5. **Phone**: Validates the property has a telephone format.

6. **Compare**: Validates two properties in a model match.

7. **EmailAddress**: Validates the property has an email format.

8. **Url**: Validates the property has a URL format.

In ASP.NET Core, Model Validation happens before even reaching the controller action and all the model validation errors will be present in ModelState. In controller action, we need to inspect ModelState. IsValid to check if there are any model validation errors and take appropriate action.

Sometimes the default ASP.NET Core provided validation attributes will not suffice to achieve the business validation requirements. Those custom validations can be achieved by creating custom validation attributes from ValidationAttribute or by implementing IValidatableObject on model. In Automobile Service Center application, we will take following uses cases to define custom validations.

1. A Service Request cannot be submitted if Requested Date is after 90 days from current date.

2. A Customer cannot submit a service request, if admin has denied his service request in past 90 days.

We will get started by creating a folder with name ValidationAttributes in ASC.Utilities project. Create a class with name FutureDateAttribute in ValidationAttributes folder as shown in Listing 10-47. This class implements ValidationAttribute and IClientModelValidator which are used to achieve server and client side validations respectively. FutureDateAttribute takes an int as a parameter through which we can specify the number of days the validation attribute should take into consideration while validating a DateTime value. We will override IsValid method of ValidationAttribute within which we check for DateTime value is in the permissible limit of the number of day's parameter from current date.

We will implement AddValidation method of IClientModelValidator interface which will help us in setting the client side data-val custom attributes through which we can achieve client side custom validation.

Listing 10-47. FutureDateAttribute class

```
using Microsoft.AspNetCore.Mvc.ModelBinding.Validation;
using System;
using System.ComponentModel.DataAnnotations;

namespace ASC.Utilities.ValidationAttributes
{
    public class FutureDateAttribute : ValidationAttribute, IClientModelValidator
    {
        private readonly int _days;
        private readonly string _errorMessage = "Date cannot be after {0} days from current
        date.";

        private FutureDateAttribute() { }
        public FutureDateAttribute(int days)
        {
            _days = days;
        }

        protected override ValidationResult IsValid(object value, ValidationContext
        validationContext)
        {
            var date = (DateTime)value;

            if (date > DateTime.UtcNow.AddDays(_days))
                return new ValidationResult(string.Format(_errorMessage, _days));

            return ValidationResult.Success;
        }

        public void AddValidation(ClientModelValidationContext context)
        {
            context.Attributes.Add("data-val-futuredate", string.Format(_errorMessage,
            _days));
            context.Attributes.Add("data-val-futuredate-days", _days.ToString());
        }
    }
}
```

Decorate the FutureDate attribute on RequestedDate property of NewServiceRequestViewModel as shown in Listing 10-48.

Listing 10-48. Usage of FutureDate attribute

```
[Required]
[FutureDate(90)]
[Display(Name = "Requested Date")]
public DateTime? RequestedDate { get; set; }
```

Run the application and navigate to New Service Request page. Enter a future date which is more than 90 days from current date and click create. We should be custom validation error message as shown in Figure 10-17.

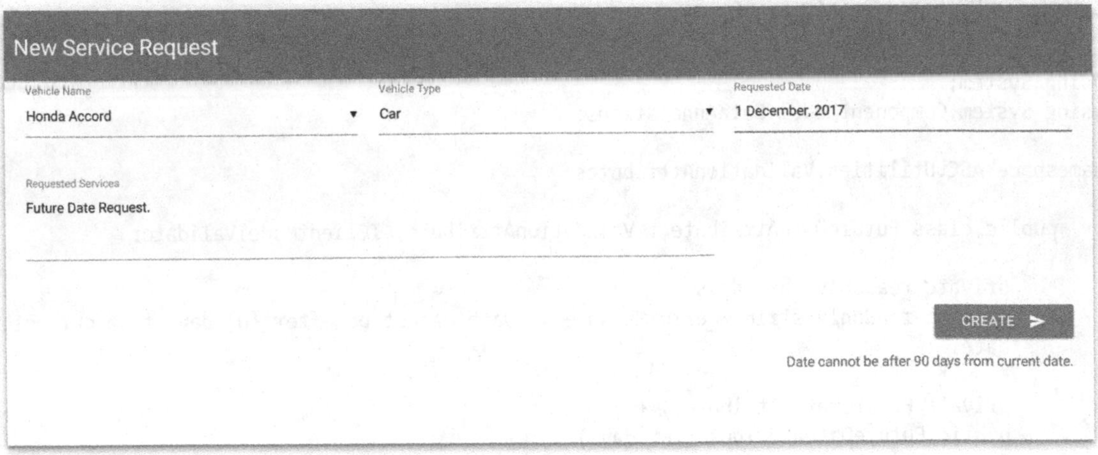

Figure 10-17. Future date validation on New Service Request screen

The validation which we have implemented is server side validation. Now we will implement client side validation. Update init.js file as shown in Listing 10-49 to include a validation method which actually performs the validation and an adapter which adds the validation function to the validation list for the input field (in our case Requested Date). The validation adapter attaches the parameters, especially days values from data-val-futuredate-days to the validation function. Validation function gets the selected requested date and compares with the computed future data (current UTC date + data-val-futuredate-days value), if the requested date is before the computed future date, then validation function returns true otherwise false. Validation error message will be pulled from data-val-futuredate attribute and will be displayed in validation summary div.

Listing 10-49. JQuery validation function for FutureDate validation

```
(function ($) {
    $(function () {
        $('.button-collapse').sideNav();
        $('.parallax').parallax();

        //Prevent browser back and forward buttons.
        if (window.history && window.history.pushState) {
            window.history.pushState('forward', '', '');

            $(window).on('popstate', function (e) {
                window.history.pushState('forward', '', '');
                e.preventDefault();
            });
        }

        //Prevent right click on entire window
        $(document).ready(function () {
            $(window).on("contextmenu", function () {
                return false;
            });
```

```
        $('#selectCulture').material_select();
    });
}); // end of document ready

// Future Date Vallidation method.
$.validator.addMethod('futuredate', function (value, element, params) {
    var selectedDate = new Date(value),
        now = new Date(),
        futureDate = new Date(),
        todaysUtcDate = new Date(now.getUTCFullYear(), now.getUTCMonth(),
          now.getUTCDate(), now.getUTCHours(), now.getUTCMinutes(), now.getUTCSeconds());
    futureDate.setDate(todaysUtcDate.getDate() + parseInt(params[0]));
    if (selectedDate >= futureDate) {
        return false;
    }
    return true;
});

// Add Future Date adapter.
$.validator.unobtrusive.adapters.add('futuredate',
    ['days'],
    function (options) {
        options.rules['futuredate'] = [parseInt(options.params['days'])];
        options.messages['futuredate'] = options.message;
    });
})(jQuery); // end of jQuery name space
```

Run the application and navigate to new service request screen. Enter a future date which is greater than 90 days from current data and click create. We should see validation error message as shown in Figure 10-18.

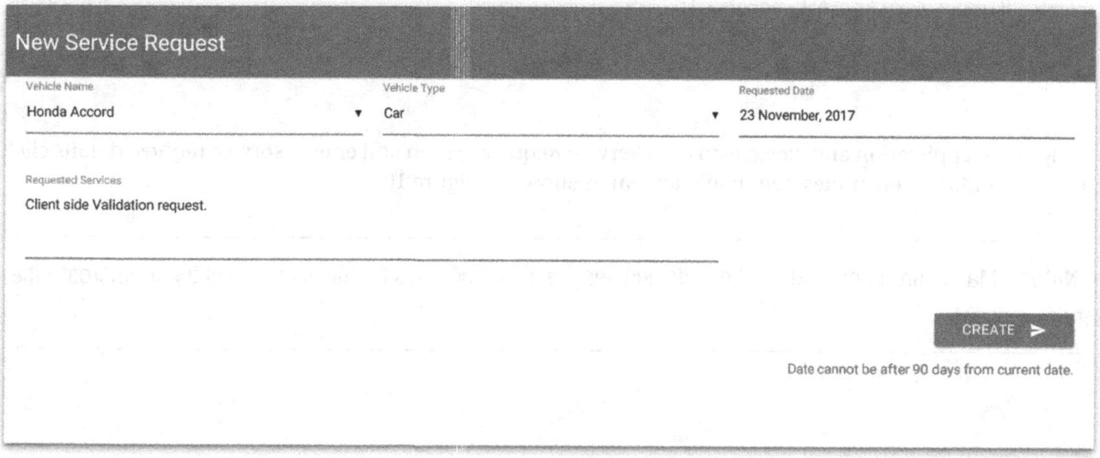

Figure 10-18. *Client side future date validation on New Service Request screen*

The next validation which we will implement will check if the customer who is about to submit a new service request has a service denial in last 90 days. If there is a denied service request, then customer needs to contact Automobile Service Center to process the new service request. We will use ASP.NET Core's Remote validation feature to achieve this validation.

Decorate RequestedDate property of NewServiceRequestViewModel with RemoteAttribute as shown in Listing 10-50. RemoteAttribute takes action, controller and area as parameters, this configuration tells remote validation to use the specified action for validating data.

Listing 10-50. Usage of Remote attribute

```
[Required]
[FutureDate(90)]
[Remote(action: "CheckDenialService", controller: "ServiceRequest", areaName:
"ServiceRequests")]
[Display(Name = "Requested Date")]
public DateTime? RequestedDate { get; set; }
```

Now we will create the action in ServiceRequest controller of ServiceRequests area as shown in Listing 10-51.

Listing 10-51. CheckDenialService action

```
public async Task<IActionResult> CheckDenialService(DateTime requestedDate)
{
    var serviceRequests = await _serviceRequestOperations.
    GetServiceRequestsByRequestedDateAndStatus(
        DateTime.UtcNow.AddDays(-90),
        new List<string>() { Status.Denied.ToString() },
        HttpContext.User.GetCurrentUserDetails().Email);

    if (serviceRequests.Any())
        return Json(data: $"There is a denied service request for you in last 90 days.
        Please contact ASC Admin.");

    return Json(data: true);
}
```

Run the application and navigate to New Service Request screen and enter a service request details click create. A Validation error message should appear as shown in Figure 10-19.

■ **Note**   Make sure to have at least one denied service in last 90 days for the user who is trying to create the service request.

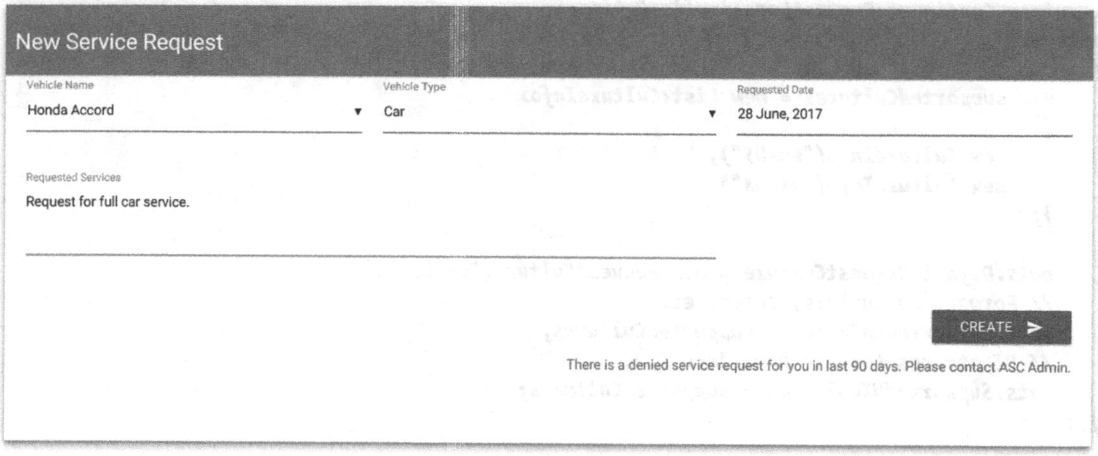

Figure 10-19. *Denial Service Validation*

Adding Internationalization Support

Automobile Service Center application is a system designed for a fictitious US Automobile servicing company. Even though English is the primary language which is supported by the application, to reach broader audience, Automobile Service Center application should be extended for multiple cultures and languages.

Internationalization is the process of converting a web application into a global application by adding multilingual support. Internationalization is a combination of two main important process, Globalization and Localization. Globalization is the process of extending an application to support multiple cultures (languages and regions). Localization is the process of customization of application for a particular culture. ASP.NET Core provides good support to create localized web applications. For Automobile Service Center application, we will configure US English (en-US) and Mexican Spanish (es-MX).

We will get start by configuring Localization in ConfigureServices method of Startup class as shown in Listing 10-52. AddLocalization adds localization services to the services container and configure the Resources path to Resource folder in the project. AddViewLocalization is used to support localized view files (for example Index.es.cshtml file). AddDataAnnotationsLocalization adds support for localized DataAnnotation validation messages. The list of cultures which are supported by the application are also configured at ConfigureServices method of Startup class. The default culture for every request is configured to en-US.

Listing 10-52. Add Localization Service in Startup class

```
services.AddLocalization(options => options.ResourcesPath = "Resources");

services
    .AddMvc(o => { o.Filters.Add(typeof(CustomExceptionFilter)); })
    .AddJsonOptions(options => options.SerializerSettings.ContractResolver = new
    DefaultContractResolver())
    .AddViewLocalization(LanguageViewLocationExpanderFormat.Suffix, options => { options.
    ResourcesPath = "Resources"; })
    .AddDataAnnotationsLocalization();
```

345

```
services.Configure<RequestLocalizationOptions>(
opts =>
{
    var supportedCultures = new List<CultureInfo>
    {
        new CultureInfo("en-US"),
        new CultureInfo("es-MX")
    };

    opts.DefaultRequestCulture = new RequestCulture("en-US");
    // Formatting numbers, dates, etc.
    opts.SupportedCultures = supportedCultures;
    // UI strings that we have localized.
    opts.SupportedUICultures = supportedCultures;
});
```

We use RequestLocalization middleware as shown in Listing 10-53 to configure the default providers to preserve the culture. The RequestLocalization middleware supports three default culture providers. The middleware is configured in Configure method of Startup class.

1. QueryStringRequestCultureProvider

2. AcceptLanguageHeaderRequestCultureProvider

3. CookieRequestCultureProvider

Listing 10-53. RequestLocalization middleware configuration

```
var options = app.ApplicationServices.GetService<IOptions<RequestLocalizationOptions>>();

app.UseRequestLocalization(options.Value);
```

Now we will add separate resource files, one for English and other for Spanish content. By default we will use English language throughout the application and we will hold all the corresponding Spanish translated text in Spanish resource file. So whenever a new user with es-MX culture uses the application, all the English text will be replaced with its corresponding Spanish version.

Create a folder with name Resources in ASC.Web Project. Right click the folder and select add new item, select Resource file and give it a name SharedResources.es.resx. Add an entry with name SectionHeader_ServiceRequests_Text and add 'Solicitudes de servicio' (Spanish translation of 'Service Requests') as its corresponding value as shown in Figure 10-20.

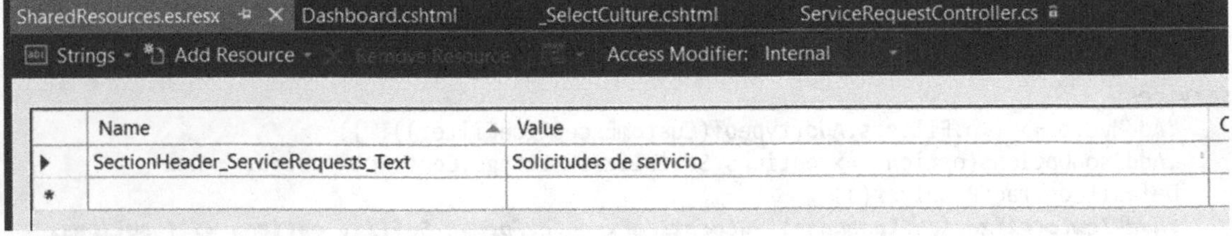

Figure 10-20. Spanish Resource File

Similarly add a resource file for English with name SharedResources.resx as shown in Figure 10-21.

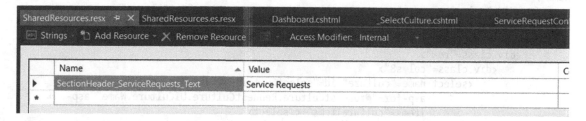

Figure 10-21. *English Resource File*

Create a class at the root of the project with name SharedResources as shown in Listing 10-54. This is required for resources which are being shared across multiple pages and across entire application.

Listing 10-54. SharedResources class

```
namespace ASC.Web
{
    public class SharedResources
    {
    }
}
```

■ **Note** The SharedResources class should have the same namespace as of root of the project. One more important point to remember is that resource files should have the same name as of SharedResources class.

We will create a simple partial view which will allow users to select a culture of their interest, so that it will be applied throughout the application. Create _SelectCutlure.cshtml in ASC.Web project under Views/Shared folder as shown in Listing 10-55. In the partial view, we will get all the SupportedUICultures (which was configured at Startup class) and display them in the Select tag. When we click on save button, the selected culture will be posted to SetCulture action of Home controller.

Listing 10-55. Select Culture partial view

```
@using System.Threading.Tasks
@using Microsoft.AspNetCore.Builder
@using Microsoft.AspNetCore.Localization
@using Microsoft.AspNetCore.Mvc.Localization
@using Microsoft.Extensions.Options

@inject IViewLocalizer Localizer
@inject IOptions<RequestLocalizationOptions> LocOptions

@{
    var requestCulture = Context.Features.Get<IRequestCultureFeature>();
    var cultureItems = LocOptions.Value.SupportedUICultures
        .Select(c => new SelectListItem { Value = c.Name, Text = c.DisplayName })
        .ToList();
}
```

```
<div title="@Localizer["Request culture provider:"] @requestCulture?.Provider?.GetType().
Name">
    <form id="selectLanguage" asp-controller="Home" asp-action="SetCulture" asp-area=""
    asp-route-returnUrl="@Context.Request.Path@Context.Request.QueryString"
        method="post" role="form">
        <div class="row">
            <div class="col s8">
                <select name="culture" id="selectCulture" class="col s12"
                    asp-for="@requestCulture.RequestCulture.UICulture.Name" asp-
                    items="cultureItems"></select>
            </div>
            <div class="input-field col s4 right-align">
                <button class="btn waves-effect waves-light btnSubmit" type="submit"
                name="action">
                    Save
                    <i class="material-icons right">send</i>
                </button>
            </div>
        </div>
    </form>
</div>
```

To initialize the Material style for select tag. Make the following code change in init.js file as shown in Listing 10-56.

Listing 10-56. Material style for Select tag of Culture

```
//Prevent right click on entire window
$(document).ready(function () {
    $(window).on("contextmenu", function () {
        return false;
    });

    $('#selectCulture').material_select();
});
```

Now we need to update _Layout.cshtml and _SecureLayout.cshtml to include select culture partial view. We will include the partial view in the footer section of layouts. _Layout.cshtml is modified as shown in Listing 10-57.

Listing 10-57. Updated layout to include Select Culture partial view

```
<div class="footer-copyright">
    <div class="container row">
        <div class="col s8">
            Powered by <a class="brown-text text-lighten-3" href="http://materializecss.com">
            Materialize</a>
        </div>
        <div class="col s4">
            @await Html.PartialAsync("_SelectCulture")
        </div>
    </div>
</div>
```

_SecureLayout.cshtml is modified as shown in Listing 10-58.

Listing 10-58. Updated secure layout with Select Culture partial view

```
<div class="footer-copyright row margin-bottom-0px">
    <div class="col s12">
        <div class="col s8">
            Powered by <a class="brown-text text-lighten-3" href="http://materializecss.
            com">Materialize</a>
        </div>
        <div class="col s4">
            @await Html.PartialAsync("_SelectCulture")
        </div>
    </div>
</div>
<div class="footer-copyright row margin-bottom-0px"></div>
```

■ **Note**   In _SecureLayout.cshtml, I have used one more footer-copyright css style (from MaterializeCSS) to avoid a small css glitch of having white space at the bottom of the screen. There is no other specific reason for the extra footer div tag.

The SetCulture action of Home controller is shown in Listing 10-59. The action takes culture and return url as parameters, it sets the Culture cookie and redirects to the return url.

Listing 10-59. SetCulture action

```
[HttpPost]
public IActionResult SetCulture(string culture, string returnUrl)
{
    Response.Cookies.Append(
        CookieRequestCultureProvider.DefaultCookieName,
        CookieRequestCultureProvider.MakeCookieValue(new RequestCulture(culture)),
        new CookieOptions { Expires = DateTime.UtcNow.AddYears(1) }
    );

    return LocalRedirect(returnUrl);
}
```

The last change which is required is to be done is at View where we should use localized string (string content from Resource file) to render the text. We will use created localized string in Dashboard view. Add the Localization namespace and inject IHtmlLocalizer in Dashboard.cshtml as shown in Listing 10-60.

Listing 10-60. Localization namespace

```
@using Microsoft.AspNetCore.Mvc.Localization
@inject IHtmlLocalizer<SharedResources> SharedLocalizer
```

To consume the localized key, change the Service Requests grid section name in Dashboard.cshtml as shown in Listing 10-61.

Listing 10-61. Usage of localized key

```
@await Html.PartialAsync("_ServiceRequestGrid", Model.ServiceRequests, new
ViewDataDictionary(ViewData) {
    { "SectionName", SharedLocalizer["SectionHeader_ServiceRequests_Text"] },
    { "Id", "tblServiceRequests" },
    { "IsAudit", false }
})
```

Run the application, Culture partial should be visible as shown in Figures 10-22 & 10-23 for normal layout and secure layout respectively.

Powered by Materialize
English (United States)
SAVE

Figure 10-22. *Culture partial in Normal layout*

Powered by Materialize
English (United States)
SAVE

Figure 10-23. *Culture partial in Secure layout*

Change the culture to Spanish and click save, the section name of service requests grid will be used from Spanish resource file as shown in Figure 10-24. Switch the culture back to English, section name should be reverted accordingly. In the similar way, the entire application can be localized.

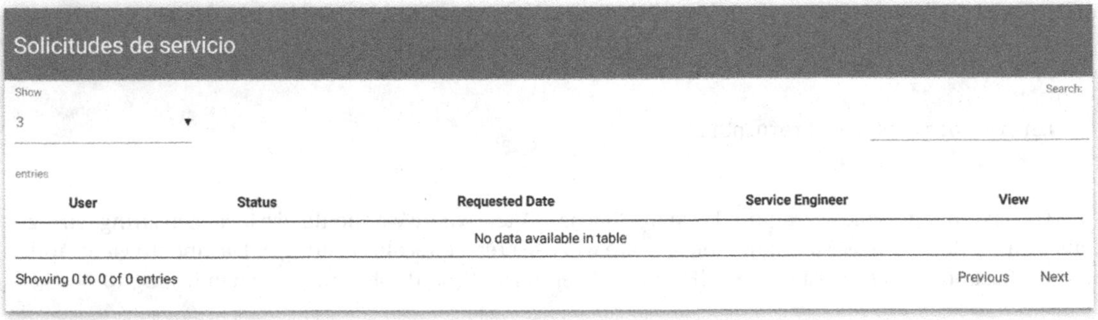
Solicitudes de servicio
Show
3
entries
Search:
User
Status
Requested Date
Service Engineer
View
No data available in table
Showing 0 to 0 of 0 entries
Previous
Next

Figure 10-24. *Localized name display in Dashboard*

■ **Note**   We used Shared Resources approach to achieve Localization for Automobile Service Center application. This way we can achieve key reusability, say for example the same string is used in multiple places on multiple pages. Also shared resources help in migrating existing resource files to ASP.NET Core application.

Another approach is to have different resource files for different views and have similar folder structure as of views for resources as well, for example HomeController Spanish resource file should be placed at Resources/Controllers/HomeController.es.resx.

We will now localize validation error messages which are displayed to user on client side or server side DataAnnotation validations. We need to configure DataAnnotation localization in ConfigureServices method of Startup class to use SharedResources as shown in Listing 10-62.

Listing 10-62. DataAnnotations localization configuration in Startup class

```
services
    .AddMvc(o => { o.Filters.Add(typeof(CustomExceptionFilter)); })
    .AddJsonOptions(options => options.SerializerSettings.ContractResolver = new
DefaultContractResolver())
    .AddViewLocalization(LanguageViewLocationExpanderFormat.Suffix, options => { options.
ResourcesPath = "Resources"; })
    .AddDataAnnotationsLocalization(options => { options.DataAnnotationLocalizerProvider =
(type, factory) =>
        factory.Create(typeof(SharedResources));
});
```

To demonstrate DataAnnotation error messages localization, we will take NewServiceRequestViewModel and update the Required DataAnnotation attribute of VehicleName property as shown in Listing 10-63.

Listing 10-63. Required attribute with SharedResource key

```
[Required(ErrorMessage = "Error_VehicleName_Message")]
[Display(Name ="Vehicle Name")]
public string VehicleName { get; set; }
```

Create the Error_VehicleName_Message key in both the SharedResources.resx and SharedResources.es.resx files as shown in respective Figures 10-25 & 10-26.

Name	Value	C(
SectionHeader_ServiceRequests_Text	Service Requests	
Error_VehicleName_Message	Vehicle Name is Required.	

Figure 10-25. *Vehicle name error messagein English resource file*

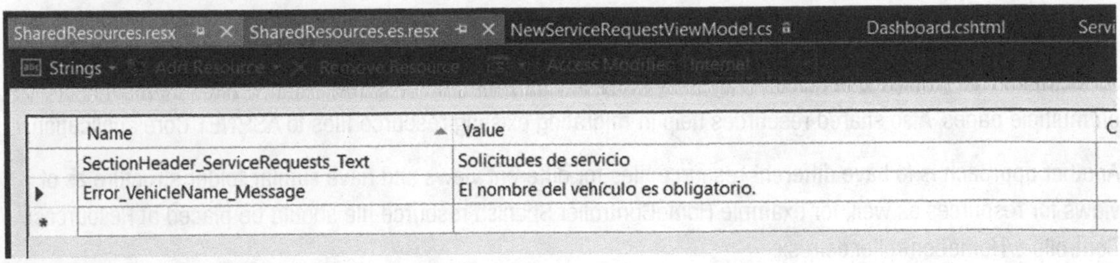

	Name	▲	Value
	SectionHeader_ServiceRequests_Text		Solicitudes de servicio
▶	Error_VehicleName_Message		El nombre del vehículo es obligatorio.
*			

Figure 10-26. *Vehicle name error message in Spanish Resource file*

Run the application and with es-US as culture we should see validation error message as shown in Figure 10-27.

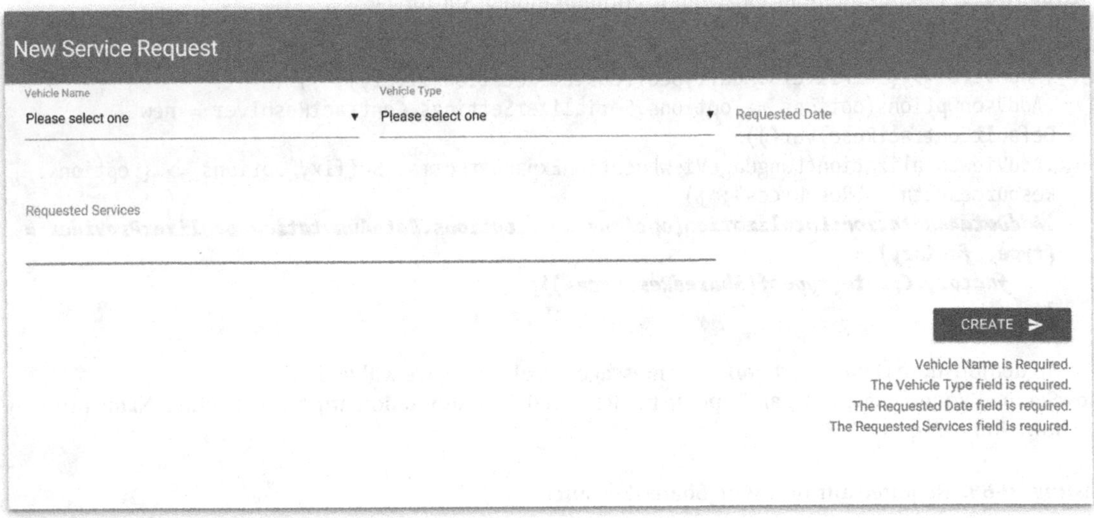

Figure 10-27. *Error message display for en-US culture*

Change the culture to Spanish and we should see Spanish error message as shown in Figure 10-28.

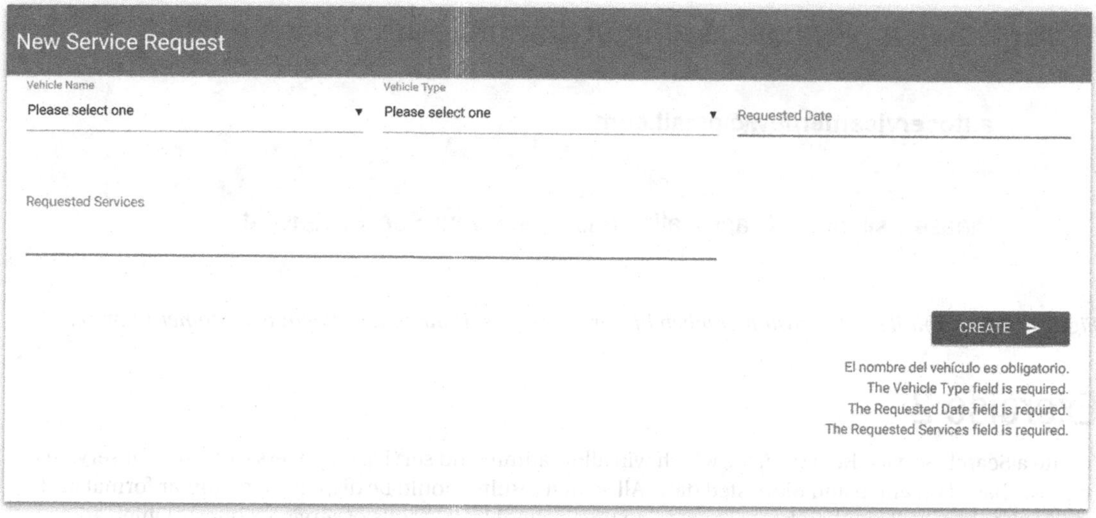

New Service Request

Vehicle Name
Please select one ▼

Vehicle Type
Please select one ▼

Requested Date

Requested Services

CREATE ➤

El nombre del vehículo es obligatorio.
The Vehicle Type field is required.
The Requested Date field is required.
The Requested Services field is required.

Figure 10-28. *Error message display for es-MX culture*

■ **Note**   We can use IStringLocalizer<SharedResources> to access localized string in Controller code. Typically we used IStringLocalizer for normal localized strings and IHtmlLocalizer for HTML content. As most of the cases, we only localize string content, IStringLocalizer is most widely used option to retrieve localized content.

Similarly we can use IViewLocalizer to find the localized content from respective view resource files.

Exercise 1

Send an Email alert to customer when his service request is marked as PendingCustomerApproval either by Admin and Service Engineer. Based on the email notification, customer can login to application and check the service updates.

■ **Note**   Solution to this problem can be found in code samples accompanied with this book. Login as Admin or Service Engineer and modify any service request status to PendingCustomerApproval and save it. Customer should receive email as shown in figure.

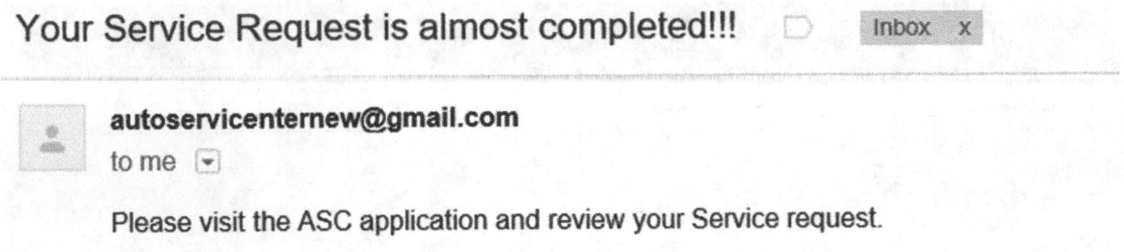

Your Service Request is almost completed!!!

autoservicenternew@gmail.com

to me ▾

Please visit the ASC application and review your Service request.

Figure 10-29. *Email alert to customer when his service request is marked as Pending customer approval*

Exercise 2

Create a Search Service Request page which will allow admin and service engineers to search for service requests based on email and requested date. All search results should be displayed in tabular format and admin should see all results whereas service engineer should see results of service requests which are associated to him. Every service request result should have view icon, clicking on which should take the user to service request details page (just like from Dashboard).

■ **Note** Solution to this problem can be found in code samples accompanied with this book. View models which are used to perform search can be found at Models folder of ServiceRequests area. Search Service Requests actions and corresponding views can be found at ServiceRequest controller and views of ServiceRequests area. Left navigation is configured at Navigation.json file. Search Service Requests view is as shown in Figure 10-30.

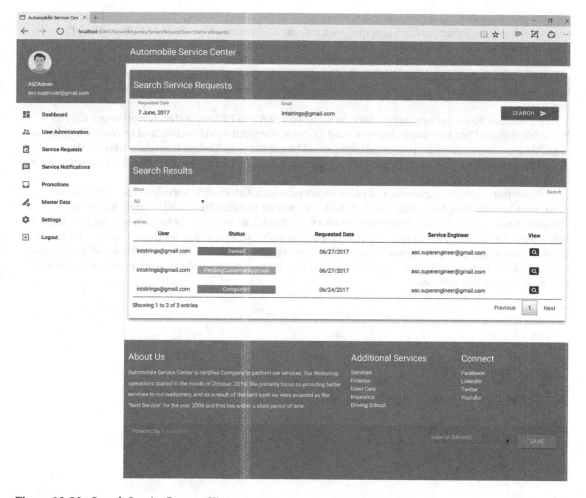

Figure 10-30. *Search Service Request View*

Summary

We started of this chapter by understanding the importance of data input forms which are traditionally used by web applications to capture information related to the user or to a particular event. In context of Automobile Service Center application, forms play a crucial role in establishing an effective communication channel between customers, service engineers and administrator. We defined a custom workflow to manage the life cycle of a service request between customers, service engineers and administrator.

We have implemented the service request workflow through the new service request screen and its associated details screen which is accessible to all user roles. Custom logic is implemented on service details screen to restrict access to update certain fields (for example a service engineer cannot assign a service request to another service engineer, customer cannot change the status of service request until it is in PendingCustomerApproval state).

We created a Dashboard view which is common to all users but displays different sets of information based on user role. To support different queries for Azure Table Storage, we extended IRepository<T> implementation with FindAllByQuery method which is primarily used by Dashboard controller to fetch different sets of information based on different conditions. A common partial view is created to display list of service requests, which is used in Dashboard to present both service requests and latest audit information to user. We also provided statistics to admin with number of active service requests handled by each service engineer.

We learned about performing validations using default ASP.NET Core's DataAnnotation attributes. We wrote custom DataAnnotation attribute and its client side validation function and unobtrusive adapter to validate the new service for requested date cannot be greater than 90 days from current date. We implemented remote validation which will prevent user to submit a new service request, if in case he got a service denial in last 90 days.

To support multiple languages and cultures, we extended Automobile Service Center application to support Localization. We configured ASC.Web solution for Localization with US English and Mexican Spanish as supported cultures. We created a shared Resource files to maintain English and Spanish texts. We then created a partial view and its corresponding action to create a provision for user to update the culture anytime and anywhere in the application. We also learned how to localize DataAnnotation validation error messages from Resource files based on selected culture. We tested the localization changed on Dashboard and New Service Request views.

CHAPTER 11

∎∎∎

Real-Time Communication with SignalR

Advancements in software solutions that have been provided by modern technology have not only revolutionized business workflows and collaborations, but also improved communication between businesses and customers. Providing a sophisticated communication platform boosts the success of software solutions by passing the right information to all business stakeholders on a timely basis and by establishing interactive channels of communication with customers in order to provide better support and services. Effective communication helps improve the efficiency and productivity of employees as well as their decision-making capabilities by enabling them to exchange critical information.

Real-time communication includes many channels, including telephone, instant messaging, VoIP, and live chat. As part of addressing the Automobile Service Center's business requirements, we'll define a scope item to provide a reliable and effective communication channel that customers and service engineers can use to exchange information about ongoing service request. The affordable and cost-optimized communication solution for the Automobile Service Center is to have a web-based instant messaging system within the Automobile Service Center application.

A real-time web-based instant messaging system can be developed using SignalR, an open source (under .NET Foundation) library that enables servers to push content to all connected clients instantly, as and when data becomes available, rather than the client making a request for new data. SignalR maintains a persistent connection between the server and clients and subsequently pushes notifications to all or specific clients by using remote procedure calls (RPCs).

In this chapter, we are going to use the SignalR library to build a real-time communication system between customers and service engineers in the Automobile Service Center application.

∎ **Note**   The traditional ASP.NET's SignalR will not work with ASP.NET Core applications because of the groundbreaking changes in .NET Core application models. At the time of writing this book, SignalR for ASP.NET Core is still in the development stage. A stable version of SignalR for ASP.NET Core is expected after the ASP. NET Core 2.0 release, which means there is still a long way to go before getting a stable version.

For the Automobile Service Center application, we will use the `0.2.0-preview2-22683` version of `Microsoft. AspNetCore.SignalR.Server` from the MyGet feed of the ASP.NET Core team. The ASP.NET Core team uses MyGet repositories to push their nightly builds (bits from latest source, which might be unstable). We will also use Microsoft's SignalR JavaScript Library (`jquery.signalr-2.2.0`), which is primarily to build a JQuery client for the Automobile Service Center application.

R. Vemula, *Real-Time Web Application Development*, https://doi.org/10.1007/978-1-4842-3270-5_11

Because we are using a preview version, some functionalities could break, and it is not advisable to go to a production release with this solution without proper testing. Knowing the cons of the preview version, we will still build a two-way communication channel in the Automobile Service Center application to showcase the potentiality of SignalR. Also, expect groundbreaking changes in the SignalR Core version (for example, implementing transport channels using duplex communication, working along with ASP.NET Core's dependency injection, and having a JavaScript client rewritten in TypeScript).

Introducing SignalR

SignalR is a library from Microsoft that offers real-time web development for ASP.NET applications. SignalR is primarily used by applications that require push notifications from server to client; for example, applications such as chat, stock market, gaming, and dashboards. Prior to SignalR, application developers used to implement real-time web functionalities by using pooling methods such as long/short polling in which a client will poll the server for new information based on a time interval. This approach is always performance intense, network offensive, and requires more hardware. SignalR solves the problem by providing a persistent connection between the client and the server. It uses the Hubs API to push notifications from server to client, and it supports multiple channels such as WebSocket, server-sent events, and long polling. SignalR supports multiple clients ranging from C#/C++ to JavaScript. SignalR supports SQL Server, Redis, Azure Service Bus, and more to achieve scalability.

As the development paradigm shifts toward ASP.NET Core, Microsoft is redesigning and rebuilding its traditional SignalR to support a new ASP.NET Core framework. The new SignalR is a complete rewrite from scratch, because ASP.NET Core has a lot of new features such as new HttpContext, dependency injection, and configuration. At the same time, the .NET Core's SignalR version should be portable with the .NET Standard. Some of the new changes in the latest SignalR for .NET Core are as follows [1].

- No dependency on JQuery. This will make the new SignalR run on the client side without JQuery references. The ASP.NET Core team plans to use most of the default features of the latest browsers.

- Hubs are mapped to routes, through which the single connection dependency was removed. Different clients can connect to hubs of their choice through different URLs.

- Just like traditional SignalR, the new version also supports WebSocket, server-sent events, and long polling transport types.

- Extensive support for binary data.

- The new SignalR will implement a new scale-out design that is more flexible than the existing one.

- User presence support, which can be used to track a user's lost or idle connections.

- The reconnection feature from traditional SignalR has been removed because of memory leaks and complicated unnecessary logic inside SignalR to make sure messages are durable.

- Traditional SignalR was used to allow clients to change servers between reconnections, but in new SignalR except WebSocket, all other connections require sticky sessions.

The ASP.NET Core SignalR high-level architecture is shown in Figure 11-1. At a high level, SignalR is host agnostic and supports numerous transports. Microsoft replaced the traditional connection API with hub endpoints, which are generic endpoints on the server. These endpoints are flexible, because the same endpoint can be leveraged across multiple transports and hosts. ASP.NET Core applications use HTTP transport to communicate with different hub endpoints.

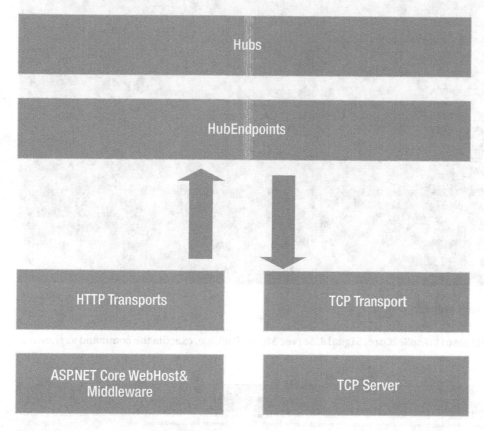

Figure 11-1. *High-level architecture of SignalR*

■ **Note** As we already discussed in the introduction, most of the new SignalR changes are still under development. We will not be implementing all of these concepts for the Automobile Service Center application.

Enabling Two-Way Communication Between Customers and Service Engineers

In this section, we will implement basic two-way communication between the customer and service engineer in the context of the service request. We will use SignalR and WebSocket to achieve this functionality.

Configure Automobile Service Center with SignalR

We will start by adding SignalR and WebSocket MyGet packages. Open the Package Manager console, shown in Figure 11-2.

Figure 11-2. Package Manager console

To add the `Microsoft.AspNetCore.SignalR.Server` MyGet Package, execute the command as shown in Figure 11-3.

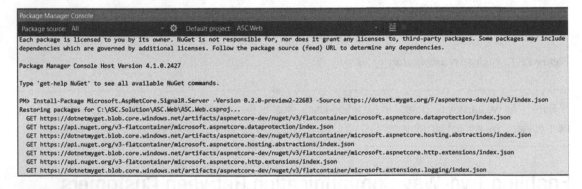

Figure 11-3. Installing the Microsoft.AspNetCore.SignalR.Server package on the ASC.Web project from the MyGet feed

Similarly, install the `Microsoft.AspNetCore.WebSockets` MyGet Package by executing the command shown in Figure 11-4.

```
PM> Install-Package Microsoft.AspNetCore.WebSockets -Version 1.0.1 -Source https://dotnet.myget.org/F/aspnetcore-dev/api/v3/index.json
Restoring packages for C:\ASC.Solution\ASC.Web\ASC.Web.csproj...
  GET https://dotnetmyget.blob.core.windows.net/artifacts/aspnetcore-dev/nuget/v3/flatcontainer/microsoft.aspnetcore.dataprotection/index.json
  GET https://api.nuget.org/v3-flatcontainer/microsoft.aspnetcore.dataprotection/index.json
  GET https://dotnetmyget.blob.core.windows.net/artifacts/aspnetcore-dev/nuget/v3/flatcontainer/microsoft.aspnetcore.hosting.abstractions/index.json
  GET https://api.nuget.org/v3-flatcontainer/microsoft.aspnetcore.hosting.abstractions/index.json
  GET https://dotnetmyget.blob.core.windows.net/artifacts/aspnetcore-dev/nuget/v3/flatcontainer/microsoft.aspnetcore.http.extensions/index.json
  GET https://api.nuget.org/v3-flatcontainer/microsoft.aspnetcore.http.extensions/index.json
  GET https://dotnetmyget.blob.core.windows.net/artifacts/aspnetcore-dev/nuget/v3/flatcontainer/microsoft.extensions.logging/index.json
  GET https://api.nuget.org/v3-flatcontainer/microsoft.extensions.logging/index.json
  GET https://dotnetmyget.blob.core.windows.net/artifacts/aspnetcore-dev/nuget/v3/flatcontainer/microsoft.extensions.options/index.json
  GET https://api.nuget.org/v3-flatcontainer/microsoft.extensions.options/index.json
  OK https://api.nuget.org/v3-flatcontainer/microsoft.aspnetcore.dataprotection/index.json 935ms
  GET https://api.nuget.org/v3-flatcontainer/microsoft.aspnetcore.dataprotection/1.1.0/microsoft.aspnetcore.dataprotection.1.1.0.nupkg
  OK https://api.nuget.org/v3-flatcontainer/microsoft.aspnetcore.hosting.abstractions/index.json 1171ms
```

Figure 11-4. *Installing the Microsoft.AspNetCore.WebSockets package to the ASC.Web project from the MyGet feed*

■ **Note** The same MyGet packages can also be restored by using the `dotnet restore` command. To restore the MyGet packages, we need to configure the MyGet repository in `Nuget.Config`. Add `Nuget.Config`, as shown in Listing 11-1. This configuration is useful at the time of the build and continuous integration.

Listing 11-1. Nuget.config configured with ASP.NET Core's MyGet feed

```xml
<?xml version="1.0" encoding="utf-8"?>
<configuration>
    <packageSources>
        <clear/>
            <add key="aspnetcidev" value="https://dotnet.myget.org/F/aspnetcore-dev/api/v3/
            index.json"/>
            <add key="api.nuget.org" value="https://api.nuget.org/v3/index.json"/>
    </packageSources>
</configuration>
```

Now we will configure SignalR and WebSocket at the ASC.Web project. Add the SignalR service to `IServiceCollection` in the `ConfigureServices` method of the `Startup` class, as shown in Listing 11-2.

Listing 11-2. Configure SignalR in Startup class

```
services.AddLocalization(options => options.ResourcesPath = "Resources");

services.AddSignalR(options =>
{
    options.Hubs.EnableDetailedErrors = true;
});

services
    .AddMvc(o => { o.Filters.Add(typeof(CustomExceptionFilter)); })
    .AddJsonOptions(options => options.SerializerSettings.ContractResolver = new
    DefaultContractResolver())
    .AddViewLocalization(LanguageViewLocationExpanderFormat.Suffix, options => { options.
    ResourcesPath = "Resources"; })
    .AddDataAnnotationsLocalization(options => { options.DataAnnotationLocalizerProvider =
    (type, factory) =>
```

```
            factory.Create(typeof(SharedResources));
    });
```

We will add SignalR and WebSocket to the HTTP pipeline through the Configure method of the Startup class, as shown in Listing 11-3.

Listing 11-3. Configure HTTP pipeline with WebSockets and SignalR

```
app.UseMvc(routes =>
{
    routes.MapRoute(name: "areaRoute",
        template: "{area:exists}/{controller=Home}/{action=Index}");
    routes.MapRoute(
        name: "default",
        template: "{controller=Home}/{action=Index}/{id?}");
});

app.UseWebSockets();
app.UseSignalR();

await storageSeed.Seed(app.ApplicationServices.GetService<UserManager<ApplicationUser>>(),
    app.ApplicationServices.GetService<RoleManager<IdentityRole>>(),
    app.ApplicationServices.GetService<IOptions<ApplicationSettings>>());
```

Create SignalR Hub to Enable-Two Way Communication Using JQuery

To create a SingalR hub, we first must focus on creating back-end data models. We create a ServiceRequestMessage model in the Models folder of the ASC.Models project. This class will be used to persist all the communication messages to Azure Table storage. The ServiceRequestMessage model is shown in Listing 11-4. It contains properties that will hold information about the message's sender, content, and date.

Listing 11-4. ServiceRequestMessage entity

```
using ASC.Models.BaseTypes;
using System;

namespace ASC.Models.Models
{
    public class ServiceRequestMessage : BaseEntity
    {
        public ServiceRequestMessage() { }

        public ServiceRequestMessage(string serviceRequestId)
        {
            this.RowKey = Guid.NewGuid().ToString();
            this.PartitionKey = serviceRequestId;
        }
```

```
        public string FromDisplayName { get; set; }
        public string FromEmail { get; set; }
        public string Message { get; set; }
        public DateTime? MessageDate { get; set; }
    }
}
```

■ **Note**   We are not going to store to whom the message is sent, because all the messages will be running in the context of a service request. If a customer sends a message on a service request, it will be pushed to the administrator and the service engineer handling that service request. Similarly, the messages from the administrator and service engineer will be broadcasted to customer.

We will create the IServiceRequestMessageOperations interface in the Interfaces folder of the ASC.Business project to handle all service request message operations related Azure Table storage. IServiceRequestMessageOperations is shown in Listing 11-5.

Listing 11-5. IServiceRequestMessageOperations interface

```
using ASC.Models.Models;
using System;
using System.Collections.Generic;
using System.Threading.Tasks;

namespace ASC.Business.Interfaces
{
    public interface IServiceRequestMessageOperations
    {
        Task CreateServiceRequestMessageAsync(ServiceRequestMessage message);
        Task<List<ServiceRequestMessage>> GetServiceRequestMessageAsync(string
serviceRequestId);
    }
}
```

Create a class named ServiceRequestMessageOperations in the ASC.Business project. We will implement IServiceRequestMessageOperations on the ServiceRequestMessageOperations class, as shown in Listing 11-6.

Listing 11-6. ServiceRequestMessageOperations class

```
using ASC.Business.Interfaces;
using ASC.DataAccess.Interfaces;
using ASC.Models.Models;
using System.Threading.Tasks;
using System.Collections.Generic;
using System.Linq;

namespace ASC.Business
{
    public class ServiceRequestMessageOperations : IServiceRequestMessageOperations
```

```
{
    private readonly IUnitOfWork _unitOfWork;
    public ServiceRequestMessageOperations(IUnitOfWork unitOfWork)
    {
        _unitOfWork = unitOfWork;
    }

    public async Task CreateServiceRequestMessageAsync(ServiceRequestMessage message)
    {
        using (_unitOfWork)
        {
            await _unitOfWork.Repository<ServiceRequestMessage>().AddAsync(message);
            _unitOfWork.CommitTransaction();
        }
    }

    public async Task<List<ServiceRequestMessage>> GetServiceRequestMessageAsync(string
    serviceRequestId)
    {
        var serviceRequestMessages = await _unitOfWork.Repository<ServiceRequest
        Message>()
            .FindAllByPartitionKeyAsync(serviceRequestId);
        return serviceRequestMessages.ToList();
    }
}
}
```

Resolve the dependency of IServiceRequestMessageOperations in the ConfigureServices method of the Startup class at the ASC.Web project, as shown in Listing 11-7.

Listing 11-7. Resolve the dependency of IServiceRequestMessageOperations

```
services.AddScoped<IServiceRequestMessageOperations, ServiceRequestMessageOperations>();
```

Now we will focus on constructing the view and its associated JQuery code. The real-time communication will be enabled on the Service Request Details view, and it supports two basic operations:

- Providing a chat area where users can have real-time communication

- Showing online/offline status of the user

■ **Note** Using SignalR, we can achieve more functionalities and real-time features. In the Automobile Service Center application, we will limit the scope to support basic features.

As we will be using the Service Request Details view to display real-time communication, we can remove the Service Notifications menu item from the left navigation pane (Navigation.json):

```
{
  "DisplayName": "Service Notifications",
  "MaterialIcon": "message",
```

```
    "Link": "/ServiceRequest/Dashboard/Dashboard",
    "IsNested": false,
    "Sequence": 4,
    "UserRoles": ["User", "Engineer", "Admin"],
    "NestedItems": []
},
```

To get started, we will first update ServiceRequestController to get
IServiceRequestMessageOperations and IConnectionManager dependencies in the constructor, as shown
in Listing 11-8. IConnectionManager is part of the SignalR API, which is used to manage connections.

Listing 11-8. Inject dependencies into ServiceRequestController class

```
private readonly IServiceRequestOperations _serviceRequestOperations;
private readonly IServiceRequestMessageOperations _serviceRequestMessageOperations;
private readonly IConnectionManager _signalRConnectionManager;
private readonly IOptions<ApplicationSettings> _options;
private readonly IMapper _mapper;
private readonly IMasterDataCacheOperations _masterData;
private readonly UserManager<ApplicationUser> _userManager;
private readonly IEmailSender _emailSender;
public ServiceRequestController(IServiceRequestOperations operations,
    IServiceRequestMessageOperations messageOperations,
    IConnectionManager signalRConnectionManager,
    IMapper mapper,
    IMasterDataCacheOperations masterData,
    UserManager<ApplicationUser> userManager,
    IEmailSender emailSender,
    IOptions<ApplicationSettings> options)
{
    _serviceRequestOperations = operations;
    _serviceRequestMessageOperations = messageOperations;
    _signalRConnectionManager = signalRConnectionManager;
    _mapper = mapper;
    _masterData = masterData;
    _userManager = userManager;
    _emailSender = emailSender;
    _options = options;
}
```

Create an action named ServiceRequestMessages that will retrieve all the messages of that service
request, as shown in Listing 11-9. This action method will be invoked by the Service Request Details view,
using a JQuery Ajax call to display all the messages.

Listing 11-9. ServiceRequestMessages action

```
[HttpGet]
public async Task<IActionResult> ServiceRequestMessages(string serviceRequestId)
{
```

```
        return Json((await _serviceRequestMessageOperations.GetServiceRequestMessageAsync(servic
        eRequestId)).OrderByDescending(p => p.MessageDate));
}
```

Now we will update ServiceRequestDetails.cshtml to display the messages associated with a service request. Append the HTML shown in Listing 11-10 to ServiceRequestDetails.cshtml. We hold the current customer e-mail in the hidden field, which will be used later in JQuery to show different color themes for messages sent by a customer, administrator, or service engineer. We fix the height of the message div and use overflow-y to get a scrollbar when more messages are being exchanged. All messages will be displayed in a list format using standard li HTML tags. When there are no messages, a No Messages text will be displayed (which is by default hidden in the UI and will be toggled based on the message count).

To post a message, we have a simple HTML input text tag. When the user enters a message and presses Enter on the keyboard, the message (using the JQuery Keypress event) will be transmitted to other users.

Listing 11-10. Service Request messages HTML code

```
@* Messages Section *@
<input type="hidden" id="hdnCustomerEmail" value="@Model.ServiceRequest.PartitionKey" />
<div class="row">
    <div class="col s6">
        <ul class="collection with-header">
            <li class="collection-header"><h5>Service Request Messages</h5></li>
            <li class="collection-item height-300px overflow-y messages">
                <ul id="messagesList"></ul>
                <div class="card-panel teal lighten-2 white-text noMessages hide">No
                Messages.</div>
            </li>
        </ul>
        <div class="input-field col s12">
            <input type="text" id="txtMessage" />
            <label for="txtMessage">Type message here and press enter.</label>
        </div>
    </div>
</div>
```

■ **Note** The following styles should be added to Style.css and are used in the service request messages section.

```
.padding-10px{
    padding: 10px;
}
.font-size-12px{
    font-size : 12px;
}
.padding-top-10px{
    padding-top: 10px !important;
}
```

```
.padding-left-50px{
    padding-left: 50px;
}
```

To get the SignalR functionality on the client side, we need to refer to jquery.signalr-2.2.0.min. js and /signalr/hubs (which is an autogenerated SignalR script). We will refer to the scripts in _SecureLayout.cshtml, as shown in Listing 11-11. We have to start the SignalR connection by using the $.connection.hub.start() method.

Listing 11-11. SignalR JQuery library reference

```
@section Scripts{
@RenderSection("Scripts", required: false)
<script src="http://ajax.aspnetcdn.com/ajax/signalr/jquery.signalr-2.2.0.min.js"></script>
<script src="/signalr/hubs"></script>
    <script type="text/javascript">
        $(function () {
            $('#ancrLogout').click(function () {
                $('#logout_form').submit();
            });

            $('#ancrResetPassword').click(function () {
                $('#resetPassword_form').submit();
            });

            @* Start the client side HUB *@
            $.connection.hub.start();
        });
    </script>
}
```

Now update ServiceRequestDetails.cshtml with the JQuery code shown in Listing 11-12. This code is required to broadcast and display messages.

Here, we make an Ajax call to the ServiceRequestMessages action, which will pass all the messages in the system for that particular service request till date. The message's response is processed on the client side and displayed in the list by using the displayMessage function. The displayMessage function will construct dynamic HTML based on the user who sent the message (a different style is applied for the customer and service engineer/Admin) and appends to the messsageList unordered list.

If there no messages are available, a No Messages text will be displayed by removing the hide CSS class of noMessages div.

The client-side JQuery SignalR hub proxy can be retrieved from $.connection.serviceMessagesHub, and then we will associate the addMessage function that will be invoked when a new message is broadcasted from server to this client. The addMessage function will check whether the PartitionKey that is returned in the message is equal to the service request's RowKey. If it matches, then only the message will be displayed; otherwise, the message is ignored. A common function, scrollToLatestMessages, is used to set the focus to the latest message on the client side. This function is called whenever a new message is added and also on the page load, when we load all the previous messages.

Listing 11-12. JQuery code to handle service request messages

```
@section Scripts{
    <script>
        $(document).ready(function () {
            // Initialize DataTable to show list of Service Requests
            var table = $('.tblServiceRequests').DataTable({
                'pageLength': 3,
                // Number of records to be displayed per page
                'lengthMenu': [[3, 5, 10, -1], [3, 5, 10, 'All']],
                // Remove default Sorting
                'sorting': [],
                'columns': [{ "visible": false }, { "visible": false }, null, { "width":
                "20%" }, null, null, null, { "visible": false }]
            });

            // Set Styles for DataTable and Number of Records to be displayed in drop-down
            $('.tblServiceRequests').css("width", "100%");
            $('select[name$="ServiceRequests_length"]').material_select();

            // Initialize DatePicker
            $('.datepicker').pickadate({
                selectMonths: true,
                selectYears: 15
            });

            // initialize Material Select
            $('select').material_select();
            $("select[required]").css({ display: "block", position: 'absolute', visibility:
            'hidden' })

            @* Need to pass Verification Token to get Request Validated for Forgery *@
            var token = $('input[type=hidden][name=__RequestVerificationToken]', document).
            val();
            $.ajaxSetup({
                // Disable caching of AJAX responses
                cache: false,
                headers: { 'RequestVerificationToken': token, 'ServiceRequestId':
                $('#ServiceRequest_RowKey').val() }
            });

            @* Get all previous messages for the service request *@
            $.get('/ServiceRequests/ServiceRequest/ServiceRequestMessages?serviceRequestId='
            + $('#ServiceRequest_RowKey').val(),
                function (data, status) {
                    addMessagesToList(data);
                });

            @* Function to scroll the messages panel to latest message *@
            function scrollToLatestMessages() {
                $('.messages').animate({ scrollTop: 10000 }, 'normal');
            };
```

```
@* Function which is used to list of messages to UI *@
function addMessagesToList(messages) {
    if (messages.length === 0) {
        $('.noMessages').removeClass('hide');
    }

    $.each(messages, function (index) {
        var message = messages[index];
        displayMessage(message);
    });

    scrollToLatestMessages();
};

@* Function which is invoked by SignalR Hub when a new message is broadcasted *@
function addMessage(message) {
    if (message.PartitionKey !== $('#ServiceRequest_RowKey').val()) {
        return;
    }

    if (message !== null) {
        $('.noMessages').addClass('hide');
    }
    displayMessage(message);
    scrollToLatestMessages();
};

@* Function used to display message on UI *@
function displayMessage(message) {
    var isCustomer = $("#hdnCustomerEmail").val() === message.FromEmail ? 'blue
    lighten-1' : 'teal lighten- 2';

    $('#messagesList').append(
        '<li class="card-panel ' + isCustomer + ' white-text padding-10px">' +
        '<div class="col s12 padding-0px">' +
        '<div class="col s8 padding-0px"><b>' + message.FromDisplayName + '</
        b></div>' +
        '<div class="col s4 padding-0px font-size-12px right-align">' + (new
        Date(message.MessageDate)).toLocaleString() + '</div>' +
        '</div><br>' + message.Message + '</li>'
    );
};

@* Get the proxy of SignalR Hub and associate client side function. *@
$.connection.serviceMessagesHub.client.publishMessage = addMessage;

@* Function used to post message to server on keypress *@
$('#txtMessage').keypress(function (e) {
    var key = e.which;
    if (key == 13) {
        var message = new Object();
```

```
            message.Message = $('#txtMessage').val();
            message.PartitionKey = $('#ServiceRequest_RowKey').val();

            $.post('/ServiceRequests/ServiceRequest/CreateServiceRequestMessage',
                { message: message },
                function (data, status, xhr) {
                    if (data) {
                        $('.noMessages').addClass('hide');
                        $('#txtMessage').val('');
                    }
                });
            scrollToLatestMessages();
        }
    });
});
</script>
}
```

Now we need to create a server-side SignalR hub that is used to broadcast messages to different connected clients. Create a folder named ServiceHub in the ASC.Web project and create a class named ServiceMessagesHub inside the ServiceHub folder, as shown in Listing 11-13. ServiceMessagesHub is derived from the SignalR Hub class in which we can create any number of methods that can be accessed from the client side to send information.

Listing 11-13. ServiceMessagesHub class

```
using Microsoft.AspNetCore.SignalR;

namespace ASC.Web.ServiceHub
{
    public class ServiceMessagesHub : Hub
    {
    }
}
```

We need to finally create an HTTP POST action named CreateServiceRequestMessage that will be invoked from the client side whenever a user creates a new message. CreateServiceRequestMessage validates the message, retrieves the Service Request Details, and associates the message with the service request by populating the details of the user who created the message and message date. Then the message is saved to Azure Table storage by using the CreateServiceRequestMessageAsync method of the IServiceRequestMessageOperations contract.

Finally, the message is broadcasted to clients by getting a hub context of type ServiceMessagesHub and calling the associated publishMessage method (which is associated with the addMessage function on the client-side JQuery). SignalR can push a message to all clients that are connected to the hub, but the messages on a particular service request should be sent only in the context of a service request, so we filter the client by specifying customer, service engineer, and admin names as users. Once the message is broadcasted, the action method returns a true value to the client.

Listing 11-14. CreateServiceRequestMessage action

```
[HttpPost]
public async Task<IActionResult> CreateServiceRequestMessage(ServiceRequestMessage message)
{
    // Message and Service Request Id (Service request Id is the partition key for a
    message)
    if (string.IsNullOrWhiteSpace(message.Message) || string.IsNullOrWhiteSpace(message.
    PartitionKey))
        return Json(false);

    // Get Service Request details
    var serviceRequesrDetails = await _serviceRequestOperations.GetServiceRequestByRowKey
    (message.PartitionKey);

    // Populate message details
    message.FromEmail = HttpContext.User.GetCurrentUserDetails().Email;
    message.FromDisplayName = HttpContext.User.GetCurrentUserDetails().Name;
    message.MessageDate = DateTime.UtcNow;
    message.RowKey = Guid.NewGuid().ToString();

    // Get Customer and Service Engineer names
    var customerName = (await _userManager.FindByEmailAsync(serviceRequesrDetails.
    PartitionKey)).UserName;
    var serviceEngineerName = string.Empty;
    if (!string.IsNullOrWhiteSpace(serviceRequesrDetails.ServiceEngineer))
    {
        serviceEngineerName = (await _userManager.FindByEmailAsync(serviceRequesrDetails.
        ServiceEngineer)).UserName;
    }
    var adminName = (await _userManager.FindByEmailAsync(_options.Value.AdminEmail)).
    UserName;

    // Save the message to Azure Storage
    await _serviceRequestMessageOperations.CreateServiceRequestMessageAsync(message);

    var users = new List<string> { customerName, adminName };
    if (!string.IsNullOrWhiteSpace(serviceEngineerName))
    {
        users.Add(serviceEngineerName);
    }
    // Broadcast the message to all clients asscoaited with Service Request
    _signalRConnectionManager.GetHubContext<ServiceMessagesHub>()
        .Clients
        .Users(users)
        .publishMessage(message);
    // Return true
    return Json(true);
}
```

Run the application. Open three browsers and log in as admin, customer, and service engineer in each browser. Navigate to a particular Service Request Details screen. On the details screen, for all users, we should see a messages panel with no messages, as shown in Figure 11-5.

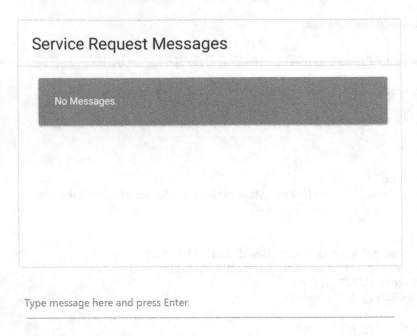

Figure 11-5. *No Messages text in the Service Request Messages section*

Now the customer can type in a message to the service engineer, as shown in Figure 11-6, and press Enter on the keyboard.

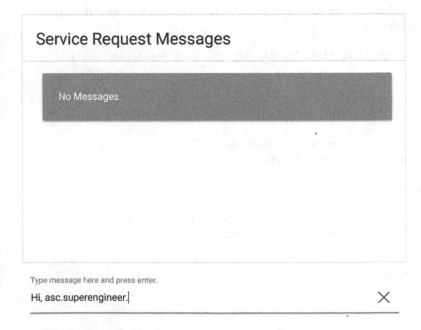

Figure 11-6. *Customer typing a message to a service engineer*

The message will be posted to the service engineer who is associated with the service request, as shown in Figure 11-7. At the same time, the message will be posted to the administrator as well for his reference. After a successful message, the customer's messages panel will be refreshed with the latest message.

Service Request Messages

intstrings	7/10/2017 10:27:59 AM
Hi, asc.superengineer.	

Type message here and press enter.

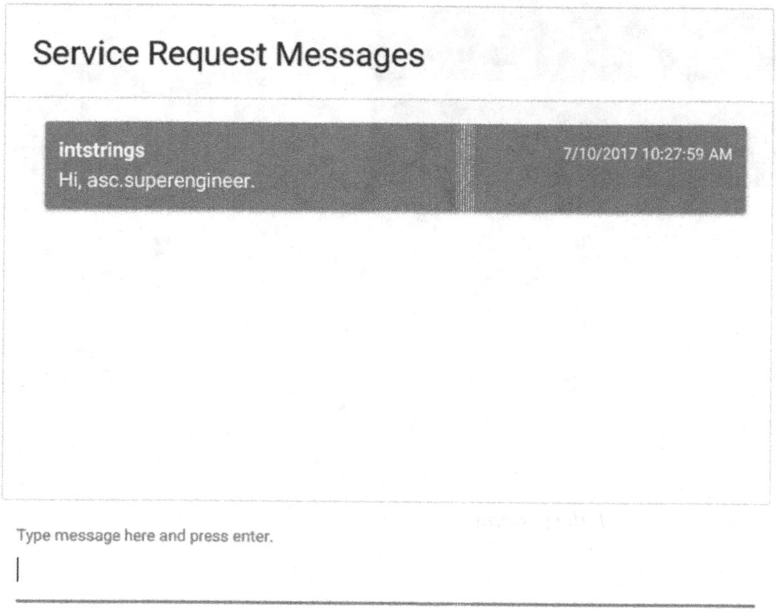

Figure 11-7. Customer posted message

Now the service engineer or administrator can post their messages, and those messages will be posted to the customer. At the same time, the service engineer and admin messages panel will be refreshed with the latest messages, as shown in Figures 11-8 and 11-9.

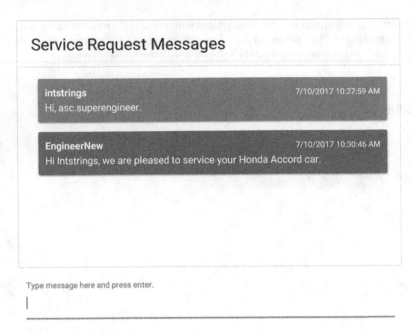

Figure 11-8. *Service engineer communicating with the customer*

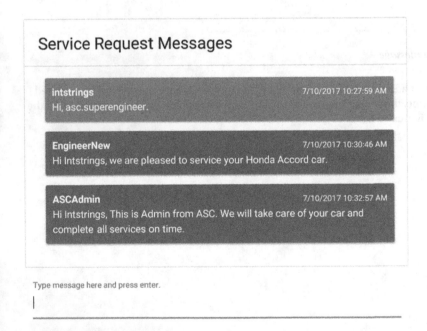

Figure 11-9. *Admin sent message to customer*

The overall screen will look like in Figure 11-10.

Figure 11-10. Service Request Details view with messages section

Enable User Online/Offline Notifications Using SignalR

In this section, we will work on showing the online/offline status of Admin, Service Engineer, and Customer on a given Service Request Details page. There are many ways to push online/offline notifications to various SignalR clients; for example, sending a notification to all clients who are connected to a hub, creating a persistent connection, and broadcasting the message to all clients. For the Automobile Service Center application, we will use the following approach.

Whenever a user navigates to the Service Request Details view, we will capture user details by using SignalR Hub's OnConnected event and store the details of the user (can be admin, service engineer, or customer) who came online to Azure Table storage. Finally, we will send the push notification, which consists of the status of each user who is associated with the service request, to other users (admin, service engineer, and customer). On receiving the notification, the client-side JQuery will flip the status of the respective user to online/offline based on the notification data.

To notify the user of offline status, we will handle SignalR Hub's OnDisconnected event, in which we will mark the corresponding OnlineUser entity's IsDeleted flag to true and send the push notification to the remaining users who are associated with the service request.

■ **Note**　The online/offline status notifications can be made more exhaustive to cover each and every screen of the Automobile Service Center application. This book limits the scope to show the online/offline status only when a user navigates to a Service Request Details view and to send push notifications to all other users who are associated with that particular service request.

Create the OnlineUser entity in the Models folder of ASC.Models project, as shown in Listing 11-15. It is used to persist the user who came online to Azure Table storage. This entity consists only of the name of the user who visited a Service Request Details screen, and it is mapped to the PartitionKey of the entity. RowKey is assigned with an autogenerated GUID value.

Listing 11-15. OnlineUser entity

```
using ASC.Models.BaseTypes;
using System;

namespace ASC.Models.Models
{
    public class OnlineUser : BaseEntity
    {
        public OnlineUser() { }
        public OnlineUser(string name)
        {
            this.RowKey = Guid.NewGuid().ToString();
            this.PartitionKey = name;
        }
    }
}
```

To perform Azure storage operations for the OnlineUser entity, create an interface named IOnlineUsersOperations in the Interfaces folder of the ASC.Business project, as shown in Listing 11-16. This interface contains basic methods to create, delete, and get an online user based on the name.

Listing 11-16. IOnlineUsersOperations interface

```
using System.Threading.Tasks;

namespace ASC.Business.Interfaces
{
    public interface IOnlineUsersOperations
    {
        Task CreateOnlineUserAsync(string name);
        Task DeleteOnlineUserAsync(string name);
        Task<bool> GetOnlineUserAsync(string name);
    }
}
```

Create a class named OnlineUsersOperations in the ASC.Business project and implement IOnlineUsersOperations, as shown in Listing 11-17. The CreateOnlineUserAsync method will create the user with the IsDeleted flag set to false in Azure Storage. If there is an existing user, it will flip the IsDeleted flag to false. The DeleteOnlineUserAsync method will soft-delete the OnlineUser entity by setting the IsDeleted flag to true. The GetOnlineUserEntity will return true if the user exists in Azure Table storage and the status of the IsDeleted flag is false; otherwise, it will return false.

Listing 11-17. OnlineUsersOperations class

```
using ASC.Business.Interfaces;
using ASC.DataAccess.Interfaces;
using ASC.Models.Models;
using System.Linq;
using System.Threading.Tasks;

namespace ASC.Business
{
    public class OnlineUsersOperations : IOnlineUsersOperations
    {
        private readonly IUnitOfWork _unitOfWork;
        public OnlineUsersOperations(IUnitOfWork unitOfWork)
        {
            _unitOfWork = unitOfWork;
        }

        public async Task CreateOnlineUserAsync(string name)
        {
            using (_unitOfWork)
            {
                var user = await _unitOfWork.Repository<OnlineUser>().FindAllByPartitionKey
                Async(name);
                if (user.Any())
                {
                    var updateUser = user.FirstOrDefault();
                    updateUser.IsDeleted = false;
                    await _unitOfWork.Repository<OnlineUser>().UpdateAsync(updateUser);
                }
                else
```

```
            {
                await _unitOfWork.Repository<OnlineUser>().AddAsync(new OnlineUser(name)
                { IsDeleted = false });
            }
            _unitOfWork.CommitTransaction();
        }
    }

    public async Task DeleteOnlineUserAsync(string name)
    {
        using (_unitOfWork)
        {
            var user = await _unitOfWork.Repository<OnlineUser>().FindAllByPartitionKey
            Async(name);
            if (user.Any())
            {
                await _unitOfWork.Repository<OnlineUser>().DeleteAsync(user.ToList().
                FirstOrDefault());
            }
            _unitOfWork.CommitTransaction();
        }
    }

    public async Task<bool> GetOnlineUserAsync(string name)
    {
        var user = await _unitOfWork.Repository<OnlineUser>().FindAllByPartitionKeyAsy
        nc(name);
        return user.Any() && user.FirstOrDefault().IsDeleted != true;
    }
  }
}
```

■ **Note** We store the user status in Azure Table storage to support the online/offline status push notifications in a multiserver environment.

Having users connect from multiple browser tabs in the same browser window is beyond the scope of this book.

Resolve the dependency of IOnlineUsersOperations in the ConfigureServices method of the Startup class at the ASC.Web project, as shown in Listing 11-18.

Listing 11-18. Resolve the dependency of IOnlineUsersOperations

```
services.AddScoped<IOnlineUsersOperations, OnlineUsersOperations>();
```

Now we will update ServiceMessagesHub to handle connected and disconnected events, as shown in Listing 11-20. ServiceMessagesHub will get all the dependencies from its constructor through ASP.NET Core's dependency system. The constructor also fetches ServiceRequestId from the HTTP request headers.

■ **Note**   For a demonstration of how to pass service-related information in each and every request, I included `ServiceRequestId` as one of the headers in the HTTP request. On the Service Request Details screen, we included this header as part of the Ajax setup, as shown in Listing 11-19. This ensures that on every Ajax call to the server, `ServiceRequestId` will be passed, and we can retrieve this information from the server by using `HttpContext.Request.Headers["ServiceRequestId"]`.

Listing 11-19. Passing ServiceRequestId in HTTP header

```
@* Need to pass Verification Token to get Request Validated for Forgery *@
            var token = $('input[type=hidden][name=__RequestVerificationToken]', document).
            val();
            $.ajaxSetup({
                // Disable caching of AJAX responses
                cache: false,
                headers: { 'RequestVerificationToken': token, 'ServiceRequestId':
                $('#ServiceRequest_RowKey').val() }
            });
```

ServiceMessagesHub will have OnConnected and OnDisconnected events that will create and delete the user from Azure Table storage and call the UpdateServiceRequestClients method, which will send notifications to all users who are associated with the service request. UpdateServiceRequestClients will check the details of the customer, service engineer, and admin who are associated with the service request and check their status in the OnlineUser Azure table. Based on the status, it will send the notifications to connected users by invoking the client-side JQuery's online method (we will see this method in the later part of the section). The data in the push notification will hold the separate Boolean flags isAd, isSe, and isCu, respectively, for admin, service engineer, and customer, which will reflect the current status of the user.

Listing 11-20. Updated ServiceMessagesHub class with OnConnected and OnDisconnected events

```
using ASC.Business.Interfaces;
using ASC.Utilities;
using ASC.Web.Configuration;
using ASC.Web.Models;
using Microsoft.AspNetCore.Http;
using Microsoft.AspNetCore.Identity;
using Microsoft.AspNetCore.SignalR;
using Microsoft.AspNetCore.SignalR.Infrastructure;
using Microsoft.Extensions.Options;
using System.Collections.Generic;
using System.Threading.Tasks;

namespace ASC.Web.ServiceHub
{
    public class ServiceMessagesHub : Hub
    {
        private readonly IConnectionManager _signalRConnectionManager;
        private readonly IHttpContextAccessor _userHttpContext;
        private readonly IServiceRequestOperations _serviceRequestOperations;
```

```csharp
private readonly UserManager<ApplicationUser> _userManager;
private readonly IOnlineUsersOperations _onlineUserOperations;
private readonly IOptions<ApplicationSettings> _options;
private readonly string _serviceRequestId;
public ServiceMessagesHub(IConnectionManager signalRConnectionManager,
    IHttpContextAccessor userHttpContext,
    IServiceRequestOperations serviceRequestOperations,
    UserManager<ApplicationUser> userManager,
    IOnlineUsersOperations onlineUserOperations,
    IOptions<ApplicationSettings> options)
{
    _signalRConnectionManager = signalRConnectionManager;
    _userHttpContext = userHttpContext;
    _serviceRequestOperations = serviceRequestOperations;
    _userManager = userManager;
    _onlineUserOperations = onlineUserOperations;
    _options = options;

    _serviceRequestId = _userHttpContext.HttpContext.Request.
    Headers["ServiceRequestId"];
}

public override async Task OnConnected()
{
    if (!string.IsNullOrWhiteSpace(_serviceRequestId))
    {
        await _onlineUserOperations.CreateOnlineUserAsync(_userHttpContext.
        HttpContext.User.GetCurrentUserDetails().Email);
        await UpdateServiceRequestClients();
    }
    await base.OnConnected();
}

public override async Task OnDisconnected(bool stopCalled)
{
    if (!string.IsNullOrWhiteSpace(_serviceRequestId))
    {
        await _onlineUserOperations.DeleteOnlineUserAsync(_userHttpContext.
        HttpContext.User.GetCurrentUserDetails().Email);
        await UpdateServiceRequestClients();
    }
    await base.OnDisconnected(stopCalled);
}

private async Task UpdateServiceRequestClients()
{
    // Get Hub Context
    var hubContext = _signalRConnectionManager.GetHubContext<ServiceMessagesHub>();

    // Get Service Request Details
```

```
        var serviceRequest = await _serviceRequestOperations.GetServiceRequestByRowKey(_
        serviceRequestId);

        // Get Customer and Service Engineer names
        var customerName = (await _userManager.FindByEmailAsync(serviceRequest.
        PartitionKey)).UserName;
        var serviceEngineerName = string.Empty;
        if (!string.IsNullOrWhiteSpace(serviceRequest.ServiceEngineer))
        {
            serviceEngineerName = (await _userManager.FindByEmailAsync(serviceRequest.
            ServiceEngineer)).UserName;
        }
        var adminName = (await _userManager.FindByEmailAsync(_options.Value.
        AdminEmail)).UserName;

        // check Admin, Service Engineer and customer are connected.
        var isAdminOnline = await _onlineUserOperations.GetOnlineUserAsync(_options.
        Value.AdminEmail);
        var isServiceEngineerOnline = false;
        if (!string.IsNullOrWhiteSpace(serviceRequest.ServiceEngineer))
        {
            isServiceEngineerOnline = await _onlineUserOperations.GetOnlineUserAsync(ser
            viceRequest.ServiceEngineer);
        }
        var isCustomerOnline = await _onlineUserOperations.GetOnlineUserAsync(serviceReq
        uest.PartitionKey);

        List<string> users = new List<string>();
        if (isAdminOnline) users.Add(adminName);
        if (!string.IsNullOrWhiteSpace(serviceEngineerName))
        {
            if (isServiceEngineerOnline) users.Add(serviceEngineerName);
        }
        if (isCustomerOnline) users.Add(customerName);

        // Send notifications
        hubContext
            .Clients
            .Users(users)
            .online(new
            {
                isAd = isAdminOnline,
                isSe = isServiceEngineerOnline,
                isCu = isCustomerOnline
            });
    }
  }
}
```

Update the ServiceRequestDetails.cshtml with the messages section, as shown in Listing 11-21.
We have added extra div tags that are decorated with Materialize CSS chips, which are used to display
the online/offline status of the customer, administrator, and service engineer. The image tags inside each

individual div are initiated with a red dot, indicating that by default all are offline. Based on the data received from SignalR's push notification, we will toggle the red dot with a green dot. A custom data-id attribute is used for image tags, through which we can identify which image tag corresponds to which user.

■ **Note** Add the images of the green dot and red dot to the images folder of the wwwroot folder in the ASC. Web project. These images are used to display the status of online/offline.

Listing 11-21. User online/offline status HTML code

```
@* Messages Section *@
<input type="hidden" id="hdnCustomerEmail" value="@Model.ServiceRequest.PartitionKey" />
<div class="row">
    <div class="col s8">
        <ul class="collection with-header">
            <li class="row collection-header">
                <div class="col s6"><h5>Service Request Messages</h5></div>
                <div class="col s6 padding-top-10px right">
                    <div class="col chip right">
                        User
                        <img src="/images/red_dot.png" data-id="isCu">
                    </div>
                    <div class="col chip right">
                        Admin
                        <img src="/images/red_dot.png" data-id="isAd">
                    </div>
                    <div class="col chip right">
                        Engineer
                        <img src="/images/red_dot.png" data-id="isSe">
                    </div>
                </div>
            </li>
            <li class="collection-item height-300px overflow-y messages">
                <ul id="messagesList"></ul>
                <div class="card-panel teal lighten-2 white-text noMessages hide">No
                Messages.</div>
            </li>
        </ul>
        <div class="input-field col s12">
            <input type="text" id="txtMessage" />
            <label for="txtMessage">Type message here and press enter.</label>
        </div>
    </div>
</div>
```

Finally, the JQuery code in `ServiceRequestDetails.cshtml` should be updated as shown in Listing 11-22. First the SignalR Hub's online method is mapped to the `updateUserStatus` function in JQuery. In the `updateUserStatus` method, we will simply get the image tags for corresponding individuals and toggle the `src` attribute based on the SignalR notification data.

Listing 11-22. JQuery code to toggle user online/offline status

```
$.connection.serviceMessagesHub.client.online = updateUserStatus;

@* Function which will toggle the status of online/offline of users. *@
function updateUserStatus(data) {
    $('div.chip img[data-id="isAd"]').attr('src', data.isAd ?
        '/images/green_dot.png' : '/images/red_dot.png');

    $('div.chip img[data-id="isCu"]').attr('src', data.isCu ?
        '/images/green_dot.png' : '/images/red_dot.png');

    $('div.chip img[data-id="isSe"]').attr('src', data.isSe ?
        '/images/green_dot.png' : '/images/red_dot.png');
}

@* Unload function to make sure the user is marked as offline. *@
$(window).unload(function () {
    $.get('/ServiceRequests/ServiceRequest/MarkOfflineUser',
        function (data, status) {
        });
});
```

■ **Note** Sometimes in this SignalR implementation (especially on the initial load of the service request screen), the disconnected event doesn't get called immediately when a user navigates away from the page or closes the browser. To provide a concrete solution, I handled the window's unload JQuery event to make an Ajax call to the `MarkOfflineUser` action of the Service Request controller, which typically runs the same code as the `OnDisconnected` event.

The `MarkOfflineUser` action of the `ServiceRequest` controller is shown in Listing 11-23. The code in the `MarkOfflineUser` action is similar to SignalR Hub's `OnDisconnected` event, where we check the Azure online storage for the service request associated with the user's status and then send a push notification with data containing the status of the users associated with that service request to online users.

Listing 11-23. MarkOfflineUser action

```
[HttpGet]
public async Task<IActionResult> MarkOfflineUser()
{
    // Delete the current logged-in user from OnlineUsers entity
    await _onlineUsersOperations.DeleteOnlineUserAsync(HttpContext.User.GetCurrentUser
    Details().Email);
```

```
string serviceRequestId = HttpContext.Request.Headers["ServiceRequestId"];
// Get Service Request Details
var serviceRequest = await _serviceRequestOperations.GetServiceRequestByRowKey(serviceR
equestId);

// Get Customer and Service Engineer names
var customerName = (await _userManager.FindByEmailAsync(serviceRequest.PartitionKey)).
UserName;
var serviceEngineerName = string.Empty;
if (!string.IsNullOrWhiteSpace(serviceRequest.ServiceEngineer))
{
    serviceEngineerName = (await _userManager.FindByEmailAsync(serviceRequest.
    ServiceEngineer)).UserName;
}
var adminName = (await _userManager.FindByEmailAsync(_options.Value.AdminEmail)).
UserName;

// check Admin, Service Engineer, and customer are connected.
var isAdminOnline = await _onlineUsersOperations.GetOnlineUserAsync(_options.Value.
AdminEmail);
var isServiceEngineerOnline = false;
if (!string.IsNullOrWhiteSpace(serviceRequest.ServiceEngineer))
{
    isServiceEngineerOnline = await _onlineUsersOperations.GetOnlineUserAsync(serviceReq
    uest.ServiceEngineer);
}
var isCustomerOnline = await _onlineUsersOperations.GetOnlineUserAsync(serviceRequest.
PartitionKey);

List<string> users = new List<string>();
if (isAdminOnline) users.Add(adminName);
if (!string.IsNullOrWhiteSpace(serviceEngineerName))
{
    if (isServiceEngineerOnline) users.Add(serviceEngineerName);
}
if (isCustomerOnline) users.Add(customerName);

// Send notifications_signalRConnectionManager.GetHubContext<ServiceMessagesHub>()
    .Clients
    .Users(users)
    .online(new
    {
        isAd = isAdminOnline,
        isSe = isServiceEngineerOnline,
        isCu = isCustomerOnline
    });

    return Json(true);
}
```

Run the application and log in as Customer. Navigate to a specific Service Request Details screen. You should see a green dot indicating online status for the user, as shown in Figure 11-11.

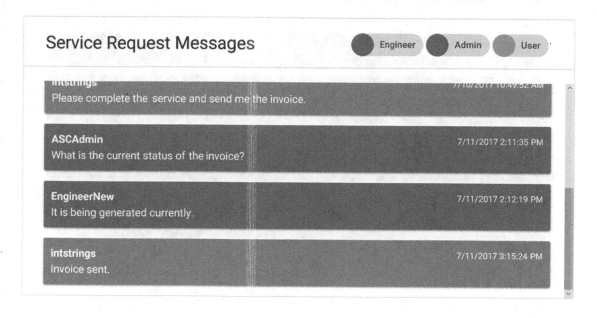

Figure 11-11. *Customer online status*

Now log in as Admin and Service Engineer in different browsers. You should see the online status for all users, as shown in Figure 11-12.

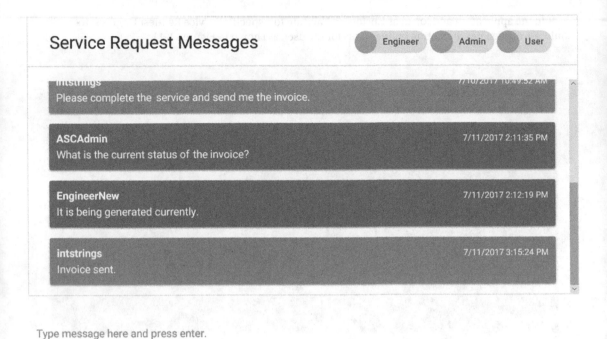

Figure 11-12. Status of Admin, Service Engineer, and Customer when they are online

Similarly, if any user navigates away to a different view from the Service Request Details view, then that user's online status is flipped to offline for this Service Request Details view.

Providing Service Updates via Text and Web Notifications

This section shows how to send SMS and web notifications to customers to keep them informed about the progress of their service requests. The built-in configurable HTTP pipeline and dependency injection system of ASP.NET Core provides an easy way to configure and send notifications. ASP.NET Core by default has no support to send SMS messages, but by using third-party communication provider Twilio, we can use SMS notifications with much less effort.

■ **Note**   Twilio is a cloud-based communications company that allows software developers to make and receive phone calls and send and receive text messages by using its web service APIs. Twilio offers a pay-as-you-go pricing model, which makes it easy to get the required services at the right time. Twilio also offers volume pricing for high-volume requirements.

Send SMS Notifications to Customers by Using Twilio API

To achieve SMS notifications, we need to capture the user's phone number. We will use the Profile view, which we already created, to capture the phone number. Update the Profile view model as shown in Listing 11-24.

Listing 11-24. Phone property in ProfileViewModel

```
public class ProfileViewModel
{
    [Required]
    [Display(Name = "Username")]
    public string Username { get; set; }

    [Required]
    [Display(Name = "Mobile")]
    public string Phone { get; set; }

    public bool IsEditSuccess { get; set; }
}
```

Now update the GET and POST actions of Profile in AccountController under the Accounts area, as shown in Listing 11-25. We included phone information to be sent to the screen in a GET action call, and update the same in a POST action call.

Listing 11-25. Updated profile actions

```
[HttpGet]
public async Task<IActionResult> Profile()
{
    var user = await _userManager.FindByEmailAsync(HttpContext.User.GetCurrentUserDetails().
    Email);
    return View(new ProfileViewModel { Username = user.UserName, Phone = user.PhoneNumber,
    IsEditSuccess = false });
}

[HttpPost]
[ValidateAntiForgeryToken]
public async Task<IActionResult> Profile(ProfileViewModel profile)
{
    var user = await _userManager.FindByEmailAsync(HttpContext.User.GetCurrentUserDetails().
    Email);
    user.UserName = profile.Username;
    user.PhoneNumber = profile.Phone;
    var result = await _userManager.UpdateAsync(user);
    await _signInManager.SignOutAsync();
    await _signInManager.SignInAsync(user, false);

    profile.IsEditSuccess = result.Succeeded;
    AddErrors(result);

    if(ModelState.ErrorCount > 0)
    {
        return View(profile);
    }

    return RedirectToAction("Profile");
}
```

Finally, update Profile.cshtml to capture the phone number, as shown in Listing 11-26.

Listing 11-26. Updated profile view

```
@* Details Section *@
<div class="row z-depth-3">
    <div class="col s12 padding-0px">
        <div class="section white-text padding-left-10px blue-grey lighten-1">
            <h5>Profile</h5>
        </div>
        <div class="divider"></div>
        <form asp-controller="Account" asp-action="Profile" method="post" class="col s12"
        id="fromUser">
            <div class="input-field col s4">
                <input asp-for="Username" class="validate" />
                <label asp-for="Username"></label>
            </div>
            <div class="input-field col s4">
                <input asp-for="Phone" class="validate" />
                <label asp-for="Phone"></label>
            </div>
            <div class="input-field col s4 right-align">
                <button class="btn waves-effect waves-light btnSubmit" type="submit"
                name="action">
                    Save
                    <i class="material-icons right">send</i>
                </button>
                <button class="btn waves-effect waves-light reset  red lighten-1"
                type="button" name="action">
                    Reset
                </button>
            </div>
            <div class="row col s12 right-align" asp-validation-summary="All"></div>
        </form>
    </div>
    <div class="row"></div>
</div>
```

Run the application and log in as a Customer. Navigate to the Profile view. You should see a phone field, as shown in Figure 11-13. Enter a phone number and click Save. The updated details should persist in the ASCAspNetUsers Azure table.

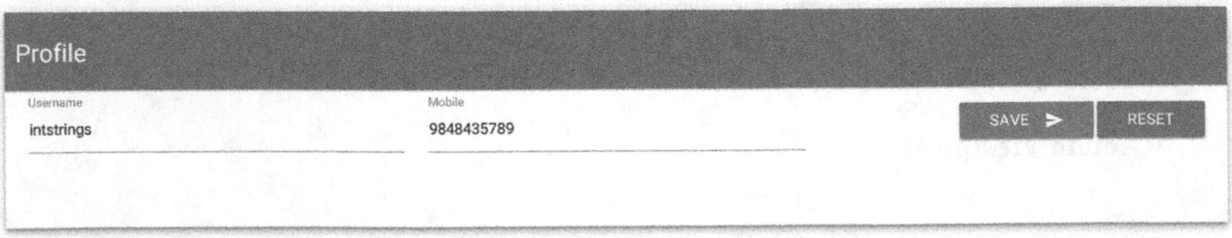

Figure 11-13. *Capturing the user's phone number*

Now we will create an account at Twilio. Go to Twilio.com and click Sign Up. Then fill in the details and click Submit, as shown in Figure 11-14.

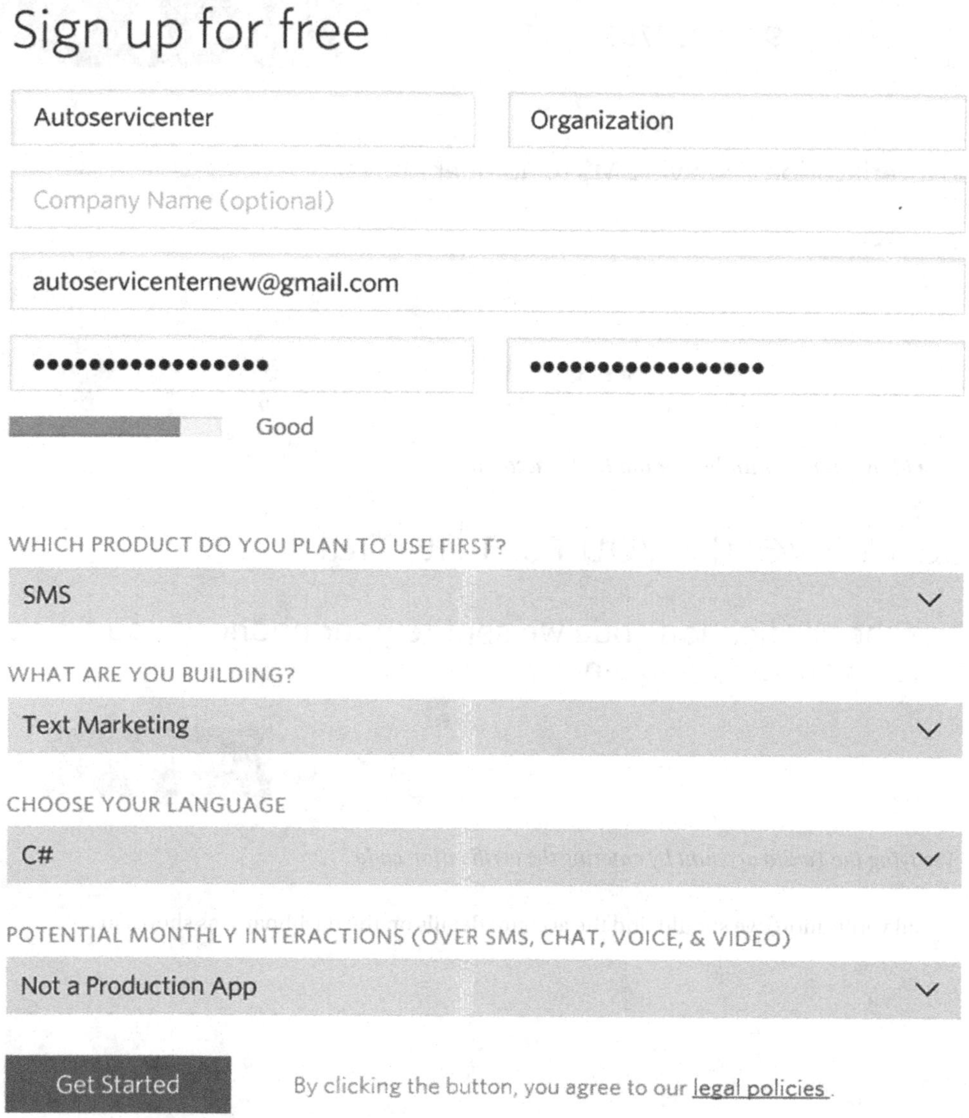

Sign up for free

| Autoservicenter | Organization |

| Company Name (optional) | |

| autoservicenternew@gmail.com |

| •••••••••••••••• | •••••••••••••••• |

████████████░░░░   Good

WHICH PRODUCT DO YOU PLAN TO USE FIRST?

SMS   ⌄

WHAT ARE YOU BUILDING?

Text Marketing   ⌄

CHOOSE YOUR LANGUAGE

C#   ⌄

POTENTIAL MONTHLY INTERACTIONS (OVER SMS, CHAT, VOICE, & VIDEO)

Not a Production App   ⌄

Get Started   By clicking the button, you agree to our legal policies.

Figure 11-14. *Signing up at Twilio*

We have to verify the account by providing a valid phone number, as shown in Figures 11-15 and 11-16.

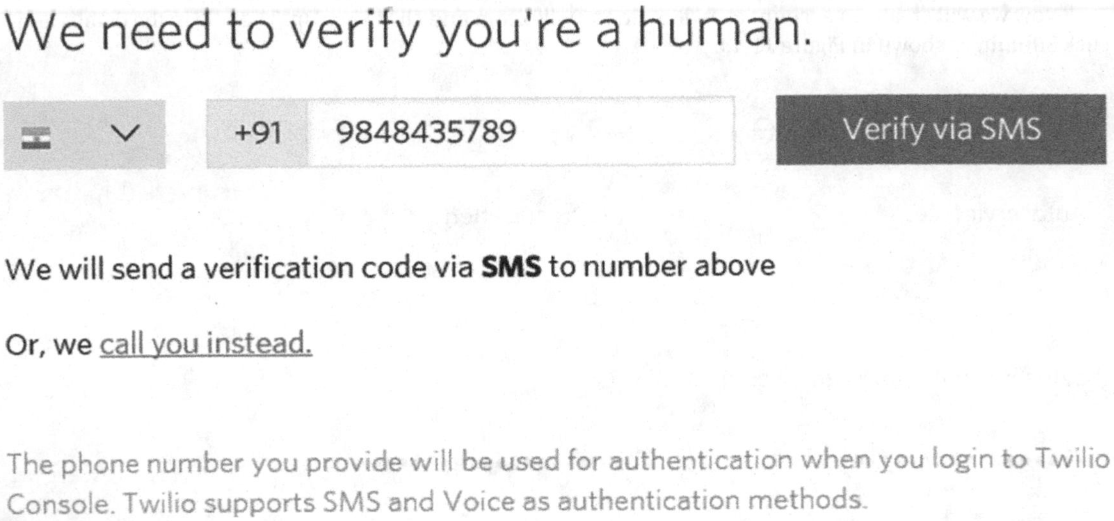

We need to verify you're a human.

We will send a verification code via **SMS** to number above

Or, we <u>call you instead.</u>

The phone number you provide will be used for authentication when you login to Twilio Console. Twilio supports SMS and Voice as authentication methods.

Figure 11-15. *Providing a phone number for the Twilio account*

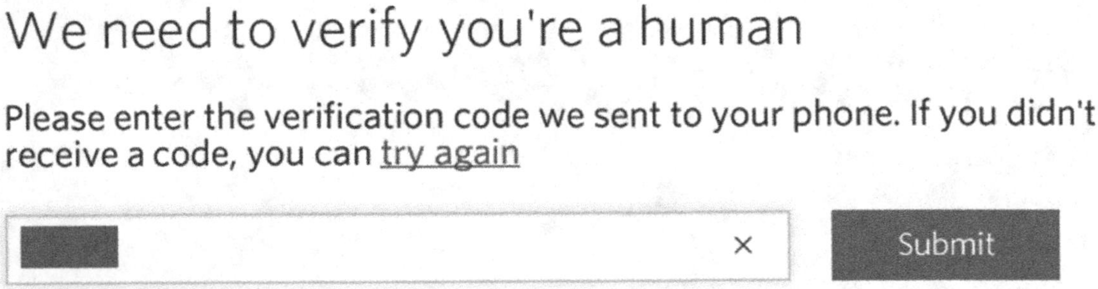

We need to verify you're a human

Please enter the verification code we sent to your phone. If you didn't receive a code, you can <u>try again</u>

Figure 11-16. *Verifying the Twilio account by entering the verification code*

Upon successful verification, we should find the account details on the dashboard, as shown in Figure 11-17.

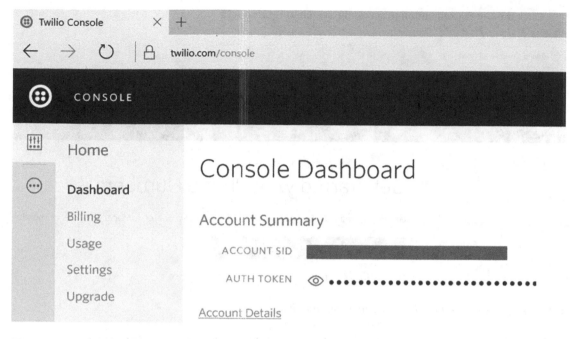

Figure 11-17. *Account details on the Twilio dashboard*

■ **Note** For security reasons, I have masked the secured information from the screenshot.

Navigate to www.twilio.com/console/phone-numbers/incoming to create a Twilio account and associate it with a phone number, as shown in Figure 11-18.

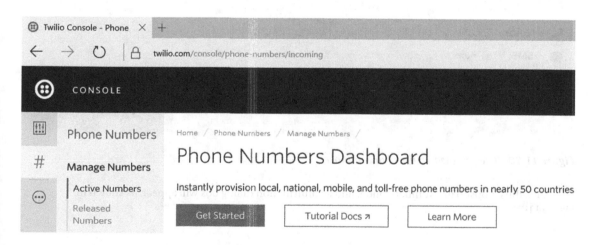

Figure 11-18. *Twilio Phone Numbers dashboard*

Click the Get Started button to access the screen in Figure 11-19.

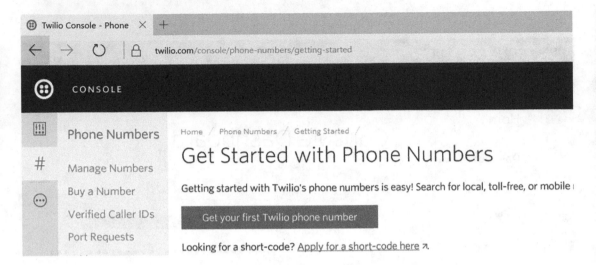

Figure 11-19. *Getting started with Twilio phone numbers*

Click the Get Your First Twilio Phone Number option, which will create a Twilio phone number, as shown in Figure 11-20.

Figure 11-20. *The assigned Twilio phone number*

Click the Choose This Number option, and a confirmation dialog box will appear, as shown in Figure 11-21.

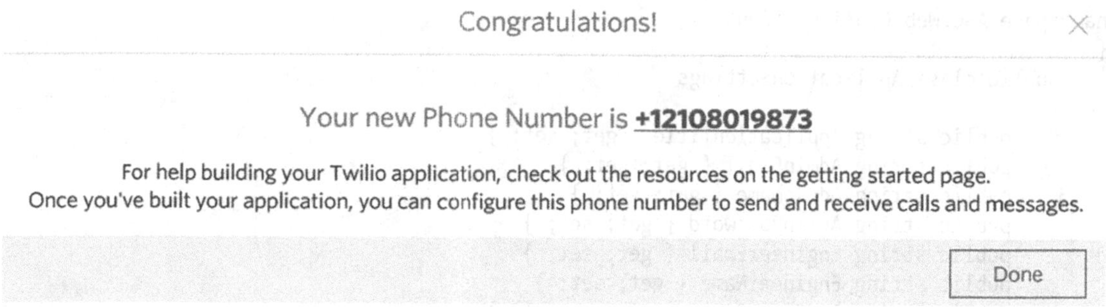

Congratulations!   ✕

Your new Phone Number is **+12108019873**

For help building your Twilio application, check out the resources on the getting started page.
Once you've built your application, you can configure this phone number to send and receive calls and messages.

Done

Figure 11-21. *Twilio phone number confirmation*

Now store the Account SID, auth token, and phone number in the appsettings.json file, as shown in Listing 11-27.

Listing 11-27. Twilio configuration in appsettings.json file

```json
"AppSettings": {
  "ApplicationTitle": "Automobile Service Center Application",
  "AdminEmail": "asc.superuser@gmail.com",
  "AdminName": "Admin",
  "AdminPassword": "P@ssw0rd",
  "EngineerEmail": "asc.superengineer@gmail.com",
  "EngineerName": "Engineer",
  "EngineerPassword": "P@ssw0rd",
  "Roles": "Admin,User,Engineer",
  "SMTPServer": "smtp.gmail.com",
  "SMTPPort": "587",
  "SMTPAccount": "autoservicenternew@gmail.com",
  "SMTPPassword": "P@ssw0rd!@#",
  "TwilioAccountSID": "XXXXXXXXXXXXXXXXXXXXXXXXXX",
  "TwilioAuthToken": "e3XXXXXXXXXXXXXXXXXXXXXXXXXX",
  "TwilioPhoneNumber": "+12108019873"
},
```

──

■ **Note**   I have masked the secured information from the code to protect the integrity of the book. In reality, it should have actual values.

──

Modify the ApplicationSettings class to have Twilio properties from appsettings.json, as shown in Listing 11-28.

Listing 11-28. Updated ApplicationSettings class with Twilio configuration properties

```
using System;
using System.Collections.Generic;
using System.Linq;
using System.Threading.Tasks;
```

```
namespace ASC.Web.Configuration
{
    public class ApplicationSettings
    {
        public string ApplicationTitle { get; set; }
        public string AdminEmail { get; set; }
        public string AdminName { get; set; }
        public string AdminPassword { get; set; }
        public string EngineerEmail { get; set; }
        public string EngineerName { get; set; }
        public string EngineerPassword { get; set; }
        public string Roles { get; set; }

        public string SMTPServer { get; set; }
        public int SMTPPort { get; set; }
        public string SMTPAccount { get; set; }
        public string SMTPPassword { get; set; }

        public string TwilioAccountSID { get; set; }
        public string TwilioAuthToken { get; set; }
        public string TwilioPhoneNumber { get; set; }
    }
}
```

As the next step, install the Twilio NuGet package on the ASC.Web project, as shown in Figure 11-22.

Figure 11-22. Installing Twilio NuGet package to the ASC.Web project

Now update the AuthMessageSender class in the Service folder of the ASC.Web project to include the SendSmsAsync method, as shown in Listing 11-29. SendSmsAsync will accept two parameters: the number to which the SMS message needs to be sent, and the message itself. Then the method will create a TwilioClient and call its Init method with the configuration values of AccountSID and AuthToken from the appsettings.json file. Finally, it will call Twilio's MessageResource.CreateAsync method to send the message. *From phone number* is passed to the CreateAsync method from the configuration value.

Listing 11-29. SendSmsAsync method

```
using ASC.Web.Configuration;
using MailKit.Net.Smtp;
using Microsoft.Extensions.Options;
using MimeKit;
using System.Threading.Tasks;
using Twilio;
```

```csharp
using Twilio.Rest.Api.V2010.Account;
using Twilio.Types;

namespace ASC.Web.Services
{
    public class AuthMessageSender : IEmailSender, ISmsSender
    {
        private IOptions<ApplicationSettings> _settings;
        public AuthMessageSender(IOptions<ApplicationSettings> settings)
        {
            _settings = settings;
        }

        public async Task SendEmailAsync(string email, string subject, string message)
        {
            var emailMessage = new MimeMessage();
            emailMessage.From.Add(new MailboxAddress(_settings.Value.SMTPAccount));
            emailMessage.To.Add(new MailboxAddress(email));
            emailMessage.Subject = subject;
            emailMessage.Body = new TextPart("plain") { Text = message };

            using (var client = new SmtpClient())
            {
                await client.ConnectAsync(_settings.Value.SMTPServer, _settings.Value.
                SMTPPort, false);
                await client.AuthenticateAsync(_settings.Value.SMTPAccount, _settings.Value.
                SMTPPassword);
                await client.SendAsync(emailMessage);
                await client.DisconnectAsync(true);

            }
        }
        public async Task SendSmsAsync(string number, string message)
        {
            TwilioClient.Init(_settings.Value.TwilioAccountSID, _settings.Value.
            TwilioAuthToken);

            var smsMessage = await MessageResource.CreateAsync(
                to: new PhoneNumber(number),
                from: new PhoneNumber(_settings.Value.TwilioPhoneNumber),
                body: message);
        }
    }
}
```

Make sure to resolve the ISmsSender dependency in the ConfigureServices method of the Startup class, as shown in Listing 11-30.

Listing 11-30. Resolve the dependency of ISmsSender

```
services.AddTransient<ISmsSender, AuthMessageSender>();
```

We will update ServiceRequestController to have the ISmsSender dependency injected to the constructor, as shown in Listing 11-31.

Listing 11-31. Inject ISmsSender dependency into ServiceRequestController class

```
private readonly IServiceRequestOperations _serviceRequestOperations;
private readonly IServiceRequestMessageOperations _serviceRequestMessageOperations;
private readonly IConnectionManager _signalRConnectionManager;
private readonly IMapper _mapper;
private readonly IMasterDataCacheOperations _masterData;
private readonly UserManager<ApplicationUser> _userManager;
private readonly IEmailSender _emailSender;
private readonly IOptions<ApplicationSettings> _options;
private readonly IOnlineUsersOperations _onlineUsersOperations;
private readonly ISmsSender _smsSender;
public ServiceRequestController(IServiceRequestOperations operations,
    IServiceRequestMessageOperations messageOperations,
    IConnectionManager signalRConnectionManager,
    IMapper mapper,
    IMasterDataCacheOperations masterData,
    UserManager<ApplicationUser> userManager,
    IEmailSender emailSender,
    IOptions<ApplicationSettings> options,
    IOnlineUsersOperations onlineUsersOperations,
    ISmsSender smsSender)
{
    _serviceRequestOperations = operations;
    _serviceRequestMessageOperations = messageOperations;
    _signalRConnectionManager = signalRConnectionManager;
    _mapper = mapper;
    _masterData = masterData;
    _userManager = userManager;
    _emailSender = emailSender;
    _onlineUsersOperations = onlineUsersOperations;
    _options = options;
    _smsSender = smsSender;
}
```

Create a private method named SendSmsAndWebNotifications in ServiceRequestController, as shown in Listing 11-32. This method sends the actual notifications to the customer. To send an SMS notification, we will call the SendSmsAsync method with the customer's phone number and a status change message.

Listing 11-32. SendSmsAndWebNotifications method

```
private async Task SendSmsAndWebNotifications(ServiceRequest serviceRequest)
{
    // Send SMS Notification
    var phoneNumber = (await _userManager.FindByEmailAsync(serviceRequest.PartitionKey)).
    PhoneNumber;
```

```
    if (!string.IsNullOrWhiteSpace(phoneNumber)) {
        await _smsSender.SendSmsAsync(string.Format("+91{0}", phoneNumber),
                    string.Format("Service Request Status updated to {0}", serviceRequest.
Status));
    }
}
```

Finally, update the UpdateServiceRequestDetails POST action to include a call to the
SendSmsAndWebNotifications method, as shown in Listing 11-33. We will track the service request
status change by using the isServiceRequestStatusUpdated flag. Based on the flag, we will call the
SendSmsAndWebNotifications method by passing the ServiceRequest object that is in context.

Listing 11-33. Updated UpdateServiceRequestDetails action

```
[HttpPost]
public async Task<IActionResult> UpdateServiceRequestDetails(UpdateServiceRequestViewModel
serviceRequest)
{
    var originalServiceRequest = await _serviceRequestOperations.GetServiceRequestByRowKey(s
erviceRequest.RowKey);
    originalServiceRequest.RequestedServices = serviceRequest.RequestedServices;

    var isServiceRequestStatusUpdated = false;
    // Update Status only if user role is either Admin or Engineer
    // Or Customer can update the status if it is only in Pending Customer Approval.
    if (HttpContext.User.IsInRole(Roles.Admin.ToString()) ||
        HttpContext.User.IsInRole(Roles.Engineer.ToString()) ||
        (HttpContext.User.IsInRole(Roles.User.ToString()) && originalServiceRequest.
        Status == Status.PendingCustomerApproval.ToString()))
    {
        if (originalServiceRequest.Status != serviceRequest.Status)
        {
            isServiceRequestStatusUpdated = true;
        }
        originalServiceRequest.Status = serviceRequest.Status;
    }

    // Update Service Engineer field only if user role is Admin
    if (HttpContext.User.IsInRole(Roles.Admin.ToString()))
    {
        originalServiceRequest.ServiceEngineer = serviceRequest.ServiceEngineer;
    }

    await _serviceRequestOperations.UpdateServiceRequestAsync(originalServiceRequest);

    if(HttpContext.User.IsInRole(Roles.Admin.ToString()) ||
        HttpContext.User.IsInRole(Roles.Engineer.ToString()) || originalServiceRequest.
        Status == Status.PendingCustomerApproval.ToString())
    {
        await _emailSender.SendEmailAsync(originalServiceRequest.PartitionKey,
                "Your Service Request is almost completed!!!",
                "Please visit the ASC application and review your Service request.");
    }
```

```
if (isServiceRequestStatusUpdated)
{
    await SendSmsAndWebNotifications(originalServiceRequest);
}

return RedirectToAction("ServiceRequestDetails", "ServiceRequest",
    new { Area = "ServiceRequests", Id = serviceRequest.RowKey });
}
```

Run the application and log in as Admin. Navigate to any Service Request Details view and change the status. The customer should get a text message, as shown in Figure 11-23.

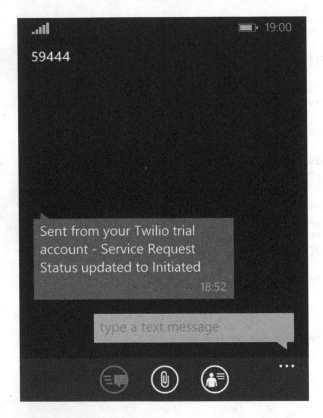

Figure 11-23. Text message received on mobile phone

■ **Note**   I have prefixed +91 to all the phone numbers because I am testing this functionality with mobile numbers issued from Indian mobile providers. For the US mobile numbers, we'd have to use +1.

We have used Twilio's free account for the entire demonstration. For a real-world production, it is advisable to get a subscription from Twilio and use it accordingly.

Enable Web Notifications to Customers by Using SignalR

Now we will work on enabling web notifications for service request status changes. Primarily, we will send notifications to the customer if he is active in the Automobile Service Center application (on any screen on the application) at the time of event (we will not store the notification messages in Azure Storage). Update the SendSmsAndWebNotifications private method in ServiceRequestController, as shown in Listing 11-34.

Listing 11-34. Updated SendSmsAndWebNotifications method

```
private async Task SendSmsAndWebNotifications(ServiceRequest serviceRequest)
{
    // Send SMS Notification
    var phoneNumber = (await _userManager.FindByEmailAsync(serviceRequest.PartitionKey)).
    PhoneNumber;
    if (!string.IsNullOrWhiteSpace(phoneNumber)) {
        await _smsSender.SendSmsAsync(string.Format("+91{0}", phoneNumber),
                    string.Format("Service Request Status updated to {0}", serviceRequest.
                    Status));
    }

    // Get Customer name
    var customerName = (await _userManager.FindByEmailAsync(serviceRequest.PartitionKey)).
    UserName;

    // Send web notifications
    _signalRConnectionManager.GetHubContext<ServiceMessagesHub>()
        .Clients
        .User(customerName)
        .publishNotification(new
        {
            status = serviceRequest.Status
        });
}
```

We will use the feature discovery concept of Materialize CSS to show a bubble notification to the end user. (Even though feature discovery is used to showcase new features to users, we will use the same concept to display notifications.) We have to include tap target HTML in _SecureLayout.cshtml, as shown in Listing 11-35, which is hidden by default. The HTML contains static text with a {$} placeholder that will be filled with push notification data from the server.

Listing 11-35. Tap Target HTML code

```
<!-- Tap Target Structure -->
<div class="tap-target cyan hide" data-activates="serviceNotification">
    <div class="tap-target-content white-text" >
        <h5 class="padding-left-50px">Status Updated!!!</h5>
        <p class="white-text padding-left-50px divNotification">The Status of your Service
        Request has been changed to {$}.</p>
    </div>
</div>
```

Finally, we have to create a client-side JQuery function that will be invoked by the SignalR hub when broadcasting a message to the client. Create the showNotification JQuery function in _SecureLayout. cshtml, as shown in Listing 11-36, and associate it with the hub by assigning it to the publishNotification proxy. The showNotification method fetches the data from the push notification and replaces the {$} placeholder with the data, removes the hide class, and finally calls Materialize CSS's tapTarget JQuery extension with open as a parameter to show the notification bubble. The notification will be displayed for 5 seconds; later it will be closed through a close operation by using the same tapTarget method. Finally, the tap target is hidden in HTML.

Listing 11-36. JQuery code to show tap target notification

```
$.connection.serviceMessagesHub.client.publishNotification = showNotification;

function showNotification(data) {
    var notificationText = $('.divNotification').html();
    $('.divNotification').html(notificationText.replace('{$}', data.status));
    $('.tap-target').removeClass('hide');

    $('.tap-target').tapTarget('open');
    setTimeout(function () {
        $('.tap-target').tapTarget('close');
        $('.tap-target').addClass('hide');;
    }, 5000);
};
```

Run the application, and log in as Admin and Customer in two different browsers. Let Admin change the service request status to any value. The customer should see the notification shown in Figure 11-24.

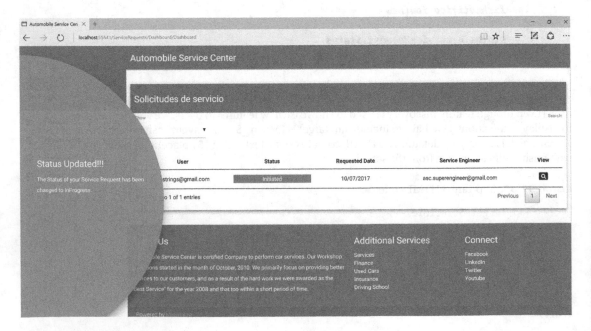

Figure 11-24. Web notification of the service request status change

Notifying Customers with Promotions

One of the important challenges that the Automobile Service Center is facing with its traditional marketing strategies is its inability to effectively promote discounts and offers to its customers. We are going to solve this challenge by providing an intuitive way to showcase all discounts, offers, and promotions through the Automobile Service Center application. In this section, we are going to build a promotions functionality for our application. The Admin user will be able to input promotional offers from time to time, and customers will receive web notifications of those offers. A common view for both the administrator and customers will be developed so they can glance at all the promotional offers.

Build the Promotional Offers Capability

We will start by creating a Promotion entity class in the Models folder of the ASC.Models project, which will serve as an Azure Storage entity, shown in Listing 11-37. It contains Header and Content properties that will hold the text displayed as the header and main body content for a promotion. The Promotion entity takes type as a parameter, which it uses as PartitionKey; the type can represent various types of promotions such as Discount or Voucher.

Listing 11-37. Promotion entity

```
using ASC.Models.BaseTypes;
using System;

namespace ASC.Models.Models
{
    public class Promotion : BaseEntity
    {
        public Promotion() { }
        public Promotion(string type)
        {
            this.RowKey = Guid.NewGuid().ToString();
            this.PartitionKey = type;
        }

        public string Header { get; set; }
        public string Content { get; set; }
    }
}
```

Now we will create IPromotionOperations in the Interfaces folder of the ASC.Business project, as shown in Listing 11-38. This interface will serve for all Azure Storage—related operations on the Promotion entity.

Listing 11-38. IPromotionOperations interface

```
using ASC.Models.Models;
using System;
using System.Collections.Generic;
using System.Threading.Tasks;
```

```
namespace ASC.Business.Interfaces
{
    public interface IPromotionOperations
    {
        Task CreatePromotionAsync(Promotion promotion);
        Task<Promotion> UpdatePromotionAsync(string rowKey, Promotion promotion);
        Task<List<Promotion>> GetAllPromotionsAsync();
    }
}
```

Create a class named PromotionOperations in the ASC.Business project, as shown in Listing 11-39. We will implement IPromotionOperations on the PromotionOperations class. The CreatePromotionAsync method creates a promotion, UpdatePromotionAsync updates a promotion based on RowKey. The GetAllPromotionsAsync method will return all promotions.

Listing 11-39. PromotionOperations class

```
using ASC.Business.Interfaces;
using ASC.DataAccess.Interfaces;
using ASC.Models.Models;
using System.Linq;
using System.Threading.Tasks;
using System;
using System.Collections.Generic;

namespace ASC.Business
{
    public class PromotionOperations : IPromotionOperations
    {
        private readonly IUnitOfWork _unitOfWork;
        public PromotionOperations(IUnitOfWork unitOfWork)
        {
            _unitOfWork = unitOfWork;
        }

        public async Task CreatePromotionAsync(Promotion promotion)
        {
            using (_unitOfWork)
            {
                await _unitOfWork.Repository<Promotion>().AddAsync(promotion);
                _unitOfWork.CommitTransaction();
            }
        }

        public async Task<List<Promotion>> GetAllPromotionsAsync()
        {
            var promotions = await _unitOfWork.Repository<Promotion>().FindAllAsync();
            return promotions.ToList();
        }

        public async Task<Promotion> UpdatePromotionAsync(string rowKey, Promotion
        promotion)
```

```
{
    var originalPromotion = await _unitOfWork.Repository<Promotion>().
    FindAsync(promotion.PartitionKey, rowKey);
    if(originalPromotion != null)
    {
        originalPromotion.Header = promotion.Header;
        originalPromotion.Content = promotion.Content;
        originalPromotion.IsDeleted = promotion.IsDeleted;
    }
    using (_unitOfWork)
    {
        await _unitOfWork.Repository<Promotion>().UpdateAsync(originalPromotion);
        _unitOfWork.CommitTransaction();
    }
    return originalPromotion;
}
}
}
```

Resolve the dependency at the ASC.Web project by adding PromotionOperations to IServiceCollection at the method of the Startup class, as shown in Listing 11-40.

Listing 11-40. Resolve the dependency of IPromotionOperations

```
services.AddScoped<IPromotionOperations, PromotionOperations>();
```

Before we proceed to creating the controller actions and views, we will update the Navigation.json file in the ASC.Web project to hold the Promotions left navigation menu item, as shown in Listing 11-41. This Promotion menu item will have options to create a new promotion and view all active promotions.

Listing 11-41. Promotions left navigation menu items

```
{
  "DisplayName": "Promotions",
  "MaterialIcon": "inbox",
  "Link": "",
  "IsNested": true,
  "Sequence": 4,
  "UserRoles": [ "User", "Engineer", "Admin" ],
  "NestedItems": [
    {
      "DisplayName": "New Promotion",
      "MaterialIcon": "insert_invitation",
      "Link": "/Promotions/Promotions/Promotion",
      "IsNested": false,
      "Sequence": 1,
      "UserRoles": [ "Admin" ],
      "NestedItems": []
    },
    {
      "DisplayName": "All Promotions",
      "MaterialIcon": "search",
```

```
            "Link": "/Promotions/Promotions/Promotions",
            "IsNested": false,
            "Sequence": 2,
            "UserRoles": [ "User", "Engineer", "Admin" ],
            "NestedItems": []
        }
    ]
},
```

We will create a new area inside the ASC.Web project named Promotions and create corresponding Controllers, Views, and Models folders, as shown in Figure 11-25.

Figure 11-25. *Promotions area folder structure*

■ **Note** Make sure to place _ViewImports.cshtml at the root of the Promotions area (just as in other areas).

We will create new view models named PromotionsViewModel and PromotionViewModel that will be used by the controller and view to display a list of promotions and add/update a new/existing promotion. Create a PromotionsViewModel class under the Models folder of the Promotions area of the ASC.Web project, as shown in Listing 11-42.

Listing 11-42. PromotionsViewModel class

```csharp
using System.Collections.Generic;

namespace ASC.Web.Areas.Promotions.Models
{
    public class PromotionsViewModel
    {
        public List<PromotionViewModel> Promotions { get; set; }
        public PromotionViewModel PromotionInContext { get; set; }
        public bool IsEdit { get; set; }
    }
}
```

Create a `PromotionViewModel` class under the `Models` folder of the `Promotions` area of the `ASC.Web` project, as shown in Listing 11-43.

Listing 11-43. PromotionViewModel class

```
using System.ComponentModel.DataAnnotations;

namespace ASC.Web.Areas.Promotions.Models
{
    public class PromotionViewModel
    {
        public string RowKey { get; set; }
        public bool IsDeleted { get; set; }

        [Required]
        [Display(Name = "Type")]
        public string PartitionKey { get; set; }

        [Required]
        [Display(Name = "Header")]
        public string Header { get; set; }

        [Required]
        [Display(Name = "Content")]
        public string Content { get; set; }
    }
}
```

■ **Note** We use `AutoMapper` to map business models to our web view models. `AutoMapper` is an object-to-object mapper that uses a fluent configuration API to define an object-to-object mapping strategy.

Create a class named `MappingProfile` under the `Models` folder of the `Promotions` area in the `ASC. Web` project, as shown in Listing 11-44. It will contain `AutoMapper`'s mappings for the `Promotion` entity and `PromotionViewModel`.

Listing 11-44. AutoMapper's Promotion mappings in MappingProfile class

```
using ASC.Models.Models;
using AutoMapper;

namespace ASC.Web.Areas.Promotions.Models
{
    public class MappingProfile : Profile
    {
        public MappingProfile()
        {
```

```
            CreateMap<Promotion, PromotionViewModel>();
            CreateMap<PromotionViewModel, Promotion>();
        }
    }
}
```

■ **Note**   Add `PromotionType` in the `MasterKeys` enum, as shown in Listing 11-45. This will be used to prepopulate the Promotions type combo box. Use the `MasterKeys` and `MasterValues` screens to create values for PromotionType (for example, Discount and Voucher).

Listing 11-45. PromotionType in MasterKeys enum

```
public enum MasterKeys
{
    VehicleName, VehicleType, PromotionType
}
```

Now we will create `PromotionsController` in the Promotions area of the `ASC.Web` project, as shown in Listing 11-46. All the dependencies are injected into the constructor of `PromotionsController`, especially `IPromotionOperations`, which is used to perform Azure Storage operations on the `Promotion` entity, and `IMasterDataCacheOperations`, which is used to retrieve the promotion types.

The GET operation gets all the promotions from Azure Storage and maps the list of promotions to `PromotionViewModel`. It also fetches the `PromotionType` reference data from the master data cache and holds it in, which can be used in the view. Finally, the view model is stored in the session, and `Promotion.cshtml` is returned with the consolidated model.

The POST action will first check for `ModelState`, and in case of any errors, the same model is returned to the view with errors. If `ModelState` succeeds, based on the mode of the operation, the `Promotion` entity is either inserted or updated. Finally, the control is redirected to the GET action.

Listing 11-46. GET and POST actions of PromotionsController

```
using Microsoft.AspNetCore.Mvc;
using ASC.Web.Controllers;
using ASC.Business.Interfaces;
using ASC.Web.Data;
using System.Linq;
using System.Threading.Tasks;
using AutoMapper;
using System.Collections.Generic;
using ASC.Utilities;
using ASC.Models.Models;
using System;
using ASC.Models.BaseTypes;
using ASC.Web.Areas.Promotions.Models;

namespace ASC.Web.Areas.Promotions.Controllers
{
    [Area("Promotions")]
    public class PromotionsController : BaseController
```

```csharp
{
    private readonly IPromotionOperations _promotionOperations;
    private readonly IMapper _mapper;
    private readonly IMasterDataCacheOperations _masterData;
    public PromotionsController(IPromotionOperations promotionOperations,
        IMapper mapper,
        IMasterDataCacheOperations masterData)
    {
        _promotionOperations = promotionOperations;
        _mapper = mapper;
        _masterData = masterData;
    }

    [HttpGet]
    public async Task<IActionResult> Promotion()
    {
        var promotions = await _promotionOperations.GetAllPromotionsAsync();
        var promotionsViewModel = _mapper.Map<List<Promotion>, List<PromotionViewModel>
        >(promotions);

        // Get All Master Keys and hold them in ViewBag for Select tag
        var masterData = await _masterData.GetMasterDataCacheAsync();
        ViewBag.PromotionTypes = masterData.Values.Where(p => p.PartitionKey ==
        MasterKeys.PromotionType.ToString()).ToList();

        // Hold all Promotions in session
        HttpContext.Session.SetSession("Promotions", promotionsViewModel);

        return View(new PromotionsViewModel
        {
            Promotions = promotionsViewModel == null ? null : promotionsViewModel.
            ToList(),
            IsEdit = false,
            PromotionInContext = new PromotionViewModel()
        });
    }

    [HttpPost]
    [ValidateAntiForgeryToken]
    public async Task<IActionResult> Promotion(PromotionsViewModel promotions)
    {
        promotions.Promotions = HttpContext.Session.GetSession<List<PromotionView
        Model>>("Promotions");
        if (!ModelState.IsValid)
        {
            return View(promotions);
        }

        var promotion = _mapper.Map<PromotionViewModel, Promotion>(promotions.
        PromotionInContext);
        if (promotions.IsEdit)
```

```
            {
                // Update Promotion
                await _promotionOperations.UpdatePromotionAsync(promotions.
                PromotionInContext.RowKey, promotion);
            }
            else
            {
                // Insert Promotion
                promotion.RowKey = Guid.NewGuid().ToString();
                await _promotionOperations.CreatePromotionAsync(promotion);
            }

            return RedirectToAction("Promotion");
        }
    }
}
```

The `Promotion.cshtml` view will consist of two sections: one to display the list of promotions, and the other to display the details of a particular promotion, as shown in Listing 11-47. An HTML table has been defined, and all the promotions are iterated and rendered in the same table. By default, we will show Type, Header, IsDeleted, and Edit action columns in the table. If no promotions are available, a No Records message will be displayed in the table.

The details section of the view contains a `form` tag with the required elements for `PartitionKey` (promotion type), Header, Content, and `IsDeleted` flags. We also maintain a hidden field inside the form to identify `RowKey` on the POST action.

Listing 11-47. Promotions View

```
@model ASC.Web.Areas.Promotions.Models.PromotionsViewModel
@{
    Layout = "_SecureLayout";
}

<div class="row"></div>
<div class="row padding-top-20px">
    <div class="row z-depth-3">
        <div class="section white-text padding-left-10px blue-grey lighten-1">
            <h5>Promotions</h5>
        </div>
        <div class="divider"></div>
        <div class="col s12 padding-bottom-15px">
            @if (Model.Promotions != null)
            {
                @* Display List of Promotions *@
                <table class="highlight centered" id="tblPromotions">
                    <thead>
                        <tr>
                            <th data-field="RowKey">Row Key</th>
                            <th data-field="PartitionKey">Type</th>
                            <th data-field="Header">Header</th>
                            <th data-field="Content">Content</th>
                            <th data-field="IsActive">Is Deleted</th>
```

```
                    <th data-field="IsActiveImg">Is Deleted</th>
                    <th data-field="Actions">Edit</th>
                </tr>
            </thead>
            <tbody>
                @foreach (var promotion in Model.Promotions)
                {
                    <tr>
                        <td>@promotion.RowKey</td>
                        <td>@promotion.PartitionKey</td>
                        <td>@promotion.Header</td>
                        <td>@promotion.Content</td>
                        <td>@promotion.IsDeleted</td>
                        <td><img src="@(promotion.IsDeleted ? "/images/green_tick.
                        png" : "/images/red_cross.png")" /></td>
                        <td><i class="small material-icons edit cursor-hand">mode_
                        edit</i></td>
                    </tr>
                }
            </tbody>
        </table>
    }
    else
    {
        @* In case of No records, display no records message *@
        <div class="card blue-grey lighten-1">
            <div class="card-content white-text">
                <span class="card-title">No Promotions!!!</span>
                <p>
                    No Promotions found, please add a Promotion to system.
                </p>
            </div>
        </div>
    }
    </div>
</div>

<div class="row"></div>

@* Details Section *@
<div class="row z-depth-3">
    <div class="col s12 padding-0px">
        <div class="section white-text padding-left-10px blue-grey lighten-1">
            <h5>Promotion Details</h5>
        </div>
        <div class="divider"></div>
        <form asp-controller="Promotions" asp-action="Promotion" method="post"
        class="col s12" id="formPromotion">
            <div class="row">
                <input type="hidden" asp-for="IsEdit" />
                <input type="hidden" asp-for="PromotionInContext.RowKey" />
```

```
            <div class="input-field col s4">
                <select id="PromotionInContext_PartitionKey"
                    asp-for="PromotionInContext.PartitionKey"
                    asp-items="@(new SelectList(ViewBag.PromotionTypes,"Name","
                    Name"))"
                    required="required">
                    <option value="">--Select--</option>
                </select>
                <label>Type</label>
            </div>
            <div class="input-field col s4">
                <input asp-for="PromotionInContext.Header" class="validate" />
                <label asp-for="PromotionInContext.Header"></label>
            </div>
            <div class="input-field col s4">
                <div class="switch">
                    <label>
                        Is Deleted
                        <input asp-for="PromotionInContext.IsDeleted"
                        class="validate" />
                        <span class="lever"></span>
                    </label>
                </div>
            </div>
        </div>
        <div class="row">
            <div class="input-field col s12">
                <textarea asp-for="PromotionInContext.Content" class="materialize-
                textarea validate"></textarea>
                <label asp-for="PromotionInContext.Content"></label>
            </div>
        </div>
        <div class="row">
            <div class="input-field col s12 right-align">
                <button class="btn waves-effect waves-light btnSubmit" type="submit"
                name="action">
                    Create
                    <i class="material-icons right">send</i>
                </button>
                <button class="btn waves-effect waves-light reset  red lighten-1"
                type="button" name="action">
                    Reset
                </button>
            </div>
            <div class="row col s12 right-align" asp-validation-summary="All"></div>
        </div>
    </form>

</div>
<div class="row"></div>
</div>
</div>
```

The Promotion.cshtml view also contains JQuery code, as shown in Listing 11-48, which is primarily used to configure DataTables by initializing it with page size and length options. In JQuery code, we also set the required styles of DataTable and hide the RowKey, Content, and IsDeleted columns. Instead of showing the IsDeleted Boolean flag, we will show green tick or red X.

We will also handle the reset button functionality in JQuery, through which user changes will be discarded. Finally, an Edit click event is handled, in which we will populate the details section with the promotion information that is under edit mode. JQuery code is also used to populate the RowKey hidden field that is used by the POST action to identity the entity being edited.

Listing 11-48. JQuery code on Promotions view

```
@section Scripts{
    <script>
        $(document).ready(function () {
            // Initialize DataTable to show list of Promotions
            var table = $('#tblPromotions').DataTable({
                'pageLength': 3,
                // Number of records to be displayed per page
                'lengthMenu': [[3, 5, 10, -1], [3, 5, 10, 'All']]
            });

            // Set Styles for DataTable and Number of Records to be displayed in drop-down
            $('#tblPromotions').css("width", "100%");
            $('select[name="tblPromotions_length"]').material_select();

            $("select[required]").css({ display: "block", position: 'absolute', visibility:
            'hidden' });
            // Initialize Select
            $('select').material_select();

            // Get the column API object
            var rowKeyColumn = table.column(0);
            rowKeyColumn.visible(false);

            var contentColumn = table.column(3);
            contentColumn.visible(false);

            var isActiveColumn = table.column(4);
            isActiveColumn.visible(false);

            // Handle Reset functionality
            $(document).on('click', '.reset', function () {
                $('#formPromotion')[0].reset();
                $('.btnSubmit').text('Create');
                $('#IsEdit').val('False');

                // Remove Partition key disabled attribute
                $('#PromotionInContext_PartitionKey').material_select('destroy');
                $('#PromotionInContext_PartitionKey').removeAttr('disabled');
                $('#PromotionInContext_PartitionKey').material_select();
```

```
                // Remove the validation error messages.
                $('.validation-summary-valid').find("ul").html('');
            });

            // On click of Edit icon, populate the details section with details of service
            engineer
            $(document).on('click', '.edit', function () {
                var promotion = $('#tblPromotions').DataTable().row($(this).parents('tr')).
                data();

                $('#IsEdit').val('True');
                // Map Row Key
                $('#PromotionInContext_RowKey').val(promotion[0]);

                // Set Partition Key Dropdown and re-initialize Material Select
                $('#PromotionInContext_PartitionKey').material_select('destroy');
                $('#PromotionInContext_PartitionKey option:contains(' + promotion[1] + ')').
                prop('selected', true);
                $('#PromotionInContext_PartitionKey').material_select();

                // Map Header
                $('#PromotionInContext_Header').val(promotion[2]);
                $('#PromotionInContext_Header').addClass('valid');
                // Map Header
                $('#PromotionInContext_Content').val(promotion[3]);
                $('#PromotionInContext_Content').addClass('valid');
                // Map IsActive
                $('#PromotionInContext_IsDeleted').prop('checked', promotion[4] === 'True' ?
                true : false);

                $('.btnSubmit').text('Save');
                Materialize.updateTextFields();
            });

        });
    </script>
}
```

Run the application and log in as Admin. You should see New Promotion in the left navigation menu, as shown in Figure 11-26.

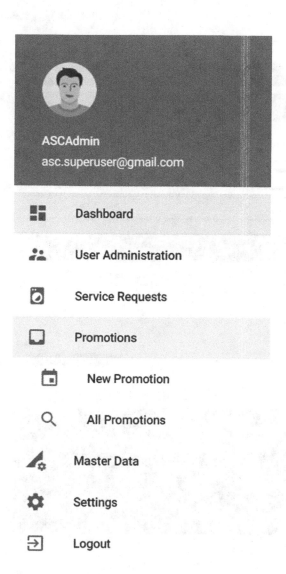

Figure 11-26. *Promotion menu items in the left navigation pane*

Click the New Promotion menu item. You should see all existing promotions, as shown in Figure 11-27.

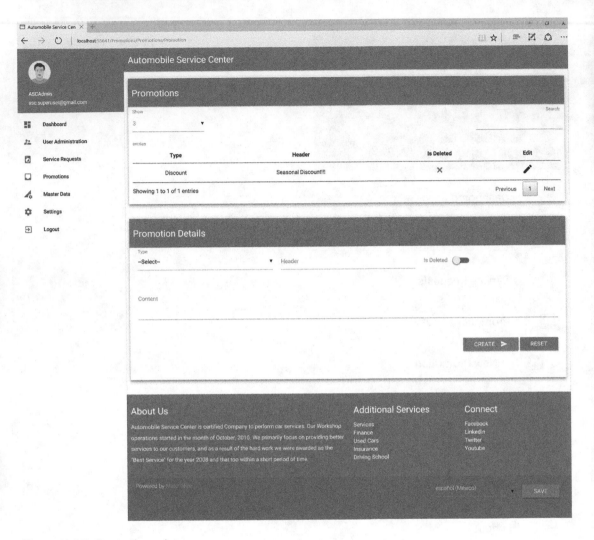

Figure 11-27. *Promotions view*

Enter a new promotion in the bottom section and click Create, as shown in Figure 11-28.

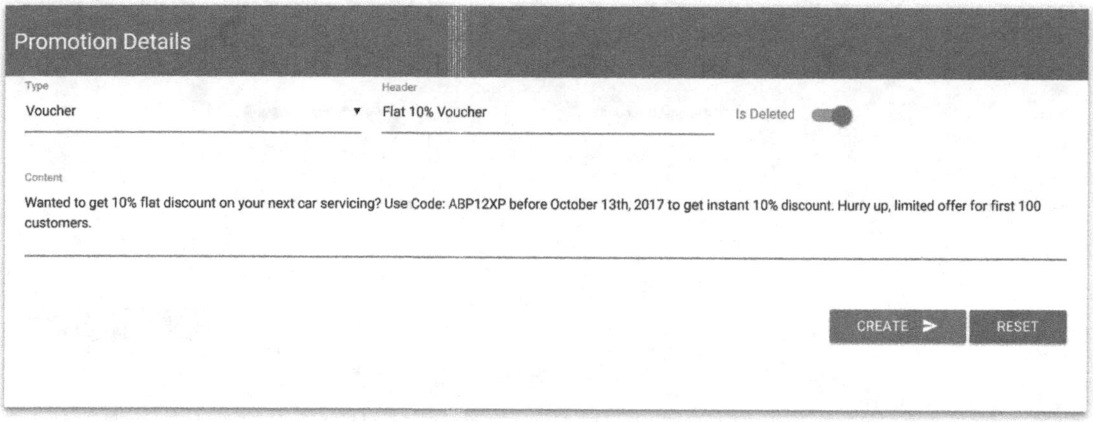

Promotion Details		
Type	Header	
Voucher ▼	Flat 10% Voucher	Is Deleted ⬤
Content		
Wanted to get 10% flat discount on your next car servicing? Use Code: ABP12XP before October 13th, 2017 to get instant 10% discount. Hurry up, limited offer for first 100 customers.		
		CREATE > RESET

Figure 11-28. *Creating a new promotion*

We should see the newly created promotion in the top section of the Promotions list, as shown in Figure 11-29.

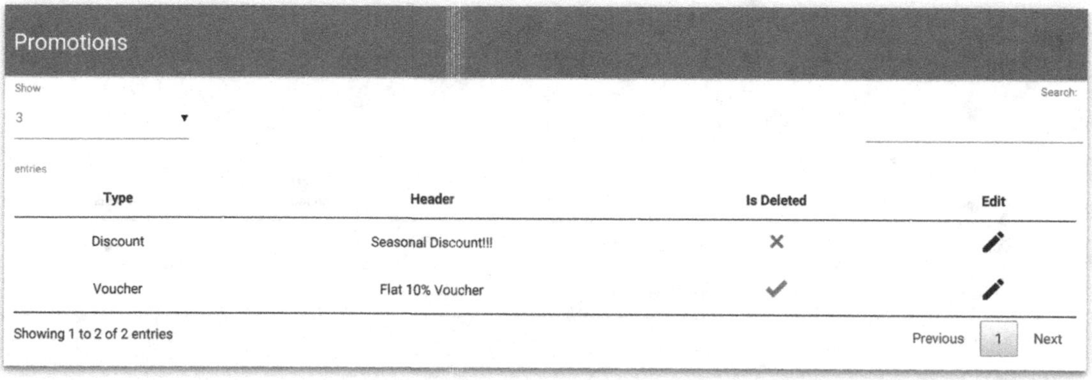

Promotions			
Show			Search:
3 ▼			
entries			
Type	**Header**	**Is Deleted**	**Edit**
Discount	Seasonal Discount!!!	✕	✎
Voucher	Flat 10% Voucher	✓	✎
Showing 1 to 2 of 2 entries		Previous 1 Next	

Figure 11-29. *Newly added promotion in list of promotions*

Now we will edit an existing promotion, and details will be displayed in the details section, as shown in Figure 11-30.

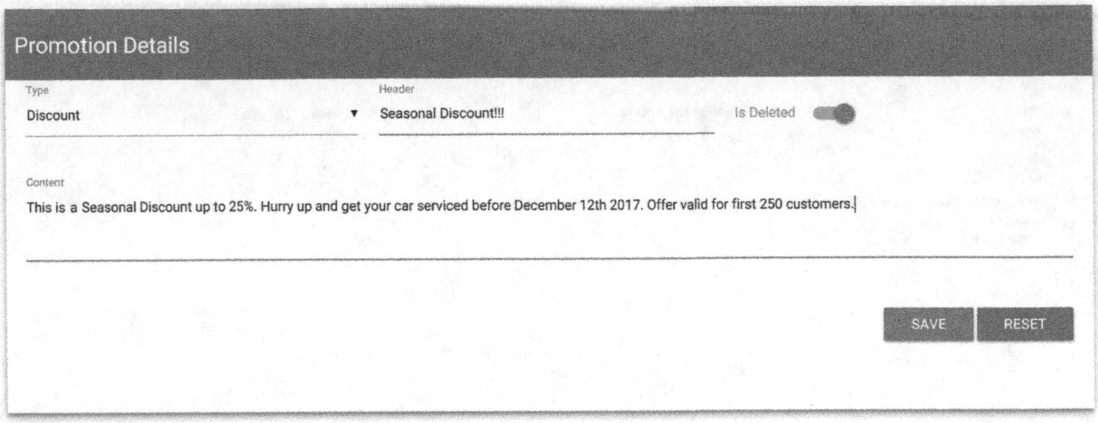

Figure 11-30. *Updating an existing promotion*

Edit the record and click Save. The updated record will be shown in the list of promotions, as shown in Figure 11-31.

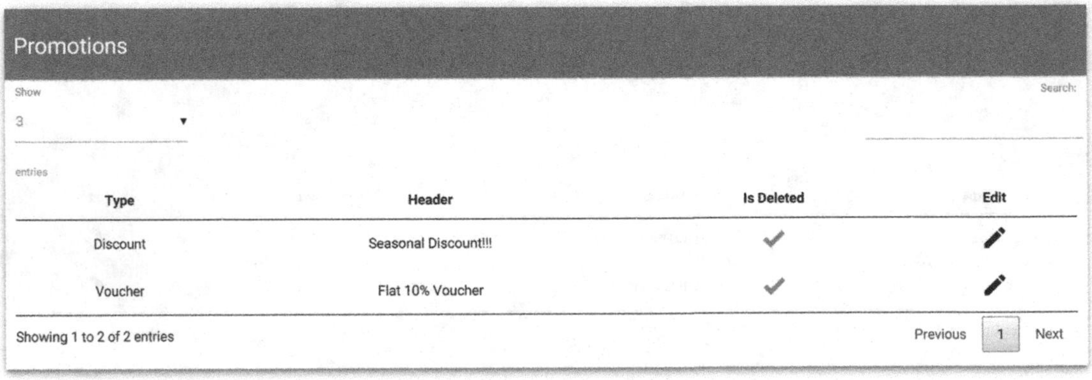

Figure 11-31. *Updated promotion in list of promotions*

If we look at the Promotion Azure table, the created entities are persisted, as shown in Figure 11-32.

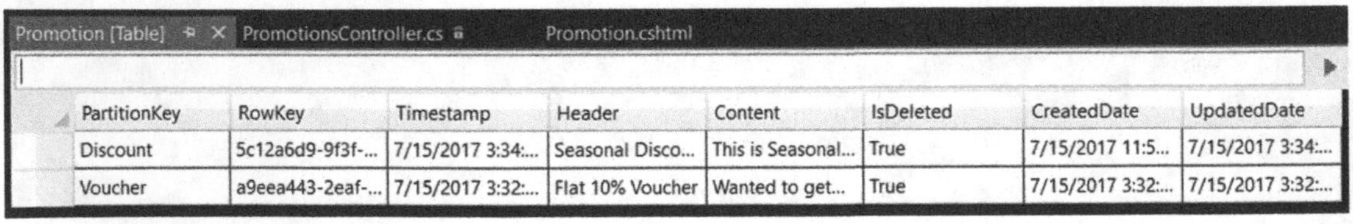

PartitionKey	RowKey	Timestamp	Header	Content	IsDeleted	CreatedDate	UpdatedDate
Discount	5c12a6d9-9f3f-...	7/15/2017 3:34:...	Seasonal Disco...	This is Seasonal...	True	7/15/2017 11:5...	7/15/2017 3:34:...
Voucher	a9eea443-2eaf-...	7/15/2017 3:32:...	Flat 10% Voucher	Wanted to get...	True	7/15/2017 3:32:...	7/15/2017 3:32:...

Figure 11-32. *Promotion Azure Storage table*

Display Promotional Offers to Customers

In this section, we will create a view for customers so they can view all the promotions. Create the Promotions action in PromotionsController, as shown in Listing 11-49. This action gets all promotions, filters them based on the IsDeleted flag, and sorts the results based on an entity's Timestamp property. Finally, the action method returns the results to the Promotions.cshtml view.

Listing 11-49. Promotions action

```
[HttpGet]
public async Task<IActionResult> Promotions()
{
    var promotions = await _promotionOperations.GetAllPromotionsAsync();
    var filteredPromotions = new List<Promotion>();
    if(promotions != null)
    {
        filteredPromotions = promotions.Where(p => !p.IsDeleted).OrderByDescending(p =>
        p.Timestamp).ToList();
    }

    return View(filteredPromotions);
}
```

We will create Promotions.cshtml, which will display all the promotions as shown in Listing 11-50. If there are any promotions, we will display them in chronological order using Materialize CSS Card styles. If there are no styles, no promotion messages will be displayed.

Listing 11-50. Promotions view

```
@model IEnumerable<ASC.Models.Models.Promotion>
@{
    Layout = "_SecureLayout";
}

<div class="row"></div>
<div class="row padding-top-20px">
    <div class="row z-depth-3">
        <div class="section white-text padding-left-10px blue-grey lighten-1">
            <h5>Promotions</h5>
        </div>
        <div class="divider"></div>
        <div class="col s12 padding-bottom-15px divPromotions">
            @if (Model != null && Model.Any())
            {
                foreach (var promotion in Model)
                {
                @* Display List of Promotions *@
                    <div class="col s12 m5">
                        <div class="card @(promotion.PartitionKey == "Discount" ? "light-
                        green darken-2" : " light-blue darken-2") ">
                            <div class="card-content white-text">
                                <span class="card-title">@promotion.Header</span>
                                <p>
```

```
                            @promotion.Content
                    </p>
                </div>
            </div>
        </div>
    }
}
else
{
    @* In case of No records, display no records message *@
    <div class="card blue-grey lighten-1">
        <div class="card-content white-text">
            <span class="card-title">No Promotions!!!</span>
            <p>
                No Promotions found.
            </p>
        </div>
    </div>
}
        </div>
    </div>

    <div class="row"></div>
</div>

@section Scripts{

}
```

Run the application, log in as a Customer, and navigate to the All Promotions navigation menu item. The promotions should be displayed, as shown in Figure 11-33.

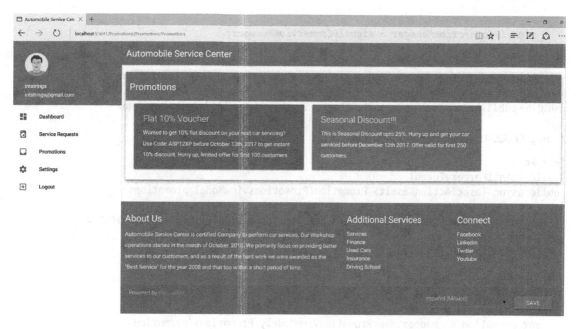

Figure 11-33. *Promotions view*

Enable Web Notifications to Customers on New Promotions

Now we will work on displaying web notifications for new promotions that are added by the administrator. Whenever a new promotion is added, we will show a notification number on the Promotions left navigation menu item, and it also will be appended to the Promotions list.

■ **Note**   The notification number that we display in the left navigation menu will not be persisted upon screen refresh or navigation to any other screen.

As a first step, we have to inject SignalR's `IConnectionManager` into `PromotionsController`, as shown in Listing 11-51.

Listing 11-51. Inject IConnectionManager dependency into PromotionsController

```
private readonly IPromotionOperations _promotionOperations;
private readonly IMapper _mapper;
private readonly IMasterDataCacheOperations _masterData;
private readonly IConnectionManager _signalRConnectionManager;
public PromotionsController(IPromotionOperations promotionOperations,
    IMapper mapper,
    IMasterDataCacheOperations masterData,
    IConnectionManager signalRConnectionManager)
{
    _promotionOperations = promotionOperations;
    _mapper = mapper;
```

```
    _masterData = masterData;
    _signalRConnectionManager = signalRConnectionManager;
}
```

To send a push notification to all SignalR clients, we need to update the POST action of Promotion, as shown in Listing 11-52. We will get the SignalR hub context and then send a push notification to all clients by using the publishPromotion proxy method by passing the newly added promotion data.

Listing 11-52. Updated Promotion action

```
[HttpPost]
[ValidateAntiForgeryToken]
public async Task<IActionResult> Promotion(PromotionsViewModel promotions)
{
    promotions.Promotions = HttpContext.Session.GetSession<List<PromotionViewModel>>
    ("Promotions");
    if (!ModelState.IsValid)
    {
        return View(promotions);
    }

    var promotion = _mapper.Map<PromotionViewModel, Promotion>(promotions.
    PromotionInContext);
    if (promotions.IsEdit)
    {
        // Update Promotion
        await _promotionOperations.UpdatePromotionAsync(promotions.PromotionInContext.
        RowKey, promotion);
    }
    else
    {
        // Insert Promotion
        promotion.RowKey = Guid.NewGuid().ToString();
        await _promotionOperations.CreatePromotionAsync(promotion);

        if (!promotion.IsDeleted)
        {
            // Broadcast the message to all clients associated with new promotion
            _signalRConnectionManager.GetHubContext<ServiceMessagesHub>()
                .Clients
                .All
                .publishPromotion(promotion);
        }
    }

    return RedirectToAction("Promotion");
}
```

Now update _SecureLayout.cshtml to hold a promotion HTML template that is hidden by default, as shown in Listing 11-53. The promotion template contains placeholders for header, content, and style information. Whenever a push notification comes from the server, we use JQuery code to retrieve the promotion template, clone it, and then replace the placeholder information with actual information. Finally, we will prepend the updated promotion div on the promotions screen.

Listing 11-53. New Promotion HTML template

```
<!-- Promotion Template -->
<div class="promotionTemplate hide">
    <div class="col s12 m5">
        <div class="card {Style}">
            <div class="card-content white-text">
                <span class="card-title">{Header}</span>
                <p>
                    {Content}
                </p>
            </div>
        </div>
    </div>
</div>
```

Finally, we will update the JQuery code in _SecureLayout.cshtml to hook up publishPromotion with the showPromotion JQuery function, as shown in Listing 11-54. We declare the counter variable, which is used to track the number of promotion updates published to the client. This counter variable is incremented in the showPromotion function. The function will also get the promotion template that we defined earlier and replaces the Header and Content placeholders with the newly added promotion data. The function also replaces the style for different types of promotions and finally prepends to the promotions div tag.

Listing 11-54. showPromotion JQuery function

```
$.connection.serviceMessagesHub.client.publishPromotion = showPromotion;

var counter = 0
function showPromotion(data) {
    counter++;
    var promotionTemplate = $('.promotionTemplate').clone().html();
    promotionTemplate = promotionTemplate.replace('{Header}', data.Header);
    promotionTemplate = promotionTemplate.replace('{Content}', data.Content);
    promotionTemplate = promotionTemplate.replace('{Style}', data.PartitionKey ==
    'Discount' ? 'light-green darken-2' : 'light-blue darken-2');

    // Prepend newly added promotion to to divPromotions on Promotions view.
    $('.divPromotions').prepend(promotionTemplate);

    // show notification counter on the left navigation menu item.
    $('#ancrPromotions .badge').remove();
    $('#ancrPromotions').prepend('<span class="new badge">' + counter + '</span>');
};
```

Run the application and log in as an administrator and customer on different browsers. Let the administrator add a promotion by using the New Promotion screen. The customer should see the notifications in the left navigation Promotions menu item, as shown in Figure 11-34.

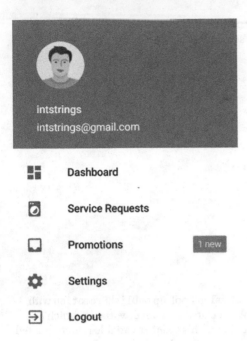

Figure 11-34. *Promotion notification to the customer*

If the customer is on the Promotions screen, he should see the left navigation count notification along with the new promotion listed with other promotions, as shown in Figure 11-35.

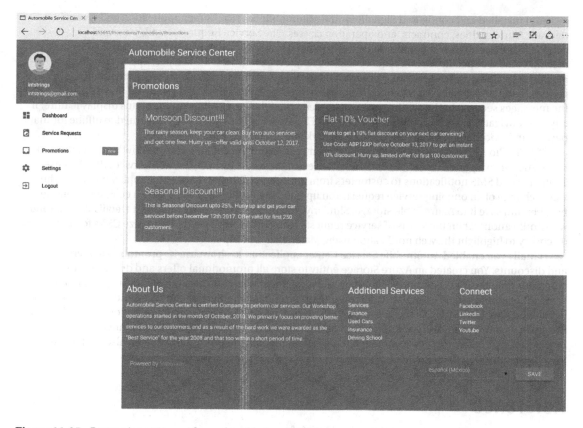

Figure 11-35. *Promotions view with newly added promotion*

Summary

You started this chapter by learning about the importance of real-time communication between businesses and their customers. Real-time communication will empower businesses to reach their customers at the right time and with the right information. It also helps businesses gain more insight and perform powerful analysis to build next-generation features for their customers. For Automobile Service Center application, real-time communication helps service engineers and customers exchange service request information. The real-time notifications about the progress of service requests will help customers know more about their car's service requirements and help them to be more confident with the Automobile Service Center's work capabilities. On the other end, real-time communication helps administrators and service engineers reach out to their customers on a timely basis and share crucial updates about the ongoing service request.

SignalR is an open source library from Microsoft that offers real-time web development features for ASP. NET applications. You used SignalR to build real-time communication for our Automobile Service Center application. SignalR uses the Hubs API to push notifications from the server to the client and supports multiple channels such as WebSocket, server-sent events, and long polling. Older versions of SignalR are not compatible with the ASP.NET Core platform, so Microsoft is in the process of developing and delivering a ground-up version to support new features of .NET Core and .NET Standard. As the stable version of the new SignalR will be available soon, you used preview versions (0.2.0-preview2-22683) to develop real-time communication for our application.

You installed and configured SignalR for the Automobile Service Center application and created relevant Azure entities, contracts, and operation classes. The Service Request Details view and corresponding controller action methods were updated to store and push notifications to all other users associated with a specific service request. Service Request Details view HTML was updated to display messages section, where users can type and send messages to other users. The corresponding JQuery code was updated to receive push notification data from the SignalR hub and process it and display it in the messages section. In the similar way, you implemented the user online/offline status display feature; if any user navigates away from the Service Request Details screen, his status will be turned to offline for that particular service request, and otherwise he is marked as an online user.

The Twilio API from Twilio, a cloud-based communications company, allows software developers to make and receive phone calls and send and receive text messages by using its web service APIs. You used Twilio to send SMS notifications to customers from our Automobile Service Center application upon the status change of an ongoing service request. You updated the Profile view to capture a customer's phone number and save it to Azure Table storage. Similarly, you updated the Service Request Details view to send web notifications when the status of service request changes. You have used Materialize CSS's feature discovery to highlight the web notification using Materialize CSS tap target styles.

Finally you enabled Automobile Service Center application to showcase its promotional offers and discounts. You created an Azure Storage entity to store all promotional offers and developed the corresponding business component contract and implementation. You also developd a new promotion screen that administrators can use to add or manage promotions in the system. A common view has been developed that will display all the active promotions in the system. When a new promotion is added to the system, a web notification is issued by using the SignalR hub, which will notify the customer by showing a new promotion badge on the Promotion left navigation menu;a the promotions screen also is updated with the latest promotion details.

Reference

1. www.youtube.com/watch?v=1TrttIkbs6c&t=96s

CHAPTER 12

■ ■ ■

Code Version Control Using GitHub Platform

As we enter a new era of software development, the complexity of business requirements is growing exponentially because of the very nature of exploring new business opportunities, which requires collaboration and integration among different systems. With increased demand for connectivity between business systems and for potential automation, managing and maintaining source code has become increasingly complex. Version-control systems play a crucial role in managing and tracking artifacts of source code. The technical advancements in code version-control systems and tools not only has made software development more resilient and effective, but also opened new global opportunities for people across the world to collaborate without worrying about source-code dependencies.

A version-control system (VCS) can make a project self-sufficient in the following ways:

- It helps effectively manage and maintain a code repository across large teams

- Version change history can be used to compare and revert code changes.

- Branching and merging source code helps maintain different versions of code for different environments and releases.

- Associating code artifacts and versions with specific business requirements and defects helps in easily identifying and tracing the code.

Many code version-control systems are on the market. Some of the popular VCSs are Git, Team Foundation Server, and Subversion. Git, one the most powerful and popular version-control systems, was created by Linus Torvalds in 2005. The power of Git comes when dealing with decentralized repositories: a developer can work on a local repository, and after the code is stable in that repository, the developer can push the code to a remote repository. Any organization can have its own infrastructure and manage Git repositories internally or can subscribe to online providers that provide Git services.

GitHub is a hosting service for Git repositories. In addition to providing source-code management, GitHub also provides collaboration features such as bug tracking, feature requests, task management, wikis, and access control for all projects. GitHub is free to use for public and open source projects. It also offers paid plans to support developers, teams, and businesses with unlimited private repositories. GitHub allows developers to fork a project repository and create their own centralized repository from the source code of the forked project. From a forked project, developers can modify code and send pull requests with updated code to the main project, which can be merged to the main project based on the project owner's decision.

In this chapter, we are going to use the GitHub platform to version the Automobile Service Center's source code. You will see how to use Git commands from Windows to manage and version source code.

© Rami Vemula 2017

R. Vemula, *Real-Time Web Application Development*, https://doi.org/10.1007/978-1-4842-3270-5_12

Getting Started with GitHub

In this section, we will create a GitHub account for the Automobile Service Center application. After the account is created, we will install GitHub for Windows and configure it to manage code versions from the command line.

Go to GitHub.com and sign up for a new account, as shown in Figure 12-1.

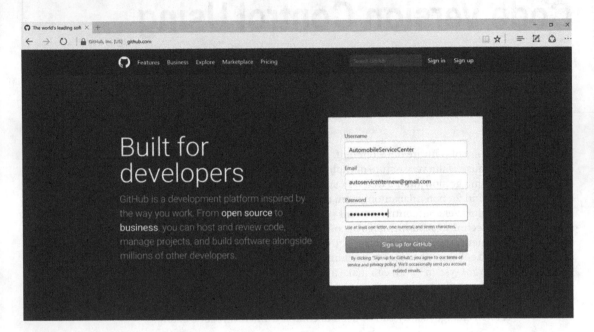

Figure 12-1. *Signing up at GitHub.com*

GitHub will prompt you to select a plan. For now, leave it as Unlimited Public Repositories for Free. Click the Continue button, shown in Figure 12-2.

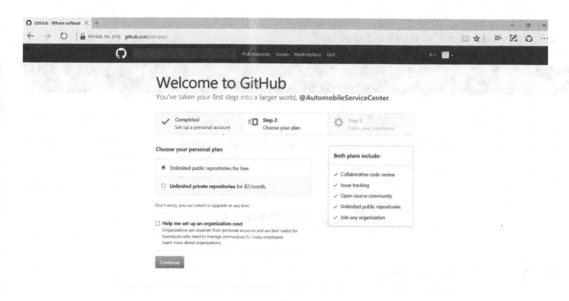

Figure 12-2. *Selecting a GitHub plan*

The next step would be to enter preliminary information about the developer experience, but this is not mandatory. Click the Skip This Step option, shown in Figure 12-3.

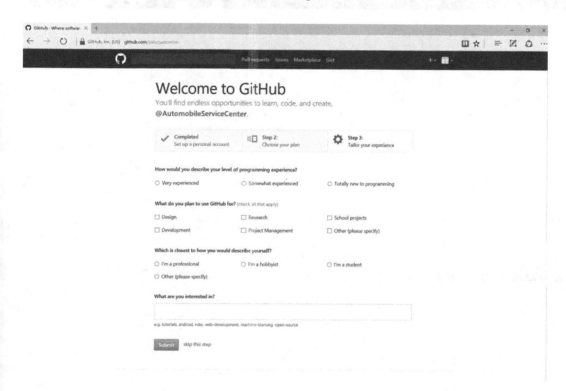

Figure 12-3. *GitHub.com capturing a developer experience*

Now that we have a GitHub account, we can navigate to our GitHub profile by choosing Your Profile from the drop-down menu, as shown in Figure 12-4.

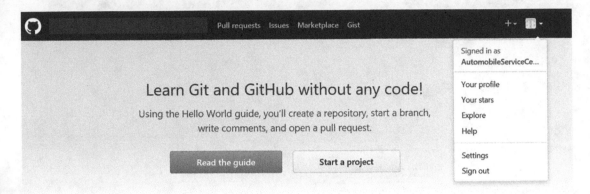

Figure 12-4. Profile navigation at GitHub.com

Because we do not have any repositories yet, we will have an empty view, shown in Figure 12-5.

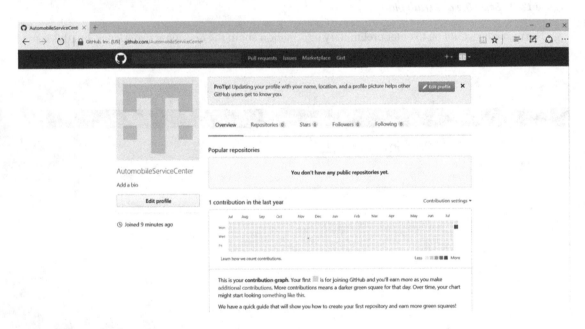

Figure 12-5. GitHub profile

■ **Note** We need to validate the e-mail address that we have used to create the account. There should be an e-mail from GitHub with a link to verify our e-mail address. Proceed with the link and verify the e-mail.

In the Profile view, navigate to the Repositories tab. You should see a No Public Repositories message, as shown in Figure 12-6.

Figure 12-6. GitHub repositories

Click the New button to create a new public repository. We are going to use this repository to store the source code of the Automobile Service Center application. Enter the name as `AutomobileServiceCenter.Core` and a description of the repository, and click Create Repository, as shown in Figure 12-7.

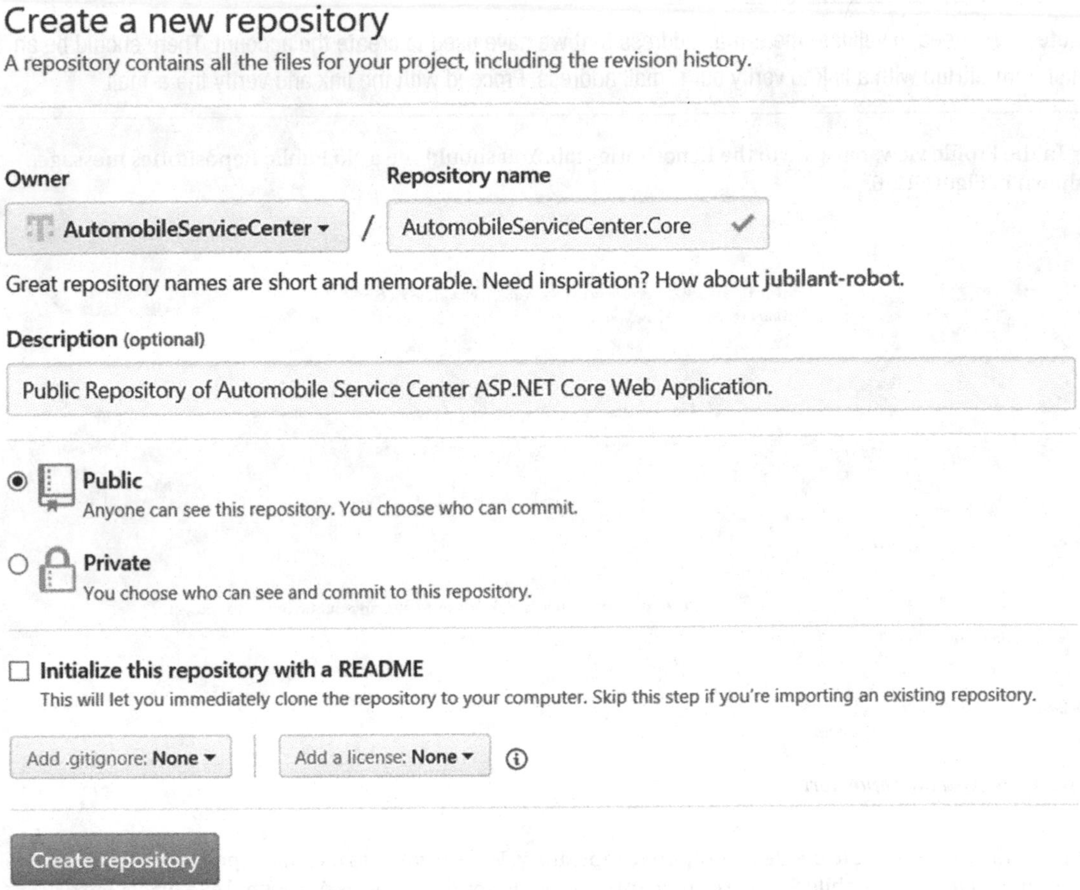

Create a new repository

A repository contains all the files for your project, including the revision history.

Owner **Repository name**

[T: AutomobileServiceCenter ▾] / [AutomobileServiceCenter.Core   ✓]

Great repository names are short and memorable. Need inspiration? How about **jubilant-robot**.

Description (optional)

[Public Repository of Automobile Service Center ASP.NET Core Web Application.]

◉ ▯ **Public**
     Anyone can see this repository. You choose who can commit.

○ 🔒 **Private**
     You choose who can see and commit to this repository.

☐ **Initialize this repository with a README**
     This will let you immediately clone the repository to your computer. Skip this step if you're importing an existing repository.

[Add .gitignore: **None** ▾] | [Add a license: **None** ▾] ⓘ

[Create repository]

Figure 12-7. Creating a new repository for the Automobile Service Center source code

Upon successful creation of the repository, we will find the Git HTTPS path (`https://github.com/AutomobileServiceCenter/AutomobileServiceCenter.Core.git`), which we will use later in this chapter to push code from the local machine to this remote repository. We can also see quick code setup guidelines, as shown in Figure 12-8.

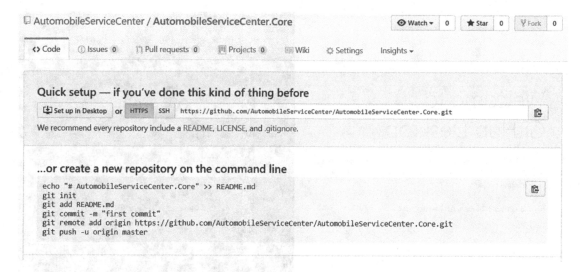

Figure 12-8. GitHub quick setup guidelines

Now we will set up Git Bash on the local machine (Windows environment). Download the GitHub for Windows executable from https://desktop.github.com/. After the download is complete, run the executable.

■ **Note** There might be no confirmation upon a successful installation, but there will be a GitHub desktop icon created on Windows Desktop. Restart the machine, and everything should be good.

Open GitHub Desktop by clicking the Windows Desktop icon. You should see the GitHub Desktop application, as shown in Figure 12-9.

Figure 12-9. *The GitHub Desktop application*

■ **Note** We will not use the GitHub Desktop GUI to manage the Automobile Service Center application's source code. We will use Git commands to perform all the necessary code-versioning tasks. The last section of this chapter shows how to perform the same code versioning by using Visual Studio. This way, we can explore both Git commands and Visual Studio interaction with GitHub.

Managing Local GitHub Credentials and Adding Collaborators to GitHub Repository

Before we proceed with Git Bash and start committing the code to a GitHub repository, make sure to remove the cached GitHub credentials (if any) from Windows Credential Manager, as shown in Figure 12-10. This will ensure that we display the login prompt on the first commit (after we enter credentials in the login prompt, they will again be cached by Credential Manager).

Figure 12-10. Cached GitHub credentials in Windows Credential Manager

---

■ **Note** I created a new GitHub account named AutomobileServiceCenterDev, which will be used to simulate a dev user who will make code commits.

We need to add an AutomobileServiceCenterDev account as one of the collaborators to the AutomobileServiceCenter.Core repository. Navigate to the Settings tab and then click Collaborators in the left navigation menu, as shown in Figure 12-11.

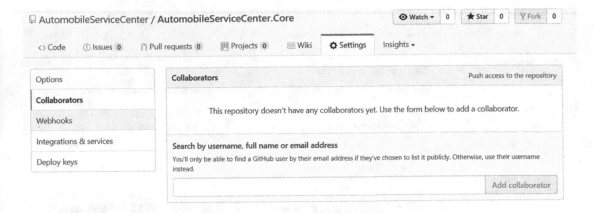

Figure 12-11. *Project collaborators*

Enter `AutomobileServiceCenterDev` in the search box and click Add Collaborator, as shown in Figure 12-12.

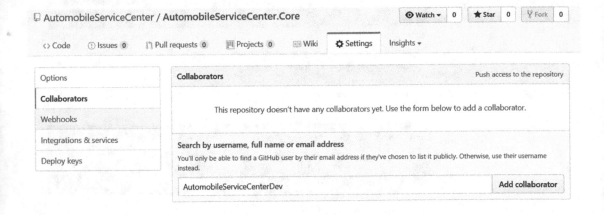

Figure 12-12. *Adding AutomobileServiceCenterDev as a collaborator*

After the collaborator is added, an e-mail will be sent to `AutomobileServiceCenterDev`'s e-mail, which he needs to accept to contribute to the repository. Until he accepts the invitation, he cannot perform any activities on the remote repository, and his status in the collaborator's section is maintained at Awaiting Response, as shown in Figure 12-13.

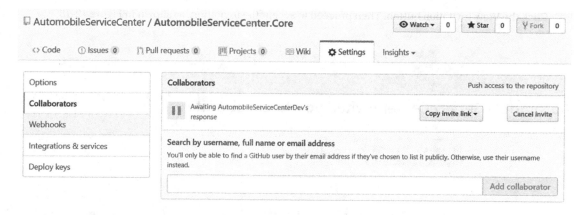

Figure 12-13. *Awaiting the collaborator's response*

The e-mail sent to the collaborator from GitHub will look like Figure 12-14.

@AutomobileServiceCenter has invited you to collaborate on the **AutomobileServiceCenter/ AutomobileServiceCenter.Core** repository

You can accept or decline this invitation. You can also head over to https://github.com/ AutomobileServiceCenter/AutomobileServiceCenter.Core to check out the repository or visit @AutomobileServiceCenter to learn a bit more about them.

Figure 12-14. *Collaborator e-mail invitation*

Click the View Invitation button. Then proceed to accept the invitation, as shown in Figure 12-15.

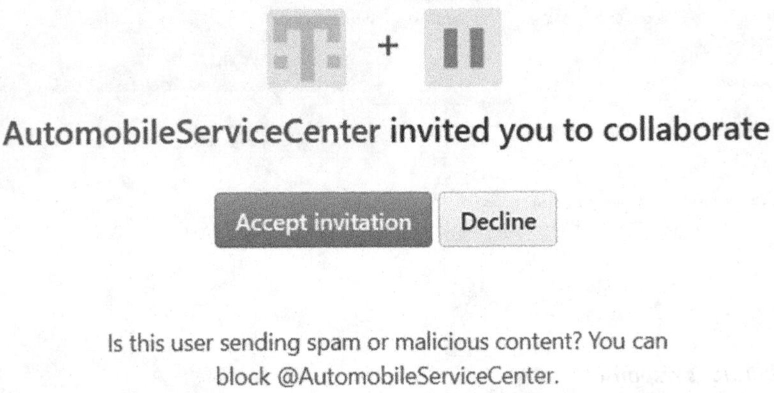

AutomobileServiceCenter invited you to collaborate

Is this user sending spam or malicious content? You can
block @AutomobileServiceCenter.

Figure 12-15. Accepting a collaborator invitation

If we now look at the Collaborators tab in the AutomobileServiceCenter.Core repository, we should
see that the newly added collaborator is active, as shown in Figure 12-16.

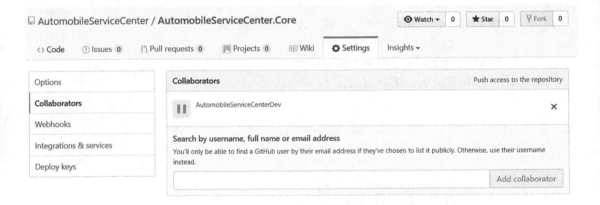

Figure 12-16. Activated collaborator

■ **Note**   Before we start committing the changes to the public repository (in our case,
AutomobileServiceCenter.Core), we have to make sure secure information is not present in the appsettings.
json configuration file (for example, password or keys). Replace the secure settings with placeholders (such as
##########).

Managing Automobile Service Centre source code using Git Bash

Create and commit source code to a Local Git Repository

Open Git Bash by searching for *Git Bash* in Windows Search, as shown in Figure 12-17.

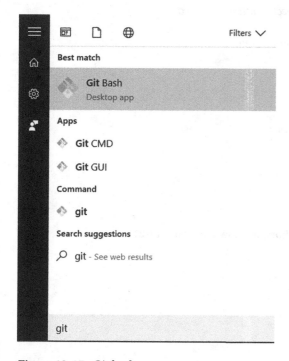

Figure 12-17. *Git bash*

Click the Git Bash option to open a Bash shell, as shown in Figure 12-18.

Figure 12-18. *Git Bash shell*

Navigate to the Automobile Service Center project location in the Bash shell, as shown in Figure 12-19.

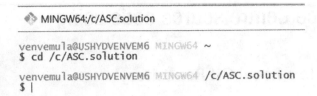

```
MINGW64:/c/ASC.solution

venvemula@USHYDVENVEM6 MINGW64 ~
$ cd /c/ASC.solution

venvemula@USHYDVENVEM6 MINGW64 /c/ASC.solution
$ |
```

Figure 12-19. *Setting the Automobile Service Center project location in context*

We will create a local Git repository, as shown in Figure 12-20.

```
MINGW64:/c/ASC.solution

venvemula@USHYDVENVEM6 MINGW64 /c/ASC.solution
$ git init
Initialized empty Git repository in C:/ASC.solution/.git/

venvemula@USHYDVENVEM6 MINGW64 /c/ASC.solution (master)
$ |
```

Figure 12-20. *Creating a local Git repository*

Set up the Git user local configuration for the repository, as shown in Figure 12-21.

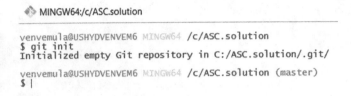

```
MINGW64:/c/ASC.solution

venvemula@USHYDVENVEM6 MINGW64 /c/ASC.solution (master)
$ git config user.name AutomobileServiceCenterDev

venvemula@USHYDVENVEM6 MINGW64 /c/ASC.solution (master)
$ git config user.email automobileservicecenterdev@gmail.com

venvemula@USHYDVENVEM6 MINGW64 /c/ASC.solution (master)
$ |
```

Figure 12-21. *Git user configuration*

Now we will add a .gitignore file that we can configure to exclude certain folders and files from remote repository commits. This feature is extremely useful in ignoring the bin, obj, and packages folders. Run the touch command, as shown in Figure 12-22, to create a .gitignore file at the root of ASC.Solution.

```
MINGW64:/c/ASC.Solution

venvemula@USHYDVENVEM6 MINGW64 /c/ASC.Solution (master)
$ touch .gitignore

venvemula@USHYDVENVEM6 MINGW64 /c/ASC.Solution (master)
$ |
```

Figure 12-22. *Creating the .gitignore file*

Add the content shown in Listing 12-1 to the .gitignore file by using any text editor (for example, Notepad++). These entries will ignore bin, obj, and packages folders and any other solution and user files.

Listing 12-1. gitignore file

```
*.suo
*.user
bin
obj
packages
```

We can now add all the code artifacts to stage a subsequent commit to the master branch on the remote Git repository, as shown in Figure 12-23.

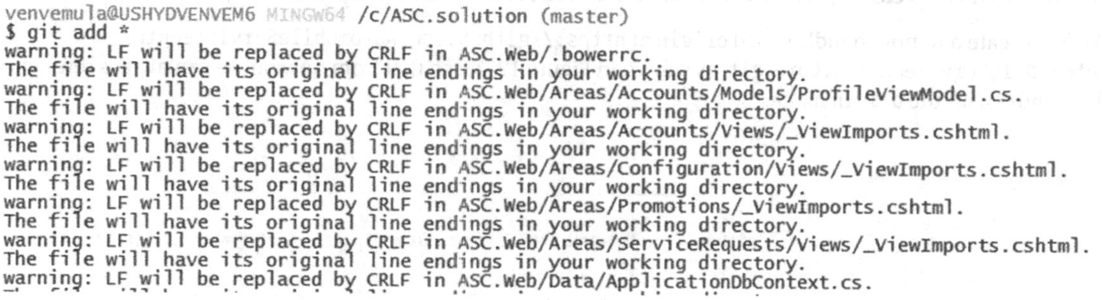

```
venvemula@USHYDVENVEM6 MINGW64 /c/ASC.solution (master)
$ git add *
warning: LF will be replaced by CRLF in ASC.Web/.bowerrc.
The file will have its original line endings in your working directory.
warning: LF will be replaced by CRLF in ASC.Web/Areas/Accounts/Models/ProfileViewModel.cs.
The file will have its original line endings in your working directory.
warning: LF will be replaced by CRLF in ASC.Web/Areas/Accounts/Views/_ViewImports.cshtml.
The file will have its original line endings in your working directory.
warning: LF will be replaced by CRLF in ASC.Web/Areas/Configuration/Views/_ViewImports.cshtml.
The file will have its original line endings in your working directory.
warning: LF will be replaced by CRLF in ASC.Web/Areas/Promotions/_ViewImports.cshtml.
The file will have its original line endings in your working directory.
warning: LF will be replaced by CRLF in ASC.Web/Areas/ServiceRequests/Views/_ViewImports.cshtml.
The file will have its original line endings in your working directory.
warning: LF will be replaced by CRLF in ASC.Web/Data/ApplicationDbContext.cs.
```

Figure 12-23. *Adding all files to stage a Git commit*

We can check the status of all files on the master branch, as shown in Figure 12-24.

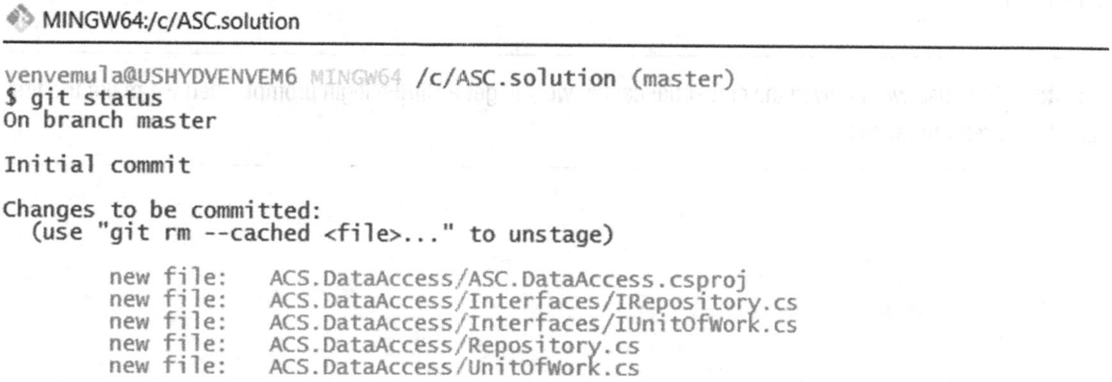

MINGW64:/c/ASC.solution

```
venvemula@USHYDVENVEM6 MINGW64 /c/ASC.solution (master)
$ git status
On branch master

Initial commit

Changes to be committed:
  (use "git rm --cached <file>..." to unstage)

        new file:   ACS.DataAccess/ASC.DataAccess.csproj
        new file:   ACS.DataAccess/Interfaces/IRepository.cs
        new file:   ACS.DataAccess/Interfaces/IUnitOfWork.cs
        new file:   ACS.DataAccess/Repository.cs
        new file:   ACS.DataAccess/UnitOfWork.cs
```

Figure 12-24. *Git status*

Now we will commit the changes to the local repository's master branch, as shown in Figure 12-25.

```
⬥ MINGW64:/c/ASC.solution

venvemula@USHYDVENVEM6 MINGW64 /c/ASC.solution (master)
$ git commit -m "Initial Commit"
[master (root-commit) a57370a] Initial Commit
 484 files changed, 137791 insertions(+)
 create mode 100644 ACS.DataAccess/ASC.DataAccess.csproj
 create mode 100644 ACS.DataAccess/Interfaces/IRepository.cs
 create mode 100644 ACS.DataAccess/Interfaces/IUnitOfWork.cs
 create mode 100644 ACS.DataAccess/Repository.cs
 create mode 100644 ACS.DataAccess/UnitOfWork.cs
```

Figure 12-25. *Commiting changes to the Git local repository*

Create and push source code to a Remote Git Repository

We will create a remote handle called origin at https://github.com/AutomobileServiceCenter/
AutomobileServiceCenter.Core.git, as shown in Figure 12-26, so that from now on we can always refer to
the remote with the origin name.

```
⬥ MINGW64:/c/ASC.solution

venvemula@USHYDVENVEM6 MINGW64 /c/ASC.solution (master)
$ git remote add origin https://github.com/AutomobileServiceCenter/AutomobileServiceCenter.Core.git

venvemula@USHYDVENVEM6 MINGW64 /c/ASC.solution (master)
$ |
```

Figure 12-26. *Adding a remote repository named origin*

Finally, we will push the commits from the master local branch to the remote named origin, as shown
in Figure 12-27.

■ **Note**   Because we removed the credential cache, we will get a GitHub login prompt when we make the first
push to the remote repository.

Figure 12-27. *Pushing changes to a remote repository*

After successful login, all the changes are pushed to the remote repository, as shown in Figure 12-28.

■ **Note**   If the login is unsuccessful or the user is not authorized, an Unable to Access 403 error message will be displayed on the bash.

```
venvemula@USHYDVENVEM6 MINGW64 /c/ASC.Solution (master)
$ git push -u origin master
Counting objects: 422, done.
Delta compression using up to 4 threads.
Compressing objects: 100% (404/404), done.
Writing objects: 100% (422/422), 3.76 MiB | 268.00 KiB/s, done.
Total 422 (delta 61), reused 0 (delta 0)
remote: Resolving deltas: 100% (61/61), done.
Branch master set up to track remote branch master from origin.
To https://github.com/AutomobileServiceCenter/AutomobileServiceCenter.Core.git
 * [new branch]      master -> master

venvemula@USHYDVENVEM6 MINGW64 /c/ASC.Solution (master)
$ |
```

Figure 12-28. *Successful Git push to a remote repository*

If we go to the `AutomobileServiceCenter.Core` repository at GitHub, we should see that all the code is available in the repository. It also shows that the user `AutomobileServiceCenterDev` makes the commit with the comment *Initial Commit*.

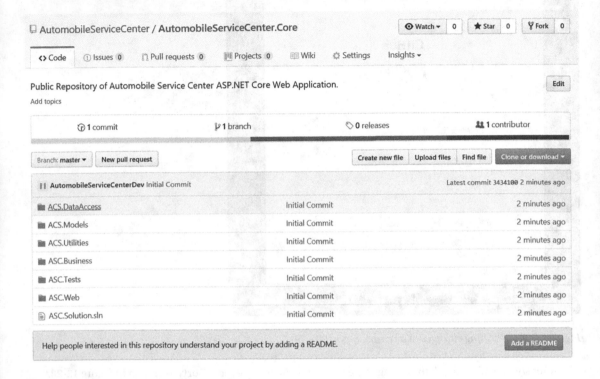

Figure 12-29. *Latest code at the GitHub repository*

Branching and merging source code

We have the latest code in the master branch in the `AutomobileServiceCenter.Core` repository. In large projects, we cannot maintain all of the code base in one branch. For example, let's say that version 1 (v1) of the code is deployed to production from the master branch, and developers start their work toward version 2 (v2) of the application. And let's assume there is a sudden issue in production, and we have to provide a hotfix right away. In this scenario, we cannot push a build to production from the master branch, because it contains unfinished work of V2, so we will hit a roadblock. So it is always advisable to have a master and multiple other branches to support releases and ongoing development and merge them accordingly, based on a release schedule.

For the Automobile Service Center application, we will create a Dev branch, and all developers will work on that branch. After we decide to push a production build, we will have to merge dev to the master branch and take a build from the master branch.

We will create a dev branch from the existing master branch, as shown in Figure 12-30.

◆◇ MINGW64:/c/ASC.Solution

```
venvemula@USHYDVENVEM6 MINGW64 /c/ASC.Solution (master)
$ git checkout -b dev
Switched to a new branch 'dev'

venvemula@USHYDVENVEM6 MINGW64 /c/ASC.Solution (dev)
$ |
```

Figure 12-30. *Dev local branch*

Now we will push the newly created dev branch to a remote repository, as shown in Figure 12-31.

```
venvemula@USHYDVENVEM6 MINGW64 /c/ASC.Solution (dev)
$ git push -u origin dev
Total 0 (delta 0), reused 0 (delta 0)
Branch dev set up to track remote branch dev from origin.
To https://github.com/AutomobileServiceCenter/AutomobileServiceCenter.Core.git
 * [new branch]      dev -> dev

venvemula@USHYDVENVEM6 MINGW64 /c/ASC.Solution (dev)
$ |
```

Figure 12-31. *Pushing the dev branch to the remote repository*

We can check the GitHub repository and see the dev branch, as shown in Figure 12-32.

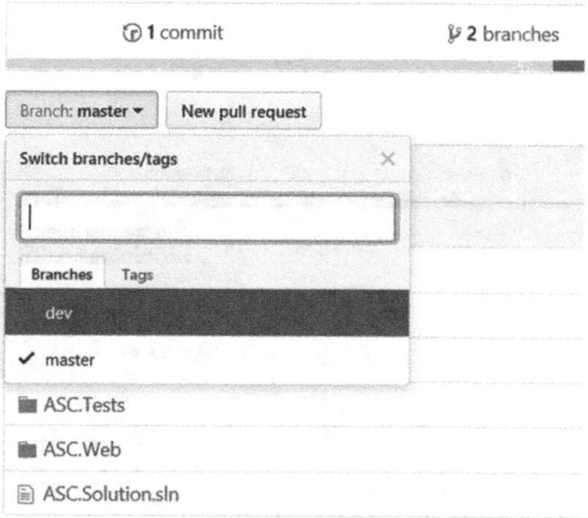

Figure 12-32. *Dev branch at GitHub repository*

We have both master and dev branches pointing to the same version of code, as shown in Figure 12-33.

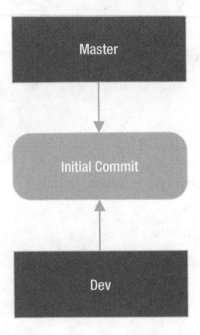

Figure 12-33. *Status of master and dev branches*

Now let's say some other developer added a README file to the dev branch, as shown in Figures 12-34 and 12-35. In the context of the dev branch, we can click the Add a README button to add a README document to the existing code.

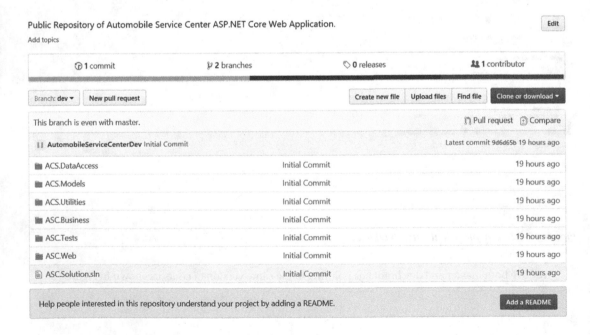

Figure 12-34. *Adding a README file at the GitHub respository*

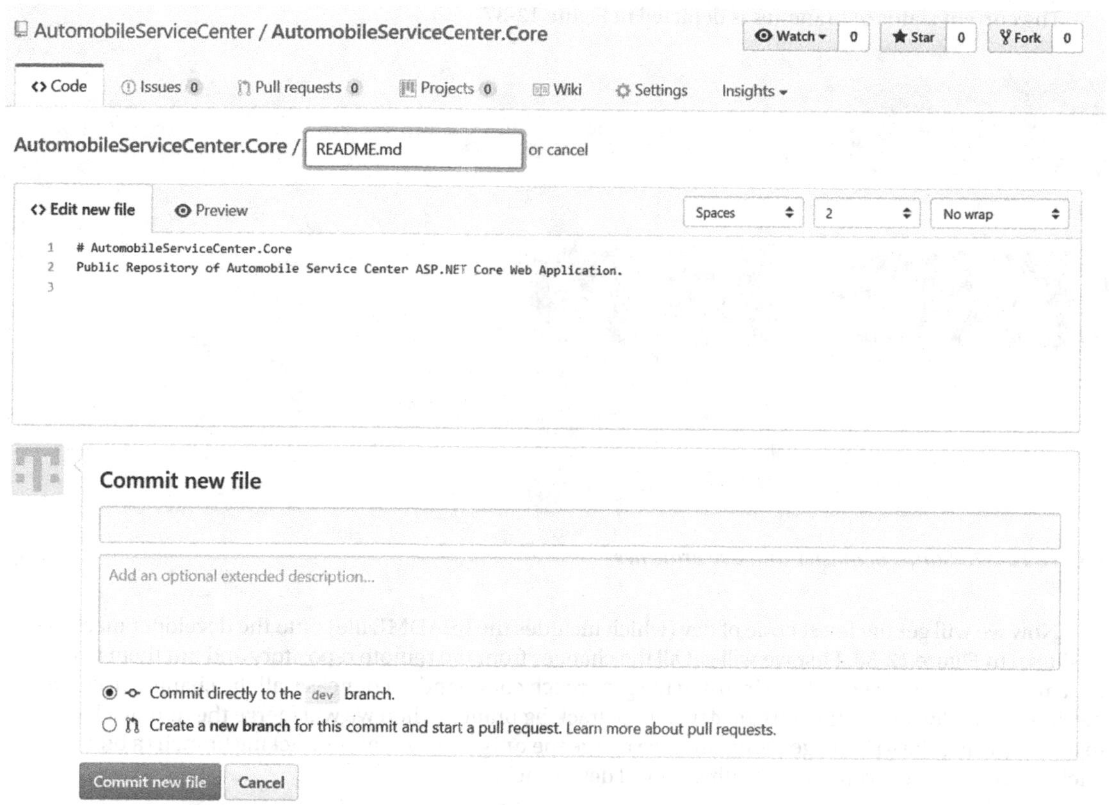

🖵 AutomobileServiceCenter / **AutomobileServiceCenter.Core**

| ⊙ Watch ▾ | 0 | ★ Star | 0 | ⑂ Fork | 0 |

| ‹› Code | ⓘ Issues **0** | ⏱ Pull requests **0** | ▦ Projects **0** | ▦ Wiki | ⚙ Settings | Insights ▾ |

AutomobileServiceCenter.Core / `README.md` or cancel

| ‹› Edit new file | ⊙ Preview | | Spaces ⬍ | 2 ⬍ | No wrap ⬍ |

```
1   # AutomobileServiceCenter.Core
2   Public Repository of Automobile Service Center ASP.NET Core Web Application.
3
```

🔳 **Commit new file**

[   ]

[Add an optional extended description...   ]

◉ ⚡ Commit directly to the `dev` branch.

○ ⌥ Create a **new branch** for this commit and start a pull request. Learn more about pull requests.

[Commit new file] Cancel

Figure 12-35. Adding content to the README file at the GitHub repository

After we have updated the README text, enter a title and description of the commit and click Commit New File. Because the option Commit Directly to the Dev Branch is selected, the new file will be added only to the dev branch but not to the master branch, as shown in Figure 12-36.

| Branch: **dev ▾** | New pull request | | | Create new file | Upload files | Find file | Clone or download ▾ |

This branch is 1 commit ahead of master. | ⏱ Pull request | ☷ Compare

🔳 **AutomobileServiceCenter** committed on **GitHub** README File | Latest commit 32e43b9 just now

🗀 ACS.DataAccess	Initial Commit	19 hours ago
🗀 ACS.Models	Initial Commit	19 hours ago
🗀 ACS.Utilities	Initial Commit	19 hours ago
🗀 ASC.Business	Initial Commit	19 hours ago
🗀 ASC.Tests	Initial Commit	19 hours ago
🗀 ASC.Web	Initial Commit	19 hours ago
🖹 ASC.Solution.sln	Initial Commit	19 hours ago
🖹 README.md	README File	just now

Figure 12-36. README file committed to the dev branch

The current status of branches is depicted in Figure 12-37.

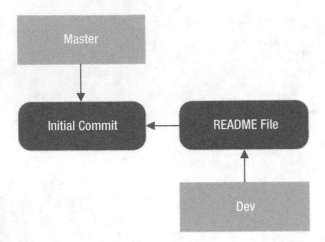

Figure 12-37. *Status of master and dev branches*

Now we will get the latest code of dev (which includes the README file) onto the developer machine, as shown in Figure 12-38. First we will get all the changes from the remote repository and put them in the local repository's object database by using the `git fetch` command. In our case, all the changes from the dev branch are located at the `origin/dev` remote tracking branch. Then we will merge the remote changes to local by using the `git merge` command. We merge the `origin/dev` remote-tracking branch (a branch fetched from a remote repository) with our local dev branch.

```
venvemula@USHYDVENVEM6 MINGW64 /c/ASC.Solution (dev)
$ git fetch origin
remote: Counting objects: 3, done.
remote: Compressing objects: 100% (3/3), done.
remote: Total 3 (delta 1), reused 0 (delta 0), pack-reused 0
Unpacking objects: 100% (3/3), done.
From https://github.com/AutomobileServiceCenter/AutomobileServiceCenter.Core
   9d6d65b..32e4309  dev          -> origin/dev

venvemula@USHYDVENVEM6 MINGW64 /c/ASC.Solution (dev)
$ git merge origin/dev
Updating 9d6d65b..32e4309
Fast-forward
 README.md | 2 ++
 1 file changed, 2 insertions(+)
 create mode 100644 README.md

venvemula@USHYDVENVEM6 MINGW64 /c/ASC.Solution (dev)
$ |
```

Figure 12-38. *Fetching and merging remote changes to the local repository*

Now let's assume the developer made the code change in the dev branch on his local machine. The developer made the change to the `ApplicationTitle` entry in the `appsettings.json` file by changing the value from Automobile Service Center Application to Automobile Service Center App, as shown in Listing 12-2.

Listing 12-2. appsettings.json file

```
"AppSettings": {
  "ApplicationTitle": "Automobile Service Center App",
  "AdminEmail": "#######################",
  "AdminName": "Admin",
  "AdminPassword": "##########",
  "EngineerEmail": "######################",
  "EngineerName": "Engineer",
  "EngineerPassword": "#######################",
  "Roles": "Admin,User,Engineer",
  "SMTPServer": "smtp.gmail.com",
  "SMTPPort": "587",
  "SMTPAccount": "######################",
  "SMTPPassword": "######################",
  "TwilioAccountSID": "######################",
  "TwilioAuthToken": "######################",
  "TwilioPhoneNumber": "######################"
},
```

We will push this change to the dev branch on the remote repository, as shown in Figure 12-39. First we will find the status of the local repository, and then we will add all the modified/deleted files to the commit. We will do one more status check to see whether all the files are properly staged for the commit. Finally, we will do a commit followed by a push to the remote dev branch.

◆ MINGW64:/c/ASC.Solution

```
venvemula@USHYDVENVEM6 MINGW64 /c/ASC.Solution (dev)
$ git status
On branch dev
Your branch is up-to-date with 'origin/dev'.
Changes not staged for commit:
  (use "git add <file>..." to update what will be committed)
  (use "git checkout -- <file>..." to discard changes in working directory)

        modified:   ASC.Web/appsettings.json

Untracked files:
  (use "git add <file>..." to include in what will be committed)

        .gitignore
        .vs/

no changes added to commit (use "git add" and/or "git commit -a")

venvemula@USHYDVENVEM6 MINGW64 /c/ASC.Solution (dev)
$ git add -u
warning: LF will be replaced by CRLF in ASC.Web/appsettings.json.
The file will have its original line endings in your working directory.

venvemula@USHYDVENVEM6 MINGW64 /c/ASC.Solution (dev)
$ git status
On branch dev
Your branch is up-to-date with 'origin/dev'.
Changes to be committed:
  (use "git reset HEAD <file>..." to unstage)

        modified:   ASC.Web/appsettings.json

Untracked files:
  (use "git add <file>..." to include in what will be committed)

        .gitignore
        .vs/


venvemula@USHYDVENVEM6 MINGW64 /c/ASC.Solution (dev)
$ git commit -m "App Name Change"
[dev c9a7a8e] App Name Change
 1 file changed, 1 insertion(+), 1 deletion(-)

venvemula@USHYDVENVEM6 MINGW64 /c/ASC.Solution (dev)
$ git push -u origin dev
Counting objects: 4, done.
Delta compression using up to 4 threads.
Compressing objects: 100% (4/4), done.
Writing objects: 100% (4/4), 376 bytes | 0 bytes/s, done.
Total 4 (delta 3), reused 0 (delta 0)
remote: Resolving deltas: 100% (3/3), completed with 3 local objects.
Branch dev set up to track remote branch dev from origin.
To https://github.com/AutomobileServiceCenter/AutomobileServiceCenter.Core.git
   32e4309..c9a7a8e  dev -> dev

venvemula@USHYDVENVEM6 MINGW64 /c/ASC.Solution (dev)
$ |
```

Figure 12-39. Pushing changes from the local dev branch to the remote dev branch

If we look at the commit history at GitHub's `AutomobileServiceCenter.Core` repository, we will find the latest commit, as shown in Figure 12-40.

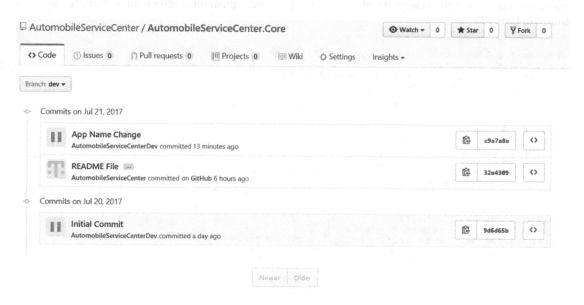

Figure 12-40. *Dev branch commit history at the GitHub repository*

The current state of all branches is shown in Figure 12-41.

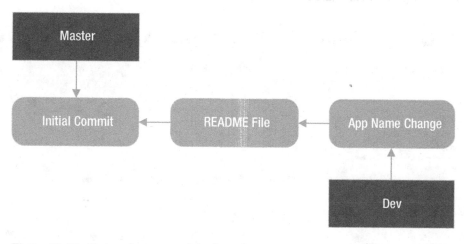

Figure 12-41. *Status of master and dev branches*

Now that we have the master and dev branches at different versions, we'll merge the dev branch with the master so that the master branch will be updated with all changes from dev. We have to first check out the master branch and then merge it with the dev branch. Finally, push the master branch to origin, as shown in Figure 12-42.

```
venvemula@USHYDVENVEM6 MINGW64 /c/ASC.Solution (dev)
$ git checkout master
Your branch is up-to-date with 'origin/master'.
Switched to branch 'master'

venvemula@USHYDVENVEM6 MINGW64 /c/ASC.Solution (master)
$ git merge dev
Updating 9d6d65b..c9a7a8e
Fast-forward
 ASC.Web/appsettings.json | 2 +-
 README.md                | 2 ++
 2 files changed, 3 insertions(+), 1 deletion(-)
 create mode 100644 README.md

venvemula@USHYDVENVEM6 MINGW64 /c/ASC.Solution (master)
$ git push -u origin master
Total 0 (delta 0), reused 0 (delta 0)
Branch master set up to track remote branch master from origin.
To https://github.com/AutomobileServiceCenter/AutomobileServiceCenter.Core.git
   9d6d65b..c9a7a8e  master -> master

venvemula@USHYDVENVEM6 MINGW64 /c/ASC.Solution (master)
$ |
```

Figure 12-42. *Merging dev with the master branch*

If we go to the `AutomobileServiceCenter.Core` repository at GitHub and explore the master branch, we should see the latest commits, as shown in Figure 12-43.

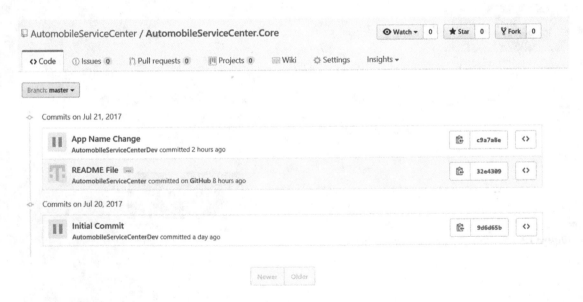

Figure 12-43. *Master branch commit history at GitHub*

The current state of all branches is shown in Figure 12-44.

Master
Initial Commit
README File
App Name Change
Dev

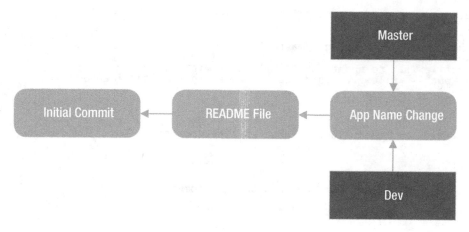

Figure 12-44. *Status of master and dev branches*

Reset an unwanted commit from Local Repository

Now let's say the developer makes a mistake with a file and accidently commits the changes to the local branch (but never pushes the changes to the remote). We will see how to revert the changes to the previous version. Let's assume the developer made a mistake in the `appsettings.json` file, as shown in Listing 12-3.

Listing 12-3. Application title mistake

```
"ApplicationTitle": "Automobile Service Center Appp",
```

To find out which files have been changed from the last commit, we can use the `git diff` command, as shown in Figure 12-45.

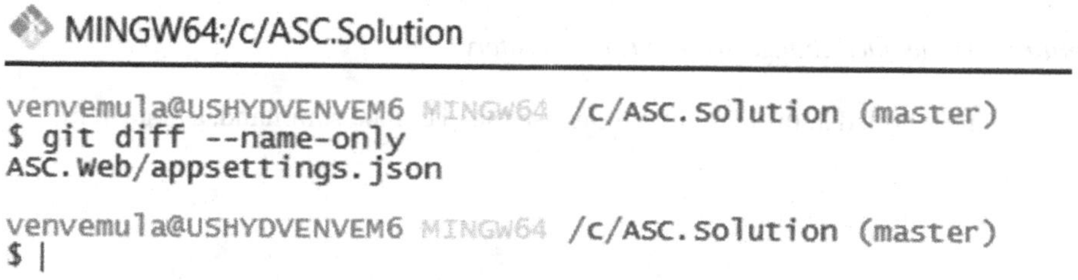

MINGW64:/c/ASC.Solution
venvemula@USHYDVENVEM6 MINGW64 /c/ASC.Solution (master)
$ git diff --name-only
ASC.Web/appsettings.json
venvemula@USHYDVENVEM6 MINGW64 /c/ASC.Solution (master)
$ |

Figure 12-45. *Finding files that are modified*

The developer accidently commits the code, as shown in Figure 12-46.

◆ MINGW64:/c/ASC.Solution

```
venvemula@USHYDVENVEM6 MINGW64 /c/ASC.Solution (master)
$ git status
On branch master
Your branch is up-to-date with 'origin/master'.
Changes not staged for commit:
  (use "git add <file>..." to update what will be committed)
  (use "git checkout -- <file>..." to discard changes in working directory)

        modified:   ASC.Web/appsettings.json

Untracked files:
  (use "git add <file>..." to include in what will be committed)

        .gitignore
        .vs/

no changes added to commit (use "git add" and/or "git commit -a")

venvemula@USHYDVENVEM6 MINGW64 /c/ASC.Solution (master)
$ git add -u

venvemula@USHYDVENVEM6 MINGW64 /c/ASC.Solution (master)
$ git status
On branch master
Your branch is up-to-date with 'origin/master'.
Changes to be committed:
  (use "git reset HEAD <file>..." to unstage)

        modified:   ASC.Web/appsettings.json

Untracked files:
  (use "git add <file>..." to include in what will be committed)

        .gitignore
        .vs/


venvemula@USHYDVENVEM6 MINGW64 /c/ASC.Solution (master)
$ git commit -m "Settings Change"
[master f6e4fc9] Settings Change
 1 file changed, 1 insertion(+), 1 deletion(-)
```

Figure 12-46. *Commiting an unwanted change to the master repository*

To find out which files are included in the commit, we can use the git show command, as shown in Figure 12-47.

MINGW64:/c/ASC.Solution

```
venvemula@USHYDVENVEM6 MINGW64 /c/ASC.Solution (master)
$ git show --name-only
commit f6e4fc9f2249d4557d1b04cd1770d19f2aab7c60
Author: AutomobileServiceCenterDev <automobileservicecenterdev@gmail.com>
Date:    Sat Jul 22 09:09:55 2017 +0530

    Settings Change

ASC.Web/appsettings.json

venvemula@USHYDVENVEM6 MINGW64 /c/ASC.Solution (master)
$ |
```

Figure 12-47. *Finding the included files in the commit*

To revert the changes in the commit to the previous state, we need to use the git reset command, as shown in Figure 12-48. --hard tells Git to discard the changes. If we do not want to discard the changes, we should use --soft. HEAD~1 tells Git to move to one before the current revision, which means undoing the current commit.

 MINGW64:/c/ASC.Solution

```
venvemula@USHYDVENVEM6 MINGW64 /c/ASC.Solution (master)
$ git reset --hard HEAD~1
HEAD is now at c9a7a8e App Name Change

venvemula@USHYDVENVEM6 MINGW64 /c/ASC.Solution (master)
$ |
```

Figure 12-48. *Undoing the latest commit from the local branch*

Reset an unwanted commit from Remote Repository

Now let's say we pushed a wrong commit to the GitHub remote repository, as shown in Figure 12-49. The Settings Change commit is the wrong commit that got pushed to the master branch.

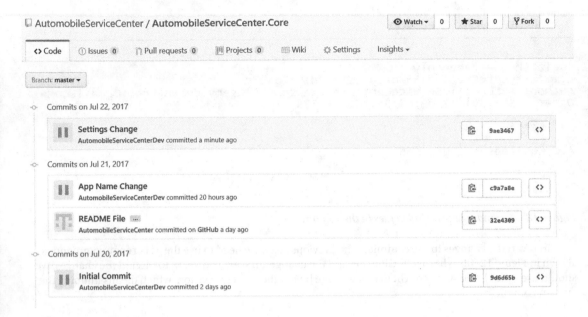

Figure 12-49. *Unwanted commit in the remote repository*

If we want to revert that commit from the remote repository, we can use the git reset and push commands.

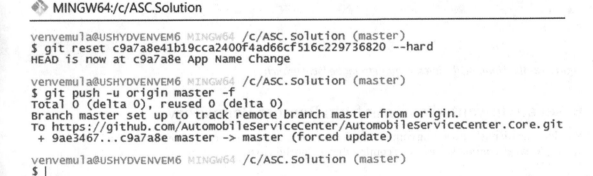

Figure 12-50. *Undoing the commit at the remote respository*

If we now check GitHub's AutomobileServiceCenter.Core repository, the wrong commit is reverted, as shown in Figure 12-51.

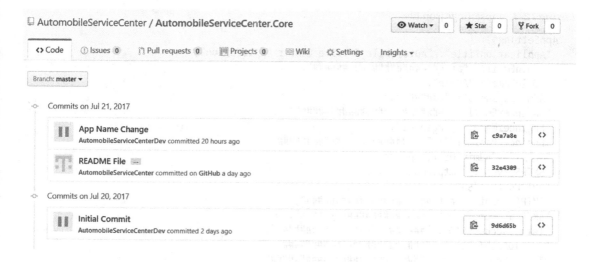

Figure 12-51. *Unwanted commit is reverted at the GitHub repository*

Resolve merge conflicts in source code

Now we will see how to resolve merge conflicts. When a developer changes a code file in his local respository that was also changed and pushed to a remote branch by another developer, there will be conflicts at the time of the code merge. When the first developer fetches the latest code from the same branch, he will be prompted with conflicts. The developer should then decide which changes he wants to persist in the code base.

Let's assume one developer commits the `appsettings.json` file with the application title set to ASC App to the dev branch of the remote repository, as shown in Figure 12-52.

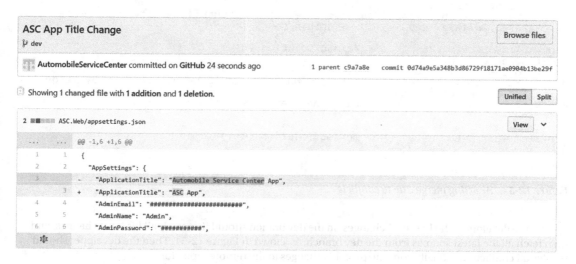

Figure 12-52. *First developer commits the application title*

At the same time, another developer changes the same setting of the `appsettings.json` file to Automobile Service Center Application, as shown in Listing 12-4.

Listing 12-4. appsettings.json file

```
"AppSettings": {
  "ApplicationTitle": "Automobile Service Center Application",
  "AdminEmail": "#######################",
  "AdminName": "Admin",
  "AdminPassword": "###########",
  "EngineerEmail": "######################",
  "EngineerName": "Engineer",
  "EngineerPassword": "#######################",
  "Roles": "Admin,User,Engineer",
  "SMTPServer": "smtp.gmail.com",
  "SMTPPort": "587",
  "SMTPAccount": "######################",
  "SMTPPassword": "######################",
  "TwilioAccountSID": "######################",
  "TwilioAuthToken": "######################",
  "TwilioPhoneNumber": "######################"
},
```

When the developer who has local changes on the dev branch tries to fetch changes from the remote origin and merge them with his local code, he will get an Operation Aborted message, as shown in Figure 12-53.

◆ MINGW64:/c/ASC.Solution

```
venvemula@USHYDVENVEM6 MINGW64 /c/ASC.Solution (dev)
$ git fetch origin
remote: Counting objects: 4, done.
remote: Compressing objects: 100% (4/4), done.
remote: Total 4 (delta 3), reused 0 (delta 0), pack-reused 0
Unpacking objects: 100% (4/4), done.
From https://github.com/AutomobileServiceCenter/AutomobileServiceCenter.Core
   c9a7a8e..0d74a9e  dev          -> origin/dev

venvemula@USHYDVENVEM6 MINGW64 /c/ASC.Solution (dev)
$ git merge origin/dev
Updating c9a7a8e..0d74a9e
error: Your local changes to the following files would be overwritten by merge:
        ASC.Web/appsettings.json
Please commit your changes or stash them before you merge.
Aborting

venvemula@USHYDVENVEM6 MINGW64 /c/ASC.Solution (dev)
$ |
```

Figure 12-53. *Aborting merge due to conflicts*

So the developer who has local changes on the dev branch should first stash all his local changes, and then fetch all the latest sources from the dev branch, as shown in Figure 12-54. Then the developer should resolve all conflicts and finally commit/push his changes to the remote repository.

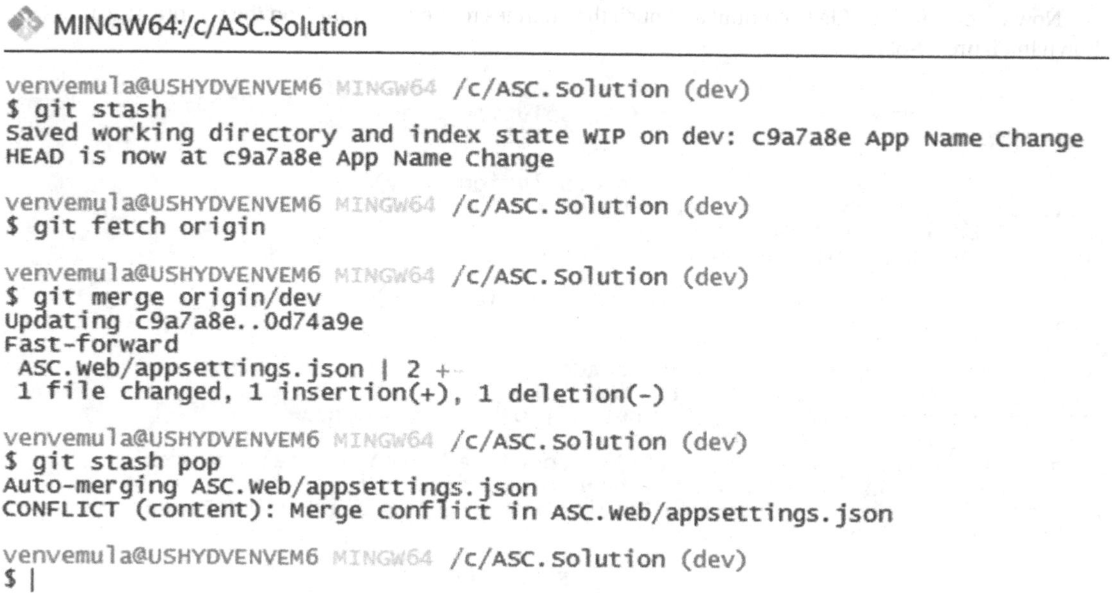

◆ MINGW64:/c/ASC.Solution

```
venvemula@USHYDVENVEM6 MINGW64 /c/ASC.Solution (dev)
$ git stash
Saved working directory and index state WIP on dev: c9a7a8e App Name Change
HEAD is now at c9a7a8e App Name Change

venvemula@USHYDVENVEM6 MINGW64 /c/ASC.Solution (dev)
$ git fetch origin

venvemula@USHYDVENVEM6 MINGW64 /c/ASC.Solution (dev)
$ git merge origin/dev
Updating c9a7a8e..0d74a9e
Fast-forward
 ASC.Web/appsettings.json | 2 +
 1 file changed, 1 insertion(+), 1 deletion(-)

venvemula@USHYDVENVEM6 MINGW64 /c/ASC.Solution (dev)
$ git stash pop
Auto-merging ASC.Web/appsettings.json
CONFLICT (content): Merge conflict in ASC.Web/appsettings.json

venvemula@USHYDVENVEM6 MINGW64 /c/ASC.Solution (dev)
$ |
```

Figure 12-54. *Stashing local changes and retrieving the stashed changes*

■ **Note**   Stashing will get work-in-progress changes and staged changes from the working directory and save them on the stack of unfinished changes. The changes stored in the stack can later be retrieved and applied at any time.

We need to manage the conflict by visiting the source code file and selecting the appropriate content to persist. Stashed and upstream changes are shown in Listing 12-5.

Listing 12-5. Conflicts in source code file

```
  "AppSettings": {
<<<<<<< Updated upstream
    "ApplicationTitle": "ASC App",
=======
    "ApplicationTitle": "Automobile Service Center Application",
>>>>>>> Stashed changes
    "AdminEmail": "#######################",
    "AdminName": "Admin",
```

Provide the resolution by updating the conflicting code, as shown in Listing 12-6.

Listing 12-6. Resolving conflict in source code

```
  "AppSettings": {
    "ApplicationTitle": "Automobile Service Center App",
    "AdminEmail": "#######################",
    "AdminName": "Admin",
```

Now we can add the file to commit and push the changes to the dev branch on the remote origin, as shown in Figure 12-55.

```
venvemula@USHYDVENVEM6 MINGW64 /c/ASC.Solution (dev)
$ git add -u

venvemula@USHYDVENVEM6 MINGW64 /c/ASC.Solution (dev)
$ git commit -m "Title conflict merged"
[dev e9278df] Title conflict merged
 1 file changed, 4 insertions(+)

venvemula@USHYDVENVEM6 MINGW64 /c/ASC.Solution (dev)
$ git push -u origin dev
Counting objects: 4, done.
Delta compression using up to 4 threads.
Compressing objects: 100% (4/4), done.
Writing objects: 100% (4/4), 480 bytes | 0 bytes/s, done.
Total 4 (delta 3), reused 0 (delta 0)
remote: Resolving deltas: 100% (3/3), completed with 3 local objects.
Branch dev set up to track remote branch dev from origin.
To https://github.com/AutomobileServiceCenter/AutomobileServiceCenter.Core.git
   0d74a9e..e9278df  dev -> dev

venvemula@USHYDVENVEM6 MINGW64 /c/ASC.Solution (dev)
$ |
```

Figure 12-55. *Committing and pushing merged code to the remote repository*

We can check the history of commits at GitHub and should see both commits, as shown in Figure 12-56.

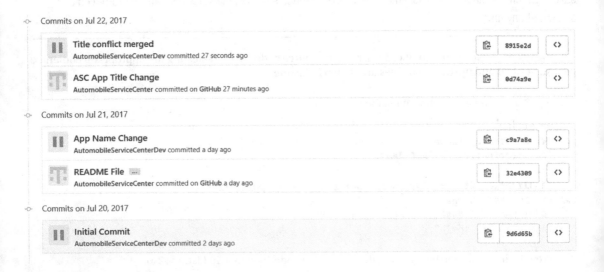

Figure 12-56. *Dev branch commits history at GitHub*

Now we will set up a GUI-based tool to resolve conflicts. We will use the KDiff3 tool, an open source diff tool. Download and install the latest version of KDiff3 from `https://sourceforge.net/projects/kdiff3/files/`. When installation is completed, we can open the KDiff3 tool from the Windows Start menu, and it should look like Figure 12-57.

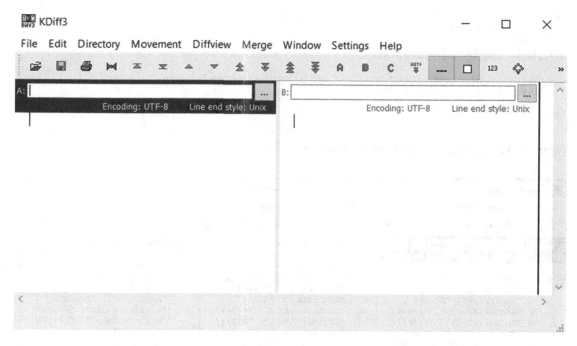

Figure 12-57. KDiff3 tool

We need to configure Git to use the KDiff3 tool as the default diff tool. Run the `git config` commands as shown in Figure 12-58.

◆ MINGW64:/c/ASC.Solution

```
venvemula@USHYDVENVEM6 MINGW64 /c/ASC.Solution (dev)
$ git config --global --add merge.tool kdiff3

venvemula@USHYDVENVEM6 MINGW64 /c/ASC.Solution (dev)
$ git config --global --add mergetool.kdiff3.path "C:/Program Files/KDiff3/kdiff3.exe"

venvemula@USHYDVENVEM6 MINGW64 /c/ASC.Solution (dev)
$ git config --global --add mergetool.kdiff3.trustExitCode false

venvemula@USHYDVENVEM6 MINGW64 /c/ASC.Solution (dev)
$ git config --global --add diff.guitool kdiff3

venvemula@USHYDVENVEM6 MINGW64 /c/ASC.Solution (dev)
$ git config --global --add difftool.kdiff3.path "C:/Program Files/KDiff3/kdiff3.exe"

venvemula@USHYDVENVEM6 MINGW64 /c/ASC.Solution (dev)
$ git config --global --add difftool.kdiff3.trustExitCode false

venvemula@USHYDVENVEM6 MINGW64 /c/ASC.Solution (dev)
$ |
```

Figure 12-58. Configuring the KDiff3 tool with Git

Let's simulate the same scenario of merge conflict that we dealt with previously. This time we will merge the conflicts in the KDiff3 tool. After we pull the local changes by using git stash pop, we have to use the `git mergetool` command to open KDiff3, as shown in Figure 12-59. KDiff3 will open the file compare view with the file in context, as shown in Figure 12-60.

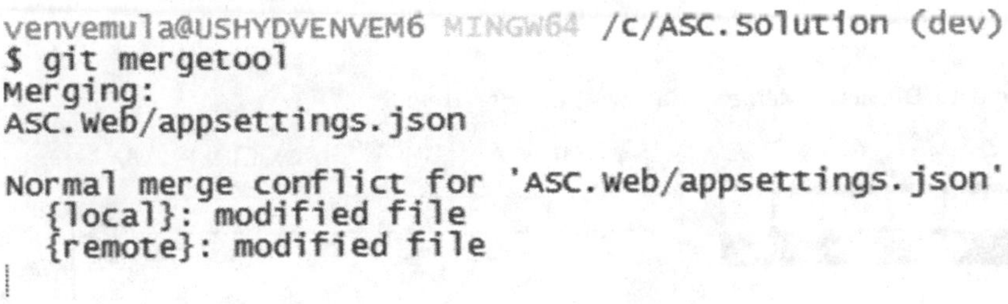

venvemula@USHYDVENVEM6 MINGW64 /c/ASC.Solution (dev)
$ git mergetool
Merging:
ASC.Web/appsettings.json

Normal merge conflict for 'ASC.Web/appsettings.json':
{local}: modified file
{remote}: modified file

Figure 12-59. Opening the KDiff3 tool to resolve conflict

appsettings.json (Base) <-> appsettings.json (Local) <-> appsettings.json (Remote) - KDiff3
File Edit Directory Movement Diffview Merge Window Settings Help
A (Base): ASC.Web\appsettings.json (Base)
B: ASC.Web\appsettings.json (Local)
C: ASC.Web\appsettings.json (Remote)
Top line 2 Encoding: UTF-8-BOM Line end style: DOS
Output: C:\ASC.Solution\ASC.Web\appsettings.json
Encoding for saving: Codec from C: UTF-8-BOM Line end style: DOS (A, B, C)
{
"AppSettings": {
<Merge Conflict>
"AdminEmail": "#########################",
"AdminName": "Admin",
"AdminPassword": "###########",
"EngineerEmail": "#########################",
"EngineerName": "Engineer",
"EngineerPassword": "########################",
"Roles": "Admin,User,Engineer",
"SMTPServer": "smtp.gmail.com",

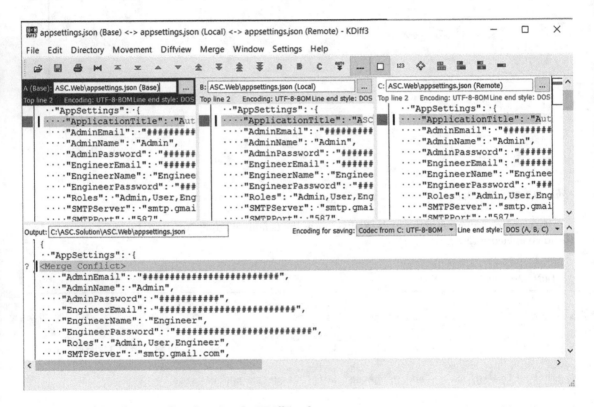

Figure 12-60. Resolving conflicts by using the KDiff3 tool

We can now use shortcuts such as Ctrl+1, Ctrl+2, or Ctrl+3 to merge the appropriate change, and the same will be reflected in the output pane, as shown in Figure 12-61.

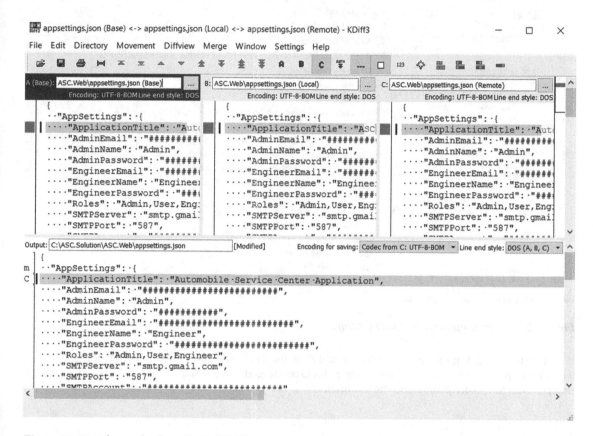

Figure 12-61. *The resolved conflict in KDiff3*

KDiff3 supports other options, shown in Figure 12-62, that can be used to merge files in different combinations.

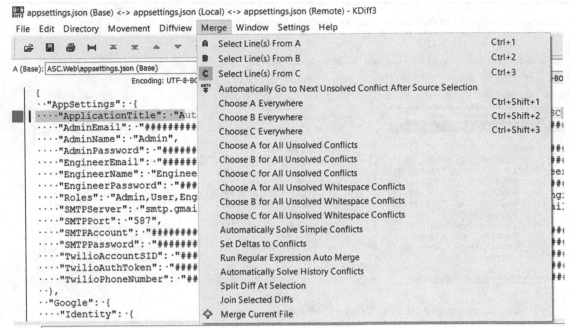

Figure 12-62. *Merge options provided by KDiff3*

After the merge is performed, save the file and close the KDiff3 window. If we use `mergetool` again, we will get a message that there are no pending files to be merged, as shown in Figure 12-63. Now we can proceed with the push operation on the dev branch.

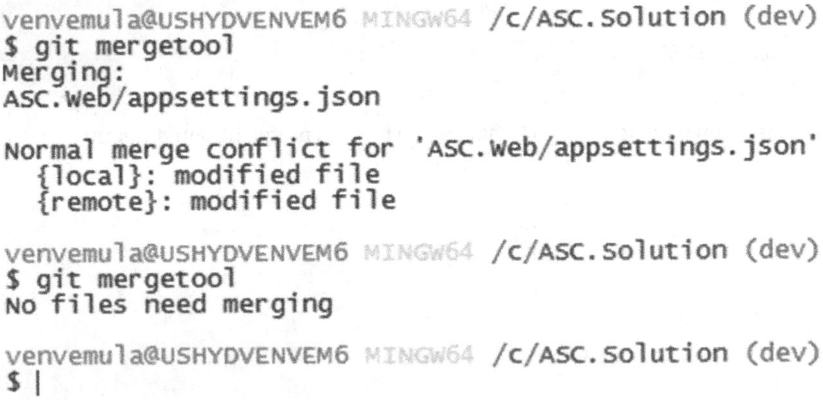

```
venvemula@USHYDVENVEM6 MINGW64 /c/ASC.Solution (dev)
$ git mergetool
Merging:
ASC.Web/appsettings.json

Normal merge conflict for 'ASC.Web/appsettings.json':
  {local}: modified file
  {remote}: modified file

venvemula@USHYDVENVEM6 MINGW64 /c/ASC.Solution (dev)
$ git mergetool
No files need merging

venvemula@USHYDVENVEM6 MINGW64 /c/ASC.Solution (dev)
$ |
```

Figure 12-63. *Checking pending files to merge*

Figure 12-64 shows the status of all branches of the `AutomobileServiceCenter.Core` repository at GitHub.

462

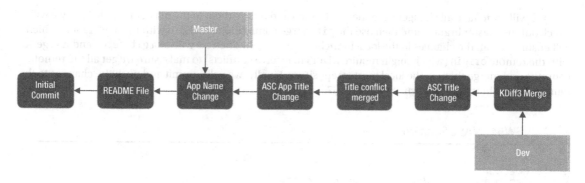

Figure 12-64. *Status of master and dev branches at GitHub*

As the last part in this section, we will merge the master and dev branches when both branches are moved forward with commits. Let's update and commit the `appsettings` title setting on the master branch, as shown in Figure 12-65.

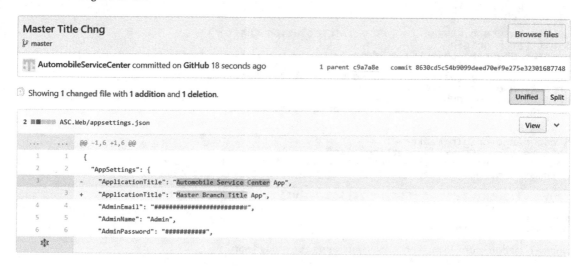

Figure 12-65. *Updating and committing appsettings.json to the master branch*

Now the status of branches on the `AutomobileServiceCenter.Core` repository is shown in Figure 12-66.

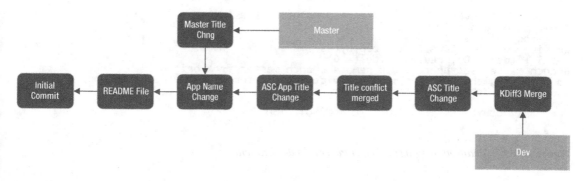

Figure 12-66. *Status of the master and dev branches at GitHub*

We will try to take all changes from the dev branch and merge them to the master branch. First we will check out the master branch, and then use the git merge command to merge it with the dev branch, which will ensure that all the changes in the local branches are merged. Then we will do a git fetch and merge with the remote origin (which might require KDiff3 to resolve conflicts) to make sure we get all the remote commits and merge them in the local master repository. Finally, we will commit and push the changes to the remote master branch, as shown in Figure 12-67.

◆◇ MINGW64:/c/ASC.Solution

```
venvemula@USHYDVENVEM6 MINGW64 /c/ASC.Solution (dev)
$ git checkout master
Your branch is up-to-date with 'origin/master'.
Switched to branch 'master'

venvemula@USHYDVENVEM6 MINGW64 /c/ASC.Solution (master)
$ git merge dev
Updating c9a7a8e..8307cbc
Fast-forward
 ASC.Web/appsettings.json | 2 +-
 1 file changed, 1 insertion(+), 1 deletion(-)

venvemula@USHYDVENVEM6 MINGW64 /c/ASC.Solution (master)
$ git fetch origin
remote: Counting objects: 4, done.
remote: Compressing objects: 100% (4/4), done.
remote: Total 4 (delta 3), reused 0 (delta 0), pack-reused 0
Unpacking objects: 100% (4/4), done.
From https://github.com/AutomobileServiceCenter/AutomobileServiceCenter.Core
   c9a7a8e..8630cd5  master     -> origin/master

venvemula@USHYDVENVEM6 MINGW64 /c/ASC.Solution (master)
$ git merge origin/master
Auto-merging ASC.Web/appsettings.json
CONFLICT (content): Merge conflict in ASC.Web/appsettings.json
Automatic merge failed; fix conflicts and then commit the result.

venvemula@USHYDVENVEM6 MINGW64 /c/ASC.Solution (master|MERGING)
$ git mergetool
Merging:
ASC.Web/appsettings.json

Normal merge conflict for 'ASC.Web/appsettings.json':
  {local}: modified file
  {remote}: modified file

venvemula@USHYDVENVEM6 MINGW64 /c/ASC.Solution (master|MERGING)
$ git commit -m "master merge with dev"
[master debc3a6] master merge with dev

venvemula@USHYDVENVEM6 MINGW64 /c/ASC.Solution (master)
$ git push -u origin master
Counting objects: 1, done.
Writing objects: 100% (1/1), 238 bytes | 0 bytes/s, done.
Total 1 (delta 0), reused 0 (delta 0)
Branch master set up to track remote branch master from origin.
To https://github.com/AutomobileServiceCenter/AutomobileServiceCenter.Core.git
   8630cd5..debc3a6  master -> master

venvemula@USHYDVENVEM6 MINGW64 /c/ASC.Solution (master)
$ |
```

Figure 12-67. Advanced merging between master and dev branches

■ **Note** In this demo, we have only one file in the dev branch to be merged with the master (appsettings. json). But in reality, you might have different files.

Instead of using the merge command, we can also use the rebase command, which performs the same merging operation but in a different way. With rebase, we will patch one of the branch's commits, and that patch will be reapplied on top of the other branch commit. This command is beyond the scope of this book; you can find more information at the Git SCM web site, https://git-scm.com.

If we look at GitHub's AutomobileServiceCenter.Core repository, we will have a combined history of commits, as shown in Figure 12-68.

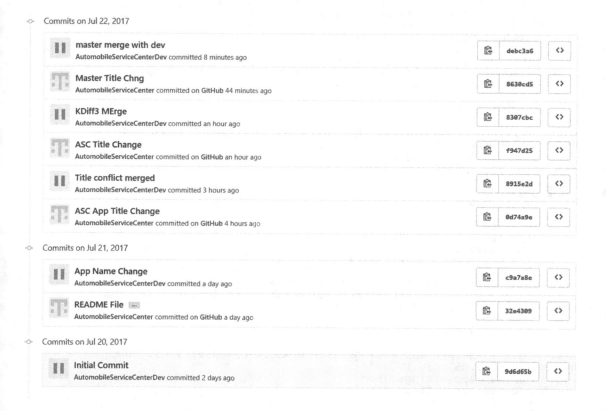

Figure 12-68. Master branch commit history at GitHub

If we want to look at the history of a particular file, we can use the git log command, as shown in Figure 12-69.

```
venvemula@USHYDVENVEM6 MINGW64 /c/ASC.Solution (dev)
$ git log -p ASC.Web/appsettings.json
commit 8307cbcd033678aa13c15e4baab08e016b722745
Author: AutomobileServiceCenterDev <automobileservicecenterdev@gmail.com>
Date:   Sat Jul 22 19:29:59 2017 +0530

    KDiff3 MErge

diff --git a/ASC.Web/appsettings.json b/ASC.Web/appsettings.json
index 4613a71..9fcbcc6 100644
--- a/ASC.Web/appsettings.json
+++ b/ASC.Web/appsettings.json
@@ -1,6 +1,6 @@
 <U+FEFF>{
   "AppSettings": {
-    "ApplicationTitle": "ASC App",
+    "ApplicationTitle": "Automobile Service Center Application",
     "AdminEmail": "#####################",
     "AdminName": "Admin",
     "AdminPassword": "###########",

commit f947d2521c6dfffc49ffa3c8e7f9ae387f518532
Author: AutomobileServiceCenter <autoservicenternew@gmail.com>
Date:   Sat Jul 22 19:16:53 2017 +0530

    ASC Title Change

diff --git a/ASC.Web/appsettings.json b/ASC.Web/appsettings.json
index d57ac3d..4613a71 100644
--- a/ASC.Web/appsettings.json
+++ b/ASC.Web/appsettings.json
@@ -1,6 +1,6 @@
 <U+FEFF>{
   "AppSettings": {
-    "ApplicationTitle": "Automobile Service Center App",
+    "ApplicationTitle": "ASC App",
     "AdminEmail": "#####################",
     "AdminName": "Admin",
     "AdminPassword": "###########",

commit 8915e2d170692dd4e7f60a71a7ad59fb712e304a
Author: AutomobileServiceCenterDev <automobileservicecenterdev@gmail.com>
Date:   Sat Jul 22 17:22:17 2017 +0530

    Title conflict merged

diff --git a/ASC.Web/appsettings.json b/ASC.Web/appsettings.json
index 4613a71..d57ac3d 100644
--- a/ASC.Web/appsettings.json
+++ b/ASC.Web/appsettings.json
@@ -1,6 +1,6 @@
 <U+FEFF>{
   "AppSettings": {
-    "ApplicationTitle": "ASC App",
+    "ApplicationTitle": "Automobile Service Center App",
     "AdminEmail": "#####################",
     "AdminName": "Admin",
     "AdminPassword": "###########",

commit 0d74a9e5a348b3d86729f18171ae0904b13be29f
Author: AutomobileServiceCenter <autoservicenternew@gmail.com>
Date:   Sat Jul 22 16:56:07 2017 +0530
```

Figure 12-69. *Version history of a specific file*

■ **Note**   If we want to delete a branch from the system, we can use the `git branch -d <branch name>` command.

By default, the `.gitignore` file is not checked in to the remote repository. Use `git add .gitignore` and later commit/push changes to the remote origin.

Using GitHub with Visual Studio

The preceding section showed how to manage code with the help of the GitHub repository, using Git Bash and Git commands. Git Bash is a good option in a development environment when we do not have a sophisticated IDE that provides a graphical user interface to interact with GitHub repositories. Fortunately, Visual Studio has good compatibility with GitHub tools and commands. This section demonstrates how to use the Visual Studio IDE and perform GitHub operations.

Open Visual Studio and expand Team Explorer, as shown in Figure 12-70.

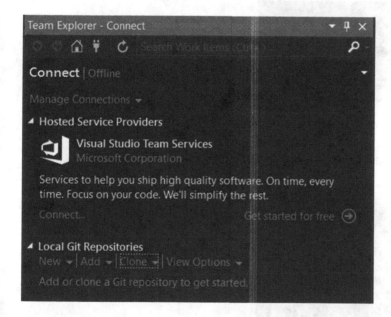

Figure 12-70. Visual Studio Team Explorer

Click the Clone option in the Local Git Repositories section and enter the `AutomobileServiceCenter.Core` GIT URL (which we got while setting up the GitHub repository), as shown in Figure 12-71.

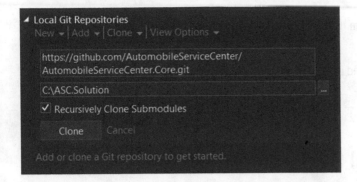

Figure 12-71. Cloning the Automobile Service Center GitHub repository

After the solution is cloned, we have the `ASC.Solution` listing in the Git repositories, as shown in Figure 12-72.

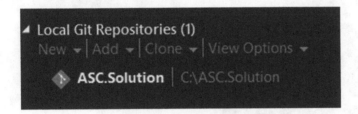

Figure 12-72. Automobile Service Center solution in the local Git repositories

Double-click `ASC.Solution`. You should see project's home screen, as shown in Figure 12-73.

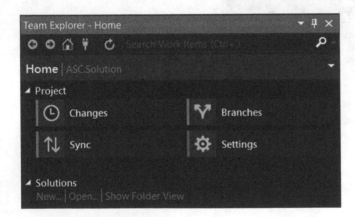

Figure 12-73. Git project home screen in Team Explorer

From the project home screen, we can perform multiple operations such as `git push` and `fetch`, maintain branches, and manage settings. First we will set the user settings by navigating to the Settings tab, as shown in Figure 12-74.

Figure 12-74. *Setting up Git user settings*

Navigate to Global settings, and enter the `AutomobileServiceCenterDev`'s credentials, as shown in Figure 12-75. Click the Update button.

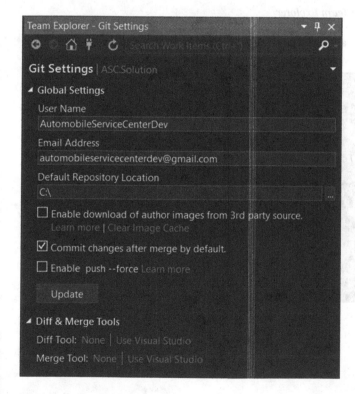

Figure 12-75. *Updating the user configuration*

We can open `ASC.Solution` in Visual Studio and explore the code. We can switch branches by using the Branches tab, as shown in Figure 12-76. We need to double-click the branch to set the focus for that branch.

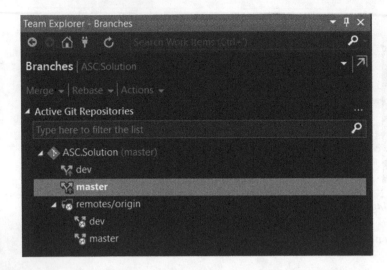

Figure 12-76. *Local and remote branches in Team Explorer*

All the Git remote repository operations are performed from the Sync tab, as shown in Figure 12-77.

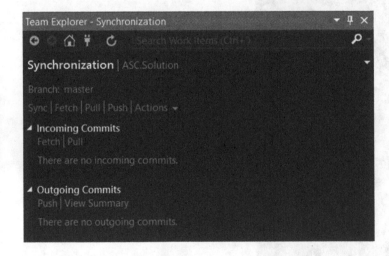

Figure 12-77. *Sync tab in Team Explorer*

Now we will see how to make code changes in Visual Studio and make the commit to the dev branch. Open ASC.Solution in Visual Studio and make a change in HomeController by removing the about action and delete About.cshtml from the Views folder. All the changes are displayed in the Changes tab, as shown in Figure 12-78.

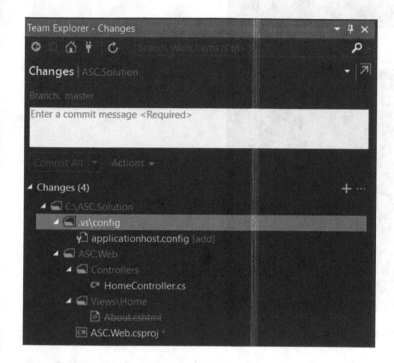

Figure 12-78. *Changes tab in Team Explorer*

We can ignore files in the .vs folder from the commit by right-clicking and selecting the Ignore These Local Items option, as shown in Figure 12-79. After ignoring the .vs folder, Visual Studio will automatically update the .gitignore file.

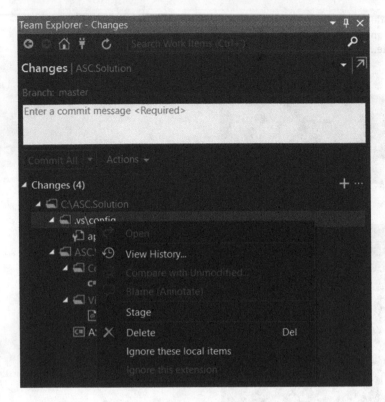

Figure 12-79. *Ignoring unwanted files from the commit*

We can also manually modify the `.gitignore` file to ignore the `.vs` folder, as shown in Listing 12-7.

Listing 12-7.

```
*.suo
*.user
bin
obj
packages
.vs
```

Enter the commit comments and click the Commit All button, shown in Figure 12-80.

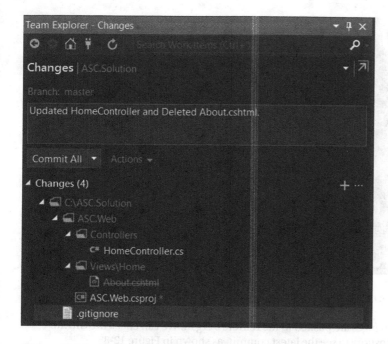

Figure 12-80. *Committing the pending changes*

The code is committed to the local repository, as shown in Figure 12-81.

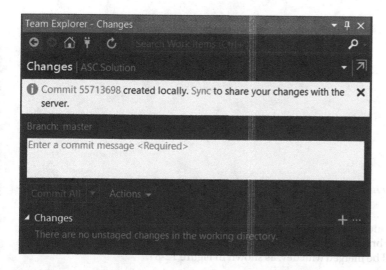

Figure 12-81. *Successful commit to the local repository*

If we go to the Sync tab, we should see that the commit is staged and we can push the change to the remote repository, as shown in Figure 12-82.

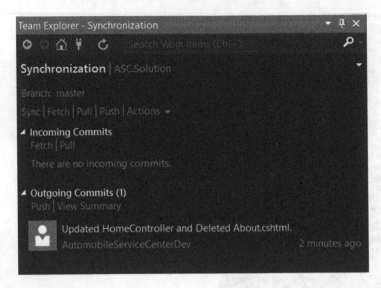

Figure 12-82. Commit staged in the Sync tab for a remote repository push

Click the Push option, and the changes are pushed to the remote origin. We can check the GitHub AutomobileServiceCenter.Core repository to see the latest commit, as shown in Figure 12-83.

Figure 12-83. Master branch commit history at GitHub

Now we will see how to merge code from the master to the dev branch from Visual Studio. Navigate to the Branches tab and click the dev branch to be the focus. In the Merge from Branch option, select the master to indicate that master should be merged with dev, as shown in Figure 12-84.

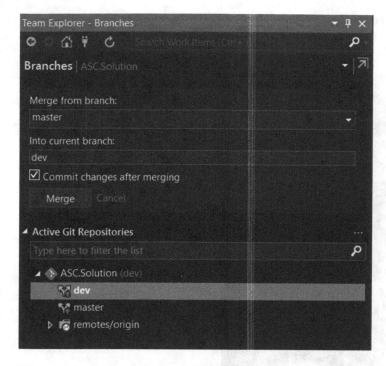

Figure 12-84. *Master branch merge into dev branch*

Click the Merge button, and we'll get a confirmation after the merge is completed, as shown in Figure 12-85.

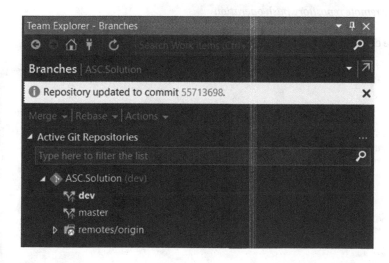

Figure 12-85. *Successful merge of master to dev branch*

The changes are merged locally, and we need to push those changes to the dev branch. Navigate to the Sync tab, and we should see all the pending commits (due to the merge) to the dev branch, as shown in Figure 12-86.

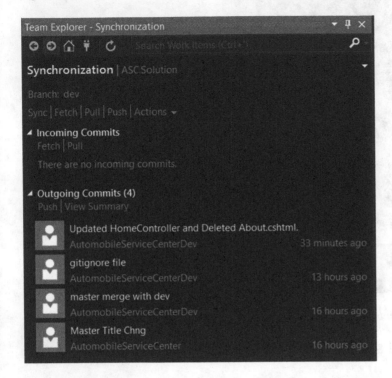

Figure 12-86. *Pending commits to the remote repository push operation*

Click the Push option, and all the changes will be pushed to the remote repository. All commits for the dev branch are shown in Figure 12-87.

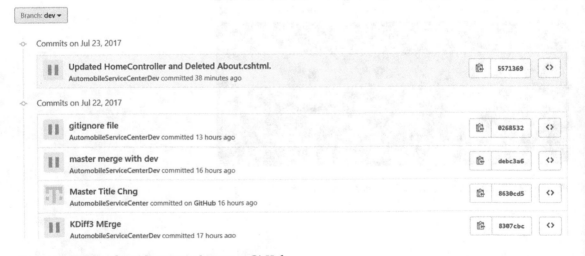

Figure 12-87. *Dev branch commits history at GitHub*

Now we will see how to resolve merge conflicts by using Visual Studio. Let's assume that another developer changed the text in the `contact` action of `HomeController` in the dev branch, as shown in Figure 12-88.

Figure 12-88. Contact action changes at the GitHub dev branch

At the same time, another developer made a different change to the same text of the `contact` action in `HomeController` in his local repository, as shown in Listing 12-8.

Listing 12-8. Contact action

```
public IActionResult Contact()
{
    ViewData["Message"] = "ASC contact page.";
    return View();
}
```

Now navigate to the Sync tab and click the Fetch option. This should fetch the remote commits, as shown in Figure 12-89.

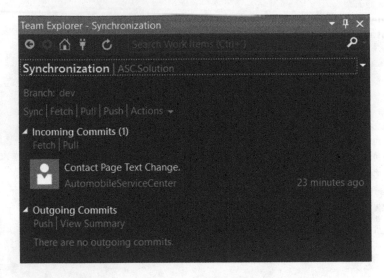

Figure 12-89. Fetching remote commits from the dev branch

We need to create a commit for the changes that we had in the local Visual Studio instance. Navigate to the Changes tab and create a commit as we did earlier. Now get back to the Sync tab and click Pull. We should see the conflicts shown in Figure 12-90.

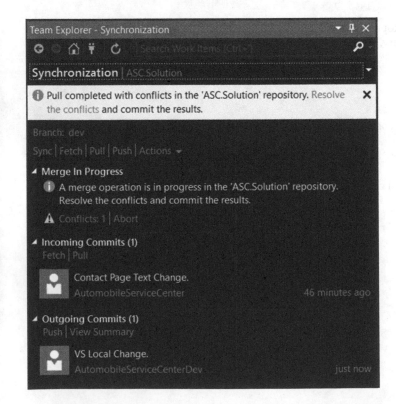

Figure 12-90. Merging conflicts between outgoing and incoming commits

Click the Conflicts option, which should open the Resolve Conflicts section with HomeController listed in the Conflicts section, as shown in Figure 12-91.

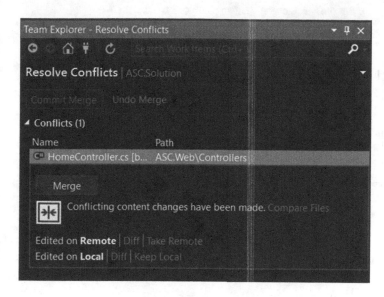

Figure 12-91. *Resolving conflicts on HomeController*

Select HomeController and click the Merge button to open KDiff3 (which we already configured for Git at Git Bash), as shown in Figure 12-92.

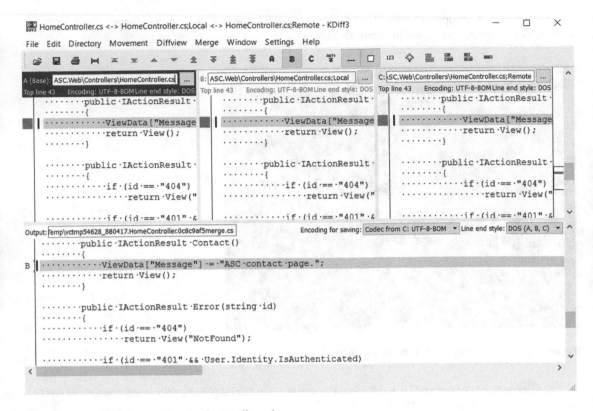

Figure 12-92. Merging conflicts in the KDiff3 tool

Complete the merge in KDiff3, save the file, and close the tool. The merge will be resolved at Visual Studio, and the Resolve Conflicts section shows no remaining conflicts message, as shown in Figure 12-93.

Figure 12-93. No pending conflicts message in the Resolve Conflicts section

Click the Commit Merge button, and this will take us to the Changes section. Enter the comment and click the Commit All button, as shown in Figure 12-94.

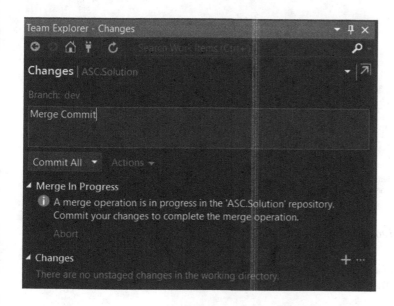

Figure 12-94. Committing merged changes

All the merge changes are staged in a commit. Now we can go to the Sync tab and see all the pending commits, as shown in Figure 12-95.

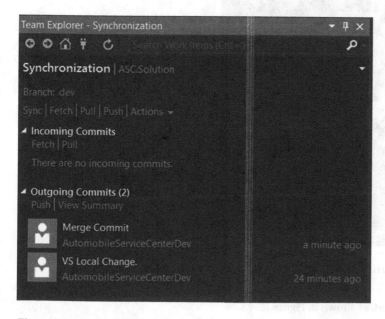

Figure 12-95. Pushing the merged commit to the remote repository

Click the Push option. All the commits are pushed to the remote origin, and we can verify the commits, as shown in Figure 12-96.

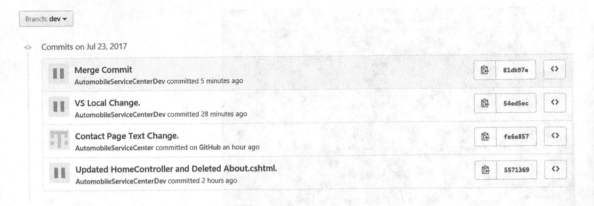

Figure 12-96. Dev branch commit history on GitHub

If we have to look at the history of a particular code file, we right-click the file in Visual Studio and select View History, as shown in Figure 12-97.

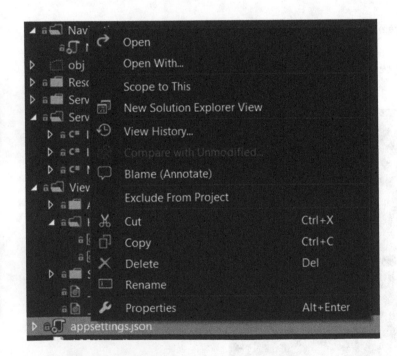

Figure 12-97. Version history of a particular file

The History view will be displayed, as shown in Figure 12-98.

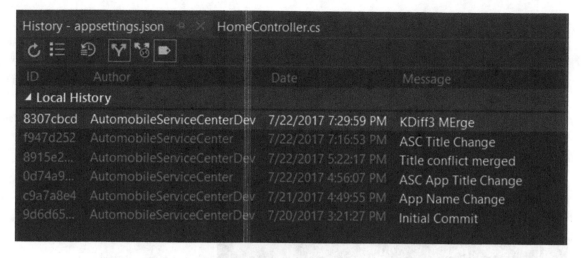

Figure 12-98. *Displaying the history view*

Now let's assume there are some changes on the remote repository and we want to fetch the latest to our local branch. The dev branch of the remote repository has a commit on the appsettings.json file, as shown in Figure 12-99.

Figure 12-99. *appsettings.json file changes on the dev branch*

To fetch this change to the local repository, navigate to the Sync tab and click the Pull option in the Incoming Commits section. The changes will be retrieved from the remote repository and merged to the local repository, as shown in Figure 12-100.

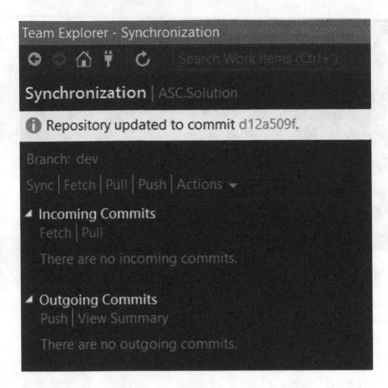

Figure 12-100. Pull the latest changes to the local repository from the remote

Now we will see how to revert the changes that are pushed in a commit to the remote repository. Navigate to the Changes section and select the View History options from the Actions menu, as shown in Figures 12-101 and 12-102.

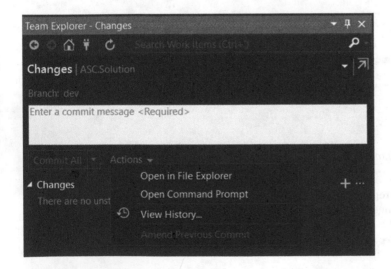

Figure 12-101. View history of changes

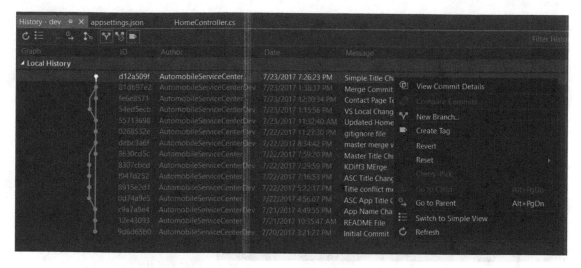

Figure 12-102. *History of all commits*

In history mode, right-click a particular commit that we want to revert and select the revert option. There will be a confirmation dialog box. Select yes, as shown in Figure 12-103.

Figure 12-103. *Confirmation for reverting a commit*

The revert operation will be completed, and the corresponding commit will be performed. Now if we navigate to the Sync tab, we should see the reverted commit in the Outgoing Commits section, as shown in Figure 12-104.

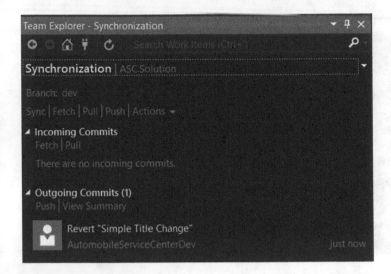

Figure 12-104. *Commit created due to revert operation*

Click the Push option, and the commit will be reverted on the remote `origin`.

■ **Note** GitHub also supports forking a repository; GitHub makes a copy of the original repository and associates the copy with the individual account owner who forked the repository.

Repository fork concepts are beyond the scope of this book. For more information, visit `https://help.github.com/articles/fork-a-repo/`.

Similarly, a lot of other features and functionalities are supported by both Git Bash and Visual Studio Git tools. This book shares the basic operational knowledge that every developer should possess to perform day-to-day activities with code maintenance and management. For more details and advanced concepts related to Git operations, I advise you to go through the following documentation:

Git with Visual Studio: `www.visualstudio.com/en-us/docs/git/gitquickstart`

Git with Git Bash: `https://git-scm.com/book/en/v2`

Summary

In this chapter, you learned the importance of having a sophisticated and reliable version-control system to manage and maintain source code. Today's code-versioning systems provide resilient and effective solutions to deal with business requirements and integrations that are highly complex. Version-control systems provide mission-critical features such as branching and merging, revising and reverting to historical versions, and collaborating with project management tools to map business requirements with code artifacts.

Git, one of the most popular version-control systems, is capable of providing decentralized repositories in which a developer can maintain multiple local and remote repositories. GitHub is a hosting service for Git repositories that is free for public and open source projects. GitHub, in addition to providing source code management, provides other features such as bug tracking, feature requests, task management, wikis, and access control for projects.

For our Automobile Service Center application, you created a new GitHub account with a new public repository. You installed GitHub for Windows, which provides both Git Bash and a graphical user interface to manage source code. You focused on the Git Bash shell to perform Git operations. You added a developer account as a collaborator for the `AutomobileServiceCenter.Core` repository and followed the developer invitation acceptance flow.

You performed the following operations by using Git Bash:

- Configured Git Bash with developer details.

- Configured a `gitignore` file to ignore folders such as `bin` and `obj`.

- Initiated Git, committed all changes, and pushed to the remote repository.

- Created dev and master branches.

- Fetched and merged the latest changes from the remote `origin` to the local branch.

- Merged the master and dev branches when they are on different commits.

- Reset commits in both local and remote.

- Configured the KDiff3 merge tool, which you used to resolve merge conflicts by stashing the local changes.

- Merged branches when all the branches are fast-forwarded with commits.

- Checked version logs and deleted a branch.

In the last section of this chapter, you configured Git in Visual Studio 2017. You learned about the sections provided by Visual Studio, such as Sync, Changes, and Settings. You performed operations such as fetching from the remote, committing to a branch, merging branches with and without merge conflicts, filing historical versions, reverting a commit on the remote `origin`.

Code version management using Git is a vast topic that can't be completely covered in one chapter of any book. I advise you to go through specific Git-related books to gain more expertise. *Pro Git* by Scott Chacon and Ben Straub (Apress, 2014) provides in-depth knowledge on performing advanced operations using Git.

References

1. `https://git-scm.com/`

2. `www.visualstudio.com/en-us/docs/git/overview`

CHAPTER 13

■ ■ ■

Configuring a Continuous Build with Travis CI

The increasing complexity of business requirements not only increases the complexity of code but also creates numerous challenges in delivering exceptional code quality along with stability. As you saw in the preceding chapter, source-code version-control systems help projects in code maintenance through local and remote repositories by providing good control for managing different versions of code through branches. Having a source version-control system alone is not enough to achieve code stability. With ever-changing business requirements and development team dynamics, managing code stability in version systems is a challenging task.

Many modern tools and platforms provide continuous integration (CI) with various version-control repositories, through which we can configure automatic builds and tests to run on the source code. *Building* is the process of compiling the source code to get an executable package, which can then be used to run the application on either a server or a client. *Testing* is the process of running automated unit-test cases (for example, xUnit tests) as part of the build to make sure the source code is properly aligned with its business and technical objectives.

Without continuous integration for building and testing, we can commit bad code to the repository—which poses a serious threat to the entire development team, because anyone can fetch committed code and assume it to be a stable version. With new continuous integration platforms, we can configure the repository with a CI provider to validate each commit and notify all the stakeholders if the build or test fails. Continuous integration ensures good code quality, minimizes the impact of build errors in code, and automates repetitive tasks.

Many third-party providers offer online services for building and testing source code. *Travis CI* is a hosted and distributed continuous integration provider for GitHub projects.

The key features of Travis CI are as follows:

- Is easy to get started. Because Travis is a hosted service, there is no need to install and configure any other tools or components.

- Builds, tests, and deploys the source code.

- Provides notifications when the build or test fails.

- Provides static code analysis.

- Offers good support for applications based on .NET Core.

- Provides out-of-the-box support for multiple languages.

In this chapter, we are going to use the Travis CI platform to build and test the source code of the `AutomobileServiceCenter.Core` GitHub repository.

© Rami Vemula 2017

R. Vemula, *Real-Time Web Application Development*, https://doi.org/10.1007/978-1-4842-3270-5_13

Introducing Travis CI

Travis CI is a distributed and hosted continuous integration service for building and testing the source code of software projects hosted at GitHub. Travis CI builds can be enabled on GitHub public repositories for free. For private repositories, Travis CI offers paid subscriptions. Apart from supporting build and test functionalities, Travis CI is capable of deploying builds to various environments from different branches of GitHub. Travis CI supports several providers for deployments, including AWS, Azure, Heroku, and npm.

Travis CI is capable of running builds concurrently (this can be limited though settings). It also is capable of automatically cancelling builds when new commits arrive as well as supporting multiple languages.

The Travis CI build process is shown in Figure 13-1. When a commit is pushed to a GitHub branch, GitHub triggers the Travis CI build process. Travis CI will then check out the relevant branch and run the commands specified in .travis.yml to execute automated builds and tests.

Figure 13-1. Travis CI workflow

.travis.yml is a YAML text file that should be configured at the root directory of the GitHub repository. This configuration file specifies the programming languages that are used in the project, the dependencies that need to be installed before the build process starts on the source code, the desired environment specifications where the build should happen, and the branches from which the source code should be used to execute the build.

Typically, a Travis YAML file consists of the following steps:

1. Before Install

2. Install

3. Before Script

4. Script

5. After Success/Failure

6. Before Deploy

7. Deploy

8. After Deploy

9. After Script

Travis uses the Before Install and Install steps to fetch all the dependencies. The Before Script and Script steps are used to set up the environment and run the build script. The After Success/Failure step is useful if you want to perform any operation—for example, creating log files for a successful or failed build. The Before Deploy, Deploy, and After Deploy steps are used to prepare and deploy the generated build packages to Travis-supported deployment providers. The After Script step is the last step, which runs after the entire script is executed.

■ **Note** For more information on customizing the `.travis.yml` file, visit `https://docs.travis-ci.com/user/customizing-the-build/`.

If deployment is configured in the YAML file, Travis CI will deploy the generated build package to the specified environment. Finally, Travis CI notifies all the stakeholders (primarily developers and project managers) about the status (success or failure) of the build/test execution.

■ **Note** We will use Travis CI only to build and test the source code of the `AutomobileServiceCenter.Core` repository's Dev branch. Even though Travis CI supports continuous deployment, we are not going to use its deployment feature. We will use Docker containers (which are described in later chapters) to achieve continuous deployment through containerization.

Creating a Travis CI Account and Associating It with the GitHub Repository

In this section, we will integrate the `AutomobileServiceCenter.Core` repository with the Travis CI build. Let's get started by creating an account at Travis CI. Visit `https://travis-ci.org/`, as shown in Figure 13-2.

Figure 13-2. *Travis CI sign-up*

Click the Sign In with GitHub button and enter the same credentials that you used to create the GitHub account. Then click the Sign In button, shown in Figure 13-3.

Sign in to **GitHub**
to continue to **Travis CI**

Username or email address

autoservicenternew@gmail.com

Password   Forgot password?

••••••••••••

Sign in

New to GitHub? Create an account.

Figure 13-3. Signing in to Travis CI by using GitHub credentials

GitHub will display an authorize prompt that allows Travis CI to access account information from GitHub, as shown in Figure 13-4. Click the Authorize travis-ci button.

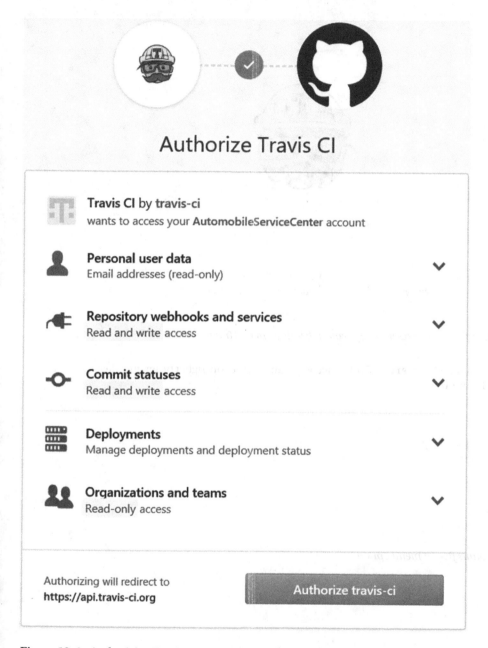

Figure 13-4. Authorizing Travis CI to access GitHub account information

Upon successful authorization, a success message will be displayed, as shown in Figure 13-5.

Great news!

We've successfully synchronized your details from GitHub.
We will redirect you to your profile in a few seconds.

Figure 13-5. *Successful synchronization of account details from GitHub to Travis CI*

Hover over the `AutomobileServiceCenter` account name at the top-right corner and click the Accounts option, shown in Figure 13-6.

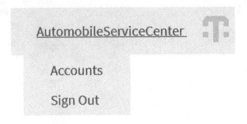

Figure 13-6. *Accounts fly-out menu option*

You will see all the public repositories of the GitHub account, including AutomobileServiceCenter.Core, as shown in Figure 13-7.

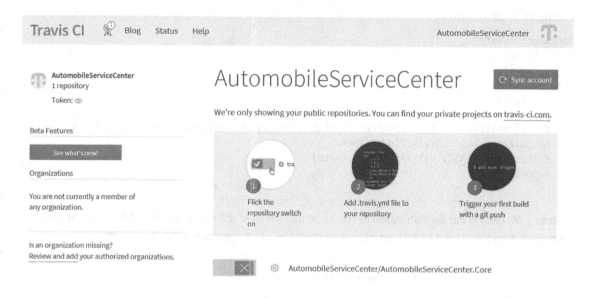

Figure 13-7. *GitHub public repositories listed at the Travis CI platform*

■ **Note** If you are not able to see the public repositories, click the Sync Account button, which will fetch all the public repositories from the GitHub account.

You can activate the AutomobileServiceCenter.Core repository with the Travis CI build by toggling the status, as shown in Figure 13-8.

 ⚙ AutomobileServiceCenter/AutomobileServiceCenter.Core

Figure 13-8. *Activating the Travis CI build for the AutomobileServiceCenter.Core GitHub repository*

Configuring the GitHub Repository with Travis.yml

In this section, we will create a .travis.yml file at the root of the GitHub's AutomobileServiceCenter.Core repository in the Dev branch, as shown in Listing 13-1.

We first set the language to C# and set the Linux distribution to trusty. We then give access to sudo and turn off mono because we are running on .NET Core. We need to specify the Dotnet Core version as 1.0.3, so the build will happen on the specified version.

The important section is the script section, where we specify the commands that will be run as part of the build process. First we do a dotnet restore (we need to specify both NuGet and MyGet source feeds because we need to get the SignalR dependency from MyGet repositories), followed by dotnet test, which will run all the xUnit test cases in the specific project (which is ASC.Tests). Lastly, we will run dotnet build, which will build the entire solution.

Listing 13-1. .travis.yml file

```
language: csharp
dist: trusty
sudo: required
mono: none
dotnet: 1.0.3
script:
  - dotnet restore -s https://dotnet.myget.org/F/aspnetcore-dev/api/v3/index.json -s
    https://api.nuget.org/v3/index.json
  - dotnet test ./ASC.Tests/ASC.Tests.csproj
  - dotnet build
```

■ **Note**   We need to set the distribution to trusty so that the build will run on Ubuntu 14.04, because .NET Core doesn't work on Ubuntu 12.04 (which is the default Linux build environment on Travis right now).

Commit the .travis.yml file, as shown in Figure 13-9.

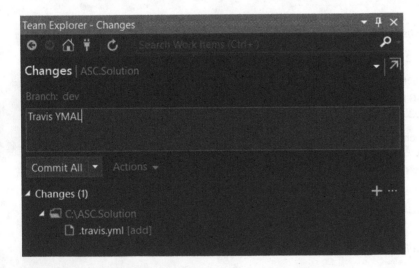

Figure 13-9. Committing Travis CI to the GitHub repository

Push the change to the remote origin from Visual Studio, as shown in Figure 13-10.

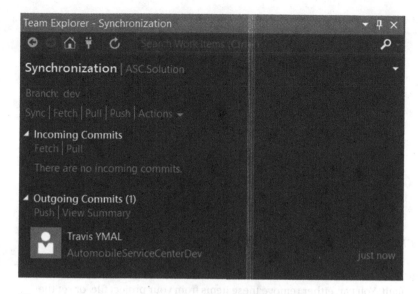

Figure 13-10. Pushing the commit to the GitHub repository

Immediately after the push operation is completed, Travis CI will trigger a build, as shown in Figure 13-11.

Figure 13-11. Travis CI build in progress

After some time, we can check the progress of the Travis build. When you check, you'll see that the build failed, as shown in Figure 13-12.

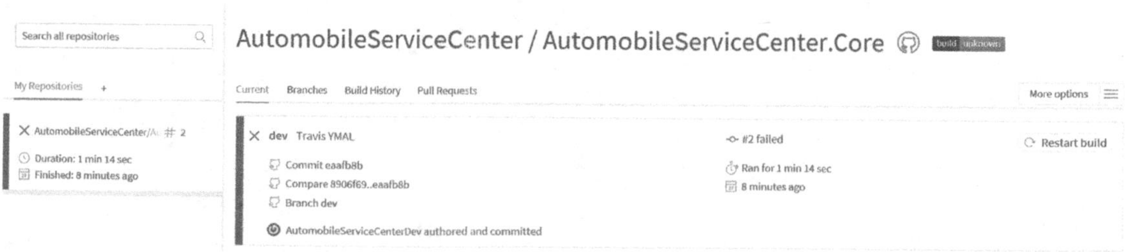

Figure 13-12. Travis CI build failure

We can check the job log at the bottom of the page, where we can find the details about the build failure, as shown in Figure 13-13.

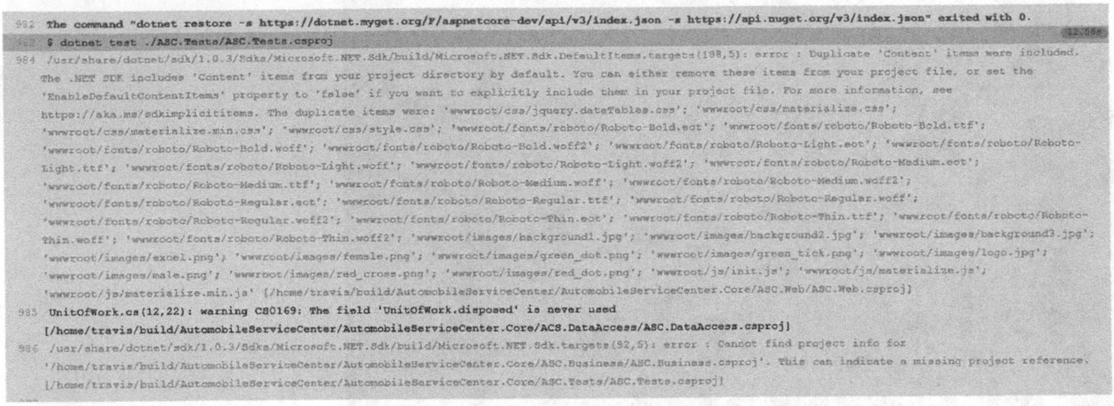

Figure 13-13. *Job log of Travis CI build*

As the error says, Duplicate 'Content items were included. The .NET SDK includes Content items from your project directory by default. You can either remove these items from your project file, or set the EnableDefaultContentItems property to false if you want to explicitly include them in your project file. We need to set the EnableDefaultContentItems property to false in ASC.Web.csproj as shown in Listing 13-2.

■ **Note**   Edit the CSPROJ file by right-clicking the ASC.Web project in Visual Studio and selecting the Edit ASC.Web.csproj option.

Listing 13-2. Setting EnableDefaultContentItems to false

```
<PropertyGroup>
  <TargetFramework>netcoreapp1.1</TargetFramework>
  <UserSecretsId>aspnet-ASC.Web-9D645DBB-9112-4508-9007-84D07A1B38F0</UserSecretsId>
  <PackageTargetFallback>portable-net45+win8</PackageTargetFallback>
  <EnableDefaultContentItems>false</EnableDefaultContentItems>
  <PreBuildEvent></PreBuildEvent>
</PropertyGroup>
```

Commit and push the CSPROJ change to the Dev branch. You should see the Travis build triggered, as shown in Figure 13-14.

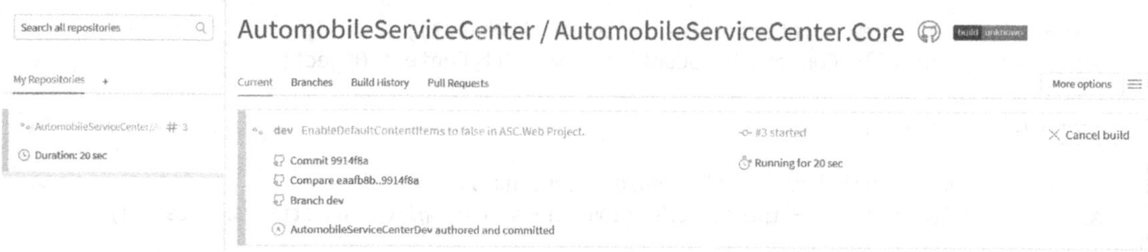

***Figure 13-14.** Travis CI build in progress*

■ **Note** To simulate other types of build fails, especially failing a build on running an xUnit test case, explicitly comment out the session-related code in the `Index` action of `HomeController`.

After some time, we can see that the build still fails, as shown in Figure 13-15. If we analyze the job details, we can see the `dotnet test` command is exited with code 1. The root cause is that one of the four xUnit test cases failed, and the failed test case is `HomeController_Index_Session_Test`.

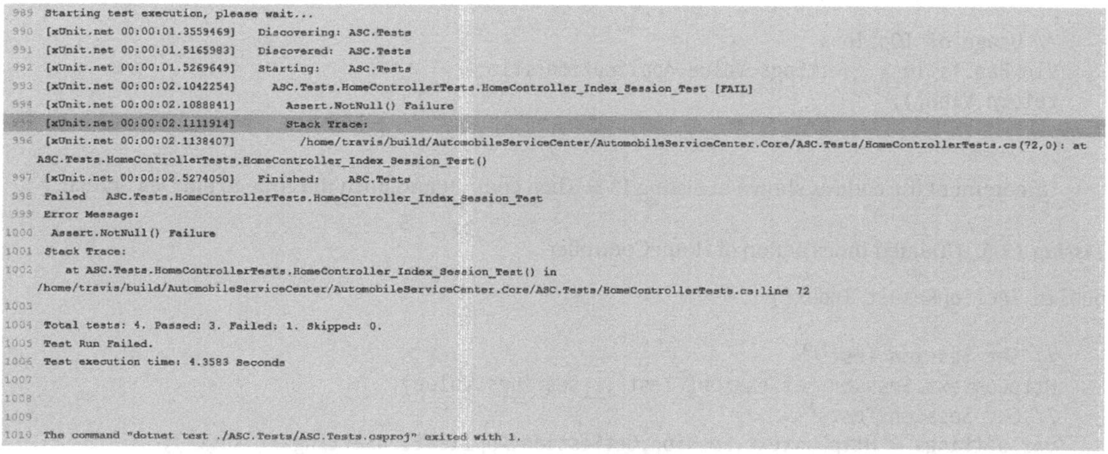

```
Starting test execution, please wait...
[xUnit.net 00:00:01.3559469]   Discovering: ASC.Tests
[xUnit.net 00:00:01.5165983]   Discovered:  ASC.Tests
[xUnit.net 00:00:01.5269649]   Starting:    ASC.Tests
[xUnit.net 00:00:02.1042254]     ASC.Tests.HomeControllerTests.HomeController_Index_Session_Test [FAIL]
[xUnit.net 00:00:02.1088841]       Assert.NotNull() Failure
[xUnit.net 00:00:02.1111914]       Stack Trace:
[xUnit.net 00:00:02.1138407]         /home/travis/build/AutomobileServiceCenter/AutomobileServiceCenter.Core/ASC.Tests/HomeControllerTests.cs(72,0): at
  ASC.Tests.HomeControllerTests.HomeController_Index_Session_Test()
[xUnit.net 00:00:02.5274050]   Finished:    ASC.Tests
Failed   ASC.Tests.HomeControllerTests.HomeController_Index_Session_Test
Error Message:
 Assert.NotNull() Failure
Stack Trace:
   at ASC.Tests.HomeControllerTests.HomeController_Index_Session_Test() in
  /home/travis/build/AutomobileServiceCenter/AutomobileServiceCenter.Core/ASC.Tests/HomeControllerTests.cs:line 72

Total tests: 4. Passed: 3. Failed: 1. Skipped: 0.
Test Run Failed.
Test execution time: 4.3583 Seconds



The command "dotnet test ./ASC.Tests/ASC.Tests.csproj" exited with 1.
```

***Figure 13-15.** Travis CI build failed because of failed xUnit test cases*

The `HomeController_Index_Session_Test` test method is shown in Listing 13-3. It checks for a not-null assertion on the session variable `Test`, but in reality we are getting the `Test` session variable as null.

Listing 13-3. HomeController Index action Session test

```
[Fact]
public void HomeController_Index_Session_Test()
{
    var controller = new HomeController(optionsMock.Object);
    controller.ControllerContext.HttpContext = mockHttpContext.Object;

    controller.Index();

    // Session value with key "Test" should not be null.
    Assert.NotNull(controller.HttpContext.Session.GetSession<ApplicationSettings>("Test"));
}
```

Now let's check the actual method under test (the Index action of HomeController), as shown in Listing 13-4. The code related to the session is in a commented state, which is why the Test session variable is not getting set, and that results in the test failing.

Listing 13-4. Index action of HomeController

```
public IActionResult Index()
{
    // Set Session Test
    // HttpContext.Session.SetSession("Test", _settings.Value);
    // Get Session Test
    // var settings = HttpContext.Session.GetSession<ApplicationSettings>("Test");

    // Usage of IOptions
    ViewBag.Title = _settings.Value.ApplicationTitle;
    return View();
}
```

Uncomment the code as shown in Listing 13-5. Then commit and push the code to the Dev branch.

Listing 13-5. Updated Index action of HomeController

```
public IActionResult Index()
{
    // Set Session Test
    HttpContext.Session.SetSession("Test", _settings.Value);
    // Get Session Test
    var settings = HttpContext.Session.GetSession<ApplicationSettings>("Test");

    // Usage of IOptions
    ViewBag.Title = _settings.Value.ApplicationTitle;
    return View();
}
```

Now the build will be passed, as shown in Figure 13-16.

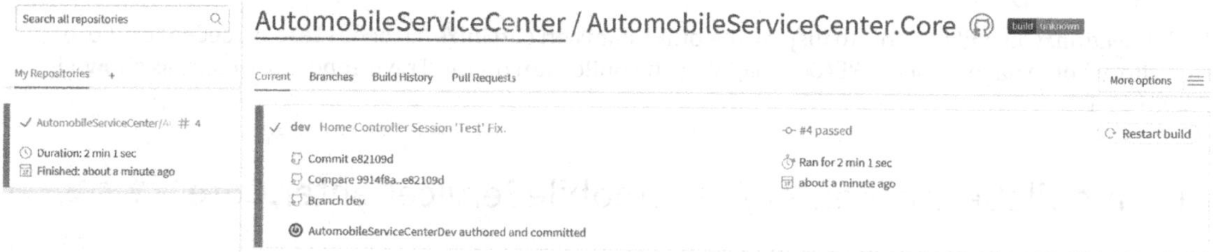

Figure 13-16. *Travis CI build success*

If you look at the job log, you should see that dotnet build is completed, as shown in Figure 13-17.

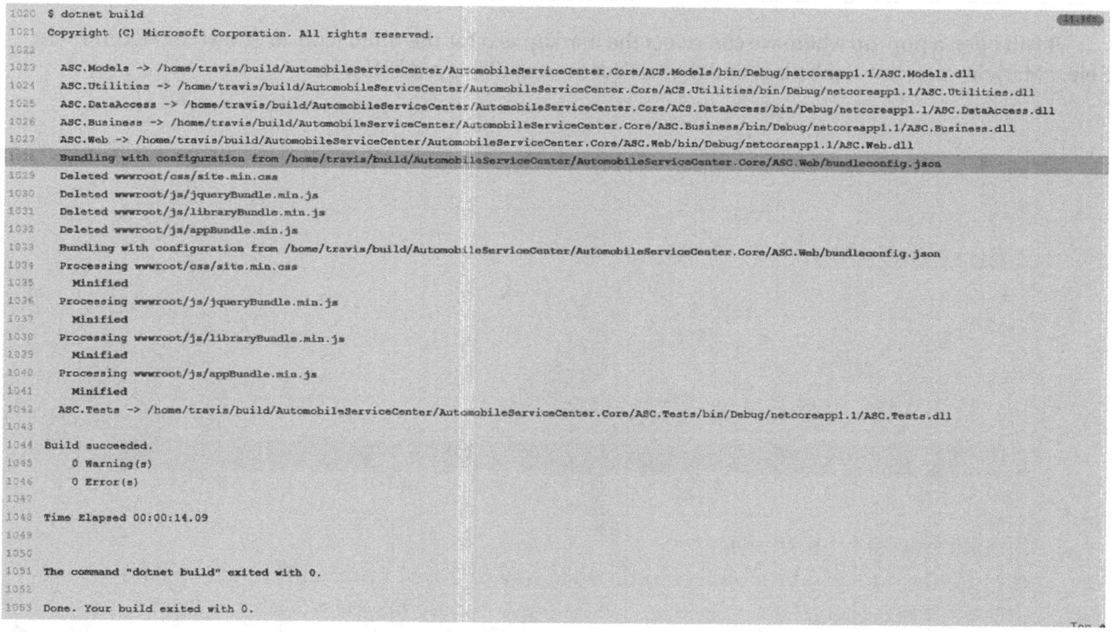

Figure 13-17. *Job log of a successful Travis CI build*

Displaying the Travis Build Status at the GitHub Repository Home Page

In this section, you will see how to display the build status on GitHub's AutomobileServiceCenter.Core repository home page, which is README.md. Click the Build icon on the Travis repository page, as shown in Figure 13-18.

AutomobileServiceCenter / AutomobileServiceCenter.Core ⬡

Figure 13-18. *Build icon at Travis CI portal for the AutomobileServiceCenter.Core repository*

■ **Note** Sometimes the build status will not be properly reflected at Travis-CI.org. This issue is being tracked at https://github.com/travis-ci/travis-ci/issues/3996.

It will open a pop-up where we can select the markup text for the Build icon, as shown in Figure 13-19. Select Markdown in the combo box and then select the text displayed below it.

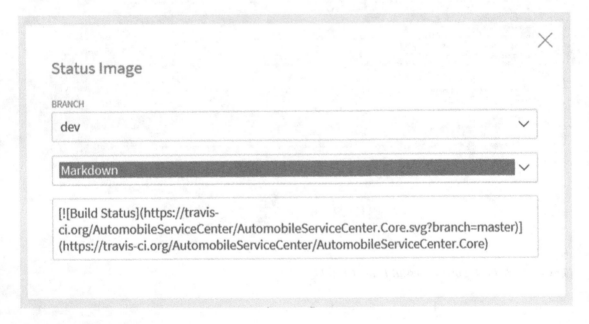

Figure 13-19. *Build icon markup text*

Change the branch name from master to dev, as shown in Listing 13-6.

Listing 13-6. Changing the source code branch name in markdown

```
[![Build Status](https://travis-ci.org/AutomobileServiceCenter/AutomobileServiceCenter.Core.
svg?branch=dev)](https://travis-ci.org/AutomobileServiceCenter/AutomobileServiceCenter.Core)
```

Now go to the Dev branch of the `AutomobileServiceCenter.Core` repository in GitHub and edit the `README.md` file in the web browser itself, as shown in Figure 13-20.

Figure 13-20. *Updatig the README.md file with the Build icon markup text*

Enter a commit comment and click the Commit Changes button.

Figure 13-21. *Committing the README.md changes to the GitHub repository*

Committing the change to the Dev branch will again trigger the Travis build, and it will be completed as shown in Figure 13-22.

Figure 13-22. *Travis CI build success*

The Travis build status is updated in the Dev branch of GitHub's `AutomobileServiceCenter.Core` repository, as shown in Figure 13-23.

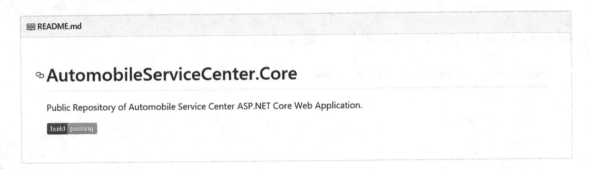

Figure 13-23. *The build status at the AutomobileServiceCenter.Core GitHub repository*

■ **Note** It might take some time for the correct build status to be reflected on the GitHub repository.

Simulate a build failure by explicitly making an xUnit test case fail. Then the failed build status would be as shown in Figure 13-24.

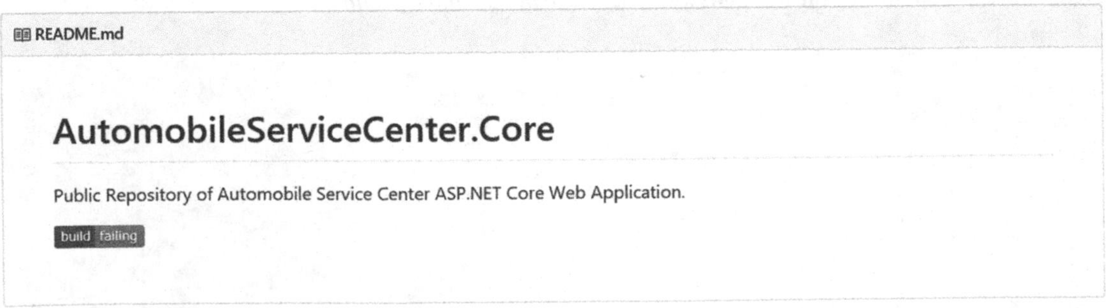

README.md

AutomobileServiceCenter.Core

Public Repository of Automobile Service Center ASP.NET Core Web Application.

build failing

Figure 13-24. *The build's failed status at the AutomobileServiceCenter.Core GitHub repository*

Enabling Travis Build Notifications to Users

This section demonstrates how to send notifications to specific users on the events of successful and failed builds. By default, a build e-mail is sent to the committer and the author, but only if they have access to the repository that the commit was pushed to, and they should be registered on the Travis CI system. To send e-mail to different users, regardless of whether they have a registered account, we can update .travis. yml as shown in Listing 13-7. In the notifications section, we need to specify all the e-mail recipients' addresses. We can also configure Travis to always send e-mail notifications on a notification event such as on_success and on_failure.

Listing 13-7. Email notification configuration in .travis.yml file

```
language: csharp
dist: trusty
sudo: required
mono: none
dotnet: 1.0.3
script:
  - dotnet restore -s https://dotnet.myget.org/F/aspnetcore-dev/api/v3/index.json -s
https://api.nuget.org/v3/index.json
  - dotnet test ./ASC.Tests/ASC.Tests.csproj
  - dotnet build
notifications:
  email:
    recipients:
    - autoservicenternew@gmail.com
    - automobileservicecenterdev@gmail.com
    on_success: always
    on_failure: always
```

Commit and push the .travis.yml file to the Dev branch. A Travis build will be triggered, and the status would be sent in an e-mail as shown in Figure 13-25.

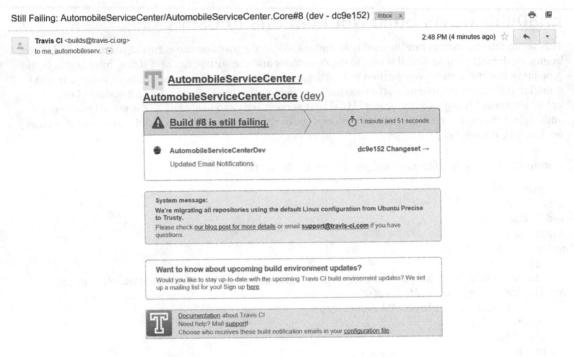

Figure 13-25. Failed Travis CI build e-mail notification

■ **Note** The Travis build is failing because to test the build status, we simulated a failed build scenario.

Now we will fix the build issue and push to the remote repository. We should get a success e-mail as shown in Figure 13-26.

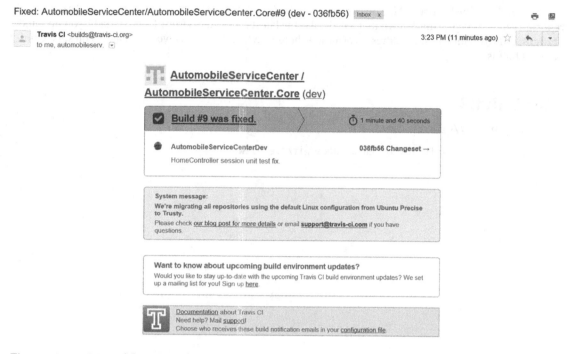

Figure 13-26. *Successful Travis CI build e-mail notification*

Summary

You started this chapter by learning about the importance of continuous integration tools and platforms in maintaining code quality for complex applications. Even though version-control systems help applications maintain and resolve issues for large code bases, managing code stability is always a challenge. This challenge can be overcome by leveraging platforms such as Travis CI, which is an online hosted and distributed continuous integration provider for GitHub. Travis CI can build, test, and deploy the source code and can send notifications on build success and fail events.

Travis CI is primarily based on a .travis.yml configuration file through which the entire build script can be configured for various program languages, dependencies, and environment specifications. The Travis configuration file contains events such as Before Script, After Success, and After Failure, through which you can perform specific actions.

You created an account for the Automobile Service Center at the Travis platform by using the same credentials that you used to create a GitHub account. Upon successful creation of an account, Travis pulls the details of public repositories that can be activated for continuous integration. You then proceeded to activate the CI for the AutomobileServiceCenter.Core repository at the Travis platform. Later you created the .travis.yml file for the Automobile Service Center application with dotnet commands and committed the code to the remote repository. after the commit was pushed, Travis automatically started the build process, which included restoring the dependencies, running the xUnit tests, and building the source code. In the process of achieving a successful build, you configured ASC.Solution to not include default content items and fixed the broken xUnit tests.

507

You updated the README.md file on the Dev branch of GitHub's AutomobileServiceCenter.Core repository to include the markdown that will display the latest build status from Travis. Finally, you updated .travis.yml to include e-mail addresses of all stakeholders who need to receive notifications on successful or failed builds.

References

1. https://git-scm.com/

2. www.visualstudio.com/en-us/docs/git/overview

CHAPTER 14

∎∎∎

Preparing an Application for Production and Creating a Docker Image

The *build* and *deployment* are two crucial phases in the software development life cycle. In these phases, the product is released not only to different stakeholders for evaluation, but also to the market, where customers can adopt and use the product. Even though the terms *build* and *deployment* are often used interchangeably, they are quite different. The *build* is the process of compiling the source code and associated artifacts, thereby generating deployment-ready packages. *Deployment* is the process of copying the package that was generated by the build to the server (or any targeted machine) and making it available for customers or stakeholders.

In the preceding chapter, we explored build concepts through Travis CI integration, and you became familiar with how to trigger automated builds for our Automobile Service Center application. In this chapter, we'll focus on the deployment strategy for our application. There are many ways to deploy an application to servers; for example, we could use modern continuous integration services from hosted providers such as Travis CI, or we could integrate source version-control repositories such as GitHub directly with Azure Cloud.

A typical problem faced during most deployments is packaging both the application and environment dependencies and making sure they are available on the targeted server. A successful deployment strategy should ensure that the targeted server is equipped with all the necessary dependencies and artifacts so that the application works seamlessly, just as it did on the developer's machine. In these scenarios, we can use container technology to plan a deployment strategy to ensure that all the required environmental dependencies (such as runtimes and tools) are packaged along with the compiled code and shipped to the server in small, executable units called *containers*. On the server, the containers are isolated from other software and run independently by using container technology.

In a way, containers abstract the application from the operating system and infrastructure. Even though containers are similar to virtual machines, there are significant differences. The major difference is that containers share the same kernel from the host machine, whereas virtual machines have kernels of their own. The key advantages of container technology are as follows:

- Containers are isolated units, so the crashing of one container will not impact other containers on the same server.

- Containers are lightweight compared to virtual machines.

- Creating and deploying a new container is quick, which provides more horizontal scalability on higher loads.

© Rami Vemula 2017

R. Vemula, *Real-Time Web Application Development*, https://doi.org/10.1007/978-1-4842-3270-5_14

- Containers are less intensive than virtual machines, so more containers can be provisioned on the same server.

- Containers are more reliable in delivering stable applications because they can package all dependencies of the application.

- They are cost-effective.

- Containers improve development team productivity because they remove the operational overhead of environment inconsistencies.

In this chapter, we will use the Docker container platform to build, ship, and run the Automobile Service Center application on a server. You will first learn about Docker and its associated concepts (including Docker images and Docker Hub). Then we will build and test a Docker image for the Automobile Service Center source code.

Exploring Docker

Docker is an open source container technology platform promoted by the Docker company. It provides isolation, abstraction, and automation to software applications by using virtualization concepts on Linux and Windows operating systems. In short, Docker isolates the applications from infrastructure and host operating systems. When an application is "Dockerized," all the required libraries, dependencies, environment runtimes, and configuration files are packaged into a container. Docker containers can be taken to any Dockerized environment and can run seamlessly without users worrying about installation of any prerequisites. Because containers are lightweight and don't require a hypervisor (which is required for VMs), we can run more containers on a given host machine.

Docker uses a client/server architecture, as shown in Figure 14-1. The Docker client is the primary system where users interact with Docker through commands. The Docker client talks to the Docker daemon, which does the heavy lifting of building, running, and distributing the Docker containers. The Docker client and daemon can run on the same system, or a Docker client can connect to a remote Docker daemon. When the Docker client sends a docker pull command to the daemon, the Docker daemon interacts with a Docker registry to fetch the required Docker images. Similarly, when we use the docker push command, the Docker daemon will save the image to a Docker registry. Docker Hub is a publicly available Docker registry and is the default option configured for Docker images. Docker Cloud is one more such registry.

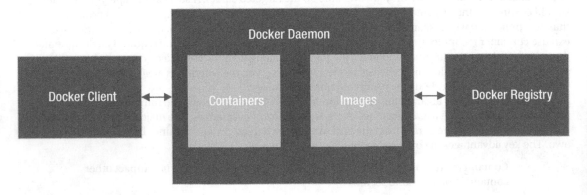

Figure 14-1. Docker architecture

A *Docker image* is a read-only template with instructions for creating a Docker container. We can use an existing Docker image or create a new one from an already existing Docker image by using a Dockerfile. When we change the Dockerfile and rebuild the image, only those layers that have changed are rebuilt, making the images lightweight, small, and fast when compared to other virtualization technologies.

A *Docker container* is a runnable instance of an image. Docker commands can be used to manage containers. A Docker container can connect to one or more networks, can have storage attached to it, and can be used to create a new Docker image based on the container's state.

Docker Swarm provide cluster management and orchestration features that are required to manage multiple Docker engines in a cluster. This feature is used to provide high scalability and reliable service through Docker integration.

■ **Note**   Docker Swarm is beyond the scope of this book.

Installing Docker and Reviewing Prerequisites

In this section, we will install Docker for Windows. Docker for Windows should be installed to configure a Docker development environment on Windows 10 and on Windows Server 2016 (at the time of writing this chapter, Docker supports only these two Windows OS variants). We can develop both Linux and Windows containers by using Docker for Windows.

■ **Note**   Before we proceed with installation, read the installation requirements at `https://docs.docker.com/docker-for-windows/install/#what-to-know-before-you-install`. (My machine meets the requirements; I am using Windows 10 Enterprise, 64-bit, Build 10586).

Download a stable version of Docker for Windows from `https://docs.docker.com/docker-for-windows/install/`, as shown in Figure 14-2.

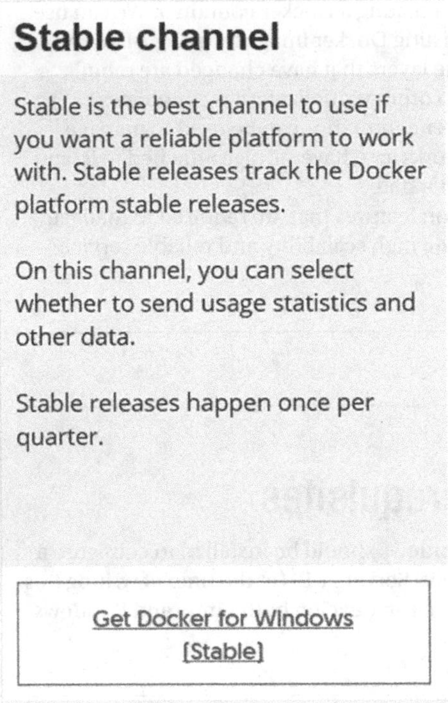

Stable channel

Stable is the best channel to use if you want a reliable platform to work with. Stable releases track the Docker platform stable releases.

On this channel, you can select whether to send usage statistics and other data.

Stable releases happen once per quarter.

Get Docker for Windows
[Stable]

Figure 14-2. *Downloading Docker installation for Windows*

Before installation, make sure Hyper-V is enabled on your machine, as shown in Figure 14-3.

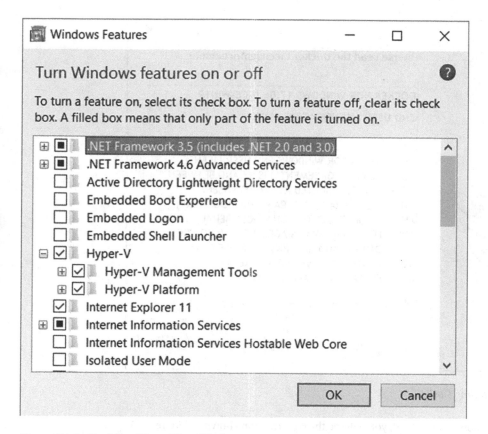

Figure 14-3. Enabling Hyper-V on Windows

■ **Note** If you have a development environment on Azure, you need to have nested virtualization enabled on your virtual machine to install Docker. Nested virtualization is supported in Azure from Dv3 or Ev3 virtual machines (`https://azure.microsoft.com/en-in/blog/nested-virtualization-in-azure/`).

Double-click the Docker installation file and intall it as shown in Figure 14-4.

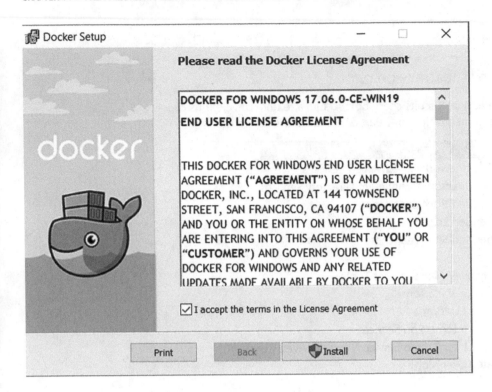

Figure 14-4. Installing Docker

Once installation is completed, you will see the confirmation shown in Figure 14-5.

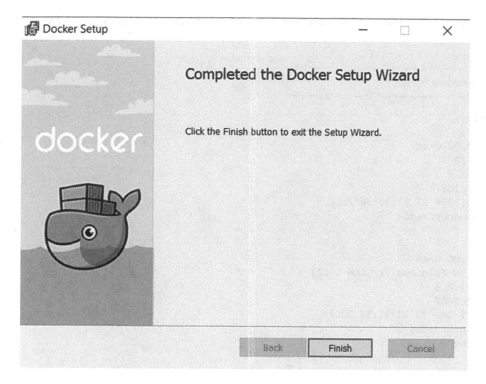

Figure 14-5. Docker installation confirmation

Restart the machine and then click the Docker shortcut that is created on the desktop as part of the installation. It might take some time for Docker to start. After it is started, a stable Docker tray icon appears, as shown in Figure 14-6.

Figure 14-6. Docker icon in the Windows tray

To make sure Docker is installed, open the command-line prompt and execute docker version, as shown in Figure 14-7.

■ Administrator: Command Prompt

```
C:\>docker version
Client:
 Version:       17.06.0-ce
 API version:   1.30
 Go version:    go1.8.3
 Git commit:    02c1d87
 Built:         Fri Jun 23 21:30:30 2017
 OS/Arch:       windows/amd64

Server:
 Version:       17.06.0-ce
 API version:   1.30 (minimum version 1.12)
 Go version:    go1.8.3
 Git commit:    02c1d87
 Built:         Fri Jun 23 21:51:55 2017
 OS/Arch:       linux/amd64
 Experimental: true

C:\>
```

Figure 14-7. *Docker version command*

Preparing the Application with an Azure Key Vault Configuration

In this section, we will prepare the Automobile Service Center application to have all its configuration details maintained at Azure Key Vault. This Azure-hosted service helps safeguard configuration data such as passwords and keys. The Automobile Service Center application is dependent on many configuration settings that are driven from the appsettings.json file. It is a security threat to have a production configuration defined in the physical appsettings.json file for the following reasons:

- The appsettings.json file version is controlled using GitHub; by having production settings in source version control, they are open to everyone and can be updated by mistake.

- The application's production configuration should be stored safely and securely in a centralized vault with limited user access.

- The production configuration should be updated and invalidated easily.

- Some of the configuration (for example, passwords) should not be stored in plain text.

■ **Note** To create a free Azure subscription, visit `https://azure.microsoft.com/en-us/`.

Set Up Azure Key Vault and Configure the Access Policy

We will start by creating an Azure Key Vault instance at the Azure portal, as shown in Figure 14-8.

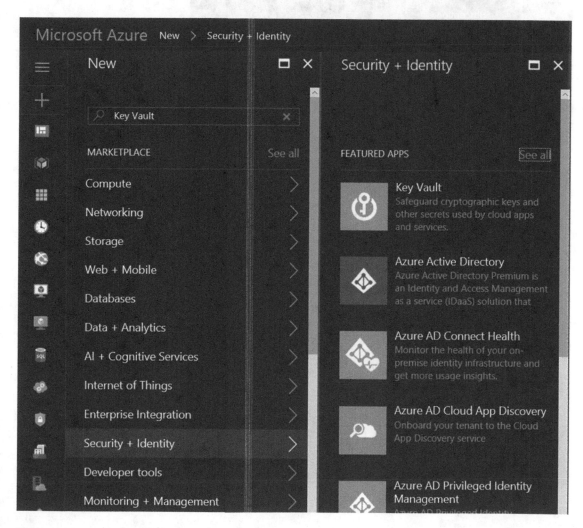

Figure 14-8. Azure Key Vault service

Select Key Vault to access the Create Key Vault dialog box, shown in Figure 14-9. Create a new instance by specifying the Name as ASCVault; set the Location to East US and the Resource Group name to ASC.

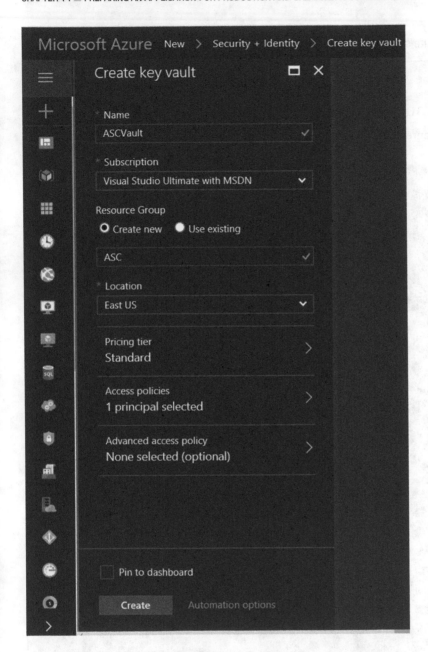

Figure 14-9. Creating a new Azure Key Vault service

■ **Note** The ASC resource group will be used to group all Automobile Service Center Azure resources. Later in the chapter, we are going to create Azure Storage and Azure Redis cache instances, and these are tied to the ASC resource group.

We can navigate to ASCVault from the Resource Groups tab. Select the ASC resource group and finally select ASCVault, as shown in Figure 14-10.

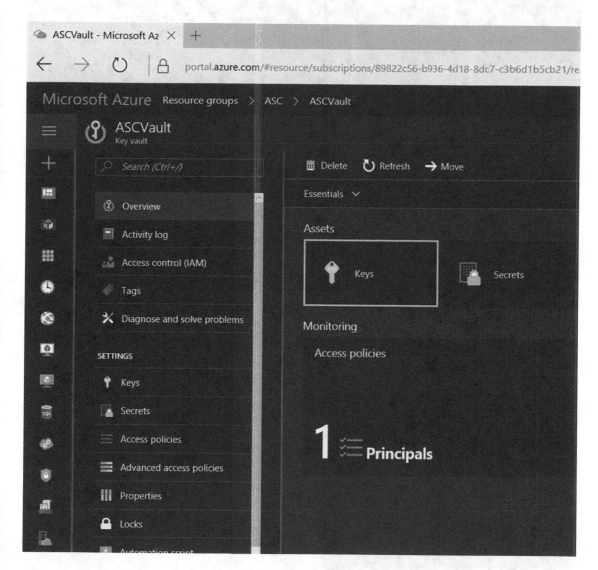

Figure 14-10. *Exploring the newly created Azure Key Vault instance*

To access Azure Key Vault from the Automobile Service Center application code, we need to first register the hosted ASC application. From Azure Active Directory, click App Registrations and then click New Application Registration, as shown in Figure 14-11.

Figure 14-11. *Application registration at the Azure portal*

In the Create dialog box that opens, enter the application details as shown in Figure 14-12. Then click Create.

Figure 14-12. *Creating a new application registration for the Automobile Service Center application*

■ **Note** Because we never hosted the application, we provide a random sign-on URL.

Now we need to generate security keys for the registered application. Using the keys, our application code can connect to Azure Key Vault and resolve the application settings. Navigate to the registered application and click Keys, as shown in Figure 14-13.

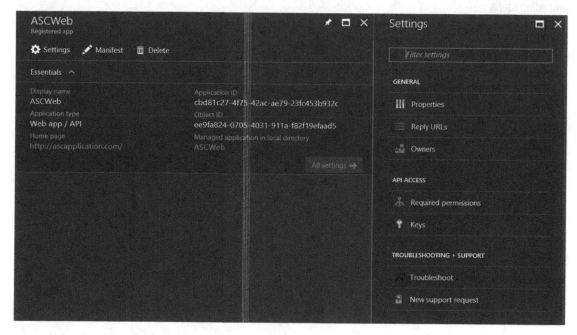

Figure 14-13. The Keys section of our registered application

Enter the Description as ASCKey and select a one-year expiration, as shown in Figure 14-14. Click Save. The key will be generated. Copy the key, so we can use it in our application code.

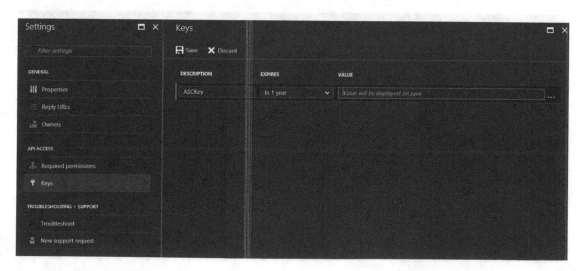

Figure 14-14. Creating a new key for the registered application

■ **Note**   Do not forgot to copy the key, because after you leave this page, you cannot retrieve the key again. If you lose a key or forget to copy it, you can delete the key and create a brand-new one by repeating the preceding steps.

The security key we created is listed in the Keys section, as shown in Figure 14-15.

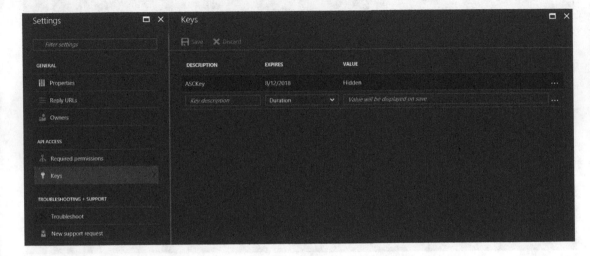

Figure 14-15. *List of security keys*

In addition to a security key, we also need an application ID. We can retrieve the application ID from the Overview section of the registered application, as shown in Figure 14-16.

Figure 14-16. *Registered application overview section*

Now that we have a registered application, we need to configure ASCVault with the registered ASCWeb application as a principle for authentication. This step is required to grant access for the security key and application ID (of the registered application) to ASCVault.

Navigate to ASCVault and go to the Access Policies tab, as shown in Figure 14-17.

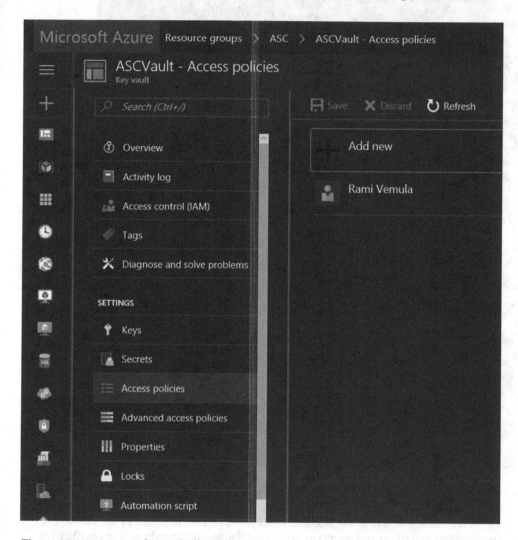

Figure 14-17. Access policies of ASCVault

Click Add New. Select the ASCWeb registered application from the options and then click the Select button, as shown in Figure 14-18.

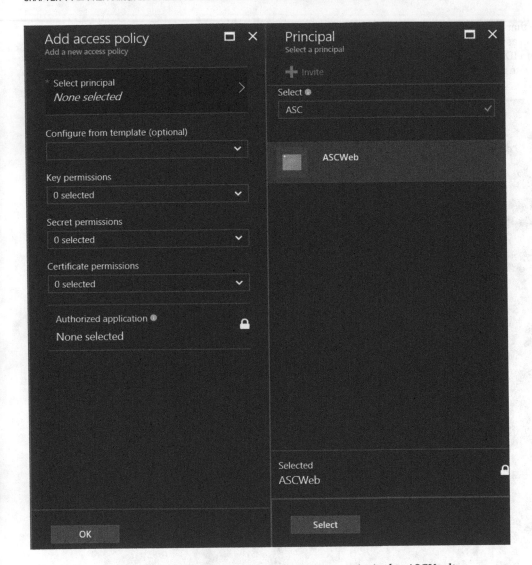

Figure 14-18. *Adding the ASCWeb registered application as a principal to ASCVault*

Select Key & Secret Management from the available templates, as shown in Figure 14-19. This will provide access permissions to the keys and secrets in Azure Vault for the configured application. Click OK.

Figure 14-19. *Setting key and secret permissions to the ASCWeb principal*

After the access policy is added, click Save.

Set Up Azure Table Storage and Azure Redis Cache Services

Now that we have created the Azure Key Vault instance, we need the following services and credentials to be configured at Azure Key Vault instead of in the appsettings.json file.

- Azure Table storage
- Azure Redis cache
- Google Identity—client ID and secret
- Twilio account
- SMTP credentials

■ **Note** We will use SMTP credentials and Twilio account details, which we created in Chapter 6 and Chapter 11, respectively.

For Google Identity, we will follow the instructions listed in Chapter 6 and create a different client ID and client secret for the production host's IP address. (For now, use localhost as one of the redirected URIs because we do not know the production details yet. When we host the application in Linux Ubuntu Azure Virtual Machine in Chapter 15, we will take that IP and configure it back at Google Identity.).

We can also make other application settings such as Admin credentials as part of the Azure Key Vault configuration.

Let's start by creating a new Azure Table storage service, as shown in Figure 14-20.

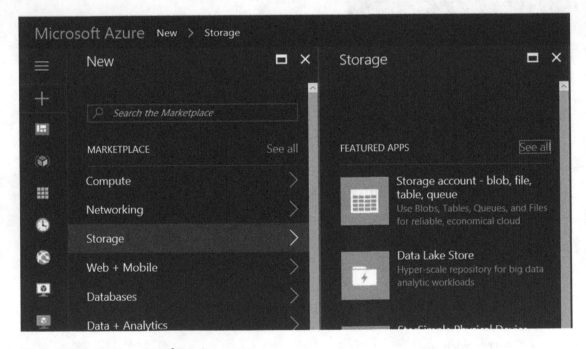

Figure 14-20. *Provisioning of new Azure storage*

Enter the name and other details, as shown in Figure 14-21, and click Create to create a new storage service.

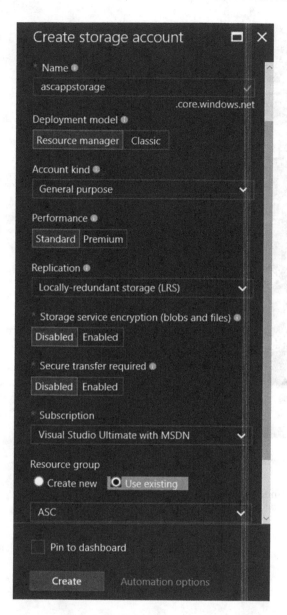

Figure 14-21. Entering details for new Azure storage

Once the new service is created, we can go to the Access keys tab of the created storage and find the connection string.

Now we will create an Azure Redis Cache instance, as shown in Figure 14-22.

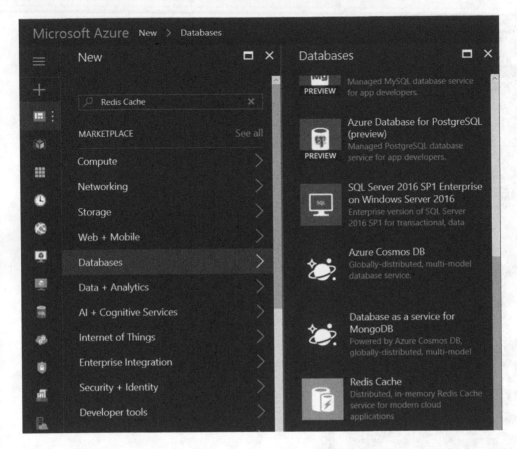

Figure 14-22. *Provisioning of new Azure Redis Cache instance*

Select Redis Cache. Then enter ASCCache as the Name, ASC as the Resource Group, and opt to unblock port 6379, as shown in Figure 14-23. Click Create.

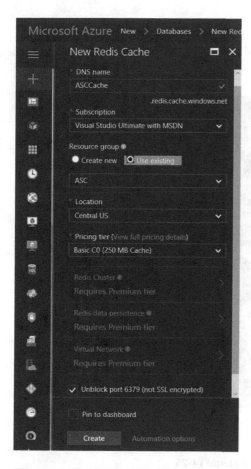

Figure 14-23. *Entering details for the new Azure Redis Cache instance*

Once the instance is created, we can go to the Access keys tab of the created Redis cache and find the connection string.

■ **Note**   There is a known issue of getting a DNS resolution exception when trying to connect to Azure Redis Cache from a Linux environment. The workaround involves configuring Azure Redis Service to unblock port 6379 (not SSL encrypted).

The ConnectionString should include resolveDns=true, as shown here:

sample.redis.cache.windows.net:6379,password=[Encrypted password],ssl=False,abortConnect= False,resolveDns=true

---

Create Secrets at Azure Key Vault

As the last step in securing application settings, we will create all secrets in Azure Key Vault, as shown in Figure 14-24.

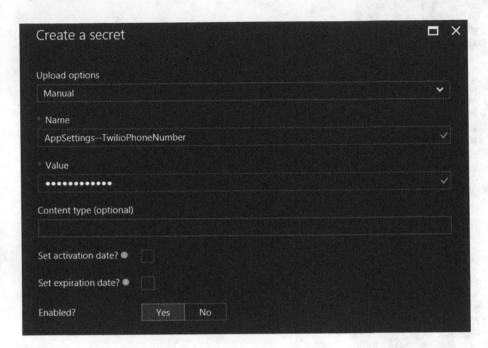

Figure 14-24. *Adding a new secret in Azure Key Vault*

The created secrets are listed in the Secrets tab, as shown in Figure 14-25.

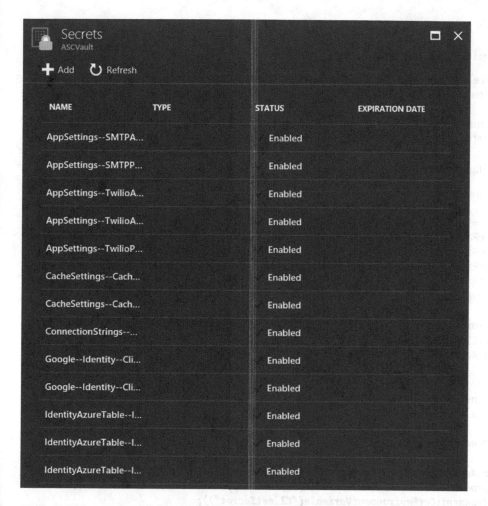

Figure 14-25. Listing of secrets that are created at Azure Key Vault

---

■ **Note**   The keys of nested section settings should be created by using the -- separator.

Integrate Application Code with Azure Key Vault

Now we have to make changes to the Automobile Service Center application code in order to read the configuration from Azure Key Vault. First, we need to add a reference of the Microsoft.Extensions. Configuration.AzureKeyVault NuGet package to the ASC.Web Project.

■ **Note**   We need to add the NewtonsoftJson NuGet package to the ASC.Web project to get Azure Key Vault working in the ASP.NET Core application.

Add the NuGet packages to the ASC.Web.csproj file, as shown in Listing 14-1.

Listing 14-1. Nuget package references

```
<PackageReference Include="Newtonsoft.Json" Version="10.0.2" />
    <PackageReference Include="Microsoft.Extensions.Configuration.AzureKeyVault" Version="1.0.0" />
```

Update the constructor of the Startup class, as shown in Listing 14-2. We will read the vault URL, client ID, and client secret of the Azure Key Vault from the environment variables.

Listing 14-2. Configure Azure Key Vault in Startup class

```
public Startup(IHostingEnvironment env)
{
    var builder = new ConfigurationBuilder()
        .SetBasePath(env.ContentRootPath)
        .AddJsonFile("appsettings.json", optional: false, reloadOnChange: true)
        .AddJsonFile($"appsettings.{env.EnvironmentName}.json", optional: true);

    if (env.IsDevelopment())
    {
        // For more details on using the user secret store see https://go.microsoft.com/
        fwlink/?LinkID=532709
        builder.AddUserSecrets<Startup>();
    }

    builder.AddEnvironmentVariables();
    Configuration = builder.Build();

    if (env.IsProduction())
    {
        builder.AddAzureKeyVault(Environment.GetEnvironmentVariable("VaultUrl"),
            Environment.GetEnvironmentVariable("ClientId"),
            Environment.GetEnvironmentVariable("ClientSecret"));
        Configuration = builder.Build();
    }
}
```

We will add the environment variables in the Debug tab of Project Properties in Visual Studio, as shown in Figure 14-26.

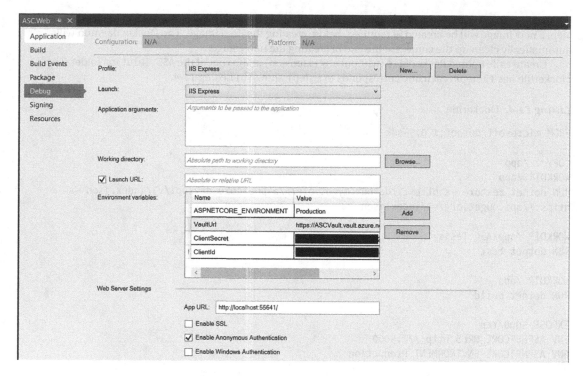

Figure 14-26. *Adding environment variables in the Debug configuration of the ASC.Web project*

▓ **Note** We maintain the environment variables in debug mode of Visual Studio Project in order to simulate a production environment while running the project on a local machine. In production, we will set these values through the deployment configuration.

Run the application in local. The application should run smoothly based on the Azure Key Vault configuration.

Creating a Docker File

In this section, we will create a Docker file for the Automobile Service Center application. A *Dockerfile* is a text document with a set of commands that are executed to build a Docker image. To build a Docker image, we need a Dockerfile along with a context. A *context* is nothing but a set of files that get the required functionality from a Docker container. We use the `docker build` command to build an image from the Dockerfile; the actual building of the image will be done by a Docker daemon. A typical `docker build` command is shown in Listing 14-3. The period (`.`) gives the current directory as the context, and `-t ascapp` gives a name to the image.

Listing 14-3. Docker build command

```
docker build -t ascapp .
```

The Docker daemon runs the instructions in the Dockerfile in sequence, from top to bottom. At each step, a new image will be created, if required, before creating the final image. The Docker daemon will automatically clean up the context at the end of creating the new image.

Create a file named `Dockerfile` (without any extension) at the root of the `ASC.Solution` folder. The Dockerfile has 13 steps (each line corresponds to a step), shown in Listing 14-4.

Listing 14-4. Dockerfile

```
FROM microsoft/dotnet:1.0.5-sdk

COPY . /app
WORKDIR /app
RUN dotnet restore -s https://dotnet.myget.org/F/aspnetcore-dev/api/v3/index.json -s
https://api.nuget.org/v3/index.json

WORKDIR /app/ASC.Tests
RUN dotnet test

WORKDIR /app
RUN dotnet build

EXPOSE 5000/tcp
ENV ASPNETCORE_URLS http://*:5000
ENV ASPNETCORE_ENVIRONMENT Production

WORKDIR /app/ASC.Web
ENTRYPOINT dotnet run
```

The steps are as follows:

1. The Docker daemon fetches `microsoft/dotnet:1.0.5-sdk` from the Docker repository to serve as the base image for the Automobile Service Center application's Docker image. Microsoft manages public images at Docker Hub (`https://hub.docker.com/r/microsoft/dotnet/`) that can serve as base images for various requirements. The base image (microsoft/dotnet:1.0.5-sdk) that we are going to use will come with the preinstalled dotnet 1.0.5 SDK (the latest stable .NET Core SDK from Microsoft).

2. Copy all the current directory folders and files recursively from the host to the Docker container. In our case, this copies all the code artifacts to the `/app` directory.

3. WORKDIR sets the working directory for the subsequent commands. We set `/app` as the working directory, as we have all the code artifacts in that location.

4. Run `dotnet restore` to restore all the NuGet and MyGet package dependencies for all projects in the Automobile Service Center solution.

5. Change the working directory to `/app/ASC.Tests`. This is required to run xUnit test cases.

6. Execute the `dotnet test` command to run all the xUnit test cases that are found at the `ASC.Tests` project.

7. Change the working directory to `/app`. This is required to build the entire solution.

8. Execute the dotnet build command, which will build the entire solution.

9. The EXPOSE instruction is used to configure the Docker container to listen to a specific port. We specify port 5000.

10. We set the environment variable ASPNETCORE_URLS to http://*:5000, the port that the Kestrel server used to host the Automobile Service Center application inside the Docker container.

11. Set the ASPNETCORE_ENVIRONMENT environment variable to Production.

12. Change the working directory to /app/ASC.Web. This is required to run the application.

13. Configure the application to run by pointing the entry point to the dotnet run command.

To build the Docker image, open the command-line prompt and navigate to the root of the project. Execute the docker build command, as shown in Figure 14-27. This command will process all the steps, as shown in Figures 14-28 to 14-33.

```
C:\WINDOWS\system32\cmd.exe - docker build . -t ascapp

c:\ASC.Solution>docker build . -t ascapp
Sending build context to Docker daemon    26.9MB
Step 1/13 : FROM microsoft/dotnet:1.0.5-sdk
1.0.5-sdk: Pulling from microsoft/dotnet
ad74af05f5a2: Downloading [========>                           ]  8.649MB/52.61MB
2b032b8bbe8b: Downloading [======>                             ]  2.555MB/19.26MB
a9a5b35f6ead: Downloading [=================================>  ]  30.52MB/43.23MB
afe9e8b5d24a: Waiting
b98971848faf: Waiting
460bb64b8b7e: Waiting
```

Figure 14-27. Executing the docker build command

```
Step 1/13 : FROM microsoft/dotnet:1.0.5-sdk
1.0.5-sdk: Pulling from microsoft/dotnet
ad74af05f5a2: Pull complete
2b032b8bbe8b: Pull complete
a9a5b35f6ead: Pull complete
afe9e8b5d24a: Pull complete
b98971848faf: Pull complete
460bb64b8b7e: Pull complete
Digest: sha256:9f37dc8bde185246bf70dd4eafd1e7971b29eab236bbc14e7e3f3c825ba8cd94
Status: Downloaded newer image for microsoft/dotnet:1.0.5-sdk
 ---> 96085c6f5594
```

Figure 14-28. Output status of step 1

535

```
Step 2/13 : COPY . /app
 ---> 68b11cf3624b
Removing intermediate container ca66e7367625
Step 3/13 : WORKDIR /app
 ---> 227a2c9fbbd5
Removing intermediate container c46c69eac9c3
Step 4/13 : RUN dotnet restore -s https://dotnet.myget.org/F/aspnetcore-dev/api/v3/index.json -s https://api.nuget.org/v3/index.json
 ---> Running in 2839233ed56c
  Restoring packages for /app/ACS.DataAccess/ASC.DataAccess.csproj...
  Restoring packages for /app/ACS.Models/ASC.Models.csproj...
  Installing Microsoft.Data.Edm 5.8.2.
  Installing Microsoft.Data.OData 5.8.2.
  Installing System.Spatial 5.8.2.
  Installing WindowsAzure.Storage 8.1.1.
  Generating MSBuild file /app/ACS.Models/obj/ASC.Models.csproj.nuget.g.props.
  Writing lock file to disk. Path: /app/ACS.Models/obj/project.assets.json
  Restore completed in 16.99 sec for /app/ACS.Models/ASC.Models.csproj.
  Restoring packages for /app/ACS.Utilities/ASC.Utilities.csproj...
  Installing Microsoft.DotNet.PlatformAbstractions 1.1.1.
  Installing Microsoft.Net.Http.Headers 1.1.1.
  Installing Microsoft.AspNetCore.Razor 1.1.1.
  Installing Microsoft.AspNetCore.WebUtilities 1.1.1.
```

Figure 14-29. *Output status of steps 2 to 4*

```
Installing Microsoft.Extensions.CommandLineUtils 1.0.1.
Installing NuGet.Frameworks 3.5.0.
Installing Microsoft.VisualStudio.Web.CodeGeneration.Tools 1.0.0.
Restore completed in 9.35 sec for /app/ASC.Web/ASC.Web.csproj.

NuGet Config files used:
    /root/.nuget/NuGet/NuGet.Config

Feeds used:
    https://dotnet.myget.org/F/aspnetcore-dev/api/v3/index.json
    https://api.nuget.org/v3/index.json

Installed:
    4 package(s) to /app/ACS.Models/ASC.Models.csproj
    49 package(s) to /app/ACS.DataAccess/ASC.DataAccess.csproj
    45 package(s) to /app/ACS.Utilities/ASC.Utilities.csproj
    49 package(s) to /app/ASC.Business/ASC.Business.csproj
    175 package(s) to /app/ASC.Web/ASC.Web.csproj
    149 package(s) to /app/ASC.Tests/ASC.Tests.csproj
 ---> bbbc028938da
Removing intermediate container 2839233ed56c
```

Figure 14-30. *Completion status of step 4*

```
Step 5/13 : WORKDIR /app/ASC.Tests
 ---> 3064798a3f3c
Removing intermediate container 8b3f83ccd484
Step 6/13 : RUN dotnet test
 ---> Running in 049f2502bbef
Build started, please wait...
UnitOfWork.cs(12,22): warning CS0169: The field 'UnitOfWork.disposed' is never used [/a
Filters/CustomExceptionFilter.cs(21,36): warning CS1998: This async method lacks 'await
.Run(...)' to do CPU-bound work on a background thread. [/app/ASC.Web/ASC.Web.csproj]
Controllers/HomeController.cs(60,17): warning CS0162: Unreachable code detected [/app/A
Build completed.

Test run for /app/ASC.Tests/bin/Debug/netcoreapp1.1/ASC.Tests.dll(.NETCoreApp,Version=\
Microsoft (R) Test Execution Command Line Tool Version 15.0.0.0
Copyright (c) Microsoft Corporation.  All rights reserved.

Starting test execution, please wait...
[xUnit.net 00:00:01.8410488]   Discovering: ASC.Tests
[xUnit.net 00:00:02.0299963]   Discovered:  ASC.Tests
[xUnit.net 00:00:02.0525007]   Starting:    ASC.Tests
[xUnit.net 00:00:02.8481968]   Finished:    ASC.Tests

Total tests: 4. Passed: 4. Failed: 0. Skipped: 0.
Test Run Successful.
Test execution time: 5.0963 Seconds


 ---> 5e3ba0cdc7ad
Removing intermediate container 049f2502bbef
Step 7/13 : WORKDIR /app
 ---> 13f925da485f
Removing intermediate container f91ba6a8e213
```

Figure 14-31. *Output status of steps 5 to 7*

```
Step 8/13 : RUN dotnet build
 ---> Running in 0a9c3ef19c11
Microsoft (R) Build Engine version 15.1.1012.6693
Copyright (C) Microsoft Corporation. All rights reserved.

  ASC.Models -> /app/ACS.Models/bin/Debug/netcoreapp1.1/ASC.Models.dll
  ASC.Utilities -> /app/ACS.Utilities/bin/Debug/netcoreapp1.1/ASC.Utilities.dll
  ASC.DataAccess -> /app/ACS.DataAccess/bin/Debug/netcoreapp1.1/ASC.DataAccess.dll
  ASC.Business -> /app/ASC.Business/bin/Debug/netcoreapp1.1/ASC.Business.dll
  ASC.Web -> /app/ASC.Web/bin/Debug/netcoreapp1.1/ASC.Web.dll
  Bundling with configuration from /app/ASC.Web/bundleconfig.json
  Deleted wwwroot/css/site.min.css
  Deleted wwwroot/js/jqueryBundle.min.js
  Deleted wwwroot/js/libraryBundle.min.js
  Deleted wwwroot/js/appBundle.min.js
  Bundling with configuration from /app/ASC.Web/bundleconfig.json
  Processing wwwroot/css/site.min.css
    Minified
  Processing wwwroot/js/jqueryBundle.min.js
    Minified
  Processing wwwroot/js/libraryBundle.min.js
    Minified
  Processing wwwroot/js/appBundle.min.js
    Minified
  ASC.Tests -> /app/ASC.Tests/bin/Debug/netcoreapp1.1/ASC.Tests.dll

Build succeeded.
    0 Warning(s)
    0 Error(s)

Time Elapsed 00:00:25.34
 ---> 7ab1087def24
Removing intermediate container 0a9c3ef19c11
Step 9/13 : EXPOSE 5000/tcp
 ---> Running in 2855836b3028
 ---> 93a81d63fc2a
Removing intermediate container 2855836b3028
Step 10/13 : ENV ASPNETCORE_URLS http://*:5000
 ---> Running in 3653c72a8f64
 ---> b6c0b5e04534
Removing intermediate container 3653c72a8f64
Step 11/13 : ENV ASPNETCORE_ENVIRONMENT Production
 ---> Running in 5b392dad43c9
 ---> f44acf1f8f9f
Removing intermediate container 5b392dad43c9
```

Figure 14-32. Output status of steps 8 to 11

```
Step 12/13 : WORKDIR /app/ASC.Web
 ---> b94a8d840788
Removing intermediate container d6cee6ce86d9
Step 13/13 : ENTRYPOINT dotnet run
 ---> Running in 0d9b8c3448ac
 ---> 8c41436cd7bc
Removing intermediate container 0d9b8c3448ac
Successfully built 8c41436cd7bc
Successfully tagged ascapp:latest
SECURITY WARNING: You are building a Docker image from Windows against a non-Windows Docker host.
 check and reset permissions for sensitive files and directories.

c:\ASC.Solution>
```

Figure 14-33. *Output status of steps 12 to 13*

We can check the created Docker image by running the docker images command, as shown in Figure 14-34.

```
C:\WINDOWS\system32\cmd.exe

c:\ASC.Solution>docker images
REPOSITORY           TAG              IMAGE ID          CREATED           SIZE
ascapp               latest           8c41436cd7bc      About an hour ago 1.21GB
microsoft/dotnet     1.0.5-sdk        96085c6f5594      14 hours ago      883MB

c:\ASC.Solution>
```

Figure 14-34. *Created Docker image*

To create a container (on a local machine and test the Docker image) out of the Docker image and run the application, we should execute the docker run command, as shown in Listing 14-5. -p 55641:5000 is used to bind port 55641 of the host machine with the exposed port 5000 of the Docker container. -e is used to set the environment variables. We need to set the Azure Key Vault URL, client ID, and client secret to the Automobile Service Center application to retrieve all the secrets (such as connection strings and Redis configuration) from Azure Key Vault. The last parameter of the docker run command is the docker image name that should be used to create the container. Run the command as shown in Figure 14-35.

Listing 14-5. Docker run command

```
docker run -p 55641:5000 -e "ClientSecret=[Your app Secret]" -e "ClientId=[Your app Id]" -e
"ASPNETCORE_ENVIRONMENT=Production" -e "VaultUrl=https://[Vault Name].vault.azure.net/" ascapp
```

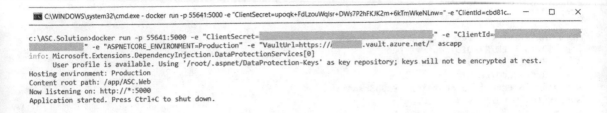

Figure 14-35. *The docker run command*

Now we can access the application via http://localhost:55641, as shown in Figure 14-36.

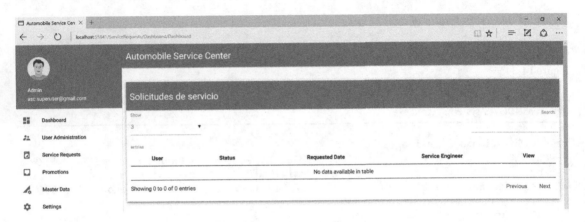

Figure 14-36. *The Automobile Service Center application running inside the Docker container*

To check the list of containers created, we can run the docker ps- a command, as shown in Figure 14-37.

```
c:\ASC.Solution>docker ps -a
CONTAINER ID       IMAGE          COMMAND                CREATED         STATUS          PORTS                      NAMES
6f602b6e8cbc       ascapp         "/bin/sh -c 'dotne..." 6 minutes ago   Up 6 minutes    0.0.0.0:55641->5000/tcp    tender_]
eavitt
```

Figure 14-37. *List of Docker containers*

To find out the Linux distro and version that is running the Docker container, we need to run the docker exec container_name cat /etc/os-release command, as shown in Figure 14-38.

```
c:\ASC.Solution>docker exec tender_leavitt cat /etc/os-release
PRETTY_NAME="Debian GNU/Linux 8 (jessie)"
NAME="Debian GNU/Linux"
VERSION_ID="8"
VERSION="8 (jessie)"
ID=debian
HOME_URL="http://www.debian.org/"
SUPPORT_URL="http://www.debian.org/support"
BUG_REPORT_URL="https://bugs.debian.org/"
```

Figure 14-38. *Checking the OS version of the Docker container*

Now we are running a Debian GNU/Linux 8 distro-based Docker container and hosting an ASP. NET Core–based Automobile Service Center application that is configured with Azure Key Vault secrets to connect with Azure Table storage and Azure Redis Cache.

Summary

You started this chapter by learning about the basic concepts of build and deployment in the software development life cycle. A build is the process of compiling the source code and generating a package, whereas deployment copies the build package to the hosted environment. You explored the traditional problem of environment inconsistencies across various machines, which can make an application unstable. Modern-day container technology solves the problem by packaging all the required environmental dependencies along with compiled code into small container units that are shipped to the targeted machine for deployment. You evaluated the potential advantages of containers over traditional VMs.

Docker is an open source container technology platform that provides isolation, abstraction, and automation for software applications from infrastructure and host operation systems. You learned about the client/server architecture of Docker, where a Docker client interacts with the Docker daemon, which does the heavy lifting of building, running, and distributing Docker containers. The Docker daemon interacts with the Docker registry (for example, Docker Hub) to pull and push various Docker images. A Docker image is a read-only template with instructions for creating a Docker container. A Docker container is a runnable instance of the environment with an application on it (based on the configuration specified in the Docker image). You installed Docker on a local machine to begin the containerization process of the Automobile Service Center application.

As the first step in preparing the Automobile Service Center application for production deployment, we moved all the configuration to Azure Key Vault. Otherwise, configuration details would be prone to security threats if stored in a physical configuration file such as appsettings.json. Azure Key Vault is a Microsoft Azure-hosted secure service that protects all the configuration data including passwords and connection strings. You then created the Azure Table storage, Azure Redis Cache instance, and Google Identity configuration and stored all the settings in Azure Key Vault. Later, the Automobile Service Center application code was upgraded to read the configuration from Azure Key Vault by installing the Microsoft. Extensions.Configuration.AzureKeyVault NuGet package and calling its AddAzureVault extension on ConfigurationBuilder in the constructor of the Startup class.

You created a Dockerfile that uses `microsoft:dotnet:1.0.5-sdk` as the base image and creates a Docker image for the Automobile Service Center application. The Dockerfile will restore, test, build, and run the Automobile Service Center application. You built the Docker image by using the `docker build` command. Finally, you ran the Docker image by using the `docker run` command and passing the Azure Key Vault's URL, client ID, and client secret as environment variables. You were able to access the Automobile Service Center application, which is hosted in a Debian GNU/Linux 8 distro-based Docker container and is configured with Azure Key Vault secrets to connect with Azure Table storage and Azure Redis Cache.

Reference

1. https://docs.docker.com/

CHAPTER 15

■ ■ ■

Continuous Deployment to Azure Linux Virtual Machines by Using Docker Cloud

Deployment, a crucial phase in the software development life cycle, is considered almost the last step in the process of making software available to end customers and stakeholders. The process of deployment has evolved and matured over the last decade, with the invention of sophisticated automated tools and platforms. Today's deployment technologies not only provide reliable automation techniques but also improve overall system performance by reducing build/deployment time with minimal resource consumption. Some of the key advantages of automated build systems are as follows:

- Reliable with less proximity to errors because of less manual intervention.

- One-click deployments are easy and simple to manage by any stakeholder in the project.

- Quite a few redundant tasks.

- Accurate and time-effective.

- Easy-to-manage multiple environment deployments.

- Effortless management of environment dependencies and prerequisites.

- Version history and logs for traceability.

- Quick dev builds and deployments, and an automated process of unit testing.

Continuous integration is the process of building and testing the source code whenever a commit happens in a source version-control system such as GitHub. *Continuous deployment* is the process of propagating successful build output to different environments such as test, staging, and production. Many continuous deployment platforms are available to automatically deploy the build to host machines that have continuous integration with a source version-control system. Travis CI, Circle CI, and Docker Cloud are some of the continuous deployment providers. The deployment strategy for the Automobile Service Center application includes building the latest source code from GitHub and creating Docker containers that are subsequently deployed to Azure-based Linux virtual machines.

In the preceding chapter, we prepared the Automobile Service Center application to easily cater to production deployments and explored the basic concepts of Docker containerization. We created a Dockerfile through which a Docker image was generated and ran it in a local environment to create a Docker container. We successfully ran the application in a Debian Linux-based container connected to Azure Storage.

© Rami Vemula 2017
R. Vemula, *Real-Time Web Application Development*, https://doi.org/10.1007/978-1-4842-3270-5_15

In this chapter, we will use Docker Cloud to build Docker images and containers on the fly, based on continuous integration with GitHub commits. The generated containers will be deployed to Linux-based Azure virtual machines through continuous deployment from Docker Cloud.

■ **Note**   This chapter is a continuation of the previous chapter. I advise you to go through Chapter 14 in order to understand the basic concepts of the Docker containerization process for the Automobile Service Center application.

Introduction to Docker Cloud

Docker Cloud is a service provided by the Docker platform that primarily helps orchestrate build and deployment pipelines. Docker Cloud provides services to create Docker images, generate Docker containers, deploy containers to different nodes, integrate security into an automation pipeline, and more. Its major services are as follows:

- *Continuous integration*: Build Docker images from the latest source code from various source version-control systems such as GitHub. Configure automated tests with notifications to monitor the quality of the build.

- *Cloud registry*: Create public or private repositories of images and configure automated builds for images.

- *Continuous deployment*: Set up automated deployments to host nodes by creating containers. Send notification when deployments succeed or fail.

- *Teams and organizations*: Create teams with different roles and responsibilities. Grant permissions to different users. Maintain separate projects for different teams.

- *Application deployment*: Link to cloud services such as AWS and Azure as infrastructure for deployments. We can bring our own host machines as well.

Docker orchestration for the Automobile Service Center application is shown in Figure 15-1. The developer commits the code to GitHub, which triggers the orchestration process. Docker Cloud will check out the code from the GitHub branch and autobuild the image and store it in the Docker repository. The Docker service kicks in immediately and generates the containers, and then finally autodeploys the containers to various nodes that are configured at Docker Cloud.

Figure 15-1. *Docker orchestration for the Automobile Service Center application*

Let's get started by creating a Docker cloud account. Visit `https://cloud.docker.com/`, as shown in Figure 15-2.

Figure 15-2. *Docker Cloud home page*

Upon successful sign-up, an activation link will be sent to the registered e-mail account, as shown in Figure 15-3.

Figure 15-3. *Docker Cloud activation e-mail*

Click the Confirm Your Email link and activate the account by signing into Docker Cloud, as shown in Figure 15-4.

Figure 15-4. *Successful login at Docker Cloud*

Turn off Swarm mode by toggling the Swarm Mode option (to the left of the Docker cloud logo, as shown in Figure 15-5). We won't be working with Docker Swarm in this book.

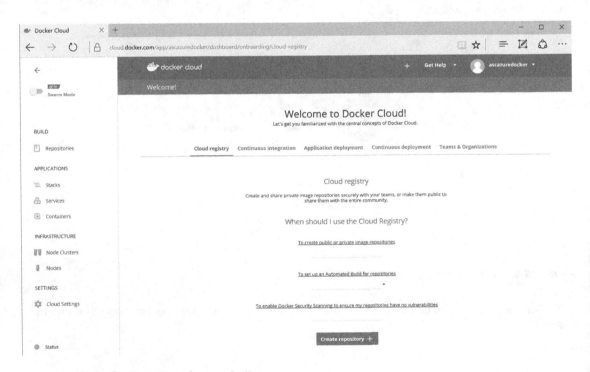

Figure 15-5. *Docker Swarm mode turned off*

Create Azure Nodes for Continuous Deployment

In this section, we will create an Azure virtual machine that will serve as a host machine for the Automobile Service Center application. First, we need to activate an Azure account at Docker Cloud. Go to the Cloud Settings tab, shown in Figure 15-6.

docker cloud
Cloud Settings
Cloud providers
Source providers

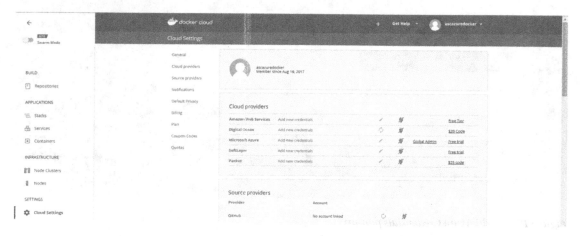

Figure 15-6. *Docker Cloud settings*

Click the Connect Provider option for Microsoft Azure, as shown in Figure 15-7.

Cloud providers
Amazon Web Services
Add new credentials
Free Tier
Digital Ocean
Add new credentials
Connect provider
$20 Code
Microsoft Azure
Add new credentials
Global Admin
Free trial
SoftLayer
Add new credentials
Free trial
Packet
Add new credentials
$25 code

Figure 15-7. *Connecting with the Microsoft Azure provider*

The Add Azure Credentials pop-up opens, as shown in Figure 15-8.

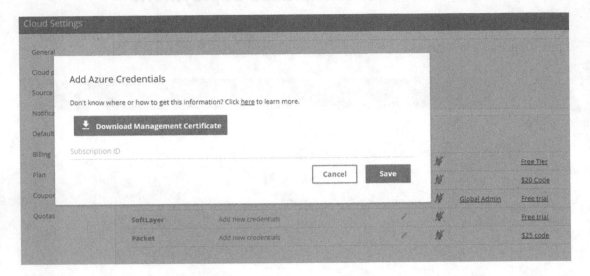

Figure 15-8. *Add Azure Credentials pop-up*

Click the Download Management Certification, which will download a certificate file. Log in to the Azure portal and upload the downloaded certificate under the Subscriptions tab, as shown in Figure 15-9.

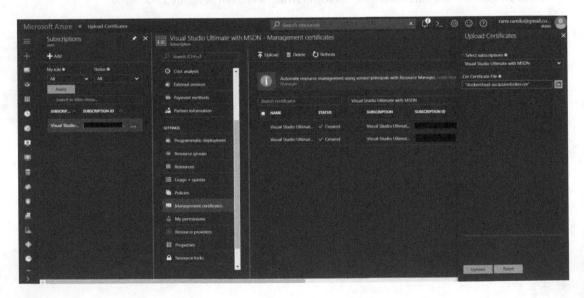

Figure 15-9. *Uploading the certificate to Azure Subscription Management Certificates*

Once uploaded, copy the Azure subscription ID and paste it in the Subscription ID field of the pop-up at the Docker portal, as shown in Figure 15-10.

Figure 15-10. *Azure subscription ID configuration at Docker Cloud*

Click Save. Upon a successful save, the Azure subscription is enabled at the Docker portal, as shown in Figure 15-11.

Cloud providers

Amazon Web Services	Add new credentials		✎	⚡	Free Tier
Digital Ocean	Add new credentials		↻	⚡	$20 Code
Microsoft Azure	▬▬▬▬▬▬▬▬▬▬		✎	⚡	Global Admin	Free trial
SoftLayer	Add new credentials		✎	⚡	Free trial
Packet	Add new credentials		✎	⚡	$25 code

Figure 15-11. *Azure connection enabled at Docker Cloud*

Now we will create Azure VM node, which can be used as a host machine to the Automobile Service Center application. Navigate to the Node Clusters tab, as shown in Figure 15-12.

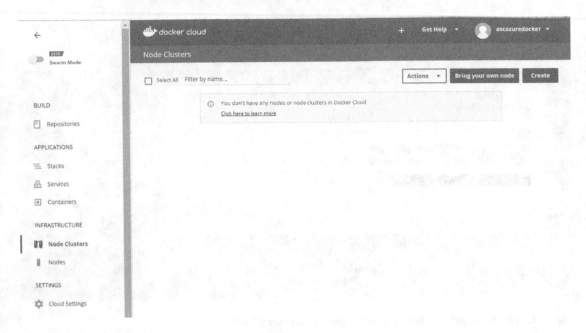

Figure 15-12. *Node Clusters tab at Docker Cloud*

Click the Create button to access the Node Clusters/Wizard page, shown in Figure 15-13, and to start creating a node at the Azure cloud. Type in the name of the cluster, set the Provider to Microsoft Azure, and set the Region to East Asia (or select any other region). We will create a Basic A0 virtual machine. Select the default size of 60GB and set the number of nodes to 1.

Figure 15-13. *Creating a new Node cluster at Docker Cloud with Azure as the infrastructure provider*

■ **Note**   Docker Cloud will prompt for payment information for additional nodes. In a free plan, we can set up only one managed node. For now, provision only one node.

Click the Launch Node Cluster button. Docker will start provisioning Azure nodes, as shown in Figure 15-14.

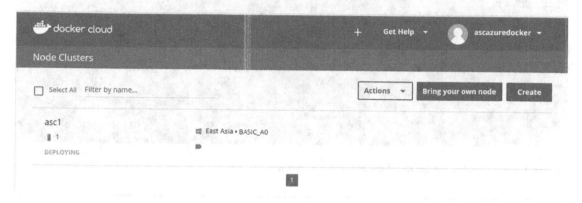

Figure 15-14. *Status of setting up a new Node cluster at Azure*

It will take some time to set up a node. After it is done, we will see a Deployed message, as shown in Figure 15-15. If we want to terminate this node, we click Terminate.

Figure 15-15. *Successful provision of new Node cluster at Azure*

If we visit the Azure portal, we should see the created virtual machine along with its cloud service and storage, as shown in Figure 15-16.

Figure 15-16. *Created virtual machine at the Azure portal*

■ **Note** By default, the virtual machines that are created through Docker Cloud do not have any credentials to access through SSH, so we will not be able to SSH into VM.

Docker Cloud Continuous Integration with GitHub Repository

In this section, we will configure Docker Cloud to connect with the Automobile Service Center source code that is versioned at GitHub. Go to the Cloud Settings tab in Docker Cloud and check the Source Providers section, as shown in Figure 15-17.

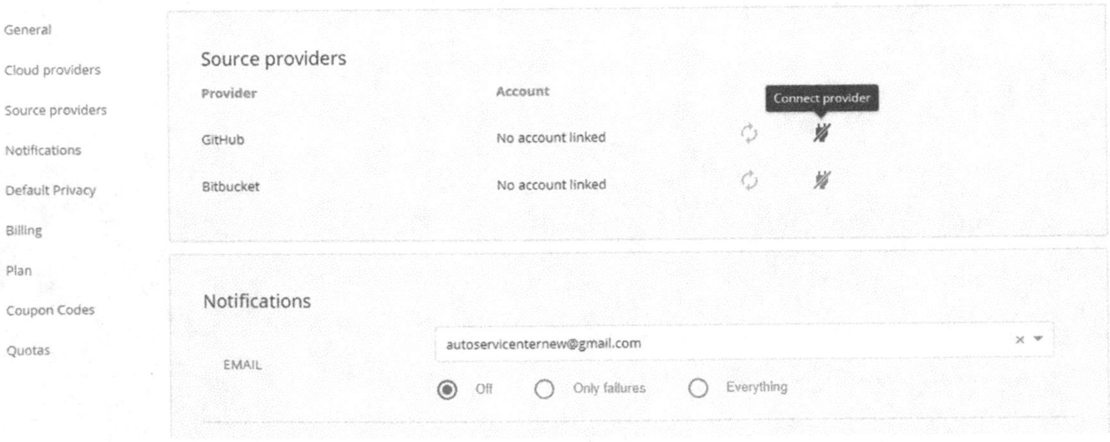

Figure 15-17. *Source providers at Docker Cloud settings*

Click the Connect Provider option. The GitHub login screen opens, as shown in Figure 15-18. Enter the credentials for the Automobile Service Center repository's owner and login.

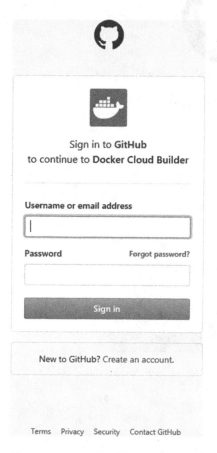

Figure 15-18. *GitHub login prompt for associating GitHub with Docker Cloud*

Upon successful login, an Authorize consent page will be displayed. Click the Authorize Docker button, shown in Figure 15-19.

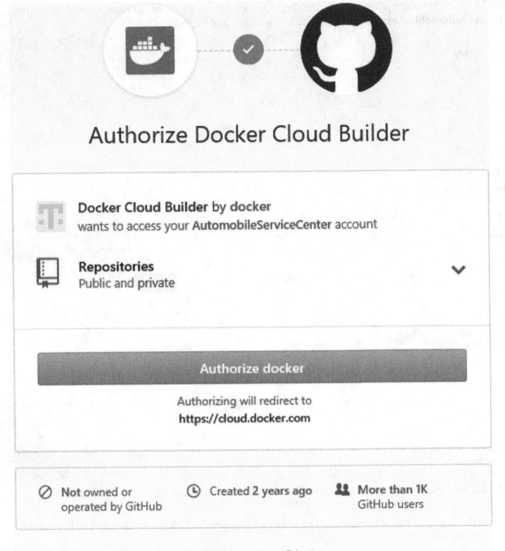

Figure 15-19. *Authorizing GitHub to allow access for Docker Cloud*

Upon successful authorization, we will see GitHub connected to Docker Cloud, as shown in Figure 15-20.

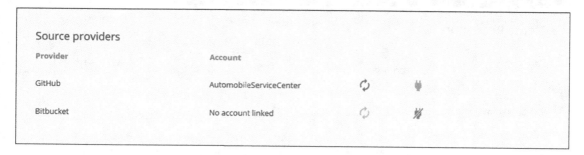

Figure 15-20. *GitHub associated with Docker Cloud*

Continuous Deployment to Azure Nodes from Docker Cloud

In previous sections, we created an Azure node to serve as a host machine, and integrated Docker Cloud with GitHub to fetch the latest source code of the Automobile Service Center application. In this section, we will build an image from the GitHub source code and hold it in the Docker repository. We will also build a Docker container from the created image and push it to the Azure node.

Let's start by creating a Docker repository. Navigate to the Repositories tab and click Create, as shown in Figure 15-21.

Figure 15-21. *Repositories tab at Docker Cloud*

Enter the name, description, and visibility of the image, as shown in Figure 15-22. Select the AutomobileServiceCenter.Core GitHub repository as the repository from which this image should be built. Click the Create button.

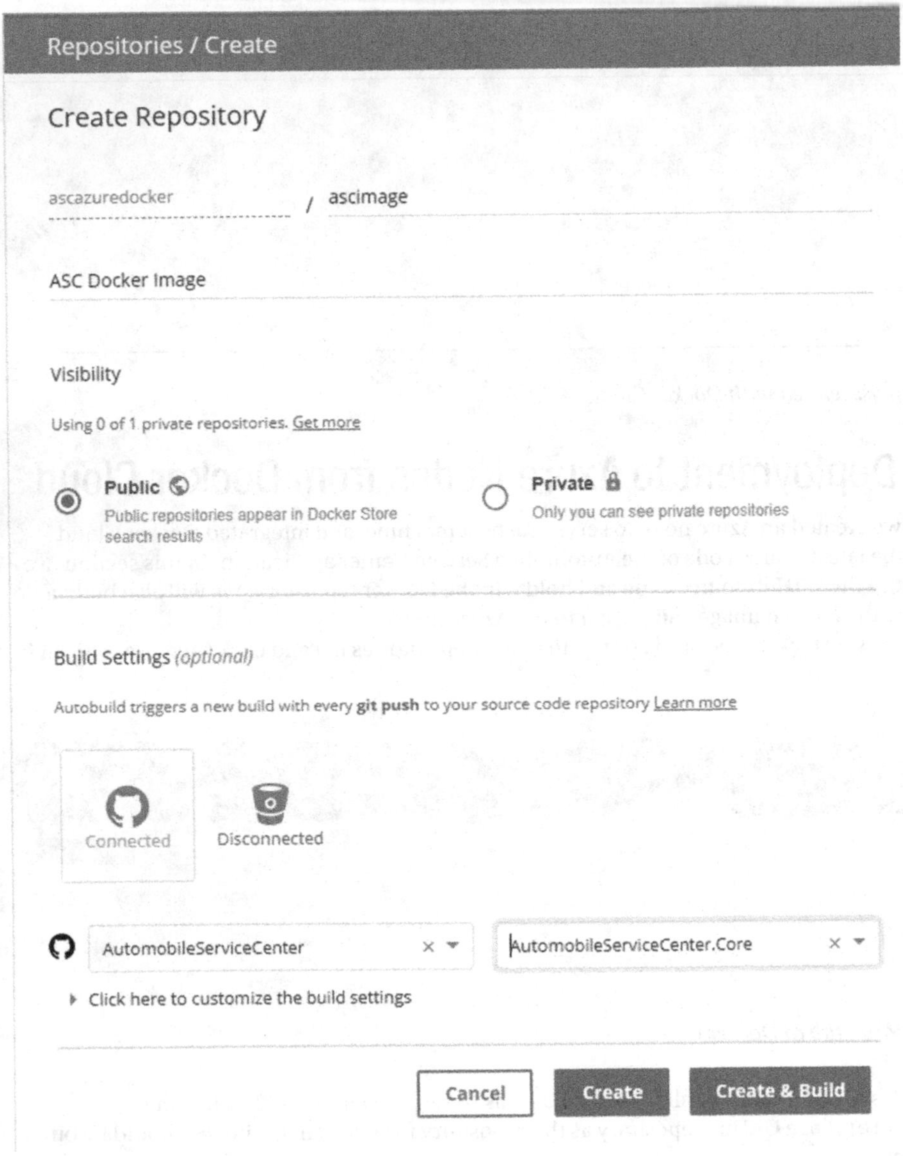

Repositories / Create

Create Repository

ascazuredocker / ascimage

ASC Docker Image

Visibility

Using 0 of 1 private repositories. Get more

◉ **Public** 🌐
Public repositories appear in Docker Store search results

○ **Private** 🔒
Only you can see private repositories

Build Settings *(optional)*

Autobuild triggers a new build with every **git push** to your source code repository Learn more

[Connected]   [Disconnected]

AutomobileServiceCenter   × ▾   AutomobileServiceCenter.Core   × ▾

▸ Click here to customize the build settings

[Cancel]   [**Create**]   [**Create & Build**]

Figure 15-22. *New Docker repository details*

Now we will configure an automated image build on every GitHub repository commit or push. Navigate to the Builds tab of the created ascimage Docker repository, as shown in Figure 15-23.

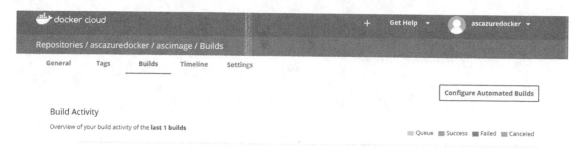

Figure 15-23. *Build tab of the Docker repository*

Click the Configure Automated Builds button. Select the Build On My Own Nodes option. Make sure to select the master branch as the source, set the Build Context to a period (.), and turn on Autobuild. Turn off Build Caching, which is enabled by default. Enter all the environment variables that the Automobile Service Center application is dependent on—ClientSecret, ClientId, ASPNETCORE_ENVIRONMENT, and VaultUrl—as shown in Figure 15-24. The environment variable configuration is required for the application to fetch all the configuration information from Azure Key Vault. Click Save.

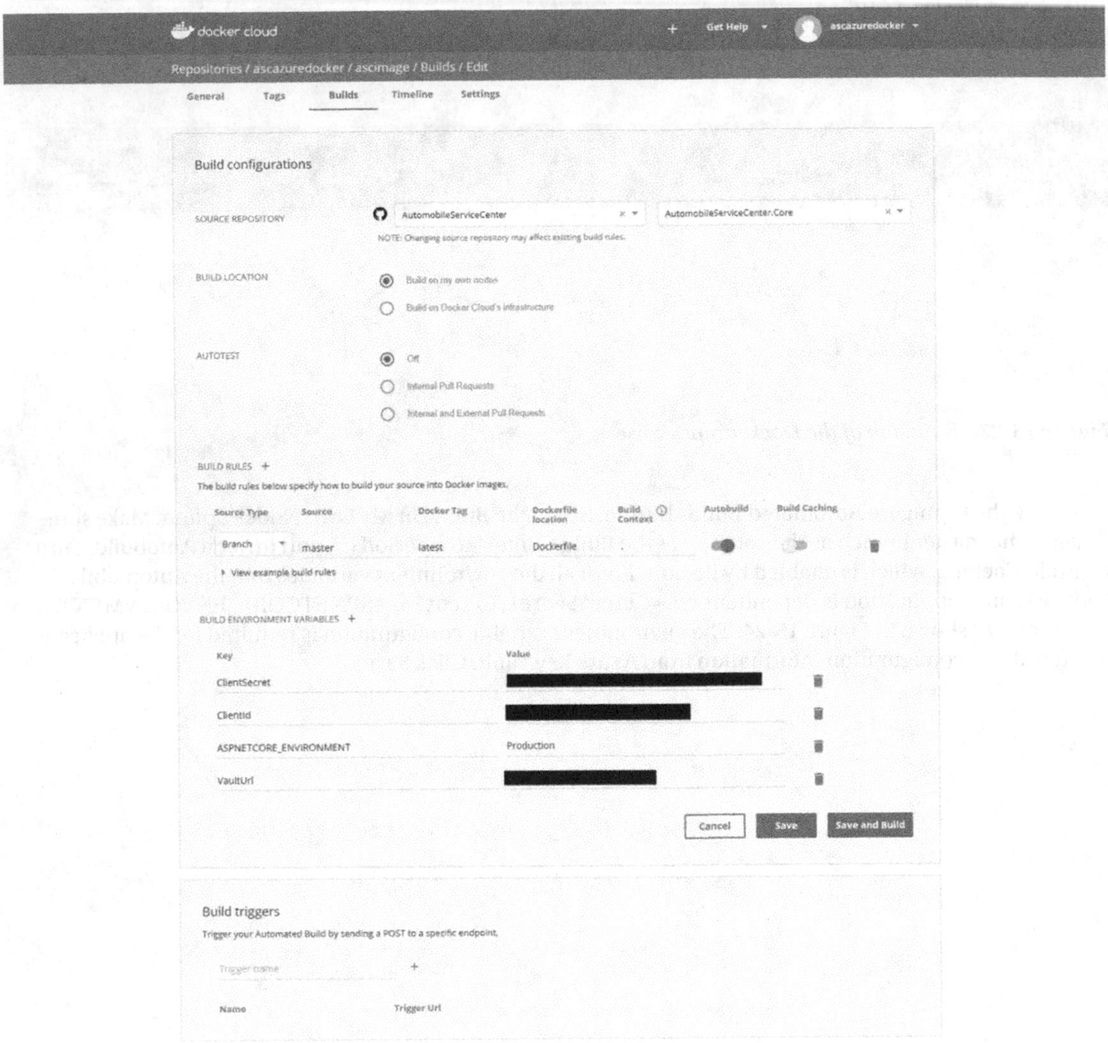

Figure 15-24. Automatic builds for the Docker repository

At this logical point, we can test the build process. Merge the `AutomobileServiceCenter.Core` repository's dev branch with the master branch at GitHub, and it should trigger a Docker build, as shown in Figure 15-25.

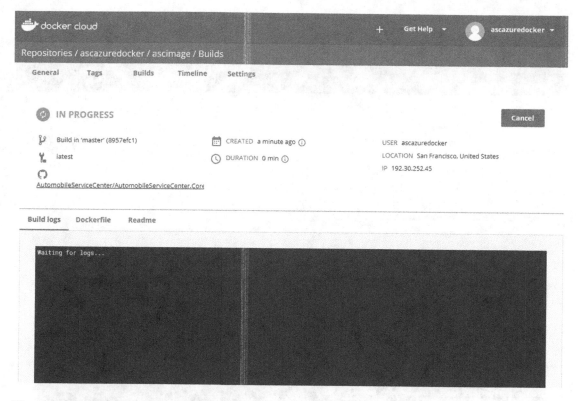

Figure 15-25. Build in progress at Docker Cloud that is triggered by a GitHub commit

Once the build starts, we will have intermediate status, as shown in Figure 15-26.

Figure 15-26. *Intermediate Docker repository build status*

And once it is completed, we have the status shown in Figure 15-27.

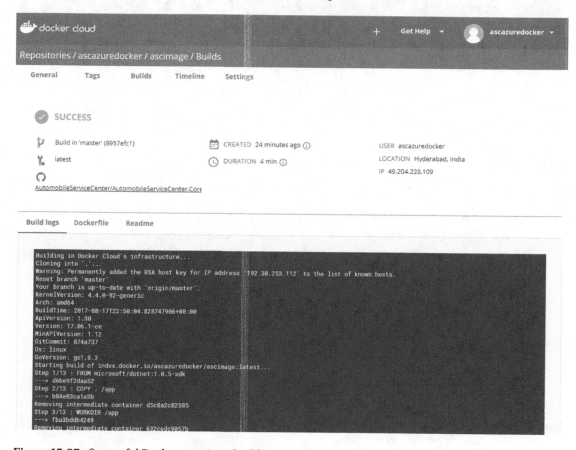

Figure 15-27. Successful Docker repository build status

The overall build status is shown in Figure 15-28. The builds that are marked in red are failed ones from my earlier tries.

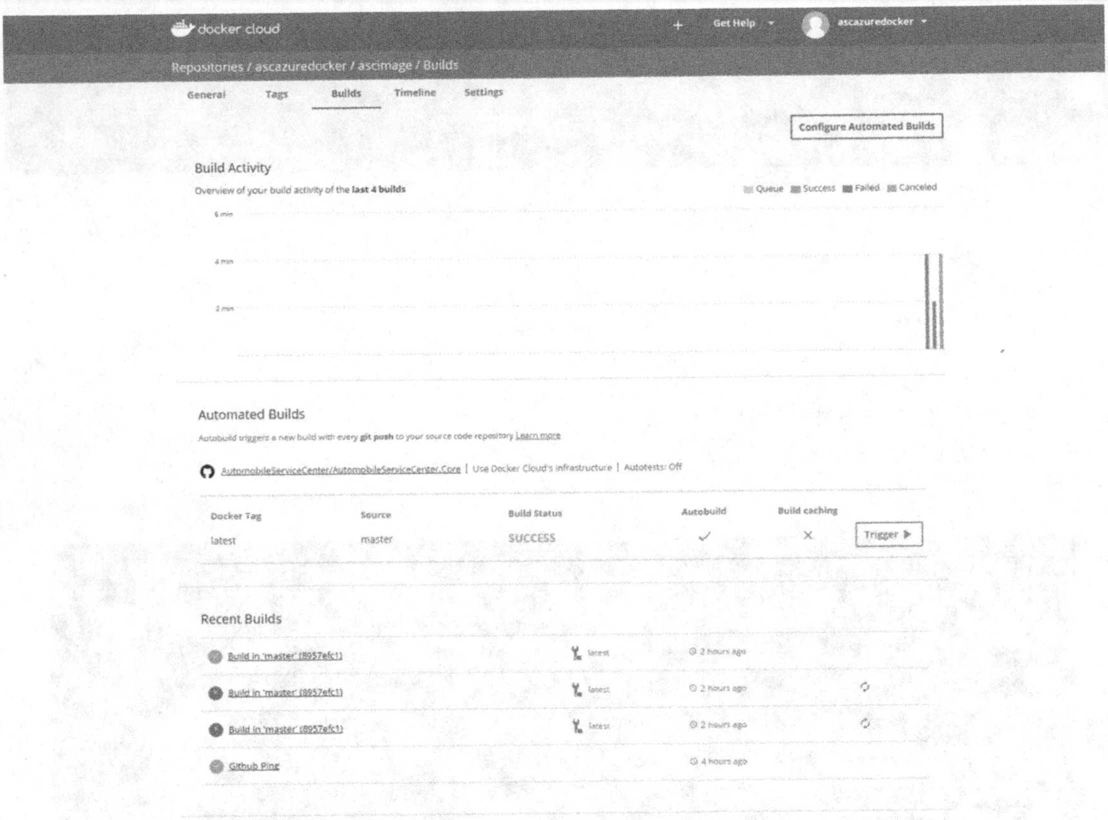

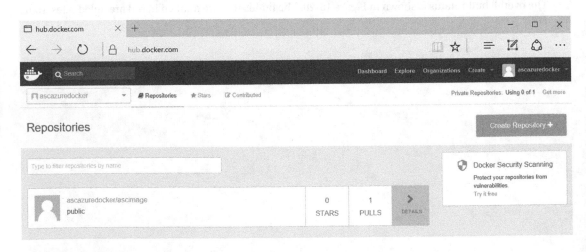

Figure 15-28. *Build activity of the Docker repository*

On successful build, we should find the Docker image in Docker Hub, as shown in Figure 15-29. Docker Hub is the cloud-based registry that holds all the Docker images and links them to code repositories.

Figure 15-29. *Docker image listed at Docker Hub*

Now we will deploy the container that is built using the Docker image. To deploy a container, we need to create a service. Navigate to the Services tab, as shown in Figure 15-30.

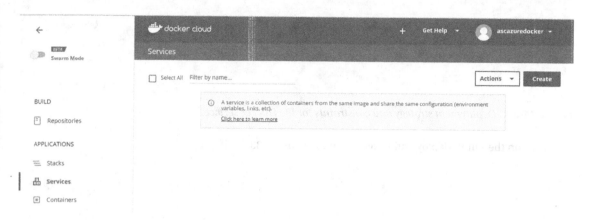

Figure 15-30. *Services tab at Docker Cloud*

Click the Create button and then navigate to the My Repositories tab. Select `ascimage`, as shown in Figure 15-31.

Figure 15-31. *Creating a Docker service with ascimage*

Set the Deployment Strategy to Every Node and set Deployment Constraints to nodecluster-name=asc1, as shown in Figure 15-32.

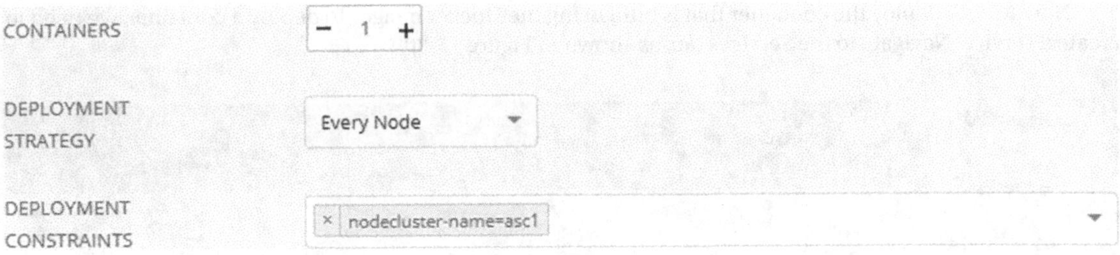

CONTAINERS	− 1 +	
DEPLOYMENT STRATEGY	Every Node ▾	
DEPLOYMENT CONSTRAINTS	✕ nodecluster-name=asc1	▾

Figure 15-32. *Deployment strategy and constraints for the Docker service*

Turn on the Autoredeploy option, as shown in Figure 15-33.

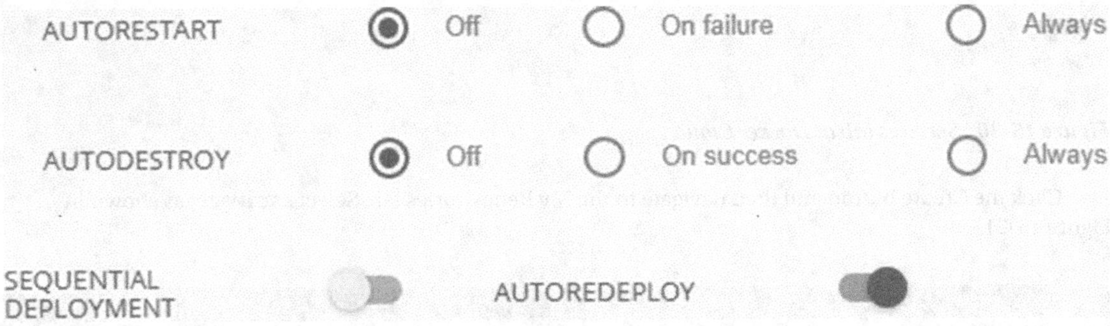

Figure 15-33. *Turning on the Autoredeploy option for the Docker service*

Enter port 80 as the published port, as shown in Figure 15-34. The container's port 5000 is mapped to the node's port 80.

Ports

Container port	Protocol	Published	Node port	
5000	tcp ▾	☑	80	↻

Use image values   Add Port

Figure 15-34. *Configuring 80 as the node port*

Enter the Automobile Service Center application's environment variables, as shown in Figure 15-35.

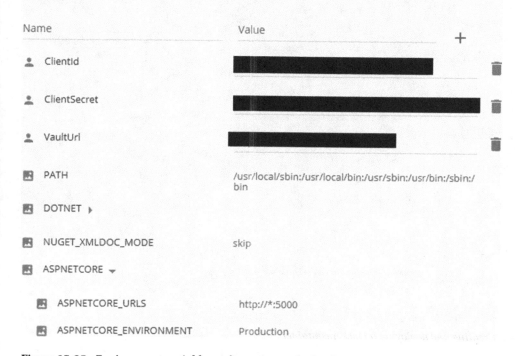

Figure 15-35. *Environment variable configuration at the Docker service*

Click the Create and Deploy option. Navigate to the Containers tab, and you should see the container being created, as shown in Figure 15-36.

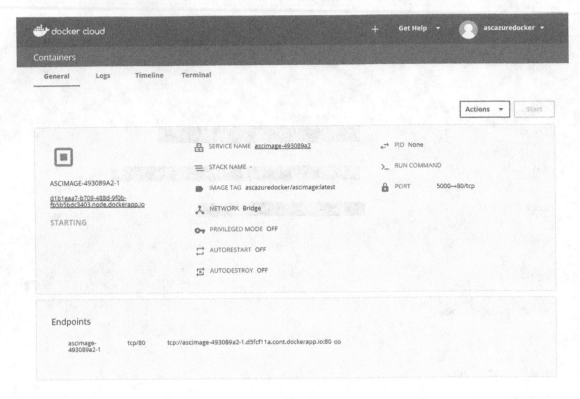

Figure 15-36. *Creating and deploying a Docker container*

After some time, the container will be up and running, as shown in Figure 15-37.

Figure 15-37. *Created container at Docker Cloud*

Find the virtual machine IP address in the General settings of the node, as shown in Figure 15-38.

Figure 15-38. *Node details at Docker Cloud*

Navigate to the IP address. You should see the hosted application, as shown in Figure 15-39.

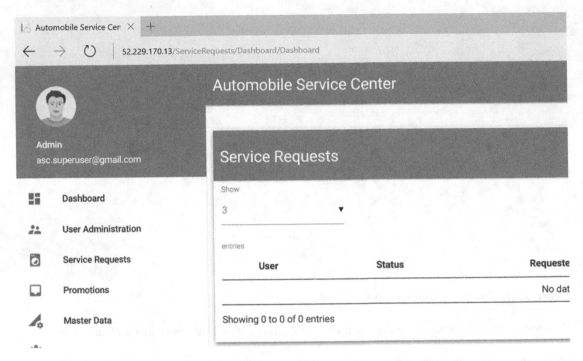

Figure 15-39. Automobile Service Center application hosted at the Azure node

At the same time, we can also access the application by using the DNS name, which we can get from an overview of the virtual machine from the Azure portal, as shown in Figure 15-40.

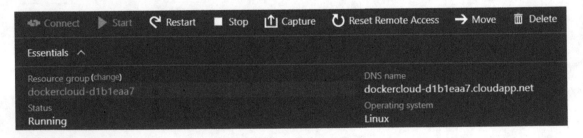

Figure 15-40. Virtual machine details at the Azure portal

Now that we know the domain name, we can update the Google Identity settings with the DNS name, as shown in Figure 15-41.

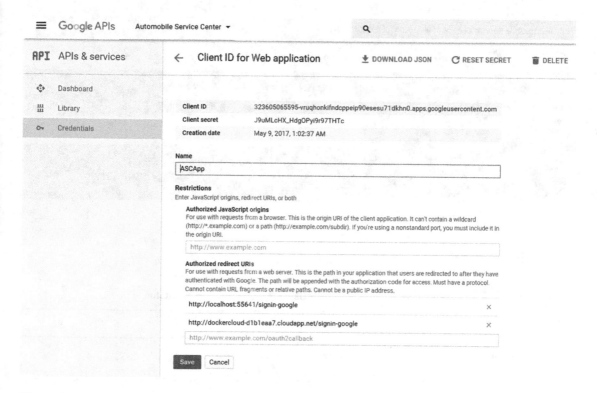

Figure 15-41. *Updating the Google Identity redirect URIs*

Now we can access the application with the DNS name and can log in with Google Identity, as shown in Figure 15-42.

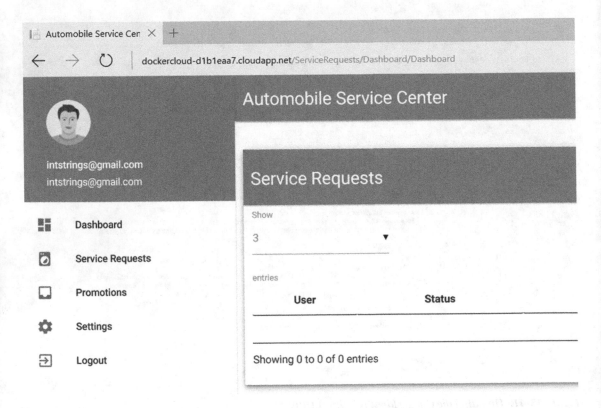

Figure 15-42. *Accessing the Automobile Service Center application through Google single sign-on*

We can now perform commits to the master branch of the AutomobileServiceCenter.Core repository at GitHub. Immediately, the entire continuous integration and continuous deployment orchestration will kick off. In no time, the latest code will be deployed to the Azure node and will be available for customers.

Bring Our Own Node for Docker Integration

In the previous section, we created an Azure virtual machine from Docker Cloud and orchestrated the entire continuous integration and continuous deployment workflow. In this section, we will bring our own host machine (any machine on any network). To simulate our own machine, we will create an Azure-based Ubuntu virtual machine, as shown in Figure 15-43.

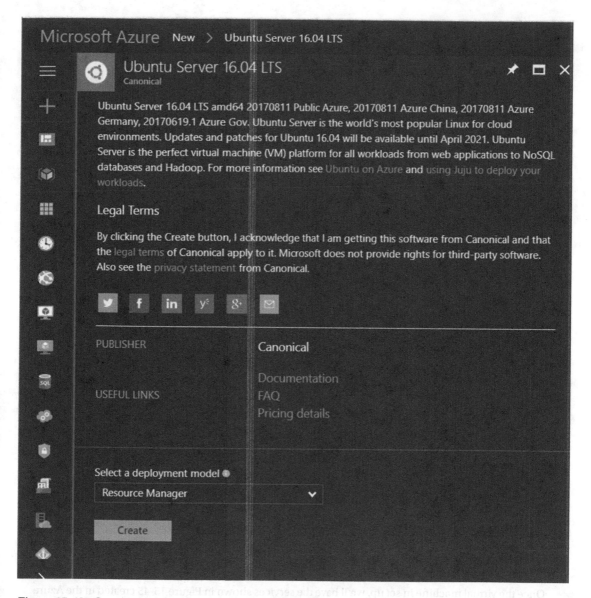

Figure 15-43. *Creating an Ubuntu server at the Azure platform*

Enter basic information, as shown in Figure 15-44. We are configuring the virtual machine with a username and password. Select the DS1_V2 Standard 1 Core 3.5GB RAM virtual machine template for the size. Leave all the other default settings to create the virtual machine.

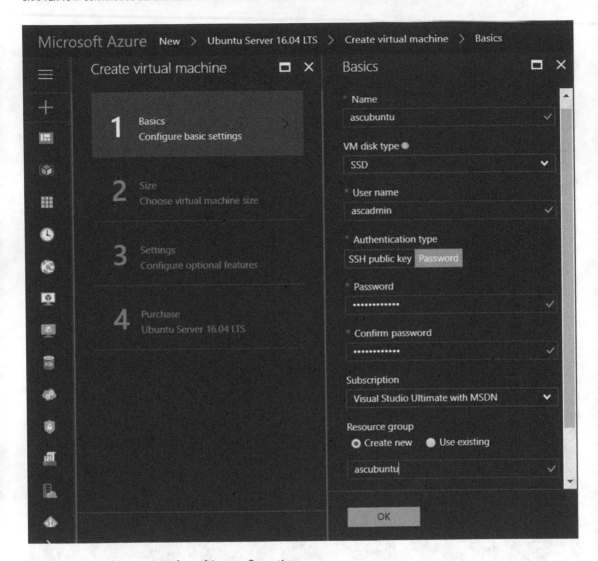

Figure 15-44. *Ubuntu virtual machine configuration*

Once the virtual machine in set up, we'll have the services shown in Figure 15-45 created in the Azure portal.

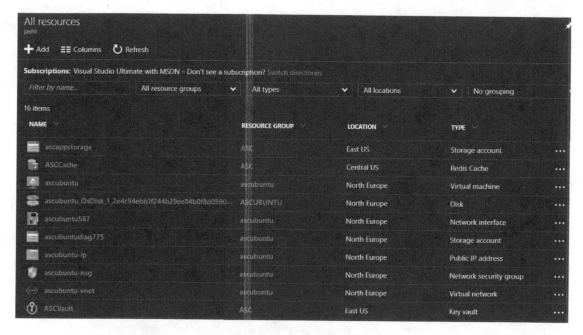

Figure 15-45. *Created virtual machine at the Azure portal*

Now that we have the Azure virtual machine created, we can bring that as a node into Docker Cloud. Navigate to the Nodes section, as shown in Figure 15-46.

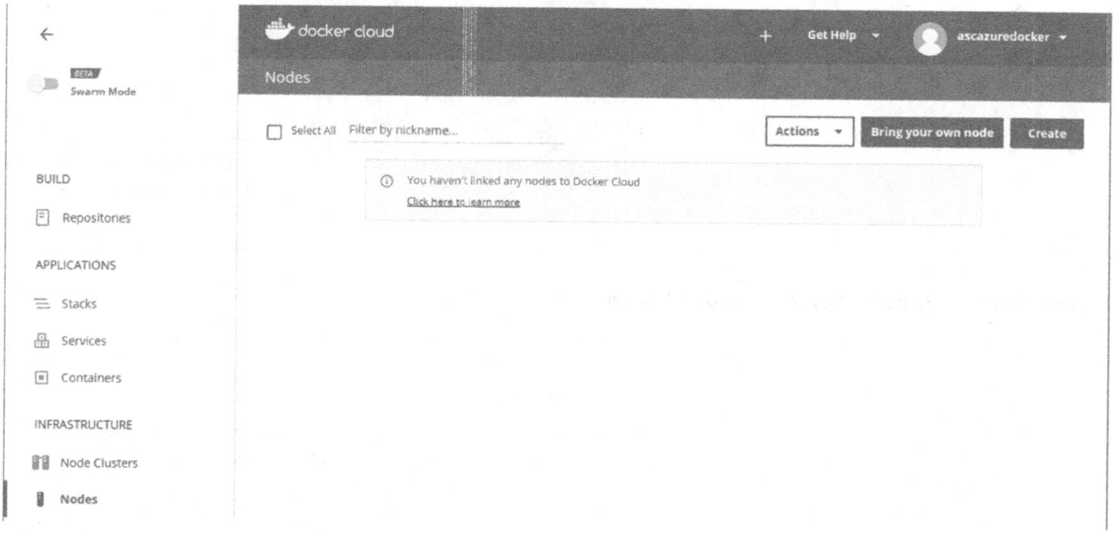

Figure 15-46. *Nodes section at Docker Cloud*

■ **Note** I deleted the Azure node that we created in the previous section to demonstrate how to bring our own node into Docker Cloud.

Click the Bring Your Node button.. A pop-up with a curl command opens, as shown in Figure 15-47. It also recommends to open ports 2375, 6783/tcp, and 6783/udp at the virtual machine. Along with these ports, we add port 80, which will serve HTTP traffic.

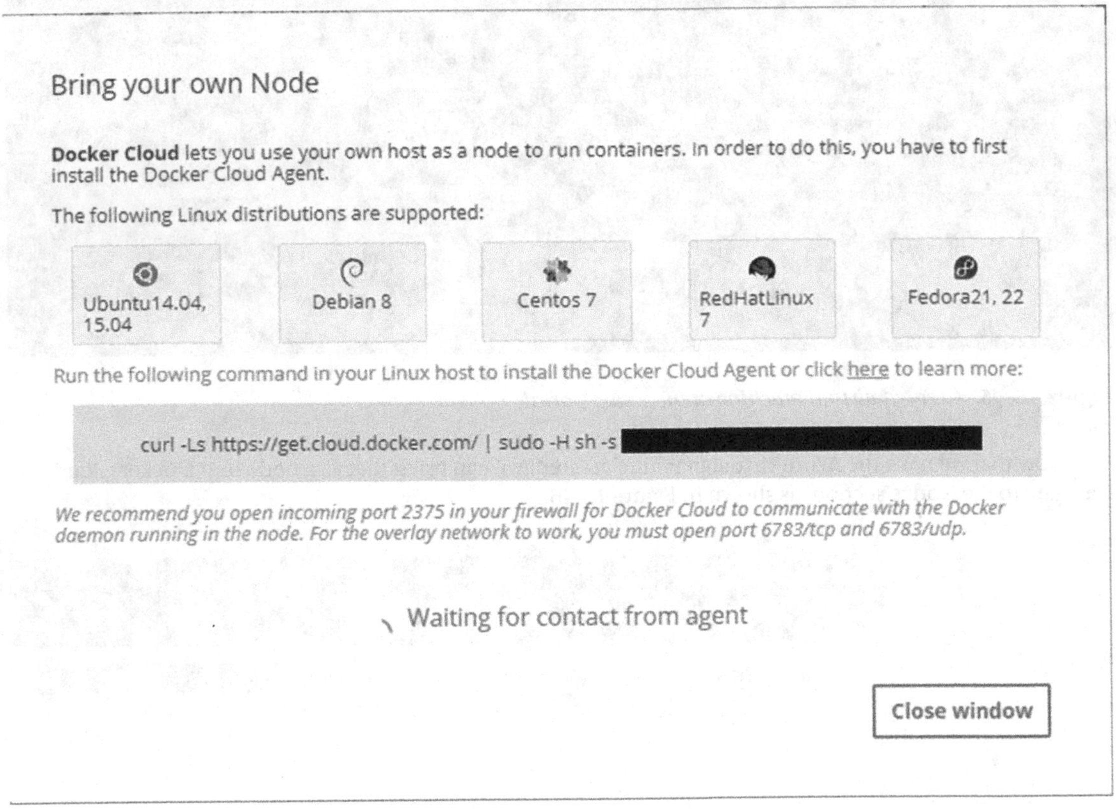

Bring your own Node

Docker Cloud lets you use your own host as a node to run containers. In order to do this, you have to first install the Docker Cloud Agent.

The following Linux distributions are supported:

| Ubuntu14.04, 15.04 | Debian 8 | Centos 7 | RedHatLinux 7 | Fedora21, 22 |

Run the following command in your Linux host to install the Docker Cloud Agent or click here to learn more:

```
curl -Ls https://get.cloud.docker.com/ | sudo -H sh -s
```

We recommend you open incoming port 2375 in your firewall for Docker Cloud to communicate with the Docker daemon running in the node. For the overlay network to work, you must open port 6783/tcp and 6783/udp.

＼ Waiting for contact from agent

Close window

Figure 15-47. Generated curl command at Docker Cloud

To add ports for the Azure virtual machine, navigate to Network Security Group (associated with our newly created virtual machine), as shown in Figure 15-48.

***Figure 15-48.** Network Security Group of the Ubuntu virtual machine*

Select Inbound Security Rules. Click Add to add a new inbound rule. Add ports 2375, 6783/tcp, 6783/udp and 80, as shown in Figures 15-49 to 15-52; then click OK.

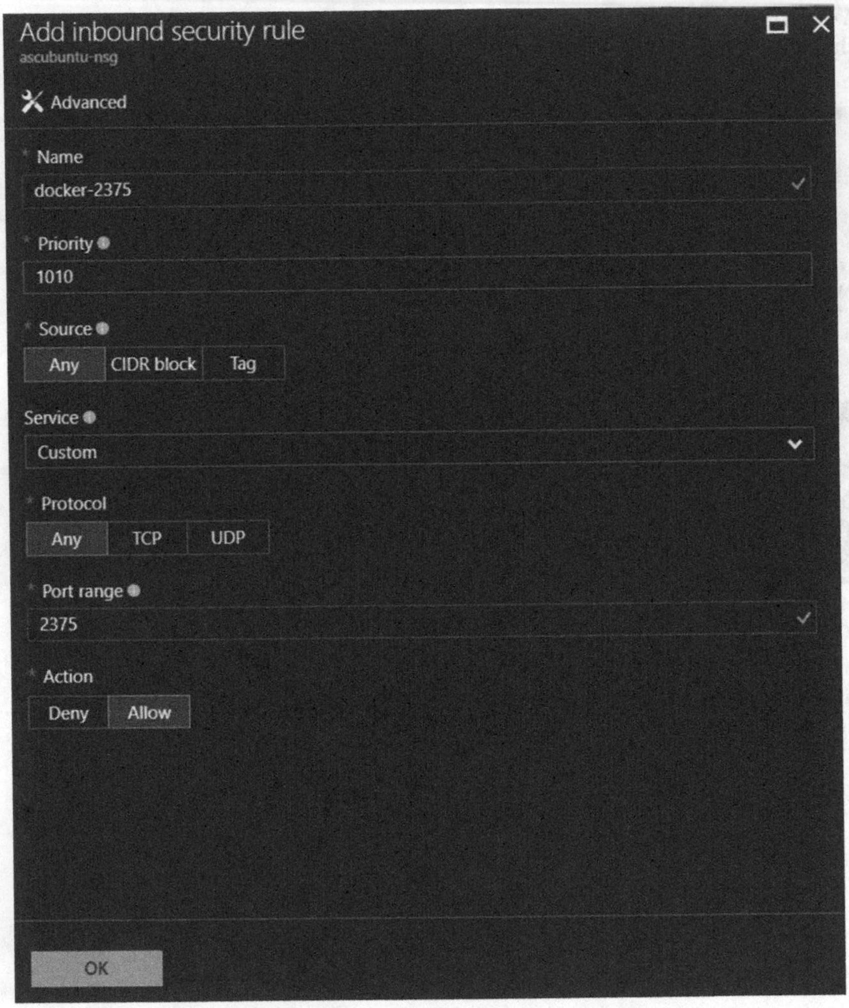

Figure 15-49. *Creating inbound rules for port 2375 for the Ubuntu virtual machine*

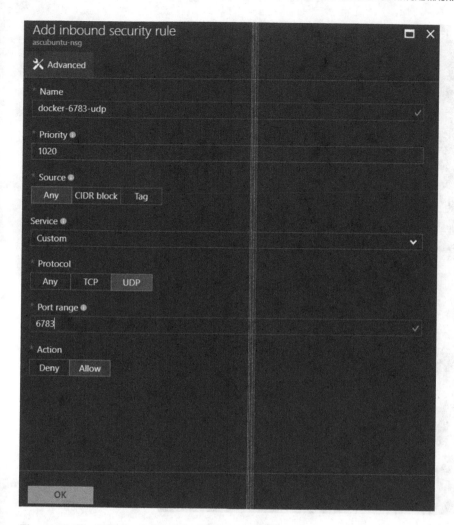

Figure 15-50. Creating inbound rules for port 6783/UDP for the Ubuntu virtual machine

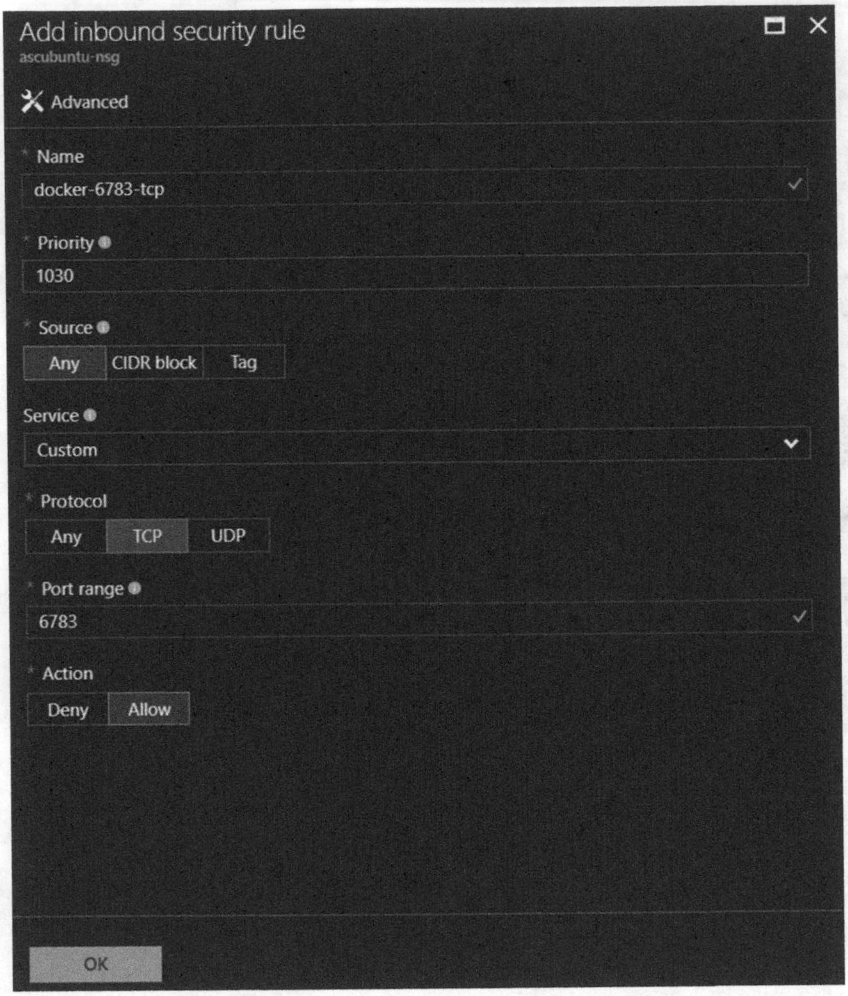

Figure 15-51. *Creating inbound rules for port 6783/TCP for the Ubuntu virtual machine*

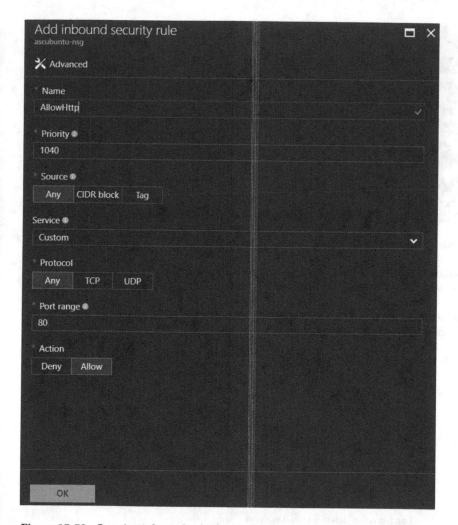

Figure 15-52. *Creating inbound rules for HTTP port 80 for the Ubuntu virtual machine*

All the ports that are added are displayed, as shown in Figure 15-53.

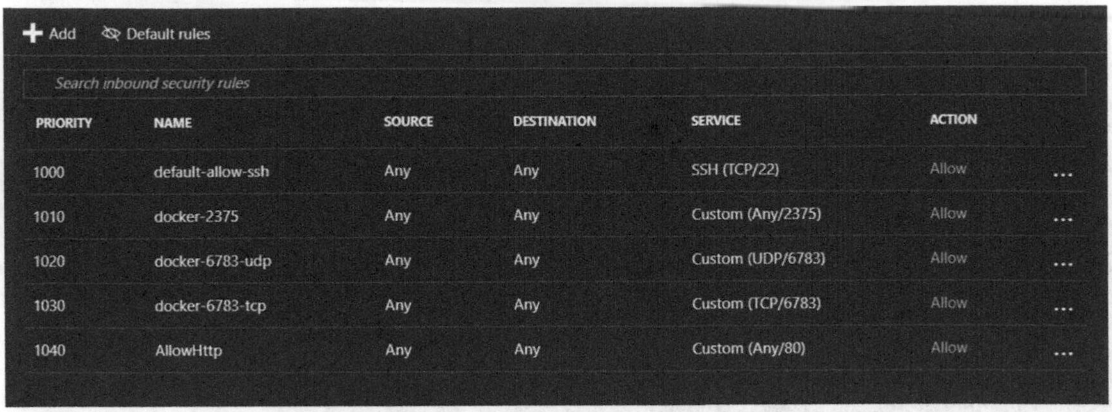

PRIORITY	NAME	SOURCE	DESTINATION	SERVICE	ACTION	
1000	default-allow-ssh	Any	Any	SSH (TCP/22)	Allow	...
1010	docker-2375	Any	Any	Custom (Any/2375)	Allow	...
1020	docker-6783-udp	Any	Any	Custom (UDP/6783)	Allow	...
1030	docker-6783-tcp	Any	Any	Custom (TCP/6783)	Allow	...
1040	AllowHttp	Any	Any	Custom (Any/80)	Allow	...

Figure 15-53. Created inbound port rules for the Ubuntu virtual machine

To run the `curl` command that we got from Docker, we need to access the virtual machine terminal. To access the terminal, download and install Putty SSH and the Telnet client (`www.putty.org`) to the local environment.

Run the Putty client and enter the VM IP address (which can be found in the Overview tab of the virtual machine), as shown in Figure 15-54. Then click Connect.

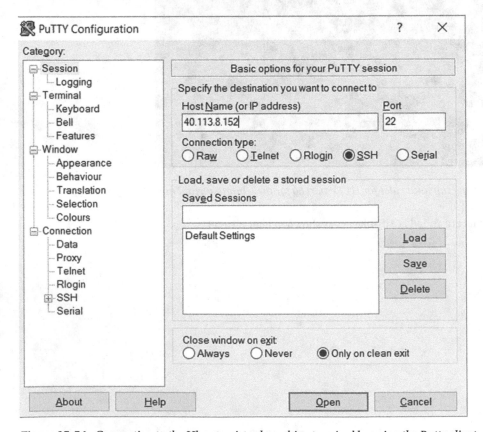

Figure 15-54. Connecting to the Ubuntu virtual machine terminal by using the Putty client

We will get an alert to cache the virtual machine's host key, as shown in Figure 15-55. Click No.

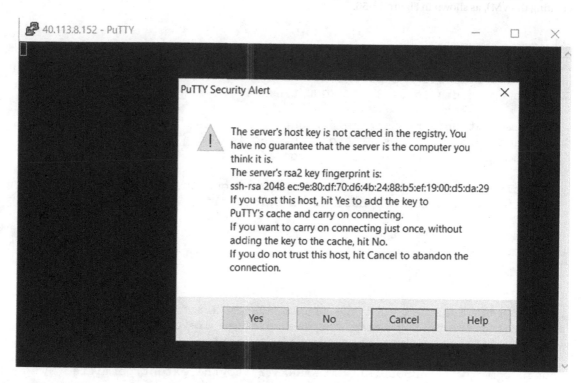

Figure 15-55. *Alert displayed to cache the virtual machine's host key*

Log in to the console by providing the username and password (which we provided at the time of creating the VM), as shown in Figure 15-56.

🖳 ascadmin@ascubuntu: ~
_____

```
login as: ascadmin
ascadmin@40.113.8.152's password:
Welcome to Ubuntu 16.04.3 LTS (GNU/Linux 4.4.0-92-generic x86_64)

 * Documentation:  https://help.ubuntu.com
 * Management:     https://landscape.canonical.com
 * Support:        https://ubuntu.com/advantage

  Get cloud support with Ubuntu Advantage Cloud Guest:
    http://www.ubuntu.com/business/services/cloud

2 packages can be updated.
0 updates are security updates.



The programs included with the Ubuntu system are free software;
the exact distribution terms for each program are described in the
individual files in /usr/share/doc/*/copyright.

Ubuntu comes with ABSOLUTELY NO WARRANTY, to the extent permitted by
applicable law.

To run a command as administrator (user "root"), use "sudo <command>".
See "man sudo_root" for details.

ascadmin@ascubuntu:~$ ▮
```

Figure 15-56. *Ubuntu virtual machine terminal after successful login*

To become the root user on the virtual machine, run the sudo -s command, as shown in Figure 15-57.

```
ascadmin@ascubuntu:~$ sudo -s
root@ascubuntu:~# ▮
```

Figure 15-57. *Becoming the root user at the terminal*

Now run the curl command, which we got from Docker Cloud, as shown in Figure 15-58. It will download and install the Docker Cloud agent on the virtual machine.

```
root@ascubuntu:~# curl -Ls https://get.cloud.docker.com/ | sudo -H sh -s 8361e29922bb48578beb9350130f980d
-> Adding Docker Cloud's GPG key...
gpg: directory '/root/.gnupg' created
gpg: new configuration file '/root/.gnupg/gpg.conf' created
gpg: WARNING: options in '/root/.gnupg/gpg.conf' are not yet active during this run
gpg: keyring '/root/.gnupg/secring.gpg' created
gpg: keyring '/root/.gnupg/pubring.gpg' created
gpg: /root/.gnupg/trustdb.gpg: trustdb created
gpg: key EF170D1C: public key "Tutum Inc. (tutum) <info@tutum.co>" imported
gpg: Total number processed: 1
gpg:               imported: 1  (RSA: 1)
OK
-> Installing required dependencies...
-> Installing dockercloud-agent...
W: http://repo.cloud.docker.com/ubuntu/dists/dockercloud/InRelease: Signature by key 278FE7333CFF7F8B60B677E85DD27147EF170D1C uses weak digest algorithm (SHA1)
Reading package lists...
Building dependency tree...
Reading state information...
The following additional packages will be installed:
  aufs-tools cgroup-lite libnih-dbus1 mountall
The following NEW packages will be installed:
  aufs-tools cgroup-lite dockercloud-agent libnih-dbus1 mountall
0 upgraded, 5 newly installed, 0 to remove and 5 not upgraded.
Need to get 2,855 kB/2,948 kB of archives.
After this operation, 9,902 kB of additional disk space will be used.
Get:1 http://repo.cloud.docker.com/ubuntu dockercloud/main amd64 dockercloud-agent amd64 1.1.0 [2,780 kB]
Get:2 http://azure.archive.ubuntu.com/ubuntu xenial/main amd64 libnih-dbus1 amd64 1.0.3-4.3ubuntu1 [14.1 kB]
Get:3 http://azure.archive.ubuntu.com/ubuntu xenial/main amd64 mountall amd64 2.54ubuntu1 [56.8 kB]
Get:4 http://azure.archive.ubuntu.com/ubuntu xenial/universe amd64 cgroup-lite all 1.11 [4,192 B]
Fetched 2,855 kB in 0s (11.7 MB/s)
Selecting previously unselected package libnih-dbus1:amd64.
(Reading database ... 61478 files and directories currently installed.)
Preparing to unpack .../libnih-dbus1_1.0.3-4.3ubuntu1_amd64.deb ...
Unpacking libnih-dbus1:amd64 (1.0.3-4.3ubuntu1) ...
Selecting previously unselected package mountall.
Preparing to unpack .../mountall_2.54ubuntu1_amd64.deb ...
Unpacking mountall (2.54ubuntu1) ...
Selecting previously unselected package aufs-tools.
Preparing to unpack .../aufs-tools_1%3a3.2+20130722-1.1ubuntu1_amd64.deb ...
Unpacking aufs-tools (1:3.2+20130722-1.1ubuntu1) ...
Selecting previously unselected package cgroup-lite.
Preparing to unpack .../cgroup-lite_1.11_all.deb ...
Unpacking cgroup-lite (1.11) ...
Selecting previously unselected package dockercloud-agent.
Preparing to unpack .../dockercloud-agent_1.1.0_amd64.deb ...
Unpacking dockercloud-agent (1.1.0) ...
Processing triggers for libc-bin (2.23-0ubuntu9) ...
Processing triggers for man-db (2.7.5-1) ...
Processing triggers for dbus (1.10.6-1ubuntu3.3) ...
Processing triggers for ureadahead (0.100.0-19) ...
Processing triggers for systemd (229-4ubuntu19) ...
Setting up libnih-dbus1:amd64 (1.0.3-4.3ubuntu1) ...
Setting up mountall (2.54ubuntu1) ...
Setting up aufs-tools (1:3.2+20130722-1.1ubuntu1) ...
Setting up cgroup-lite (1.11) ...
Setting up dockercloud-agent (1.1.0) ...
sent invalidate(passwd) request, exiting
sent invalidate(group) request, exiting
sent invalidate(group) request, exiting
Processing triggers for libc-bin (2.23-0ubuntu9) ...
Processing triggers for dbus (1.10.6-1ubuntu3.3) ...
Processing triggers for ureadahead (0.100.0-19) ...
Processing triggers for systemd (229-4ubuntu19) ...
-> Configuring dockercloud-agent...
-> Enabling dockercloud-agent to start on boot on systemd...
Synchronizing state of dockercloud-agent.service with SysV init with /lib/systemd/systemd-sysv-install...
Executing /lib/systemd/systemd-sysv-install enable dockercloud-agent
-> Starting dockercloud-agent service...
-> Done!

***************************************************************
Docker Cloud Agent installed successfully
***************************************************************

You can now deploy containers to this node using Docker Cloud

root@ascubuntu:~# █
```

Figure 15-58. *Executing the curl command at the Ubunti virtual machine's terminal*

The pop-up at the Docker Cloud portal will detect the curl command execution, as shown in Figure 15-59.

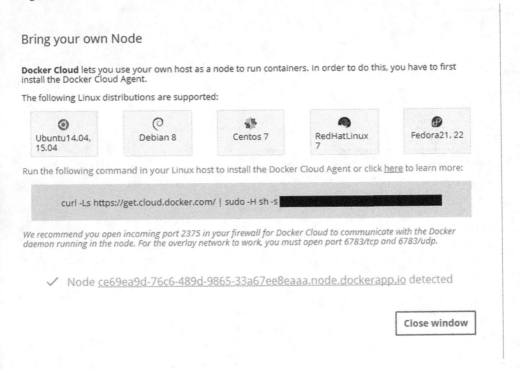

Figure 15-59. *Docker Cloud detects the node connection.*

The newly created node is shown in the Nodes tab, as shown in Figure 15-60.

Figure 15-60. *Onboarded node listed in the Nodes section of Docker Cloud*

Click the Labels icon and add *asc1* as the label, as shown in Figure 15-61.

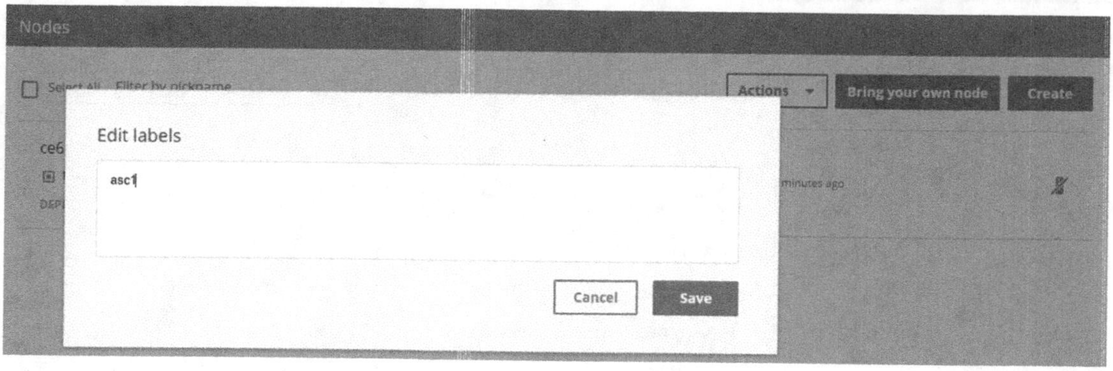

Figure 15-61. *Adding a label to the node at Docker Cloud*

Now we will associate the newly added node to the Docker service. Edit the Docker service and add the asc1 label as a deployment constraint, as shown in Figure 15-62.

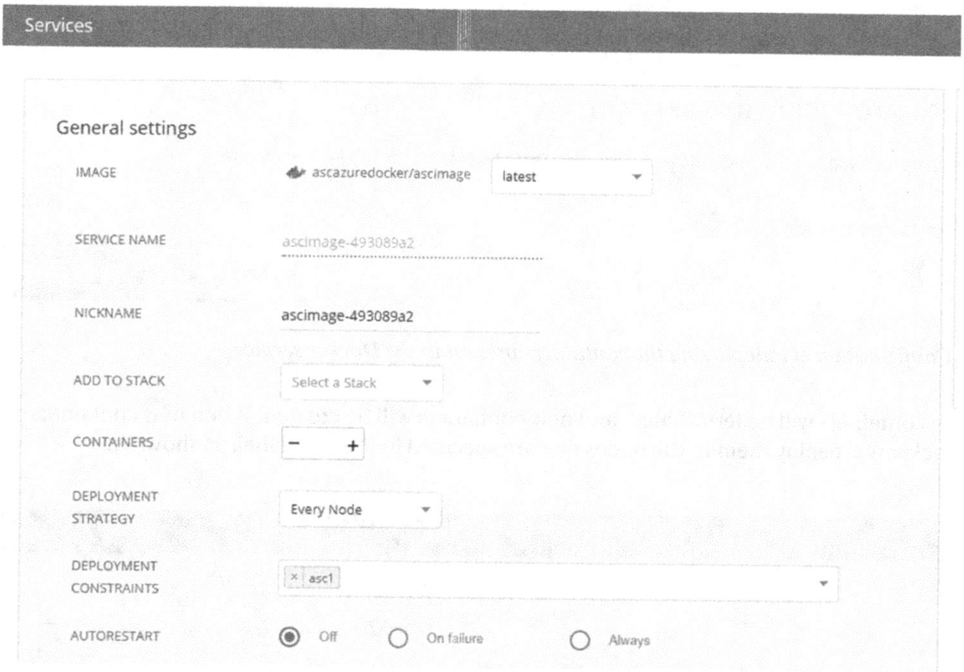

Figure 15-62. *Configuring the Docker service with the asc1 label as a deployment constraint*

Save the changes. From the Action menu, select the Redeploy option, as shown in Figure 15-63.

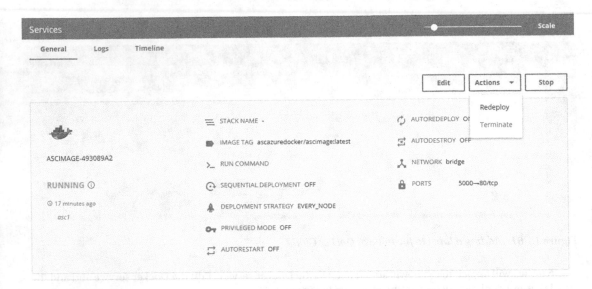

Figure 15-63. *Redeploying the containers present in the Docker service*

A confirmation pop-up appears, as shown in Figure 15-64. Click the Redeploy button.

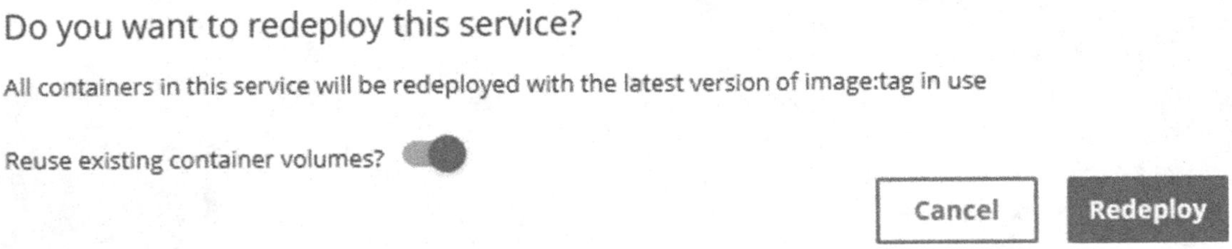

Do you want to redeploy this service?

All containers in this service will be redeployed with the latest version of image:tag in use

Reuse existing container volumes?

Cancel   **Redeploy**

Figure 15-64. *Confirmation of redeploying the containers present in the Docker service*

The existing containers will be terminated, and new containers will be created. When new containers are available, Docker will deploy them to the nodes that are specified in the asc1 label, as shown in Figure 15-65.

Figure 15-65. *New containers deployed to nodes*

586

Access the Automobile Service Center application by using the virtual machine IP address. You should be able to see the application, as shown in Figure 15-66.

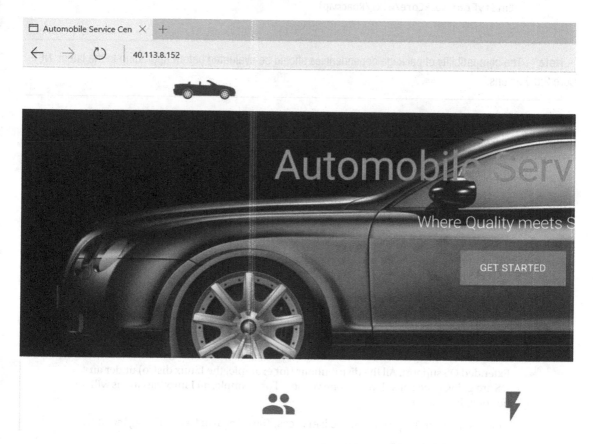

Figure 15-66. *Access ing the Automobile Service Center application with the Ubuntu server virtual machine's IP address*

Automobile Service Center and .NET Core 2.0

The incredible pace of technical shifts in technology is inevitable in the process to equip developers with new tools and platforms to solve complex problems. We started this chapter with .NET Core 1.0.3 as the base version, and now we have 1.1.2 as the Long Term Support version. Microsoft also shipped the next major release of .NET Core, which is 2.0.

We have the following major roadblocks to upgrading the Automobile Service Center application to .NET Core 2.0:

- ASP.NET Core SignalR is not yet released. Based on the latest information on GitHub, it will be released in the next few weeks (https://github.com/aspnet/SignalR/iss ues/429#issuecomment-323562878).

- We have used the ElCamino NuGet package to integrate ASP.NET Core Identity with Azure cloud storage. This NuGet package is not compatible with ASP.NET Core Identity 2.0 (https://github.com/dlmelendez/identityazuretable/issues/23).

- The Entity Framework Core team is still working on including a provider for nonrelational databases such as Azure Table storage (`https://github.com/aspnet/EntityFrameworkCore/wiki/Roadmap`).

■ **Note** The compatibility of package dependencies should be evaluated before upgrading to the latest .NET Core 2.0 versions.

Because of the preceding roadblocks, we are not going to upgrade the Automobile Service Center application to .NET Core 2.0.

ASP.NET Core 2.0 has a lot of new features, including the following:

- Support for .NET Standard 2.0, which gives access to broader APIs.

- The ASP.NET Core metapackage will house all the required ASP.NET and EF Core packages.

- ASP.NET Core Razor pages can be used to create pages without controllers.

- Option to configure Razor and view compilation to an assembly instead of CSHTMLs.

- Improvements to Kestrel server that make it more suitable for Internet-based applications.

- `IConfiguration`, `ILogger`, and `IHostingEnvironment` can be configured at the web-host layer.

- Extended OS support. All the distributions (for example, the Linux distro) under an OS are going to be considered as one version. For example, all Linux variations will be considered as Linux.

- Improvements to `TempData`, `IHostedServices`, `IHostingStartup`, and `Logging` APIs.

- Support for the Visual Basic language.

- Great support for application insights without even needing to write a single line of code in the application.

We can plan an Automobile Service Center code upgrade to .NET Core 2.0 in Q1 of 2018 or later only when we get support for SignalR and other required dependencies. Until then, we can explore the new features of .NET and ASP.NET Core.

Recommended Exercises

I propose the following exercises to extend the Automobile Service Center application which will give you more technical exposure:

1. Develop a module to manage a spare parts inventory. These pages can be similar to the master data management module. Associate the created spare parts with a particular service request.

2. Create a screen that displays an invoice generated for a service request based on spare parts and labor costs. Notify the customer with the overall detailed invoice.

3. Integrate service engineer accounts with two-factor authentication.

4. Explore the Azure container service and transform the Automobile Service Center application's deployment strategy to support Docker Swarm.

5. Complete xUnit test cases to cover the entire code base.

6. Integrate single sign-on with Facebook and Twitter authentication providers.

■ **Note**   The solutions to the preceding proposed exercises are beyond the scope of this book.

Summary

In this chapter, you learned about the relevance and importance of automated deployment systems in the software development life cycle. The new automated deployment systems provide easy, reliable, and accurate deployment strategies that support multiple environments with minimal redundant manual tasks to maximize overall system productivity. Many continuous deployment platforms are available to automatically trigger deployment to host machines with continuous integration and source version-control systems. We are going to use the Docker platform for the Automobile Service Center application to build the latest source code from GitHub and deploy it to Azure-based Linux virtual machines.

Docker Cloud is a service provided by the Docker platform that primarily helps orchestrate the build and deployment pipelines. You learned about the Docker orchestration, which is initiated by fetching the latest source code from the source version-control system, followed by autobuilding the Docker image from source code with specifications mentioned in the Dockerfile. Upon a successful image build, Docker services will kick in and generate Docker containers, which are finally deployed to host machines configured with the Docker engine. You then proceeded to create a free subscription account at Docker Cloud.

You connected Docker with an Azure subscription, which helps set up new nodes or onboard existing nodes to the Docker platform. Later you proceeded to create a new node cluster with a single node in the East Asia Azure datacenter. This node can be maintained at the Azure portal, and at the same time, the node can be terminated from the Docker portal. You then connected Docker with GitHub, and created a Docker repository with GitHub's `AutomobileServiceCenter.Core` as the source code repository. The Docker repository is configured with the master branch of the GitHub repository, and autobuild is turned on. The environment variables required for the Automobile Service Center application are specified as parameters with values. You triggered a Docker build by merging the dev with the master branch at GitHub. Upon the successful Docker build, the generated image will be available at Docker Hub.

You created a Docker service from the Docker image and configured the service to deploy the container on every node with a specific label. You also configured other options including autoredeploy, HTTP port, and environment variables. Once configuration was completed, the container was deployed to the virtual machine node. You were able to access the Automobile Service Center application by using the virtual machine's IP address.

In the final section of the chapter, you learned how to bring our own node to Docker Cloud. To simulate our own host machine, you created an Azure-based Ubuntu server and configured it with the required ports for Docker integration. Using Putty, you ran the `curl` command given by Docker at the virtual machine's terminal, which installed the Docker Cloud agent. You then triggered a Docker service redeploy, which regenerated and deployed the container of the Automobile Service Center application to the virtual machine. By using the virtual machine's IP address, you are able to access the application.

The Final Word

The key mantra for the success of any business lies in providing the right solutions to the right problems with a customer-centric approach. The software industry is no exception. The exceptional pace of progress in the software industry not only opens different business opportunities but also provides exceptional solutions to technical challenges. Understanding and implementing the right technologies to enrich a business solution and building eminence around current technologies have been the most common problems faced by most organizations in the recent past. This book showcases one software development approach to providing end-to-end application development, and thereby building eminence capabilities around some of the modern technologies.

Throughout the journey of this book, you have seen various technologies used for different purposes, to cater to the overall business workflow: performing authentication with the Google platform and storing user information in Azure storage, running an ASP.NET Core application by using Docker containers, sending SMS notifications by using Twilio and sending web notifications with SignalR, and maintaining the master data cache in Azure Redis Cache. These integrations became a reality through the evolution of strong open source technologies and communities.

I sincerely thank the developers at Microsoft and in the open source communities for providing a great platform and toolkits that are continuously used in this book. I hope you enjoyed the content and have learned something new and interesting. I hope to see you soon in another interesting venture.

Reference

1. https://docs.docker.com/

Index

Get the eBook for only $5!

Why limit yourself?

With most of our titles available in both PDF and ePUB format, you can access your content wherever and however you wish—on your PC, phone, tablet, or reader.

Since you've purchased this print book, we are happy to offer you the eBook for just $5.

To learn more, go to http://www.apress.com/companion or contact support@apress.com.

Apress®

Printed in the United States
By Bookmasters